Strictly a Musician

Dick Cary

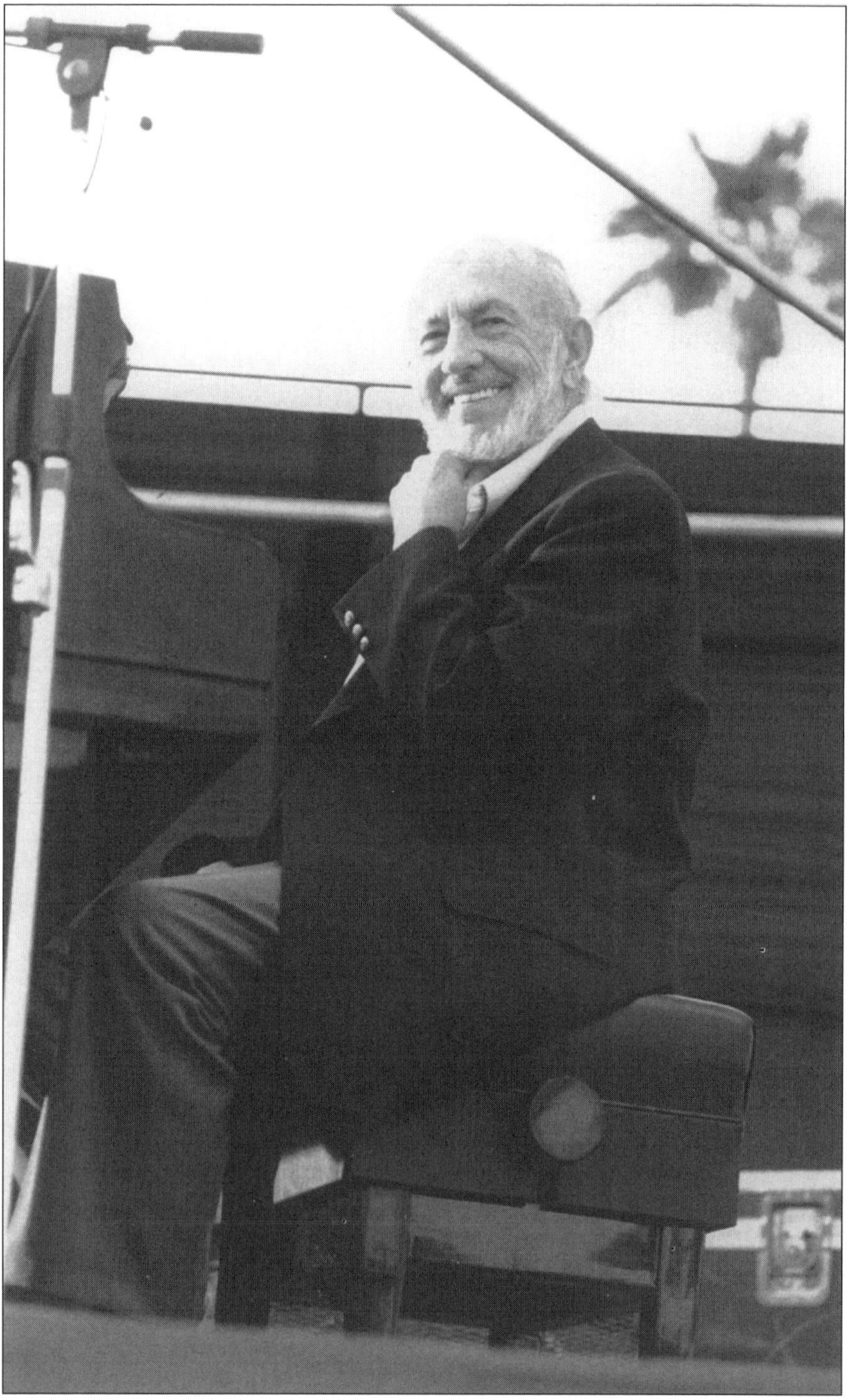

Strictly a Musician

Dick Cary

A Biography and Discography

by

Derek Coller

A Dick Cary Music Company Publication

Dick Cary Music Company
9828 Wornom Avenue, Sunland, CA 91040, U.S.A.

© 2012 published by Dick Cary Music Company,
and the author, © Derek Coller

First printing March 2012
Printed in the United States of America by BookMasters, Inc.

Library of Congress Cataloging-in-Publication Data

Derek Coller, 1926–
Strictly a Musician—Dick Cary

Biography: p   Discography: p   Includes index.

1. Dick Cary 1916–1994
2. Jazz musician / arranger / composer—United States.

Library of Congress No. PCN 2011938499

ISBN No. 978-0-615-53867-9

Drawings by Rich Normandin
www.normandinart.com

All rights reserved. No part of this publication may be reproduced,
published or transmitted in any form or by any means, electronic, mechanical,
or otherwise, without the prior written permission of the
Dick Cary Music Company and the author.

*To my children, Judith, Brenda and Simon,
to my grandchildren
and to
Jim Turner, custodian of the Dick Cary legacy*

Contents

Introduction ... to Dick Cary xi
Introduction ... to the author's connection with Dick Cary xii
Foreword (A Memoir) xiii
Acknowledgements xiv
The Dick Cary Diaries xviii

The Biography

Chapter 1   School Days and the Wesleyan Serenaders 2
Chapter 2   Nick's, Eddie Condon and Uncle Sam 25
Chapter 3   Billy Butterfield, Amusement Parks and Polish Hops .. 56
Chapter 4   With Louis Armstrong and the All Stars 66
Chapter 5   Composition and Condon 86
Chapter 6   Jimmy Dorsey, Jingles and Television 107
Chapter 7   "We'll send you to Lake Placid" 130
Chapter 8   Joy Ride 153
Chapter 9   Bobby Hackett at the Henry Hudson 177
Chapter 10 Georgia Sketches 198
Chapter 11 Interlude—Blackberry Brandy
            and Peppermint Schnapps 221
Chapter 12 9828 Wornom Ave., Sunland, CA 226
Chapter 13 Down Under and Disneyland 244
Chapter 14 Blue Angels and the World's Greatest 266
Chapter 15 Slings and Arrows 281
Chapter 16 Interlude—Hi Hat and Merry-Go-Round 296
Chapter 17 Europe Beckons 298
Chapter 18 Brisbane, The Red Lion and The Revolution Club 318
Chapter 19 Tours, Festivals and Disc Troubles 339
Chapter 20 Louis Tributes, Harry James, Banjos and Tubas 358
Chapter 21 "We never did play *In the Mood*" 377
Chapter 22 Interlude—The Rehearsal Bands 398
Chapter 23 Final Notes 406
Chapter 24 Tributes and Memories 416

The Appendices

Appendix One:	Cary's Views	424
Two:	At Rehearsal: Musicians' Biographies (The Tuesday Night Friends)	436
Three:	Bandleaders and singers for whom Dick Cary made arrangements	441
Four:	Original Compositions: Recorded and/or Published	444
Five:	A Survey of Dick Cary's Recordings	450
	Important Ten	463
Six:	Dick Cary—Other Sources	464

The Discography

The Dick Cary Discography 479
The Merry-Go-Round and Hi Hat Records 554
Dick Cary's Recorded Arrangements 560

The Indexes

Name Index to Biography 570
Name Index to Discography 595

Introduction ... to Dick Cary

Dick Cary was a master musician in the world of jazz. He could play most instruments, but concentrated on piano, trumpet and alto horn. On the alto horn, also called the peck horn, he was unique. He was an arranger and a composer who was highly respected within his own circle but unconsidered beyond.

As a player he was associated early on with that group of jazzmen who gathered around Eddie Condon, guitarist, bandleader, organiser and wit, but he deplored the connection with the word "Dixieland." Like Condon, he preferred to call it music.

He was no showman and had no concern for his appearance. He was an eccentric, but more to some than to others. He was a man of decided opinions. He would have appreciated wider recognition for his music but had no burning ambition beyond that. Above all, he loved to play and especially to write.

His career had a number of highlights, but in the main he was a jobbing musician. Big Band or studio work did not appeal to him, and in any event the days of the swing bands were numbered by the time he was discharged from the U.S. Army. As a result much of his life was spent playing short-lived gigs or one-night stands. This was true particularly of his years in Los Angeles, when he could find himself playing for a senior citizens' party, a mannequin show, a circus or the opening of a car dealership. But there were also the jazz clubs and the recordings, the latter for companies both major and minor. In later years there were solo tours, jazz parties and jazz festivals.

The peaks in his career were his seven months with the original Louis Armstrong All Stars and his longer stay with Bobby Hackett's band, the one featured at the Henry Hudson Hotel, when he could compose and arrange, knowing his work would be played. He also had great pride in the rehearsal band which met weekly at his home in Sunland and later became known as his Tuesday Night Friends.

Looking back, Cary was grateful to have met and worked with so many jazz greats he could call friends: Louis Armstrong, Jack Teagarden, Art Tatum, Bobby Hackett, Billy Butterfield, Sid Catlett, Willie "The Lion" Smith, Eddie Condon, Eddie Miller, Jimmy and Tommy Dorsey and many more. They, of course, were fortunate to have worked with him.

Dick Cary was the archetypal musicians' musician.

Introduction ... to the author's connection with Dick Cary

As a teenager I had a keen interest in jazz records and in discography, which meant that I was aware of Dick Cary's name during the 1940s, but it was not until the Eddie Condon albums on Columbia, in the 1950s, that I came to realise just how good a musician he was.

In 1976 I was gathering material for an article about the Bobby Hackett band which had been featured at New York's Henry Hudson Hotel in 1956. Dick Cary was one of the members of that band to whom I wrote and his help was readily given. Our spasmodic correspondence continued long after the story of that unique Bobby Hackett sextet was published in the *IAJRC Journal*.

Dick always wrote interesting letters, willing to answer questions, telling of his current activities, complaining about the state of the music business, praising fellow musicians. From time to time in these letters Dick would mention his interest in documenting his life story or in talking about the men with whom he had played. He spoke of sitting down with a tape-recorder for a series of interviews. In those years I was pre-occupied with work on a biography of the pianist Jess Stacy, but did endeavour to find someone willing to cooperate with Dick on his project. Unfortunately, the authors I approached were also unable to help. Looking back, this was an important opportunity missed; I should have helped him myself, regardless of other commitments. Fortunately, Floyd Levin was not as tardy and conducted a lengthy and detailed interview with Dick in 1991. After Dick's death the treasure trove of his diaries also became known.

In 1979 Bert Whyatt, a life-long friend and fellow researcher, and I visited Los Angeles, where we met Dick at his home in Sunland. Thirteen years later we returned to Los Angeles and our visit to see Dick coincided with a rehearsal by the Tuesday Night Friends, which was quite a revelation. There were also brief meetings when Dick was touring Britain, either solo or with the Keith Smith "Wonderful World of Louis Armstrong" package.

Correspondence with Jim Turner, who inherited Cary's estate, proved to be a boon, resulting in the golden opportunity to scour Dick's diaries.

From all these contacts with Dick Cary and as a result of listening to so many of his recordings, it was clear that his wish to have his story told should be fulfilled. It is hoped that the reader will feel that this aim has been achieved. —*Derek Coller*

Foreword (A Memoir)
by Jessie Buster (formerly Mrs. Jessie Cary)

Dick and Jessie—1969

There's not a lot I can contribute except to tell you we had a very loving and compatible relationship for the majority of our years together.

One thing I feel should be included in a Dick Cary story is our mutual love and interest in animals. When he moved in with me I had two Cocker Spaniels—mother and daughter—Tinker and Nana. Nana immediately fell in love with Dick and was his shadow from then on. One time I came out of the bathroom to find Nana sitting patiently, waiting for Dick. She gave me a startled look and took off to find him. Any time we visited friends who had cats or dogs the animals were immediately in Dick's lap.

Dick and Rick Fay and I visited the San Diego Zoo one time and as we passed the various caged animals Rick and I realized that Dick was not with us. We retraced our steps and found him sitting on the ground communing with a capybara (a not very handsome hog-size animal). They were just sitting—admiring each other.

We had a happy assortment of dogs (not all at the same time) and two horses.

My eldest daughter, Judy, was married. My other daughter, Kathie, and son Paul were still at home. Except that I am such a neat-nick and he was not, our life was pleasant.

Dick's brass quartette was always fun—Betty and Barrett O'Hara, Dick and me. They were evenings of many laughs. One year during Christmas holidays we took the quartette (Dick's versions of Christmas carols) up to the local business corner, playing on each of the corners. The last was at a gas station. Someone took our picture and we were all amused and elated to see a neon sign behind us, over our heads, that said: TUNE UP.

Acknowledgements

The major sources of information for this biography were:

1. The Dick Cary Diaries, which are described in more detail on pages xviii–xix. These are copyright 2006, The Dick Cary Music Company, and were made available to me through the generosity of the Dick Cary archivist, Jim Turner.

2. An interview which Dick Cary gave to the late FLOYD LEVIN on July 8, 1991. Mr. Levin's kindness in allowing unlimited quotation from this long interview cannot be overstated. The interview was transcribed by Richard Miller.

3. A radio interview with Dick Cary by SCOTT ELLSWORTH on his show, "Scott's Place," on station KFI-LA, June 11, 1971.

4. 18 letters, written by Dick Cary to Ken Gallacher between April 1959 and 1978, quoted by permission of Mr. Gallacher's widow, Moraig.

5. Personal correspondence with Dick Cary between 1976 and 1993.

6. Letters from Dick Cary to Jessie Cary, written between May 1972 and October 1974, 14 in total. Quoted by permission of Jessie (Cary) Buster.

7. Interview articles published in the following magazines:
    - Ken Gallacher in *Jazz Journal*, September 1964
    - Gudrun Endress in *Jazz Podium*, June 1976 and February 1978. English translation by Manfred Selchow. Note this interview has been translated twice—English into German, then German into English.
    - Alan Stevens in *Crescendo International*, October 1977
    - Chuck Conklin & Al Reimen in *Jazz Forum*, September 16, 1990

8. Various magazines, particularly *Down Beat*, as listed in the Source Notes.

9. Conversations and correspondence with the following musicians and collectors:

Ernie Anderson
Anthony Barnett
Dan Barrett
Dave Bennett
Joe Boughton
Dave Bourne
Roy Bower
Jessie Buster (Cary)
Geoff Cole
Bill Crow
Charlie Crump
John Dengler
Bob Enevoldsen
Gudrun Endress *(Jazz Podium)*
Banu Gibson
Jim Gordon
Tommy Gwaltney
Friedrich Hackenberg
Gösta Hägglöf
Peter Hanley
Mike Hart (Edinburgh Jazz Festival)
Stan Hester
Steve Hester
Franz Hoffmann
George Hulme
Gunnar Jacobsen
Conrad Janis
David Jessop
Wolfram Knauer (Jazzinstitut Darmstadt)
Roger Krum (Sacramento Traditional Jazz Society)
Floyd Levin
John McMahon (AFM Local 47)
Barry Martyn
Axel Melhardt (Jazzland Club, Vienna)
Dr. Heiner Muckenberger
Jost Münster
David Nathan (National Jazz Archive, U.K.)
Dieter Nentwig
Barrett and Betty O'Hara
Lino Patruno (Milan College Jazz Society)
Brian Peerless
Ron Rubin

Amy Rule (Center for Creative Photography, University of Arizona)
Howard Rye
Bo Scherman
Mannie Selchow
Hal Smith
John Smith
Keith Smith (Hefty Jazz)
Sam Stephenson (Center for Documentary Studies, Durham, NC)
Dick Sudhalter (notes for Mosaic MD80206)
Jim Turner (Dick Cary Archive)
Peter Vacher
Ken Vail (relevant section of as yet unpublished Louis Armstrong Diary)
Johnny Varro
Reimer von Essen (Barrelhouse Jazz Band)
Arnt Weidler (Jazzinstitut Darmstadt)
Bob Weir
Bert Whyatt
Bob Wilber
Jos Willems (relevant section of "All of Me," the Louis Armstrong Discography, publisher Scarecrow Press.)
Art Zimmerman

The willingness of so many collectors, researchers and musicians to help with their recollections, to delve into their files and into their record collections is gratefully acknowledged. Their help is so typical of the generous spirit and camaraderie which exists within the world of jazz research.

My apologies if, due to the haphazard nature of my filing, there is anyone I have failed to acknowledge.

One other radio interview has been heard, entitled "We Call It Music," July 24, 1969, but this was short and added little new information. Of general interest is the publication "The Jazz Loft Project: Photographs and tapes of W. Eugene Smith from 821 Sixth Avenue 1957–1965" by Sam Stephenson, published by Alfred A. Knopf, 2009. The Jazz Loft Project is at the Center for Documentary Studies at Duke University, Durham. N.C.

www.jazzloftproject.org. e-mail: lauren.hart@duke.edu

In addition to Dick Cary's diaries, Jim Turner was more than generous in his help with cuttings, photographs, programmes, etc, from the Dick Cary Archive. The archive web site is at:
> *www.dickcary.com*

With love and thanks to my wife, Phyllis, for patience above and beyond.

And finally, grateful acknowledgements to Mike Hazeldine and Lynn Lanning. Mike died shortly before he had finished designing this book and it was his expertise which converted my plain manuscript into a real book. Lynn continued where Mike left off and seamlessly completed his work.

—Derek Coller

The Dick Cary Diaries

The Dick Cary diaries are a fascinating glimpse into the life of a professional jazz musician, his hopes, his fears, his hobbies and his working life. Cary kept a diary between 1931 and 1994 and there are 56 diaries in existence. The years which are missing are 1936 to 1939, 1944, 1970, 1972, 1988 to 1990 and 1992.

Details for 1931 to 1935, plus a few days in 1936, are written in a five-year diary, followed by a four-year gap until he resumed in 1940. Thereafter he was diligent for many years, except when a major upheaval interfered. For example, there is no diary for 1944, covering his first full year in the army.

It was 1940 when Cary decided: "I'm ready to start another diary. It's been five years since I finished the five-year diary I kept in high school, prep school and college, but this is one of the most important times in my life and I'll be glad in a few years to know what jobs I played and what I made. The best of this is keeping track of musicians. It's an interesting and valuable thing to do."

In later years there are many gaps and towards the end of his life the diaries were treated as date books. Future jobs are entered but comments on them are infrequent; the detail of the earlier diaries is missing.

The 5-year diary is difficult to read. The spacing is narrow and the writing, mainly in pencil, is not always clear. From 1940 on, the writing is legible until towards the end of his life, when age and illness take their toll. There is also the occasional day when he attempts to make an entry during or after a drinking spell.

Other problems with the entries are the use of abbreviations and other references, the meaning of which are now lost. The names of movie stars are generally given in full, but musicians and friends are referred to by their Christian names only and often there is no mention of instruments played, making identification difficult—or impossible. When the references in Los Angeles are to "Ray," then it is relatively easy to decide between Ray Sherman the pianist or Ray Leatherwood the bassist, but elsewhere it is to be hoped that this writer has not jumped to any hasty identifications. Cary's spelling of names was sometimes inaccurate, which is not surprising when he was often naming musicians met just once or twice on a gig. Many incorrect spellings have been corrected, but others may remain.

Entries were made, or so it would seem, on a day-to-day basis, though not always. Where he does have to catch up from memory some inaccuracies may have crept in. For example, his 1948 diary was in a suitcase which was stolen while Cary was napping on Grand Central Station, so the first eight weeks in the replacement diary were entered from memory.

The earlier diaries are full of sports news, usually heard on the radio, in addition to notes on good meals eaten, films seen, bars visited and music events, plus thoughts on friends and people in the jazz and dance music business.

It was a privilege, thanks to Jim Turner, to be allowed to read the Dick Cary diaries and to use extracts in this book. Quotes from the diary entries have been included in the text in quotation marks and should be readily identifiable. [Any other use of Cary's own words, from letters, interviews or conversations, are in italics and inset. Quotations of the words of other musicians or critics are either identified in the text or in the "Sources" listed after the biography.]

The diaries are an amazing treasure trove of information—quotations from them virtually doubled the size of this book—and it is gratifying that Jim Turner intends to make them available to future researchers.

The Biography

1. School Days and the Wesleyan Serenaders (1916–1940)

Dick Cary's father, Albert Ely Cary, was born in Old Lyme, Connecticut, on March 26, 1876. At the age of 38, on June 24, 1914, in Wellesly, Maryland, he married Lois Pierson Durant, who had been born in St. Paul, Maryland, on January 7, 1890. They were living at 137 Edgewood Street, Hartford, Connecticut, when their first-born child arrived on July 10, 1916—Richard Durant Cary, now better known as Dick Cary. There were four other children, a son William (Bill), and two daughters, and another boy who died in infancy. "Bill was a musician of sorts, he played trumpet, but never was as good as Dick."* (Bill died in 2003 and one daughter, Phyllis, in July 1955.)

The family home, listed in the 1920 Census, was at 70 Kenyon Street, Hartford. "It is in a nice area on a nice quiet street." By the time of the 1930 Census the house, valued at $18,000, was owned by Dick Cary's father, who was a dentist in general practice.

Cary family residence.

70 Kenyon Street, Hartford, Connecticut.

(Photo: September 2005 by Abel Tangarone)

*Unattributed quotations are identified in "Other Sources" beginning on page 464.

The children were shown as Richard D. Cary, son, aged 13, William B. Cary, son, aged 10, Lois E. Cary, daughter, age 7, Phyllis A. Cary, daughter, aged 3. Also resident were Lucy Durant, mother-in-law, age 74, and Stella Budzinski, servant, age 24.

> *Durant. That was my mother's maiden name. She was a good pianist and she taught. She had ambitions to be a professional, until she got married and had five children. I was the first and she took it all out on me: started me at the age of four and desperately wanted me to be a concert violinist. I had to practice all during my childhood, two hours a day on the violin and one hour a day on the piano. I never could get out of it, even for baseball tryouts. She sent me to the best violin teacher in Hartford, Harold Berkely, a very good violinist himself. He was at the Hartford School of Music.*
>
> *There's a theory among a lot of parents these days that you shouldn't force the little dears to do anything. That's a lot of crap. My mother forced me for ten years and I fought all the way, but you've got to do it. There are very few people I know who were born with something. It's a matter of interest and concentration and being forced to practice. The lucky people are the ones who like it so much, the jazz players, that they do it by themselves.*

Dick Cary.

(Courtesy: Dick Cary Archive)

She didn't approve of jazz at all. There was never any jazz in the house but she was pianist for a local women's club and they started asking for popular songs, gradually. She hadn't any experience with that. The only time I played them was when I was in high school or when she was out of the house. I memorised all these things so I wouldn't have to bring any music home. So she started bringing song sheets home. She'd sit down and play them and then she'd say, "Now you play them." And I'd play them and she'd say, "Why does it sound so different when you play them?"

I can remember the first time that I ever improvised. It was when I was seven or eight years old, on a popular song of the day, in the key of G. One day at the piano I started to play this without any music and it was like some kind of a light being turned on. It was amazing.

My mother would have me give little recitals. The first time I got money I played for a bridge club somewhere. A friend of my mother gave me a dollar and I thought, "My, my, I did something I enjoyed and got a dollar for it!" I played in the Hartford Symphony when I was eleven years old. If you start at the age of four then you have seven good years of practice in back of you.

An incomplete, unidentified and undated (though probably early 1928) newspaper clipping refers to "... Cary, 11.... in fine recital." It describes Richard Durant Cary, a student, giving an informal recital in his home on Tuesday afternoon for a group of invited guests:

L-R: Dick, Albert Ely Cary (Father), Bill and Lois   *(Courtesy: Dick Cary Archive)*

The young musician, who is not quite 12 years old, gave a varied program on both violin and piano. The opening number was a Handel Sonata for violin and piano in four movements with Richard at the violin and Mrs. Cary at the piano. The boy then gave a group of five piano numbers, Handel's Gigue *and* Sarabande, *MacDowell's* From an Indian Lodge *and two numbers by Debussy,* Little Shepherd *and* Dr. Gradus ad Parnassum. *As his concluding piano number, the* 26th Air Varie *by De Bériot was chosen.*

Cary continued:
There were three enormous high schools in Hartford, four, five thousand kids in each, awful big schools—Buckley, Weaver and Hartford. [Cary was in Hartford.] Each had a senior orchestra and from each orchestra they picked the "Inter-High Orchestra," which was the best players from the three and I was the first violinist.

Our first year we entered and won—there wasn't anyone near us—the New England contest in Pawtucket,

L-R: Dick Cary, Bill Cary and Lois Cary.
(Courtesy: Dick Cary Archive)

(Courtesy: Dick Cary Archive)

Rhode Island. We played the Cesar Franck Symphony and Finlandia by Sibelius and a couple of other things.

I didn't graduate high school, because I didn't get along in high school very well. I flunked out my second year, so they sent me away to prep school in the early 1930s for three years. Got a chance to play baseball and all the sports. [I] graduated in 1934 and then I went to college, Wesleyan University in Middletown, Connecticut. There were so few people of any artistic ability in that college. They were all future insurance people!

His mother, Lois Cary, died on July 15, 1930.

If my mother had lived she would have sent me to Juilliard and I would have had a wholly different path. When I was fourteen my mother died and I gave up the violin, because it had been a constant struggle to make me practice. I appreciate it now but at the time it was difficult to do. I still have the fiddle but it stays in the case! My father didn't think being a musician was anything worthwhile, so he made me go to college. I'm not saying I wasted four years at Wesleyan, but it was pretty much of a waste because I didn't care for most of the people there.

Cary began writing a diary in 1931, a routine he was to follow with varying degrees of determination for the next sixty years. Early entries for 1931 refer to the playing of two solos, two consecutive weeks, during a recital at the Hartford School of Music. In September of 1931 he entered Tabor Academy in Marion, Massachusetts, about 12 miles from New Bedford, where he was to remain for three years, studying, playing sports (he was in the baseball squad), listening to the radio (Mills Brothers, Boswell Sisters, Ted Weems, the Casa Loma Orchestra), singing in the glee club and playing. Tabor students wore sailor suits, studied navigation and learned to sail. To his wife, Jessie, he said: "It was a good place to go to school. The first year was rough for certain reasons, but the second and third were fine." To quote his diary for October 20, "Had first meeting of orchestra. Lousy. I play piano" and on January 17, 1932, "I'm kicked out of the jazz orch." No reason is given, though he was soon back as a violinist when the band went to New York to play a night at somewhere called Hoyt's—"I also had a couple too many champagnes." The following month the orchestra played a club at Boston University.

College restarted in September. Events deemed worthy of mention included playing trombone in the band for at least one football game, and working again with the jazz orchestra. An entry on December 9 states: "Jazz orchestra's first rehearsal tonight—it went pretty well—much better than last year." It would appear that this group was proficient, though one is left wondering about the jazz content.

1933 continued in the same routine until Cary graduated ("satisfactorily completed course of study," achieving excellent results in English, Latin, French, Solid Geometry, Trigonometry and Seamanship) from Tabor in June 1934. He entered Wesleyan University in Middletown, Connecticut, on September 13. Musical activities that fall, mentioned in his diary, include hitching to Hartford to hear Duke Ellington; hearing the Mal Hallett orchestra at Travellers; playing *Sweet and Slow* on piano for a WTIC amateur show; sitting in with Johnny Green's orchestra; practising in a flute trio; and travelling to New York with the glee club to appear on WTZ in Radio City and on WOTL. Towards the end of 1935 he found more and more work as a musician:

October 31:   Got $5 playing at Yacht Club with 5-piece job. I hope there are many more of these.
November 6:   Played at Falcon House for two bucks.
November 23:   Serenaders at Meriden Community Hall —good job.
December 13:   Job at Edgwood Club—only 8 pieces tonight.
December 26:   Played (5 piece) at Bond for Jewish dance.

On December 27, 1935, he rehearsed with a band which was booked for a New Year's trip to Bermuda. Two days later he boarded the SS N.Y. in New York and, to quote his diary: "Played afternoon and evening—beer. Lousy storm—was very sick after finishing." He was poorly all the following day and illness no doubt explains his reference to "3 piece band instead of 7." They arrived in Bermuda on the 31st and, after a spell ashore, they "played two hours in the evening. A Mr. Brown bought us all champagne. Much merriment." On New Year's Day he "played in afternoon and evening till my digits almost dropped. Up drinking with Beeb till 5:30." The ship docked back in New York about 10 a.m. on January 2nd and Cary concluded his adventure by going to see Glen Gray and his Orchestra at the Paramount Theatre.

When asked about his influences at the piano Cary always spoke of Fats Waller, Earl Hines, Teddy Wilson, Art Tatum and Bob Zurke, though stylistically it is evident that it was Teddy Wilson who had the greatest affect on the young pianist.

Cary said:

I got a lot from Fats Waller. I used to memorise his solos. When I was a kid I used to copy Teddy Wilson's solos off and learn them. I liked Bob Zurke very much when I was young. He was a good friend of mine. Anytime the Bob Crosby band was in New England I'd go and see them. I used to bring him a jug, because in Connecticut you couldn't buy one on Sundays, so he was always glad to see me.

Art Tatum influenced everybody, except NOBODY can play like him.

When I went to college there was a fantastic piano player who lived in Middletown named Jack O'Brien [b. 1906]. He was a very close friend of Dave Tough and Bud Freeman's. They went all over Europe, but mostly France, they lived there. Every Sunday while I was in college people would pick me up and we'd go try to find Jack someplace.

The point was to get him to the piano, because once you got him there it was marvellous. I'd always start playing and after a few minutes I'd hear, "For Chrisake, Cary, get the hell out of there!" He was very profane, a very outspoken, immensely bright, brilliant man. One of the most unusual persons I've ever met in my life. He got offers all the time but he'd never leave Middletown, Connecticut.

He was a big fan of Willie "The Lion" Smith. He could play The Lion's pieces better than The Lion could. There's a piece The Lion wrote called Love Remembers. *I'd never heard anybody play it except Jack. It's a very difficult piece and it has about five parts to it. I know it, very sloppily. Jack could play the hell out of those things. Not only that, he studied Bach a couple of years with the man who was the father of the man in charge of our glee club at Wesleyan. Old man Daltry was the conductor, an old man from England. So [Jack's] playing was all counterpoint. His left hand would be playing lines the same as the right hand, but interweaving them. It was like composition. I had the band, after the first year. I played in the local saloons and I had the college orchestra. I found I could make five dollars in the saloons, playing piano.*

We had a dance orchestra called the Wesleyan Serenaders and something very interesting happened to us when I was a sophomore. I think it was 1936. The Camel Caravan was Benny Goodman's first big radio programme. The second year they decided to put a gimmick in it, a college

> glee club. They sent John Hammond as the intermediary and he came to Wesleyan to make the arrangements. He didn't want to hear the glee club because that was all cut-and-dried. He wanted to hear our orchestra and he put three of us on the show — the trumpet player, John Griffin, our tenor player and myself. The tenor man and the trumpet player played with the Goodman Trio. I didn't play. They [the Benny Goodman orchestra] played an arrangement of mine, Exactly Like You. That was a big thrill for me.
>
> It had an introduction which sounded more like Jimmy Dorsey and I told John Hammond, "You won't like the introduction because it doesn't sound like Benny Goodman." He heard it and he said, "You're right! Change the introduction."

A non-vocal version of *Exactly Like You* was played by the Benny Goodman orchestra on a December 29, 1936, broadcast and this is probably the Dick Cary arrangement. Cary recalls the arrangement being introduced on the air as his. What does not fit is the fact that an augmented trio version of *I Can't Give You Anything But Love* is listed with Ziggy Elman, trumpet, and Vido Musso, tenor, as the added players. Perhaps Cary's memory is at fault or the listing is wrong, there being no known aircheck to verify it. At this time the show was the "Camel Caravan: The Jack Oakie College of Musical Knowledge," with Goodman providing four musical numbers.

That Cary's stay in New York was during the last week of December 1936 is confirmed by the fact that Count Basie's first engagement at the Roseland Ballroom was from December 24, 1936, to January 20, 1937, with Woody Herman as one of the bands playing opposite, both of whom Cary recalls seeing:

> Another thing that happened in New York; it was the first year he [John Hammond] got Count Basie to play the Roseland Ballroom and the band on the opposite stage was the old Isham Jones band, which Woody Herman had taken over.
>
> It was still being fronted by Nick Hupfer, a very good fiddle player.
>
> Allan Reuss, the guitar player, came over to me during the rehearsal and said, "There's one thing you have to learn. You gotta write all the chords that the saxophones are playing for the guitar." I took that as gospel truth at the time. A star telling me this and I found out later he was lying! You believe all these things when you are young. The guys in the band

were very, very pleasant to me, all except one. We went over to 52nd Street one night, with John Hammond, and Ziggy Elman was very rude to me.

    I spent a whole week in New York with John Hammond and he took me all over the place. I had already learned Teddy Wilson's piano solos by memory, I knew a lot of them, and I got to see him.

    We were going to stay in New York for a couple of days after the broadcast and then go back home. A friend who was in CBS had a chance to get us on the Saturday Night Swing Program with Bunny Berigan and I was all excited about that. We were supposed to meet him at CBS at eleven in the morning. I couldn't get these guys up! I got so goddamn mad at them. We got down the street, were just about to get a cab and one of them said, "I'll go and have some breakfast!" With that I got in the cab and went over to see Ted Wick, [and told him] "I can't get these guys over here!" So that fell through. I hated those two bastards.

All too soon the bright lights of Broadway were left behind: I went back to school, finished my education, graduated.

Dick Cary
1934—Prep School

(Courtesy:
Dick Cary Archive)

Cary had no formal training in the art of writing arrangements until after he left the army in 1946. Eddie Durham's chart of *Running a Temperature* for the Jimmy Lunceford orchestra was one of his favourite arrangements from 1936. Of his own arrangements from the 1930s, he told Floyd Levin:

> *I'd copy things off records. A good friend of mine, Bill Beebe, was a fine musician. He got me started in arranging in college. He was writing for a guy who was orchestrating for Andre Kostelanetz in New York.*

Or as he told Scott Ellsworth:

> *I started by copying arrangements off records. We had all the Benny Goodman, Fletcher Henderson arrangements in our college band, so I knew that style fairly well.*
>
> *We had a pretty good band in Connecticut when I was in college and I continued afterwards [after graduation]. We didn't have enough musicians in the college at that time. Our dance band had to call on about half the guys from the surrounding towns. So it continued after that and it was called the Carter Brothers. We had some pretty good kids in there. One was Conrad Gozzo, from New Britain, Connecticut, and he played with us when he was very young, 14, 15, 16 years old. He was asking me to write him high F's at that time. He loved that. Then he went with Tommy Reynolds.*
>
> *We had another kid, he was a wonderful trumpet player named Pete Brownlow [or Brownall?].*

Conrad Gozzo (1922–1964) is reported to have played with the Carter Brothers Orchestra, out of Meriden, Connecticut, in late 1938. He went on to become one of the great trumpet section men in the big bands and in the studios, working with Bob Chester, Claude Thornhill, Benny Goodman, Artie Shaw's Navy Band, and Woody Herman, among others.

Cary's father wanted him to study mathematics and he did later graduate from Wesleyan University with a degree in that subject. When Albert Cary died on August 4, 1937, Aunt Helen, Albert's sister, moved into the house to take care of the family.

The Archivist at Wesleyan University confirms that Cary, who was a member of Delta Tau Delta, "graduated with the class of 1938 as a math major and listed field (ie, marching) band as activities from his freshman and sophomore years. There is no mention in the archives of his being involved in any other Wesleyan musical groups, such as orchestra. Anything else he would have been involved with at Wesleyan may have been informal with other students or in the outside community. We do not have alumni brothers by the name of Carter who were at Wesleyan when he was. Perhaps their orchestra was a local or regional one." (Bachelor of Arts was granted to Cary on June 19, 1938.)

Years later Cary spoke of his envy of the older musicians, men such as Rex Stewart, who, to quote, "Missed their later schooling and instead spent their nights in joints and ballrooms, getting the invaluable playing experience necessary to be a stand-out jazz artist. How I wish I'd done that!" [Instead of] "wasting four years in college, living with a bunch of America's future business men and educators."

All through his school days Cary had nurtured his interest in sports. In his early teens he had helped two friends to build a clay tennis court, spending countless hours practising on it. He might even have tried for a career in baseball if he had not become overweight during one summer of drinking and eating while playing with various bands. For the rest of his life sport remained a major attraction, both participating and watching.

In his diary Cary lists leaders named Sage, Westman, Boynk and Corvo as men he worked for prior to moving to Albany. It is probable that these were short-term jobs or, perhaps, involved arranging only. He may also have played, in 1938, for Tommy Reynolds.

> [The Carter band] was good but there was no work around Connecticut. I played bass in a band for a while. There wasn't any other job. So I went to Albany in New York. I got a job in a saloon up there and we worked from nine [p.m.] to five every morning, seven nights a week. The joint was called The Frolics. In south Pearl Street. In those days there was a saloon on every corner. [The leader] was a drummer, Al something [Al Gordon]. It was just a band to play a show and play for dancing. My first wife was singing. I think my salary at that time was $23.50 a week for 56 hours. The tips were pretty good then. There was a big kitty and my wife made much better tips than I did. She'd get as much as fifty dollars sometimes for one song if a guy was loaded both ways. We had some guys come in and spend fifty dollar bills and get rid of a thousand dollars in one evening. It wasn't exceptional.

Cary's marriage to his first wife, Rose, had taken place on

either May 4th or August 24th, 1938, with the latter seeming more likely. Cary's diary gives both these dates for the anniversary. There was no wedding certificate in his effects to confirm details. The first of their two daughters, Judy, was born February 20, 1939. His comment in his diary ten years later was: "I was a drunken, wild, stupid and very immature college boy when Judy was conceived... we both agree that if it weren't for Miss J. we would have led different lives in much different directions."

On June 2nd, the move to Albany, New York, took place, with Cary working in Al Gordon's five-piece group alongside trumpeter John 'Tweet' Peterson, Stan Steveburg and Matt Fiorito. This was at a show bar called The Frolics ("the four brothers who ran that place couldn't reach the top of a Division Street gutter"). There were frequent changes of personnel and two newcomers were Dick Anderson and reedman Freddy Johnston, with whom Cary became especially friendly.

Some forty years later Cary was in a band playing a country club where singer Herb Jeffries came on to do his night club act. Jeffries described the singular way broads picked up folded bills and silver dollars, saying one got so good she could pick up quarters and give you 15¢ change. Which reminded Cary "of Big Charlie's and the Swing Club [sic] in Albany. I had an abrupt entrance into that life. First time away from Connecticut. Good experience."

About this time there was a short connection with Glenn Miller:

I came perilously close to working for Glenn Miller and I'm so glad I didn't. I spent a whole evening with him in 1939, when I was out of college, at the Glen Island Casino in New York. He wanted me to write something and told me his ideas about the way to voice the saxophones, the idea of something blue and something borrowed. So I did an arrangement of East of the Sun *and sent it in. Then that job in Albany came up and I disappeared. After I'd been in Albany a few months they said, "Glenn Miller was looking for you and was wondering where you went." So I guess he liked my arrangement.*

Cary has a note in his diary for May 5, 1940, that he was supposed to see Glenn Miller but the contact, Sal, did not turn up.

On October 1st, 1939, the Frolics closed and Cary moved to a bar called Skippy's, staying there for four months. Other members of the band included Red Ives ("fine alto") and Freddy Johnston.

("Freddy and I are trying to learn to play in all the keys and are playing tunes in A, E, B, and G. Probably doesn't sound too good but is fine practice.") Touring musicians would visit when in town and Cary mentions the bands of Larry Fink and Emery Deutsch. From the latter frequent sitters-in included Sam Levine, trombone, Clarence Willard (trumpeter for many years with Isham Jones and then Woody Herman) and "especially Rollo Laylan, a marvelous drummer and guy, now a grand friend of Rozee's and mine." Laylan played with Paul Whiteman and Eddie Condon, as well as leading a popular Dixieland band in Miami. Alto player Larry Molinelli was also in the Deutsch band. In his diary Cary notes: "Am doing a little work for Emery Deutsch, who is now at the Kenmore ... They played *Oh Johnny* on all broadcasts, which Rollo Laylan and I made in two hours one afternoon in Skippy's." Deutsch was a violinist whose orchestra's theme was *When a Gipsy Makes His Violin Cry!* Cary's arrangements also included *Stop It's Wonderful, Fit to be Tied* and *Blue World*. But back to Skippy's, where he was working long hours for low pay.

> These places were all run by hoods. They paid for elections and kept a certain family in power in Albany until Mr. Dewey got rid of them and changed the curfew. At that time bars were open 24 hours a day. Albany was quite a place in those days, but when Dewey removed the O'Connell family from Albany it became like other cities.
>
> After five we'd go out and play in a little place called the Bon-Ton Bar, for fun. We'd come home sometimes eleven [a.m.], twelve [noon]. It was wonderful. There were some wonderful black places like The Rhythm Club. Big Charlie's was a notorious place where a lot of unusual things took place. But the Rhythm Club—every Sunday morning, everybody in the vicinity would gather at six o'clock [a.m.] after they were through work. One weekend I heard Roy Eldridge was going to be there, so I ran as fast as I could from my job. I got the piano first and I stayed there for six hours with Roy. I don't know if either of us got off the stand (except for the can) and I've never heard trumpet playing like this before or since.
>
> I was fooling around with a lot of the instruments. God, I bought my first cornet for four bucks and my first clarinet for three dollars. Albert system, like Barney [Bigard] used to play. I bought a guitar for four dollars and I had a soprano sax for two or three dollars. You could go to hock shops and just pick all these things up. I fooled around with the cornet all this time.

I practiced trombone years ago one whole summer when I was in college. I played saxophone one summer and, of course, violin and bass and everything.

I left Albany with Art Mooney, who had all kinds of bands at that time. I went to the Benjamin Franklin, Philadelphia, with him. He had a so-called hotel band with a Hammond organ and a steel guitar; sounded like a cat-fight all night.

At the end of January 1940, Deutsch was replaced at the Kenmore by Art Mooney and his orchestra (3 brass, 3 tenor saxes, 4 rhythm including the Hammond organ and steel guitar) and Mooney began asking for arrangements. Among those Cary mentions are *To You Aloha, Gaucho Serenade* and Cary's own *Now's the Time*. When Mooney left after five weeks Cary was with him for the opening at the Benjamin Franklin Hotel in Philadelphia on March 6th. The band played 7 to 9 and 10 to 1 each evening, except Friday and Saturday when they finished at 2 a.m., and had three 15-minute broadcasts on local radio during the week, plus a Columbia network broadcast on Mondays 11.30 to midnight. It is not clear which instrument Cary played in the band, in addition to his arranging duties—trumpet or piano.

Cary soon had complaints to enter into his diary: "They've put the damn organ speakers next to my left ear and that's all I can hear." "I find I'm only to get $3 per score, but can do nothing about it." "*Starlit Hour* and *Wind and Rain in Her Hair* too 'jazzy' for the bastard, so must do over." "Copied and scored *Too Romantic* off [Everett] Hoagland record. Stinks but will be well liked." Despite these problems the wage was welcome, even when it was paid late. While still at Skippy's, on February 15th, Cary had noted in his diary, "We are absolutely broke now. $5 on rent is paid though and we're owed $11.60."

The band was paid on March 21, a day late, and Cary wrote: "$56.50 (4 for tax) + $10 for arranging. Amazing thing happened on job—Mooney gave notice to whole band." But two days later, "It developed tonight that Mooney … is not to give up music, but he swears he has no job yet after this one. He is trying to get rid of certain members." When the Benjamin Franklin engagement ended, on either April 5 or 6, the band drove to New York on the 7th for an audition in Nola Studios. This may have been for Decca Records.

While in New York Cary was unimpressed by the Bud Freeman Summa Cum Laude Orchestra's performance at the Brick Club, but thought that the Will Bradley Orchestra at the Famous Door was "really terrific."

After a few days in Middletown, Cary returned with Rose to New York and rejoined Mooney for a 10 day job at Santilla Gardens in Richmond, Virginia, commencing April 13. Of the first 9:30 to 1 a.m. session Cary wrote: "Good—rhythm separated from organ and very solid." On the 23rd Cary returned to New York "to wait orders," but he had already played his last job with Art Mooney and he soon returned to Middletown.

While there he saw pianist Jack O'Brien at the Mark Twain in Hartford—"as good as ever. I sat in several sets." He also heard the Bobby Byrne orchestra, commenting "[Byrne] is a remarkable trombonist and band is very good." While employed by Mooney, Cary bought several records, including three Commodores by Bobby Hackett—"latter are beautiful. *Embraceable You* is the prettiest thing I've ever heard. Spent all afternoon practising cornet and copying BH solos."

Cary's last pay cheque was for $23.50 ($35 less $8 advance and $3.50 tax) and before long he complained, "No work and money going." Movies and golf kept him occupied during the slow days, as it was not until the middle of May that he found a gig. Gradually, from then on, odd dates (a wedding; a school) came along, until two nights at a club called Friars, with Joe Richards and Johnny Ribera, turned into a four-nights-a-week booking. As well, at the beginning of June, leader Joe de Fazio agreed to buy 15 arrangements for $40.

After five weeks at Friars it was on to the Embassy Club in Leeds, playing piano in a six-piece show band, which included, at various times, Bob Quinn, trumpet, Ray Ostman, Eddie Stivola, Freddy Johnston, reeds, Lennie Oders, piano, and Johnny Vine or Bob Desbois, drums. Cary played piano initially, but perhaps switched to other instruments when Oders joined. When Johnston was off sick for a few nights Cary played clarinet in his place. This engagement lasted from June 28 to September 14, with Cary becoming the leader on July 22. Each Friday they rehearsed a new show and each Friday Cary commented, "another stinker."

Cary tried to obtain $150 a week for the six men but had to compromise on $140—"I'll pay $20 to guys, get $26 myself and $14 tax to union." But from September 2 the band was down to four men, receiving a total of $75.00, though there were occasional tips. On the 1st Cary had noted: "Band sounds real good, just as we must stop."

Odd gigs followed and Cary's bank balance was improved by a cheque for $388 from his grandmother's estate. He noted: "I feel like a different person with a few dollars," and the following day put down a deposit on a car.

On September 30 he was in Windsor, New York, to start a week of rehearsals before opening October 7 with the Bill Tasillo band at The Wayside. Tasillo said the job would last until June, which was typical leader's wishful thinking. The band was Tasillo, trumpet, with two tenors (Ray Ostman was one) and the rhythm section, including Cary, piano and arranger, Henry Garcia, steel guitar, a bassist, and a drummer doubling vibes, with Lorraine Barre the vocalist. Cary thought Tasillo was a nice fellow. "I think I was getting three bucks an arrangement in those days—if I got it!"

Sunday was their day off and on October 20 Cary visited New York to hear Joe Marsala with Dave Tough at the Hickory House and Bobby Hackett ("best thing I've ever heard") at Nick's. The following day, before returning to Windsor, he went to Leed's Music to meet Lou Levy, Vic Schoen and Don Raye. A diary entry refers to "new song from Sy called *Yiddishe Blues* (for Andrews Sisters, we hope)," but this meeting with the singers' associates is not mentioned again. Neither is the comment, "Levy might get me with Abe Lyman!!"

The Tasillo job petered out early in November and on the 17th Cary started a job at the Brigham Hotel in Boston, playing trumpet in a five piece band, as well as piano for the singers in the show. The band included Joe Taylor, tenor, and Al Scully, drums and leader. There were five sets a night between 6:20 p.m. and about 1:00 a.m., including a show and dancing. Sometimes Cary also played afternoons, presumably as solo pianist. Then, on Saturday, December 7, the band was told it was their last night or, as Cary put it, "usually even non-union rats give some notice."

Cary, intrigued by Joe Taylor's stories of working on the boats travelling between Boston and New York and New York and Nassau, gained employment on the Boston to New York run starting December 23, $30 plus room and board. In between he found casual work, a few days with Duke Davis at the Ken Club, even playing cornet in a brass band, as well as writing arrangements for several now forgotten performers—Al Scully, Gertie Hayes, Jimmy Johnson, Ernie Bell and Harden Downing. But when the 23rd came there was a strike in progress and he was not wanted until the 26th, which gave him three days in Middletown with Rose and Judy—"Marvellous to be at home with Rose and the imp." At Boston docks on the 26th he was told they would sail on the 30th, but it appears that the strike continued, for he hitched and bussed his way home that same day.

As 1941 was ushered in Cary no doubt played *Auld Lang Syne* or, as he put it, "at midnite I was playing piano at the Concord Country Club—pretty nice job." A few days later he was offered work with Al Johns at the Biltmore Hotel in Providence, Rhode Island, starting January 13.

Johns led a large orchestra with three or four trumpets, three trombones, five saxophones, two or three violins, and rhythm, with Cary playing piano and sometimes violin. He was expected to provide three arrangements a week and he also refers to rehearsing Arthur Murray dance shows for Thursday and Saturday nights. The band played for shows and dancing, between 7:15 and 1:00 a.m., with regular broadcasts over station WEAN. Each show played for one or two weeks and Cary's first ("not a bad one") featured a magician, a singer and a contortionist, while the second starred a comedy team, a dog act and a singer. Later shows had dance acts, a performing seal, a rope-twirling tap-dancer, Swiss bell-ringers, and Dixie Dunbar and her Rhythmaires. All of show business was there.

Reactions to his arrangements were mixed. Referring to his first three offerings he wrote, "My three last week seemed to baffle everybody. I get rather disgusted at musicianship of many bandsmen I work with." But the following day he reported the three charts were "sounding better now," and later he commented that "*There Was a Little Girl* going over big." On the broadcast of February 19 he soloed on *I Hear a Rhapsody*, "my first yet."

By the end of March he could write, "I want to get on boats. I'm so disgusted after rehearsals these days. I dislike Johns' attitude ... and the general, bad musicianship of much of the band."

The first Sunday of his engagement Cary returned home to Middletown, but on the second he attended the afternoon session at the Crown Hotel, becoming a regular participant at these weekly affairs:

> *Every Sunday I'd go to the Crown Hotel and hear this jazz band and sit in. There were people like Bernie Billings [tenor saxophonist], Rico Vallese [cornet], who sounded a great deal like Hackett, and a guy named Johnny Tortolla, a clarinet player. They had arrangements that Brad Gowans had given them. When I first walked in that place one Sunday afternoon I heard this band playing* That Da-Da Strain *of Brad Gowans' and these guys were imitating Bobby Hackett, Pee Wee Russell and a little Bud Freeman, it sounded like a second-string band at Nick's. (I'd been to Nick's of course and heard Bobby Hackett.)*

Other guests when Cary visited the Beachcomber Room read like a who's who of the New York jazz scene. They included Bobby

Hackett, Hot Lips Page, Muggsy Spanier, Joe Bushkin, Buddy Rich, Max Kaminsky, Buzzy Drootin, Joe Sullivan ("bad"), Pee Wee Russell, Marty Marsala, Coleman Hawkins, and Sid Catlett. With Hawkins and Catlett "I played *Body and Soul* and *Sheik of Araby*." On Sunday, March 30th, he complained, "I didn't play at all today. Guess I'm not as good as three they had. Very discouraging." Despite this setback, playing with top musicians was good experience and a start to making his name known in such circles.

The Biltmore job finished April 12 but Cary scuffled in Providence for a little longer, playing four days with a quartet at the Moderne Theatre in Brockton—shows at 1:30, 5:15 and 9:00—under conductor Jay Riseman. "Stinking piano—if that's what it is." He experienced three "nightmare jobs on horrible piano" at the Balalaika Club in a trio, but one of two nights at the Valley Club he described as "marvellous." On the new novachord, after a few days of practice, he auditioned for a leader called Pratt, for whom he also wrote a few arrangements. Just before returning to Middletown he agreed to write thirteen scores for trumpeter Tommy Di Carlo, ex-Artie Shaw and Gene Krupa, who was forming a new band. The scores were written but it is not known if the Di Carlo venture got beyond the rehearsal stage.

It is unclear when the Cary family moved to New York. It may have been towards the end of April 1941 or perhaps a little later. Dick had to establish residence there for six months in order to qualify for membership in Local 802 of the American Federation of Musicians. What is unexplained is that he did not apply for his 802 card until July 14th.

Cary was home from the Providence venture for only two full days and he spent both evenings at the Higgins Inn listening to Jack O'Brien. Then it was off to New York on May 10, 1941, to fulfill his wish to play on the cruise ships, though working for the Alcoa Line soon showed that the grass is not always greener on the other side. (The Alcoa Line is mentioned in Cary's diary, not the Eastern Steamship as he later recalled.)

> *We had a place up in West 85th Street, my wife and kid, and my best friend, who I'd been working with in Albany, with his wife and kid. We had 1 1/2 rooms for six of us.*
>
> *It was a madhouse. So I got a job working for the Eastern Steamship Line for the Al Donahue office. He booked a lot of cruises. We'd go to Bermuda each time [but] every third trip we'd go down to the Virgin Islands and Trinidad. I played with a trio on the boat, violin, baritone saxophone and piano.*

Enough for a three-handed pinochle game every night.
These guys did a lot of smuggling at that time. Employees coming off the boats [weren't searched], so they'd bring all kinds of stuff back. At the rate of exchange they'd make a hundred percent down there and a hundred percent back here, so they didn't pay us a hell of a lot.

Al Donahue was a popular society band leader, though he did experiment with a swing band in the early 1940s. For a time he had one the largest agencies providing bands for hotels and steamship lines.

Cary's first trip lasted five days, sailing to Bermuda, and arriving back in New York on May 15. On the 17th he was away for two weeks, visiting Bermuda and then various ports in the Leeward and Windward Islands before returning to New York on May 30. The next day they set forth for an eleven day cruise, arriving back in the home port on June 11, before departing again at 5:15 p.m. on June 12. His final sailing, which ended on June 27, included stops at St. Thomas, Antigua, Trinidad, Grenada, St. Vincent, St. Dominica and St. Croix.

The playing conditions on board were not arduous. On Cary's first trip the band played a set for the sailing at 4:00 p.m. and the night session was from 9:30 to 12:15. The following day, a Sunday, he played hymns at 11:00 and the band worked two hours in the evening. In Bermuda he got badly sunburnt. (It was not unusual for Cary to suffer sunburn, which probably contributed to his health problems later in life.) Shortly after the cruise, which began on May 17, he wrote: "Then regular routine started again—one which I dislike very much. Horrible crowd of drunks, loud-mouthed, stupid bastards." And again, "What horrible monotony!! I hope I don't have to do this for long—it's awful." He came to hate the cruises, being away from everything, arranging at a standstill, the restrictions and rules—and the rough seas. "Cards—eat—sleep—read—or play" became the routine, with the card sessions often lasting until 4:00 or 5:00 a.m.

On June 11, after sitting-in with the band, he was offered a job at Cobb's Mill in Westport, Connecticut, but he couldn't find a substitute to take his place on the boat. Fortunately, when he returned on June 27 the vacancy was still open and he started that same night.

The personnel was Cary, trumpet, violin, tenor, Fred Williams, tenor, Carl Corelli, trombone, accordion, Irv Olton, piano, leader, Mike Storm, bass, Whitey Olton, drums. Cary wrote: "Band is pretty good. Agreeable group and I'm finally playing what I want," but after three days Irv called him aside to say his fiddle didn't satisfy and he was on two weeks notice. This seems to have been withdrawn after Cary put in some concentrated violin practice.

On August 8, Lenny Goldstein joined the band on alto saxophone and Cary was playing piano while Irv Olton was away ill. Four days later he could write: "I think that some of the jazz we played was pretty good." (Goldstein had played lead alto with Red Norvo and was a good friend of arranger Eddie Sauter. Cary noted "only 22 and teaches at Juillard.") This is how Cary remembered it many years later:

> *Finally this best friend of mine got a summer job in Westport, Connecticut, at a very snooty society place called Cobb's Mill Inn. He got me on it playing violin, saxophone and cornet. Mostly saxophone. We had three horns and were playing this soupy dance music. It was out in the country, right on a beautiful pond. We played on a porch at night with coloured lights and the swans in the pond.*
>
> *Right next door to us lived [the film stars] Tyrone Power and Annabella. They were renting a cottage next to ours, but I never saw them for a whole month. The shades were always down. As I remember, they gave him a cocktail party one afternoon and he showed up about an hour late, stayed about ten minutes and disappeared.*
>
> *We played there the whole summer. When the union guy would check on me [in New York], my wife would call me up right away. I'd take the next train in and be there [when he'd] come back to check on me. Then I'd get the next train back to Westport. I had to make a living [but] it was against the rules to work a steady job the first six months.*
>
> *After I got through with Westport, I came back to New York without a job and so I'd take anything. I was broke until I was in my forties. I had a lot of disappointments when I was young, naturally, but it is hard to believe I spent so many years financially broke, just living from day to day. But it didn't seem to worry me. I thought as long as there's someplace with a free lunch and a piano in it, I could go in and survive.*
>
> *We would go to the union three days a week, an enormous hall with all these guys waiting to get a call for a job. After that we'd go over to a place called Beefsteak Charley's on*

50th Street. They had a free lunch there and beer was a dime and a shot was fifteen, twenty cents. For a buck you could eat and drink, spend a nice afternoon with friends and smoke a joint in the men's room. There's nothing like that now.

On 52nd Street there were two blocks between 5th and 7th, they were all solid jazz places, except The Club 18. That was a comedy place and I played the regular piano player's night off every week. That was a wonderful experience. The main comedian was a marvellous old man named Jack White, very well-known then. Every time I'd come in—and he really didn't know me—he'd buy me a double at the start of the evening. He was such a gracious man. There were three other comedians and they just got up there and winged it. They didn't know what they were going to do, but there was never a dull moment, and woe be it to any lady who went to the lady's room during that!

I would go up to Harlem quite often to see either the Lion [Willie "The Lion" Smith] or Fats Waller or a wonderful boogie woogie piano player, Albert Ammons. [Willie "The Lion" Smith was] fascinating, very marvellous. He had the relief band at the Vanguard every Monday for Harry Lim. Every jazz player in New York would be there. I think the most important thing about him is the influence he had on Duke Ellington. Everything I hear Duke play on records in the 'twenties is derivative of The Lion. He [Ellington] came to New York in the 'twenties and I guess The Lion took him under his wing, more or less.

Just three days after he finished at Cobb's Mill Cary worked at Club 18 on September 4th, subbing for pianist Doug Wark. The following night he received a call at 11:20 p.m. to sub again and he notes that he played 1:45 to 2:45 a.m. for three bucks. This led to regular relief work on Monday nights, 9:00 p.m. to 3:00 a.m. for $12.

Other activities during September included an engagement at the 19th Hole in the Village, but this lasted only four days, as the boss wanted an "accordion double"; a trio date on the 6th at Leon and Eddie's, which he considered important; on the 13th he travelled to the Larchmont Lodge in Larchmont for an unsuccessful audition for Abe Levine; he finished copying *Sugar* for Muggsy Spanier; and he heard Art Tatum—"at last, only for one tune but !!!"

In October Cary received union permission to play in Brooklyn, at the 52nd Street Cafe. He was there from the 12th to the 19th ($4.80, working 9 to 3), but on the 16th, "Dewey informs me I'm fired. This is really something—not being good enough for the 52nd St. Cafe, Brooklyn." He watched a Pee Wee Erwin band rehearsal and was impressed by Deane Kincaide's arrangements; sat-in at the Howdy Club. There was a one nighter with drummer Danny Alvin at the Tough Club; and rehearsals, starting October 9, with the Charles Margulis orchestra. Of Margulis he commented, "bad saxes, bad arrangements," but he thought that trumpeter Carl Poole was a "nice chap, good ear, plays fine." At one rehearsal he met Jerry Jerome, tenor, Hank Wayland, bass, and Ralph Muzzillo, trumpet; Jerome was to prove a useful contact. At another Cary was impressed by trombonist Jack Satterfield and by Eddie Rosa who, he said, "plays very fine lead alto and clarinet and has good ideas."

Margulis liked an arrangement of *Jim* which he had asked Cary to write, so Dick was assigned part of *Hildur* [spelling?] to be scored. This was to be used on NBC's Chamber Music Society of Lower Basin Street broadcast on October 15. Cary also rehearsed with the Charles Paley orchestra, which appeared to have some connection with Margulis. But for all the many rehearsals, and the arrangements which Cary supplied, Margulis failed to find the work he was hoping for, despite an audition at the Roseland Ballroom on December 15.

Bandleaders were rarely quick to pay for arrangements and Margulis was no exception. In January 1942 Cary signed a union claim for $347, and on February 10 he was awarded $172. Some payments of $25 were noted, but it is not known if the balance was cleared.

During 1940 and 1941 Cary wrote over 130 arrangements for 20 or more bands and singers. These charts were a mixture of popular songs of the day (for example, *I Got It Bad, Yes, My Darling Daughter)* and standards *(Stardust, Night and Day).* There are two originals mentioned, one titled *Bar Fly* and the other *Tabs*. When Cary was in Windsor he had sat-in at a club called Tabs.

Towards the end of October Cary survived a boat trip to Boston, playing piano on the way out and trumpet for the return. In November there were odd dates at Club 18, the Nut Club and the Met Club, and he was paid for rehearsing singers Belle Sloan and Jerry Scott. On November 25 he started "officially" at the Nut Club, playing with clarinetist Bill Reinhardt, trumpeter George Stacey, tenor man Frank Horrington, and trombonist Frank Orchard, working there for just over two weeks. One night he tried vibes for the first time, commenting, "really enjoy them." Also he was a frequent sitter-in at Nick's, where the band was Wild Bill Davison, cornet, George Brunis, trombone, Pee Wee Russell, clarinet, Earl Murphy, bass, and Danny Alvin, drums, with Charlie Queener the regular pianist.

Domestically there were perhaps more downs than ups in his marriage. Musicians' working hours did not help with family life and Cary was absent for weeks at a time during the early months of 1941. Taken together with their money problems it is not surprising that Rose was not happy. Dick's diaries for this time contain few entries about his home life, mainly negative. For example:

July 21, 1941: "Rose very hard to get along with these days."

September 7, 1941: "Domestic trouble as usual lately— money big reason, I guess."

His grandmother's legacy of nearly $400 had helped, though two months after its receipt, in November 1940, he noted: "Drew $20 from bank, leaving $60 in." Income became more regular in January 1941, but from September he was scuffling again and by November 2nd his comment was: "Pretty near broke." On the 4th he received an overdue cheque for $30, so the following day he bought a topcoat for $25. One hopes that Rose was consulted on this! If she wasn't, she had forgiven him by mid-December when they went to the theatre together to see "Arsenic and Old Lace."

A trained musician from an early age, Cary was evidently an accomplished jazz player at this stage in his career, despite the fact that so much of his work had been with show and dance bands. Listening to records and the radio had been part of his education, as was informal tuition from a pianist like Jack O'Brien. No doubt there were jam sessions late at night when few customers remained in the clubs where he was playing and such events as the Beachcomber swing club sessions would have allowed him to compare his abilities with the best musicians. Nevertheless, very shortly, his talents were to be tested in one of the major jazz venues in New York City.

It was December 7, the day when Japan attacked Pearl Harbour, that Cary was asked to join the band at Nick's, starting on the 14th. One diary entry on December 10 suggests both his wish to take the offer and his reservations about accepting: "Guess I'll start Sunday. Maybe it's the right thing to do," and on December 13: "I start at Nick's tomorrow. Wonder what will come of it."

2. Nick's, Eddie Condon and Uncle Sam (1941–1946)

Nick Rongetti was a mediocre pianist who opened a bar in Greenwich Village in 1936. The following year he moved into new premises at West 10th Street and Seventh Avenue, "the home of Dixieland jazz and sizzling steaks." The bands for the opening engagement were led by trumpeters Bobby Hackett and Sharkey Bonano. Occasionally other regular bands would appear (Muggsy Spanier's Ragtime Band and Bud Freeman's Summa Cum Laude Orchestra had notable gigs there), but the usual arrangement was for an evolving personnel with one of the regulars acting as leader. Over the years these leaders included Miff Mole, Muggsy Spanier, Pee Wee Russell, Billy Butterfield, Yank Lawson, Pee Wee Erwin and Billy Maxted.

Guitarist Eddie Condon was an irregular regular at Nick's from the time it opened in 1937 until he moved into his own club in December, 1945. He probably spent as much time talking to customers as he did playing, so Rongetti would fire him on a routine basis and then reinstate him just as often. As Condon put it: "For the next eight years I was in and out of Nick's more often than the mailman. He fired me regularly ... and sent for me on schedule."

Wild Bill Davison replaced Marty Marsala, another trumpeter, as leader of the band in November 1941. It was with this group (Davison, trumpet, Brad Gowans, who had replaced George Brunis, valve-trombone, Pee Wee Russell, clarinet, Danny Alvin, drums) that Dick Cary found his first permanent work in New York City. Earl Murphy the bassist was also in the band but left a week or so after Cary joined.

Cary's first night at Nick's was Sunday, December 14, and it was not auspicious, as his diary entry indicates: "Entire group, except maybe Murphy, very drunk—loud, meaningless evening. Disliked it until proper nip." Fortunately things improved. Monday was their day off and of Tuesday he noted, "I enjoyed Nick's tonight." By the 22nd he could write: "Some wonderful sets—band is really sounding like a unit," while on Christmas Eve it was "One continuous ball all evening."

And a week later: "I've learned more in the last couple of weeks than I would in three months elsewhere. I understand why these guys like Pee Wee, Brad and Danny are really outstanding in their particular line. Davison is erratic but gets a wonderful ensemble beat as, of course, Pee Wee does. So glad Brunies left. Brad much more of a musician and much more agreeable to work with from all I've seen. My hands are going to get very strong— already have a couple of slight bone bruises from trying to keep up with Danny.

"What a year [1941] for getting started. Two weeks to go on my 802 card. Know many good guys now and have got as far as Nick's. Pee Wee tells me it won't be long now and we get along fine. He's really a good-hearted guy and really rates his reputation. All looks very encouraging. A year ago these events would have seemed unbelievable. But it still takes a little time to have people used to seeing you around; planting an impression in the very thin soil around here."

The reference to his 802 card is interesting as he has earlier noted receiving union dispensation to work anywhere without permission.

Three decades later Cary looked back on the circumstances which led to his employment at Nick's:

> I was out of work, only getting an occasional gig, and living on almost nothing. But still I'd go down to listen to Art Tatum or watch the Sunday afternoon sessions Milt Gabler organised in Jimmy Ryan's. There was a nice bar across the street called Reilly's where Eddie Condon hung out all the time. By hanging out there every Sunday I got to know Eddie and those other guys that way. They were very hard to get to know.
>
> Once in a while Joe Sullivan wouldn't show up and I'd get a chance to sit in. I became Joe Sullivan's substitute. He drank a great deal and wasn't always reliable. Some nights he just wouldn't show up on jobs and I'd work for him.

Joe Sullivan, of course, was not the only hard drinker in the Eddie Condon group of strolling players. In addition to Condon himself, the best known imbibers included Wild Bill Davison, Pee Wee Russell and, later, Billy Butterfield, Tony Parenti and Cliff Leeman.

Cary's views were:

> When we were young we were doing all the different things like smoking shit and drinking and whatever else. Luckily I came before the heroin stage. Thank God for that. I never tried coke, I never tried the hard things. I was very lucky I didn't.

But I drank as much as anybody, including Wild Bill and Eddie Condon and everybody else and we all survived a pretty long time. It was amazing how long Wild Bill survived! But I quit in time.

One gig which Joe Sullivan missed was remembered by Cary: *At that time Art Hodes had a jazz radio programme on the New York station, WNYC. We had met up at Reilly's Bar and took a cab from there. Everybody's got a jug and we're smoking shit on the way down. I didn't know Eddie very well and at one point I timorously asked him, "Eddie, what are we going to play?" He looked at me in amazement and said [sternly], "You'll find out when we get there!" I never asked him again. That was the way he'd lead things. He'd just get on the stand and call something off, never planned anything.*

But at Christmas in 1941 I got my first break ... a two week spell [at $35 a week] with Brad Gowans, Pee Wee Russell and Wild Bill Davison at Nick's. I went in on piano because Charlie Queener wanted to spend Christmas at home, but Queener never came back and I stayed until I was drafted in 1943.

Fifty years later, to *Jazz Forum*, Cary was less complimentary

Postcard of Nick's in Greenwich Village—1950. *(Derek Coller Collection)*

about Wild Bill, saying that his horn sounded like a woman screaming, and he was loath to take Queener's place for two weeks for that reason. He finally said "OK, but hurry back." Queener didn't and Cary said it was fun, especially when Gowans was there and "taught us all those great songs."

That job was the hardest I ever worked in my life. Bill could never remember the songs by name so I made out a special master sheet for him ... just the first bar of each tune with the title. It was all he needed. He's a really hard working guy. By some standards he may be a terrible musician but all these guys are specialists and must be judged that way.

We used to get together two or three afternoons a week to expand our repertoire. It was really hard work while that front line was there but it was a lot of fun. Pee Wee had only one piece of clothing, a beat-up tuxedo with frayed lapels. His afternoon wear differed from his evening wear only in the tie ... long during the day, when he wore one!

When I met him he [Pee Wee Russell] was down to rock-bottom. He hardly ate any more and his clothes hung on him. At that time we played at Nick's. Every night he got a hamburger and he needed almost a whole bottle of ketchup to gulp that thing down. A great ensemble musician, Pee Wee heard every note the other instruments played and filled the gaps.

When I first went into Nick's we played ten sets a night. Twenty on, twenty off, until four o'clock in the morning ... then they changed it to seven. When we were working every night, seven or eight hours a night, after a while you get pretty efficient and you all know what you're doing together. When it jells on the right thing and you're playing well, everybody at the same time, something happens. It's a feeling that I never got in anything else in my life. If that happens once in those seven hours, or maybe twice, it's wonderful. I can't explain what it is. Everything was flowing and it's the greatest thrill that I've ever had.

The best band in that two years was led by Brad Gowans, with Pee Wee Russell, Wild Bill Davison, Danny Alvin [Viniello] and me. No bass until the second year, so my left hand got damn strong for awhile. I played my night off for Harry Lim at The Village Vanguard, which he ran every Monday and [they] were marvellous nights, with so many New York musicians showing up each week. Before Lim started I played Mondays at Nick's, solo piano.

Brad Gowans was a marvellous, talented guy; very abrasive to some, but I love people like this. He taught us a lot, including Hackett, who worked with him in Boston. I was at Nick's for two years and he was there about three-quarters of that time. The other trombone was George Brunis. I loved working with Brad and I still use a lot of his phrases on the alto horn. He was a good athlete, and inventor, and had the most comprehensive memory of the Original Dixieland Jazz Band; knew everything each horn played. Brad played saxophone, trumpet, clarinet, before he stayed on the valve-trombone (in C), and invented the combination valve and slide trombone (the valide).

He got in the habit of playing fours with himself! He'd take four on the slide and four on the valves. Later on he had a couple of others made that were full-length. Bob Enevoldsen used to play one of those but not anymore. Nobody knows that Brad actually invented that, but he never got anything for it. He invented a lot of things. He invented a very scientific pinball machine one time and got a patent from the government for it. He was a remarkable guy and not enough has been known about him.

Brad Gowans could play [clarinet] like Larry Shields, too. He was a big student of the Original Dixieland Jazz Band and he knew every part they played by memory and he had them all written down. Nappy Lamare was with Gowans the day before he died; he said Brad had a big bonfire and burned all his music. He became kind of strange when he came out [to Los Angeles]. He came back to New York ... and he lived with me for a while and I had to kick him out. He was too nutty.

When he was at Nick's we had the most extensive repertoire of any jazz band I've ever been with, by far. With Brad, Condon and Hackett around, everyone knew the correct harmony to hundreds of pieces. Eddie Condon knew a hell of a lot more than some gave him credit for. I [came to know] Eddie very well. I worked on and off with him at Nick's and at his own club and made trips with him. He was a very interesting guy. We used to walk three blocks home after Nick's sometimes and take over an hour to make those three blocks. That's if he was drinking. If he was sober he wouldn't talk much. He would stop. He'd put a little pressure on your arm, then he'd adopt his regular stance and tell a story. You had to stay there and listen, but it was worth it.

The two years I was there Nick only wanted two people, it was either Brad Gowans or George Brunis. It was fun with Brad but a bore with Brunis, because he was kind of a knucklehead. When Brad was there, every once in a while Brunis would stick his head in the door and see how things were going. Brad had a habit of taking his loose tuning slide and putting it to his lips and making a raspberry at Brunis. Brunis would then disappear and about five minutes later he would sneak back in and have a beer, to see when Nick was going to have him back.

The partnership with Brad Gowans was short-lived, with the valve-trombonist leaving the club in February 1942. Cary said that when Gowans left the job became "just hard, unpleasant work." In "The Wildest One," Hal Willard says that Gowans had an argument with Pee Wee Russell; Nick Rongetti decided that Gowans was in the wrong and told Wild Bill to sack him. Davison refused, so he was fired as well. Davison and Gowans left together, going to Chicago for a time. When they returned Nick wanted them back, but only Davison went. Instead Gowans joined the big band then being formed by drummer Ray McKinley. Cary auditioned for the McKinley band, on saxophone, but without success.

Dick Cary and Pee Wee Russell.

Providence, R.I. 1940s

(Courtesy: Dick Cary Archive)

Bill Davison was replaced by Max Kaminsky and Brad Gowans by Frank Orchard, leading Cary to comment: "I really know now what a good guy Max is. I've heard a sample of his seldom heard best playing." and "Max is really marvellous on some ensembles." But on the other hand: "Disgusted with band—Pee Wee no leader, Orchard no leader," "Orchard very annoying at times" and "Band nothing like it was—not for me."

When Wild Bill Davison returned to Nick's, starting March 21, 1942, his contract was for $55 a week, with Pee Wee Russell, clarinet, Frank Orchard, trombone, Dick Cary, piano, and Danny Alvin, drums, receiving $40. There was an extra $10 for Cary when he worked his night off and a further $10 when he worked a Harry Lim session on Mondays at the Village Vanguard.

> Cary said:
> *I was broke until I was in my forties. When I worked at Nick's I think I finally saved a hundred dollars in the bank. You know what they paid at Nick's, thirty-five bucks a week. I just wanted to work. I just liked that life.*

It took a long time for the Carys' finances to stabilise. On January 13, 1942, he recorded the fact that "Rose had to pawn her wedding ring to pay doctor" [four injections for 15 bucks] and on the 15th, "Are we broke!" In April he was able to visit the pawnbroker to redeem his camera and Rose's watch, but in June he was writing "Now I'm broke again," modified to "Very happy days lately, though less dough than usual." (This last was probably a reference to Nick's being closed on Sundays during the summer.) On July 11 he notes that the "band is sore at so much being spent on decorating but not improving pay" and on the 12th refers to the "usual strenuous weekly argument with R. [Rose, no doubt] over dough."

Things were not perfect at home and there are `other diary references to this, including "Awful argument with Rose over nothing"; "Arguments growing serious and lasting longer"; and "One of our money arguments got me out of the house." With precarious finances and with Cary devoting so much time to music it was inevitable that his relationship with Rose would be under stress.

However musically there were some encouraging signs. He played a Sunday session at the Vanguard with Charlie Shavers, Ed Hall and Sid Catlett, but it was taking time to be accepted at Ryan's. He rehearsed with pick-up bands led by Frank Orchard and clarinetist Bill Reinhardt for possible off-night engagements. Sidney Bechet visited Nick's and, Cary reported, "complimented me." There were arrangements at $10 each to write for Enoch Light and there was talk about joining the Chico Marx orchestra which was being organised by Ben Pollack. Cary saw Marx and Pollack at Nola's rehearsal rooms on January 7, followed a few days later by an enigmatic note that on the 12th he was evicted from a Pollack rehearsal!

Late payments for arrangements continued to irk Cary: "I'm so disgusted now I feel like giving up arranging till I get with McKinley or someone. I'm going to laugh in these bastard's faces soon." A few days later McKinley left a message at Nick's, "but I didn't call back. It's going to complicate everything now I know."

Two more orchestras for which Cary wrote were led by trumpeter Lee Castle and guitarist Bobby Day. "I'm learning things and knowing people more every day. Must carefully consider my treatment of everyone. Glad to know Lee C., one of chosen few who know about Bud, Louis, etc." Adding, "Castle will give me $15 for 2 [arrangements]." On April 29 Cary heard the band at Roseland "murdering" his score for *Skylark*. If he said this to Castle it would explain why the leader later gave Cary the brush-off he mentions.

He was not impressed by the Day band, which began a run at the Arcadia Ballroom on April 16, though his version of *Summertime* drew a compliment from fellow-arranger George Handy, who also worked briefly with the band. (Handy was sacked shortly after spending over an hour rehearsing one arrangement. Cary commented, "Good but not worth an hour.") A Metronome review for June 1942 mentions "...some fine arranging by Edgar Sampson, Pat Inzintare and Dick Carey [sic] ...."

During this time Cary saw Nat 'King' Cole at Kelly's Stables, commenting "wonderful" and he also liked pianist Frank Signorelli. He went to the Arcadia Ballroom to see the Muggsy Spanier big band, which he considered a "waste of a buck. Band stunk. Muggsy not even on stand more than three or four tunes." At Nick's Rod Cless subbed on at least two occasions for Russell and Cary thought his playing was impressive. The programme for an Eddie Condon Town Hall concert on April 11 made a reference to Cless and the legendary Chicago clarinetist Frank Teschemacher. "Rod wondered what he should do to be like Teschemacher—I suggested long underwear and a jug of gin. Pee Wee enjoyed that."

Things were now going well at Nick's, with Davison and Russell in the band. On April 10 Cary wrote: "Had a wonderful night at Nick's and played as well as I ever have. Ernie Anderson down—Eddie [Condon] wants me at Town Hall in case any writing is necessary. I'm an awful sucker maybe and Eddie probably understands this. I don't mean this in a nasty way; I enjoy their company." George Brunis returned to the band at Nick's on the 16th—"Brunies [sic] very good, though really he should be in vaudeville. What a loud braggart at times. But if he can play as he does it's alright." The previous month Cary had written: "I'm doing about what I like and am in no hurry to advance until I learn more about playing and arranging." [On the advice of an astrologer Brunies had changed his name to Brunis.]

Of their sets on May 15 Cary wrote: "I'm sure I never played better ensemble—that's what I like anyway—the hell with solos—I don't like my solos—I enjoy accompanying the great guys—Brunis, Alvin, Russell, Davison—the finest four of their kind (Brad Gowans doesn't play slide)." Cary's praise for Danny Alvin ("the greatest I'll ever hear") is indeed surprising.

The routine after a day at home, usually spent writing, was for Cary to leave his apartment about 9 p.m., catch the 9:08 local at 86th Street, then the express at 72nd to the 14th, and walk from there to Nick's. At times Cary had been constrained to tune the old piano in Nick's, so May 26 was a special day with the arrival of a new piano—"and a pretty good one, action and tone much better." Just a week later he would write: "Working at Nick's so long makes me feel as if I was caught in quicksand and sinking deeper and deeper. It seems that any other piano player at Nick's has made a little dough in the last year. Not me." He had written to the singer Buddy Clark, who was seeking a pianist, and at the interview was told that the job was his "if present pianist is drafted. But I don't like dough. I find that the sucker gets about $30 less than scale ($87)."

Sitters-in at Nick's during Cary's tenure included the best of the New York musicians, men like Sidney Bechet ("marvelous"), Duke Ellington ("did beautiful job on Nick's piano"), Woody Herman, Billy Butterfield ("terrific"), Muggsy Spanier, Joe Rushton, Lou McGarity, Red Allen, Rex Stewart, Fats Waller ("always a sensation. Wish I had what he has" or "played a couple—what a show"), Bobby Sherwood, Sterling Bose, Mel Powell, Dave Bowman, Joe Bushkin, Bobby Hackett, Ben Pollack and even actress/singer Martha Raye and actor Pfc Dan Dailey. Cliff Jackson was the intermission pianist and once or twice Cary "got four pianos going for an intermission"—Cary, Jackson and Rongetti with, on one occasion, Mel Powell and Art Hodes on another. (Presumably Cary means 4 pianists on two pianos.)

During April he had met with Eddie Condon and learned

Eddie's composition *Wherever There's Love*, noting "Not too good though the idea has possibilities." He and Condon then went to music publishers Jack and Leo Robin but Jack Robin wouldn't listen to the tune. (With lyrics by Johnny DeVries, *Wherever There's Love* continues to be played and sung.) The following month he copied down another Condon/DeVries song, *Back in Arkansas.* "DeVries will take it to Sinatra tomorrow!" Later he played "DeVries song *G.I. Dream* for a guy at Dorsey Bros. Embassy Music." Early in 1943 there is a reference that Cary wrote a tune for DeVries called *Franklin and Winnie and Joe.* He also "wrote down music for DeVries' song *Rainbow in My Heart*—nice melody."

That summer Johnny DeVries began to put together a musical show to be called "Louder and Funnier" and he persuaded Cary to help him. Joe Bushkin was the main composer, with DeVries the lyricist. Between August and December Cary got four of the DeVries/Bushkin songs down on paper, composed a setting for a poem by Edwin Arlington Robinson (1869–1935) entitled *Richard Cory*, and rehearsed all five songs with singer Mary Lou Howard. On January 6, 1943, Cary accompanied Howard when she previewed the show songs at Helen and Herbert Asbury's home, with the John O'Haras, the George Fraziers, Min Pious, and Eddie Condon in the literary audience. Cary's comments include: "Saw John's sets," which presumably means they were shown sketches for same and "They still all like *Richard Cory*." The other songs included *Ain't Love a Mess, Tortured* and *New York a Nice Place*. DeVries hoped to sell the score to Sid Perelman but a presentation to him at Cheryl Crawford's apartment on January 10, 1943 raised only, in Cary's words, "stoney, mild approval." On March 5 Howard and Cary recorded *Ain't Love a Mess, New York a Nice Place, Used to You, Things I Know, Richard Cory* and *New Routine*, though whether the records were for audition purposes or just for DeVries' library is unstated. Cary's entry infers that the accompaniment was by Bobby Hackett, cornet, Carl Kress and Eddie Condon, guitars, with DeVries and Zutty Singleton also present. Cary played novachord on *Things*.

It was in July 1942 that Cary made his first commercial recording, as a member of clarinetist Joe Marsala's band on Decca records, recreating four early jazz tunes alongside such veterans as Max Kaminsky, trumpet, George Brunis, trombone, Carmen Mastren, guitar, Haig Stephens, bass, and Zutty Singleton, drums. Cary sounds quite at home, contributing satisfactory solos and accompaniments. At the rehearsal on July 2 he had "to do some writing and much figuring out of the trio parts," while at the actual date on the 6th, 1:30 to 5:15, "Rhythm seemed bad. Zutty certainly has played better—I only depend on drums. Mastren and Stephens good—but we never played together." Cary's remuneration was $28.80. Perhaps this session led to:

> About 1942 George Avakian gave me one vote in Esquire (I think) for being "promising."

Regarding the hard work at Nick's—ten sets a night—Cary said:

> The sets lasted only for twenty minutes, but it was always a hard twenty minutes. The room was noisy and there was no amplification; so we had to play loud. I used to bang away so hard that, one night, Eddie leaned across and said: "Cary, will you please stop pounding that anvil?!"

Cary was generally unhappy with the band at Nick's, during July, 1942, making such comments as: "Brunis doing odd stupid things now that he's leader"; "Brunis [has] become the most ridiculous, stubborn, disagreeable bastard yet. Chelsea [Quealey] stinks at times. I hate that type of lead. Rod out-of-tune"; "The sound of the band now by comparison is dull, colorless, blendless—no lead, not

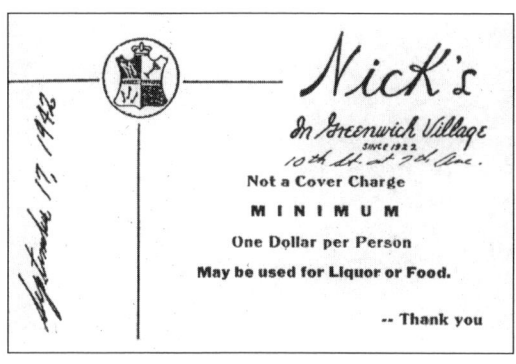

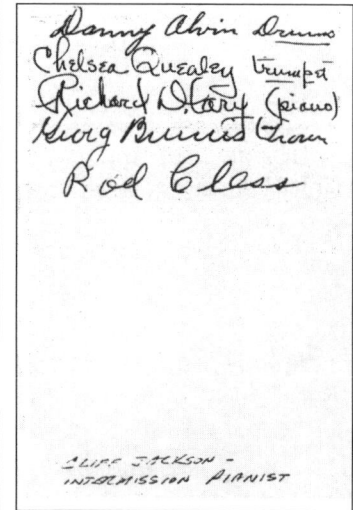

Above left: Table card from Nick's—17 September 1942.
Above: signed reverse of card.
(Art Pilkington collection)
Left: Chicago Jazzmen—1940s.

35 : 1942

the best intonation, no clarity. It's like working an entirely different job." But a month later he noted, "Chelsea and Rod improving steadily."

Other employment Cary mentions includes playing with a girl vocal trio, apparently managed by Arnie Freeman, Bud's brother. This meant rehearsals, making demo records and auditioning for G.A.C. and for Frederick Brothers. When the trio broadcast a few weeks later, with just clarinet (Jimmy Lytell), guitar and bass accompaniment, they were introduced as the Barrie Sisters. On August 8, 1942, Cary earned $11.60 playing a fashion show for Gimbels, with Joe Marsala and Eddie Condon. (At Christmas he was back in Gimbels with Condon and Pee Wee Russell.) There was the occasional private party and he wrote arrangements for Joe Marsala, Art Paulson, someone called Rhodis and began a long association with Charles Peterson, for whom he scored about 40 songs.

There were more moans in October. Rod Cless was ill and Garon Moore subbed for him on clarinet and tenor, but when Cless returned six days later Moore stayed on, playing, to quote Cary, "horrible" tenor. On November 11 Cary noted: "Garon Moore through tonight!! Hurray."

The complaints continued and in November he wrote: "Danny [Alvin] brought me down tonight by saying my tempos bad lately. He is under impression ... that he can't be wrong. I will admit I may be wrong 50% or more of the time, but not 100%. After all the shit I take and don't mention, it annoys me a great deal. Am in awful rut lately, listening to the trite C. Quealey, the exercise man. He has as little imagination as anyone." He also refers to George Brunis' "limited ways and repertoire."

It was in November that Cary bought himself a recording machine, apparently a Federal recorder, using 7-inch discs. Thereafter he made records both at Nick's and at home, as well as from the radio. Some of these records still exist but in unacceptable sound. On February 18 the Nick's band, less Brunis, who failed to appear, did a 30-minute broadcast over WNYC and Rose missed recording the first two of the four tunes played. Whether the purchase was the sign of a general improvement in the Cary's finances or was just an extravagance on Dick's part is uncertain.

"Finally," as Cary put it, he played one of Eddie Condon's Town Hall concerts. On December 5, 1942, there was a rehearsal at Nola's studio, followed by the concert at 5 p.m. His duties included backing Benny Morton's trombone feature on *Body and Soul* and working in a group with trumpeter Hot Lips Page.

With Christmas came a warning. He was home all day on the 25th with a very swollen throat, but staggered to Nick's on the 26th. At 2 a.m. he returned home. "Woke at 5:00 feeling as bad as I've ever felt—very scared ... my mind in an awful state and terrible nightmares." Despite this he was back at work as usual the next few days until, on the 31st, he suffered "another awful mental spell." He was in St. Vincent's Clinic for 90 minutes after being "taken ill for nervous spell, worst of three in last week. Doctor reassured me a lot and I passed rest of night easily, aided by M and M."

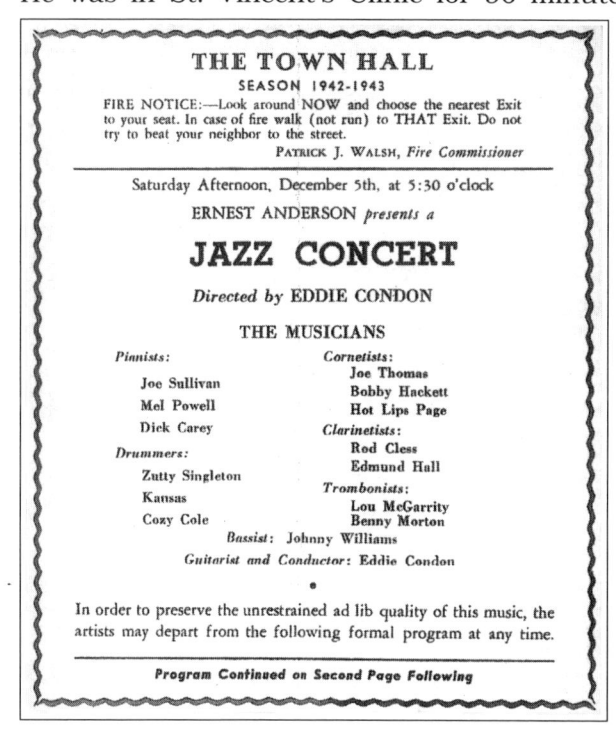

On January 10, 1943, he visited a doctor again and was told that physically he was OK but "nerves shot to pieces" and a change of job was suggested. This advice was ignored and Cary continued at Nick's for most of 1943. No reason for his "nervous spells" are given, but it is difficult to discount the probability that regular, heavy drinking was to blame. The evening of the 10th he was back at work at Nick's, noting "no mootah or whiskey, only beer."

It is not surprising that Cary's entry for January 30, 1943, is "January stunk." He writes: "If there's any truth at all to 'a bad start means a good finish' or 'a bad rehearsal means a good performance,' I should have a wonderful year. January stunk, for outside work [but] for my mental condition mostly. Nick's became unbearable at times. If someone had told me a couple of years ago that making 50 or 60 per, working at Nick's with Pee Wee and Brunis and living in a cozy joint on 13th Street could be disagreeable, I would have been sure they were crazy. It is a fine example of how little anyone knows about their own minds and adaptability of them. I don't know whether it's a good thing to be continually dissatisfied with position.

THE TOWN HALL
SEASON 1942-1943

FIRE NOTICE:—Look around NOW and choose the nearest Exit to your seat. In case of fire walk (not run) to THAT Exit. Do not try to beat your neighbor to the street.
PATRICK J. WALSH, *Fire Commissioner*

Saturday Afternoon, December 5th, at 5:30 o'clock

ERNEST ANDERSON *presents a*

JAZZ CONCERT

Directed by EDDIE CONDON

THE MUSICIANS

Pianists:
Joe Sullivan
Mel Powell
Dick Carey

Drummers:
Zutty Singleton
Kansas
Cozy Cole

Cornetists:
Joe Thomas
Bobby Hackett
Hot Lips Page

Clarinetists:
Rod Cless
Edmund Hall

Trombonists:
Lou McGarrity
Benny Morton

Bassist: Johnny Williams
Guitarist and Conductor: Eddie Condon

•

In order to preserve the unrestrained ad lib quality of this music, the artists may depart from the following formal program at any time.

Program Continued on Second Page Following

Rose and I both are to some extent. I know I should study arranging and make some money at it, but at the same time I hate the process of rehearsing a dozen half-wits when it's disagreeable to talk with them (with few exceptions)."

In January 1943 Pee Wee Russell returned to the band and late in February there were more changes. On the 25th Brad Gowans replaced George Brunis and two days later Eddie Condon was added on guitar, but Cary was still unhappy—"Somehow going to this joint gets more disagreeable every night, despite Pee Wee."

In February Cary wrote, "I can feel satisfied at 4:00 and come home not ready to die or to curse job and everything in general .... Wonder if I'll be playing, working in a factory or wearing a uniform, say, three months from now. I think it's the uncertainty that is making me so nervous or discouraged lately. It's a sad life when you know you could or should be making money and are not. Maybe I should be a Forest hotel type or a Hodes type. These are two extremes. I like both styles, the best of each, I mean, but can't be an extreme. So will I ever make much of self?"

Other diary entries from this period confirm the ups and downs of music-making at Nick's:

February 26: Very good night—Brad's a wonderful leader.

February 27: Brad got too drunk, bass too loud, Condon knows chords that Brad and I don't play, so there was conflict.

March 1: Much griping by Condon and Brad about rhythm dragging. Alvin has been let alone so long that he sulked part of night [over] couple of Brad's comments.

March 4: Bass player [Fowler Hayes] dragged as usual—makes one feel like not trying anymore. Condon amazing for his alertness to some things and his blind ignorance of others.

March 5: Condon drove me nuts—drunk, critical, dissatisfied, insulting and the most opinionated, stubborn bastard. Criticized my playing, how I beat my foot, how I lifted my fingers, "anvil touch," wrong chords, but after a few quick boilermakers I laughed it off. This is good training and it doesn't bother me too much. Brad has the problem. Rhythm is poor however.

March 7: Enjoyed job. Condon easier to take the more I get used to him. Brad is a wonderful fellow with a very enviable sense of humor. Pee Wee did a few things tonight no one could follow. My best thrill was getting attention on two choruses. Everyone on stand listened, even Ed, to O'Brien's *If You'll Just Say*. [Cary classifies himself as only a half-ass imitation of Jack O'Brien in Hartford.]

March 10: Not a very good night—rigor mortis seemed to set in.
March 17: Band sober tonight and sounded fine at times.
March 21: Music incidental to Condon's chatter tonight.
April 11: Felt good all night and played best horn on last set that I ever have, while Condon played piano in F.

Another complaint about Nick's was Cary going to the club when it was closed for piano practice, only for the chef to complain about the music because he had a headache. Despite this, Cary wrote: "Nick's has a certain hypnotic power over everyone, perhaps because it's only place that [this] type of jazz can be heard or played." One Monday night Cary sat-in when the Bobby Hackett band was playing and indulged himself—"No trombone so I played Brad's. Got along fine."

By April he writes of little prospect of leaving Nick's. "No big bands clamoring for R. Cary. Would like to get out of New York for summer but what is more important—health or music—can't have both. Piano is improving gradually and perhaps I had better stay and use Park Central pool and gym again this summer if nothing else happens. Am sure my arrangements will make some dough some day. No fear of draft for two or three months." Then [in one of his few entries about the war itself], "Newscasters talking of Germany trying to bargain with Russia, also of invasion of Europe soon. How long will this nightmare go on?"

During the year there were occasional war jobs, playing for Russian War Relief or for servicemen at Camp Kilner, the Valley Forge Military base, the Merchant Marine Canteen or the Brewster airplane factory. He also played what he called "lull" (ie, intermission) piano on some of the Monday off-nites at Nick's.

There is a dramatic entry in the diary for Friday, May 21, 1943: "This is a horrible nightmare of a day. Awakened at 11.00 by Judy announcing two male visitors. In they came ... asked for some moo. After I refused, informed me I was arrested ... we went downtown, photographed, printed, questioned by several men." Rose arranged bail and Cary was home by 4:30, "very shaken, as if in a bad dream." Cary infers that he was with someone who bought "shit" from a dealer who had an agent with him. After initially pleading "not guilty," Cary later changed his plea to "guilty," receiving a three-month suspended sentence and a year's probation.

Pee Wee Russell spent the last week of May 1943 in St. Vincent's hospital. Clarinetists who subbed for him included Al Klink (ex-Glenn Miller), Slats Long and Joe Dixon (ex-Tommy Dorsey, with Fred Waring). Cary noted: "Klink best tone, good technique and a bit stereotyped; Dixon amazingly fast and interesting, good to accompany; Long the best experienced in jazz of our type, much like Noone at times. All agreeable to work with. Klink plays Brad's [Larry] Shields' clarinet parts the best and so pleases Brad most."

On May 7 the picture magazine *Life* appeared, containing a photograph of Nick Rongetti with the band. The month also featured Cary, with a dozen other musicians, in two concerts promoted by the pianist Sammy Price, the 15th in Philadelphia and the 17th in Washington.

An uncredited, undated newspaper clipping, from around this period, and illustrated in Eddie Condon's Scrapbook of Jazz, states: "Nick's, at Seventh Avenue and 10 Street in Greenwich Village, is still smoky, crowded and wonderful. The band, which is led by valve trombonist Brad Gowans, has Pee Wee Russell, playing better than he has in ages, on clarinet, Eddie Condon on guitar, Chelsea Quealey on trumpet, Danny Alvin on drums and Dick Carey (sic) on piano. Night in, night out, it seems to me the most satisfying band working in Manhattan at the moment. Beer costs 20 cents, the

Brad Gowans and Dick Cary—1940s   *(Courtesy: Dick Cary Archive)*

musicians fear nobody (especially Nick) and the whole atmosphere is conducive to the right jazz."

Bassist Warren Vache, Sr. never had the opportunity to play with Dick Cary, but he recalled one particular conversation. "On a visit to Nick's in Greenwich Village I found him sitting at a little table next to the bandstand scribbling on manuscript paper, completely oblivious of the sounds being pounded in his ears by the relief band. When I expressed wonder, he told me the noise didn't bother him, but he had promised Billy Maxted, who had a band at a spot in Westchester with a radio wire, that he would have an arrangement ready for the next broadcast. 'But how can you write without a piano and with all that noise going on?' I asked. Without a pause in his writing, he shrugged and said, 'No problem.'"

Jimmy Johnson, who had played bass with Cary in Albany, was working with the Will Osborne orchestra (this was June, 1943) and said he would try to get Cary a job with Osborne. After hearing the band at the Pennsylvania Hotel Cary wrote: "Pretty good band, arrangements good. Osborne a bit of an asshole, I couldn't enjoy working for him; knows very little music." But he did contribute at least one arrangement, *Judy*, for which he received $30.00, and this sum earned ten exclamation marks in Cary's diary.

On July 27 Davison and Alvin left Nick's, with Quealey returning and the old O.D.J.B. drummer Tony Sbarbaro joining. Cary was ambivalent about the latter. Of opening night he wrote: "Sbarbaro a wonderful drummer—delicate and rhythmical. Morris Rayman good bassist." A week later: "Sbarbaro seems to drag at times, maybe because our uptown bassist is playing ahead of him."

Towards the end of 1943 Brad Gowans was involved in another project:

> *Wild Bill and I were supposed to go on a tour with Brad Gowans with the Katherine Dunham Dancers. She used to come down to Nick's. We had a lot of dancers who used to come down there. We had dancing in Nick's in those days and we liked to play for dancing. I liked it much better than just playing for people who are sitting on their hands. Professional dancers from the Paramount Theatre would come down to practice. They said it was the best dance music in town. And it was. It was swinging music. My God, here's guys working together seven nights a week, it ought to be pretty good.*

In actual fact, Wild Bill Davison did work with Katherine Dunham for a few weeks prior to entering the army, but Cary seems to have missed out. The Gowans band, with the leader playing clarinet, performed two numbers in Miss Dunham's show on Broadway in the style of the Original Dixieland Jazz Band. Two founder members of the O.D.J.B. were present, Eddie Edwards on trombone and Tony Sbarbaro (Spargo) on drums.

During the months at Nick's a number of alternative jobs were talked about. Cary's attitude was that he would accept an offer from "any good big band, not necessarily a swing type." In June, 1942, Muggsy Spanier visited Nick's looking for a pianist to replace Charlie Queener, but Cary's reaction was, "Wouldn't join him even if I was asked." Then, in July, Milt Gabler put him in touch with Charlie Spivak's manager, Bill Downer, who visited Nick's to hear him. Cary noted that Downer and his companions "put me very ill-at-ease and heard wrong sets." They informed him, not surprisingly, that their band played a different style from Nick's. Despite this Cary was still hoping to hear from Spivak—it would be "fine to play with Dave Tough; Spivak's band as good as any right now." The last entry on this quotes Gabler: "Politics got relative in Spivak's band."

Milt Gabler, in January 1943, thought he might get Cary with Woody Herman, but the job did not materialise. At about the same time Bobby Hackett recommended Cary to Louis Prima and a 5 p.m. appointment was arranged at the President Hotel. After fifty minutes Prima had not appeared so Cary left a note and departed. In February he wrote out his two weeks notice, possibly because George Brunis wanted him for his U.S.O. tour, but there is no further mention of this. In May Art Hodes said he would "steer a $100 per [week] Venuti job" in Cary's way and in July "Bill Davison convinced me I should put in notice and start with him at the Famous Door on the 27th. Think I will." He did hand in his notice, but Gowans persuaded him to withdraw it. The next month Cary noted: "Joe Carroll, new manager of Capitol Hotel, may hire me to provide music in new room he is planning."

In July came the opportunity to score for a major name in big bands:

> I finally got to write for Benny Goodman, background voices, dance music, in 1943 and that was the year I was drafted. He said, 'If you get deferred we'll talk about a contract and all that.' I can't remember [the arrangements]. All the ones for the nice, pretty little vocalist and I could never remember her name. [It was Carole Kaye.]
>
> [Goodman] wasn't too happy then, because that was a time when everybody was getting drafted. He had a hell

of a time getting a good band. The best band he had was about 1941, with Billy Butterfield. It was wonderful—Lou McGarity, Cutty Cutshall, Cootie Williams and Mel Powell and those guys. I loved Eddie Sauter's work better than anybody. Sauter was always my favourite jazz composer. It was marvellous to watch that band rehearse a Sauter thing. I learned a lot in one afternoon. I took an arrangement up to the Astor Roof, I think it was. I didn't get to hear my arrangement because they spent three hours on one ballad that Sauter wrote, In the Blue of the Evening. The first hour sounded like a big mess, a big jumble, and I think most leaders would have said, "Get out of here with that thing," but Benny spent three hours on that and it was a masterpiece. Of course, it was very difficult and they could never use it.

During a Danny Kaye rehearsal for an hour and 25 minutes at the Paramount, I was sitting in the back behind the curtain with Benny. We did not speak a word and he just did finger exercises on his clarinet. Because I was very young I didn't dare to talk. Then he walked out on stage to play his final numbers. However, after that we [Cary, Goodman, his wife and Fred Goodman] played bridge in the dressing room and it was like nothing had happened before.

On the telephone he is very charming but seems to have trouble standing face to face with people and looking into their eyes. One time Benny came into Eddie Condon's and just said "Hi, Ed" and did not speak one further word. I don't know why he was that way. He was so very successful but very shy.

Carole Kaye and Ray Dorey were the two singers for whom Cary wrote arrangements, in addition to one which Goodman himself sang. There is just one arrangement by Cary in Yale University's Benny Goodman Archive. It is dated 1943 and is for the tune *You Better Give Me Lots of Loving, Honey*. Cary himself lists eight other titles. Four are known to have been broadcast, one of which, *Do Nothing Till You Hear From Me*, with a Goodman vocal, appeared on record. On July 12 he was given his first arrangement to write for Goodman and just ten days later he wrote: "Heard my *Thank Your Lucky Stars* on B.G. air tonight, one of biggest thrills of my musical life so far. I sounded good." In August Cary noted: "B.G. says he wishes to hire me steadily—will discuss after these two arrangements," but there is no further mention of this.

As well as his arrangements for Goodman, Cary also wrote at least five for Carmen Cavallaro's big band, which was playing at the Statler Hotel in Washington, though it is not certain that all were used.

After threatening to leave Nick's a number of times during the year, Cary finally did it, albeit briefly. He finished at the club on August 15th and, through the good offices of Milt Gabler, joined Glen Gray and his Casa Loma Orchestra on the 18th for $100 a week. Cary was recruited to replace pianist Joe "Horse" Hall, who had been with the band since 1927, but the signs indicated that Cary would be lucky to stay 16 weeks, much less 16 years. In the event it was just four weeks! Prior to joining he went to the Hotel Pennsylvania to collect his uniform where he "met most of band and was impressed—mostly unfavorably. These fellows look and sound very dull."

A week later he heard the band on the radio, commenting: "they may have some lovely pipes and the best hair-dresser in town, but where's the music. Uniforms are shabby and bad-fitting but I don't expect to do it long." (In fact he had already received an A1 classification from his local draft board in Windsor.) That same evening he visited Nick's, where Brad Gowans and Pee Wee Russell did a vocal blues in their last set:

>Pee Wee in a coma
>If he doesn't snap out of it
>We'll send him to the Casa Loma

Cary's comments on the Casa Loma after his first night were in a similar vein. "Bad arrangements, a puking tenor, wild, phoney trumpet, fair trombone, drums mediocre." After a break following the evening performance they played again from 10:30 p.m. to 1:30 a.m. Cary had a drink with Red Ogle, presumably the "fair" trombonist, and then the band rehearsed from 2 a.m. to 4:30 a.m., with Leonard Whitney doing most of the conducting. (Whitney was a saxophonist and arranger.)

The band broadcast regularly on WOR and WABC. A few of the band members mentioned by Cary are John Owens, trumpet, George Jean, Red Ogle, trombones, Clarence Hutchenrider, Conn Humphreys, Ted McKay, Bunny Bardock, reeds, Herb Ellis, guitar, Stan Dennis, bass, Tony Briglia, drums, Eugenie Baird, vocalist, "and a lost piano player named Cary."

Things did not improve. On August 25 he noted: "Eugenie Baird and I went over some old tunes—she's alright and stupid. Bill Challis and Whitney rehearsed three arrangements and I enjoyed

Challis telling a couple of ass-holes off, including a sax guy named Ted McKay." On the 28th, "Just as dull for me as ever—band out-of-tune, no rhythm, horrible arrangements, some of them." Two days later he stated: "Glen Gray said 'Just oom-pah' tonight and that's the last straw—I go." But a hangover meant that he missed two sets the following day and Gray gave him notice. That evening he visited Nick's and got his old job back, so he finished with the Casa Loma on September 14th and was back at Nick's the following night. His replacement with Gray was Lou Carter.

While working his notice with the Casa Loma he wrote on September 6 about one of the off-night sessions at Nick's: "Played a hell of a set about 2:30. One tune lasted about a half-hour—unusual for Nick's and its bored, lazy, jazzboys—as I am most of the time." A week later he was again at Nick's, on piano—"Can't remember playing better than one tune" with band which included Bobby Hackett, Ray Conniff, Rufus Pepper, Bob Haggart and George Wettling. After work on September 8 he visited the Three Deuces—"Art Tatum amazing, astounding—clean, fast and interesting—kept me there until 4:00."

Work at Nick's continued as before, with its ups and its downs. On September 28, when Wild Bill Davison replaced Quealey: "Davison wonderful. Pee Wee claimed he was in terrible shape and as usual played ass off. Gowans unusually agreeable. He makes me most uncomfortable when he's not insulting me." On October 8 it was "another wonderful night," but on the 9th it was a "terrible band tonight; pretty drunk as a result."

Other occasional engagements included:

- September 27: played intermission piano at Nick's. "Brought Willie "The Lion" Smith from Vanguard to Nick's. Played with him after getting Hoagy Carmichael off the third piano."
- September 28: trio with Johnny Windhurst at Merchant Marine canteen.
- October 1: played Brewster airplane factory with Bobby Hackett, Vernon Brown, Pee Wee, Jerry Jerome.
- October 4: with Jerry Jerome, ts, Sandy Williams, tb, Al Lucas, b, Specs Powell, d, at The Hurricane.
- October 5: trio with Wild Bill Davison and Eddie Condon at Merchant Marine canteen.
- October 19: with Davison, Pee Wee Russell, Condon at Merchant Marine canteen.

October 23:   On Leonard Feather's Platterbrains radio show, with Condon, Milt Gabler, and critic George Frazier.

At times there were feelings of depression about his imminent induction. He commented in one entry: "My mental state is awful." With the draft in mind Cary wrote: "This winter, if all goes well, I'll be working 4 jobs—Nick's, defense, B.G. [arranging] and one programme for Harry Sosnick on the 'Beat the Band' show. I might make more than $200, but I won't plan this." A few days later he noted: "Dave Bowman has 'Beat the Band' show—curses. Sosnick critical of my score—changes and then??"

He also said, "The army will be well off if it doesn't get me." Almost certainly he was right, but the army didn't know that, and its ignorance ruined the rest of his plans.

Cary was inducted into the U.S. Army on October 28, 1943, reporting to Fort Dix, New Jersey.

It is unfortunate that Dick Cary did not keep a diary for 1944, so we have no direct comment on his initial reaction to becoming a soldier, how he fared in basic training or felt about army discipline. Reaching Fort Dix he spent, reason unknown, four weeks in hospital and on the day he got out Wild Bill Davison arrived. As Cary told Ken Gallacher, "The usual procedure at Fort Dix was to process and send us along in about a week or less. But the New York columnist Hy Gardner was Lt. of special services and he was quite impressed with a jazz band Wild Bill and I put together. He kept cancelling our orders to leave and we stayed until after the New Year's Eve officers' club dance. Then Bill and I went our respective ways."

He also recalled an occasion when Davison was assigned to play 'retreat.' "I never heard a rendition of 'retreat' like that in my life. They never let him play it again."

> *I went to a Glenn Miller unit at Fort Slocum, New York, very briefly, then I ended up at Camp Shanks, 20 miles north of N.Y.C. on the west side of the Hudson River. This was the largest embarkation camp in the U.S. and our 28-piece band played the guys off on the N.Y.C. piers, as they loaded 24,000 men on the Queen Elizabeth like cattle. This picture made me physically sick my first job, but we got used to it. We gave a spirited send-off to the troops being shipped to Europe.*
>
> *I played trumpet in the 28 piece band. I'd fooled*

around with the old cornet but playing in the army for two years gave me a lip I'd never had before. I also started to play my peck horn at this time. The alto horn was assigned to a brilliant French horn player who'd been with the Philadelphia Symphony Orchestra, but he refused to play it. In fact, he threatened to throw it in the Hudson River, but I persuaded him to let me borrow it. From then on I guess I just sort of took to the instrument. It's an army instrument and I still use my army horn. It's gone somewhat out of tune now and has to be lipped up or down, but it's such an easy blowing horn. It went through two world wars without getting a dent in it and it took Lufthansa Airlines to damage it!

Cary also told Ken Gallacher: "At Shanks were our own band, a Negro band and a special service show band led by Walter Gross. He'd been a conductor and pianist at CBS in N.Y.C. before the draft. We saw and worked with the colored band just once in my year there. Two fellows I knew in it were Jimmy Crawford and Sy Oliver [both ex-Jimmy Lunceford]. It was a tremendous post and they were housed miles away—talk about segregation."

The alto horn is the American term for a valved brass instrument pitched in E-flat below the cornet, like a small euphonium in shape. It is sometimes called an E-flat horn or a peck horn. It is equivalent to the English tenor horn and is intermediate in pitch between the cornet and the euphonium, though the tenor horn is in B-flat, along with the euphonium and the baritone horn.

The horn which Cary "rescued" from the army was, as he told *Jazz Forum*, "an old Reynolds. It's older than me, and I've been looking for another for over 40 years. The closest thing I've been able to find is a Czech horn called a Le Fleur ... and I found that in Stockholm, Sweden." To Ken Gallacher he confided: "I get the feeling sometimes that I'm a different person on each instrument and think the peck horn may be the best expression so far."

Eddie Condon referred to the alto horn as a valve bedpan, while Nick Fatool called it a raincatcher. Or to quote Dick Cary again:
It's an old rhythm instrument. The tuba does the "oom" and the peck horn does the "pah." That's all they ever wrote for it. They never wrote anything more than a quarter note. It really doesn't get the nice sound that the French horn has, but in some way it's easier to get around on it because it hasn't got those treacherous [rotary] valves. A French horn is really a life work.

> I was at Camp Shanks, near Nyack, New York, and I could hitchhike every day after duty. I'd take off my army cap and tie. Although I was in the army I spent every night in New York jamming at the Pied Piper with Max Kaminsky and his band, which included Willie "The Lion" Smith and Rod Cless. James P. Johnson played intermission piano on his own Steinway. Eddie Condon's became my home-away-from-home, or rather camp! I would ... stay at Eddie's apartment on weekends.
>
> Shanks, being the largest embarkation camp in the world, avoided any and all publicity. While there, a group I put together won a Major Bowes contest, with a sort of Spike Jones version of Farewell Blues and then they cancelled all radio performances by the group.
>
> Billy Butterfield was at ABC [American Broadcasting Company] and he had an excellent little jazz band with five horns and three rhythm, with Hank D'Amico [clarinet] and Vernon Brown [trombone] [and George Wettling, drums] and I did a whole library for him there. Then I took that library on the road with me and used it in the army for dances, playing Billy's parts ... That's when I got serious about the trumpet, in the army, [who] issued me with a beautiful Bach cornet, brand new.
>
> I was doing all the things that Eddie Condon needed every Saturday at Town Hall when I was in the army. I did every bit of writing that he needed. All Lee Wiley's things, Bobby Hackett's—anything that they needed, I did it. On rare occasions Bobby Hackett would make a very simple arrangement but the rest are mine, although Condon didn't need too many—mostly for vocals and some backgrounds for instrumental ballads.

The Eddie Condon Blue Network broadcasts are important in jazz history. These unsponsored, thirty minute radio programmes took place on Saturday afternoons starting at 1 p.m. Produced by Ernie Anderson, they featured the very best musicians appearing in New York at the time. Originally broadcast from the Town Hall and then from a studio in the Ritz Theatre, the shows ran for almost a year, from May 1944 to April 1945. Most of them were recorded by AFRS (the Armed Forces Radio Services) and 16-inch $33^1/3$rd transcriptions were sent to services radio stations overseas. Eleven volumes of this music have been released on the "Jazzology" label.

> **THE TOWN HALL.**
> SEASON 1943-1944
>
> FIRE NOTICE:—Look around NOW and choose the nearest Exit to your seat. In case of fire walk (not run) to THAT Exit. Do not try to beat your neighbor to the street.
> PATRICK WALSH, *Fire Commissioner*
>
> Saturday Afternoon, February 19th, at 5:30 o'clock
>
> ERNEST ANDERSON *presents a*
>
> # JAZZ CONCERT
>
> Directed by EDDIE CONDON
>
> A program note by Gilbert Seldes will be found on page 7
>
> THE MUSICIANS:
>
> PIANISTS: James P. Johnson, Gene Schroeder
> DRUMMERS: Cosy Cole, Joe Grosso, Sidney Catlett, George Wettling (and Dave Tough if we can find him.)
> CORNETISTS: Sterling Bose, Hot Lips Page, Dick Carey
> CLARINETISTS: Joe Marsala, Edmund Hall, PeeWee Russell
> TROMBONISTS: Wilbur De Paris, Benny Morton, Miff Mole
> BASSIST: Bob Casey
> GUITARIST AND CONDUCTOR: Eddie Condon
>
> *In order to preserve the unrestrained ad lib qualities of this music, the artists may depart from the following program at any time.*
>
> **Program Continued on Second Page Following**

Cary quickly fitted into the Eddie Condon routine. He is known to have appeared on at least three of Condon's Carnegie Hall concerts —on February 19, 1944, December 2, 1944, and January 20, 1945 — and was scheduled to appear on October 16, 1944. These, plus his work for the Eddie Condon Blue Network broadcasts, made him even better known in the New York jazz field.

In addition to sketching out backgrounds for the singers on the broadcasts, usually Lee Wiley or Red McKenzie, Cary also played trumpet on some numbers. For example, the closing *Impromptu Ensemble* on the November 4, 1944, broadcast features a powerful solo in the company of such men as Muggsy Spanier, Billy Butterfield and Lou McGarity. Cary is announced as arranger for the March 10, 1945, show, though by then he was stationed at Lake Placid.

Despite being a G.I., Cary's growing status on the New York jazz scene was confirmed by the gradual increase in his recording opportunities. During February 1944 he recorded with Joe Marsala again, for World Transcriptions, and in April there were three sessions with Muggsy Spanier for Commodore Records and for World Transcriptions. He did a solo piano session for the Black and White label in March, though only two of the four sides were issued. [Cary bought the 78 of *I Thought About You* and *You Took Advantage of Me* in March, 1947, and commented "Pretty awful, tired, monotonous, scared!" To this writer's ears these sound perfectly acceptable jazz solos—and Cary was competing with a score or two of fine pianists.] In January 1945, on the 19th, he recorded, again for Commodore, with Wild Bill Davison, though this was as a substitute for George Zack. As Cary said, "I think Zack was pretty fractured when he arrived and I was always available then ... so I made last three sides."

By the time Cary resumed his diary in 1945 the war with Germany was drawing to a close and American attention was being focused on the enemy in the east, Japan. As a result activity in Shanks was being reduced, as his first entry indicates: "January 1: Yesterday Azzolina and his 523rd AAF band left this camp for overseas. Up at 10:30 today, wakened by prowling prickish captain." After a large turkey dinner Cary was told to get the furnace going: "No axe around so gave up and listened to the radio." At 4:30 he caught the bus to New York, went to the cinema, then visited Nick's, noting: "Made 20 at Nick's and 20 from Ernie [Anderson] for Christmas Carnegie [concert]. I worked years on the piano and now appear only on the cornet."

He slept at Eddie Condon's, rose at noon and returned to camp. There he "hung around" until 4:00, then hitched a lift back to New York!

After another night spent at Condon's he returned early to Shanks and a very cold barracks. He practised to mid-afternoon, when he again hitched to New York, visiting Rickey's to see Billy Butterfield's Wednesday night band and sitting-in at Kelly's Stables, before returning to camp. Thursday the 4th he was up in time to eat at 11 a.m., and practised all afternoon. On Friday he was "awakened by a prowling, surly sergeant asking questions and criticizing condition of joint!" After more practice he left at 3 p.m. for a weekend in Middletown, though the atmosphere with Rose seems to have been frosty.

Another proof of his comment "I know I'm more harm than good in the army" is Tuesday, January 9th. He returned to camp at 8:30 a.m. after spending the night in New York, snatched about two hours sleep and at 3 p.m., after further practice, headed once more for N.Y.C. The following day he was back in Shanks at 6:30 a.m., rose for lunch, then set off for New York at 3 p.m. There he went to the theatre for a film and Lionel Hampton's "wild band," then subbed for pianist Marty Napoleon in Billy Butterfield's small group. He stayed at Butterfield's apartment "with no thought of returning to that horrible camp." He was AWOL on the 11th, visiting various bars and seeing the Willie "The Lion" Smith Trio and the James P. Johnson band (including Sidney and Wilbur DeParis, Franz Jackson, Israel Crosby) at the Pied Piper. He returned to Shanks to sleep and the following day noted, "Looks like I was not missed yesterday." He cut out just after noon for the weekend, attending the Eddie Condon NBC rehearsal in New York, then travelling to Middletown.

Cary spent both the Saturday and the Sunday evenings at a

local club, so perhaps it was not surprising that relations with his wife continued to be cool. (On February 28 he wrote: "I've never yet lost the feeling of anticipation when I'm to see Rose again, but on arrival the bubble breaks and only Judy seems glad to welcome me and treat me halfway decently.")

He was back in camp at 5:30 a.m. on Monday, sleeping in until 9 a.m. "No one to report to still, so got in town early afternoon." Similarly on Tuesday morning, he "found nothing doing" and returned to New York. He did not return to Shanks until Friday morning, where no one seemed concerned that he missed a roll-call or two, though he did discover that he was being transferred to Lake Placid. On Wednesday the 17th he had noted: "Didn't bother to go to camp today—good sleep but still those hangovers. The present situation at camp isn't as good as it sounds. Nothing to do there so it's unbearable hanging around, but when away I'm always wondering when I'll be called for something."

These activities came to an end shortly after the Davison recording session, when the army relocated him. On the 20th of January, 1945, Cary played piano for an Eddie Condon concert at Carnegie Hall; then, three days later, he arrived in Lake Placid, which he called a "redistribution center."

> *In 1945 the army sent me to Lake Placid for nine months— special services, playing and writing, and I ended up at Fort Devens near Boston in another army band. I didn't see Condon again until sometime in 1946 and by this time his club was established in the Village on 3rd Street.*

Lake Placid, in Essex County, New York State, provided entertainment for the troops resting there, with many musicians employed. For Cary most days centred on movies, sport and music. He was able to indulge his liking, depending on the weather, for baseball, basketball, skating, golf, tennis, riding and swimming, while his military duties consisted of playing trumpet with a big band for shows and dances, for both officers and enlisted men, writing arrangements and rehearsing them, and playing solo piano. There were also opportunities to sit-in, with the Marcy club frequently mentioned, and there was the occasional arranging comission, such as those used by Thelma Carpenter and Bud Freeman on their Majestic recordings. In addition there were other occasions when he played in the military band, on peck horn, in a hillbilly group at a horse show, "third cornet" in a Gay Nineties show and even fifth trumpet in the big band.

Cary had a telephone call from Ernie Anderson on August 31, 1945, asking if he would write four arrangements for a Majestic recording session by vocalist Thelma Carpenter with Bud Freeman's orchestra. He received the songs on September 2 and mailed the charts to Anderson by special delivery on September 4. Presumably they were considered satisfactory because three days later he was commissioned to do four for Bud Freeman. When Cary heard Carpenter's recording of *Foolish Things* and *Guy's Come Back* on the last day of the year, he commented: "They chopped off most of arrangement on first, using about 16 bars in all." The *Down Beat* reviewer (November 15, 1945) said: "..the band could have been stronger, trouble lies mainly with the average arrangements."

Relations with Rose continued to be fractious, except for a short time during 1945. On March 20 he refers to a "nice discussion with Rose" and it appears that she and Judy came to live in Lake Placid shortly afterwards. On April 18 he refers to Rose enjoying her stay and in June she was working 6 p.m. to 2:30 a.m. in Sam's diner.

Diary entries from June onwards are spasmodic. In one he refers to "usual routine—wrote, ate all day—played during evening from 9–12 at Copa Club." Others refer to typical army situations or highlight his seniors' opinion of Pfc Cary:

"Helped clear up joint for tomorrow's inspection. Worked trumpet relief on stage of theatre." "Played piano in tea room."

"Convinced the idiot Sergeant Stone that I should be able to write when and where I liked."

"Chief announced at roll call that he didn't want Cary on parade again."

"Colonel McGregor told me, 'I'm still in the army. I owe the government a good job.'"

"Retreat parade as ridiculous, childish, scoutish, idiotic as ever."

"What an assinine, stupid, sickening, childish, idiotic, moronic disagreeable class—about saluting and not calling corporals by their first name, but by rank, just because you may be jealous of their exalted position in this world. Get rid of every uniform in the world, cover them with miscarriage and burn!"

Another entry (August 27) indicates that for the past week or so Cary had been spending time moving stones and wheeling barrows of cement. No reason is given, but perhaps one of Cary's transgressions caught up with him?

42045443 Private First Class Dick Cary, circa 1944 *(Courtesy: Dick Cary Archive)*

On November 1, 1945, after nine months at Lake Placid, Cary was transferred to Fort Devens, Massachusetts, to play with the 320th Army Band. Again this involved, to quote, a "lot of hanging around," but proximity to Boston meant frequent trips into that city to hear and sit-in with old colleagues Brad Gowans and Pee Wee Russell who were playing in Max Kaminsky's band which had opened at the Copley Terrace Hotel in October. A few days later he played an afternoon session with a "good young trumpet, good ear," called Ruby—though his opinion of Ruby Braff was to change in later years.

Of his four months at the camp he comments, "usual routine of bed all day, beer in the evening" and "this existence is merely that. Jobs too short at night, days drag and make sleeping the only out." The army stated that he "played trumpet in military and dance bands. Played piano at United Service Organization Club and Service Clubs. Led dance band for four months using own orchestrations." One musician in the band for a time was altoist Toots Mondello and he did meet arranger Paul Villepigue (sometimes spelt Villepique, 1920–1953), reporting an "interesting talk. He will do well I think, will make up in mechanical ability what his ear lacks. He's the plugging, piano-pounding type of arranger."

There are several references to recording transcriptions, presumably with the 320th Army band, as shown in the discography. He mentions gigs at various services club, including the U.S.O. in Shirley (where he met trumpeter Lou Columbo, back from Japan), as well as dates at a hospital and at least two jobs playing bass, sitting-in "with a lousy band at a WAC club" and at an officers' club. Outside jobs included playing a jazz concert for promoter Bob Harrington in Middletown on December 3, alongside Wild Bill Davison, Albert Nicholas, Art Hodes, Danny Alvin, Joe Sullivan and Cow Cow Davenport, plus two paid appearances at the Copley Terrace, one with a small group and the other playing solo piano.

After one trip into Boston he stayed there overnight, returning to the barracks at 9:30 the following morning. He noted, "Conte questioned me—had him apologetic before I was through." One week later, in Middletown on the final day of a four-day pass, he wrote: "Couldn't sleep late, as always on last day before return to jail."

Inevitably thoughts were turned towards demob, including "The next year will be a wondrous one. [This] one started and ended badly. Placid was enjoyable at times. It's been a pleasure knowing some of these boys. Schroeder is soloing at Eddie's, about the only piano job I'd take. So what will it be, some joint, big band, small band, club dates, arranging??? It all has an intriguing air of discovery and mystery—but will common-sense prevail in any job? It has to." And on another occasion, "It will be a severe shock to be free, but keep that thought along the right lines and maybe I can do something after all. If I could only lead a sober life at Nick's or maybe Eddie's new joint." [Eddie Condon had opened his own club at 47 West 3rd Street on December 20, 1945.] Early in December Cary had petitioned the Personnel Office for his discharge but, though he was feeling hopeful, it did not come through until late in February.

He was able to spend Christmas week at home with Rose and Judy, then saw the New Year in "playing stocks with Joe Conte in officers' club—was quite drunk, as were many others, of course." 1946 began with another trip to Boston on January 3, followed by a weekend pass to go home and to fit in a visit to Eddie Condon's. Then on the 11th there was a ten-day furlough, which involved several visits to Condon's (he was hired as relief pianist on the Monday), Jimmy Ryan's or Nick's.

The Max Kaminsky band had moved from the Copley Terrace and opened on February 3 in "a little cellar joint" called "Maxie's," Kaminsky's short-lived club venture. Cary's visits to Boston in early February allowed him to sit-in with the band. The first weekend in February Cary also travelled to Middletown and on the Monday he sent a telegram to Sergeant Fish—"Wife ill—be in tomorrow." The sergeant's views are not reported, but two weeks later, with his discharge imminent, Cary was late returning to the camp after another weekend pass. He noted with satisfaction: "W.O. Hickok excited over my late arrival but can do nothing."

Cary's diary entry for February 20, 1946, was, "The day has arrived." And so Private Richard D. Cary had his honorable discharge from the Center Service Command Unit #1160, Fort Devens, Mass. He reached Middletown at 6:50 p.m., as a civilian and an out-of-work musician.

3. Billy Butterfield, Amusement Parks and Polish Hops (1946–1947)

> *I was living in Middletown, Connecticut, with my wife and child, but when I got through with the army in 1946 I went down to New York as much as I could to try and find some work.*

In fact Cary found a job within a few days of his discharge, although there would be no immediate regular wage. He travelled into New York on February 26 to look for work and in Charlie's Tavern chanced to meet Billy Butterfield, who offered him the piano chair in the big band he was starting. Cary declined as pianist, but accepted on trumpet and peck horn. A number of rehearsals followed, with fluctuating personnels, and Cary started to write arrangements for the band.

During the weeks of rehearsal, and before the band's first tour, which began on May 15, Cary found occasional gigs wherever he could. He wrote arrangements for clarinetist Hank D'Amico's band, plus two for an Eddie Condon record session. At Condon's club he subbed for pianist Gene Schroeder or for cornetist Wild Bill Davison, while on May 13 he played one number on trumpet at Condon's Carnegie Hall concert. Commenting on sitting-in at Condon's on March 7 he wrote: "[Joe] Bushkin and I cornetted on last set" and on May 1 he mentions "some guitar player from coast— Barney Kessel—fairly fast." He was in the Monday-night (March 11) group at Nick's and one night he played at Jimmy Ryan's with Johnny Windhurst "and young jazz band."

Closer to home he played on four Monday-night sessions at The Paddock in Meriden, where the guest stars included Brad Gowans, Joe Marsala and Pee Wee Russell. At the end of April he played seven or eight nights at Otto's in Hartford. In Middletown there was at least one wedding engagement and one shower job, plus two dates at St. Sebastien's, probably showers or weddings. The day before the Butterfield tour started Cary wrote: "Up to date again. Wish I had ambition to write several pages a day—or the talent."

All these weeks it appears that Rose was suffering a difficult pregnancy and on Sunday, March 25th, she gave birth to a premature boy, who lived only a short time. She returned home on the 31st, to be looked after by her mother, after a stay in hospital of more than two weeks.

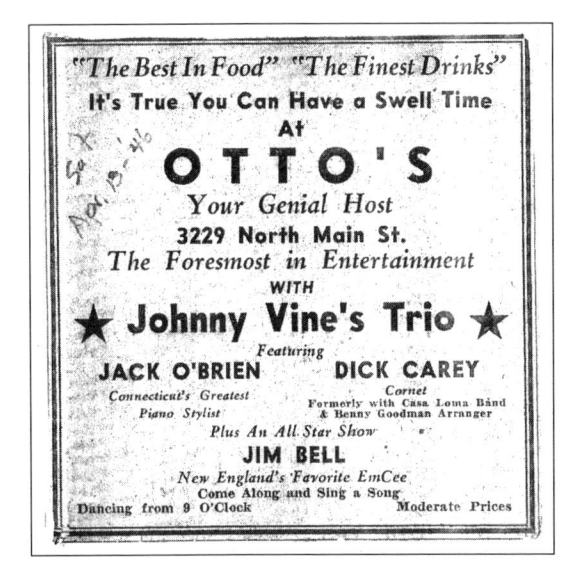

> "The Best In Food" "The Finest Drinks"
> It's True You Can Have a Swell Time
> At
> **OTTO'S**
> Your Genial Host
> 3229 North Main St.
> The Foremost in Entertainment
> WITH
> ★ **Johnny Vine's Trio** ★
> Featuring
> JACK O'BRIEN   DICK CAREY
> Connecticut's Greatest   Cornet
> Piano Stylist   Formerly with Casa Loma Band
>   & Benny Goodman Arranger
> Plus An All Star Show
> **JIM BELL**
> New England's Favorite EmCee
> Come Along and Sing a Song
> Dancing from 9 O'Clock   Moderate Prices

Although unable to accept a three day tour with Condon at the end of April Cary was free to fly to New Orleans with a Condon unit, on May 5th, for a concert at the Municipal Auditorium at 8:30 that evening, followed by an afternoon concert in Baton Rouge the next day, before flying back to New York. The band also included Wild Bill Davison, cornet, Jack Lesberg, bass, Tony Parenti, clarinet, George Wettling, Dave Tough, drums, Gene Schroeder, piano, Max Kaminsky, trumpet, and George Brunis, Vernon Brown, trombones.

After the 8:30 concert Cary, Davison, Lesberg, Parenti and Wettling, found their way to the Plaza Club in Kenney, a New Orleans suburb, to jam with the unique New Orleans-style clarinetist, Irving Fazola.

* * * * * * *

Billy Butterfield (1917–1988) was one of the finest trumpet players of the big band era. He joined the Bob Crosby orchestra as a twenty-year-old and was featured on Bob Haggart's composition, *I'm Free* (later, with words added, *What's New?*). With Artie Shaw his introductory statement to the orchestra's version of *Stardust* was widely admired, as was his work with Benny Goodman during the Eddie Sauter period. He also worked in studio orchestras, as well as playing and recording with Eddie Condon and, later, The World's Greatest Jazz Band.

In 1946, despite warning signs that the swing era was ending and that audiences were turning their attention to singers, Butterfield foolishly decided to become a bandleader. As he told John Chilton, "I suppose it cost me about $35,000, which in the 1940s was a lot of money."

Cary played his first rehearsal with Butterfield on the last day of February, 1946. Bill Stegmeyer, best remembered as a member of the pre-war Bob Crosby orchestra, was the straw boss and chief arranger, as well as playing clarinet and alto. The band had a contract with Capitol Records. For the initial recordings the rhythm section, guitar, bass and drums, was, to quote *Down Beat*, "unset," so studio musicians filled these chairs.

> Urbie Green's brother, Jack, sat next to me in the trombone section and was always bragging about some kid brother. I doubled on alto horn and fifth trumpet.

By May the rhythm section positions were settled.
> Stegmeyer hired his brother-in-law [George Ryan] to play bass because he was his copyist and our drummer [Bob Dickenson] was a very pleasant crippled fellow from Detroit, neither of whom belonged in a band like this. Actually this was a group of young guys, not used to recording, all just out of the army and experience was woefully lacking.

On March 23 Cary reported that they played "for stuffed shirts" at the Merchant Marine Academy—"band bad, drums awful," and on April 29 and May 14 they recorded for Capitol Records and Capitol Transcriptions. On May 15 the band set off on tour, starting in Manchester, or to quote Cary: "9 p.m. to 1:00 the BB band struggled through their first club date." Locations which followed included New Bedford, New London, Canobie Lake and ten days at the Palace in Old Orchard. The band returned to New York on June 11 for another recording session and to begin rehearsals with Jerry Colonna, the comedian-singer best remembered for his comedy sketches with Bob Hope.

Cary was not impressed with Colonna's act, except for a surprising remark about his singing. He noted that Colonna rushed his lines and had no control over the audience until he sang. "Doubt if his mind will ever be quick enough for a single [act]. He will remain a stooge but also a favorite singer of mine."

On June 14 the band set out on this six-week tour, which was scheduled to be:
> one-nighters from New England thru Canada towards the coast. The fact that they put a Hollywood show with us for several months (sic) kept Billy out of the red for a short time. The show was fronted by Jerry Colonna, with [singer] Tony Romano and assorted singers and dancers from California. All mostly unknown to eastern seaboard merry-go-round

lovers. I think we played every amusement park from Maine to Texas.

The band played two nights in Houston, Texas, and after the show on July 9 Cary and Bob Peck, one of the trumpet players, went to the 'Southern' where pianist Peck Kelley worked. (Kelley was often given the description of 'legendary.') "We had no coats and they wouldn't let us in, but I got a glimpse of Peck and met him after. I knew he reminded me of Jack O'Brien; resemblance in hands and spidery way they work over middle of piano. But Peck leans more to the [Eddie] Duchin a bit."

Never happy when on tour, Cary was also displeased with his lack of solo opportunity: "I play once or twice a night and find it a strain this way and not much comes out." Later he added: "I haven't made the peck horn a must in B.B.'s mind. He professes to like my musicianship but more from a distance, like an arranger can stay. I'm a little disappointed about this horn setback but welcome the thought of returning to small bands. This trip not successful for me at all. Talked it over with R. and am trying to make up my mind whether to quit or not." He also noted that Butterfield was fed up: "I know why he really hates this routine—no output for his wonderful talent."

Rose accompanied her husband for most of July, but their marital problems continued. ("I wonder if Rose is right when she says, 'No one else could stand you.'") Two days after she returned home, on the 22nd, Cary wrote: "Pretty lonesome these days. Trip wearing on all nerves. No enjoyment in playing at all." The following day his entry is: "BB and I got jug after [the show] and he fired me in the nicest way and seemed relieved that I seemed relieved. Says he never wants to lose touch and 'keep writing.' Now it's settled and it is such a relief."

The Colonna tour ended in St. Paul on July 24, but the band remained there until the 29th when it took the train to St. Louis for a week long engagement at the Tune Town Ballroom. Cary completed his notice on the 3rd August and returned to New York.

In later interviews Cary considered the Butterfield interlude: *The situation was this: Stegmeyer ran the band and did all the arrangements to be recorded, then he gave those left over to either Bob Peck [trumpeter] or myself. I have very little memory of what I wrote.* More Than You Know *was one for sure. I know I didn't do* Rumors Are Flying, *which was titled on our* parts *as* Landlady's Lament. *Billy liked something I did on Cheatin' on Me which I once told him I did for a big army band as a joke and he used to ask me to do more "jokes" for him.*

Billy Butterfield on tour, 1946

Cheatin' on Me was recorded for a transcription, with a Butterfield vocal, after Cary left the band, as was *More Than You Know*, though the CD notes credit the arrangement to Bob Peck. Cary has an alto horn solo on another of his arrangements, *Thou Swell*. Although Stegmeyer arranged nearly all the Capitol recordings, Cary said he did most of the writing for the transcriptions the band made when he was present. Only a few titles from these transcriptions, with Cary, have been traced, as the discography shows.

> *We did quite a few transcriptions in New York, before going on the road, and I did a lot of those and wish I had them. Billy played so much better on [them]—less pressure, etc. He was quite a drinker and never got over it. That was the most beautiful trumpet sound I ever heard. He was not the greatest improvisor—but that pure sound, range and impeccable intonation!!!!*

Cary commented on one title which was recorded for Capitol Transcriptions:

> *This Believing World was an Eddie Sauter original—very difficult but once in a while, when they got close, it was the most enjoyable ballad of the night. I copied the score and still have it.*
>
> *Stegmeyer was a fine arranger—later doing mostly radio studio work in New York, but he ran the band on the*

> road and acted like a very disagreeable, overbearing first sergeant. He was the main reason I left the band in St. Louis, just before they came to California. [The orchestra was due to start a four-week engagement at the Avalon Ballroom in Los Angeles on August 14th.]
>
> Several months later, when Billy appeared in Connecticut, they'd reduced the band to three trumpets, two trombones and three saxes, and I could see the end was in sight. Billy was never suited to run a band; he was an artist and far from any kind of business man and, of course, he enjoyed the spirits, as all my friends did in those days, including me as much as anyone. We enjoyed small bands a hell of a lot more—no bus rides, same arrangements, singers, and all the monotonous junk one has to play in ballrooms. Even the Ellington band could get terribly bored.

On another occasion, asked about going on the road, Cary replied:

> I didn't play with very many big bands. I liked the little ones and I liked to stay in one saloon at a time. I only made $110 a week with Billy Butterfield. He couldn't afford any more. But I loved Billy.

Butterfield told Max Jones, jazz writer for *The Melody Maker*, that Cary was "a good pianist, but he didn't like to play the piano and I could never understand that. He was always grabbing a trumpet or that E-flat horn or something and saying, 'I don't like to play the piano.' Quite a strange guy. He was in my big band in 1946; used to play alto horn."

Butterfield's big band struggled on until late in 1947. On November 25 Butterfield went into Nick's to lead the band there, but even then his agent was claiming, "This is just a temporary thing to get over what is a temporary rough spot for the whole business." But the big band never reformed.

When he left Butterfield Cary was hoping to join the band which accompanied the Braves baseball team, until being told a trombonist was required, not a horn player. [But Cary could play trombone!] Instead he decided: "This is a new era—a reconditioning period of relaxation and writing." At the same time he started a new regimen: "Started on a diet today (August 29). To eat very little, drink only milk, and a minimum of before-bed meals. Feel effects already.

Hope to make this a real reconversion year, with an attempt at moderation and common sense—plus work on original arranging."

Relaxing on August 27 could have been serious: "About 3 a.m. I woke in my usual chair by the radio—Rose shaking me, room full of smoke, rug smouldering with foot-wide hole. So I've been lucky again. Why can't I ever learn?"

Two days later he was back in his favoured "one saloon," beginning a three nights a week engagement at the Ridgeway Inn, near Meriden, Connecticut, with a quartet which he and drummer Johnny Vine put together. They worked Thursdays, Fridays and Saturdays through September, then Wednesdays, Fridays and Saturdays, even for a time stretching to four nights a week. After the first night Cary noted: "Band may be mediocre if we try hard." The personnel changed frequently, with a tenor player called Cubeta leaving after three nights, his replacement Fromica being "much better." Pianist Pete Foster lasted two weeks, replaced by "Ollie," soon replaced by Gus Weber. Two high quality bassists were used. For a time one was Neidlinger, presumably the formidable Buell Neidlinger, and the other was John Giuffrida, but nothing is known of Ernie Russo who came in later. In September Cary wrote: "Job griped me at night. I've done all the 80 arrangements for nil." But it was regular work and he noted on October 8 that his week's salary was pretty fair:

Ridgeway	40
Shurer (arrangements)	30
D'Agostino (arrangements)	20
Democratic Victory Party	12 = $102.00

Russ Shurer, a drummer-leader in Meriden, and Joe D'Agostino ("runs music store, teaches two days a week and has band at Wonderbar") had started ordering arrangements from Cary. These were followed by requests from other local leaders, including Paul Lauderman, Eddie Miranda, Al Gentile and Murray Gottfried (Godfrey). Cary noted that the Gentile band included his friends John 'Tweet' and Betty Peterson, and that Lauderman had "really a nice hotel band."

For two Sundays, September 22 and 29, he played at the Three Oaks, "mostly Polish hops" and "Job awful—most moronic of all music—piano terrible." On October 28 and November 1 he appeared at concerts in Bristol and Bushnell, promoted by Bob Harrington. Other occasional jobs including working "a shower at St. Sebastien," and a wedding at the Rose Garden. Early in November

Cary was pleased to see himself featured in an article, with photograph, which appeared in *The Clarion*—"Frances Migliori wrote a very nice thing about me...."

On Saturday, January 4, 1947, "[Owner Ernie] Rousseau said 'two nights next week,' we said 'no,' and our Ridgeway days are over." Only a few days before Cary had noted, "What a germ that Ernie Rousseau is. The type of small-time gangster with a lying put-up front who fools only the average who stooge for him .... You can't believe a word he utters. Those are the ones who should be used to test atom bombs on." So four months of regular work came to an end, but the following Thursday the band opened at the Rose Garden. Cary could write: "We feel more comfortable. No scum like that Rousseau and his petty would-be racketeers." And, "Another successful evening. Get 9 per night and no publicity." The band seems to have varied in size, but included Johnny Vine, drums, and Sal(?) Giacco, alto. It began by working Thursday, Friday and Saturday nights, and Sundays 5 pm to 9 pm, but the Thursdays were soon cancelled. Cary even mentions "doing a bit of crooning"!

There were occasional trips into New York, when he usually sat-in at Condon's. On November 25 he drove in with Johnny Vine. They met Hank D'Amico who said he was studying music with Paul Creston, as was Gene Schroeder, and Cary bore this in mind. On January 10, before going to Condon's, he visited the 18 Club to hear the Joe Mooney Quartet, "latest musicians' sensation—a very sensitive unit."

From February 17, 1947, Cary was involved in the Monday night jam sessions at Matarese's Circle Bar supper club in Hartford, Connecticut. A seven-piece local band (Glenn Pierce, Eddie Flanagan, "boy pianist,"—Zabidis, "awful bass," and others), led by a clarinetist called Gage, provided support for the guests, who during the year included Bobby Hackett, Bud Freeman, J.C. Higginbotham, Hot Lips Page, Max Kaminsky, Bill Harris, Rex Stewart and Roy Eldridge. After two weeks Gage was fired so that Joe Marsala could lead, with Cary organising the band. His March 10 diary entry refers to a wonderful session with guests Jack Teagarden, Johnny Windhurst and Brad Gowans, plus Joe Marsala.

He was on piano for an Eddie Condon concert at Symphony Hall in Boston on March 21, plus "cornet on finale." Teagarden, Kaminsky, Hucko, Hackett and James P. Johnson were also there. After the show they went to the Ken Club, where Buzzy and Al Drootin played drums and reeds respectively. He was back at Symphony Hall on April 11, playing piano, including a duet with Cliff

Jackson, alongside Kaminsky, Hackett, Hucko, Joe Dixon and George Wettling among the other participants. He played with Hackett, Hucko and Kaminsky again on the 19th at the Plandome Country Club on Long Island.

The trips to Boston perhaps eased the way for other work there. April 20 he played a private party in Everett with Ruby Braff, Frank Orchard, John Field and the Drootin brothers. Four days later there was a Princeton concert with Hackett, Kaminsky, Hucko, Miff Mole, trombone, Jack Lesberg, bass, Specs Powell, drums, and Cliff Jackson, solo piano. Afterwards it was back by train to New York and Eddie Condon's, before catching the 4:45 a.m. train to Meriden. Sunday sessions in Boston included, on April 27, Braff and Hackett, Orchard, Hucko, Tortolla, clarinet, and the Drootins. The following week guest Max Kaminsky failed to appear ("I never knew him to do this before"), so the band was Braff, Orchard, Tortolla, Cary, John Field, bass, and Don Marino, drums. Frankie Newton was the guest on May 11.

Cary's fortunes had stabilised by this time, with the three nights a week at the Rose Garden, and the Sunday job at the Matarese Circle, plus the incidental gigs and the income from arranging. Most of his writing now was for Al Gentile, but other leaders he mentions are Russ Shurer and Lesniak and his Polish band ($10 for two arrangements).

On April 30 he played piano and trumpet at a Portland High P.T.A. dance; he did the announcing and judged a waltz competition. In the meantime business at the Rose Garden was declining and Cary's last night there was in May, probably on the 16th. Prior to this he had rehearsed with a Joe Marsala group, which opened at Ferdinand's Club in Hartford on Thursday, May 8. The band was nine strong, including Marsala, clarinet, Fred and Lou Bredise (instruments not known), John Giuffrida, bass, and Johnny Vine, drums, but Marsala seems not to have continued, due to illness, and after three weekend gigs, ending May 31, there is no further mention of Ferdinand's. There are two mentions of sessions at the Palmetto Club, one with Hot Lips Page on May 12, and on May 26 he was again at the Matarese Circle when James P. Johnson was the guest, though he thought that James P. was "playing very sloppy these days."

All through these early months of 1947, when not playing or writing, Cary had occupied his time with his other interests—movies, sport (playing golf and tennis), listening to the radio, choir practice and, unfortunately, drinking. The family also acquired a pup who was named Bix.

It was in May that Cary wrote that Rose was pregnant. And it was on Sunday, May 10, that Ernie Anderson telephoned to say the Cary was to play "the Louis Armstrong concert next week! Must learn tunes. Hal Lowey probably has all of 'em." Four days later he visited Lowey, who had been manager at the Matarese Circle, and listened to Louis Armstrong records. Cary's short but momentous association with the greatest of jazz trumpeters was about to begin.

Ernest Anderson presents
FRED ROBBINS'
ONE-NITE STAND
A Midnight Variety Concert
starring

Eleven-Thirty Saturday Night
At **TOWN HALL**
All Seats Reserved

May 17, 1947

4. With Louis Armstrong and the All Stars—and Jean Goldkette (1947–48)

Louis Armstrong, apart from a period spent in Europe, had been fronting a big band since 1929. Through the 1930s and into the 1940s he was a star popular entertainer, a majestic trumpet player and a unique singer, who appeared in movies and on records, and tirelessly toured the country. In all these years his big band, despite the presence of several superior musicians, was there solely to provide a backdrop to Louis' inimitable talents.

Not that he had been lost entirely to small band jazz. In 1940 there was a New Orleans style recording session with Sidney Bechet for Decca, followed the next year by Decca sessions with a contingent from his big band. There were jam sessions at the *Esquire* award ceremonies in January 1944 and the superb V-Disc recordings of December that same year.

Towards the end of 1946 Louis was featured in the filming of "New Orleans," in which he played with Kid Ory, the trombonist on his legendary Hot Five and Seven records of the 1920s, and Barney Bigard, clarinetist famous for his long association with Duke Ellington. As part of the publicity for the movie they recorded four of its songs for Victor in October 1946.

The previous month writer and critic Leonard Feather had organised a small band session for Louis on the French "Swing" label and he continued to press for Armstrong to abandon the large orchestra. Then, in February 1947, he arranged a Carnegie Hall concert, to feature Louis with Ed Hall's small band in the first half and with the big band after the interval. Inexorably, Louis was being edged towards the All Stars format.

On April 26th Louis starred in the "This Is Jazz" radio show, backed by a sextet which included Wild Bill Davison, cornet, George Brunis, trombone, Albert Nicholas, clarinet, Art Hodes, piano, Pops Foster, bass, and Baby Dodds, drums.

Three weeks after this, on May 17th, 1947, came the famous Town Hall concert promoted by Ernie Anderson, later to be the personal representative for such stars as Artie Shaw, John Huston and Charles Bronson. Anderson was always happy to tell how he arranged for this event to take place. Anxious to feature Louis Armstrong with a small band, his trump card was knowing that Joe

Glaser hated more than most to return money once he had it in his hand. To quote Anderson: "In 1947 Louis Armstrong's career had stalled. He had an inferior big band and travelled all over the country in a beat-up bus, working one nighters in dance halls. You could buy the band for $350 per night and the most they ever were guaranteed was $650 for a Saturday night.

"I handed Joe Glaser, Louis' manager, a certified check for $1,000. 'That's for Louis for one night without the band,' I told Glaser. I booked Town Hall, set Bobby Hackett as Louis' musical director. With Bobby I laid out a program which Louis approved and then I set Dick Cary, George Wettling, Sidney Catlett, Jack Teagarden, Peanuts Hucko and Bob Haggart as his sidemen, with Bobby Hackett. The concert, which I had privately arranged to have recorded, was a smash success. The day after the concert Joe Glaser gave their notices to everyone in the big band, made a seven year contract with Teagarden, and began booking Louis as a small band."

Different stories have been told about the rehearsals for the Town Hall concert. Armstrong was too busy to rehearse until the day of the concert and, according to Anderson, when he arrived at the Hall he greeted each of the musicians, saying, "We don't have to rehearse. We'll just hit at eleven thirty and play the show!" Anderson said: "Dick Cary knew everything Louis ever played and he rehearsed the musicians a day or two before the concert, with Hackett playing Louis' parts." Cary himself recalled to both Ken Gallacher and Scott Ellsworth:

> This was the first time I met Louis. It was at Town Hall and it was the thrill of my life. I was pretty young then and we didn't even rehearse [but see quote below]. We got together in some studio at ABC and talked it over. And the concert came out very well.

On the day itself he was up at 11:30 and was visited by Fred Williams. They listened to a few of Louis' records, then at 2 p.m. set off for New York, he, Rose and Fred. His entry for the rest of the day is: "Hangover bad but I have something important to do and forget it. Wonderful rehearsal with Louis, Hackett, Peanuts, Teagarden, Haggart, Big Sid and Stud (Wettling?). Two hours of solid, good rehearsal. Then with Rose and Fred to Costello's—several doubles, ate, back to Town Hall at 11:00 and concert at 11:30. Wonderful, hall jammed, people loved it. Everybody there; fine programme without a hitch, except when Louis started *Monday Date* again in place of *Big Butter and Egg Man*. After the concert we went to Big T's job at the Famous Door." Cary was paid $50 for the concert. On June 4 he met Ernie Anderson who "gave me a large signed picture of Louis A. saying 'to a man can play anything on piano.'"

The concert and the subsequent records were a great success at the time and the recordings continue to be highly rated. The opening four numbers, first made famous by Armstrong twenty years before, featured him with the rhythm section and allowed a small amount of solo space for Cary.

Ernie Anderson also commented: "Dick Cary was a dear friend of mine. Always a very accomplished musician. He knows our music inside out. When I set up the 1947 Louis small band concert ... Bobby Hackett agreed that the best choice for Louis was Dick, who played the concert perfectly. Then he was hired for the band and he played throughout the rest of 1947 as Louis' only piano player."

The *Down Beat* review of the concert included the comment that "Dick Carey (sic), while playing conservatively styled piano, supported Louis in excellent taste." Critic Max Harrison, reviewing the records, went so far as to write: "*St. James Infirmary* is in both instrumental and vocal terms quite simply one of [Jack Teagarden's] greatest recordings, with an imaginative accompaniment from Cary."

There was another Armstrong small band recording session

Town Hall concert, N.Y.C.—May 17, 1947.
l-r: Teagarden, Cary, Armstrong, Hackett, Hucko, Haggart, Catlett.
(Courtesy: Dick Cary Archive)

for Victor on June 10th (including Teagarden, Hucko, Ernie Caceres on baritone saxophone, and Johnny Guarnieri, not Cary, on piano), followed on the 19th by a Winter Garden Theatre concert to celebrate the opening of the film "New Orleans." This featured the same personnel as the Town Hall engagement, except that the bassist was Jack Lesberg. Cary recalled:

> Louis was in bad shape that night. Had trouble with his lip in the first part.

The film itself failed to live up to its hype. Good musical interludes could not disguise a ludicrous script, but the film did generate a lot of favourable publicity for Louis Armstrong.

In his diary Cary wrote: "I can't forget May 17 or June 19—two dates with Louis—real events in my life and many thanks to Ernie Anderson."

Jean Goldkette, a famous pioneer bandleader from the 1920s when his sidemen included Bix Beiderbecke, Frankie Trumbauer, the Dorsey brothers, Joe Venuti and Eddie Lang, had been persuaded to form another big band, although his name would mean little to the dancers of 1947. As *Down Beat* reported: "Jean Goldkette due to open on or about June 25 at the Million Dollar Pier, Atlantic City, for five weeks, with a five week option."

Goldkette telephoned Cary on May 28 to ask him to join his new band, with the first rehearsal taking place on June 9, Cary stating: "4th trumpet, motley group, Jim Johnson on bass, arranging by Leon Magerian [sp?] of Lucky Millinder's band." There was a second rehearsal the following day "for Mr. Hamid of the Pier, Atlantic City; different group, terrible, drummer good, Irving Kluger of [Boyd] Raeburn band." Another rehearsal was held June 19, after which Cary hurried to NBC for a Louis Armstrong rehearsal prior to playing a Runyon Cancer Fund benefit at a private house in Columbus Circle, and then the concert at the Winter Garden Theatre. Cary recalled: "Louis getting a rub-down in nude in dressing room after concert in mixed company, a sight I'll never forget. What a guy, anything goes but nicely!!"

The next day, after another Goldkette rehearsal, Cary says: "We heard records of last night's concert, done at Nola's. Not bad at all."

During the Goldkette rehearsal period Cary took the usual variety of jobs. On Sunday, June 1, he played alto horn with Rex Stewart at Bible Rock, a venue he has mentioned once or twice before. There was a wedding job at the Garde Hotel, a little [trio] job at Sunset, a shower at St. Mary's and a couple of gigs at Avon's Laurel House, as well as two references to "Sons of Italy," one mentioning "for Franco shower!" On June 23 Cary had stayed overnight at Johnny Windhurst's mother's, who was a teacher, and the next morning he and Windhurst played for her school's assembly.

The Pier engagement started on June 27 and Cary mentions his roommate Chas McAmish, trombonist, and Don Joseph, 3rd trumpet and jazz trumpet. "I dislike first trumpeter [Magerian] extremely—a loud, overbearing, young, opinionated jerk with an iron lip and a head to match." But the following night, "Seems that Hamid complained about triple fortissimo of band and especially of the first trumpet man, so we played in hats and mutes and things sounded much better, more rhythmical."

In his diary Cary also recorded thanks to Ernie Anderson for recommending him for the job with Goldkette: "a nice salary at 200 per, though it should be 300. But times for entertainers on the average are a bit bad. Anyway, it's back to work for me and perhaps the start of a very healthy summer. I have a very kind boss, though a bit eccentric and confused at moment." That was on June 30th, but on July 31 he wrote of much confusion in his work. "Trumpet lip terrible, breathing bad, headaches. Arrangements I thought about and tried on were usually most badly played. Quickies on pops worked out best—*Alamo, Mardi Gras, Kate*. Band completely disintegrated; not entirely Goldkette's fault but an awful lot due to his ignorance and stubbornness." This despite the rhythm section featuring such excellent players as Eddie Safranski on bass and Cliff Leeman on drums.

Of the band Cary also wrote: "Very little to say—it stinks!" He also noted: "When Jean G. is in New York and returns late, the band, under Safranski, plays easily and the best they are capable of. Jean arrives and a tension and hostility sets in, also childish kidding and intentional clinkers." There were some good occasions: "*Summertime* of George Handy is a very controversial arrangement. I enjoyed playing it because it is different. Aside from that I can't say—it's impressionistic to a small percentage of what Stravinsky is." Nonetheless, Cary was not unhappy when the engagement ended on July 31, 1947.

Cary gave his salary as $90 for three arrangements a week, $110 for playing, minus $1.10 social security, $9.90 union tax, $4.76 withholding. At the weekends the band played 3 p.m. to 5 p.m., then 8:30 p.m. to around 1 a.m. There was a half-hour broadcast over WOR at 12:15 or 12:30. On July 3 he spent too long on the beach and missed a couple of sets because of sunburn.

In retrospect Dick Cary recalled:
Jean Goldkette was a real gentleman. His last orchestra was put together short term for a guest performance in Atlantic City by Ernie Anderson.

Goldkette came to New York and we got a few so-called all-stars, put a band together for him and we worked Atlantic City for five weeks. Eddie Safranski was one of the all-stars [and he] became a very good friend of mine and we played shuffleboard every night after work in a little beer bar. Jean would come along and talk to us, which was very pleasant. We talked until 4 a.m. many times. He had no music of his own. I played fourth trumpet and alto horn and did a lot of arranging for them. The other people you've never heard of.

He was up in his sixties [in fact, Goldkette was 48], smoked cigars continuously, was quite nervous. One night they put one of these stinkers in his cigar; they stink like hell. It was the same night that an agent came down from New York to talk to him and he picked up the cigar after the set and was talking to the agent and the place stunk like hell! He put it in an ashtray and didn't even let on that he had noticed anything; never said a word about it.

That's the only engagement we had and the only reason we were there was that the guy who owned the ballroom was trying to be a band agent. He was Jean's agent. That's the only reason we got into this, his father owned the ballroom! Anyway, that only lasted five weeks and then I was out of a job again and I went back to Connecticut.

The following August when the All Stars were being formed, Louis said he'd like 'the kid who did the concert.' I was so thrilled at the thought of playing with Pops, with Jack Teagarden and with Sid Catlett, the greatest drummer of all time.

Cary quoted a variation on this, with Louis saying, "...that little ofay who played Town Hall would be pretty good."

Armstrong himself recalled: "I never picked my own bands—too many good musicians around, makes bad friends." And, "Joe [Glaser] picked them and sent them out to me in California where I was just finishing the film, 'A Song Is Born.' Let me see, we had that trumpet man on piano, Dick Cary ... and Morty Corb, he played real good bass, came from out on the coast." However, Cary said that

Ernie Anderson put the first All Stars together for Glaser.

After leaving Goldkette Cary spent August 1 in New York, staying with Johnny Windhurst, then went home to Middletown where, on August 4, Ernie Anderson telephoned him about going to Hollywood with the All Stars, the first date by Louis' new band. On the 6th he was back in New York to meet Joe Glaser and at 11:30 that night he, along with Jack Teagarden, Sid Catlett, Ernie Anderson and his friend, Lee Sheridan, left La Guardia on an American Airways flight to Los Angeles, with just one stop in Chicago.

His entry for August 7 is: "At 6048 Hollywood Boulevard in a wild house with Jack Tea. His son lives there with a seven-piece band." There was a visit to Billy Berg's, where the All Stars were booked, then on to the Hangover "where good ol' Lou McGarity playing in a five-piece band," then to Nappy Lamare's joint [Club 47], meeting Rico Vallese, Nick Pelico and Doc Rando. The next day Teagarden moved in with his ex-wife, Addie, and Cary joined him. It was here that Cary first met Nicky Allen, a medical technician and budding painter.

The five days prior to the Billy Berg's opening were occupied by two or three rehearsals, sitting-in at the Hangover with Warren Smith and Matty Matlock ("two of my kid idols when they were big guys with Bob Crosby") and going to hear Phil Moore's "fine little band at Rounders on Sunset." Of the rehearsals, on the 11th Cary noted that Louis was making a film "but tired only when not playing," and on the 12th, "Louis' ulcers bad but how he could still play!" Earlier in the day Cary had visited the Goldwyn Studios to watch some of the filming of "A Song Is Born," in which Louis was featured with Danny Kaye, Benny Goodman, Tommy Dorsey, Lionel Hampton and others. He refers to "a wild rendition of *Anvil Chorus*."

The All Stars first booking began at Billy Berg's nightclub in Los Angeles on August 13th, 1947, where the band played from 9 p.m. to 2 a.m. nightly. The personnel was Louis, trumpet, Jack Teagarden, trombone, Barney Bigard, clarinet. Dick Cary, piano, Morty Corb, bass, and Sid Catlett, drums. *Down Beat* reported that "Louis Armstrong gave Billy Berg's the most jam-packed opening the Vine Street nitery has seen since war days." Cary remembered:

> *We opened at Billy Berg's in Hollywood and people queued outside every night for four weeks.*

In his diary Cary refers to "The Opening—hundreds turned away—many musicians—Kenton, Woody Herman, Bunk, Frank

Sinatra, Tatum, etc, etc. People looked rapt, mouths open, while Louis sang. A wonderful, beautiful, heart-warming experience to be a part of. Thank you, Ernie. Never saw more people feeling happier together at one time. What a remedy for the world; violence and hate were completely left out of tonight's mood. Then over to 6048, played a bit [with] Jack T. and Artie Lyons, good clarinet." Cary also said: "Opening night was one of my biggest thrills in the music business. It seemed no one could have dreamed of being a jazz pianist and spending a more ideal night. I was accompanying Louis Armstrong and Jack Teagarden and being assisted—or being an assistant to— Sid Catlett and Morty Corb."

Nicky Allen pleased Dick by contacting his sister, Lois, so that she could be present on the opening night.

Also on the bill at Billy Berg's was singer/pianist Nellie Lutcher, another highly popular artist of the period. She was an added factor in the success of the engagement, during which Billy Berg's became the place for Hollywood celebrities to be seen and, of course, old friends of Louis such as Bing Crosby, Hoagy Carmichael and Johnny Mercer were warmly welcomed.

During this hectic four weeks Cary kept a varied schedule. He managed a few trips to the movies and even a game of golf, plus

Louis Armstrong All Stars, 1947   l–r: Velma Middleton, Dick Cary, Jack Teagarden, Sid Catlett, Louis Armstrong, Barney Bigard, Arvell Shaw.
(Courtesy: Dick Cary Archive)

the usual parties and visits to clubs. Visitors to Berg's mentioned by Cary include Jimmy Dorsey, Johnny Mercer ("sang a couple") and Harry Barris ("sat-in one tune—what a little fireball"). On August 17 Norma Teagarden, Jack's sister, played piano, as did Art Tatum. In fact Tatum visited a number of times, leading Cary to write: "How can anyone play that much—very discouraging" and "Art Tatum sat-in, amazes always. Louis kept growling 'Out' but couldn't stop him" and again, "No one can do on an instrument what he does to the piano—a wonder of the world."

Cary's sit-ins included the Brass Rail, where Wingy Manone, Brad Gowans and Zutty Singleton were working, Club 47 where he played with Rico Vallese, Mahlon Clark, Brad Gowans, Doc Rando and Morty Corb, and the Ja Da Club on Sunset, on trumpet this time, with Johnny Windhurst and Joe Rushton (Vallese, Bill Campbell, Bud Wilson and Matty Matlock were in regular band). Cary noted: "Trumpet is the instrument I'm interested in."

One of the parties was at 504 Woodlawn "where Armstrong had a lawn party at Major Louis Brooks' fine home. A very amiable time. Jo Stafford, Paul Weston, Bill Goodwin, Bob Crosby there, among others."

There was another visit to the Goldwyn Studios on August 20. "Louis showed me around studio and was wonderful. Got in trucks and had parade around Hollywood—Lionel Hampton, Danny Kaye and car-full, Louis, Virginia Mayo, Steve Cochran, Kid Ory, Tommy Dorsey and Benny Goodman. On way to Casino Gardens Louis and I played old songs at upright in front of truck. Then we did set at [Tommy] Dorsey's Casino, to a huge mob [before] back to Berg's for night's work."

Cary was guilty of two slip-ups during the engagement. He was late for the afternoon show at Bill Berg's on Sunday the 17th ("did not get up in time") and on September 1st he was at the Rounders listening to Phil Moore, which made him late for the second set. "Louis pretty nice considering; think we get along pretty well. He's a remarkable man, basically one of the most good-hearted, rich-souled, simple and sincere people I have ever had fortune to know."

On August 22 the big news was Tommy Dorsey twice hitting Benny Goodman on the chin. "Everyone got a bang out of it, though the bang would have been bigger if Tommy had been the one clipped. Louis said, 'Benny was fightin' like a sissy, trying to kick him.'"

After the tumultuous reception which the band received during the four weeks at Billy Berg's it was clear that it would continue as a regular outfit, though perhaps no one foresaw that

Louis would still be leading his All Stars for more than two decades on, until ill-health forced him to stop playing, prior to his death on July 6, 1971.

Not that everyone was enthusiastic. Critic Ralph Gleason wrote in *Down Beat* that there were only two men in the band, Louis and Big Sid. He suggested that "the band stinks" and asked what was being done to the greatest trumpet player in the world. But Gleason's view was a minority one. Another *Down Beat* critic, George Hoefer, reviewing a Chicago concert, agreed there were too many novelties and disliked singer Velma Middleton, but he was generally impressed, particularly with Armstrong's singing and playing.

Velma Middleton, who had been with Armstrong's big band, had been added to the party. She was a moderate singer, but Louis enjoyed clowning with her and she was undoubtedly a crowd-pleaser.

Armstrong's appearances during 1947, at Town Hall, Billy Berg's, the Rag Doll and Carnegie Hall, for example, were reviewed country-wide, in such publications as *Variety, Fortune, The New York Daily News* and *The New Yorker*. *Variety* reported that the police had to be called to the Rag Doll to regulate the mobs, while *Down Beat* said that "cheering customers jammed Harry Greenbach's Burma Club all shows December 3, despite threat of rain, to welcome Louis Armstrong," though it later advised that Greenbach lost money on the booking!

In most reviews Cary was lucky to be mentioned as the pianist and luckier still if his name was spelt correctly.

September 8 was their final night at Billy Berg's. On the 9th they played a concert at the Civic Auditorium in Pasadena, followed by two days off. They caught the train for Chicago on the 12th, arriving in the Windy City on Friday, the 15th, a journey of around 60 hours. The following night they opened at the Rag Doll (6335 N. Western Avenue), where they worked 9:30 p.m. to 3:30 a.m., and until 4:30 a.m. on Saturday. Arvell Shaw was now the bass player. "RC on a lousy little spinet. Madhouse—hot—jammed—no dressing room—no place to stand except out in back. But business being good is some compensation for all of us."

Cary was to spend six months with the All Stars, during which time they travelled from coast to coast:

4 weeks August 13–September 8:	Billy Berg's, Hollywood
5 weeks September 16–October 19:	Rag Doll, Chicago
1 week October 21–26:	Tune Town Ballroom, Chase Hotel, St. Louis
3 weeks:	on tour for A.B.C.

1 week November 17–26:		Frolics, Detroit
3 weeks December 3–23:		Burma Club, San Francisco
4 weeks December 24–January 19:		Billy Berg's, Hollywood ("on KMPC every night 12:30")

3 weeks January 28–February 17: Roxy Theatre, New York (The All Stars left Los Angeles by train on the 21st, arrived in New York on the 24th, rehearsed at the Roxy on the 26th, and opened on the 28th.)

A.B.C. was the Associated Booking Corporation, Joe Glaser's organisation. The one-nighters from the end of October included the following concerts:

October	27:	Kansas City, Missouri ("small crowd")
	28:	Cedar Rapids, Iowa ("¼ house")
	29:	Rockford, Illinois (Masonic Temple)
	30:	Masonic Auditorium, Davenport, Iowa (big barn, bad crowd)
	31:	Quimby (?) Auditorium, Fort Wayne
November	1:	Dayton, Ohio ("bad house")
	2:	Indianapolis, Indiana ("half a house")
	4:	Milwaukee, Wisconsin (Pabst Theatre) ("best yet")
	7:	Madison ("two good receptive houses")
	8:	Civic Opera House, Chicago
	9:	Severance Hall, Cleveland (two concerts)
	11:	Brodhill Naval Armory (one hour concert, then dancing)
	15:	Carnegie Hall, NY (a midnight concert)

The days not shown were either rest or travel days.

There were also concerts during the club dates, including appearances at the Civic Auditorium in Pasadena on September 9, a plane trip for a benefit at Percy Jones Hospital in Battle Creek on November 20, the Academy of Music, Philadelphia on November 28 and at Symphony Hall in Boston on November 30. The latter concert was recorded and issued on Decca. These recordings confirm that Cary is a junior member of the group, given few solo opportunities and rarely shining in this company. It does not help that the recording balance is unkind to Cary, though writer Dr. Heiner Mückenberger refers to his "poetic introduction" to *Sunny Side of the Street*.

A session in Chicago for Victor Records, at 445 Lake Shore Drive, on October 16 found him in similar mode on four lacklustre songs which featured the singing of Armstrong and Teagarden. Cary

Louis ARMSTRONG
and His Concert Group

The Players

trombone and voice	JACK TEAGARDEN
clarinet	BARNEY BIGARD
drums	SIDNEY CATLETT
bassist	ARVELL SHAW
piano	DICK CARY
voice	VELMA MIDDLETON
trumpet and voice	LOUIS ARMSTRONG

The Program

Due to the ad lib quality of this music no formal program is possible. It is likely, however, that the following numbers will be heard.

High Society
Cornet Chop Suey
Dear Old Southland — an instrumental duet with Mr. Cary
Monday Date
Big Butter and Egg Man
Struttin' With Some Barbecue
That's For Me
Pennies From Heaven
St. Louis Blues
Ain't Misbehavin'
Rockin' Chair — a vocal duet with Mr. Teagarden
Rose Room — featuring Mr. Bigard
St. James Infirmary Blues — featuring Mr. Teagarden
Do You Know What It Means to Miss New Orleans — from the United Artists release of Louis Armstrong's life story, New Orleans a duet with Mr. Teagarden
The Jack Armstrong Blues — an impromptu composition in which the entire orchestra improvises

Confessin'
Royal Garden Blues
Back O'Town Blues
I Can't Give You Anything But Love
Mop Mop — featuring Mr. Catlett
Save It Pretty Mama
Muskrat Ramble
At the Jazz Band Ball
Velma's Blues — featuring Miss Middleton
Some Day — a new ballad written by Mr. Armstrong
Basin Street Blues — a duet with Mr. Teagarden
Sugar

Credits

The piano is a Steinway. Mr. Armstrong's trumpet is a balanced action model, designed by him, and made by the famous French instrument maker, Selmer. It was imported for Mr. Armstrong by the firm of G. Schirmer, Inc., 3 East 43rd Street, New York City 17.

Mr. Armstrong, Mr. Teagarden and the other members of this company are represented exclusively by Associated Booking Corp., Joe Glaser, president, 745 Fifth Ave., New York City, PL 5-5572.

This concert was produced by Ernest Anderson.

Symphony Hall concert programme, excerpt *(Courtesy: Dr. Heiner Mückenberger)* wrote: "I played an awful release" on *A Song Was Born* (theme from New World Symphony), but he thought Sid Catlett's song, *Before Long*, was pretty. He also noted: "... Jug arrived and last three sides done faster."

Cary had no illusions about his place in the band. "The members, except me, are soloists and great applause-getters. But when we got in the Victor Studios in Chicago to attempt four sides, the truth was out—the horrible blend and intonation was set down."

Also during the Rag Doll engagement, on October 19, the band gave a concert at the Highland Park High School, with Cary reporting, "Kids very appreciative." On two occasions he sat-in at Jazz, Ltd., Bill and Ruth Reinhardt's club, where Doc Evans was leading the band, and he visited Squirrel Ashcraft's home on October 12, where he "played with Jack T. for Squire's tape machine."

An entry for October 9 advises: "Louis has had a bad week, lip swollen, but last night he was back in form again, at times amazing with speed of ideas and drive, combined with beautiful, simple melodies."

During the St. Louis date Cary writes that a local enthusiast, John Phillips, recorded almost all of the October 25 programme at Tune Town, only to find that the records were under-recorded—"almost quiet. He must have been brokenhearted." Phillips had arranged a party for the band the previous night which had lasted until dawn. Illustrating the variation in working hours, the sets at Tune Town were 8:30 to 10:00 p.m.; 10:20 to 11:20 p.m.; and 11:40 p.m. to 12:30 a.m.

After the concert on October 29 Cary attended a jam session which featured "Bobby Nichols, 22-year old ex-Tex Beneke trumpet player." A revealing comment was: "Jack Teagarden was there too—he'll play anywhere."

One recording opportunity which caused Cary a great deal of disappointment was scheduled for Victor in December. This session, mentioned in *Down Beat*, was to be held in Los Angeles, reputedly of twelve titles. Cary told Swedish promotor Gösta Hägglöf that a Victor representative visited Armstrong to discuss recording a large number of songs during the last week of December. This was prior to the second recording ban called by the AFM, the musicians' union, due to come into effect on January 1, 1948. During the conversation the Victor man said that the Chicago recordings of October 16th were unsatisfactory and would have to be remade. "Louis became furious and shouted at the man, who listened quietly, then said: 'You may shout at Joe Glaser but not at me,' left and slammed the door. No recordings were made."

Perhaps the Victor executive had heard of the scheduled rehearsal at 2:30 p.m. on November 14 at Meridan and Havan Studios, presumably in New York City, which was aborted due to a slanging match between Armstrong and Glaser. Cary said: "Listened to L.A. and Joe yelling at each other. No sense made, only openings for pent-up feelings, long awaiting expression [but] getting nowhere and meaning nothing as a result. Only loud steam escaping. Ernie Anderson, a rather soft-spoken guy, got snowed-under, rudely treated. Whole thing amusing but regrettable."

Of the Frolics in Detroit Cary said, "a very noisy colored place on John R."—"noisy but agreeable enough"—"a barrelhouse place to play—Louis really got blowing."

At the Burma Club the All Stars played four sessions at 9:00, 10:25 and 11:50 p.m. and 1:20 to 2:00 a.m. In listing their routine for each set Cary comments, "and it's a real monotonous one too." For examples, the first set began with *Muskrat Ramble, Black and Blue* and *Royal Garden Blues*; the second set with *Mahogany Hall Stomp, Sunny Side of the Street* and *St. Louis Blues*. And one can sympathise, recognising many of the tunes that would continue to be featured in All Stars programmes for years ahead. His comments years later to Whitney Balliett on this subject, given on the next page, were more generous when discussing the Louis programmes.

The All Stars and friends, possibly at Burma Club, December 1947
Shaw on left; Bigard standing behind Armstrong and Teagarden; Catlett standing, in white jacket; Cary on right, with Virginia Allen   *(Courtesy: Dick Cary Archive)*

Barry Martyn, who cooperated with Barney Bigard on his autobiography, "With Louis and the Duke," recalled how he had to tone down Bigard's comments on Earl Hines who, after all, had provided the foreword for Barney's book! Bigard said of Hines, "He couldn't accompany crap. He wasn't as good as Dick Cary. Cary was ten times better for the band." In the book this became, "Earl Hines was so different from our first pianist, Dick Cary. I mean, Dick is a great band piano player and plays all the right stuff but he is strictly a musician. Absolutely no showmanship."

> Cary told *The New Yorker*'s Whitney Balliett:
> *There was not a harsh word among us and we never knew what we were going to do musically. The band hadn't become a vaudeville show yet. [In this context Cary would claim that Louis played* Indiana *as an opening number for about 18 years.] We hung out all the time. Sid Catlett took us to a big ballroom in Minneapolis and Jack and I were the only whites there. We sat in and when they turned the lights way down, the music got very soft and you could hear this enormous sound of dancing.*
>
> *Sid and Jack were wary of each other at first, but one night they got drunk and after that they were buddies. Louis and Jack really got on together. When we were on the bus out in the midlands, Louis used to play practical jokes on us.*

One which Louis played happened September 26 at the Rag Doll when he gave Cary a high quality joint, saying it was made from mild marijuana. Dick floated onto the stage, feeling no pain until, after a feature number by Barney Bigard, Louis announced: "And now our piano player, Mr. Dick Cary, will play a solo on *Chloe*!" And the band walked off stage, leaving Dick to play his way out of his predicament. "I felt lost—terrible spot—I'm not used to it—have nothing prepared for a solo and furthermore don't want to do these."

> Despite this, Cary could say,
> *I spent the best time of my life when with him [Armstrong], not least because Jack Teagarden introduced me to the woman who later became my wife. I am very proud that I was allowed to play with him.*

Armstrong did have one complaint about Cary, according to Ernie Anderson. "You have to understand Louis' almost mystic attitude about improvisation. He truly believed there was something magical, or even religious, about it. Once something good was improvised you were supposed to remember it in every detail and play it that way every time. When Dick played *West End Blues* he just improvised his own blues solo chorus. Louis thought he should have played the chorus Earl Hines played on the original record. Louis' mind was rigidly fixed on this. He admired Dick but couldn't understand why he didn't play it just the way Earl had done."

It was at Billy Berg's that Cary had his first, but not his last, insight into the character of the band's road manager, Frenchy (Pierre Tallerie). This initial upset involved Frenchy and bassist Morty Corb. Cary considered Morty Corb to be an excellent bassist (until he became involved with the fender bass). With Armstrong, Corb was getting $100 a week, but he wanted $150 for the trip east, so that his wife could accompany him. Frenchy refused Corb's request and instead hired Arvell Shaw for $85 a week. To Frenchy this must have seemed a good financial move, and Shaw had been with the Armstrong big band during the last months of its existence, but Cary considered Corb was unfairly treated.

> *They had a big argument downstairs in the basement about taking him [Corb] to Chicago. Louis really fought to get him. [Frenchy was] one of the slimiest sonofabitches I ever knew... a horrible man. He started more trouble in that band between people. And that was his job, to do it. I got a glimpse of how they do things like that.*

Other references to Frenchy included, "Talking to him makes me feel like trying to sidestep a poisonous snake" and "one of nature's most deplorable efforts." Another Frenchy incident involved Sid Catlett:

> *That's when I met my second wife out there, Virginia. We were downstairs one night after we were all through at Billy Berg's and it wasn't really fixed up for guest rooms, they just had cloth separations. We were in the back part of the thing and we hear this argument. Frenchy starts this big thing between Louis and Sid Catlett and then leaves. And they get into a big fight on account of what Frenchy said. At one point Sid had Louis round the neck and was choking him. Then he stopped and he was weeping. It was very embarrassing and Virginia and I didn't want anybody to know that we were there, so we huddled in the back until they left. [Frenchy] gave out this*

propaganda about people. They were trying to get rid of Sid Catlett too. They had no idea he was a great drummer because they didn't know anything about music. But he had borrowed money ahead of his salary and they had to get rid of him. Frenchy had this story where they gave Louis his head one time and let him hire a big band and he went ahead and got a bunch of people and went way over budget, so they took it away from him and never let him do it again.

[Louis] fought for Catlett ... he did keep him. Anybody who got rid of Sid was out of their mind. He was the greatest drummer I ever heard. Greatest soloist anyway.

Cary was unimpressed by Joe Glaser.
Whatever the stories are about Glaser, the truth is really that he was a loud-mouthed, obscene gangster, who had nothing but contempt for the blacks and became a multimillionaire on their talents. He did get Louis out of a couple of busts (maybe more) but it is obvious it was for his benefit.

He noted that 1947 "has been an important year in my life," except "Don't feel right playing piano and not trumpet [and] no arranging." Also, "Another wonderful thing, I met a girl I was already sure I was in love with. She had ... several names, the latest being Nicky Allen. Dorothy Virginia Boyd has been twice married and luckily divorced the same number of times. With her was her daughter, Leslie, aged five." (Nicky is sometimes spelt Nickie.)

"Of course I was still married, with a wonderful daughter almost nine, a very nice girl for a wife and to make it even more complicated, a new daughter two days before Christmas, 1947." The new daughter was named Janet.

Virginia Allen & Josh Billings, North Hollywood, January 1948 with Johnny Windhurst's Ford automobile

In January 1948 the All Stars arrived in New York and Cary's final date with them was at the 5,900-seat Roxy Theatre at 153 W. 50th Street. The feature film showing was "You Were Meant for Me," starring Jeanne Crain and Dan Dailey.

There was one thing about the Roxy, everything had to be on schedule. So one night Jack Teagarden sang a different song from the one he usually did. Instead of St. James Infirmary *he sang* Basin Street, *his other one and all hell broke loose. They had meetings and memos that you have to notify us a week in advance and all that stuff.*

I shared a room with Jack at the time. They were paying him only $500 a week and they were taking $410 of it [because] they lost money with his band and things like that. Addie [Mrs. Teagarden] and Glaser were handling his debts and she would grab the rest of it. He was in such a low state he used to say to me, 'Dick, if I don't have enough to buy a pint of Four Roses every day I'm going to quit playing.' And he went to Europe completely broke, for Chrisake, the poor son-of-a-gun.

Dick Cary and Virginia Allen, circa January 1948

French jazz critic Hugues Panassie was organising an international jazz festival to be held in Nice between the 22nd and 28th of February, and he booked the All Stars to be the headline act. However, he wanted Earl Hines, another big name in France, to be the pianist with the band. In preparation for this Hines was also on stage when the All Stars began their engagement at the Roxy on January 28th.

Cary recalled:
We had two pianos on the stage, one on each end, Earl here and me there. Earl was going to Europe with them and I was going to stay behind—with pay—and then rejoin them after a couple of weeks. We were going to have two pianos, which I could never figure how they were going to do that, unless they were just going to invite Earl up to play solos or something. He didn't like to play in someone else's band, never did.

Cary's remark is a little puzzling. After the weeks at the Roxy one would have expected a routine with the two pianists to have evolved and there is a diary note, "Earl Hines and I both play, two pianos throughout." Later he mentions that the Hines feature number, *Boogie Woogie on St. Louis Blues*, is on the programme. Four sets were played each day, except Saturday when it was five.

But the Panassie proposal seems to have been quite acceptable to Cary.

> They [the Nice Festival committee] had specifically asked for Hines and I was to get a two week vacation.
>
> Before they went to Europe I was in the process of getting a divorce and I was drinking too much and I was getting cramps in my legs. It happened that one of the cramps grabbed me one night and there was nothing I could do but wait until the spotlight [moved] and [I could] duck into the wings. Luckily they had another piano, but here's one vacant piano. All you can do is walk it off and it was horrible. Just the thought of getting one, the anxiety, is paralysing, almost. So they issued a memo to me that if I had to leave the stage I better get a sub, so I did for one day. I went to a doctor and he gave me some sedatives. I was still getting the huge sum of $150 a week—my starting salary. I'd been promised an immediate raise at the start if the thing was a success and nothing could have been more successful. I never thought very much about money as long as I was working and happy. I didn't give a damn because I just enjoyed it so much. So the band went to Europe and I went up to Joe Glaser's office to see about a bit more money. I thought it was time. I was getting a divorce and was going to need some money.
>
> So I'm sitting in the office and Frenchy (who I can truthfully say was as scummy a bastard as anyone in the music business) comes in and he tells Joe Glaser that I'm a drug addict. That was absolutely false and I got mad as hell. I absolutely blew up. I told him what I thought of him and I left the office and that was the end of that. I've always wondered if that was these assholes' method of getting rid of me.

The All Stars played several benefits during the run at the Roxy. Cary also mentioned on February 14 that he had not even had a beer since the earlier attack of leg cramps. That same day he saw the Stan Kenton orchestra at Carnegie Hall: "These guys have nerve and lungs—no one has taste, although their rhythm section is good. Safranski no fake, Shelly Manne a clever drummer."

> *Years later, after Louis' death, Bobby Hackett, who was as close to Louis as anyone, told me that Louis was very hurt at my leaving and I felt terrible that he'd never known what had really taken place.*

It was on the last day of their Roxy engagement, February 17, that Cary spoke to Joe Glaser about a raise. "He was his usual loud, profane, disagreeable, obscene, dirty self. No result—I'm to call tomorrow." "I want 200 a week or I'm through." "I went off the wagon." On telephoning the next day Cary was told to call about March 8 or 9. When he spoke to Glaser on the 9th the message was: "They're going to use Hines for a month or two—so I'm free to find work and study here in New York! Feels good." He celebrated by going to the cinema and guesting on trumpet at Eddie Condon's.

Louis Armstrong arrived in France on February 20th and *Down Beat* for March 10, 1948, reduced these events to the single comment: "Dick Cary, pianist-arranger, split with Louis Armstrong just before Satchmo's flight for France."

5. Composition and Condon
(1948–1949)

So I went back up to Connecticut to settle the divorce, then get my girl, Virginia, and settle down in New York. I wanted to stay in New York and study composition. Through the G.I. Bill of Rights, I was able to have four years study free of charge with Stefan Wolpe. Previous students of his were Eddie Sauter and John Carisi. He was a marvellous teacher. People just couldn't understand why I didn't stay with Louis, but I wouldn't have traded the experience with Wolpe for anything.

He [Wolpe] had a thing called the Contemporary Music School and he had a lot of pupils and fine instructors and he was a great composer. He was an inspiration to be with every week. He had taught Eddie Sauter a lot and that's why I went to him, because I liked Eddie's music so much. It pulls you away from a lot of things you're doing and puts you in whole new areas—atonal music and serial music, which is very difficult to write. All composers have a desire to be up-to-date. They hate to be considered old-fashioned. I remember Wolpe had a thing of his [A Man From Midian, a series of nine short things about the life of Moses] done at Carnegie Hall. It had been written in the thirties and he went around apologising to everybody that it was old fashioned.

Stefan Wolpe [pronounced Vol-pee] (1902–1972) had fled Berlin in 1933. Arriving in the U.S.A. in 1938, by way of Palestine, he worked at various musical academies and was considered an influential teacher. Joe Bushkin was another of his pupils. His influence on Cary was clearly considerable, though one wonders if, from a jazz point of view, this influence was entirely benign. Eddie Sauter was arranging for big bands like Benny Goodman and then Ray McKinley, and could hear his charts played by young, eager musicians who wanted to play jazz, but for Cary such opportunities were very limited.

Through the 1950s Cary continued to study composition as much as he could.

Then I had a year [1954] with a man named Tim Timothy, who

> a lot of people went to. The guy who wrote Stompin' at the Savoy [Edgar Sampson] went to him and he [Timothy] said he wrote it initially, but I don't know. I studied the Schillinger System. George Gershwin and a lot of studio musicians, arrangers used that system. Schillinger was a scientist and he connected mathematics to music. He had an enormous fat book, The Schillinger System, explaining how to use mathematics to write music. It was very useful to some people in television. Anyway, Tim Timothy taught a sort of watered-down version of it, but I really didn't go for writing with mathematics. So I had about a year with him and a year with Paul Creston [1906–1985], who was a rather famous American composer, but I didn't really get much from him. Then [in Los Angeles in the 1960s] I studied with a man named Dr. Joseph Wagner for about two or three years and I did get something out of that. I also studied with another man [in Los Angeles] who was a very good movie scorer, but I can't think of his name.

Another reported to have studied with Paul Creston was Gene Schroeder, pianist at Condon's club for many years. The "movie scorer" Cary mentions may have been Albert Harris.

Cary was accepted by Wolpe as a student and had his first lesson on April 6, 1948. The lessons took an hour each week. On April 20 he noted: "Met Eddie Sauter, taking hour after mine." He also heard David Tudor play Wolpe's *Passacaglia for Piano*—"I can't hear these things but am willing to learn." A few weeks later he saw John Carisi and "talked of Wolpe and his critics like Joe Bushkin, who's levelled his talent off with fear and reactionary feeling."

One lesson with Wolpe was "about phrases—focal points—relation of ideas—intervals—rhythmic ideas—difference of levels. I did a thing in 7ths yesterday which he seemed to like, suggested I use it for first movement of some work."

Work was elusive when Cary and Virginia Allen arrived in Middletown and then New York. (It was about this time that Nicky became Virginia.) He played twice at Matarese's Circle at the end of February, once on piano with Muggsy Spanier and once on piano, trumpet and alto horn with Tony Parenti. On piano he was at Club Ferdinand on March 1, but not all may have been paying jobs. Gradually, however, the number of such gigs began to increase. A date with Muggsy Spanier at the Tip Toe Club in Bridgeport on March 18 was followed by a series of one or two nights a week at the club with a number of guests, including Hot Lips Page, Sol Yaged, Max Kaminsky, etc. He played sets with singer Chippie Hill at Jimmy Ryan's on April 4 and 18, and on the 19th at Phil Becker's in Waterbury. He had been scheduled to play a Jack Crystal session on the 18th, but Crystal called that afternoon—"Cancelled me, saying that he'd got too many guys and I was the only one he could talk to. So if I'm the nice guy, I'm also the broke fellow, while the ones you can't talk to, make it."

Other gigs were two dates at the Rustic Cabin, one where he played piano in a quartet with clarinetist Tony Parenti and played bass with the second band, while at the Matarese Circle (run by Roc Matarese) on April 16 he played trumpet, peck horn and clarinet. On May 2 and 3 he accompanied singer Gweneth Omeron at Friehofer Bread dinners, and on the 5th subbed for an ill James P. Johnson at a Schubert Theatre, New Haven, concert.

Contemplating his situation on April 11 Cary wrote: "I'm lucky, but I've always believed in small bands and improvising and I'm starting to realize a little from several years of effort. He lists his earnings for the week as $116, adding, "Nickie gets $50, making 166 bucks between us, which is just a start here in the greatest city in the world—for my business anyway, though at times I hate the place."

He was a member of a Condon group, alongside Bobby Hackett, cornet, Peanuts Hucko, clarinet, Bud Freeman, tenor, Irv Manning, bass, and Zutty Singleton, drums, which played a four-week engagement (May 10–June 6) in 1948 at the Blue Note in Chicago. They flew to Chicago on Sunday, May 9, and soon visited clubs. "Heard band at Blue Note—mediocre bebop (Red Rodney, Bill Harris, George Auld, Lou Levy, Chubby Jackson, Shelly Manne). Then to Brass Rail for one awful set with Mike Riley, Rico Vallese, Hank Wayland and three others in funny costume, then Jazz, Ltd. Played one on trumpet—terrible." On the 17th Louis and Lucille Armstrong, Sid Catlett and Arvell Shaw came in to hear the band, and the following day Cary went "to Riptide, Calumet City, to catch one set by Louis' All Stars."

"What a day off" is how Cary referred to May 25. "To Charles Creath's for gumbo and Charles' talk of his past and present philosophy. Has white Polish wife and 10-year-old nice boy, Richard. Pretty nice folks, I guess. Zutty ate five plates and beat me by one." Then it was off to Squirrel Ashcraft's until 8:30 the next morning— "lots of taping." [Charlie Creath—1890–1951—was a trumpet player who was active in St. Louis in the 1920s and worked with riverboat pianist Fate Marable.]

Back in New York there were many gaps in Cary's calendar, but he had occasional gigs at Condon's. June 18 he visited the Royal Roost to hear Dizzy Gillespie's band and the Thelonious Monk Quartet—"Felonious is ridiculous! Absolutely." The next day he was at the Tip Toe club in Bridgeport, playing with Tony Parenti, Miff Mole and Ralph Sutton—"the latter quite a pianist—full—sort of ragtime style but strong and moving." And on the 22nd he worked at Condon's with guest Ed Hall—"a real gentleman and what clarinet!"

On the day that Cary got a job at the Ha Ha club he met Charlie Parker—"Had couple with 'Yardbird.' He has terrible persecution complex, naturally, having done so much time in hospital and jail. I was English, Russian, FBI, psychiatrist—in that order."

The job, five nights a week, at the Ha Ha club began on July 2 at "$85 a week, 10:30 to 4, three shows of awful singers and dancers. Fairly easy, dull job." Of one Saturday session he recalled: "Ha Ha very noisy tonight. Many of the thugs around. During Winnie's last strip they got a fight going and no one watched Winnie." Later he remarked, "This Ha Ha joint is a front for gambling." He finished there on August 12 and started at Eddie Condon's the following night as intermission pianist for four weeks. Joe Sullivan had left and Ralph Sutton was not due to replace him until September. As Cary told Sutton's biographer, Jim Shacter,

> *I sat in a lot with the band when I wasn't actually working at the [Condon] club and sometimes I sat in on trumpet with Ralph. So did Johnny Windhurst and we used to comment that very few pianists could provide such a fine rhythmic accompaniment without bass and drums.*

Cary and Sutton established a rapport which was to continue for the rest of their lives. Cary also recalled how, when he was playing with the Condon band,

> *I'd sometimes see Ralph at a nearby table and catch his eye and get a small grin of appreciation. Ralph never talked much, but that grin was a lot more meaningful than any words. I recall it with pleasure. Of course, if you think you're playing badly, you avoid those glances. But if you think you might have done something that Condon would have called 'fairly respectable,' you may look about to see if one of your peers will offer some small confirmation.*

A couple of upsets with Virginia are mentioned. There was "a hell of an argument" over money one evening, but next day all was agreeable until late evening, when there was another argument and Virginia almost walked out—"The result of a couple of stubborn tempers and bad moods acting up at the same time."

The four weeks at Condon's passed smoothly, though Sutton was back in town before the end of August. Cary specifically mentions that Jack Teagarden sat-in one night and that Bobby Hackett and Tony Parenti were the guests on August 31. That was the day he and Virginia moved to 273 West 47th Street. His final night at Condon's was on September 9.

During the Condon's booking he played two concerts at the Red Coach Inn in Middletown, on August 25 with Johnny Windhurst and Jack Teagarden, and on September 1 with Max Kaminsky. The Inn was advertised as New England's Famous Dine and Dance Spot, with "Max Kaminsky assisted by Dick Cary, Henry Martin, Johnny Vine, Bill Leukhardt, Johnny Giuffrida." There were three more dates at the Red Coach during September, with familiar names like Wild Bill Davison, Muggsy Spanier, and Ed Hall/Lips Page/Eddie Condon guesting. Cary received $15 for each gig and $10 for the occasional Matarese Circle appearance.

JAZZ CONCERT
TONIGHT
9 P.M. to 1 A.M.
THE RED COACH INN
New England's Famous
Dine and Dance Spot Presents
MAX KAMINSKY
Jazz Trumpet Artist
Direct from Bar Harbor, Boston
Assisted by Dick Cary, Henry Martin,
Johnny Vine, Bill Leukhardt,
Johnny Giuffrida
No Cover Charge
For Res. Call Middletown 5191

On September 7, 1948, the first of the Eddie Condon Floor Shows was televised by the New York City station WPIX, channel 11. As always, Ernie Anderson was the driving force behind the scenes.

Condon had pioneered jazz on television as early as 1942. As he put it: "I accidentally had the first jazz concert on television, in April 1942 .... We broadcast four shows before Federal Communications Commission wartime restrictions shut us down, along with almost everyone else. It was no loss; there were probably about three people watching us on three-inch televisions."

Anderson commented: "After the war we had our next TV show series on WPIX ... the show was a hit in the newspapers, the critics loved it and gave it big space. NBC bought the show because they thought they'd sell it to a sponsor [but they didn't!]. I was the sole producer of all the Eddie Condon shows on radio and on TV."

There were a total of 49 known Eddie Condon Floor Show programmes between September 7, 1948, and September 17, 1949, the first twelve on WPIX on Tuesday evenings and the balance on WNBT (Channel 4) and the NBC network on Saturday evenings. In addition there were perhaps six or seven shows produced by CBS in May and June 1950.

As with the earlier Blue Network radio programmes, the Floor Shows featured the best jazzmen in New York. In addition to the usual Condon faces there appeared such stars as Louis Armstrong, Jack Teagarden, Gene Krupa, Count Basie, Woody Herman, Cootie Williams, Hot Lips Page and Mary Lou Williams. Dancers who performed included Pearl Primus, Baby Lawrence and Bunny Briggs; among the singers were Ella Fitzgerald, Lee Wiley, Maxine Sullivan, Thelma Carpenter, Sarah Vaughan, Rosemary Clooney, Pearl Bailey and Billie Holiday; and celebrity guests included film stars Kirk Douglas, Zero Mostel and Jackie Cooper.

Dick Cary appeared on a number of these shows, playing piano, trumpet or alto horn, and was almost always present to write any backgrounds which might be required. Many titles were issued on LPs, some serving as good examples of Cary's work at this time. He plays excellent piano behind a Red Allen vocal on *I Told Ya I Love Ya, Now Get Out,* and behind Sidney Bechet and Wild Bill Davison on the November 16, 1948, telecast. The following week he was reunited with Armstrong and Teagarden, taking a fine piano solo on *King Porter Stomp*. On a March 26, 1949, broadcast, during a George Gershwin medley, he takes a typically out-of-the-ordinary approach in his solo piano version of *The Man I Love*.

> Cary told Bert Whyatt:
> *At that time all the guests—no matter who—would do that show for a 100 bucks just to do TV which was so new to everyone. It was one big party each week with the old Pathe studio uptown full of friends for the rehearsal all day and the show in early evening, done live, of course.*

> And as he told Floyd Levin:
> *I did all the arrangements for that just to stay on the show, because there was no budget.*

Available but incomplete details of the Floor Shows including

Dick Cary's work are listed in the discography. However, it is worth mentioning that in addition to trumpet and piano, he played organ on some titles, accompanying Lee Wiley or Bobby Hackett, and later in the series, his work on alto horn was a feature. During the April 16, 1949, show, devoted to George Gershwin's music, he played two piano duets with Joe Bushkin, *Ain't Necessarily So* and *Liza*.

Writing arrangements had taken a back seat in recent months and opportunities for such work were scarce. He had written three, including two originals, for an eight-piece band which drummer Morey Feld had been rehearsing, plus two for "the blonde Quinn Sisters" when they were working at the Ha Ha club. On September 23 he accompanied singer Liza Morrow when she recorded his tune *Richard Cory*. Presumably this was a "demo" record as a week later he wrote: "Gave *R. Cory* tune to Milt Gabler." That same day he enrolled at the Contemporary Music School.

He did miss the Condon shows for the four weeks when he played for $200 a week with cornetist Muggsy Spanier's group, which opened at the Blue Note in Chicago on October 11, 1948. Also in the band were Miff Mole, trombone, Pee Wee Russell, clarinet, Herb Ward, bass, and Eddie Phyfe, drums. Art Tatum ("as unbelievable as ever") was the intermission pianist. Spanier collected Russell and Cary in his 1948 white De Soto at 6:30 on Friday, October 8, and they arrived in Chicago at 7 a.m. on the Saturday. Cary spent his two free days before the band's opening visiting the Louis Armstrong All Stars at the Oriental Theatre and looking in at Jazz, Ltd.

Cary found himself replacing Spanier on trumpet for a day or two:

> *What happened was: Muggsy did the Dave Garroway Show with a large studio orchestra. I think it was our second or third night in the Blue Note. I did two or three arrangements for the show and went along, I guess to play piano and rehearse the band. Muggsy hadn't done much of that type of work and was very happy about the whole thing. On the way to work he stopped the cab about three times at inviting-looking saloons and the driver came in with us and we arrived at the Blue Note with Mr. Spanier not able to do his best, so Frank Holyfiend [Frank Holzfeind, the owner] sent him home. So for four or five days I played trumpet and we had a different piano player each night and I never could remember any of these later on. [Cary's diary lists Tut Soper, Steve Freedman and Shelley Robin, plus one night Doc Evans played trumpet. Cary had arranged* Relaxin' at the Touro *for Spanier, with six clarinets,*

three trombones and rhythm, "but then Spanier got drunk and was a fool on the broadcast."]

Also, Mr. A. TATUM was in there. Pee Wee and I stayed in every interval to hear this great man and when I was back on piano I played way over my head. I think Mr. T. provided me with more great pleasure than anyone I ever heard on any instrument. I often thought he was such a pleasant guy because there was none [for him] to be jealous of. What a position to be in!

Dave Garroway, a popular radio presenter, promoted a concert at the Opera House on October 16, featuring the Spanier band—"We played second part ... for 4,500 people who seemed to like the band very much." The band members were less happy when they discovered that Spanier had received $250 and had paid each musician $20.

Johnny Windhurst arrived in Chicago October 13 to open at Jazz, Ltd. that evening, though Cary later commented, "It's a terrible band." There was a party there on November 5 to celebrate Windhurst's 22nd birthday. Another interlude was seeing a performance of "A Streetcar Named Desire," with Anthony Quinn in the lead and Arnie Freeman as a Mexican poker-player.

While in Chicago Cary had written an arrangement of *My Old Flame* for Woody Herman, presumably on spec, but Herman's booking at the Sherman Hotel fell through and Cary did not see him.

Cary travelled with Pee Wee and Mary Russell on the Greyhound bus back to New York on November 8/9, only to be concerned about the future again: "Can't overcome uneasiness produced by no job and owing Rose $30 a week." Fortunately Virginia was "getting a lot of medical illustrating." She was also painting portraits of various musicians, including Louis Armstrong and Sid Catlett, though of the Armstrong Cary wrote: "looks like a Dorian Gray-Mr. Hyde thing. Ugh!"

But more work soon began coming his way. On November 14 he played trumpet at Jimmy Ryan's with Brad Gowans, Pee Wee Russell and Ralph Sutton, and piano with Wild Bill Davison, Benny Morton and Tony Parenti. That paid $10, as did an arrangement of *Trees* for a Polish band in Middletown. On the 16th and the 23rd he played piano for Eddie Condon Floor Shows on television [The October 23 show was scheduled for 9:05 to 9:30 p.m. "Louis scared hell out of all of us by arriving at 9:03."]; on the 17th he subbed for Charlie Queener at Nick's; and in the meantime Milt Gabler put him in touch with organist Ethel Smith for a week's work.

To jump forward to the Ethel Smith job, after three rehearsals with her Cary commented: "She's a technician though and I'll conceal no admiration for that quality." On November 30 he flew to Norfolk, Virginia, then on to Plymouth, where they opened for a week, starting the next day. The first show was at 2:20. "I play, with Jim Johnson, bass, and Nat Ray, drums, *Lucky Day* bringing Ethel on. By the fourth show we were well into rut, where we'll remain for the rest of the week." The last show was at 9:35, with five appearances on Saturday, and all for $125 a week. Cary was back in New York on December 8 to carry on working at Ryan's, which was "better than accompanying an organ." However, he continued to write for Ethel Smith, although he considered her "a tight little broad"—"We argued till I had a headache. She came down to 110 bucks for those four arrangements."

On October 12 Cary was asked to arrange *You're All I Want for Christmas* for Benny Goodman. On the 15th Cary said: "To Squibb Building and BG rehearsal at 1:00. He did my arrangement too slow and then put it aside." Cary was told that Goodman was "not impressed" by his chart, but a week later Cary was at another rehearsal where his arrangement was played, for which he received $50. There is no mention of any further writing for Goodman.

> *I went to quite a few Benny Goodman rehearsals and he had that slightly bop-orientated band, with arranger Chico O'Farrill. They had rehearsals in the Columbia Studios and John Hammond and a whole bunch of his friends would attend, which pissed Benny off, because he didn't like that at all, but he couldn't tell John that. He didn't like some of these kids [musicians] either, because they were wiseguys. They thought Benny and those people were old-fashioned. I'll never forget one day at the rehearsal. Just before they were going to pack up Benny said, "Oh, wait a minute boys, there's just one thing I want to play." They pulled out one of Eddie Sauter's marvellous pieces like* Benny Rides Again *or* Clarinet a la King *and these kids tried to play that. It was the worst thing you ever heard in your life. It was horrible. It was so bad that by the time the music died down, there was deafening silence in the room. Not a sound, for just a few seconds. Benny gradually turned around, kind of half-looked at the band and says, "Pretty square arrangement, huh?" And everybody in the room howled and I laughed the loudest of anybody.*

However, in telling this story to Gudrun Endress, for *Jazz Podium*, Cary does not mention Sauter but refers to "a new piece with a dreadful arrangement."

> *There were two people I declined to play for: Benny Goodman and Tommy Dorsey. In the first place I didn't know how to play in a big band. That's why I didn't go on the road. I wanted to work in saloons in small jazz bands. I was afraid they wouldn't like what I did and when they didn't, either one of those guys, it was rough. Especially Tommy, he could be very cruel at times. Benny was different from Tommy but he could be cruel in his own way. I liked these guys very much but would never play with either, because that was when friendship would end. I only travelled with two bands on the road, Billy Butterfield's and Jimmy Dorsey's.*

While he had been rehearsing with Ethel Smith, Cary began a regular gig at Jimmy Ryan's, with Max Kaminsky, trumpet, leader, and Art Trappier, drums, starting November 22. He put in a substitute during the week he spent with Ethel Smith and on his return found that Cecil Scott had been added, leading to a number of notes on the Ryan's personnel: "Cecil Scott ... goes from Freddy Martin to Bud Freeman, etc, to straight [Illinois] Jacquet"—"I couldn't work with a more agreeable group"—"Cecil is as out-of-tune as anyone can be, Trappier and Max mad, piano very embarrassing"— "Cecil Scott broke it up with a cadenza on *Body and Soul*—he's possessed of quite a technique." (And a wooden leg, Cary noted.)

On at least two nights Don Frye, the intermission pianist, sat-in with the quartet and Cary switched to clarinet. Other nights trumpeter Hot Lips Page came in to play, causing Cary to rave on one occasion: "Lips in. Really got going. He's sensational at times." That night Cary wrote of his own performance: "played much better than usual timorous, lazy crap I do."

New Year's Eve was one of the nights when Cary played clarinet and it was Virginia Allen's birthday. (She was born in 1922.) Her relationship with Cary also seems to have been rocky, as instanced by: "V & I had hell of an argument this p.m. on finances. Damn money and whiskey, eternally damn them." And on January 1, 1949 he notes an argument, followed by "V. making sounds like a wife." This remark, coupled with the lack of any documentary evidence, would suggest that he and Virginia never married, despite his intentions in 1947.

December 30, 1948, found Cary playing peck horn and bass

at a rehearsal of Johnny Windhurst's new band, with Ed Hubble, trombone, Sol Yaged, clarinet, Dick Hyman, piano, and Eddie Phyfe, drums. He was very impressed by Hyman: "...a very talented young pianist who graduated from Columbia last year, majoring in music. Heard him play at President Hotel bar—very fast, good harmonic sense, imagination and sense of form. Acts very old, worried and serious for his 21 years or so." [Months later Cary was playing at Nick's one evening when Willie "The Lion" Smith, Gene Schroeder and Dick Hyman came in, leading to a similar entry: "Hyman has wonderful foundation—technique, taste, ear."]

On January 15, 1949—"Tonight we got notice at Ryan's— latter was taken off if we'd take a cut of five dollars," but it was not in Cary's nature to bend to such an ultimatum. The band finished on January 29, 1949, though Cary was back the following night for the jam session "where I blew my ring off on the Martin," with Sidney Bechet, Hot Lips Page, Sammy Price, etc. On the last day of January Cary sang the blues—"Slushy, dark day in New York and I'm out of work!"

Then, on February 1, he was asked to work at Nick's for one week (Charlie Queener's father was ill), so the next night he was playing with Billy Butterfield, Cutty Cutshall, Ernie Caceres, Irving Manning and Joe Grauso. After a week's break he was back at Nick's for another seven days, playing intermission piano for Hank Duncan, whose uncle had died. Brad Gowans asked Cary, "When are you expecting the next death?" He also settled into a run of Sunday afternoon appearances at Nick's, playing trumpet from 5:30 to 8:00 p.m. or sometimes later. These lasted until May 15, though he also worked other days at the club.

All during this period Cary was continuing his studies with Wolpe and he also started, at the end of November, orchestration lessons with "little Ralph Shapey." By June of 1949 he could write: "Shapey very encouraging. Says he wouldn't be ashamed to show 'waltz' to Hindemith or Bartók." Things were more difficult with Wolpe. After one class on counterpoint he threatened: "I'll drop this nonsense," but later wrote: "I have my first 'opus' almost done—will do it for a small chamber group." (Ralph Shapey, born 1921, was a Wolpe student also. In later years he was busy as a conductor. His works remain unpublished.)

As a further example of a professional jazz musician's working life, the following are the various jobs which Dick Cary played from early January to early March, 1949. In addition he was involved with the Eddie Condon Floor Show programmes for television on Saturdays, plus rehearsals on one day during each week. He had his studies with Wolpe and Ralph Shapey and was doing a certain amount of incidental arranging work. The Floor Shows and other activities are discussed during the next few pages.

January 9: at Jimmy Ryan's, played trumpet. Roy Eldridge and Hot Lips Page sat-in. "Eldridge still the man." Then to Rustic Lodge, New Brunswick, played with Benny Morton, Tony Parenti, Johnny Windhurst, Ed Hubble, etc.
February 11: Stuyvesant Casino, with Windhurst, Brunis. "The Casino job is horrible—awful piano."
February 12: Eddie Condon TV show
February 13: Nick's—subbed for Billy Butterfield
February 18: Condon TV rehearsal, then Central Plaza (with Sidney Bechet, Brad Gowans, Joe Sullivan— "Piano was impossible.")
February 19: Condon TV show—Cootie Williams played *Cabin in the Sky* with my arrangement. To Nick's, on relief piano.
February 24: recorded two titles for Decca [unissued] with Jimmy Atkins, a cowboy singer.
February 26: Condon TV show—Cootie Williams, with the Woody Herman orchestra, played Cary's transcription of *Concerto for Cootie*. "The Herman Herd read my arrangement very poorly. Cootie loved it and wants a copy. Show ran over and they cut band off right in middle of Cootie's tune."
March 5: played a university house party in Middletown with Bobby Hackett, Brad Gowans, Hank D'Amico, clarinet, Felix Giobbe, bass, Buzzy Drootin, drums, and Bill Leukhardt, reeds.

During January, Cary had been cooperating with Johnny DeVries on five songs and early in February, they showed them to Milt Gabler, who was a&r man at Decca records, as well as the owner of Commodore Records. "Milt's plan is Ella Fitzgerald does *Rockabye Baby on the Be-bop*, Bing does *Windmill on a Hill in Heaven*, Dorothy Shay *Peanut Brittle Time*. No action on *Streetcar Named Desire* or *Sweet Daddy*." This plan is not mentioned again, nor is the success or otherwise of Cary's arrangement of *Rockabye Baby on the Be-bop* for Gene Krupa. The song did get one airing, sung and danced by Teddy Hale on the Eddie Condon Floor Show of April 2, 1949. Perhaps it was even broadcast over WNBT when Cary accompanied Teddy Hale on the Damon Runyon programme on April 9.

After one Sunday session at Nick's, 5:30 to 8:00, on March 20, with clarinetist Joe Marsala as the guest, Cary wrote: "Joe is a strange clarinet player. If he had any drive or did much practising, he'd be a bitch, but now he can play pretty, do Pee Wee, Teschemacher, Roppolo tricks." He also commented on his own use of the cornet: "Enjoyed working on my old Bach cornet. Entirely different instrument from a trumpet—lower register, more distinct notes, intervals, cleaner articulation."

Late in March he gave three trumpet lessons—"nice lad— no ear, nothing, but I get 7 bucks and he got a few nips and an enjoyable 1½ hours." The lessons continued, at growing intervals, at least until July. These, plus a couple of sessions at Condon's and the Floor Show television, were his income until on April 3 Cary was back in Nick's as a regular replacement for pianist Charlie Queener, for $125 a week, less $12.65 stoppages and he retained his regular Sunday job on trumpet.

The job at Nick's lasted nearly two months and during that time there were the usual highs and lows. A wide range of celebrities and musicians visited the saloon and one, composer Cy Walter, told Cary his playing was "fantastic!" One evening he reported on the improvement when Eddie Phyfe worked instead of Joe Grauso and at one Sunday session, "Buzzy Drootin sat-in and woke band up." Another sitter-in was trombonist and comedian Mike Riley, a visit which led to a little arranging work for Riley's band and a recording date.

Cary had a busy day on May 10. Just before noon he was in the Columbia Studios on behalf of Lees Carpets, making "two records of singing commercials, girl trio, Hammond organ, and I played celeste—came out well." Then it was over to WOR as a spectator "where March of Time filmed an Eddie Condon record date, which I wrote a march for. On date were Bushkin, Manning, Rich, Bradley, Hackett and Hucko; was a tie-up with Atlantic Records."

Two days later Joe Bushkin, Ernie Anderson and Cary met the Atlantic owners, Ahmed Ertegun and Herb Abramson, with singer Ruth Brown at Ertegun's apartment. Miss Brown, who was to record two songs with the Condon band, "'hasn't a chance,' according to Bushkin," which was another inaccurate forecast. *So Long* reached number 6 in the r&b chart and she made many successful records during the next forty years.

Above courtesy:
George Hulme

The Atlantic recording session was held on May 25, with several personnel changes from the film—Manning and Rich were replaced by Jack Lesberg, bass, and Sid Catlett, drums, while Ernie Caceres, baritone, was added. (Cary fails to mention Eddie Condon.) In addition to *So Long* and *It's Raining* for Ruth Brown, the band made *Seems Like Old Times* ("Hackett solo, he wrote arrangement") and *Time Marches On* —"my march." When released Cary's number was called *Time Carries On* and it was credited to "Condon—arr. Dick Cary."

In August, on the 13th, Ahmet Ertegun called "to order an arrangement on *So Long* for Ruth—will be played by Basie." Eight days later Cary visited Bop City and heard Count Basie play his chart—"Basie's band has pretty good reeds but sloppy brass."

During this summer Cary visited Bop City and other clubs a number of times. June 7 he saw the Milt Jackson Trio and the Charlie Barnet band at Bop City, and August 25 Louis Armstrong's All Stars and the George Shearing Quintet opened. Cary visited on the 28th and reported: "Louis as good as ever, but band is awful as an ensemble. Shearing group is wonderful." On July 19 Frank Orchard had called for him just after midnight "and we went to 52nd Street, where there was quite a session in the 3 Deuces. Crowd inside and on sidewalk. Guys that blew were Bud Powell, Shearing, DeFranco, Parker, Chuck Wayne and assorted bop drummers and bassists—Stan Getz, Tony Scott, Miles Davis. But the guys were Shearing and DeFranco ... Shearing sensational." On August 22 he and Virginia went to George "Auld's new place, Tin Pan Alley, and heard a bop session with Tadd Dameron, Alvin Stoller, Red [Mitchell] (Ventura's bass), Kai Winding, Conte Candoli, Gerry Mulligan—at least they're fast but amazingly repetitious."

May 21 had been the Billy Butterfield band's last night at Nick's—"We all got our notice, except Cutty Cutshall," wrote Cary, adding, "terrible to break this little band up." With good timing, Johnny Windhurst visited on the last night and hired Cary to play the El Morocco in New London on Fridays and Sundays. He had also been recommended by pianist Sanford Gold to register with Roy Shields' office.

> So I went to see this big fat asshole up at C.B.S. and he's sitting behind a big desk. He used to be a well-known conductor in the radio days. Roy Shields. I had to fill out a resume and ... [he] sees that I'm working with Eddie Condon once in a while. He picks up a long yellow pencil and points it and says, "You don't read, do you?" I said, "Well, I played in the Hartford Symphony when I was eleven years old." The next week I had a job doubling on violin and cornet and I hadn't played the fiddle for years. I faked it.
>
> But that's so typical. That horrible word Dixieland—it just kills your career. That's if you want to do any studio or any other kind of work. Eddie Condon hated that word and so did everybody else. Imagine calling Billy Butterfield or Bobby Hackett Dixieland trumpet players. It's an insult.
>
> There's a lot of prestige in working for someone like Louis Armstrong, of course. But it doesn't get you any more work. You get typed as a Dixieland player and you are cut off from almost everything in this business. It's a terrible stigma to get attached to your name.

Dick Cary felt very strongly about what he considered to be the damaging effect of the word "Dixieland" and it was a subject to which he would often return.

On leaving Nick's, Cary wrote: "am now unemployed, but there are many angles to work on—songs, singing commercials, radio, singers, arranging and club dates." The last included just two Sundays (May 29, June 5) at the El Morocco in Sound View, with Windhurst, trumpet, Ed Hubble, trombone, Sonny Salad, clarinet, and Johnny Vine, drums—"very hard to play on out-of-tune uprite and no bass, but job not bad. Made 12 bucks which it cost me to work." There was one gig at Eddie Condon's on trumpet and one arranging job—"Illick Kwarsczyk is having me arrange a couple for Krakowska orchestra—gave me ten as down payment on the two polkas which are for a record date—one an original, *If Only I Were Single*." He was also writing for the Eddie Condon Floor Show on television, providing backgrounds for singers Billy Eckstine, Lee Wiley, June Christy and Sara Vaughan, though payment here seemed hit-and-miss.

Each Saturday between May 28 and June 25, Cary went to station WPIX, either as a member of the audience or as a participant, for the Art Ford show. On May 28 he observed: "Art Ford show 11–12, many greats, very successful"; on June 11, "I played couple with Jack Teagarden"; on June 25, "To WPIX to see last of Art Ford show." These shows were, one assumes, a forerunner for the more famous Art Ford Jazz Party telecasts on station WNTA in 1958.

In June he rehearsed "ridiculous old crap at Nola's" with the Indiana Five and he was equally scathing about a Pete Pelizzi band ("silly crap") for which he had been persuaded to write two Dixieland arrangements for a sawbuck ("I'm nuts"). On June 10 and 24 there were jobs at Cobb's Mill Inn in Westport, where he had worked in 1941. Tony Parenti was on both dates, with Jimmy Archey, Art Hodes on the first and Hot Lips Page, Sandy Williams on the second. On the 11th Ernie Anderson asked him to bring his horns to the Floor Show Studio—"I didn't play a note and got pretty annoyed ... Teagarden home with us—tuned piano (as usual)." (Then off to the Art Ford show, as noted above.)

The weekend of June 18/19 found him at the NBC Studios ("Billy B. suggested me and I have a job for Sunday on trumpet and fiddle!"). On the Saturday he rehearsed with the leader, Larry Fuller, noting "ridiculous amateur music" and the following day rehearsing and then playing for "the Fordham revue." His cheques were for "Stop the Music," presumably the proper name for the show.

Still in June, on the 23rd, he had a late call from Bob Wilber, asking him to play with his band at Bill Green's Rustic Lodge. The band was Henry Goodwin, trumpet, Jimmy Archey, trombone, Wilber, clarinet, Pops Foster, bass, and an "awful drummer," though it is hard to believe this would have been Tommy Benford, Wilber's regular drummer. Cary said: "Wilber a nice kid—works like hell on his old-fashioned music—nice evening." The following day he played again at Cobb's Mill Inn in Westport, with Hot Lips Page, trumpet, Sandy Williams, trombone, Tony Parenti, clarinet, Bill Pemberton, "exceptional bass," and Art Trappier, drums. Cary clearly had no problems keeping up in this fast company, despite his reflection on June 29, after Gene Schroeder had hired him for three sets at Condon's, subbing for intermission pianist Sanford Gold. "I'm a horrible piano player at times. The monotony of constant rhythm and the pattern into which my fingers have been conditioned is unbearable."

Work was still irregular. At the end of June the only constant was "Condon's show on Saturday night, with enough club dates to keep existing, barely." Early in July he rehearsed with a singer, Carol Ingersoll, and thought he might have a job accompanying her. "She has a surprisingly pleasing quality." He recorded five titles with her at Hartley Studios on July 18 and 21, presumably as demonstration records, and a month later they did auditions at the Village Vanguard and Jimmy Ryan's, as well as for a Washington, D.C., club owner, presumably without success. The last mention of Carol is on October 24, when he played "a set at Nitecap with Carol Ingersoll, then she was fired."

His studies with Wolpe and Shapey continued, though on May 4 he had commented on Wolpe: "Latter was over my noggin today—way over." Lessons with both tutors continued through the year. The unofficial opening of Wolpe's Contemporary Music Scheme took place on September 29 and Cary attended, taking a tutorial with Ralph Shapey. On October 9 and 29 he refers to tuition by a Mr. Oppenheimer, while on November 16 he was at Carnegie Hall for a concert which included Mozart, Schumann and Volpe's *Sonata 1949*, followed the next day by a lesson with Arnold Copeland. He was also playing baseball on a regular basis, sometimes pushing himself too hard. Jose Ferrer the actor was another participant.

Registering with the Shields office finally paid a small dividend in August. On the 1st he received a call to do the "Easy Does It" TV show at 6:30 p.m. with Johnny Andrews and Francis Lane—"went alright." He did four shows the following week (August 8-11), with Francis Lane and Arthur Johnson—rehearse 2:00 to 4:00, show at 6:30, but then, on the 12th, he went out of town to play at the Montana Yacht Club. This was for $125, plus room and board, except that a week later, on the 19th, he was given immediate notice after lunch—"that's the shortest notice I ever got." Cary, who offered no explanation for the Montana fiasco, considered it cost him "an awful lot," losing the "Easy Does It" show and the solo job at Condon's.

Other stillborn projects included one with Jack Teagarden. Teagarden visited with the Carys in early August, telling them he was leaving Louis Armstrong in September and would start his own band, with Cary as arranger and musical director. Another project was writing two songs for Ruth Brown with lyricist Ralph Besse (sp?). No more was heard of these or of the string quartet which Cary started at the end of July.

A job with an amateur Dixieland band at the Merry Whirl on Long Island on August 26 passed without comment, while on September 1 he played with Johnny Windhurst, Ed Hubble and Johnny Vine at the Swordfish Club in Westhampton. The same band played the Pease House in Middletown the next two nights, a visit which gave Cary the opportunity to see his children again.

Eight days passed before his next job, September 12, 1949,

when he was in one of the bands at Ryan's. The following night he and Tony Parenti were the Tuesday night guests at Eddie Condon's and he was back at Condon's on the Saturday, September 17, working 9:00 to 10:30 p.m. with Johnny Windhurst, Munn Ware, trombone, Pee Wee Russell, Bob Casey, bass, and Buzzy Drootin—"Regular guys were doing Condon's last show on video." Then came two days (September 18 and 20) substituting for pianist Billy Maxted at Nick's, where the band was Phil Napoleon, trumpet, Andy Russo, trombone, Phil Olivella, clarinet, Jack Fay, bass, Tony Spargo, drums. On the 20th there were two broadcasts, "one for army overseas transcriptions." In between, on the 19th, he was at Jimmy Ryan's, with J.C. Higginbotham, trombone, and Tony Parenti, clarinet, and he was there again one week later on cornet with Parenti—"I played terribly—no tone at all."

Cary's week prior to starting a full-time job with Tony Parenti included:

October 4: at the Playgoer's Club on 51st & 6th, with Mike Riley
6/7: rehearsal with Tony Parenti band
8: playing trumpet for Italian wedding, Prospect Hall, Brooklyn
9: hired by Irving Oppenheimer for Jewish group in Mamaroneck, 4–7
10: worked at Jimmy Ryan's, with Pee Wee Russell, clarinet, Munn Ware, trombone, Don Frye, piano, Art Trappier, drums.

Opening night at Ryan's for the Tony Parenti band was Tuesday, October 11. Cary's pay was $77.50, less $4.55 tax. On the 15th Sol Yaged subbed for Parenti, which Cary called "a great improvement." Other work away from Ryan's included an M-G-M recording date on October 13 with Mike Riley and the start of rehearsals at Nola Studios with a big band led by Peanuts Hucko. Cary wrote arrangements for these rehearsals, noting early on: "My original not too satisfactory." He worked another job at Mamaroneck on the 29th, with Johnny Windhurst, trumpet, Jack Fuller, clarinet, Bob Casey, bass; and Mike Bryan (guitar?). In addition he was arranging for Jimmy Dorsey's Dixieland band, as well as playing piano on Dorsey's recording sessions of November 1 and 2. On November 3 he went to the Apollo to rehearse "George Hudson's horrible band—complete lack of any musical feeling—shading, intonation nil."

Cary attended six of the Peanuts Hucko rehearsals between the end of October and early December, in his role as arranger and not as a player. Many of the best musicians in town were at the rehearsals, including Steve Lipkins, Bernie Priven, Louis Mucci, trumpets, Cutty Cutshall, Eddie Bert, Ray Diehl, trombones, Ernie Caceres, Al Klink, reeds, Dick Hyman or Gene Schroeder, piano, Jack Lesberg, bass, and Morey Feld or Buzzy Drootin, drums. At the November 18 session "Billy Butterfield surprised me and played lousy" and, on December 1, "Zoot Sims was nowhere. What a futile character." The Peanuts Hucko rehearsals continued into 1950.

Tony Parenti's band closed at Jimmy Ryan's on November 13, with Jack Teagarden sitting-in on a couple of numbers on that final night. At the time Cary noted: "Have had my first experience on cornet on a steady, tough job and the lip comes along slowly. Band has a terrible, raucous old time sound. Parenti gets the worst flat sound on clarinet. Hodes is an absolute butcher on the piano and Trappier follows him. Ray Diehl is a very good musician."

> I played quite a bit with Parenti. One time for four weeks at Jimmy Ryan's, also Eddie Condon's and various club-dates. Tony had some technique, not the best intonation, and got that rather harsh Italian sound. He fit better with horns such as Brunis and Davison, circus players. [He] was a very amiable guy. With him at Ryan's was Art Hodes who I can report with no hesitation is one of the worst piano players I ever heard. After four weeks of that I ended up with one very swollen testicle and had to stay in bed for a week.

On another occasion Cary wrote:
> We had no bass and the rhythm was awful. Plus the fact that Mr. Hodes is one of the most inept piano players I ever worked with. It's hard for any serious musicians I know to explain how he can hoodwink the public. But then, so did an awful lot of others, including "Wild Bull" as Condon would refer to him.

Reviewing the band in *Down Beat*, John Wilson listed the personnel as Dick Carey (sic), trumpet, Ray Diehl, trombone, Tony Parenti, clarinet, Art Hodes, piano, and Arthur Trappier, drums. After kind words for Hodes and the leader, Wilson wrote: "Carey (sic), better known as a pianist, has fooled around with trumpet before, but this is the first time he has worked a steady job in New York entirely on the horn. He has a rough, exuberant style which blends well with this group despite the fact that a little uncertainty creeps into his work from time to time."

After the Parenti job there were several days of rest, though his reference to "a week in bed" was poetic licence, interspersed with the Peanuts Hucko rehearsals and visits to Nick's and Condon's. He was in a band, presumably at Ryan's, on Sunday, November 20, which included Max Kaminsky, Johnny Windhurst, Cutty Cutshall and Ernie Caceres and on the 25th he played with a Jerry Jerome Quintet (Jerome, tenor, Red Solomon, trumpet, Cary, piano, Ed Safranski, bass, Terry -----, drums) as the relief group at the Commodore Ballroom. November 30 he backed singer Teal Joy at a Cafe Society audition.

Cary's entry for December 1 suggests, presumably from something said at that day's Hucko rehearsal, that he might have a job with leader Ina Ray Hutton, but this was another dead end. That evening he sat-in at the Riviera on 7th Avenue, and at Nick's. He was at the Riviera for the following three nights, and again on December 8, presumably sitting-in, though it is not always clear which is a paid job and which is not. Presumably unpaid were two broadcasts from Nick's on alto horn on December 4 and 7 with the Bobby Hackett band. Also on the 4th he played, probably on trumpet, for an Italian welfare party at the Reuben Bleu, with unnamed piano and guitar, and Charlie Traeger on bass.

And so December 1949 continued with the usual melange— rest days, rehearsals, lessons, sit-ins and the occasional paid job. To quote Cary on the 10th: "It is a little ironic at times to be the only member of A.E. Cary's brood to be poverty stricken." But the next day he was feeling a little more optimistic, "in spite of being close to broke."

December 17: subbed for Ralph Sutton at Condon's. Paid $300 for Jimmy Dorsey recording and arranging.
    18: worked at 88 Club with regular band from Condon's
    19: to Birdland, where he was unimpressed by Billy Eckstine and Harry Belafonte, thought young Red Rodney with Charlie Parker was "disgusting, struggling along" and found the "best, cleanest, fastest music" came from "Lennie Tristano and his little school of polytonal fellows."
    20: guested at Eddie Condon's
    22: worked a Christmas party 5:00 to 8:00 at Gray O'Reilly's, then played an hour at Little Club for Joe Bushkin, "who opened tonight in 'The Rat Race.'" [This was a play written by Garson Kanin.]

23: another hour for Joe Bushkin, 10:30 to 11:30
24 and 26: subbed for Ralph Sutton at Eddie Condon's
25: spent Christmas Day at Johnny Vine's in Middletown
27: MacKay's woodwind rehearsal—"my *Elegie* sounds good now."
30: played trumpet, alto horn and piano at Central Plaza, with Wild Bill Davison, Jimmy Archey, Sidney Bechet, Johnny Windhurst, Lloyd Phillips, piano, and Freddie Moore, drums.
31: saw in the New Year at the Bayard Stockton club house at Princeton, with Sidney Bechet, Johnny Windhurst and a local band.

From a jazz point of view what better way to start the second half of the 20th Century than to play it in with a friend, a fine young trumpeter, and a veteran soprano saxophonist, one of the very greatest of the pioneer musicians.

In his summary of his year, Cary referred to his occasional steady job with Billy Butterfield at Nick's and Tony Parenti at Ryan's, and the few recordings with Ruth Brown/Eddie Condon, Mike Riley, and "the very best, the Jimmy Dorsey 8 side album, plus two other sides with Claire Hogan, which have been really plugged by the jerkeys." Following a mention of the band fronted by Peanuts Hucko he continues: "After a stagnant summer as far as composing went, Wolpe grabbed me again in September and theatrical music started to come out again. This is the hardest and most valuable work of all and the slowest for me. I am learning form the hard way. Virginia said one night, 'You're just full of anti-climaxes,' a very apt criticism. [She], incidentally, is gradually broadening her contacts and impressing different people with her ability on the canvas. We've settled down to getting along together probably better than 95 out of a 100 people, at least in this business where the hours are so unevenly matched. We've spent over a year at 273 W 47th St., just off 8th Avenue, a really old, cockroach-ridden building, housing mostly orientals, who we occasionally annoy with early a.m. noises.

"My first family—Rose, Judy and Janet—is doing alright up in Middletown, Conn. I haven't been able to send what the court decreed, but someday I hope to help them financially and perhaps other ways. Judy is a wonderful girl of almost eleven years, straight and keen and respectful, and I am glad they are not in N.Y.C."

6. Jimmy Dorsey, Jingles and Television (1950–1952)

January 1950 started slowly, with Dick Cary having just a small amount of work with singers or even, in one case, no work at all. He went to the Apex Studios to help audition a singer who did not turn up, but Herb Abramson, of Atlantic Records, paid him $5 anyway. The following day he made a test record with Jimmy Scott and the day after accompanied Don Forbes when the singer auditioned for Max Gordon, owner of the Blue Angel and the Village Vanguard, top New York clubs. As Cary put it, Forbes "didn't kill Max Gordon!"

On January 6 Cary began a job, three or four days a week, at the Casa Seville in Franklin Square, Long Island, playing piano with a septet which backed a show including a magician, a ballet dancer and an eight girl chorus line. One member of the band who impressed Cary was Mary Osborne—"she's a good singer and plays guitar, besides being built well."

His initial reaction to his employer was that "Eddie Stone is a good leader, makes a cute m.c.," but this was to change on January 15, after eight nights' work when: "Stone told me he was going to 'try a new pianist' tonight. Felt rather upset about getting fired by someone like Stone. I liked job and was trying to play as well as I could for what was necessary. Can I be that bad or what the hell was the reason? Stone said I was too busy, but was that it?"

To allay this setback there was a rehearsal and a recording session, January 16 and 17, with the Jimmy Dorsey Dixieland group, then nothing for a few days, except for lessons with Wolpe and Shapey. On the 27th trombonist Ray Diehl promoted a concert at the Westchester County Center, featuring brassmen Wild Bill Davison and Johnny Glasel, clarinetist Buster Bailey, bassist Charlie Traeger and drummer Johnny Vine, with Cary on piano. "Diehl lost his ass. Reason? No advertising in papers." Two days later he was in Bristol to play a private party with Bill Leukhardt, clarinet, and a drummer for jazz fan Bob Harrington. Friends Tweet and Betty Peterson visited and Betty played valve-trombone.

Then began, on February 1, two weeks at the Hickory Log,

working with Ernie Caceres, reeds, Sam Bruno, bass, and Joe Grauso, drums. There were various sitters-in, including Billy Butterfield and Kai Winding, "supposedly one of top trombonists in country. No! Out-of-tune, wavering tone, what standards do these bums have?" In between he subbed at a Jimmy Dorsey band rehearsal, appeared as a guest at Condon's club and led Wild Bill Davison, Bill Leukhardt and Johnny Vine at a Sunday session at the Casino Grille in Saybrook.

When the Hickory Log engagement ended on February 13 Cary returned to his job-by-job existence. There was a Peanuts Hucko rehearsal, composition and conducting lessons, the writing of some parts for the Jack Palmer band, a session in Connecticut with Ralph Sutton and Buster Bailey, a date at Condon's, "a night of raucous Dixieland" with Pete Pelizzi's Jazz Band at the Blue Moon in the Bronx, and, at the Central Plaza, "One of hardest jobs I ever played. Band indescribable—piano the worst—with Baby Dodds and Buster Bailey, and very old Negro trumpet and Negro tuba." There was another gig with trombonist Mike Riley, plus one at Princeton University with Johnny Windhurst, Frank Orchard, Bill Leukhardt and Johnny Vine where "our group, without exception, got very loaded."

On three Saturdays between February 18 and March 4, Cary, along with Cutty Cutshall and Carl Kress, played two numbers with Jimmy Dorsey's Dixieland group for broadcasts from the Statler Hotel. Then a few days later he noted in his diary: "Agreed to join J. Dorsey for $125 in New York, then $165 from then on. This will be quite a test, for staying on the wagon, putting up with musicians (of this type), putting up with repetition and being able to play with a big band. Also if I can sell an arrangement or two occasionally. Try to save some dough and send some to Middletown also. Means giving up school and I hate that idea."

So, on Monday, March 6, Cary joined the Jimmy Dorsey orchestra at the Statler Hotel, commenting "I got by better than I expected." Dorsey, the clarinet and alto playing brother of Tommy Dorsey, was continuing to lead a big band, his success with such hit tunes as *Amapola, Tangerine* and *Green Eyes* undoubtedly helping him to carry on, despite declining popular support for the swing bands. With Dorsey's expert playing, a trumpet section which included Charlie Teagarden and Shorty Sherock, and with Ray Bauduc as the featured drummer, this was still an impressive unit.

As noted in the previous chapter, Cary's association with Dorsey started towards the end of 1949. Dorsey planned to record some Dixieland numbers with a small group he called his Original Dorseyland Jazz Band. The recordings, made on November 1 and 2 and issued by Columbia Records, proved reasonably successful. The ODJB was built around members of the orchestra, with veteran jazzmen Teagarden and Bauduc at the core, with Frank Maynes, tenor, and Bill Lolatte, bass added. Dick Cary, piano, Cutty Cutshall, trombone, and Carl Kress, guitar, were brought in for the recordings.

> *I did all those arrangements and I played on them. So the piano player in the [big] band got hacked and he quit. [Dorsey] also hired another ringer, Cutty Cutshall, so the trombone player got hacked and he quit. So Jimmy asked me, as a result of these records, to go on the road with the band. I accepted and I wish I hadn't. It was a big waste of time and I drank a lot with Jimmy. I liked Jimmy very much.*

Cary also said:
> *But I had a great time with Jimmy, drinking with him after the job, 200 to 400 miles a day. I did a lot of miles with Jimmy Dorsey. They featured a small band within a band a couple of times a night. The only trouble was that Jimmy would play the same two tunes every night.*

Jimmy Dorsey Dorseylanders, March 1950
Cary; Bill Lolatte, b; Dorsey, cl; Ray Diehl, tb; Frank Maynes, ts; Charlie Teagarden, tp; Ray Bauduc, d.

The Dixieland group recorded four more titles on March 7 and there was a big band session, also for Columbia, ten days later. On the March 17 date pianist and composer, Terry Shand, sang *You Don't Have to Be a Baby to Cry*, of which title Cary noted, "I did as modern a version of a Jess Stacy background, a proven commodity."

After a month with Dorsey, Cary wrote: "I find that added years and experience have helped me put up with a thing like this. Get along fine with every member of band, command an adequate amount of respect, which anyone absolutely needs, and although the bulk of the arrangements become hideously monotonous, can almost enjoy certain moments. It teaches one to do what they do a little more accurate and consistent, both of which I can use. Doubt if J.D. will stand for what I'd like to write, so I have done *Shimme-sha-wabble* using large band and small group as an instrument." (Cary never offered his chart to Dorsey, partly because, he said, the band never had a rehearsal while he was a member.) But only a few days later, after a lesson with Wolpe, he was complaining that he was playing "a raggy, trashy piano style for $165 per so that I can send daughters money and so V and I can live in a decent place sometime. The reasons are fairly worthy I guess, but are they worth being a whore?"

In those two sentences Cary summed up the eternal quandary of the artist caught between his art and the need to earn a living.

His hopes of progressing financially had seemed justified when on March 8, 1950, he wrote: "When I bank $130 tomorrow the account will be up to 680—highest I ever earned and saved." That same day Mel Torme sat-in, singing and drumming, with the Dorsey orchestra, while on the 10th at the Hickory Log he saw Frank Sinatra and Ava Gardner, both looking thin and haggard and both very loaded. On Sunday 19th, his day off, he sat-in with Al Gentile's big band at the Ritz Theatre, followed by a gig at the Tip Toe Inn with Charlie Teagarden and Peanuts Hucko. On his next Sunday off Cary subbed with the Mike Riley band again and when the leader left early Cary took the opportunity to play his trombone.

Cary attended an Eddie Condon recording session on the 20th—he had written the arrangements for the band—and heard the Ray McKinley orchestra on stage the following day. He was not impressed with the McKinley band ("pretty bad intonation, especially reeds") or with the King Cole quartet (sic)—"good, efficient, rhythmical, but disgustingly catering to the lowest aspect of audience reaction." Artie Shaw at Bop City fared even worse ("thin band—he smells!"), but Oscar Peterson was a "wonderful pianist, Canada's Art Tatum. This 270-lb guy can do anything—amazing speed." On April 5 he saw the Count Basie octet at the Strand—Emmett Berry, trumpet, George Auld, tenor, J.J. Johnson, trombone ("half tone sharp but fast"), and Buddy DeFranco ("the most fluent modern clarinet sound")—and Billie Holiday ("moaning").

Jimmy Dorsey finished at the Statler on April 1, with two personnel changes before the band started a series of one-night stands. Ray Diehl joined as jazz trombonist and Pat O'Connor replaced Claire Hogan as vocalist, necessitating a couple of rehearsals involving O'Connor, Cary and arranger Howard Gibeling. Then, on Saturday, April 9, when they travelled to Atlantic City for a weekend at the Steel Pier, the touring began. Entry after entry in Cary's diary speaks of "bus to Rochester," "bus to Harrisburg, Pa," "bus to Raleigh, NC," "long ride to Jackson, Miss.," "bus at midnight to Charleston," "300 miles to Sioux Falls," "almost 300 miles to Montevideo, Minn.," mile after dreary mile.

On April 19 the band played at the Jewish Progressive Club ("best yet") in Atlanta, Georgia. "Armstrong group in town. Saw Jack Teagarden, who played last hour with us."

Dorsey's drinking has already been commented upon and while at the Statler Hotel Cary mentions "Jimmy very loaded tonight" and "Jimmy didn't play after 9:00—couldn't, I guess," and no doubt this continued on tour. Certainly Cary himself was drinking heavily during this time. He gave Dorsey his notice on April 29, when they were playing in Centenary, SC. On May 2, in Tulsa, Oklahoma, he overslept and missed the bus, which meant catching a plane to Kansas City and another on to Topeka to rejoin the band. On May 16 Cary wrote: "Dorsey reached the peak of his insults. This time that I play with the worst taste, etc. I can't wait to leave this boor who can be such a darling lamb to anyone who wants his autograph or who has money and plays the sycophant jazz lover. I'm praying that [pianist] Bob Carter will arrive tomorrow in St. Paul."

At the Cobblestone Inn, Storm Lake, on May 22, Cary's entry is: "Got very numb. Told Jimmy Dorsey few things. Fell down cellar stairs and don't remember much after that." It was as well that Bob Carter actually arrived the following day, though he did not replace Cary full time until they reached Lakeside Park in Denver. Cary's last day with Dorsey was May 28, after which he went by train to Chicago on the 29th, spent the 30th in Chicago, and flew to New York on the 31st. There he travelled to the new home at Hampton Hall apartments, 6D, at 43-06 46th Street, Sunnyside, Long Island.

At the beginning of June 1950, Cary was delighted to have finished his "sentence with J.D." but accepted that it had had two benefits. There was the experience gained, plus "acquired enough loot to enable us to get a wonderful new place in Sunnyside, Long Island and start sending an occasional financial help to Judy, my fine little daughter."

Back in New York he was scuffling again and things were slow to start, as indicated by the gaps in his schedule:

June 5: played 4 sets on trumpet at Ryan's with Vic Dickenson, Ed Hall, Charlie Queener, Art Trappier.

June 9: played in Bill Reid band (Lee Gifford, trombone, Jack Fuller, clarinet) at Princeton University. Other bands led by Hot Lips Page, Max Kaminsky and Red Allen.

June 10: same venue.

June 11: also Princeton, played trumpet 4 to midnight at Bayard Stockton's.

June 16: Central Plaza 9 to 1, with Ed Hall, Russell Moore, Willie "The Lion" Smith and Sid Catlett.

June 17: played with Jerry Jerome, tenor, Ed Safranski, bass, Morey Feld, drums, Nick Parito, accordion, at Englewood Athletic Club.

Two days after the Englewood session Cary met with Jerry Jerome and immediately began work at the television station WPIX ... "Did a Summer Theatre program—Glenn Powell show. 2 dancers, 3 singers." In a disgruntled moment Cary referred to "the Daily News cheap little video station WPIX," but he also called it his "new security job, a job I can double on, write and collect $126 per for as little work as I've ever done. Get home early almost every night, two days a week off and the value of being a part of video in its birth struggles."

Jerry Jerome (1912–2002) had been an impressive tenor player with several of the major swing bands, including those of Red Norvo, Benny Goodman and Artie Shaw, but in the 1940s he gradually moved into radio and television as a music director. In 1950 he started working for WPIX-TV and he was soon leading what *Down Beat* called "an all-star video band" with Nick Parito, accordion, Dick Carey (sic), piano, Don Costa, guitar, and Jack Zimmerman, bass.

Cary was with Jerome from June 1950 until January 1952. The story of his connection with WPIX during that eighteen months follows as an entity, without digressing into his other activities in that period—and with evenings and weekends free there were many. These are related after the WPIX experience has been explored.

He worked on a number of programmes at WPIX, including appearances on the Laraine Day Show and the Sister Kenney Show, as well as features with such titles as Morgan's Party, Home Town and From the Top. Music was also provided for a 1950 Miss Television competition. Through the summer of 1950, June to October, the Jerome group played the "Summer Theatre" show three days a week, until the final six weeks when it became a weekly programme as "Glenn's House." Glenn Powell was the emcee of "Summer Theatre."

There are also many mentions of the Art Ford Show between June and November 1950, but these probably had no direct connection with Jerry Jerome. One suspects that Cary was a participant—he refers to rehearsals at 9:30, prior to the one hour show starting at 10:00 p.m.—but his diary is not always clear. The Ford shows had Ray Eberle and Ann Vincent as regular singers, but jazz was included and for the one on September 25 Maxine Sullivan and Errol Garner are mentioned. On June 30 Cary noted, "Show stunk—except a singer from Cafe Society accompanied by Al Haig—good pianist." Duke Ellington's name appears in the July 18, 1950, entry, but that is the only reference. The broadcasts concluded on December 1, but there is a note of an Art Ford village barn show on January 29, 1951, for which Cary wrote piano parts for Mynell Allen.

However, the main feature on which the Jerome band appeared was the Ted Steele Show. This was a magazine programme which was televised four or five afternoons a week. A typical day was a rehearsal starting at 1 p.m., followed by a three hour broadcast. Occasionally Cary would be featured. On September 22 he played violin, and during October he performed the Willie "The Lion" Smith's piano compositions, *Echo of Spring* and *Fingerbuster*. On other occasions he played trumpet, alto horn or bass, in addition to supplying arrangements. *Brahms' Lullaby* and *Roses of Picardy* were two of his features on alto horn and it is mentioned that a horn solo was a regular.

On August 15 Jerry Jerome told Cary he was "not satisfied with music and offered some advice on my accompanying. I should be more definite on lead-ins—think fast!!! He's right. He tells people I can play 'when he wants to'—I've heard that for years, but wish I could control it, the erratic quality which so many guys I know have—Willie "The Lion," Jack O'Brien, Max Kaminsky, Pee Wee Russell, etc."

He was given eight-week's notice on September 11, 1950, at which Cary commented: "Well, it was too good to last. So it was an easy touch while it lasted. Enabled me to buy car, video [ie; a television set] and tape recorder and a temporary feeling of security, though not one of accomplishment. What next!" He also explained: "Jerry Jerome told me they wanted an organist, then this week says he's getting 'a long-hair pianist.' What can I think of all this horse shit? What is the real reason for his not wanting me around? If he had the talent and demanded any respect at all, I should worry about the musical side, but in his case, god knows. I can at least say that a good musician never fired me. Four times it's happened, 52nd Street Cafe in Brooklyn, Glen Gray, Eddie Stone and Jerry Jerome."

He did not help his cause by continuing to over-indulge and on October 23—"goofed on my studio job and missed rehearsal and show," so the next day, "Jerome called, said to take today off as well." However, it would seem that Cary's versatility was in his favour because although he finished at WPIX on Friday, November 3, Jerome telephoned him on the Sunday to say, "'Come in next week'; hasn't found a concert pianist yet. Wonder if he will." A week later Cary wrote: "Playing piano most of the time," and at the end of November, "WPIX is keeping me on to do the Steele Show with Jerry Jerome, Nick Parito, Don Costa and Jack Zimmerman. Could be a long engagement. Everything is now 20 hours a week, Monday through Friday, 1;00 to 5:00, every night off."

For his own part in the show a December entry states: "I annoy viewers with mediocre piano, cornet, alto horn, arrangements for Calella and the Southern Sisters and fiddle with Arizona Cliff Martin." He also noted: "I am appreciating the foundation of video ... all ideas are considered and tried if at all possible ... realizing that everyone is groping."

Of Jerome's personnel, Cary appears to have appreciated the singer Sonny Calella, for whom he did several arrangements, including his own compositions, *When Love Comes Along* and *Windmill on a Hill*, for use on the Steele Show. Of Nick Parito he wrote: "Steele keeps saying 'greatest accordion player in the world' and Nick undoubtedly in his heart really knows this is true." Don Costa (1925–1983) played guitar and also contributed arrangements, and about this time began a successful recording career. Cary thought that "the work Don Costa does is the best a kid could do for a horror like Vaughn Monroe, but at least Don is getting good television experience by hearing his bigger orchestral sounds, with strings and voices, once a week." Costa also scored for Steve Lawrence and Edie Gorme, which led to an a&r post with ABC-Paramount. As well as writing for movies, he was Frank Sinatra's touring conductor in the 1970s.

Highlights for Cary during January 1951 included Stanley Davis singing *R. Cory*; the scoring of one of Debussy's Children's Corner pieces, *The Show Is Dancing*; and, on the 16th, playing *Singing the Blues*. "I scored Bix's chorus four ways, guitar accompaniment, clarinet and cornet and Steele liked it. Also made my video debut singing a dog called *Roving Kind* [the Guy Mitchell song]." On January 31 he played *Cabin in the Sky* à la Cootie Williams. One popular segment which receives a mention—"models showing off slips this afternoon—the high point of the shows as a rule."

In February he "used a gag on Steele Show of playing clinkers on piano, then pulling hammers out." For two weeks during the month the Kefauver Committee investigation into organised crime was shown on WPIX ("the most sensational entertainment ever devised") and the Steele Show was only seen during the committee's lunch break, but on the 15th Cary refers to a very snappy hour; "We did *Dill Pickles*, *Mood Indigo* and *Bugle Call Rag*."

On another show he played *Concerto for Cootie*, noting, "sounds good for five men." This was shortly after Ted Steele had celebrated the show's first anniversary, on May 1. There was an evening show on June 14 which required Cary to smoke a cigar and wear a derby and another late show had him doing a "one man band act on piano, trumpet, bass and horn full of water!" In August Nancy Reed joined the show and Cary wrote of her, "first class."

Working with Jerry Jerome gave rise to other work. Jerome himself played occasional gigs and Cary also took part in some of Don Costa's recordings. One particular evening which is mentioned concerned a trip to Fort Dix—"with our own band, 15 models, etc; did a glorified burlesque show in a service club under the name of a 'fashion show.'"

Cary listed one short all-music Steele Show on August 9, 1951, at 8:30 p.m., which Virginia taped, as follows:

1. *Undecided* (theme)
2. *Tenderly* — 14-year-old trumpet
3. *Perdido* — Don Costa arrangement
4. *When Your Lover Has Gone* — guest Bobby Hackett
5. *Struttin' With Some Barbecue* — guest Bobby Hackett
6. *'S Wonderful* (Nancy Reed, vocal) — Cary arrangement
7. *Temptation* — guests Red Norvo Trio
8. *Zing Went the Strings* — guests Red Norvo Trio
9. *Honeysuckle Rose* (& theme) — Band

At the start of October the WPIX routine was "2:30 to 5:00 except on ball-game days." But this soon reverted to the one hour rehearsal, 2 $^1/_2$ hour show, 5 days per week, routine. "Home Town alternates on Wednesday evenings with From the Top." Cary continues that he is thinking of leaving WPIX and getting better work, "though this job has wonderful hours, really little work, occasionally interesting and much doubling." On October 16, WPIX signed with the union and Cary's salary was increased from $126 to $131, but on November 19 he received his notice, "so I'll be free in January." Again, the reason for receiving this notice is not given.

Prior to this he had complained in his diary about Jerome "pilfering a few bucks from your so-called friends," but without giving details, though one suspects he is referring to overtime payments. "The stagehands get each penny and there is no reason why we shouldn't. I may go to the union about the problem soon. Musicians have too much conscience about things outside union rules."

Although Cary's last working day at WPIX was on January 11, 1952, he was asked to play as a substitute for two days at the end of January, so the parting must have been fairly amicable.

Remarking on his work at WPIX during 1951, Cary thought he would stay awhile, saying: "Certain trying moments have arisen but it is too easy a job to leave yet and I've saved $1,500 so far. About the only serious thing to be remedied is lack of serious writing work. "Sometime maybe to get with a new band or singer and help each other. Could it be Sonny Calella, a wonderful guy, still in supporting Copa cast?" This was in March, while in May he wrote: "Am filling up Saturdays and occasional Sundays, so things are financially 'swinging' for the first time in my life. Someday soon we'll get a small house and not have these assholes banging on wall after 11 p.m. We both love trees and grass and freedom and will appreciate it when it finally is possible." In July he wrote of the "steadiest, most normal, clean job I've ever had, no drinking at all, losing weight and feeling a new 'on top' as the scientists put it. Going to get a car soon, get married, help my Connecticut family, and in general get the noggin above the surface for the first time."

During his time at the television station, Cary's finances improved considerably. His earnings in 1950 approached $8,000 and in 1951 more than $10,000. In August he bought his "first new car, a Ford '51, Hawaiian Bronze, convertible with white wall tyres." A few days later he noted, "our savings are almost up to 4 grand." Quite an improvement on the $680 balance in March 1950.

The association with Jerome was to be another source of work for Cary. Jerome had established a successful business as a provider of advertising jingles and was able to use Cary's arranging abilities in this field. As Jerome said of his fellow musicians, "Those guys loved doing jingles. They were making sixty bucks an hour. It was the best paying gig for sidemen in the music business." Among the many companies for whom he organised jingles were Miller Light Beer, Ballentine Ale and Winston Cigarettes.

On his "Something Old, Something New" CD Jerry Jerome said: "After a jingles session we sometimes had studio time remaining, so some of the guys would stick around and jam." A version of *I Never Knew (That Roses Grew)* is then played, featuring Jerome, tenor, Dick Cary, piano—a good solo—Phil Kraus, vibes, Allen Hanlon, guitar, and Tommy Abruzzo, bass.

Cary's memory of the jingles field is perhaps not as cheery as Jerome's!

> *About Jerome, I did a lot with him. We did a lot of jingles, mostly television and radio advertising spots. He did the business. I did all the writing and playing and I, to use one of our slang expressions, "got the business" financially.*

Scrolling back to the summer of 1950 and then through to the end of the year, we find Cary, at the weekends or evenings, working at Condon's on a number of occasions, either as a Tuesday night guest or substituting for pianist Gene Schroeder. He had several gigs at Nick's, subbing for pianist Billy Maxted or, August 1–3, for trumpeter Pee Wee Erwin, plus three days as intermission pianist when Hank Duncan broke his thumb. There were three dates at Central Plaza, with Big Sid Catlett getting a special mention each time, plus three at the Stuyvesant Casino during December. On the 15th he played piano with Wild Bill Davison, Johnny Windhurst, trumpet, Sandy Williams, trombone, and Bob Wilber, clarinet; on the 22nd he was on trumpet with Tyree Glenn, trombone, Mezz Mezzrow, clarinet, and Charlie Queener, piano; and on the 29th with Glenn, Wilber and Joe Sullivan, piano.

During this six months Cary had two regular though limited bookings, the first with a Max Kaminsky band at the Diamond Horseshoe and then the Aquarium. In his autobiography, Max Kaminsky wrote: "I had the last band in Billy Rose's Diamond Horseshoe, where we played the last two weeks before it closed." Cary joined the band on September 17, 1950, and the personnel was: Kaminsky, trumpet, Munn Ware, trombone, Harry Green, clarinet, Dick Cary, piano, Charlie Traeger, bass, and Eddie Phyfe, drums. There was a report that Cary played trombone with the Kaminsky band, but Cary denied this. He worked five nights at the Diamond Horseshoe, with Charlie Queener subbing for him on three. On September 27, the Kaminsky band ("our raucous 5-piece group") opened at the Aquarium and on October 6 Cary "gave Max notice—I'm so relieved at getting out of this delinquent hangout." Despite this notice, his final gig with the band was only three days later, on October 9, when it played, as it had on the 2nd, at the Rainbow Inn in New Brunswick.

The second regular booking was at Cafe Society with a Johnny Windhurst band (Windhurst, trumpet; Ed Hubble, trombone, Joe Barufaldi, clarinet, Cary, piano, arranger, and Eddie Phyfe, drums), for two weeks from November 23 to December 6, 9:30 to 3:30 or 4:00. Star of the show was Josh White plus Leonard Connor ("a lousy singer") and Beatrice Howell, vaudeville comedian. "Windhurst playing well—nice tone, good range."

Cary found time to visit Middletown, where he worked at the Eclectic and, at an unknown location, with the Gene Nelson bop band. In November there were a couple of visits to Princeton—on the 18th he led a band which contained Johnny Windhurst, trumpet, Ed Hubble, trombone, Bill Leukhardt, clarinet, Willie "The Lion" Smith, piano, Ed Safranski, bass, and Art Trappier, drums, and on the 26th he played in the Armory with a student band which included John Dengler, cornet and soprano, Marty Ille, trombone, and Dick Hadlock, soprano. (Dengler was to play with Cary in Bobby Hackett's band and Hadlock became well-known as a jazz writer.)

Add in a single engagement with the Pee Wee Hunt band at the Glen Island Casino, a Jewish wedding at the Henry Hudson Hotel, an Italian wedding at the St. George's, making audition records with singer Charlie Dicken, rehearsing with the Stu McKay woodwind quintet, playing a hymn at a political rally, writing the occasional arrangement, including one for a Maxine Sullivan record date, another for Hot Lips Page's opening at the Apollo, and one has a fairly busy schedule. On a rare day off he stayed home and listened to Stravinsky and Debussy!

He and Virginia saw 1951 in at "the St. Nicholas Arena, Broadway and 66th, standing in front of Stan Kenton's loud 18-piece band ... That Maynard Ferguson, greatest acrobat on trumpet in the world. How long will he last?"

1951 carried on where 1950 left off. Cary was at WPIX all

year and worked all manner of jobs when he was not needed at the television station.

> *We were busy all the time. I did a lot of arranging for people. There were an awful lot of jazz places all around Connecticut and New Jersey. We'd all go and split even on those jobs.*

In his diary he mentions playing 15 of the Bob Maltz Friday night sessions at the Stuyvesant Casino and 17 appearances at Eddie Condon's club, all spread between January and December. On occasions he would work at the Stuyvesant first, then move on to Condon's and sometimes the reverse. There were seven appearances at Matarese's Circle and four at The Embers, but only two at Nick's, during March, when he substituted for Billy Maxted. The Eclectic in Middletown is reported twice, in March and May, and there are five gigs at Princeton and seven at country clubs scattered through the year. One of the Princeton bookings was a weekend affair, playing with a Bill Reid group in a tent on Friday, until 4:15 a.m., and on Saturday until midnight. The other dates were with "all-star" personnels in the Colonial Club, the Tiger Club or the university house.

A May date at the Bay Shore Country Club is described as a "lousy job," but a "Nightmare Ball" at the Norwalk C.C. on June 22 is notable for ingenious costumes. Cary led the band, with Max Kaminsky, trumpet, Munn Ware, trombone, Peanuts Hucko, clarinet, Jack Lesberg, bass, and Morey Feld, drums. In July the Plainfield C.C. is called a "beautiful club," where he played with a small group including Ann Vincent, vocals, an accordionist called Harry, and Boomie Richman on tenor, who "made job very interesting." One of the bookings in December, at the Roslyn C.C., included two rehearsals for a Christmas show, while on December 21, at the Ardsley C.C. he played a school kids' party with chaperones, "so a bit dull, but they enjoyed a couple of short jazz concerts we put on." The "we" were Joe Ferrante, trumpet, Jerry Jerome, tenor, Dick Cary, piano, Jack Zimmerman, bass, and Don Lamond, drums. "Lamond one of really great drummers. Tells me he used to bum around with [Sid] Catlett a lot and admired him greatly."

A Battle of Music between "Two Great Dixieland Bands" was the main event for the annual Steamboat Ball to be held on June 2, 1951 in Pittsburgh. Cary flew to the city on that Saturday morning and played alongside Bud Freeman in the Max Kaminsky band on the SS Homestead in the afternoon. He was probably on alto horn, according to bassist Bob Haggart, there being no piano on the ship.

The "race" between the SS Jones, with Wild Bill Davison's band on board, and the SS Homestead "was a tie!" In the evening, 9:00 to 2:00, the bands played the Urban Room of the William Penn Hotel, where Cary worked with Davison, Cutty Cutshall, Ed Hall, Bob Haggart and George Wettling.

On July 2, a series of square dances began in Riverside Park, starting at 8:30 p.m. and ending at 11:00. Promoted by Pepsi Cola, the other parks visited each week were Central, Prospect and Forest, providing Cary with work for four nights a week during July and August. The final dance was held on August 31. Cary gives no details for the programmes or personnels, or what instrument he played, except that Arizona Cliff Martin, from WPIX, was the singer for at least one of the dances and Cary was receiving $80 a week.

During the year Cary made a number of appearances on Eddie Newman's "Record Breakers," a WPIX-TV programme chaired by Leonard Feather. For example, referring to the broadcast of October 1, Cary writes, "Did 'Record Breakers' at 8:30. Played bass with Mary Lou Williams, piano, with Lee Castle, Red Norvo and Mary Osborne. Panel was Leonard Feather and Mel Torme (who helped us on drums)."

Cary called the Red Norvo Trio (Norvo, vibes, Tal Farlow, guitar, Charles Mingus, bass) the "greatest trio ever assembled," so his feelings can be imagined when, on July 21, he had to reject Norvo's offer of a (sub's) job with them... Norvo was sick, but so was Cary: "I felt pretty bad, stomach pains, and had to refuse."

A quick scan of Cary's individual jobs for the year shows a gig with Pete Pelizzi at the Rathskeller in the Bronx; the Pee Wee Russell Benefit; a dance at a girls' college in Lakewood; a show at Camp Kelmer; a fireman's ball in Dunellen, New Jersey, with the WPIX band; and a wedding at St. George's Hotel. With Max Kaminsky there was a "wonderful job at Canton Show Shop" and another at Bryn Mawr; with Ed Hall he played the Bedford Rest in Brooklyn; with Bud Freeman he was at Hillman's and at the Beachcomber in Madison; and there was a Marty Ferricker job at Lost Battalion Hall, with 3 brass, 3 sax, 3 rhythm; in addition there were occasional dates at Matarese Circle and the Eclectic.

During April he had to have several days of dental treatment, but this did not stop him from preparing arrangements of six Dixieland tunes for Art Mooney to play at the Meadowbrook Ballroom.

Companies for which commercials were made during the year

included a dime savings bank, Tip Top Bread and "a short job accompanying Toni Southern, who sang a phone number for a clothes reconditioner!" His recordings for the year were concentrated into the month of November and were all connected with Don Costa, two sessions presumed to be under Costa's name and one by singer Tom Eldredge.

One special event which necessitated extra house-keeping occurred on August 31, 1951—"Joint all cleaned up pending arrival of Lucille Armstrong for supper, then she and Virginia to The Embers." Cary could not go as he had a date at Forest Park, the last in the series, to fulfil.

Following a break from his composition studies with Stefan Wolpe, Cary resumed them in February, calling them "the only really important thing I ever do." The lessons varied in duration from thirty minutes to more than two hours, leaving the pupil feeling either elated or bemused. After one lesson in April he writes of a "baffling discussion of intervals." There was another break in these classes from June until early October. In the first after the resumption, Wolpe "told me of using tones in repetition and not always jumping to new sounds." Later that month Cary wrote: "Stefan has been working very hard proof-reading his work *(Metropolis)* for the Philharmonic on November 1. What an unusual man—believes in greatness, including his own and no matter what the long-lasting (or not) success of his writing, he can be known to be great by a good influence on more people than any politician, entertainer, businessman, etc, etc. People of this type have no desire or inclination to fight anyone, only to produce music or art and enjoy the associations of anyone sincerely interested in the same field and appreciative of their efforts."

A later note after a "wonderful lesson" by Wolpe, was: "He showed me himself in action on one of his piano pieces for a ballet. He is years ahead of where my poor mind, ambition-drawn behind by laziness will ever take me. Spoke of formal relationship of material, using repetition of tones and not always to new areas of tones. Stefan is most stimulating personality I've ever known."

Unlike the previous year, Cary ended 1951 as a musician and not as a listener. In the company of Jerry Jerome on reeds and Don Marino on drums he played the Old Year out in the no doubt comfortable surroundings of the Roslyn Country Club.

On December 10, 1951 the New York radio station WMGM began broadcasting six nights a week a thirty-minute programme called "Dr. Jazz." Created by the enthusiasm of Aime Gauvin, a staff announcer at the station, these live remotes came from the Central Plaza (Sundays), Condon's club (Mondays), Jimmy Ryan's (Wednesdays), Lou Terassi's (Thursdays), the Stuyvesant Casino (Fridays) and Nick's (Saturdays). Having failed to find a sponsor, the series ended on June 25, 1952, but not before this representative survey of New York jazz had been put onto acetate discs by collectors.

Dick Cary was heard on "Dr. Jazz" broadcasts by the Stuyvesant Stompers on December 28, 1951 (during which he featured *Sheik of Araby* playing alto horn), January 4 and 11, 1952 and February 1,1952. He played piano with the usual suspects, including Wild Bill Davison, Hot Lips Page, Lou McGarity, Pee Wee Russell, Peanuts Hucko, and George Wettling. The Stuyvesant Casino sessions were promoted by Bob Maltz on Fridays and Saturdays, with Cary making a total of eleven appearances there during 1952.

On March 17th he was on trumpet at Eddie Condon's, with Cutty Cutshall, Ed Hall, Ralph Sutton, Bob Casey and Buzzy Drootin. Four titles from this broadcast, issued on CD, confirm John Wilson's view that Cary's trumpet work was rough and exuberant. His lead is generally strong and workmanlike, his solos are neatly constructed, close to the melody, but his tone is straight and overall his performance lacks individuality.

Cary was frequently the replacement on either trumpet or piano whenever Wild Bill Davison or Gene Schroeder were on leave from Condon's. He made two or three single appearances a month during 1952, either as a sub or as a Tuesday evening guest. The exception was in the summer, when he worked at Condon's or at Child's Restaurant on a full-time basis.

In fact his employment during 1952 consisted of steady engagements ranging in duration from one to seven weeks, interspersed with one-off gigs, recording dates and a few commissions for arrangements. His last mention of Stefan Wolpe is in May 1952, and it was more than a year before he began further study with Tim Timothy.

The first of the steady engagements was an uneventful week, January 18–24, with a Wild Bill Davison band at the Brown Derby in Washington, D.C. Cary was on piano, with Frank Orchard, trombone, Bob Wilber, clarinet, and Johnny Vine, drums.

This was followed by 2½ weeks (February 21–March 8) at the Grandview Inn, Columbus, Ohio, with Johnny Windhurst, trumpet, Ed Hubble, trombone, Jack Fuller, clarinet and Johnny

Ralph Sutton watching Dick Cary at the organ. *(Courtesy: Dick Cary Archive)*

Vine again on drums. Cary logged the drive there at 557 miles. "Grandview is one of the nicest clubs I've been in. We work 9:00 to 2:30. Place is on Dublin Road, about 4 or 5 miles from center of Columbus ... Joint was packed and very responsive to our group.

Scotch is 30¢ for us and food is good, with 20% off." During this stay Cary went to Trocaveri's to hear Lester Young's "cute" five-piece band and also enjoyed the hospitality of local jazz enthusiast Bill Culter and his wife, as well as being interviewed on Culter's radio show.

Cary's connection with Jerry Jerome meant that he was pianist on two concerts the tenorman presented on March 24 and 25, 1952 at Loew's Theatres. The first was held at the King in Brooklyn and the musicians included Billy Butterfield, Red Allen, trumpets, "Big Chief" Moore, Bill Harris, trombones, Buddy DeFranco, clarinet, Jerry Jerome, tenor, Charlie Parker, alto, Teddy Wilson, piano, Ed Safranski, bass, Don Lamond, drums. For his piano solo Cary chose *Fingerbuster*. "About 1400 people, all wild, some dancing on stage and in aisles. Benny Goodman and John Hammond there to see this; must of reminded Benny of several years ago when he incited that sort of behaviour at the Paramount." On the 25th, at the Valencia in Jamaica, NY, the line-up was similar except that Hot Lips Page replaced Butterfield—"(latter rather loaded last night and playing suffers)." One title has been issued from this concert, an 8½ minute version of *Ornithology*, with Cary adapting to the more modern leanings of the rest of the band. Cary also lists Louis Prima on the bill.

> I remember these concerts vividly. New York City had many large Loews movie houses and in the '50s, when the movie business was a bit lagging, they rented these out for jazz concerts and we did several. Charlie [Parker] was not in good health, had cut down on "everything" except large quantities of beer.

During 1952 Cary had continued his rehearsals with the Stu McKay woodwind group, though he was unhappy with the intonation and execution on the arrangements he contributed. Also he wrote arrangements for Peanuts Hucko, Lee Castle, Jimmy McPartland, Harry Lookofsky and singer Irene Manning. In March he met Anna Leas Klievert, an organist, and began rehearsing with her—"I like her work much better than Ethel Smith." On April 8 and 9 they played at the Melody Lounge, then Cary was replaced by "Graham" (presumably Graham Forbes), although he did sit-in on the 11th...

Another contact in March 1952 was Harry Lookofsky, who was guided to Cary by Billy Butterfield, who was then working at ABC (American Broadcasting Company). Lookofsky was looking for "arrangements for swing violin and small group." As Cary put it, "We talked and talked as if we'd known each other before." On April 7 they met at Nola's studio and ran over Cary's two arrangements: "He plays fiddle very well and has good jazz feeling, besides being a very affable character." Cary helped to put the small group together, which consisted of violin, clarinet, vibes, piano, guitar, bass, and drums, with a varying personnel. Cary decided that their audition records "ain't so bad after all!" Three of his arrangements which were used on broadcasts have found their way onto CD, including his original *Night Life*, played by a Lookofsky Septet, with Peanuts Hucko, clarinet, Buddy Christian, vibes, Buddy Weed, piano, and Morey Feld, drums.

> When I lived in New York I never hustled around and tried to get a job. I'd get calls from people and one thing would lead to another. At one point I was doing a lot of writing for friends of mine at ABC, because all the jazz players, like Billy Butterfield, were at ABC. There's a fiddle player named Harry Lookofsky [at ABC radio]. He was a great violinist but he couldn't improvise and I wrote all his jazz solos out for him. In fact, we did a 12-minute concerto for the Whiteman Orchestra with him. Harry was the only concert violinist I ever knew who could play written jazz and make it swing—a very rare fiddler.

The aforementioned concerto with the Paul Whiteman orchestra has not been traced. The Whiteman Collection at Williams University has no details and it was not mentioned by Lookofsky in interviews with researchers Anthony Barnett and Don Rayno. Cary's contributions to the Paul Whiteman radio shows remain to be documented.

In May he met Alice Towsley, a budding songwriter, and agreed to help her at "a saw a shot!" But this scheme folded within a month following an argument about Cary receiving credit on a song for which he wrote most of the music—"so no more of that witch."

During 1952 Cary became a familiar figure at Child's Restaurant, beginning on April 29 as intermission pianist opposite the Max Kaminsky band (Kaminsky, trumpet, Ray Diehl, trombone, Gail Curtis, clarinet, Charlie Queener, piano, Don McLean, drums). He worked 7:00 p.m. to 12:30, with an hour off, for $150 a week, ending on May 11.

May 28 found him making the long drive to Columbus, Ohio again, where he opened at the Grandview Inn the following day, with Bobby Hackett, cornet, John Giuffrida, bass, and Buzzy Drootin, drums. The club owner, Mike Flesch, said of the opening night that he had to turn away at least 200 customers. Cary's notes were: "terrific business, band kills 'em" and "we are working harder than we have in years. Hackett best I ever heard him." Sundays were days off, as Ohio was dry, and June 8 was spent at Journal Island, the retreat of multi-millionaire Edgar Wolfe. The temperatures were in the high 80s or low 90s, but Cary still played golf, reporting one occasion when "I had a 77 ... especially a birdie on 430 par 4." (His hours spent on the driving range had clearly been beneficial.) On Friday the 13th he played 36 holes, so it was not surprising that he spent Saturday, the last day of the engagement, in bed, but he still drove back to New York after the final set. "'Twas indeed a marvelous 2 ½ weeks."

Ten days after returning to New York Cary started work, on June 25, as intermission pianist, in place of Ralph Sutton, at Eddie Condon's club. He considered the nights were long, playing seven half-hour sets, but after a few days he felt that things were "getting easier as I get used to playing alone and finding out what they like." His last night was July 16, and then he was off "to the wilds of Connecticut" with Virginia and daughter Leslie for a long weekend—"three lakes, nice musical experiences and a trifle too much alcohol." The musical experience was sitting-in at the Blue Lantern where Betty Peterson (later Betty O'Hara) led a quartet.

Back in New York on Sunday, July 20, 1952, he "started week and a day at Nick's. Band is all subs except Phil Napoleon. Kenny John, drums, Joe Tarto, bass and tuba, Miff Sines (rough and flat), trombone, and Ben Parrish, clarinet. Band is most out-of-tune group I've been with in years. Long day 5:30 to 4 a.m., off from 8:00 to 9:30." Cary was pleased when trumpeter Lee Castle sat-in on two occasions. A photograph from about this time shows this band but with Cary on trumpet, Billy Maxted, piano, Joe Tarto, bass, and Phil Napoleon, tuba.

Between August 25 and September 3 he was back at Eddie Condon's, this time playing trumpet. He particularly mentions the 30th as "Quite a night ... Johnny Mercer and his mother in, then Lee Wiley and actress Signe Hasso. Bunny Shawker (drums) murdered first two sets while Leeman was doing Hit Parade."

For three nights, September 11–12–13, he worked for Max Kaminsky at Child's Paramount Grill and then, on the 16th, opened there with Bobby Hackett, whose band had Vic Dickenson, trombone, Gene Sedric, reeds, Dick Cary, piano, John Giuffrida, bass, Buzzy Drootin, drums. Cary makes a few comments about

Phil Napoleon's band at Nick's, July 1952
l-r: Cary; Ben Parrish, cl; Napoleon, tp; Kenny John, d; Miff Sines, tb; Joe Tarto, tu.
(Courtesy: Dick Cary Archive)

Phil Napoleon's band at Nick's, July 1952
l-r: Billy Maxted, p; Parrish, cl; Cary, tp; John, d; Sines, tb; Tarto, b; Napoleon, tu
(Courtesy: Dick Cary Archive)

"poor house," but presumably there were sufficient customers to keep the management satisfied until the booking ended on November 9th. Guest bands were added on Sunday evenings and Cary played opposite the Benny Waters group ("There's a sort of old charm in these guys' blatant, ugly sounds"), a Red Allen band, the Salt City Five ("loud, young, Dixie enthusiasts—what a f. racket!"), Wild Bill Davison's band ("rather sad group, terrible rhythm ... no style"), a

Yank Lawson group, and the Mary Lou Williams quartet. On the last night Lee Wiley was featured on the last set "doing about ten tunes. She went over with everyone and could have done ten more."

On November 24, 1952, Leonard Feather arranged for an M-G-M recording session to be held at Birdland. There was a regular Monday evening audience, but the session was organised as a Battle of Jazz, Jimmy McPartland and the Hot Jazz Stars versus Dizzy Gillespie and the Cool Jazz Stars. Four tunes *(Muskrat Ramble, Battle of the Blues, Indiana, How High the Moon)* were played by both bands, with cornetist McPartland leading the Hot Jazz Stars—Vic Dickenson, trombone, Ed Hall, clarinet, Jack Lesberg, bass, George Wettling, drums, and Cary on piano. Trumpeter Dizzy Gillespie and clarinetist Buddy DeFranco were added to Don Elliott's house band, Elliott playing mainly mellophone, but also trumpet. For the 'cool' version of *Battle of the Blues*, Cary played trumpet alongside McPartland, Gillespie and Elliott. Dick Cary noted: "WE LOST." He told Manfred Selchow:

> *I do remember the Hot-Cool nite. We always said that Leonard Feather stacked the cards because he added Dizzy and DeFranco to Elliott's house band. The only thing on our side was that we were slightly more organised on the repertoire, whereas Dizzy put together his pieces at the moment. I really prefer* Muskrat Ramble *as a Latin piece as Dizzy did it.*

Towards the end of November, Cary began rehearsals with a Lee Castle unit, but prior to its engagement at the Meadowbrook ballroom, he went into the same venue with drummer Ray McKinley's orchestra, with whom he played second trumpet. McKinley was in the Meadowbrook for six days, November 25–30, with Del Castle "the girl singer" and vocalist "Bob Eberle in show Friday/Saturday/Sunday." Cary commented: "Library contains some Eddie Sauter works, some very unusual, Deane Kincaide, some very strange and at times awkward, and Joe Cribari's medleys, quite simple and copies of the Miller style, which I guess is commercial but easy to play and quite uninteresting." He also noted: "We do *Da Da Strain* every night with jazz band." The Meadowbrook was followed by three one-nighters, December 1–3, in Norfolk (Navy job), Bolling Field, Washington, and Fort Dix.

Cary was back in the Meadowbrook on December 4, but this time with Lee Castle, who was leading an 11-piece band. The personnel was Lee Castle, Dick Hoffman, Roy Ray, trumpets, Paul Seldon, trombone, Sonny Salad, clarinet, alto; Monte Giest, alto and baritone; Charlie [Albertine?], tenor, Tony ----, baritone, Cary, piano, Irv Manning, bass, Nat Ray, drums. Of the first night Cary said, "not quite as bad as expected." He had brought in six arrangements, commenting: "Most of library by John Barbe and sounds like a high school band. Some old Deane Kincaide—must have been quickies, some other real old ones. Some nights I wonder how much a man can stand!!" At the start Richard Hayes was the guest singer but on the 9th Cary refers to: "Rehearsed Allan Dean, the English singer. Then we did *Easy Melody* and *Taking a Chance on Love*—latter very satisfying in spots, especially fadeout ending with two baritones, harmons, clarinets, etc. Fair sound for only eight horns. Lee likes both—now! will he want to pay for them?"

The ten days at the Meadowbrook finished on December 14 and the next day Cary was off to Holyoke for five days at Toto's ("a lavish joint") with Earl Hodges, vibes and bass, Jack Garvey, bass and fiddle, Bill Ladley, drums, "while I banged on a piano horribly out of tune." There is no explanation as to why Cary would have been offered or would have accepted such a gig, a seven hour drive from New York. However, during the engagement he did take the opportunity to visit his ex-wife, Rose, and daughters Judy and Janet in Middletown.

Back in New York on December 20 he played at The Vat in Palisades, and on the 23rd, after two rest days, he played for an office party with Don Arnone, guitar, and Bob Casey, bass. Christmas was spent at home; then on the 26th and 27th he was at the Stuyvesant Casino, playing trumpet with George Brunis, Pee Wee Russell and Joe Sullivan.

1952 ended at the Meadowbrook. Cary was in the Lee Castle band which played there on New Year's Eve to celebrate the arrival of 1953.

7. "We'll send you to Lake Placid" (1953–1954)

The first day of January 1953 was spent recovering from the efforts of the previous day, but the next two found Cary at the Stuyvesant Casino playing piano with Lee Castle, trumpet, Bill Harris, trombone, and Eddie Barefield, clarinet. Lee Wiley sat-in with the band on the first night ("she murdered them as always") and also rehearsed with Cary "downstairs." He was writing charts on *What a Difference a Day Makes* and *There Will Never Be Another You* for Miss Wiley to sing with Harry Lookofsky's group, plus English horn and harp. Reference is also made to "a couple of piano sheets" for her appearance at George Wein's Storyville club in Boston during February.

He was at Condon's club twice in January. For the 6th Condon had booked both Cary and Lee Castle, but on the day bassist Walter Page was ill, so Cary played bass. On the 9th he worked three sets on peck horn, substituting for Cutty Cutshall. The Condon band at this time was Johnny Windhurst, trumpet; Cutshall, trombone; Ed Hall, clarinet; Gene Schroeder, piano; Page, bass; Nat Ray, drums.

Canada was the next destination, travelling by train to Toronto on January 11, ready to open the following day at the Colonial Tavern for a two week engagement with cornetist Muggsy Spanier's band. After Toronto Cary remained with the band for a week starting January 26 at the Blue Mirror in Washington, D.C. and a week commencing February 3 at Eddie Leonard's Spa in Baltimore, but he was unhappy about his pay and had given Spanier his notice at the end of January. On Sunday, February 8, the band played an afternoon and an evening session; then Cary collected his pay, said his farewells and caught the 1:50 a.m. train back to New York.

Cary's comments on the band were: "...rough, raucous, fast and very crowd pleasing. That Barrett Deems quite an act on the drums. Truck Parham on bass, strong but rushes at times. Ralph Hutchinson good lip on trombone, but terribly out-of-tune from F up. Darnell Howard gets all kinds of things out of the clarinet. Very agreeable to work with. Muggsy still has about three phrases left and the people applaud them every time."

While in Canada Cary was surprised to receive a parcel from Bob Thiele containing records, music and instructions for a proposed Jimmy McPartland "Plays Bix" album. Cary was surprised because Thiele had told McPartland that Deane Kincaide would be writing the arrangements. The sessions took place between March and June, with producer Leonard Feather's sleeve notes saying: "McPartland's first move was to hire Dick Cary to sketch some arrangements. Cary, who today is better known as a trumpeter, played piano on the original sessions and worked with Jimmy on selecting the personnel."

Still a movie fan, Cary did not always mention the names of the films he had seen, but during the Baltimore booking he made the following comments: "Saw 'Detective Story' (glad Kirk Douglas got shot) and 'Yukon Gold' (everyone should have been)." The next day he watched 'Pony Soldier' ("Tyrone Power sure was brave)." Cary should have been a film critic.

Back in New York he resumed his nomadic career, playing jobs as they were offered. One small instance was an engagement at the Stuyvesant Casino on March 6, 1953, playing piano in a group which included Max Kaminsky, trumpet, Frank Orchard, valve-trombone, Albert Nicholas, clarinet and Zutty Singleton, drums. In fact, 1953 was the year when Cary's association with Kaminsky began to grow.

He was in a Max Kaminsky band, playing piano, sketching arrangements and helping the leader with two originals, which were recorded for M-G-M on March 17/18. Eighteen months later Kaminsky telephoned to say he had sold one of their originals, *Go, Go, Go*, for $500 to Ford Motors, so Cary would be receiving $125.

There were also a few college dates with Kaminsky. On February 13 they were at Dickinson College, Carlisle, Pennsylvania, with Herb Fleming, trombone, Eddie Barefield, clarinet, and Johnny Blowers, drums. "We did three 20-minute slots between Tommy Tucker." After the concert they experienced the colour prejudice so widespread then: "We were denied service in one cafe due to Eddie and Herb. Christ almighty! Can say nothing else."

He and Kaminsky were at Lancaster, Pennsylvania, for an Elks' party on the 21st (with Barefield, Tyree Glenn, trombone, Tommy Benford, drums—"latter drove me nuts—sounded like a machine gun out of control") and at Cary's alma mater, Wesleyan, on the 27th, with Fleming, Blowers, John Giuffrida, bass, Harry Green, clarinet. During March, in addition to the record dates, he played with Kaminsky in five different locations, including Child's restaurant, the Stuyvesant Casino, and The Vat. Cary played a number of engagements at The Vat between February and May and during November and December.

En route to The Blue Room in Hempstead on March 15, on Max Kaminsky's car radio, Cary heard his arrangement of *A Foggy Day* played by Harry Lookofsky at ABC—"I was quite thrilled at my first large band effort." The previous day the chart had run at 8 $\frac{1}{2}$ minutes, so Cary cut two minutes from it!

At the initial Jimmy McPartland recording session, on March 10, Bob Thiele "also told me they sent soundtrack of *Windmill* to New York for Alan Dale—that they thought it too good for Dale and sent it back to Bing Crosby." About the same time bassoonist Mel Tax "advised me to try to find record staff arranging job ... Someday I may start hustling, hardly know how yet; really a difficult thing to learn."

Cary's steady stream of one-night gigs brought him into contact with a surprising range of jazz musicians, young and old. For example:

March 6:	Stuyvesant Casino, with Max Kaminsky, trumpet, Frank Orchard, trombone, Albert Nicholas, clarinet, Zutty Singleton, a veteran New Orleans drummer.
March 8:	Child's, with Max Kaminsky, trumpet; Herb Fleming, trombone, Eddie Barefield, clarinet, and Jo Jones, drummer with Count Basie for more than ten years.
March 22:	Blue Room, Hempstead: Cary, trumpet, Herb Fleming, trombone, Eddie Barefield, clarinet, Gene Schroeder, piano, Jimmy Johnson, bass, and Sonny Greer, drummer with Duke Ellington for 30 years—"Greer is now probably the worst drummer of any."
March 28:	housing project, Manhattan Beach: "weird gig with Sol Yaged and Jimmy Dee."
March 29:	Glenview Inn, Glendale: band included Hal McKusick on tenor, who was altoist in such big bands as those led by Woody Herman, Boyd Raeburn and Elliott Lawrence.
April 10:	Glenville Inn, in sextet which included Hal McKusick and Gil Evans: "Nice to meet Gil E.—well known arranger for years, many bands, now mostly singers."

April 11:   Country club in Bronxville, with Billy Butterfield, trumpet, Ernie Caceres, Al Klink, reeds, Jimmy Johnson, bass, Ted Pashert, drums(?).
April 26:   Harbor Rest, Rockaway: with Kaminsky, Hubble, Barefield, Blowers. The other group included Howard McGhee, trumpet, and Milt Jackson, vibes, veterans of the bop movement.

The diary entry for April 15 is ... "To New Haven Arena, hung around the Louis Armstrong dressing room all evening. First concert of a six-week Armstrong-Goodman tour, under Glaser, [John] Hammond and [Norman] Granz. Louis, Joe Bushkin, Barney Bigard, Arvell Shaw, Cozy Cole and Trummy Young, plus 'ouwa vocalist, Velma Middleton.' Louis did an hour and was through. Benny Goodman then went on, later announced Louis [who] wouldn't return. Big argument in dressing room, Glaser, Hammond and Louis—wonderful scene. Louis asked me to rejoin after tour—I dunno???"

On April 21, 1953, Cary started work on piano with a Jimmy McPartland band at Child's restaurant, alongside Jeff Stoughton, trombone, Hank D'Amico, clarinet, Bob Peterson, bass, George Wettling, drums. He noted: "Not a bad band. Easy work, 6:30–8:30 and 9:30 to 12:30." McPartland appears to have been in and out of the band, with both Cary and Johnny Windhurst playing trumpet on various occasions. Another variation was Lennie Hambro playing clarinet in place of Hank D'Amico. On May 8 he reported: "Vice-president of Child's chain actually there in person and we played his favorite song, *12th Street Rag*. Quite a privilege indeed for a poor group of humble minstrels." That same night Cary finished early at the restaurant to be able to play a "wonderful evening" at the Art Students League Ball at the Plaza Hotel, in an Eddie Condon group, with Wild Bill Davison, Lou McGarity, Peanuts Hucko, Jack Lesberg, Cliff Leeman. "One night in another world!!!"

Outside events during this job included visiting Birdland with Jimmy McPartland to hear Stan Kenton's orchestra, and Cary attending a Sauter-Finegan rehearsal—"What a wonderful time these two arrangers [Eddie Sauter and Bill Finegan] are having. Sauter really the composer here. His work a bit hard for these musicians. Ferrante and brass section really blow."

The Jimmy McPartland recordings for the 10″ Bix tribute album were completed on May 14, with earlier sessions taking place on April 7 and 9. On May 28 Cary spent the afternoon at Decca checking the takes for the album, which was to be called "Shades of

Bix." He comments that "Virginia got the cover for Kurnit," though the artist is not credited on the sleeve.

The Child's engagement ended on Thursday, June 4, 1953 and the next day Cary recorded with a band partially drawn from the Child's personnel, led by Jeff Stoughton, and the four titles came out on Preview, though Cary was not among the musicians listed on the labels. He noted that the titles "came out pretty good," though one must say they sound rather ordinary now.

Cary's next settled booking was at Eddie Condon's club, commencing June 27, 1953, playing trumpet and relief on piano. For this opening night he enthuses: "Then Billy Butterfield arrived and we had a hell of a band all night—Billy, Cutty Cutshall, trombone, Ed Hall, clarinet, Walter Page, bass, and Nat Ray, drums, the only weak link, but not too bad." But a month later he said: "This job gets monotonous too" and, a little later, "No sponsors. I felt very tired and depressed." So when he finished at Condon's on August 22 his summary was: "I've enjoyed it quite a lot, especially when Leeman was drumming, but I'm through just in time."

On August 4, 1953, trumpeter and singer Wingy Manone recorded four titles in his inimitable style for Atlantic Records, though only two were released. Playing with him were Cutty Cutshall, trombone, Peanuts Hucko, clarinet, Dick Cary, trumpet and arranger, Carmen Mastren, guitar; Jack Zimmerman, bass, and Cliff Leeman, drums. Surprisingly, Cary noted: "No piano— played trumpet all way. Not a bad date." (At the time Manone was playing an engagement at the Bandbox in New York.)

During the year he also played on at least eight commercial recording sessions, the titles of which, where known, suggest they were of little consequence. Several, if not all, seem to be connected to Don Costa, though full details are still missing. There were titles such as *Ragamuffin Doll* by 10-year-old singer Jill Whitney on Coral (Cary played alto horn, piano and celeste—"Little gal sang very well") and *What Word Is Sweeter Than Sweetheart* by Buddy Greco, also on Coral (Cary on piano and celeste).

Before he left Condon's, Cary had received a call from trombonist Jeff Stoughton—"He got the job with [Guy] Lombardo. I replace him as leader at Lake Placid, $100 plus room and board, plus $70 for the Sunday concert." Lake Placid, in Essex County, New York State, and one of Cary's old army haunts, is a resort in the Adirondack mountains, some 200 miles north of New York City and about fifty miles from the Canadian border. It was the site of the 1932 and 1980 Winter Olympics, as well as featuring two golf courses and many tennis courts.

Cary flew to Lake Placid on August 26 and two days later he wrote: "Tonight was my first one standing in front of six-piece band. Paul Jouard is really leader and makes it easy for me." "I room with John Uwhiler who fiddles and plays trombone. Never improvised before and did surprisingly well for first attempt. Charley Harmon, fine tenor sound, clarinet adequate for jazz band—has studied and can teach Schillinger. He lives in adjoining room with Joe Iadone, bassist, has taught five years at University of Colorado in Denver, spent few years with Hindemith. Paul Jouard is pianist, graduate of Juilliard, composes. Tele [Lesbines] is drummer, could be alright, but never keeps time on solos and sort of a creepy little character. All-in-all, one of nicest groups I could be with."

The work included afternoon and evening concerts at what Cary calls Carriage on Sundays. "On Saturday we do white coat job in Agora theatre, rehearsing three dance teams in afternoon. Job is 9:00 p.m. to 1:00 a.m. with show." In addition there were dances, including a movie dance, and shows for the staff.

Cary was employed for only two weeks, playing his last concert on Sunday, September 13, and returning to New York the next day, but had done enough to be booked to play again over the Christmas holiday. In fact he was to spend four years working the summers at the Lake Placid Club.

September ended with a "wonderful job" on trumpet at Child's, with Lou McGarity, trombone, Bill Stegmeyer, clarinet, Lou Stein, piano, and Bunny Shawker, drums, and a guest spot at Condon's, plus a recording session, without details, for Don Costa. On October 1 he recorded with a big band led by Harry Ranch and that evening began a two week run at Terassi's with a Bud Freeman group. Cary does not list the other musicians, but mentions halfway through the date: "Bud and I had an argument—he criticized my attitude. Later he told the drummer how to play. Bud is very opinionated in what he thinks 'jazz' is—boom, boom, boom—doesn't care for subtleties or 'felt' rhythm, like the Red Norvo trio. Can't stand having music around, no arrangements. Oh, well, that's why he's an individual and a very good performer for those who like him." The last night with Freeman was on Wednesday, October 14.

On October 7 he mentions piano practice: "Lot of practising on piano; use as an exercise two choruses of *Lover Come Back to Me* as played by Oscar Peterson, whose technique and continuity is amazing." On the 9th he started lessons with Tim Timothy, studying "first essentials of Schillinger mathematical system of evaluating music. I am going to like this." Two weeks later he was writing the third movement of a woodwind quartet.

He met two more budding songwriters, Nellie Mae Leonard and Ruth Simpson—"to work on nine songs. Two were impossible, two were quite good, especially a waltz, *Bridge in the Mist.*" Nothing more came of this, though it did earn him $50. He wrote a few arrangements, for a ten-piece band, for Ernie and Angel Stewart, who were Canadian apparently, plus at least three more for Harry Lookofsky. In addition he wrote down a Bud Freeman composition entitled *You're on My Mind* which Freeman was going to give to Joe Marsala. It was Cary who organised the rhythm section for Freeman's recording sessions in December and made the outline arrangements.

Other gigs included:

October 15: Jack Dempsey's: with Pee Wee Erwin, trumpet, Ed Hubble, trombone, Teddy Roy, piano, George Wettling, drums.

October 16: Eddie Condon's: two sets for Wild Bill Davison, Stuyvesant Casino: two sets with Lou McGarity, trombone; Aaron Sachs, clarinet, Frank Signorelli, piano, Tony Spargo, drums. (Sachs born 1923; Signorelli 1901; Spargo 1897)

October 18: party, 2:00 to 9:00 p.m. for Jackie Gleason: with Max Kaminsky, trumpet, Ray Diehl, trombone, Hank D'Amico, clarinet, Jack Lesberg, bass, Cliff Leeman, drums.

October 25: Glenville, with Kaminsky, Frank Orchard, trombone, Eddie Barefield, clarinet, Johnny Blowers, drums.

October 26 –27: Eddie Condon's: replacing Wild Bill Davison.

October 30: Eddie Condon's: replacing Ralph Sutton on piano.

October 31: Meadowbrook: Cary and Kaminsky rehearsed half-hour television show with the Korn Kobblers.

November 3: Eddie Condon's: played as guest.

November 6: Eddie Condon's: replacing Wild Bill Davison, despite an earlier argument over pro-rata payment. Cary thought he should receive more than the $20 Davison was willing to pay.

November 7: The Vat: with Max Kaminsky, Eddie Barefield,

>   Johnny Blowers, Porky Cohen, vibes—"very
>   mediocre."
> November 13: Central Plaza: with Hot Lips Page, trumpet,
>   Jimmy Archey, trombone, Cecil Scott,
>   clarinet, Freddy Moore, drums.
> November 14: The Vat: with Joe Thomas, trumpet, Eddie
>   Barefield, Blowers, Porky Cohen, vibes
>   and/or trombone.
> November 15: Matarese Circle: with Frank Rehak, trombone,
>   Bud Freeman, tenor, John Giuffrida, bass,
>   Johnny Vine, drums, & blind pianist.
> November 20: Central Plaza: with Sidney Bechet, soprano,
>   Herb Fleming, trombone, Arvell Shaw, bass,
>   Panama Francis, drums.
> November 21: Princeton Tiger Club: with Kaminsky,
>   Orchard, Barefield, Shaw, Francis.
> November 25: Glenwood Manor: with Kaminsky, Jack Fuller,
>   clarinet, Dick Fales, ? , Nat Ray, drums.
> November 27: Eddie Condon's: replacing Sutton on piano.
>   "Silvana Mangano, Yul Brynner and party in."
> November 28: The Vat: with Joe Thomas, trumpet, Garvin
>   Bushell, clarinet, Porky Cohen, trombone?,
>   Johnny Blowers, drums.
> November 29: Pellegrini's, Ridgewood: with Red Allen,
>   trumpet, Frank Rehak, trombone, Ernie
>   Mauro, clarinet, Nat Ray, drums.

On November 24, 1953, there was a session with Eddie Condon for Columbia, the famous "Coast to Coast" album. Aside from some background work on a medley, Cary is impressive on just one track, the exciting *Jam Session Blues*. Often shown as playing trumpet only, he does in fact have two good solos on piano, in competition with Gene Schroeder, plus an exhilarating break and two excellent solos on trumpet. He noted that "George Avakian directed—Chivas Regal scotch played a major role."

> *We recorded this in the big Columbia church in New York on East 30th Street. I think it's a wonderful place to record. It used to be a great big church. Now Columbia use it for a studio.*

This recording was followed in December, on the 4th and 11th, by two sessions with Bud Freeman for Capitol Records.

Although the eight titles are just tenor with a rhythm section, it is the brilliant guitarist George Barnes who takes the solos when Freeman has a breather. Cary's comping in the background is good enough to make one wish he had received more solo space. *Blue Moon* closes with a riff which was later to be incorporated into a tune, *The Time Is Right*, arranged for Tommy Dorsey.

For most of the year Cary had been playing tennis on a regular basis and it is only towards the end of November that there are no further mentions of this activity. But in the weeks before Christmas, in addition to his lessons with Timothy, he worked on recordings for Ford Transcriptions and for a Pabst Beer advert. For the Ford, with a small group, Georgia Gibbs sang on two of the four titles and one was a parody on *Jingle Bells*. For Pabst's Blue Ribbon beer Bill Gale had organised a big studio band which included Yank Lawson, Andy Ferretti, Chris Griffin, Will Bradley, Cutty Cutshall, Bobby Byrne, Bill Stegmeyer, Dick Cary, Bob Haggart, Terry Snyder and others. As well Cary "wrote a fast arrangement for Jerry Jerome on a Lux commercial." Also in December there were two gigs at the Central Plaza, and single dates at Matarese Circle, Child's, The Vat, the Belvedere Room of the Astor Hotel (75 minutes with Charlie Harmon, tenor, Paul Jouard, piano), and a joint in Albany.

Cary set out for his holiday booking at Lake Placid on December 22 but his car broke down en route and as a result he did not arrive until Christmas Eve. His first job, from 10:30 p.m. to midnight, was on Christmas Day. On the 26th he played at St. Moritz, presumably a club, where "the manager irked me with his saying that jazz is sinful and ruins a place." On New Year's Eve he worked in the Agora Room of the Lake Placid Club and enjoyed playing trumpet, tenor, peck horn and second piano with the Paul Jouard band—Jouard on piano, Louis Labella, bass, John Porterfield, drums, Archie on tenor and Sam on violin. After a final gig in the Agora ("two pianos again") on January 2, he drove back to New York the following day.

During the years with Virginia their life together had been regularly disrupted by what Cary described as "terrible arguments" on the subject of money. Finally, in July 1953 they decided to part—"V. and I agreed to go different ways tonight, by at least September. I'll pay rent here through then. A new life will be stimulating and, I hope, more productive." A few days later he wrote that "since V. and I decided to part everything is so sweet!" This did not last, but he had not moved out by October, when he wrote: "V. has gone on wagon and is wonderful ... so nice to me that I'm very confused now about our agreement to separate."

The break was finally made after his return from Lake Placid. On January 6, 1954, he left Sunnyside and moved into Apartment 1C, 110 Bedford Street. He was "amazed and relieved" that trumpeter Johnny Windhurst had moved into 1D. However, this was not a complete break and his attachment to Virginia continued for many more months.

His array of unusual work continued. In January he did arrangements, at her mother's request, for Jeannine Tanzon—"She's a ballet dancer who wants night club work." After two rehearsals at Roseland he commented that she was: "17, with thighs of iron. She won't ever do much!" On January 16 he was on piano with Max Kaminsky when his band played at the Sawdust Trail ("a bucket of gore"). Also present were Ray Diehl, trombone, Harry Green, clarinet and Eddie Phyfe, drums. This gig led to four more days, January 19–22, in the Sawdust Trail, causing Cary to complain: "God, these amateur singers."

Tommy Dorsey (1906–1956) financed a number of recordings in 1954, but rather than start his own label, as later reported by *Down Beat*, he sold or leased the masters to Columbia. This was at a time when his orchestra included Lee Castle on trumpet, Louis Bellson on drums and brother Jimmy Dorsey on alto and clarinet. The band, whose book was largely by Neal Hefti and Howard Gibeling and, later, Ernie Wilkins, played long and frequent engagements at the Cafe Rouge of the Hotel Statler in New York.

The Dorseys were good friends of Bud Freeman and this led to some composing:

> *One night Bud was at Tommy's home and played a quintet album I played on and arranged for Bud. On* Blue Moon, *Bud had one of his prepared parodies, which he did on so many, and we did it for the last chorus. When Tommy heard that, he said, "Bud, play that over again." After a couple more times he said, "You're crazy if you don't make a tune out of that." So it became* The Time Is Right *and Tommy played it twice a night at the Statler. Another was called* A Junket to Plunkett's, *which was a well-known musicians' bar in New York around the 1930s.*
>
> > *Bud and I had both become single just before this and were living in the Village. He would think of something in his hotel room and come over and play it for me. Bud thought of some of the themes, I thought of some of the others and I did the writing. I'd make an arrangement out of it and I think the Dorseys must have had about ten or twelve of these in*

their library before they died. They recorded about three of them. They were extremely nice to me. They played these [arrangements] and they'd rehearse them right on the job. If Tommy wanted to hear it again, he'd play it again. He didn't care. [Charlie Shavers] wrote very interesting, very, very swinging arrangements for Tommy. But things like Rhumba Montevideo *and the things that Charlie did, they wouldn't play until after one o'clock, when a lot of the people had left the room.*

A recording of *A Junket to Plunkett's*, written by Cary alone and said to be by a small group, has not been traced, but the Freeman-Cary tune, *Rhumba Montevideo*, appeared on the Columbia album by Tommy Dorsey which also contained *The Time Is Right*. The same album included a tune entitled *Dixieland Mambo*, credited to "D[anny] Hurd." This title is allocated by Joe Davis to a tune, not too dissimilar but with a slower tempo, composed by Dick Cary and Lee Castle and recorded by Castle's Dixieland group in October, 1954. Another Cary-Freeman song played by the Dorsey orchestra was called *A Gal Has a Way*. Most of these Tommy Dorsey tunes were published by the Embassy Music Corporation.

Many of the events connected with the Dorsey brothers took place during 1954. Cary wrote on January 11: "Took *Time Is Right* to Statler at 12 [midnight]—Dorseys played at sight and then did it over again." The next day he composed, at Tommy Dorsey's request, a small band original for them. This presumably was *A Junket to Plunkett's* which Dorsey rehearsed on the 27th, together with *Rhumba Montevideo:* "likes them both … says write more." Freeman and Cary signed three contracts for their tunes, with Cary to write the stocks, following which *Time* and *Montevideo* were recorded on March 23. *Junket* and another Freeman-Cary piece, *A Gal Has a Way*, were to have been recorded in September, but things did not go as planned. Of a rehearsal Cary wrote: "Dorseys both in terrible mood, rehearsing terrible crap. Then *A Gal Has a Way* was done—too busy, too slow, too hard I guess." And on September 24, the day of recording, Lee Castle told Cary that the band had to get up at]7 a.m. to be at the studio, but the brothers got mad, "Tommy stomped out and they [the band] don't get paid."

Cary signed a contract for the above four titles with Embassy Music in 1954. No recordings have been traced for *A Gal Has a Way*, *A Junket to Plunkett's* or for a second small band number which Cary wrote for Dorsey entitled *So—What Else Is New?*

During early 1954, Bud Freeman organised a series of Saturday afternoon jam sessions at the Van Rensselaer Hotel, with Cary a regular participant between February 6 and April 17. The basic personnel was Cary, trumpet, Buster Bailey, clarinet, Freeman, tenor, Joe Sullivan then Willie "The Lion" Smith, piano, and George Wettling, drums, plus guests, who included, at various times, Buck Clayton, Jonah Jones, Steve Lacey, soprano, and singer Art Lund.

"Best I've enjoyed Central" was Cary's comment on his February 12 date at the Central Plaza, where he played with Bob Wilber and the Westchester Wildcats! Johnny Glasel, trumpet, Ed Hubble, trombone, Eddie Phyfe, drums, and Bob Peterson, bass, had been amateur musicians just ten years before. In May Phyfe, who was a member of a cooperative group called The Six, in which Bob Wilber and Johnny Glasel were prominent, played a record of the band for Cary, who commented: "Phyfe sounded well on drums. Very cute arrangements, well played. This little group should work—but one never knows who likes what these days." (The Six struggled along for two years before breaking up.)

On February 16, Cary met with Chuck Wasserman and others to watch four short army training films and to discuss background music for them. There is no further mention of this project.

Of a lesson in February with Tim Timothy, he wrote: "He started on non-harmonic elements—one of the most interesting hour or two I ever spent. This simplifies guitar writing, bass notation and backgrounds, while providing a wonderful aid in solo structure." After a lesson in May, Cary mentions "pedal tones—using system of 12–12 subdivided at will; more to my liking as a direction towards 12 tone scale which I'm too impatient about."

Cary initially played solo piano at the Sons of Italy Hall in Glen Cove on February 21, and then at 9 p.m., he was joined by four other musicians. One of them was clarinetist John LaPorta, a Lennie Tristano disciple and his presence further complicates Cary's remark: "Much griping from Dixieland fans because people were dancing."

During February and March he played twice at The Vat, including playing piano for a stag party, as well as writing arrangements for a Pee Wee Russell record session on March 4. "I brought trumpet and played ensemble background." (This session, with Doc Cheatham, trumpet, and Vic Dickenson, trombone, is usually shown as recorded in 1953, but it was actually made when the George Wein band was playing at Basin Street in New York.) On March 7, Cary worked at the Roseland ballroom with Max Kaminsky,

Joe Thomas, trumpets, Urbie Green, trombone, Buster Bailey, Cecil Scott, reeds, Arvell Shaw, bass, and Johnny Blowers, drums. Of Green he said: "best young trombone player I've heard." Barney and Dot Bigard visited—"they open Basin Street Friday with Louis."

During an intermission at The Metropole on March 12, Cary hurried to Basin Street to hear Louis Armstrong's first set. He thought the band, with Bigard, Trummy Young, trombone, Billy Kyle, piano, Milt Hinton, bass, and Kenny John [drums] ("really showing off") sounded good. "Hinton one of our very best bassists— one can hear what notes he is playing, which is rare."

There was a strange session at Earl Kennett's studio on March 11 when some kind of multi-taping was taking place. "Spent all afternoon very futilely—Oscar Pettiford [bass], Quincy Jones [trumpet?], Harry [Lookofsky?, violin] and a cellist. Nothing came out." George and Bunny Shawker (drummer) were also present for a short time.

On March 14 Jimmy McPartland led a band for the early evening sets at Child's which included Phil Olivella, clarinet, Jack Green, trombone, Dick Cary, piano, and George Wettling, drums. Cary does not say if he told Green, a colleague from Billy Butterfield's 1946 big band, that he now agreed with Jack's opinion of his younger brother, Urbie.

Jingle work, mainly provided by Jerry Jerome, continued through the first six months of 1954. Companies and products mentioned include Philip Morris cigarettes, Tip Top Bread, Ford's, RCA television, Ballantine's beer, Conoco Oil, and Halo Shampoo. The Halo jingles included vocals by Fran Warren or Dolores Hawkins, accompanied by such musicians as Jerry Jerome, Tyree Glenn, trombone/vibes, Billy Bauer, guitar, and, of course, Dick Cary. Cary observed of the Halo: "They're doing all styles now on these—we did Duke and Dixieland—tomorrow, Benny Goodman and boogie-woogledy." Jerome, Glenn and Cary were also in a small group which recorded an audition record for "a Muzak type buyer."

Cary does not list personnel for two weekends spent at Charlie Ventura's 'Open House' (April 24/25 & May 1/2), except to comment: "Jimmy Crawford rushing like so many large band type drummers." The Saturday hours were 9:00 to 3:00 and Sunday 5:00 to 7:00, including a half-hour broadcast, and 9:00 to 1:30. He reports: "Two shows with Jimmy Caesar and Jay Lester—they want arrangements."

Another example of the work on offer was a job at Greenwich Country Club on Saturday, May 29. He played trumpet and alto horn in a six-piece band led by Irving Gitlin on violin—"So-called 'show tunes' played at ridiculous tempos, all too fast for any music."

Earlier in the year, February 1954, Cary went "to see a loft with Eddie Phyfe and a Dave Young on 6th between 28th and 29th. What a joint! Dark, filthy. Three floors each at $40 a month. Agreed to take it." A few weeks later, on March 22, his large items were delivered to the 821 6th Avenue loft and on the 23rd Cary moved in. By April 5 he had finished painting the ceiling ("gave me headache, got pretty annoyed about whole goddam loft"), then he hired a floor sander and at the end of the month he "put another gallon of Tile Red on the floor—three so far."

The 821 building, dating from 1853, was in the flower district of Manhattan and had various businesses on the ground floor, with the second floor used for storage. Artist David X. Young rented the 5th floor. Pianist/composer Hall Overton and photographer Harold Feinstein shared the fourth floor and Cary had the third floor. Overton lived in the loft until his death in 1972. Photographer W. Eugene Smith replaced Feinstein in the front half of the 4th floor in 1957 and began taking thousands of photographs in and around the building, as well as taping, reel-to-reel, all the relevant activities, conversations, street sounds and jam sessions. During his 14 years in the loft Smith, who died in 1978, recorded 3,000 hours of music and conversation and took 20,000 photographs. Cary's work may yet be found among these thousands of items in Smith's archives stored at the University of Arizona in Tucson.

And so the first six months in the loft passed with the usual mixture of highs and lows:

April 10: Cary reported that a "deaf and dumb club has rented downstairs. Parties for club three nights a week" and on the 17th that the wholesale market area around number 821 was crowded with buyers wanting flowers for "Easter Sunday tomorrow."

June 7: "Dave Young had a party at night, ended up in my place, four guys playing, Hall Overton [piano], Teddy Charles [vibes], Jimmy Raney [guitar] "marvellous" and Eddie Phyfe [drums]."

June 17: "I sit in this loft with all this music, all these instruments, etc, etc, & I can't bring myself to work the way I should. When can I sluff off this laziness & inertia of accomplishment?

	Need a good job maybe—good writing commission." (Eight years and one month earlier Cary had written: "I wish I had ambition to write several pages a day—or the talent.")
June 19:	About 10:15 Windhurst, Hubble, Phyfe, Steve Lacey, Frank Orchard, Max Kaminsky, Dick Schwartz, Bill Goodall, later Tom, v-tb—played till daylight.
June 21:	Session late with JW, EH, Phyfe, Lacey, Schwartz, Goodall, piano, clarinet, until police got complaint and warned us.
June 23:	Jam session in loft later.
September 8:	I've never felt more discouragement in my life at my business, my domestic life or lack of it, that damn loft with no heat or hot water.
September 22:	Plumber finished—now have radiator, shower, hot water and water heater.

Cary's discography continued to grow during 1954. In March, on piano, he made four titles with trumpeter Lee Castle,

Loft building at 821 Sixth Avenue. *(Photograph by Scott Landis, December 2008.)*

with another four made in October to complete a 10″ LP, plus a further four fifteen months later to make up a 12″ LP! In May he was pianist and arranger for separate sessions by trumpeters Johnny Windhurst and Max Kaminsky. The Windhurst session was held at engineer Rudy Van Gelder's home in Hackensack, NJ—"No arrangements, no bass ... But what a sloppy mess ... doubt if we'll ever get paid for this crap." He cooperated with Lee Castle on two originals and with Kaminsky for a further two. In these and similar instances it appears that the leader would suggest a theme or a riff and Cary would organise and arrange this material. Pianist Johnny Varro had no doubt that this was so. He told collector Gunnar Jacobsen that Cary was the most accomplished musician of those guys (the Condon gang) and did all the writing.

In his response to Leonard Feather's questionnaire for "The Encyclopedia of Jazz," Cary named his favorite musicians as Roy Eldridge on trumpet, Art Tatum on piano, Don Elliott on mellophone, and Eddie Sauter as arranger. He also said that he had no favorite solos and that after studying with Stefan Wolpe he:

started trying to write more serious music, finally getting something performed by Rochester Symphony this year [1954].

Feather, in the "Encyclopedia," referred to Cary's "symphonic work," though Cary was at pains to stress that he had not written a symphony.

In March, opening on the 5th, Jimmy McPartland took a band into The Metropole for the late evening sets, 8:30 to 3:30 or 9:00 to 3:00 some nights. With him were "Big Chief" Russell Moore, trombone, Bud Freeman, tenor, Dick Cary, piano, Bob Peterson, bass, George Wettling, drums, though in early April Peterson and Wettling were replaced by Ron McLean and Tom O'Neill. Among Cary's comments were: "piano defies description" and: "McPartland always plays same two tunes to start, *Rose of Washington Square* and *Sentimental Journey* and I can't stand it. The old disease of monotony is gripping me and hanging anchors all over me, especially the head. How can people be content with the same thing always, always. I griped about this one day—McPartland went back to *Somebody Loves Me*, which he opened with at Child's—even worse as nightly fare. Then after two weeks it went back to *Rose*. I said, 'Even that's a relief.' My! What sensitivity!"

Cary's final date with the band was on April 22, 1954. Charlie Queener was to be his replacement, but on the last night McPartland was ill and Cary played trumpet.

Around this period a lot of time is spent watching the McCarthy Senate Hearings: "Everyone hates McCarthy except McPartland and Hackett!"

Among the one-off jobs during May was an audition for Arthur Godfrey's talent show in a band which included Joe Barufaldi on clarinet. The songs chosen were *Muskrat Ramble* and *When the Saints Go Marching In*. There is no mention that they passed the audition.

Eddie Condon's Club, June 1954
l-r: Condon, g; Urbie Green, tb; Cary, tp; Bobby Donaldson, d; Ernie Caceres, cl; Al Hall, b; Gene Schroeder, p. *(Courtesy: Peter Vacher)*

On June 22 he was photographed, on trumpet, at Condon's club in a band which included Urbie Green, trombone, Ernie Caceres, clarinet, Gene Schroeder, piano, Al Hall, bass, and Bobby Donaldson, drums. Then, on the 25th of the month, on alto horn, he took part in another admired Columbia session by Eddie Condon. Of *How Come You Do Me Like You Do*, Cary said:

> I make a very large clam in the middle of this and I've heard more about this album than anything I ever did because of

that clam and the remark that Condon made afterward. He said, "We'll send you to Lake Placid in the morning," which was true. I worked up at Lake Placid for the summer and I was leaving next day.

On the album cover it's a picture of [drummer] Cliff Leeman's foot, along with his thermos bottle, which he always carried with him. That was in his whisky sour period.

Following the Condon session Cary went to WABC radio station for a Paul Whiteman rehearsal and show. "The orchestra applauded Urbie Green who did *Skylark* and my arrangement of *Alone Together*. Urbie over at midnight, the arrangement was fine, and he brought me a record." Mention should also be made of the work which Cary did on *Flamingo* for pianist Marian McPartland to play on Paul Whiteman's ABC Show on May 13—he wrote the "introduction and one chorus for 35 men."

The day after the Condon recording, June 25, 1954, Cary was on the road at 8:30 a.m., arriving at Lake Placid at 5:00 p.m. He was to remain there until early September, playing in a small group with Paul Jouard, piano, Charlie Harmon, tenor, Jim Barton, bass, and Al Nick, presumably the drummer. There is a mention of a John Talter, probably a violinist, and also of playing a two piano set with Nick Parito. His work with the band would have been on trumpet, but on occasion he played intermission piano, and even bass with Paul Jouard.

Throughout July and August his free time was devoted to golf, tennis and the cinema, as well as a certain amount of imbibing, which led to the comment: "I've probably incurred enough displeasure this week from the powers here." The work, a continuation of that from the previous year, was not onerous, covering the usual round of playing for cocktail parties and masquerade parties, for a show followed by a dance, or for surprise nights ("It's like a big church social"). There were dances for children, for guests, for staff, and for tea, plus jazz concerts at either the Alpine club or the Majestic club on Sunday evenings. Cary also did a small amount of arranging for the Lake Placid Club bands.

One enjoyable interlude at the end of July was when Max Kaminsky and Frank Orchard were in the area for ten days, probably booked at the Alpine. They definitely played there on July 22/24/25 and at the Majestic on August 1.

Looking back at his various stays at Lake Placid, Cary was ambivalent about his feelings for the resort. In December 1954, he wrote: "This Lake Placid Club has a pretty rotten, decayed, forced type of good time ... a shame, because the country, the trees, snow, the little town, is beautiful, the lake, the white mountains—and here gather some of the dullest people I've ever seen." And in July 1954: "What a scene from my third floor corner room in the 'Overlook.' Lake is a ripply smooth deep blue, sky is perfectly clear and very light blue, the pines always reach for the sky in a wonderful loose symmetry. There's a constant flash of windshields from the town's main street and the never subsiding yells of kids from the boathouse, because it's the 4th July and everyone must observe it because it's a tradition to be as happily active as possible on this gala summer day."

Cary drove back to New York on September 7, and he and Virginia went to Jack Teagarden's opening night at Basin Street. Teagarden's band, which Cary thought was "lousy," included sister Norma on piano and Ray Bauduc on drums. Also on the bill were the Lee Konitz quartet ("quite dull") and the Johnny Hodges group. Then followed a few days of tennis and television until the 16th when he started work at Condon's on trumpet, subbing for Wild Bill Davison. The band was Cutty Cutshall, trombone, Ed Hall, clarinet, Gene Schroeder, piano, Walter Page, bass, and George Wettling, who had re-joined the previous evening, drums. His last night at Condon's was on October 2.

He stayed with Virginia for three days. September 9: "I feel awful about leaving Virginia, but really know it's for the best. So I go tomorrow. Damn couch most uncomfortable." And a few days later he was still wishing that she loved him a little, a fraction as much as he did her. In November she visited the loft to show Cary the self-portrait she had painted—and to borrow 150 bucks.

Other work during September included a session at Child's with Emmett Berry, trumpet, and Pee Wee Russell, clarinet; writing and recording a jingle for Ballentine Ale with Tyree Glenn "and the marvelous Milt Hinton," and two full days rehearsing a show for the Quality Bakers convention at the Statler Hotel. The final rehearsal and the show, with Nick Parito conducting a small band, plus five singers and four dancers, took place on September 27.

Brad Gowans, Cary's mentor from the early days at Nick's, died September 8, 1954. When he heard, Cary wrote: "...one of the musicians I enjoyed musically and personally very much—a most unusual guy—pretty rude to a lot of people, but then used to say to me, 'There are many things, Cary, that are not included in your philosophy.'" It was Gowans who told him not to become associated too closely with Eddie Condon; that he, Gowans, had been trying to break away for years.

On October 9, Cary was pianist with Max Kaminsky, trumpet, Ray Diehl, trombone, Eddie Barefield, clarinet, and Jimmy Crawford, drums, for a concert at Throggs Neck Bridge Stadium. This was followed a week later, October 17/18, by a gig playing bass in a similar Max Kaminsky group with Diehl, Hank D'Amico, clarinet, Crawford, and Bob Creash, accordion. They performed for a Jackie Gleason party held on two cars of a train, travelling to Detroit. On arriving, they "started playing about 11:00 in the Presidential Suite on 25th floor." Cary quoted Gleason as saying that "he liked peck horn, says it should be in albums, will have to remind Hackett." (Gleason's albums with strings, plus Bobby Hackett's cornet solos, were big sellers for Capitol at this time. Cary did record with Hackett and strings, but not until three years later.)

In his autobiography, Kaminsky wrote that he hired Dick Cary on piano, along with Ray Diehl, trombone, Eddie Barefield, reeds, and Jimmy Crawford, drums, for a tour of colleges in New England, Pennsylvania, New York and New Jersey. "Some were quite successful and some didn't draw so well." The tour was repeated again the following spring. Kaminsky said: "I'll never forget how wonderful Dick Cary was on these tours. He used to take half the men in his car and since he knew I was hard up for money, he never charged me for the gas or mileage." After problems with the weather, the rowdyism at some campuses and prejudice against the black musicians, Kaminsky decided to deny himself the pleasures of college tours.

On the 11th and 12th, Ed Hall was the clarinetist, replaced by Eddie Barefield for the remaining dates. The Gleason personnel is given above.

October 11:	Storrs
October 12:	John Hancock Hall, Huntington
October 17/18:	Jackie Gleason, Detroit
October 19:	McCarter Theatre, Princeton
October 24:	Child's, New York City
October 25:	Mechanic's Hall, Worcester
October 26:	The Auditorium, Bangor
October 27:	Middlebury College
October 28:	Webster Hall, Dartmouth
October 29:	University, Burlington

Of the Webster Hall concert Cary was moved to comment, "fine Steinway," while of Bangor he refers to "a mammoth old barn—small crowd but noisy. Crawford's drum solos get the kids in a frenzy. Max gives me a couple of choruses on *Ja Da* on the trumpet now and it's just a little difficult to pick it up cold after pounding (literally) on the piano up till that time."

After a couple of days of relaxation, Cary started on trumpet at Condon's on November 1, playing there until the 13th. The diary entry of the 8th is: "Sitting-in tonight were Jack Teagarden, Ray McKinley, Ray Bauduc, Peanuts Hucko, etc. Jack T. plays with the band, with Ralph Sutton, then band, etc., on and on. What a giant in his way." Rehearsals for the Society of Artists and Illustrators annual show, with "22 or 23 sketches," for which Cary provided the band and music, began on October 1, 1954. He mentions the show running for five nights from November 8–12, with two of them for "men only" at 25 bucks. While working for the show he put in a substitute for the early sets at Condon's.

In November 1954 the second part of Max Kaminsky's "Jazz on the Campus" tour got underway with a changed personnel: Max Kaminsky, trumpet, Frank Orchard, trombone, Joe Barufaldi (sometimes called Joe Barry), clarinet, Dick Cary, piano, Bob Casey, bass, and Eddie Phyfe, drums. The dates were:

November 15:	Pembroke, Providence, RI
November 16:	Hamilton
November 17:	Ogdenburg
November 19:	Lancaster, PA
November 20:	Princeton
November 29:	Jimmy Durante
December 4:	Irvington, NJ
December 5:	Child's, New York City

There was a variation in the band for November 29, when Ray Diehl was on trombone, Jack Zimmerman on bass and Morey Feld on drums. The diary notes for this date are: "Job at '21' 7–11. Texaco people. Durante marvelous, also Donald O'Connor. Band very good. Jimmy said, 'What an arrangement!' at various times and wants us on the show (I hope)." Needless to say, there is no further mention of an appearance on the Jimmy Durante Show.

The Irvington date was for an RCA factory party in a large ballroom.

Occasionally things do go well for musicians. In November Cary noted that Johnny Vine had bought 15 acres for $18,000 and in December that John Giuffrida's wife had won a contest with a prize of 100 grand.

There was a flurry of recording activity around this time. On October 21 he made four more titles with the Lee Castle band and when they were released in December he commented: "Joe Davis called one of them *Dixieland Mambo*, same name as one of Dorsey's and Lee knows Tommy will be very mad if he hears of it." A week or so later, on November 3, he recorded with Jerry Jerome ("planned three very corny arrangements for M-G-M date. Jerry on soprano"), followed by three recording sessions with Jack Teagarden for the Period label. He arranged all the material, playing trumpet on the first session and piano on the third. For the middle session Leonard Feather, who organised the recordings, said that a pianist had been booked, but on the day, when no piano player turned up, Feather said that he, Feather, would have to play. Cary also recalled that Feather had a private version of *Music to Love By* for Teagarden to sing, changing one word. He promised to send copies of this "limited edition" to each of the musicians, but never did.

Cary was also writing arrangements for the Al Gentile big band and sitting-in with it when he was visiting Middletown to see his ex-wife, Rose, and his daughters. One occasion was on November 27—he was in Middletown for Judy's high school dance at the Polish Hall in Bristol, when Gentile had five trumpets, five saxes and three rhythm. He thought the band sounded ridiculous at times. Nevertheless he sat-in on both trumpet and piano. "I wrote *More Than You Know* for solo trumpet and played it twice."

Gentile sometimes used an instrumentation of five saxophones and three rhythm, plus Betty Peterson on various brass instruments, and Cary sat in with this combination on December 11 at Crystal Lake, on the 17th in "a beautiful modern school in Wallingford," when he replaced Mrs. Peterson, and on the 18th when he heard his *Begin the Beguine* arrangement. As a Christmas present he gave Betty Peterson, later to be better known as Betty O'Hara, an arrangement of *Stella by Starlight*, scored as a trumpet feature.

In addition to the dates with Max Kaminsky, December included two gigs at Eddie Condon's, substituting for Wild Bill Davison, and one appearance at the Stuyvesant Casino, playing trumpet with Pee Wee Russell, Frank Orchard, pianist Teddy Roy and drummer Keg Purnell. On the 20th he visited the Roosevelt Hotel to hear the Guy Lombardo orchestra, noting: "Lombardo played *Saints* and room reaction was very good." What have we missed by not having the opportunity to hear Guy Lombardo playing a Dick Cary arrangement of *When the Saints Go Marching In?*

On Christmas Eve, 1954, he drove to Lake Placid for the holiday period. "We live in playhouse again—where I lived during army days." "We" included Paul Jouard, Charlie Harmon and Al Nick, plus Ken Belding. After nine days of playing and drinking ("There will be a day of reckoning after this last week"), he drove back to New York on January 3, 1955.

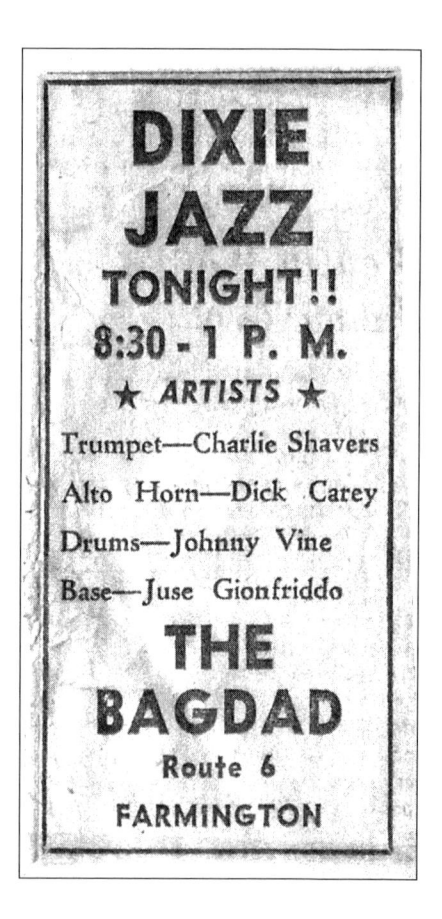

Press advertisements for the Bagdad Restuarant (See opposite page)

8. Joy Ride (1955–1956)

Through 1955 Dick Cary worked his usual quota of dates with Max Kaminsky and at Eddie Condon's club, a dozen with the former and more than thirty with the latter. These were concentrated in the early or later months of the year, his three summer months being spent at Lake Placid.

He was a guest star at Condon's on January 4; then on the 7th the Max Kaminsky band made the 305 mile trip to Syracuse for a college date — Kaminsky, trumpet, Ray Diehl, trombone, Eddie Barefield, clarinet, Cary, piano, Bill Goodall, bass, and Keg Purnell, drums. Perhaps the same personnel played the concert at Gettysburg College on January 10, though Haywood Henry was the clarinetist for the Cornell concert on the 21st.

It was in January that Cary organised a series of Monday concerts at The Bagdad restaurant in Farmington ("Dixie Jazz tonight, 8:30 to 1 P.M.") (sic) The regular bassist was John Giuffrida and the drummer Johnny Vine. Cary played alto horn and, presumably, piano.

January 17: Red Allen, trumpet, Dave McKenna, piano
January 24: Charlie Shavers, trumpet ("What a lip!")
January 31: Wild Bill Davison, trumpet, unnamed clarinet
February 7: Red Allen, trumpet ("wonderful")
February 14: Max Kaminsky, trumpet, Eddie Barefield, clarinet
February 21: Johnny Windhurst, trumpet, Bud Freeman, tenor
February 28: Coleman Hawkins, tenor
March 7:   Red Allen, trumpet ("had crowd really going tonight"). But—"Union guy came down and caused so much shit that [owner] Choolgian called it off with me and all New York guests."

On January 22 he played a "nice job at Westford 'Father's' club masquerade" with Tyree Glenn, Bud Freeman, Dave Bowman, Jack Zimmerman and Jimmy Crawford, with Barbara Lea on vocals.

There was another "Jazz on the Campus" concert on February 16, at the State College near Lewistown, with Kaminsky, Diehl, Barefield, John Field, bass, and Purnell, 7:30 to 9:30, including a half-hour broadcast. The following day he went to Condon's to meet Bud Freeman and comments, a little enviously, "Bob Wilber there practising—does this about every day." The next evening, the

Henry 'Red' Allen, tpt; Cary, alto horn.
(Photograph by Gene Marchand, Britstol, Conn.)

18th, the Matarese Circle in Meriden re-opened and Cary worked there for three weekends (Friday to Sunday) "before that squirt Giuf[frida] told me my services not wanted after two weeks." Bob Wilber, clarinet, and Benny Morton, trombone, were the guests on February 20, Bob Wilber again on the 25th, with trombonist Lou McGarity ("really blowing") the guest on February 26/27.

During the early months of 1955, Cary visited Middletown several times, to see his daughters, to visit with friends, and to play with the Al Gentile orchestra. January 8 he played a Veterans of Foreign Wars affair in Middletown, and on the 14th, he was in a five-piece group which provided the music for Judy's Junior Prom—"what a sound, like a bunch of dying calves."

His appearances with Al Gentile included:

January 11: Holyoke
January 15: Bristol (Cary, trumpet; 5 reeds; 3 rhythm)
January 25: Holyoke
February 5: Bristol (Cary, Ray Davis, trumpets)
February 6: Bridgeport (5 brass; 5 reeds; 3 rhythm)
February 8: Holyoke (small band?, including Betty Peterson)
February 11: Statler Hotel, Hartford (U. of Connecticut alumni dance—Cary, trumpet, Betty Peterson, trombone; 5 reeds; 3 rhythm)
February 12: Armory, Manchester (same)
March 6: Ritz Ballroom, Bridgeport
March 8: Holyoke
March 12: Polish Home, Bristol (Cary, Davis, Tweet Peterson, trumpets; 5 reeds; 3 rhythm)
April 3: Hamilton Park, New Britain (5 brass; 5 reeds; 3 rhythm) (drove "in heavy blinding wet snow. Played to less than 50 people.")

"I have near 20 arrangements in books now, got paid for two, but I'm not complaining. Still trying to learn how to write the most rhythmical type and get out of ruts. *Darts* is a little out of a rut."

A Wesleyan University fraternity house (Delta Tau Delta) booking took place on March 4 with Johnny Windhurst, trumpet, Ed Hubble, trombone, John Field, bass, and Walt Gifford, drums. He was a guest again at Condon's on March 15, 22 and 29, and on Sunday, the 20th, he was at Child's restaurant with Ben Ribble, trumpet, Ray Diehl, trombone, Phil Olivella, clarinet, Bob Carter, "hell of a bass player," and Moe Purtill, drums.

Charlie Parker died on March 12, 1955. When Cary read the news of his death he wrote: "Poor guy. One of really great improvisors on the alto, if not the most inventive at a rapid speed. I was lucky enough to work with him on two or three concerts and on those he was very nice, though finding sobriety pretty dull and being a loner. One of the greatest influences ever on our American jazz."

With Max Kaminsky he worked a concert at Cartland College on March 23 and, two days later, at the American Legion Hall, Harrisburg, with Ray Diehl, Eddie Barefield, John Field, and Keg Purnell. On March 26 they played a short concert in the Memorial Gym in Charlottesville, but their stay was tainted by, as Cary wrote: "No motels would take in our two Negros, Barefield and Purnell."

Other bookings with Kaminsky during the early part of the year, with Ray Diehl, trombone, Pee Wee Russell, clarinet and Cary, piano, included:

April 16: Laurel Park ("fabulous clubhouse"): (Steve Lacey, clarinet, replacing Russell, John Field, bass, Karl Kiffe, drums)

April 23: Fraternity House of the University of Pennsylvania (Field, bass, Kiffe, drums) ("I played trumpet on one tune with the Princeton kid—Stan Rubin—who has a lot of energy and very little talent.")

May 4: St. Vincent's College, Latrobe, Penn., by train (Keg Purnell, drums)

May 10: Westport: (Johnny Vine, drums)

May 13: University of Rochester (Field, bass, Purnell, drums)

He also wrote the outlines for a Max Kaminsky recording date for Jazztone held on April 11. Miff Mole, trombone, Pee Wee Russell, clarinet, Joe Sullivan, piano, Jack Lesberg, bass, and George Wettling, drums, were in the band. As Cary rightly noted: "Max had record date tonight—a mess."

In addition to Al Gentile, at this time Cary was writing arrangements for Sonny Calella, Sol Yaged and Ed Hall, as well as trying something for Woody Herman. His diary notes: "Finished *Touché* for Woody Herman and will send score to Nat Pierce." Apparently Herman did not use the arrangement, but Cary recorded *Touché* in 1957 for Stereocraft. Ed Hall's scores were for a private recording session with strings on April 1, while the Sol Yaged charts, *Oh Baby* and *After You've Gone*, were for the clarinetist to play on the Steve Allen Show on April 14. He did them "pretty well."

Also on April 1, Cary was at the Art Students League Ball, dressed as Nero! Presumably he was playing, but he only notes that the Count Basie band and Joe Bushkin group were there, that Johnny Mercer and Sylvia Sims sang and that Anita Ekberg was the ball queen.

Jingles work for the year began on February 2 when Max Kaminsky, Lou McGarity, Jerry Jerome, Don Elliott, mellophone or vibes, Cary on piano, Don Arnone, guitar, ---- Romoff, bass, Mel Zelnick, drums, made "Sell the Hell Out of Shell"—"very satisfactory date—did wild track on *Muskrat Ramble*." At Audio Video, during a three-hour session on April 12, he also played piano for a Coca Cola jingle. Supporting the singers, Bob Kennedy and a quartet, were Doc Severinsen, trumpet, Jerome, Arnone, Romoff, Zelnick, an accordionist and a harpist.

Three days later he worked with Jerry Jerome on three originals, one by Cary, for Philip Morris about "gentleness"—"I celested to a gal singing 12 second spots," and on May 3 there was a session for Hotpoint. At this time Johnny DeVries was working for the J. Walter Thompson agency and Cary "figured out the original music" for a Ford Company jingle, played by Cary, Peanuts Hucko, clarinet, and George Wettling, drums. The recording took place on April 28 at the Coastal Studios, situated next door to the Hickory House. They were back at Coastal on May 24 for a Post Bran advertisement with a jazz band front-line, plus bassoon and flute/ tenor (Phil Bodner). The band was Max Kaminsky, Lou McGarity, Jerry Jerome, Dick Cary, piano, Don Arnone, Milt Hinton and Jimmy Crawford. Next day, at Audio Video in a one-hour session, an Old Gold jingle was made with a similar personnel—Kaminsky, Cutty Cutshall, trombone, Jerome, Cary, piano, Art Ryerson, guitar, Hinton and Crawford. Such work continued throughout the year,

Music in the loft on 6th Avenue remained another feature of Cary's life during 1955. His references include, on January 15, a mention of pianist Hall Overton working upstairs, plus a Teddy

Charles rehearsal taking place, and on March 14, "Hall Overton had session" with Teddy Charles, vibes, Charles Mingus, bass, and a drummer. On April 2 Cary listened to another session in Overton's apartment, where Dave Young said that Gerry Mulligan and Stan Getz wanted to "wail" in Cary's loft—"Jeff Stoughton and Charles Harmon came, but few others."

On April 9 Cary noted: "Woken at midnight for parties in Young's and then Hall's" and on the 21st: "Felonious Monk and gang upstairs." This was about the time that Hall Overton received a Guggenheim grant "of a few thousand—so, as they say, our fourth floor is swinging ... I'm rather proud to have him above me in our loft building."

One of his few appearances at the Central Plaza in 1955 was on April 8, playing trumpet alongside Jimmy Archey, trombone, Sol Yaged, clarinet, Willie "The Lion" Smith, piano, and Jo Jones, drums. Afterwards he and Yaged went to Basin Street to see Louis Armstrong—"his lip was phenomenal."

He recorded, April 20, on alto horn, for another session by Eddie Condon, telling Floyd Levin:

This was the third in the series of Columbia albums we did with Eddie and this featured Bobby Hackett playing a bunch of songs that [Bix] Beiderbecke used to like to play. Bobby wasn't listed on the album; he was under contract to Capitol, so they used the name Pete Pesci, who was the manager of Condon's night club. Condon called him "my night damager." I did the arrangements for this album too.

Among the numerous single gigs during the year, several of which seem to have emanated from the Lester Lanin agency, there was one with an interesting personnel at Maukasset on April 11—Joe Marsala, clarinet, his wife, Adele Girard, harp, Flip Phillips, tenor, Mickey Crane, piano, Charlie Traeger, bass, Cliff Leeman, drums and Cary on alto horn, no doubt. Other dates included playing piano with the Sol Yaged Trio, subbing for Charlie Queener at The Embers on April 24.

Engagements at Princeton University were staggered through the year. On April 22 Cary played "in mud in open air, opening with *Perdido*" with an all-star group which included Jonah Jones, Al Aston, trumpets, "Big Chief" Moore, Urbie Green, trombones, Cecil Scott, Phil Olivella, clarinets, Charlie Queener, piano, Jack Zimmerman, bass, and Karl Kiffe, drums. "I played trumpet, alto horn, piano and bass. Terrible fog on way back." One week later he was playing piano in St. Mary's church gym in Manhasset with Billy

Butterfield, trumpet, Nick Caiazza, tenor, Danny Peri, guitar, and Felix Giobbe, bass. A gig no doubt inspired by the fact that Giobbe's 18-year-old daughter was a senior at the school. The next day he was at Vassar College for an outdoor concert with, among others, "Big Chief" Moore, Bob Wilber and Charlie Queener, followed by one in the theatre. Queener recommended his teacher, Paul Creston, to Dick Cary, though it was some months before Cary took action on this.

He was in the orchestra (5 brass, including Max Kaminsky, 5 sax, 3 rhythm, including Cary, piano) which Lennie Hayton conducted on the Lena Horne Show of May 6th. There were two rehearsals for the broadcast, with Cary commenting on the 5th: "Lennie Hayton rehearsal for show tomorrow. He and Billy Strayhorn on piano for Lena Horne, so I had 1 to 4 off at 5 bucks an hour … Then rehearsal for Lou Wills, Red Buttons and Charlie Applewhite."

May 14 saw the start of three weeks at Eddie Condon's, substituting for Wild Bill Davison who was working in St. Louis. This stay at the club was uneventful, the only comment being that Ed Hall was sulking because he didn't like Don Marino at the drums. During the engagement he also played a concert, May 16, in Allentown with Jimmy McPartland, Vic Dickenson, Eddie Barefield and Karl Kiffe. The supporting group was a trio of Teddy Charles, vibes, Charlie Mingus, bass, and a "good tenor." On Sunday, May 22, he was at a nightclub in Poughkeepsie with, among others, Johnny Windhurst, Johnny Glasel, trumpets, Ed Hubble, trombone, and Bob Wilber, reeds.

Closing at Condon's on June 3, he spent a weekend in Connecticut, followed by a few days of writing, interrupted by two days, June 10/11, in Princeton. On the first night, probably on trumpet, he worked with Don Kirkpatrick, piano, and John Field, bass, "while class of '40 had supper." Later, in a tent band, he played with Max Kaminsky, trumpet, Ray Diehl, trombone, Steve Lacey, clarinet, Cary, piano, Field, bass, and Jo Jones, "who was really something," drums.

An Old Gold jingle was recorded at Audio-Video on June 15, with Jerry Jerome; there was a record date with the arranger Marion Evans on June 24—"I was hired to play 'whorehouse' piano"—and he was a guest at Eddie Condon's on June 21.

Occasional engagements with the Al Gentile orchestra took place during May and June:

May 12:	taping session (probably for Al Gentile's files)
May 29:	Lake Quasipeg, Middlebury
June 4:	Polish Hall, Bristol ("band sounded very well at times, though he plays more and more

June 5:   Lake Quasipeg, Middlebury
June 18: possibly Lake Quasipeg
June 25: Palmer Casino, Indian Neck
June 26: Ivoryton (outdoor job: 5 brass; 5 reeds; 3 rhythm), then to: Lake Quasipeg, Middlebury

Half of June was spent writing, watching television and playing golf, either on the driving range or on a course in company with Jimmy McPartland and Bud Freeman. He left New York on June 30, driving to Lake Placid, ready to spend the summer there.

He started work at 8:00 p.m. on Saturday, July 2, 1955, in the Agora ballroom, playing for a "kid's dance," followed by a 9:15 to midnight general dance. Once more the pattern was set for this two-month holiday period, as it was in 1954—Sunday jazz sessions at the Alpine, "coffee hours," "surprise nights" and "stunts nights," shows, and dances for the staff, the children and the adults. When not playing there was tennis, swimming, golf and the movies.

Paul Jouard was continuing as the leader, with Charlie Harmon on reeds, and Ken Belding on drums. Cary also mentions two others, but no surnames or instruments.

On August 7 there was "a party at Dwight Mill's 'Last Chance Ranch.' I wore straw hat, ribbon tie, vest, apron, armbands and played the five octave red piano." On the 15th he appears to have imbibed too well—"boss sent waitress to tell me to quit playing piano!" Two days later they had the evening off because of a lengthy movie. And on the 22nd, after a staff dance in the boathouse, Cary was very cross because Jouard wouldn't use the event to try the numerous arrangements the band had—"When musicians have nothing to do, why can't they rehearse and try to improve themselves just a little bit?"

Cary left Lake Placid on September 7 and was soon back into the swing of things.

September 9:   Stuyvesant Casino: with Billy Butterfield, trumpet, Miff Mole, trombone, Hank D'Amico, clarinet, Nat Ray and George Wettling, drums. "The piano was terrible!"
September 10: Troton: Police ball with Al Gentile orchestra.
September 12: New London: wedding at Lighthouse, with "the very talented" Mike Giacco, alto, Al Gentile, and—Richards.
September 17: Bristol: Al Gentile (Cary, trumpet; 5 sax).

September 18:   Riverboat on the Hudson: Max Kaminsky, trumpet, Ray Diehl, trombone, Eddie Barefield, clarinet, Cary, piano, Pops Foster, bass, Panama Francis, drums. "Also Stan Rubin and Tiger Town Five—gad!"

September 23:   Princeton: Lester Lanin jazz concert—Kaminsky, "Big Chief" Moore, trombone, Phil Olivella, clarinet, Cy Baker, reeds, Cary, piano, Cozy Cole, drums, Chubby Silvers, ?, Irv [Manning?], bass.

September 24:   Holyoke: with an Al Gentile small band, though Gentile arrived 2½ hours late.

September 26:   to Atlantic City for rehearsals of "Scott Show." No other details.

September 27:   "Scott Show" 11:00 to 12:00—"went pretty well"

For September Cary wrote: "Amazing action with jingles. Am very curious, will it last? These last two weeks have been two of the busiest I've ever had." This reaction is understandable when one considers his schedule—and Jerry Jerome's—at this time. Below are recording and audition dates, which do not include the time spent preparing the material:

September 12:   recorded 2 jingles at WOR studio.
September 15:   auditions for Spree Cleaner jingle.
September 16:   recorded jingle for Tip Top Bread at WOR.
September 21:   jingle for an airline, at WOR.
September 22:   another jingle audition.
September 23:   recorded a coke jingle at Audio Video and rehearsed Knick beer jingle ("I wrote most of it") at WOR.
September 28:   recorded Knick jingle at Coastal 12–3.
September 29:   Tip Top Bread again—Cary played trumpet on *Georgia Cake Walk* and organ on a waltz. Small band also included Tyree Glenn, Jerry Jerome and Hy White, guitar.
September 30:   jingle for Spree, with small band, Jerome on clarinet, plus string quartet. Cary's arrangement "went fine indeed."
October 4:   recorded three versions of Schick 25 jingle, 5:30 to 7:00.
October 5:   Success Wax jingle.
October 10:   jingle for unnamed product, with string

	quartet, including Harry Lookofsky, violin, at Coastal.
October 18:	jingle for E & B Beer at Fine Sound.
October 25:	"Jerry, Bob Kennedy and I demo'd an air force jingle."
November 4:	more for Tip Top Bread at WOR—instrumental quartet—"Fran sang."
November 7:	"did couple of free demos for JJ—Ivory Soap and Mayofrone."
November 14:	"Jerry Jerome called. 13-piece arrangement for Eskimo Pie ditty tomorrow at noon."
November 15:	Arrangement done in middle of night. Band included Max Kaminsky, Red Solomon, John Plonsky, trumpets; saxes; and rhythm. "First we did *Flying Home*, then mine. JJ used only baritone and rhythm—arrangement went for nought!" Recorded at Fine Sound.
November 16:	jingle for unnamed product at WOR. Small unit included Eddie Costa, "quite a vibist."
November 18:	Knick Beer jingle at Coastal.
November 25:	jingle for Nabisco.

As 1955 faded away so did the jingle work, with Cary spending the early part of 1956 in Los Angeles, out of direct contact with Jerry Jerome. This fruitful source of employment gradually disappeared, though even as late as 1957 there was still occasional work. In January he was involved in "three versions of gas jingle" with three singers, followed the next month by "about eight versions of a terrible coffee jingle with Jimmy Brown for Jerry Jerome to exhibit to three Compton boys."

Reverting to September's activities, on the 12th there is an intriguing entry that George Avakian, a&r man for Columbia Records, telephoned—"Turk Murphy needs trumpet—I couldn't." Billy Butterfield played trumpet on a two-title Murphy recording date for Columbia on September 22, so did Avakian ask Cary before he spoke to Butterfield? It would have been interesting to hear Cary play with Murphy's very traditional jazz band.

Cary spent the weekend of October 1/2 in Middletown, visiting his ex-wife and playing on the Saturday at the Chippanee Country Club, near Bristol, with Johnny Windhurst, Eddie Hubble, Sam Margolis, reeds, and Johnny Vine, drums. Returning to New York on the 3rd, he played celeste for a girl vocal trio on a demonstration date. His first lesson with Paul Creston took place the next day—"Creston spoke of rhythm and assigned sub-division examples," while a later one was on "irregular subdivisions"—and that evening Cary guested at Eddie Condon's.

Middletown claimed Cary's presence the next two weekends. On Friday the 5th he was in a band at Fazzino's ("a wild joint"), which included Eddie Hubble, trombone, and Buell Neidlinger, bass, plus Dave Rich and Hoyt. The following night he was at DTD with Hubble, Rich, Hoyt and Johnny Vine. Back in Middletown for the second weekend, he spent Friday the 14th with his daughter, Janet, and on the 15th played with an Al Gentile sextet at a policemen's ball.

A diary entry after a visit to the Cafe Bohemia to hear Phil Woods is: "What alto!! fantastic. Rest of band fair, except George Wallington [pianist] appeared mad to one and all."

The end of October was quiet, until Max Kaminsky obtained a three-day booking for October 31–November 2, at the Crystal Room of the Belmont-Plaza hotel, playing for a Greybar Convention. In addition to Kaminsky and Cary the band was Ray Diehl, Phil Olivella and George Wettling. On November 7 Cary began a week at Eddie Condon's, subbing on trumpet. He received a parking ticket on his last day there, November 11—"$15 again—God, I hate this city"—and the next night he worked at the Charter Club at Princeton.

With Eddie Condon and George Wettling he travelled to the Glen Island Casino on November 13, noting: "I squeezed through three sets. Ken Kersey [pianist] late so I played a 15-minute *Oh Baby* with Sol Yaged." His next gig was again with Eddie Condon, in Fordham on the 18th, alongside Billy Butterfield, Freddie Ohms, trombone, Peanuts Hucko, Jack Lesberg and Cliff Leeman ("Condon helpless"). There was a college date in New Haven with a local group on the 19th, followed the next afternoon by a session at Yale "with Lanin's noisemakers—Max Kaminsky, Joe Thomas, trumpets, Pee Wee Russell, clarinet, Cary, piano and trumpet, Pops Foster, bass, George Wettling, drums, and Chubby Silvers, ?. 'Christ, what a din!'"

He travelled by train to Philadelphia on November 25 to take part in a concert at the Academy of Music and his diary lists the details:

1. Max Kaminsky, Conrad Janis, Hank D'Amico, Cary, John Giuffrida, Zutty Singleton
2. Ralph Sutton trio
3. Jimmy McPartland, Vic Dickenson, Peanuts Hucko, Bud Freeman, Cary, Eddie Condon, Milt Hinton! (sic), George Wettling. (Intermission)

4. Buck Clayton group
5. Coleman Hawkins, Tyree Glenn, Cary, Hinton, Wettling "on a bitch of a set."
6. Then all on blues and *Saints*.
   "Very successful concert in every way."

On November 26 he was considering an offer from Conrad Janis to spend three months in a show in California and a few days later he "agreed to go to California with 'Joy Ride,' maybe three months ... This loft is cold and lonely on occasion lately"—so he was anticipating playing golf and tennis and looking up friends in Los Angeles. His decision meant that he was away from New York for six months, losing contact with Jerry Jerome and his jingle work, and with Paul Creston, whose lessons had continued on a weekly basis. His final day with Creston, who he considered a good teacher, seems to have been on December 6. Cary was pleased it had been "possible to study with Creston and feel the slight possibility of writing a little bit of something some day."

Towards the end of November, Irving Townsend, a producer at Columbia Records, spoke to Cary about writing arrangements for Wild Bill Davison and a small group to play along with piano rolls by Fats Waller and James P. Johnson. On December 9, after a visit to Madison Square Garden to watch professional tennis, to see Pancho Gonzales show "why he's the greatest," Cary went to Condon's Club to discuss the project with Davison. On the last day of December Cary noted: "Quite a bit of writing. Finished Wild Bill's Columbia album with player piano"—and that was the last heard of that idea. Hal Willard tells the story of this unsuccessful plan in "The Wildest One: The Life of Wild Bill Davison."

On November 27 Cary drove Bud Freeman and Vic Dickenson to the Glen Island Casino for an afternoon session with Jimmy and Marian McPartland, Bill Crow, bass, and Joe Morello, drums. Of the rhythm he notes: "Fine section indeed!" Other groups playing were led by Phil Napoleon and Sol Yaged. The following night Cary started at Eddie Condon's, leading a band he had put together while the Condon mob was in Florida for three days. His personnel was Cary, trumpet, Cutty Cutshall, who did not go with Condon, trombone, Peanuts Hucko, clarinet, Dave Bowman, piano, Jack Lesberg, bass, and Cliff Leeman, drums. He commented: "First band they've heard in there in quite a while."

He also worked at Condon's on December 1/2, subbing for Wild Bill Davison. With the regulars back from Florida he wrote:

"Walter Page helpless and exhausted; Cutty mad again; Pee Wee Russell also very beat and Condon not there to turn the handle. An old time amusement park mechanical band would have a much more enthusiastic sound." And the following day—"band just terrible."

December 3 found him at Farmingdale, Long Island, playing a concert with Eddie Condon, Bud Freeman, Ralph Sutton, piano, John Giuffrida, bass, and Cliff Leeman, drums. On the 5th he was on piano in the band—including Jimmy McPartland, trumpet, Freddie Ohms, trombone, Peanuts Hucko, clarinet, and Bud Freeman, tenor—which opened an ambitious P.T.A. concert at a high school in Stamford. Also on the bill were the Marian McPartland Trio, the Mundell Lowe group ("with Al Klink, who sounded fine"), Dick Hyman plus Carmen McRae.

There was more excitement on December 11, starting with a visit with Bud Freeman to the Roseland Ballroom at 11:30 to see Tommy and Jimmy Dorsey. "Tommy played *Hanid* twice in a row—was pleased. Bud was absolutely shining... Tom took us to Birdland to hear Basie!! Benny Carter, Bill Basie sat with us, saw many others, marvelous night. Basie is going to get three arrangements a week from Wednesday—hot dog! What a band—write so simple—they take care of the swinging." Over the next few days Cary worked on the charts for the Count and talked with Bud Freeman about Bud's tune for the band. On December 21 they went to Birdland for Basie's last night there—"joint jammed. Save the arrangements. Bud will take them to the Apollo in January." Were the arrangements finished? Did Bud Freeman deliver them? Did Count Basie play them?

Clarinetist Peanuts Hucko obtained a job at the Melody Lounge, commencing December 14, with Cary on trumpet and piano, Freddie Ohms, trombone, Al Mattucci, bass, and Morey Feld, drums. The following night he mentions: "Met Pat Ward—can't sing but looks marvelous trying." Presumably Ms. Ward was not a regular member of the band.

On the 16th, when the personnel varied, with Johnny Windhurst on trumpet, Bill Byers, trombone, Bob Carter, bass, and Feld, drums, Cary had too much to drink and Hucko dropped him.

The festive season got underway on December 20 when Cary and Bud Freeman were the guests at Eddie Condon's that night, but earlier played for an affair at the Plaza for NBC public relations. On the 22nd there was an Eastern Airlines party, where the band was Jimmy McPartland, trumpet, Bud Freeman, tenor, Cary, piano, and Buzzy Drootin, drums.

Cary drove to Middletown on Christmas Eve to spend the holiday with Rose and his daughters. That night he played piano while Judy sang. Rose had re-married after their divorce but one assumes that the second marriage had also failed.

He was back in New York on the 28th, where he worked on the Wild Bill Davison arrangements already mentioned, in addition to those needed by Jimmy McPartland. These were four required to increase the "Shades of Bix" album to a 12″ LP, plus those for a Jazztone album, including several originals. Then, on New Year's Eve, after visiting Eddie Condon's, "Bud Freeman and I cabbed to Society of Illustrators," where they played from 11:15, had breakfast at 1:15, and finally stopped playing at 3:00 a.m. Or, as Cary put it, "Year ended in midst of some of most talented illustrators in the world, playing *Auld Lang Syne*...."

New Year's Day of 1956 was spent packing for the trip to Los Angeles and phoning goodbyes, followed by visits to the Hickory House ("met the McPartlands, Woody Herman, Jimmy Dorsey"), and to Basin Street ("Clifford Brown hypnotizes me—Max Roach good tonight. Then Marian's drummer, Joe Morello (!!) sat-in with George Shearing's clean but uninteresting group (all too efficient)."

The Conrad Janis band for the "Joy Ride" show was Johnny Windhurst, trumpet, Conrad Janis, trombone, Gene Sedric, reeds, Dick Cary, piano, and Nat Ray, drums. Cary travelled with Windhurst and their flight left New York at 08:40 on January 2, and arrived, after stops in Cleveland and Chicago, in Los Angeles at 06:10 on the 3rd. There was a rehearsal in the union hall, then Cary visited Zardi's to hear altoist Herb Geller and the Hangover for baritone saxist Joe Rushton. Rehearsals continued each day until the official opening night at the Huntington Hartford Theatre on January 12. The leader of the show orchestra, which included Tommy Todd on piano and Jerry Rosen on drums, was Milt Greene, while the leads were Joel Grey, Muriel Landers, Bernie West, Dorothy Greener, and Aileen Stanley.

"Only thing I do in show is sing in group on *Chiringa* from pit, then open *Hey, Chicago* with Loray White blues—this ends first act. Second number in second act is *World of Strangers* by Sammy Fain—I walk across in raincoat, then off, until finally—*Joy Ride* —play 16 fast bars on trumpet from top level—people bouncing around two slides and a trampoline." Of Miss White he remarked: "Negress singer—nice body—awful voice."

This would suggest that the jazz band was little used in the show and one can understand why Conrad Janis campaigned for it to at least play *When the Saints Go Marching In*! Rehearsals continued on into February, with at least four new directors during the first three weeks of the run. An article in the Mirror-News for February 18 stated that the original "Joy Ride" cost was $110,000 and that the losses to date were $30,000.

Conrad Janis remembered his part in "Joy Ride" as follows, although it differs in a few details from Dick Cary's recollections:

"Around 1956, I got to do one of the leading roles in the musical revue 'Joy Ride' which was a compilation of the best numbers from a group of successful Broadway Revues ('New Faces,' 'Catch a Rising Star' and so on) for a production produced by Huntington Hartford. This musical revue was scheduled to run at the Huntington Hartford Theater in Hollywood, California and then work its way across the U.S. and eventually end up on Broadway.

"My co-leads were Joel Grey (many years before his great success in 'Cabaret'), Dorothy Greener (a well known revue comedienne) and Bernie West, a very funny stand up comic who later went on to produce such TV sit-com hits as 'The Jeffersons.' Also, Huntington Hartford decided that my band would make a fresh addition to the proceedings and thus in addition to my starring role in 'Joy Ride,' he asked me to put together a 5 piece group which would appear on stage. As there was also a full orchestra in the pit, this was somewhat of an innovation and several numbers were created for the band, then known as Conrad Janis and his Tailgate 5. The group consisted of Johnny Windhurst, trumpet; Eugene 'Honeybear' Sedric, clarinet; Nat Ray, drums; and of course Dick Cary, piano. One of these production numbers consisted of a New Orleans 'Storyville' opus, complete with prostitutes and pimps and such, and the theme was the closing of Storyville and the migration North that followed. The number was called (if memory serves) *Goin' to Chicago*. Cary and the band and indeed all the dancers and singers were elaborately costumed in colorful creations of the period and Dick Cary, to top off his costume, wore wide braces and a Bowler (or as we call it a Derby, pronounced, in the US as Derr-bee not Dar Bee). At any rate it was not very convincing and eventually got cut from the show.

"'Joy Ride' ran for more than 5 months ... at the Hartford Theater until an accident to the theater closed it down for repairs and at that point we actually took off for Chicago to run there for several weeks before heading for Broadway.

"However, by then Joel Grey and Bernie West and others had left the revue for greener pastures and finally in Chicago and after many months of my futile pleas to the various directors of 'Joy Ride' to include a Jazz number in the show, only to be told over and over again that there was no place for Jazz on a legitimate stage and it would not be any good. So, finally, as a last ditch measure they concocted a number for the band which actually allowed us to blow our own style.

"Naturally we chose *The Saints* and the plot of the skit was a 'jam session' that took place in a run down street in Chicago. The band members were to show up carrying our horns, remove the instruments from their cases, and hold a jam session. Cary, who was 'late' which prompted 'comments' from the band, finally made his entrance from the wings, pushing his piano in front of him, which produced a good laugh. One night he ad-libbed 'Sorry I'm late, I had trouble getting it on the bus.' This got a really good laugh and the director told him to keep it in the skit. Well, we played the hell out of the number in a 'Damn the Torpedoes, Full Speed Ahead' Central Plaza Style, complete with a rousing drum solo and a big finish (a Hallelujah halftime ending on the last four bars). The director was astounded as the audience roared and gave us a standing ovation.

"They moved the number down to just before the finale, but Huntington Hartford had by then lost interest in being a producer and the show never made it to Broadway."

* * * * * * * *

Huntington Hartford (1911–2008) inherited $90 million at 12 years of age but died penniless, having squandered his fortune, to quote one obituary, on "a series of quixotic artistic and commercial ventures and expensive wives." But at least he had provided five musicians with regular work for a few months.

The accident to which Conrad Janis refers happened during the matinee performance on March 31. Cary says a main beam came loose and the theatre was closed for repairs. It was very fortunate that the beam slipped only a few inches—"it could have been a real mess." But the accident did provide: "Our first night off in twelve weeks!" The show re-opened on April 10 and continued until May 26. They were on the train the following day, arriving in Chicago on the afternoon of the 29th. Rehearsals began on the 31st and there was a preview for the newspapers at the Shubert Theatre on Sunday, June 3. According to Cary the resulting reviews, when published on the Tuesday were "two awful, one fair, one very good." On the Monday they spent "all afternoon getting *Saints* ready for opening ... a packed house seemed to enjoy our efforts." But despite these efforts the show closed on June 23.

Cary and Windhurst spent three days with guitarist Bill Priestley and his wife, Cricket, before catching the train back to New York on June 27, reaching there the following day.

During the months in Los Angeles, Cary visited a number of clubs and among those he commented upon were Sardi's, where he saw Stan Kenton—"some of the arrangements are marvelous—some of the young, very cocky-acting boys are lousy soloists"; Tiffany's and Shelly Manne—"good drummer, over-arty. Hampton Hawes a fast but too studious colored pianist"; the Hangover—"terrible band, George Thow lousy trumpeter"; Jazz City, to see Howard McGhee and Alan Eager; and to Zardi's again, to see Count Basie. On May 15 he commented after seeing Art Tatum—"Tatum has shed many pounds. Doesn't drink but the fingers are still working—god! No one else can move compared to this giant of all time."

Among the places he sat-in were the Tailspin and, on three occasions, the Knotty Pine: "Played with Johnny Lucas, crippled trumpet player, drums, piano [Don Owens] and Matty Matlock, who sounds fine and is hell of a nice guy." A couple of nights later, he visited again with Conrad Janis—"Janis played a loud, fast show-off set. He's a nice boy, I guess—very energetic, terrific gall."

Other events were the usual mixture of good and bad. The latter included missing the start of a show, for which his pay was docked. He was very annoyed about this! Then there was the occasion that the police found him asleep in his car after imbibing too well, causing him to spend a few hours in jail until his sister Lois arrived to pay his fine. There was also a letter from Paul Jouard to say they could not afford Cary at the Lake Placid Club this summer. And he was saddened by the death of one of his favourite radio comedians, Fred Allen.

On the plus side, Mrs. Huntington Hartford threw a party for the cast and the musicians and the stagehands; he earned a few dollars by completing two Tommy Todd arrangements for a record date for Chuck Gould (at the time of writing Mr. Gould remains a mystery); and he did play a lot of golf. It was in May that he mentions an event which contributed to his financial stability in later years—"Gave Merrill Lynch my check for $1485 for 45 shares of American Express."

In Chicago he visited the Preview (on one occasion "a rude barkeep shooed me out when I requested ginger ale"), the Cloisters (where he was most impressed by singer Lurlean Hunter) and the Brass Rail, but it was at Jazz, Ltd., owned by Bill and Ruth Reinhardt, that he was most comfortable. As well as sitting-in ("band most agreeable") he was able to talk with Ruth Reinhardt, an A.A. member for seven years—though he was not inspired to join A.A. himself.

While Cary was away from New York Jimmy McPartland recorded, on February 2, four more titles associated with Bix Beiderbecke in order to expand the Shades of Bix LP from 10″ to 12″. These included Cary's unique version of *In a Mist*. McPartland told Leonard Feather how this came about, starting with the time that he and Beiderbecke came out of a classical concert in Carnegie Hall: "I said, 'Bix, you should write a jazz symphony—something along the lines of *In a Mist*, but with other instruments to enhance the piano—maybe a bassoon, an oboe.' Bix said, 'You know, kid, I like that. It's a good idea. Why don't you write it?' And I said, 'Oh, gosh, I can't stand arranging—it takes up so much time.' ... but when this new opportunity came along I outlined the whole thing for Dick Cary and asked him to orchestrate it, telling him what I had talked to Bix about."

The result, using a standard Dixieland instrumentation, plus a bassoon and an oboe, is a minor masterpiece, completely capturing, yet enhancing, the solitary mood of Beiderbecke's sombre piano solo.

> *They wanted me to take some of the Beiderbecke introductions and little bridges and things, but everybody could play their own choruses. But in this particular case we added a bassoon and an oboe, some of the studio men. Marian McPartland played the piano part. I wanted to get some misty sounds with the reeds and the cymbals and things like that. ... I wasn't there at the time, I was [in Los Angeles] with a show at the Huntington Hartford Theatre and I was worried about it. I understand Bud Freeman conducted! I was wondering how it would come out, but it came out fairly well.*

Critic Max Harrison wrote of *In a Mist*: "Lasting the greater part of five minutes, this is an arrangement by Cary along the lines once discussed by Beiderbecke with the young McPartland ... The original piano solo is embedded in a rich fabric indeed, and here interpretation becomes a creative act on the parts of the arranger and all the performers."

In the space of a few days the McPartlands recorded the final four Bix titles for Brunswick, in addition to sessions for Grand Award and Jazztone. About the Jazztone date, *Down Beat* reported that some numbers were by McPartland and Cary. The record has no composer credits, but there are six titles which appear to be originals. The sleeve notes state that Bill Stegmeyer did all the arrangements.

Back in New York City on June 28, 1956, Cary was quickly into the old routine. On the 30th he played piano at the Central Plaza with Max Kaminsky, J.C. Higginbotham, trombone, Tony Parenti, and Arthur Trappier, and bass with Johnny Windhurst, Ed Hubble and Johnny Vine for a wedding on Long Island on July 1. He was a guest star at Eddie Condon's on the 3rd, then played on a Schaeffer beer float in a parade in Bridgeport on the 4th with a Max Kaminsky band. On the 5th he worked at Condon's while Condon, Davison and Schroeder were at the Newport Jazz Festival. Two nights at the Central Plaza were followed by a gig at Pleasure Beach in Bridgeport in a band with four trumpets, five saxes, three rhythm and "two gals." "Really enjoyed job on trumpet and alto horn." No doubt this was with Al Gentile.

He started four days at Condon's on July 10, playing piano while Gene Schroeder was at the Washington Jazz Festival, and appeared at the Central Plaza on the 14th; then the remainder of July was mainly spent either in the Middletown area or playing with Max Kaminsky. He is unforthcoming about a session at Child's on the 21st, when he played piano with Buck Clayton, trumpet, Coleman Hawkins, tenor, and Cecil Scott, clarinet. The jobs with Kaminsky were:

July 24:	Tonight Show, Morey Amsterdam, m.c. with Kaminsky, Pee Wee Russell, Lee Gifford, Dick Cary, Jack Lesberg, George Wettling.
July 27:	Lake Hopatcong, midnight concert: Kaminsky, Gifford, Russell, Cary, Charlie Traeger, bass; Johnny Vine, drums.
July 28:	Central Plaza: Kaminsky, Conrad Janis, Eddie Barefield, Arthur Herbert, drums.
July 30:	McCarthy's in Southampton with Pee Wee Russell and a 17-year-old trumpet player.
July 31:	Wes Nor diner, Westport: Kaminsky, Cary, Traeger, Vine.

During July, he and Jimmy McPartland met Herbert Marks of music publisher E.B. Marks, who "has nice deal on arranging an album, ten of their standards and four of our originals." The next day he "spent the afternoon with McPartland, thinking of tunes—at least I did." On July 12 Herbert Marks liked Cary's playing of the originals.

August 3 he was at the Central Plaza with Conrad Janis, who recalled that Cary "was well known as a very thorough musician and an excellent pianist. He worked with me in my bands at the Central Plaza, The Metropole, and God knows how many other jobs in and around New York City and environs." The next day there was a concert at Campo Beach, Westport, with Max Kaminsky, Vic Dickenson, Pee Wee Russell, Charlie Traeger, and Johnny Vine, and this was followed by appearances (7:00 a.m. local and 8:00 a.m. midwest) on the Will Rogers Jr. Show on CBS—"Programme was in memory of Bix Beiderbecke—died 25 years ago today. [Went] without a hitch and Jimmy talked very well. We played *In a Mist, Singin' the Blues, Davenport* and ended our half-hour with *Saints*, just Jim [McPartland] and I, Milt Hinton [bass] and Joe Morello [drums]. Couldn't get a much better rhythm duet to try to play with."

After a short stay in Middletown Cary started work on August 10 at Eddie Condon's for two weeks, "on the banana."

Cary had attended an abortive rehearsal with clarinetist Stan Rubin on August 2—"Wonder if I should go to Atlantic City with Rubin. Barbara Lea was there but refused to sing any of my arrangements—too high." In any event, he did decide to join Rubin and, on August 24, he and trombonist Ed Hubble drove to Atlantic

Stan Rubin's band, 1956 includes John Frost, tp, at left; Steve Philo, b, 4th from left; Ed Hubble, tb, 5th from left; Barbara Lea, Stan Rubin, Dick Cary in centre.
(Courtesy: Dick Cary Archive)

City. After a swim and a rehearsal they worked at the Steel Pier, 8:30 to 12:30, with a broadcast at 9:30. This routine ran until the last day of the job, August 30, when Cary arrived for work to discover that his tape-recorder, music and cheque book had been stolen. He had bought the Ferrograph recorder only the week previous.

Though Cary was not impressed with Rubin or his band he wrote some arrangements for him and played a few other gigs with him, including August 31 at the Parkway Casino and September 4/5 at Rogers Beach, plus a noon and supper session with Rubin's big band in the cafeteria of the Victor tube factory in Harrison, New Jersey on September 17. Working with Rubin led to a friendship with Barbara Lea, for whom he did some writing. On September 6, he accompanied her at the Wes Nor diner. This contact led to work as pianist and arranger for her recording sessions for Prestige on October 18th and 19th. Miss Lea was in a concert (A Dixieland Holiday) at Carnegie Hall towards the end of the year, when Cary was in a group led by Max Kaminsky and also including Vic Dickenson, trombone, Eddie Barefield, clarinet, Arvell Shaw, bass, and George Wettling, drums.

September was completed by:

September 8:	Central Plaza
September 10/11:	Metropole—with Conrad Janis
September 18:	Wes Nor Diner—"very nice job with Lou McGarity, George Barnes, Jack Lesberg, Cliff Leeman"
September 19:	a benefit for Jack Crystal, one set with Pee Wee Erwin, trumpet, George Stevenson, trombone, Tony Parenti, clarinet, Arthur Trappier, drums.
September 22:	The Rustic Lodge North Brunswick, New Jersey—with local band
September 25:	Eddie Condon's—as guest, with Peanuts Hucko
September 27:	Audio Show—John Hammond called, pianist Ellis Larkins had not arrived, so Cary went over and played "in the small room with cornetist Ruby Braff."
September 29:	party at Toots Shor's—"what a band" —Max Kaminsky, Ray Diehl, Pee Wee Russell, Peanuts Hucko on tenor, Cary, piano & alto horn, Don Arnone, guitar, Charlie Traeger, bass, Nat Ray, drums.

"The Loft" receives few mentions during 1956, but one September entry is: "Hall Overton spent evening with me—asked about 'Dixieland' and I played a little upstairs. He explained a little about Horace Silver and wrote a 12-bar illustration on the blues." It was also this month that Cary visited Birdland to hear both the Maynard Ferguson big band and Phineas Newborn, of whom he wrote: "Best young pianist I've heard—terrific speed and good taste." Hearing him again in December the superlatives increased—"Newborn most fantastic pianist I've ever heard—technique, terrific rhythm, imagination and all that, just amazing. His group is very fine also, especially brother Calvin on guitar."

During September Ralph Sutton had written to him about a job near San Francisco on a riverboat, details of which were to become clearer towards the end of the year. In February, while in Los Angeles, he had written: "I'm pretty sure I want to live out here within a few years." Sutton's proposal, plus his experience with "Joy Ride," caused him to write a few days later: "Am thinking a lot of California life"—though it was to be another three years before the thought became the deed.

Jimmy McPartland and Cary drove to Detroit on Sunday, September 30, to open the following day at Baker's Keyboard Lounge. McPartland's quartet consisted of himself on cornet, Cary on piano and alto horn, and unnamed bass and drums. The booking was for six nights and Cary played a "nice Baldwin Grand."

Having completed work on four Bud Freeman tunes for the Dorsey brothers, Cary went to the Statler Hotel on October 8 to meet them—"heard *Newport News*—terrible." While there he had a drink or two with Charlie Shavers ("who hates T. Dorsey and is leaving") and Gail Curtis. (Tommy Dorsey died a few weeks later, on November 26, and Cary refers to this "terrible news.")

A long weekend in Hartford followed, during which, on Saturday, October 13, he played alto horn with Al Gentile's band (five saxes) at Lake Compounce, Bristol. "[Mike] Giacco led saxes wonderfully on *The Way You Look Tonight* and Gentile liked *Newport News*. Only drawback was that stuffy bum, Gus Weber on piano." He had also worked on two other originals for Gentile, *Red Run* and *Spence de Fence*.

After the Barbara Lea recording sessions the work pattern continued much as before:

October 20:   the Central Plaza
October 21:   Connecticut University: played a "real good job" (with McPartland, Dickenson, Freeman,

	Al Hall, bass, and Buzzy Drootin, drums)
October 23:	Eddie Condon's: subbed for Jimmy McPartland (Cary, trumpet, Dickenson, trombone; Bob Wilber, clarinet)
October 24:	recording session with Don Costa Ray Conniff-type music. "I played out-of-tune piano on a Costa original"—*Everybody Loves Pierre*.
October 26:	Matarese Circle: (with McPartland, Dickenson, Freeman, Drootin)
October 27:	Pennsylvania University: (with Max Kaminsky, Ray Diehl, Eddie Barefield, Charlie Traeger, Johnny Vine—"awful job—piano way, way off, so I alto'd mostly."
October 28:`	Shakespeare Theatre, Stratford, Conn: charity concert (2 sets with McPartland, Dickenson, Pee Wee Russell, Walter Page, Bobby Donaldson)
November 3:	Hackley School, Tarrytown: Stan Rubin
November 4:	Zeta PSI, Yale University: with Jonah Jones, Max Kaminsky, trumpets, "Big Chief" Moore, Jerry Bouchard, trombones; Phil Olivella, clarinet, Irving Lang, bass, Jo Jones, drums) (Lester Lanin job)

At the October 28 concert the other artists on the programme were the Billy Taylor Trio, Jimmy Rushing, a Buck Clayton group and Barbara Lea. Cary noted that the only good set was by Buck Clayton, trumpet, Tyree Glenn, trombone, and Coleman Hawkins, tenor. The Stan Rubin concert on November 3 was described as a "very nice job for the prep school boys. Stan Rubin had best band he ever played in"—Ray Diehl, trombone, Cary, piano no doubt, a drummer, and John Dengler playing cornet, clarinet, baritone, soprano and valve trombone.

One entry states: "Bought eight Prestige albums—Clifford Brown, Miles Davis, Sonny Rollins and that ilk. Boy, some of this shit is awful! They just are badly recorded—arrangements are terrible—phrases all the same—no organization—should be so much better."

There are still occasional mentions of visits to the movies and, even more occasionally, a trip to the theatre. He had seen the Lunts earlier in the year and in November he saw Paul Muni and Ed Begley at the National Theatre in "Inherit the Wind." There is also a mention, without the title, of a George Bernard Shaw play. During this same period he was rehearsing with Barbara Lea (he worked with her at the Village Vanguard on November 6) and with Bud Freeman.

After another long weekend in the Hartford area, Cary returned to New York to find that Eddie Condon had cancelled him from one job and that Bobby Hackett wanted him for another. He was hired for Hackett's engagement at the Henry Hudson Hotel, starting November 24, 1956, a booking which was to prove to be one of the peaks of Dick Cary's career.

In the days prior to the Henry Hudson, there were two rehearsals with the Hackett band, a day with Max Kaminsky, Gene Sedric, George Wettling and Bob Cordana playing on a private train to New Haven and at St. Elmo's on November 17, a guest spot at Eddie Condon's on the 20th, and an afternoon at the Metropole, playing alongside Pee Wee Erwin, "Big Chief" Moore, Bud Freeman, Milt Hinton and Buzzy Drootin, on the 22nd. He also appeared at the Metropole on the afternoon of the 24th, finding Milton Hinton, bass, and Panama Francis, drums, "easy to play with."

Sunday, November 25, being a day off, he was able to participate in the train ride to Boston, playing again for comedian Jackie Gleason. The other musicians were Max Kaminsky, Bob Wilber, George Wettling and Dom Cortese, accordion. Arriving back in New York at 6 p.m. he was in time to attend Willie "The Lion" Smith's party at the Central Plaza.

He worked at the Metropole on the afternoons of December 1st and 2nd, first with Jimmy McPartland, Coleman Hawkins, Arvell Shaw and George Wettling, and second with Shaw and Wettling on just one number. After the December 1 session he changed, and went to Carnegie Hall for "A Dixie Holiday" concert. He played in Max Kaminsky's band, with Vic Dickenson, Eddie Barefield, Shaw and Wettling. Also on the bill were Stan Rubin's Tigertown Five, the Tony Parenti quartet, and Barbara Lea.

During December, Cary was involved in discussions about the "riverboat deal" with Ralph Sutton. He was visited twice by representatives from San Francisco and later spent time with one of them—Ned Travis, who was responsible for the project—"it's a real big deal." He was shown pictures, figures, maps, etc, of Sausalito Bay, where the plan was to build a motel, shopping centre and swimming pool, and to convert a large boat into a jazz club. Ralph Sutton, who was then living in San Francisco, and Dick Cary were to be the key musicians. Sadly, this was another good idea which never came to fruition.

Also in December Cary had four Sunday afternoon bookings, 3 p.m. to 7 p.m, the 9th to 30th, at a club called Diron's in Brooklyn. These seem to have been arranged by a Frank Carey, and the musicians invited included Sol Yaged, Harry Shepherd, vibes, Harry DeVito, trombone, Herman Autrey, trumpet, and Bud Freeman.

December 25 the band did not work and Cary had a "pretty sad Christmas." On the 30th he sat for over three hours without a drink at Birdland, hearing Count Basie and the "very inspiring" Phineas Newborn, and the 31st was spent at the Henry Hudson playing the usual New Year's Eve numbers, "followed by *The Saints* which I sang."

9. Bobby Hackett at the Henry Hudson (1956–1958)

Five months earlier, in July 1956, cornetist Bobby Hackett had organised a small band with which to tour. His personnel was Ray Diehl, trombone, Tommy Gwaltney, clarinet, vibes, Teddy Roy, piano, John Dengler, tuba, Tony Hannan, drums. Towards the close of the year he obtained a residency in the Voyager Room of the Henry Hudson Hotel in New York City. When the band opened there on November 24, 1956, it was for a two-week engagement, with a two-week option, and with two changes to the personnel. Diehl had left, replaced by Ernie Caceres, "clarinet and hydrant," and Cary was in for Roy. Cary referred to "...Bobby (enigma) Hackett on cornet and yeah's. Band unusual—gets going at times." The success of the engagement was confirmed when a *Down Beat* news item stated that: "Bobby Hackett, the first jazz combo to play the Voyager Room ... is in for an indefinite stay ... every night but Sunday 9 p.m. to 1." However, Cary lists the band's hours as 8 p.m. to 1 a.m. Monday to Friday, 9 p.m. to 2 a.m. on Saturday, with Sunday off. For his first Monday he noted: "We do half-hours at 8, 9, 10, 11, 12 and 15 [minutes] at 12.45." Probably indicating a later change, The New York Post for December 31, 1956, listed the band as playing 8 till 1 a.m. Monday to Thursday and 8 until 2 a.m. on Friday and Saturday.

About six weeks after the opening, drummer Tony Hannan left and in his January 5 diary entry Cary noted: "Nat Ray now with us and band is more solid." The remaining personnel were Bobby Hackett; Dick Cary, piano, alto horn, arranger; Tommy Gwaltney, clarinet, vibes; Ernie Caceres, baritone, clarinet; John Dengler, tuba. Gwaltney commented on the arranging and instrumentation: "Cary did most of the arranging, Hackett did a little and some were cooperative arrangements. Hackett played no guitar. Bobby would let Dengler play cornet once in a while, but John was mostly tuba. I played a little alto, but mostly clarinet. I originally started on soprano, but went to clarinet and vibes exclusively after a few months." Gwaltney credits Cary with the switch in the band's style: "The change was initiated when Dick Cary joined and began writing for us. Hackett wanted to get away from the Dixieland label." Dick Cary himself said:

I did all the arranging for the Henry Hudson band. [Hackett] gave me a small amount to write any way I wanted, knowing very well I would have done so anyway. My problem was attempting to get leaders to play what I liked to write. I can easily say that Bob [was] the only leader who tried everything I tried.

The growing length of the run in the Voyager Room resulted in newspaper reviews, regular Mutual broadcasts in the "Bandstand USA" series, and recording sessions for Capitol Records. Leonard Feather, not noted for his interest in musicians with Condon affiliations, wrote a rave review in *Down Beat* (April 4, 1957) in which he stated: "it is the most attractive and resourceful jazz group now resident in Manhattan." He went on to say: "Cary, who has written the entire eclectic book that gives the group much of its protean personality, deserves a healthy share of the credit. Dick also lends the band some of its striking coloration by playing an E-flat horn, which, blended with the tuba and baritone, sometimes gives the group a quality that recalls the Miles Davis Capitol sides. He further impresses the masses by sometimes sitting at the keyboard, playing piano with his left hand and horn with his right."

In the review Feather mentions a Cary original titled *Out Tate*, "a harmonically rich minor theme." He also comments; "If you think I swallowed this band hook, line and sinker, I must point out that on one tune Dick played eight bars of cocktail piano that I didn't dig."

Bobby Hackett sextet at Henry Hudson Hotel, c. December 1956
l-r Tommy Gwaltney, cl; Cary, p; Hackett, co; Ernie Caceres, bar;
Tony Hannan, d; John Dengler, tu.
(Bill Spilka photograph, courtesy of John Dengler.)

Pianist John Sheridan told Ken Gallacher: "Cary was an exceptional musician and when I say that I'm not just talking about his contribution to the Hackett Henry Hudson band. That group really stretched out and the writing was responsible for that because Cary made the guys work. They were not only playing the traditional material, they were into Benny Golson and Thelonious Monk tunes and some of the Willie "The Lion's" stuff too and that was not easy for a band to master!"

Tapes from the Voyager Room broadcasts are in limited circulation, and some of the Bandstand USA transcriptions were used for the Alamac and Shoestring albums released two or more decades ago.

Eleven titles by Bobby Hackett and his Jazz Band with the album title of "Gotham Jazz Scene" were well received (Jack Tracy in *Down Beat* gave it a four-star review), but there was some criticism that it was not fully representative of the band's potential. Tommy Gwaltney again: "Quite a lot of numbers were never released since Capitol wanted the Dixieland tunes released for some reason. I personally felt that some of the best material was not released. The LP was definitely not an indication of our regular programming." Dick Cary's view was:

> We [Hackett and Cary] both were tremendously disappointed when our man at Capitol was unbendingly stubborn about what was to go into the "Gotham" album. His oft-repeated phrase was "You can't fight city hall." So it was "Dixieland" and "ballads"—the only two things which they figured Bobby should be selling. Capitol wouldn't even consider our tamest things ... except one I wrote as a joke and entitled Capitol Punishment. *Of course they changed the title to* Henry Hudson.

In his diary, on April 5, he noted: "Andy Wiswall ... won't do *Handle With Cary* but wants another Dixieland, so I wrote one in five minutes and we played it last set tonight—*Capitol Punishment*." And on April 8: "He likes my new Dixieland thing we'll call *Henry Hudson*—also likes *Darts*."

John Dengler had similar feelings about Capitol's restrictions, though modifying Gwaltney's statement about the number of unissued titles: "Only one of the Capitol tunes was not released. It was *It Don't Mean a Thing*, which was a Cary arrangement. The a&r man, a New Englander of some vintage (Yale man, I think, Andy Wiswall) rushed out of the control booth blurting 'That's bop! I can't take that to the front office!' As a result we were kept completely under wraps and played nothing of the beautiful Cary book for Capitol posterity."

Among the originals issued on record, either on Capitol or from airshots, were the above mentioned *Henry Hudson, Handle With Cary* and *Spinning* (wrongly labelled *Spinney*) by Cary, *Albatross* by Jimmy McPartland with Cary, and *The Reverend's in Town* by Bud Freeman with Cary. (*The Reverend* was named for the Rev. Kershaw, who won The $64,000 Question show by answering questions on jazz.) On January 9, the band rehearsed *Out Tate, Agora, The Indubitable* and a Marian McPartland ballad. *Agora* was named for a club where Cary sometimes played when working at Lake Placid.

Clearly the musicians felt strongly about the way that Capitol controlled the numbers the band could record, but perhaps being so close to the situation they tended to overstate the case. There are four "Dixieland" titles on the album, but otherwise the range does not appear too restricted when compared with, for example, the set at the Newport Jazz Festival or many of the broadcasts.

Cary's diary thoughts were: "I'm not proud of this album—lousy songs, lousy arrangements, lousy rhythm and hardly any good solos. But this may sell a few because of the name of the leader, the ponderous tuba and amateurish blatting."

He must have been feeling liverish to make such unkind comments. The album remains an invaluable reminder of the group's superior music-making. It should be noted that a pianist

Bobby Hackett Sextet, Toronto, July 1957
Gwaltney, vb; Hackett, tp; Cary, a-h; Caceres, cl.

(Photograph by and courtesy of George Hulme)

(Mickey Crane) and a bassist (Al Hall or Milt Hinton) were added to the regular personnel solely for the recording sessions.

But though Cary was frequently critical about ventures in which he was involved, some of his diary entries for this period are more hopeful, ranging from "I'm learning a lot on this little job, writing more sparsely and rhythmically" to (optimistically) "I guess this band could become a big commercial money making thing. If we had a fine singer, any age, someone different who could maybe add an ensemble voice—but not too much. Most people way, way overdo this gimmick. I somehow have a natural distaste for the Jackie Cain's, etc." Neither was he happy about the tuba in the band, on one occasion noting: "Dengler didn't play the last set and what a relief!" On another: "Dengler a problem on tuba—he'll always be a semi-pro."

When he was played *Albatross* by the Hackett band during a Blindfold Test for *Down Beat*, trumpeter Miles Davis commented: "I'll give it five stars ... I liked that. The trombone player knocked me out ... That trombone player gassed me." So high praise for the recording and for Dick Cary (on alto horn, not trombone!) from an unexpected quarter.

At the end of April or early in May, Buzzy Drootin replaced Nat Ray as drummer with the group. Drootin's first broadcast with the band was on May 4.

After seven months, on June 27, 1957, the first engagement

Bobby Hackett sextet, Toronto, July 1957.
Gwaltney, vb; Caceres, cl; Hackett, tp; Cary, p
(Photograph by and courtesy of George Hulme)

in the Voyager Room came to an end. A week off followed, which Cary spent in Middletown, playing with local bands at such clubs as Tiny's, then he was back with the Hackett group for the Newport Jazz Festival on July 5, followed by a one-week booking from July 8 at the Rose Garden in Toronto. Collector and writer George Hulme saw the band there on several occasions and confirms the personnel with Dick Cary and Buzzy Drootin, commenting that "the repertoire was basically as on the broadcasts and the Capitol record. The venue was a licenced 'garden,' complete with trellis work around the bandstand. We were all astonished that the proprietor was taking a flyer on jazz music in such an unlikely location." With the management's failure to advertise their star attractions, George Hulme's lack of confidence was justified and the Rose Garden's jazz policy ended when Hackett left.

> Dick Cary also has memories of this venue!
> *Incidentally, that place in Toronto was somewhat unusual. It was outdoors, called the Rose Garden, and was in back of a hotel which was the largest brothel I've ever seen. Each night I would look up at all those dark, busy rooms and wonder if anyone was enjoying what we were doing. Bobby, who was quite timid about certain things, was very leery of this place, because of the occasional brawls and the type of clientele and, if not sitting at someone's table, would lock himself in the manager's office. What a place!*
>
> *I left Hackett in Toronto. I did not want to go on the road but agreed to do the Toronto job, because I liked Toronto and then I could drive over to Lake Placid, where I spent most of the summer. I worked at the Lake Placid Club four summers, besides spending nine of my army months there in 1945 and it was like a second home.*

Cary's thoughts on leaving the band ranged from: "Goodbye to band (hooray!)" and "Feel good about quitting." These views were more to do with his dislike of touring, for he rejoined Hackett at the Henry Hudson in December 1957.

Before investigating Cary's activities for the rest of the year it should noted that after further bookings in Detroit, Milwaukee and Chicago, the Hackett band, without Cary, returned to the Henry Hudson Hotel on August 30, 1957 and was to remain there for another five months. We should also spend a little time considering other aspects of Cary's stay with the Hackett band between December 1956 and July 1957.

One might think that a long residence in a venue like the Voyager Room was a sinecure, just four hours' work a night for six nights a week, plus rehearsals and recording sessions, but for an in-demand musician like Dick Cary it was not so straightforward. The Hackett band also played some outside gigs while at the hotel including, after work, four tunes on the Arthritis telethon at the Ritz theatre, plus two appearances on the Will Rogers Jr. Show, at 7 am and 8 am. The first was on December 21, 1956, with a rehearsal at 5:30 a.m. "We did *Darts*, which Bobby called *Good Morning Will*, and *Lullaby in Rhythm*. The second was on January 28, 1957, when the band played four numbers. On April 4, Cary noted: "... we did the Tonite Show and rehearsal first. So it was a fairly hectic night back and forth."

One night the band played a set for a Port Authority police party, having a police escort to get them there. On another occasion it had a Sunday engagement, a rare event, at the Villa Rosa in Milford. Cary's diary for April 18 mentions a commercial for a cigarette company: "Transcription at Coastal—did *Saints* for Spud's (daybreak fresh)—Hackett's band—3 singers, Helen Ward, Tom Feustado and Lynn Taylor."

On March 7 and April 3, 1957, Bud Freeman recorded eight titles with an octet for Victor, with Cary on piano, though *The Reverend's in Town* features him on alto horn in a more contemporary sounding sextet. "Quite a change of pace," wrote Cary. One title, *At Sundown*, with no piano solo, was played to trumpeter Donald Byrd as part of his Blindfold Test in *Down Beat* (June 26, 1958). Byrd's comments included the following: "One significant thing that got me was the piano player. He seemed to be younger than the rest of them—at least in thought. Some of his chords seemed modern!"

Cary was also kept busy with recording sessions and providing arrangements for all and sundry. He recalls bandleader Tony Pastor coming into the hotel—"loves *Touché* and ordered two more"; he notes, "wrote a piano piece for Marian [McPartland]; "wrote arrangement of *Little Girl Blue* ...—5 voices—probably be tough"; "Bud Freeman over-wrote a tune in five minutes for next Monday. Arnie [Bud's brother] over-dictated *Don't Be Ridiculous, Nikalous* and we made demo in Brill Building." On June 28 he writes: "Took arrangement *[Prince of Wails]* to Fred Reynolds for Bud's date (which I can't be on—damn)." This refers to Freeman's July 8, 1957 session for Victor.

During April Cary was writing arrangements for and

organising further recording sessions for singer Barbara Lea. These were for Prestige, using such musicians as trumpeter Johnny Windhurst, guitarist Jimmy Raney and harpist Adele Girard. He also took time out, on April 11, to play for Lea's audition for the Arthur Godfrey talent show. We do not learn if she won, though Cary did not think she would.

Shortly before the band left the Henry Hudson, Cary recorded six titles on June 11 for a small record company. Apparently bassist Jack Zimmerman was an a&r man for Golden Crest and he asked Cary to organise a band and make the arrangements for a "Dixieland Goes Progressive" album:

> This was an experimental group, from an album called "Dixieland Goes Progressive" for a little company in Huntington, Long Island, called Golden Crest. We had five or six horns, including tuba, and rhythm. It wasn't recorded very well. They were experimenting. They put a partition between each one of us. Put us in a big semi-circle, we had no rehearsal and we couldn't hear each other. I was sitting next to Urbie Green; he was the only one I could hear.
>
> The point of this was, to take the old Dixieland chestnuts and try to do a modern treatment of them à la the band that Miles Davis had, with the French horn and tuba. So this was an experimental thing.

Cary's personnel was Johnny Glasel, trumpet, Urbie Green, trombone, Cary, alto horn, Bob Wilber, reeds, Hall Overton, piano, Sal Salvador, guitar, Bill Stanley, tuba, Jack Zimmerman, bass, Jerry Segal, drums. Jim Raney was Cary's preferred choice as guitarist and he was annoyed to find Salvador on the date. The six tracks were one side of an LP, with six by trumpeter Johnny Plonsky on the reverse. The recording was made a month before Bob Brookmeyer's "Traditionalism Revisited" and almost a year before Gil Evans' "New Bottle, Old Wine" album.

Gerry Mulligan, commenting on *That's a Plenty* from "Dixieland Goes Progressive," when played this on a blindfold test, said: "That's loaded with humor, isn't it? I'd sort of guess that it might be the band that Bobby Hackett got together ... I wouldn't know how to classify this, but it was a lot of fun." The *Down Beat* reviewer, Dom Cerulli, wrote: "On the whole I found Dick Cary's set more thoroughly modern in conception and execution" and "Cary's chart on *St. James Infirmary* is very contemporary sounding." Cerulli also noted: "Cary's name is misspelled throughout. A relatively small matter, but one which shouldn't happen!"

In June 1957, Cary recorded four sessions for Joe Marsala for the Stere-O-Craft tape label. The first, on the 8th, apparently unissued, was with singer Dick Todd, the second, on the 20th, was under Cary's name, and the third, also on the 20th, was with Bud Freeman and rhythm. The fourth, on the 28th, was made with clarinetist Joe Marsala. Playing cornet on the Marsala date was Rex Stewart, with whom Cary was to forge an association over the next several months.

Excellent examples of Cary's orchestrations can be found on the June 20 recordings under his own name. There are three originals by Cary, plus another version of the Dick Cary-Bud Freeman *The Reverend's in Town*. Cary makes full use of the versatility of his musicians. Playing trumpet, alto trumpet, piano and alto horn himself, he has Bob Wilber on clarinet and bass-clarinet, Al Cohn on tenor and clarinet, and Ernie Caceres on baritone and clarinet. Cary said: "Best thing I've done yet, a lot due to the excellent playing of Cohn, Wilber, Caceres, Casamenti, Buzzy, Al Hall."

The *New York Times* critic, John Wilson, liked this album and said Cary was:

> "middle stream" which I thought was several notches up from the usual "Dixieland." Wilson was in the same fraternity at Wesleyan University. He was a senior when I was a freshman and was a pleasant man who was editor of the Wesleyan magazine "Argus." I've only seen him once since 1935, but his criticisms have been kind. I wasn't aware of any musical background but I guess that's par for a jazz critic.

In September he refers to writing new tunes like *Mars Rock, Moby, Compo Beach* and *Spence de Fence*, while for Hackett he lists *Two Beats or Not to Beat, Humphrey's House* and *Darts*.

Off days at the Henry Hudson were Sundays, when Cary was usually to be found playing dates around New York or even further afield. One such was with trumpeter Johnny Glasel and involved flying to Lake Placid and returning the next morning. Other 1957 bookings included:

January 6:	private costume party with Kaminsky, Wilber, Traeger and "an awful Bob Asher."
January 27:	White Horse Bowling Alley, with Pee Wee and Dengler—playing on stage behind bar.
February 3:	White Horse Bowling Alley, Pee Wee, Dengler, Bob Jenney

February 10:	25th anniversary party in library room of Biltmore, Pee Wee Russell, Andy Russo, Tony Spargo and Charlie Queener.
March 3:	Windhurst, Diehl, Pee Wee & Cary off to a teacher's college in New Paltz, NY. "Neil Timberlin played bass and hired us."
March 10:	"usual frantic afternoon at one of Yale's clubs" with Max Kaminsky, Jo Jones, Phil Olivella, "Big Chief," Chubby Silvers, Irv Lang.
March 17:	"Giuf's Cliff House—band awful—Coz, Hubbel (sic), Charlie Hoyt, Johnny Vine, Giuf and I (tp)."
April 21:	"Drove Wettling, Pee Wee and Cutty to Wes Nor diner."

Occasionally Cary would take a day off during the week, when he was not feeling well or when offered an attractive gig. On these occasions he would arrange for another pianist to substitute for him with Hackett. One such break, on January 11, 1957, was to allow him to travel to Savannah for a concert which featured the Max Kaminsky band (Kaminsky, Ray Diehl, Pee Wee Russell, Cary, George Wettling and a local bassist, Carl Higginbotham) with the Savannah Symphony Orchestra.

The trip to Savannah, GA, resulted in a minor tiff with his daughter, Janet. While in Atlanta he had mailed a card to his other daughter, Judy, with the inevitable complaint from Janet! A long letter was needed to placate her. Janet was training to be a nurse, leading Cary to comment:

There's a strain in my lineage which impels certain members to be ministers, missionaries, nurses, etc. Wonder if my offerings will serve anyone as well? Maybe—but I'll continue anyway.

Janet, with other trainee nurses, visited the Henry Hudson during Dick's stay with Bobby Hackett, as did Virginia. His relationship with Virginia still confused him at times, though gradually it seems to have settled into something more relaxed.

All of Cary's work was done with what many of us would consider to be far below the minimum amount of sleep required. Throughout the year there are references to going to bed in the early hours, 2 a.m., 3:30 a.m., 4 a.m., 5:30 a.m. It is not surprising that Cary enjoyed engagements in places such as Lake Placid, where the location lived up to its name, even if he did continue to stay up into the wee small hours.

Sport continued to be a major interest, whether participating or watching. He played golf regularly with Bud Freeman, Jimmy McPartland and sometimes Bill Crow. His competitive spirit can be seen in a May entry, "I had an 88," while in November "I was only 2 over on first 7 holes!" At other times he was playing tennis and his daily routine was to swim in the 60-foot-long Henry Hudson pool prior to starting work in the evening. In May he attended a pro-celeb golf tournament, following Ben Hogan one day and Sam Snead the next. In July he saw Donald Budge in a tennis doubles exhibition and in November he watched the Cleveland Browns beat the Los Angeles Rams, when Jimmy Brown gained 237 yards in 31 trys and scored 4 touchdowns.

Dick Cary's last date with Bobby Hackett's sextet was on July 12, 1957, and the following day he drove directly from Toronto to Lake Placid. There he worked with a local group at the Lake Placid Club and at Freddie's. He writes of playing for dances in the golf house and the boat house. For example:

Wednesday: Golf house 10–12, Freddie's till 2:30.
Saturday: Kids' dance at 8—regulars at 9—floor show—Freddie's till late. I played the electric keyboard which sounds mostly like a guitar and at times a harp. Really enjoyed it ... others commented most favorably.

From Lake Placid he moved to Moss Rock for two weeks of relaxation, golf and swimming, playing four nights at Freddie's. On July 30 the band gave a joint concert in Agora with a symphony group (Symphonietta). They played two of Cary's arrangements, *Full Moon* and *Reverie*.

From mid-August to mid-October he spent most of his time in the Connecticut area, working a few gigs with drummer Johnny Vine but mostly with the Al Gentile band. Gentile was a musician, but he operated mainly as a promoter and booking agent, and Cary worked for him in New Haven, Bridgeport, Hartford, Savin Rock, Waterbury and Middletown. In addition, on September 22, Cary started a month of Sunday dates at a club called Giuf's, when guests included Buck Clayton, Ed Hubble and Vic Dickenson. Giuf's was probably named for bassist John Giuffrida (Jose Giefriddio).

He was back in New York for the first twelve days of October, playing three nights, 1st to 3rd, at Jazz City, with a group including Jimmy McPartland, cornet, Vic Dickenson, trombone, Bud Freeman, tenor, and Bill Crow, bass, and substituting for trumpeter Pee Wee Erwin at Condon's club on the 4th. Then it was back to Middletown for another ten days, followed by two university dates at the weekend of November 2/3. The first of these, with McPartland and Freeman, was at the University of Virginia, alternating with Pee Wee Hunt, and the second at Yale, with a group which included Rex Stewart, cornet, Al Alston, trumpet, "Big Chief" Moore, trombone, Phil Olivella, clarinet, Irving Lang, bass, Jo Jones, drums.

On November 8 he drove to Knoxville, Tennessee, for a concert, then was back in town for a Time magazine party, playing with Jimmy McPartland, Vic Dickenson, Coleman Hawkins, tenor, Buster Bailey, clarinet, Bill Pemberton, bass, and George Wettling. This was followed by at least four nights in Condon's, substituting on trumpet or piano.

Starting November 17 he was a member of a Jimmy McPartland quintet which did a two week engagement in the Theatrical Lounge in Cleveland. Full personnel was McPartland, cornet, Vic Dickenson, trombone, Cary, piano, Buell Neidlinger, bass, and Gene Smith, drums. Cary views on the band varied throughout the booking:

> Never heard a worse group—felt like we were stealing whatever meagre salary would be paid us.
> Band getting a lot better, started to swing tonight, although McPartland downing the Scotch whiskey.
> Band pretty good at times—Vic Dickenson a bitch.
> Group is disgusting. We get going at times when Vic is playing, but sometimes we provide the most embarrassing sounds.

Back in New York, a few gigs materialised, usually at Condon's. He played piano there on December 6 and trumpet on the 10th. But it was for his work on alto horn that he was mentioned in the *Down Beat* Readers Poll, in December 1957, coming 39th in the Miscellaneous Instrument section! First place went to Don Elliott on mellophone, as it did in 1958, when Cary moved up to 22nd. Elliott had 1362 votes, Cary 21. In the same magazine's Critic's Choice poll he was named by one critic, Robert Sylvester of the *New York Daily News*, as a New Star pianist. In two instances he was still called Dick Carey. Such was the price of fame.

* * * * * * *

Meanwhile Bobby Hackett's sextet had continued at the Henry Hudson. Pinie Caceres, Ernie's brother, had taken Dick Cary's place on piano and in November, Tommy Gwaltney was replaced by clarinetist Bob Wilber, who was surprised to discover that he was expected, like Gwaltney, to play vibes. The difference was that Gwaltney was an expert and Wilber had never touched a vibraphone in his life.

Bob Wilber recalled: "Around New Year's [early December, more likely] Ernie left, to be replaced by Dick Hafer, who played tenor, baritone, clarinet, oboe and eng. horn. Then I believe Cary came back for a while." (John Dengler said, "Ernie quit in a huff.") On another occasion Wilber remembered that "The Caceres brothers roomed together and used to cook their meals in the hotel bedroom. When the neighbors complained of the strong aroma of Mexican food, Ernie was asked to leave. Pinie, in loyalty to his brother, announced he was going to leave too."

Of the Henry Hudson unit, Wilber said: "It was a very unique band, playing a tremendous variety of music, 95% of which was never recorded. The bulk of the writing was by Dick Cary and included things by Ellington, Monk, Willard Robison, and many Cary originals. I wrote some Duke things for the band and in addition to clarinet and vibes, played tenor and bass clarinet. Benny Golson also wrote some charts for the band. We had guest night once a week and feature artists included Hawk, Billy Butterfield, and Dizzy among others. In fact Dizzy was a frequent visitor. After having a swim at the health club in the basement he would come in, have dinner, dance to the band and sit in, sometimes on piano. Dick Hafer and I used to play Bach two-part inventions on tenor and baritone with the rhythm section (such as Warne Marsh and Lee Konitz used to do with the Tristano group).

"I think Bobby really enjoyed the group and regretted having to give it up when the economics made it unfeasible. I look back on those days with very pleasant memories, although truthfully I do not regret having abandoned my short-lived career as a vibraphonist!"

Cary had memories of Dizzy Gillespie coming into the Henry Hudson quite often:

> *I would arrive at the hotel two hours early every night and meet a group of guys down in the pool and practice our diving. One evening Dizzy appeared in the pool and watched our gainers and one-and-a-halfs, etc, and then started throwing himself off the board imitating some of these. He didn't score*

too well but was quite agile. It wasn't until we dressed and went upstairs that I realised he was full of martinis—and had attempted his first gainer.

On November 12 he was on piano with Jimmy McPartland again in a "Jazz at Time" concert promoted by Time-Life at the Time-Life Building. Also present were Vic Dickenson, trombone, Buster Bailey, clarinet, Coleman Hawkins, tenor, Bill Pemberton, bass, and George Wettling, drums.

Pinie Caceres may have left the Hackett band in sympathy with his brother or perhaps was fired because of his drink problem but, whatever the reason, he was replaced on December 13 by Dick Cary, who was no doubt pleased to find that the band, now with Bob Wilber and Dick Hafer, reeds, Dengler, tuba, and Drootin, drums, was as special as ever:

> Musicians and even a college jazz class under Marshall Stearns came into the Voyager Room to hear the wide variety of Bobby's repertoire. We might open with Tizol's Caravan, do one of Bob's special ballads, then Golliwog's Cake Walk by Debussy, then one of my originals, somewhat leaning toward atonality, and close with Cornet Chop Suey on which Bob would attain his one concert E-flat above the staff for the evening, to start his second chorus.
>
> Sometimes there'd be five horns and drums at one time. A big sound and it swung. We even experimented with atonal music, which is the twelve tone scale. With a jazz band that's pretty unusual to do in a hotel room, but we got away with it and people liked it just as much as Jazz Band Ball.
>
> Almost every night the manager of the room would drop in for a nightcap and tell Bob and me how much he liked us, saying we'd be there for five or ten years if he had his way.

Buoyed by this optimism, Cary said:

> I went to the Baldwin Co. and bought a new, small grand—an ambition from the first time I ever had to pound one of those saloon pianos. But the new Coliseum had just been finished, a block away, and since the hotel wanted as much of their convention trade as they could get [they] decided to remodel—so everything was changed and out we went, right after I'd bought that new Baldwin piano. Then to Boston and that was it.

It is significant that Cary's diary for December 18, which notes that pianist Bernie Leighton was a guest, that drummer Morey Feld sat-in and that Dizzy Gillespie played *Perdido*, also says: "Quite a gang in tonight—all musicians, no customers." Other comments on guests included "Ruby Brash [Braff] the guest tonight" and "Vic Dickenson was a wonderful guest." The next day Cary was in the Capitol Studios recording four duets on alto horn with Bobby Hackett. Under Hackett's name, these were very melodic ballads with backing by strings and voices.

Another Carnegie Hall appearance took place on February 1, 1958, when the band did two shows with comedienne Dody Goodman ("Dody in Dixieland") at 8:30 and 12:30.

It was on January 15, 1958, that Cary officially learned that the Hackett band's stay at the Henry Hudson was coming to an end and the band closed there on January 30. The *New Yorker* for February 1, 1958, reported: "Bobby Hackett and his rough-riders, among them Buzzy Drootin, Bob Wilber, Dick Cary and John Dengler, finish up in this colossal drill hall, which is part of the Henry Hudson Hotel, on Thursday, Jan. 30. Next evening Barbara Carroll ... will bring her trio back to the big city."

Down Beat (March 6, 1958) gave no closing date but confirmed that Barbara Carroll had replaced Hackett, saying that "Hackett's group did a week at Boston's Storyville." So, on February 9, the members of the Bobby Hackett sextet went their separate ways. Hackett himself opened at The Embers in New York on April 14, 1958, with just a rhythm section. As Bob Wilber said, "Jonah Jones had made the trumpet plus rhythm format a very saleable package at that time."

> Looking back, Cary said of Hackett:
> *A big influence is Bobby Hackett, but nobody could sound like him anyway. He was an absolute artist, through and through. He was a strange little man. He talked as if he was trying to imitate a gangster. It was funny, coming out of this little guy, who was actually very timid in lots of ways.*
>
> *He played so accurately and concentrated so much. He was a violin player and a guitar player and he couldn't stand making a mistake. You could work with him a whole night and you'd never hear a wrong note.*

And writing, nearly twenty years later, of the Henry Hudson band:

> *This all seems like sort of a wild dream now. No one should ever indulge in such a wild variety and expect to survive in our American way of music. The way things are now, at least here in Los Angeles, we must be sure to include* In the Mood *and other gems to stay in business.*

The Bobby Hackett adventure did inspire Dick Cary's first New York rehearsal band or, as Cary put it:

> *It led to Wilber, Hafer and I starting up a rehearsal group in my loft every Monday night which eventually grew to 3 brass, 4 sax plus Harvey Phillips on tuba, plus drums and bass. I've had rehearsal bands ever since—I really must thank Robert H. for so much.*

Hackett and friends.
l-r, seated: Buzzy Drootin, Hackett, unknown, Louis Armstrong, unknown, standing: Bob McCracken, John Giuffrida, Cary.
(Photograph by Bob Parent. Courtesy: Dick Cary Archive)

> *I had a loft right in the middle of Manhattan. Upstairs from me was one of the greatest composers and teachers I've ever heard of, Hall Overton. We had three floors, forty bucks a month. On the top floor was a young modern artist. There was something going on those three floors all the time. We could play all night long or into the morning, there was nobody living around there.*

Cary lived at 821 Sixth Avenue between 1954 and 1959. Bob Wilber had his own memories of the rehearsals, though he has them starting later than Cary suggested and incorrectly mentions Tuesday nights rather than Mondays: "... Dick started the Tuesday night sessions at his apartment on Sixth Avenue. Hall Overton [1920–1972] lived above Dick and on another floor was an artist who liked to have jam sessions in his pad. Fortunately for Dick the apartment below him was a meeting place for the Deaf and Dumb Society who

Hackett and friends.
l-r, seated: Drootin, Hackett, Armstrong, unknown. standing: McCracken, Giuffrida, unknown, Cary.
(Photograph by Bob Parent. Courtesy: Dick Cary Archive)

never complained about the music since they couldn't hear it! Dick was a very bohemian character—all the furniture in his loft was covered with a thick layer of dust and there was usually dirty dishes in the sink with roaches crawling around. Nevertheless we musicians looked forward to those Tuesday night rehearsals. Dick would produce at least four new charts every week, hand copied in pencil. The writing was beautiful, very contrapuntal and difficult to play. The instrumentation was trumpet (with Dick doubling on trumpet sometimes), trombone, two reeds (saxes with clarinet doubles, sometimes flute), tuba voiced with the horns like Miles' 'Birth of the Cool' and piano (Dick), bass and drums. Harvey Phillips was on tuba. He later became famous for organising the 'tubathon,' 100 or more tuba players playing Christmas carols at Rockefeller Center—an amazing sound! Buzzy Drootin was on drums, Dick Hafer on the other reed. Trumpet and trombone varied depending on who wasn't working that night. We never had a gig with the band—Dick just loved to write and wanted to hear what his latest charts sounded like. When he moved to the coast we thought he'd get into scoring for movies—he certainly had the knowledge but then Dick never pushed himself."

Bobby Hackett sextet: Gwaltney, clt; Hackett, tpt; Cary, a-h; Caceres, bar
Toronto, July 1957   *(Photograph by and courtesy of George Hulme.)*

Apropos the housekeeping, one visitor reported Cary saying that he fed the mice and rats in the loft to discourage them from eating "the real food."

In a February 10, 1957, diary entry Cary mentions: "Party in David Young's loft—a lot of nonsensical, self-conscious, small-pseudo-arty-talk. Brother David—who's much better than this (I guess, but I don't quite grasp his painting—blobs of color). Met Bob Brookmeyer whom I admire very much and couldn't stand Teddy Charles." The only mention of music in the loft is a session by Teddy Charles, vibes, and Hall Overton, piano, one evening in May. No rehearsal band is mentioned during 1957.

Another very promising project which came to nothing was that some of Cary's arrangements for the Hackett band should be recorded for Victor. This was discussed with Fred Reynolds of that company and, with Hackett under contract to Capitol, Billy Butterfield was suggested on trumpet.

Harking back to the beginning of 1957, Jimmy McPartland recorded two sessions for Epic, on February 26 and March 5, with Dick Cary on piano, alto horn and arranging. This was another unconventional Dixieland session which included four McPartland-Cary originals. Writer and cornetist Richard M. Sudhalter made some very complimentary remarks about Cary in the notes to the Mosaic reissue of these titles, commenting "McPartland, like Condon and others, swore by Cary..." and "Shy, even reclusive, Cary often reminded colleagues of Linus, the piano-playing character in the Peanuts comic strip. His piano solos often reflected his admiration for such modernists as Horace Silver and Wynton Kelly." In agreement with Sudhalter yet again was Dom Cerulli, the *Down Beat* reviewer: "The choice of Dick Cary to arrange for the date was a wise one. Cary, too, is a musician steeped in tradition but intelligent enough to assimilate what is going on about him. I've never heard Cary or McPartland do anything that was ever out of good musical taste."

Richard Sudhalter continued, "the tutelary spirit here, as on so many other New York sessions of these years, is the sometimes wayward, forever uncategorizable Dick Cary.

"Among the originals (all published concurrently as part of a 'combo-orks' folio by Edward B. Marks company) is *Third Street Blues*, an attractive 32-bar theme warranting far greater attention than it's received. Had *The Albatross* been written in the 1920s, it might have become a jazz standard."

The McPartland-Cary originals were *Lackadaisy Lazy*, *The*

Albatross, Third Street Blues and *Whistle Stop*. These were among the 14 titles published by the Edward B. Marks Music Corporation in The Jimmy McPartland Dixieland Series for Combo Orks, as arranged by Jimmy McPartland and Dick Cary and recorded by the McPartland Jazz Band on Epic records. Nine months later, Cary again recorded with Jimmy McPartland.

* * * * * * *

The musical "The Music Man," words and music by Meredith Willson, opened on Broadway on December 19, 1957. On that same day Jimmy McPartland began recording an album of the score for Epic, with arrangements by Dick Cary.

A month earlier McPartland and Cary had met Stu Ostrow at the offices of "Frank" [Loesser] Music to hear "The Music Man" score and to be asked to prepare a Dixieland album which would be issued about a month after the cast album. They travelled to Philadelphia on December 5 to see the show and to talk with Meredith Willson.

"My Fair Lady" had an album made by Shelly Manne [drums, with Andre Previn, piano] that broke all the records for a jazz album at the time, so everybody was waiting for the next big musical to hop on and make a jazz album. We assembled about fifteen or sixteen of the top so-called Dixieland musicians around New York, but by the time this came out a couple of others had beaten us to it, so it kind of got lost in the shuffle; didn't go anywhere near as well as we hoped it would. There were some marvellous players on this, like the two tenors were Bud Freeman and Coleman Hawkins. Our tuba player [was] Bill Bell. I never heard a tuba played so thunderously.

[On Marian the Librarian*] Jimmy was supposed to sing and that particular day he wasn't ready, so I played his part, on an alto-trumpet in F. It had a very unusual sound. It sounds perhaps like a big flugelhorn. It looked very much like a trumpet, but I used a big mouthpiece on it. Somebody stole it out of my loft and I could never replace a thing like that.*

Dick Sudhalter wrote: "Cary's scores are full of ensemble textures and colorations," while pianist and arranger John Sheridan said: "Cary was one of the greatest arrangers for that type of music. Just recently I caught up with the Jimmy McPartland Music Man album ... and it is wonderful. Dick's arrangement on *Marian the*

Librarian, well, that is a work of art. Believe me, the writing there is extraordinary, just wonderful."

The Music Man recording session, January 16, 1958
l-r: Jimmy McPartland, tp; Cary, tp; Gene Schroeder; x; x; Milt Hinton;
Bud Freeman, Eddie Condon, Charlie Shavers, Cutty Cutshall; Coleman Hawkins;
Cliff Leeman, d. (Peanuts Hucko, cl; hidden by mike)
(Acknowledgements to Don Hunstein and Columbia Records)

10. Georgia Sketches (1958–1959)

Eddie Condon's club at 47 West 3rd Street closed on December 28, 1957, prior to moving to a new location on 56th Street later the following year. Cary, Wilber, Drootin and Dengler rushed from the Henry Hudson to Condon's for the final hour, but were disappointed to find there was no music, just some drunks talking to Condon. In his diary Cary confided his disappointment about the evening ("ended in a big fizzle!") and about the policy at the club. He thought that Condon's attitude was influenced by talking with Pete Pesci, the club's dubious manager, along with "Farraro the cashier and first sergeant in the local mafia." He felt sympathy for the "customer who pays to hear a group of court jesters assembled to keep Joe Baggiano happy with Pesci's financial report."

He speaks of: "A 12-year-old saloon where some fairly nice jazz artists have almost killed themselves with booze, trying to sound fresh and please the lushes so many hours, while the manager walks round saying stupid things and collecting on so many people's efforts. If the man had anything to offer besides the doling out and mostly the collecting of the monies, OK, I can find a niche, but not these bums.

"I realize I'm lucky not to be killing myself for some people who are killing the guy [Condon] who would be my boss, not my friend, if I did open up the new place on trumpet, as he asked me to. I would love to try the trumpet with him, but I can't do it for his 'FRIENDS.'"

In January 1958 British critic Stanley Dance was in New York recording a number of mainstream jazz sessions for release on English Decca's Felsted label. Dance was anxious to revive the recording careers of men from the swing era who were neglected because of the emphasis on either traditional jazz or be-bop. Cary recorded on piano with Rex Stewart on January 27 and 31 at the Victor Studios, with four originals credited to Stewart and Cary.

Cary's January 29 entry reads: "Eddie Condon's new place opened tonight—under Sutton Hotel, 56th near First Avenue." The following night was the last at the Henry Hudson and on the 31st

Cary did play trumpet at the new Condon's. On their day off, February 2, he appeared at the Clover Leaf in Meriden in a band which included Max Kaminsky, Ed Hubble and Buzzy Drootin.

The Hackett sextet opened in Boston at Storyville on Monday, February 3, working 8:30 to 1:00. The one week engagement ended on the 9th, after an afternoon and evening session, plus a television appearance on WBZ. And that was the end for a wonderfully unique band.

>Back in New York on the 10th the scuffling resumed:
>February 11: recording for Eddie Condon (M-G-M)
>February 12: recording for Eddie Condon (M-G-M)
>February 14: Norwalk High School, with Max Kaminsky, Tyree Glenn, Phil Olivella, Roy Burns, drums
>February 15: Paraglide, Hempstead ("in driving snow"), with Jeff Stoughton, trombone, Charles Harmon, reeds, Jim Simmons, tuba, Buzzy Drootin.
>February 23: Clover Leaf, Meriden, with Wild Bill Davison, Buzzy Drootin
>February 25: recorded Nestle Quik jingle with Mel Davis, trumpet, piccolo, bassoon, tuba, drums. Cary on alto horn.

The Eddie Condon sessions for M-G-M included *The Albatross* and *Third Street Blues*, both by McPartland-Cary, *Ginger Brown* and *Newport News*, by Freeman-Cary, and *Eddie and the Milkman*, by Condon-Cary. This was the regular band at Condon's club, plus guests Dick Cary, Billy Butterfield and Bud Freeman. As part of his Blindfold Test for Miles Davis, Leonard Feather played *Eddie and the Milkman* to the trumpeter, who responded: "It's Don Elliott ... It has a nice beat, but it sounded like Don Elliott imitating somebody, but I know it wasn't him. I like the piece, but you know Don is, always, 'da, da, da, da, da.' I know it isn't him because he doesn't have that much feeling."

Max Kaminsky recalled in his autobiography that in mid-January 1958 he took a band into the Gothic Room of the Duane Hotel. On February 22, Cary sat-in with the group, when the musicians were Herb Fleming, trombone, Joe Barufaldi, clarinet, Charlie Queener, piano, a bassist and a drummer. Two days later Cary became a regular member of the band, with Kaminsky deciding to have Cary on alto horn, rather than employing a trombonist. That first night Cary played with Joe Barufaldi, clarinet, Red Richards, piano, Bobby Donaldson, drums, and Carl Pruitt, bass, but it was a band with a fluctuating personnel.

Work at the Duane continued for eleven weeks, until May 10, during which time, on March 17, Bob Wilber, clarinet, and Joe Benjamin, bass, joined the band for two weeks. A few days later Cary wrote: "Band was pitiful tonight—some terrible drummer named Solomon." But the next night, with Wilber, Jimmy Jones, piano, Benjamin and Donaldson, it was the "best band Max ever had—wonderful night."

Joe Barufaldi returned after Wilber's two weeks, but Benjamin must have stayed on for Cary to be able to note on April 4: "Max has been miserable all week, picking on drummers, telling everyone how to play. Fired Joe Benjamin today." Bobby Donaldson also left at the end of March to work at The Embers. On April 5 Cary thought it was "a terrible band." The next replacements were John Giuffrida on bass and Buzzy Drootin on drums, though a week later reference is made to Charlie Smith being "not the drummer he was."

From this period Art Zimmerman reports a "Bandstand USA" broadcast from the Duane Hotel, New York City, by a Max Kaminsky group which includes Cary on alto horn, Joe Barufaldi, clarinet, Charlie Queener, piano, Johnny Giuffrida, bass, and Charlie Smith, drums.

Gigs which took place during the Duane engagement included:

March 2: Clover Leaf Restaurant, Meriden, Conn.—with Max Kaminsky
March 7: recorded jingle for American Airlines on alto horn
March 9: Wes Nor diner—with Max Kaminsky, Carl Pruitt, Bobby Donaldson, et al.
March 10: Kool jingle date at Coastal with Jerry Jerome. Rhythm section was Billy Bauer, guitar, Clyde Lombardi, bass, Osie Johnson, drums.
March 13: recorded American Beer TV jingle with Bobby Hackett, trumpet, George Berg, Jerome Richardson, reeds, Billy Bauer, guitar, Jack Zimmerman, bass.
March 16: Wes Nor diner—with Hackett, Lombardi, Drootin, et al.
March 20: recorded for Muzak ("wallpaper for stores, dental offices, etc") with Bobby Hackett at Capitol ("that damn Wiswall")
March 23: Clover Leaf, Meriden—with Bobby Hackett.

	"Capacity crowd—Fats Daniel [clarinet] sat in and sounded good."
April 1:	jingle date for Jerry Jerome, with Julie Baker, "one of world's greatest flautists."
April 6:	Clover Leaf, Meriden—with Max Kaminsky and Joe Barufaldi.
April 19:	Princeton, freshman prom—with Max Kaminsky, Eddie Barefield, Charlie Queener, John Giuffrida and Charlie Smith.
April 20:	Clover Leaf, Meriden—with Peanuts Hucko.
April 21:	Condon's, subbing for Rex Stewart. "Cutty Cutshall said he enjoyed the rest, as compared to Rex who drives!"
April 26:	wrote a song, *Whatever Happened to the Big Bands?*, with Johnny DeVries.
April 28:	recorded jingles for Schick Razor. Personnel included Bill Costa and Chuck Wayne, guitar.

After the Clover Leaf date on March 23, "Arriving at loft Dave Young invited me upstairs where Bob Brookmeyer, Jimmy Giuffre, Hall Overton and Dick Lord were playing—fine evening." On April 8 Cary notes: "Hall Overton rehearsed *Histoire de Soldat*. I couldn't do fiddle part, but they got a guy." Others present included Johnny Glasel, trumpet, Aaron Sachs, clarinet and Billy Ver Planck, trombone.

During March he was active in helping singer Lee Wiley prepare for a booking she had in Chicago: "She has two weeks at Mr. Kelly's for $1500 per. She ought to get a lot more. Hope she does well. A hell of a woman." They sorted music on the 11th and rehearsed on the 18th and 22nd. He was also, from April onwards, writing and planning with Rex Stewart for a festival to be held in late July and early August and for their joint publishing venture, Cornucopia. In addition he was scoring for various recording sessions.

Early in May Cary signed with Joe Glaser to tour India as part of Jack Teagarden's band, with Max Kaminsky, but when this four month tour covering India to Japan began at the end of September, it was Don Ewell who was the pianist.

And so it continued. May 20—trip to UPI, 560 miles each way, with Jimmy McPartland, Bob Wilber, Eddie Orlino, trombone, and others. May 22—a recording session with Eddie Condon for Pacific, followed by two hours discussing jingles for Schick razors with Jerry Jerome. The next day he played solo piano for an hour (7:30 to 8:30) for the "Present Day Club" at Princeton, then (presumably) alto horn with Max Kaminsky, Bob Wilber, Charlie Queener, piano, Al Hall, bass, and Bobby Donaldson, drums. On the 24th he received "a ticket for speeding on way to tennis"; this was his second in two months.

The Schick jingles were recorded on May 26, with a personnel which included Billy Butterfield, Joe Wilder, Mel Davis, trumpets, Bill Ranch, trombone, Allan Hanlon, guitar, Clyde Lombardi, bass, Phil Kraus, drums, plus a string quartet, flute and oboe. The following day it was gig at Harold's, South Orange, New Jersey, 9:00 to 1:00 a.m.—"band rotten but nice evening."

On May 29 he appeared on the Art Ford Jazz Party on WNTA television, playing with Jimmy McPartland, Bud Freeman, Bob Wilber and others. Billie Holiday was also on the bill. The next morning he drove through terrible traffic to Atlantic City, where he worked in a Bobby Hackett quartet completed by Bob Wilber and John Giuffrida. They played on the Steel Pier, matinees and evenings, for three days, May 30 to June 1.

The following week Gene Schroeder, Eddie Condon's regular pianist, was working with the Bob Scobey band, and Cary subbed for him at the club from June 3 to 7. On June 6 he was involved with Bill Bauer, guitar, and John Drew, bass, in recording a "round" jingle for Manischewitz Wine. This had been demonstrated to an agency by "Jerry Jerome, Darlene and her three guys" and presumably Dick Cary, three days earlier.

Cary attended two more Eddie Condon recording sessions at the Capitol studios, this time for Dot Records, on June 10 and 11, and he recorded a jingle for Carling Ale on the 11th. The Dot LP consisted of a series of medleys, a total of 23 songs, with the format proving rather better than one might guess. Cary made one comment about the record:

> As an example of the genius of these record people: Condon did an album for Bob Thiele (Dot, I think). Bob called me in one afternoon to identify the titles and I discovered they'd cut 20 bars!! out of a Butterfield chorus on Be Some Changes Made—and they just stared at each other. No one took the blame and the fact was, they were not even aware of it.

He did not say if the 20 bars were reinstated, but there is no obvious flaw in the issued version of *There'll Be Some Changes Made*.

June 13 found him driving Max Kaminsky and Bob Wilber

to Princeton where they played two nights "for class of '43" and "played on truck for parade." Next, June 15, he flew to Atlanta, and then on to Panama City, Florida, for three weeks work with a band which included Johnny Windhurst, trumpet, Ed Hubble, trombone, Red Balaban, bass, and Eddie Phyfe, drums. The last day at this unknown club, where business was poor, was July 5.

More single jobs followed, but Cary was no longer consistently making daily entries into his diary. For example, the pages covering June 17 and July 3, and July 17 to 22, are blank. This may have been because he was not working between those dates.

July 8:	working on jingles with Jerry Jerome
July 9:	Roadside Rest—with Jimmy McPartland, Pee Wee Russell, Eddie Condon, et al.
July 12:	Waterbury—with Johnny Vine, et al.
July 13:	Ivoryton Inn—with same group
July 14:	job in Southampton—with Max Kaminsky, Bob Wilber, Charlie Queener
July 16:	Roadside Rest—band included Miff Mole, trombone, Al Hall, bass
July 23:	Roadside Rest—band included Bud Freeman, tenor, Johnny Rae, vibes

Three months before the second annual (1958) Great South Bay Festival on Long Island, New York, was due to take place, cornetist Rex Stewart had been asked to organise a tribute to the pioneer pianist, arranger and leader, Fletcher Henderson (1897–1952). This followed on from the success which the Henderson Alumni, also led by Stewart, had achieved the previous year. Stewart decided to write an extended work to honour Henderson and he approached Dick Cary to help him with the orchestration. The work is called *Georgia Sketches* and is in three movements: *Motion*, *Tempo Espagnole*, and *The Earth Is Good*. "The title," explained Stewart, "comes from the fact that Fletcher came from Cuthbert, Georgia. We—Dick and I, for one of the themes is his—tried to portray some of the most striking aspects of Georgia."

The Festival was held over two weekends, July 26 and 27, and August 1, 2 and 3. For a July 26 set Stewart led the South Bay Seven, which included Cary on trumpet, Benny Morton, trombone, and Garvin Bushell, clarinet, playing mainly Dixieland standards, and backing Big Joe Turner singing some of his blues hits. That opening night Cary was cross with Rex Stewart for not calling him for a solo and thought that "our 8-piece group was terrible."

On the 27th, Sunday, Cary worked the afternoon (1:15 to 7:15) at the Metropole with Max Kaminsky and a "very good drummer," before returning to the Festival. The following day he played a Lester Lanin gig at Southampton with Rex Stewart, "Big Chief" Moore and Eddie Barefield, then, on the 30th, he was again at the Roadside Rest.

The following weekend, on August 1, Cary played alto horn in the Henderson Alumni. In addition to *Georgia Sketches* the orchestra played a collection of their old leader's best known numbers. The concert was recorded and most of the set was issued on a United Artists album.

> Rex and I laboured over a three-part thing that took the whole side of an album. Originally that was a suite having five parts but on the record only three have been released and those have been shortened. The whole thing was negative for us, as they put us on as the last band in the programme, late at night. The band was over-tired and full of whisky.
>
> For the rehearsals we rented two rooms. In one Rex rehearsed the brass; in the other I did the reeds. We had planned to begin the rehearsal in the afternoon, between 2 and 5, but Garvin Bushell came only at 3, and a little later two other saxophonists turned up. But it made no sense to start before Ben Webster came. He waddled in at 4:15 p.m., put his horn on the table, hat and coat next to it, explained that he had to make an urgent phone call ... and he was gone again. The whole rehearsal went on like that, with never all the musicians there together. Ben Webster showed absolutely no interest, so finally Rex replaced him with Buddy Tate.

Organiser Francis Thorne told researcher Walter C. Allen that United Artists kept the early groups on far too long. "The Henderson reunion didn't come on until 12:30 a.m. (having been there since 8:30 p.m.) and many members were drunk by then. There were goofs and fluffs galore and many of the musicians were sore at waiting so long to go on. It just didn't jell, but U.A. did release the 'best' of it which I think should never have come out.

"Our festival was run on a shoe-string and the audiences were never large enough to recoup expenses and so we folded in 1958. However, the 1957 reunion was worth it."

Cary too complained ("very sloppy") of the other bands

over-running, but was moved to comment that "*Georgia Sketches* did not go as bad as I had expected!" Also on August 1, Dick Cary and Buddy Tate soloed on *Youth Speaks* played by the South Huntington Long Island Junior High School band.

On August 2 he was at the Cabana Club in New Jersey, working with Jerry Shard, returning to the Festival the next day to hear the bands of Charlie Mingus ("good") and Duke Ellington ("fine"). And so it continued....

August 9: Westport—with Max Kaminsky, Bob Wilber, Charlie Queener, Al Hall, Johnny Vine
August 12: jingle date with Jerry Jerome
August 13: recording session (?) with Dave Terry and singer Lou Ann Simms
August 15: recording session (?) for Bob Weil, with Bob Wilber, Barbara Lea, et al. outdoor job in carpark of Abraham Strauss, Babylon—with Rex Stewart and Bob Wilber
August 16: French Lick festival, Louisville—with Eddie Condon: Cary, trumpet, Lou McGarity, Pee Wee Russell, Teddy Napoleon, piano, Gene Krupa, drums

Cary travelled with Max Kaminsky and George Wettling to the Randall's Island Jazz Festival on August 22, playing that day on piano with Kaminsky, trumpet, Lou McGarity, trombone, Pee Wee Russell, clarinet, Jack Lesberg, bass, and Wettling, drums. The following day he was on stage with Jimmy McPartland and Bud Freeman.

Things were quiet after the festival, though he did spend the weekend of August 30/September 1 at Eddie Condon's "retreat" at Monmouth Beach. He found when he returned to the loft on the 2nd that he had been burgled and his alto horn taken.

The one-off engagements in September included:
September 2: Southampton—with Rex Stewart, "Big Chief" Moore, Jo Jones, et al.
September 4: jingles session with Jerry Jerome
September 5: Ralph Burns date—with Ray Charles Singers, Clark Terry, trumpet, and big band
September 12: recording jingle for Playtex Girdles
September 13: at Eddie Condon's—subbed on alto horn for Cutty Cutshall, who was sick
September 15: rehearsal with Sonny Dunham small band

September 17: recorded six versions of Sterling Beer jingle.

Harold's House of Dixieland in New Jersey had booked the Sonny Dunham band, which included, in addition to Cary, Dunham, trumpet, Bob Wilber, reeds, Bobby Donaldson, drums, Buddy Blacklock, piano, and Bill Stanley, bass and perhaps tuba. Of the opening night, on September 16, Cary said, "Very hard night and I got mad—ready to quit but some vodka fixed everything." As the evenings passed his mood improved. For example, "had pleasant night, though the rhythm was pretty bad!" One evening he "rode out with that awful Harvey Leon," whose drumming gave him a headache.

Sonny Dunham finished on September 28, but Cary continued to work at Harold's House of Dixieland, possibly with a similar personnel. Bud Freeman joined the band on September 30 and Cary found it took less than a week for him "to become a pain in the ass." On October 4 guitarist Bill Bauer "replaced our piano and we had best night yet—good crowd and band swung." But the entry for the next night, Sunday, October 5, is: "Last night at Harold's by mutual consent."

Intervening jobs included:

September 21: at Canton Chow Shop—with Eddie Condon band, Cary, trumpet, Elmer?, trombone, Herb Hall, clarinet, Gene Schroeder, piano, Leonard Gaskin, bass, George Wettling, drums.
September 24: recording beer jingle—with Don Arnone, Eddie Costa, Mousey Alexander, et al.
September 26: recording Good Luck Margarine jingle—with Phil Kraus, vibes, Bill Bauer, guitar, Arnold Fishkin, bass, Osie Johnson, drums.
September 29: recording Texize jingle.
October 6–7: flew to South Bend for Festival—with Eddie Condon band: Johnny Windhurst, Ed Hubble, Bob Wilber, Jack Lesberg, Buzzy Drootin.

During October, Cary and Rex Stewart consulted a lawyer "about our 'Cornucopia' publishing house. About eight numbers to be presented to ASCAP for a licence ... copied some of the originals for Hackett, hoping to get group together when Bob Wilber returns from Benny Goodman trip in five weeks." Later he mentions having twenty originals ready when Wilber gets back. Jay Feingold, Goodman's manager, had telephoned to ask Cary join the band—"I asked for $300, which I knew I wouldn't get, so I wouldn't go."

Cary, and presumably Stewart, was elected to membership of ASCAP (American Society of Composers, Authors and Publishers) on December 18, 1958. ASCAP confirmed that "Mr. Cary was at one time a member..." but could/would provide no other details. Cary said:

> *I figure I had over 120 original pieces recorded in the 50s. I was a member of ASCAP, but I never got any royalties on any of them.*

There is one ASCAP royalty statement in the Cary papers. This is for the year 1995, when he received a cheque for $4.62 for the tune *Wampum*, which he had co-written with Barney Bigard in 1973. *Wampum* had been played by someone in Britain.

He rehearsed with The Commanders, led by trumpeter Jimmy Sedlar, on October 16. On the 18th, after an afternoon with Jerry Shard at St. Elizabeth's College in Convent, New Jersey, he returned to New York and the Columbia studios for a 9:00 p.m. to 1:00 session with The Commanders, in which "were old friends Bill Stanley, bass, Charles Harmon, reeds, Ephie Resnick and Frank Rehak, trombones, and Moots. Worked pretty hard on piano, so many medleys, etc." (The Commanders was originally a Decca studio band organised by Tutti Camarata. Later it was a touring band, first with drummer Eddie Grady as leader, then with trombonist Warren Covington. It is not known if this orchestra is connected to the Columbia session, no trace of which has been found so far.)

The following day, for variety, he was at the Legion Post in Williston, "playing trumpet better than I ever did, I think," with a band of youngsters led by clarinetist Jack Sohmer. He worked the evening, 8:00 to 11:00, on October 24 for Jerry Shard at Marymount College, in a band which included Jack Honeywell, trumpet, Hank D'Amico, clarinet, Doc Solomon, and Sam Ulano, drums.

His next gig was on October 28 at Wes Nor in Westport—"most congenial group and got off ground at times"—Lou McGarity, trombone, Jack Lesberg, bass, Don Marino, drums. This was followed on November 1 by a small big-band (3 brass, 4 sax, 3 rhythm) date at City Centre. Ken Hawk on drums and "Brendan Ward works all night—sax with us, piano with Irish trio, doing the "stack-o-barley." On November 7 he worked at the Cup of Jazz with Bill Bauer, guitar, and bassist Peter Ind, "a bearded Englishman."

"No liquor, kids drink coffee and soda." Possibly he played the same location on the 10th, again with Bill Bauer, plus a tenor saxist, Jack Lesberg, bass, and Buzzy Drootin, drums. "I didn't play much, just tried to drown the pain in my leg."

Cary had been suffering from a terrible pain in his right leg for several days, for which his doctor recommended codeine and rest, advice which he finally took, though it was not until the end of the month that his leg improved, whereupon his back began to hurt. It took a visit to a chiropractor to solve the problem—"He straightened me up. Now I can walk straight up." But these pains did not stop him from working during the last two weeks of November.

With stereo the new thing in sound reproduction, the record companies were promoting it as hard as they could. On November 17 and 21 and December 1, Cary was at the Victor studios recording "Sounds of Brass"—"loud band for RCA stereo" with five trumpets and five trombones, plus a French horn and Cary on alto horn.

There was a Lester Lanin job at Yale on November 16, and another at Princeton on November 21, when Rex Stewart, trumpet, Phil Olivella, clarinet, Irving Lang, bass, and J.C. Heard, drums, were the band—"Piano in basement of club had 22 notes missing, so I used peck horn quite a bit." The following day he played trumpet at the Meadowbrook, 9:00 to 1:00, probably for Jerry Shard, and on Sunday, the 30th, he was at Buckley's, 4:00 to 8:00, in a group which included Doc Cheatham, trumpet, Eddie Barefield, reeds, and Benny Long, trombone.

The first rehearsal which Cary organised in his loft took place on Monday, November 24, 1958, and it included Bob Wilber and Dick Hafer, reeds, Sam Parkins, bass sax, Doug Mettome, trumpet, Bill Crow, bass, Harvey Phillips, tuba, and Buzzy Drootin, drums. Most Mondays thereafter, except when Cary was otherwise employed, there was a rehearsal, with the personnel varying around Cary, Wilber and Hafer. They continued through December and then spasmodically in 1959—two in January and February, four in April and one in May and June. Thus was established a rehearsal tradition which was to continue throughout Cary's life.

Also in November 1958, trombonist Al Godlis talked of a brass quintet album and Cary started to write material for this. Rehearsals, with trumpeter Johnny Glasel in the group, began on December 8, after the second of Cary's Monday night rehearsals. For a time that was the routine, for the brass quintet to play after the band rehearsal.

There are two mentions of jam sessions in the loft at the end of the year. On December 1, he reports Bob Brookmeyer, Zoot Sims, Jim Raney and "Tackus" (Bill Tackus, bass?) playing in Dave Young's apartment, while on the 15th, "session in Hall's went to 7 a.m.—Zoot Sims a hell of a blower." They were back in Young's loft on the 22nd, with Bob Brookmeyer, Dave McKenna, piano, Bill Crow, bass, Dick Scott, drums, Gerry Mulligan, baritone, and—"Zoot! who's just marvelous—a natural."

Jazz gigs in December were interwoven with meetings with Jerry Jerome to write jingles and then to record them.

December 2: jingles session with Pee Wee Erwin, trumpet, Cutty Cutshall, trombone, Bill Crow, bass, Mousey Alexander, drums, for Kentucky Fried Chicken and WOR.

December 3: jingles session for Schick razors, with Allan Hanlon, guitar, Al Lucas, bass, and Jim Brown Quartet.

December 7: at Hastings—with Ruby Braff, cornet, Vic Dickenson, trombone, Pee Wee Russell, clarinet, Whitey Mitchell, bass, Buzzy Drootin, drums.

December 9: jingles session with singer Darlene and three flutes. At Eddie Condon's—subbing on trumpet for Rex Stewart.

December 13: Lester Lanin job at Dickenson College, Carlisle, PA—Wild Bill Davison, "Big Chief" Moore, trombone, Phil Olivella, clarinet, Irving Lang, bass, leader, J.C. Heard, drums, Harry Shepherd, vibes.

December 14: at Buckley's—with Johnny Letman, trumpet, Vic Dickenson, trombone, Eddie Barefield, reeds, Jack Vogt, drums.

December 16: jingles session for Schick ("about nine versions")—with "bad quartet." Wes Nor, Westport, with Charlie Shavers, trumpet, Harry DeVito, trombone, Rex Stewart and Buzzy Drootin.

December 20: at The Vat—"awful band" with Garvin Bushell, reeds, Herb Nichols, piano, and Eddie, a drummer.

December 21: at Buckley's—with Doc Cheatham, trumpet, Sonny Russo, trombone, Eddie Barefield, reeds, Jack Vogt, drums.

December 22: Dave Allen date at Victor studios for Warner Bros.—Nick Travis, Cary, trumpets, Norman Paris, string quartet et al.
December 24: at The Embers—with Bobby Hackett, Buzzy Drootin, Bob Carter, bass—"pretty good group."
December 26: Bob Wilber recording session at Bell Sound.
December 28: Buckley's—with Johnny Letman, Benny Long, Eddie Barefield, Jack Vogt.
December 31: Brooklyn at 11:00 p.m.—with Johnny Letman, Sonny Russo, Eddie Barefield.

On January 1, 1959, Dick Cary again subbed on piano for a sick Dave McKenna at The Embers with Bobby Hackett. Carter was on bass and Cary calls the drummer "Skinny." When the club closed just before 2 a.m. Cary returned to the loft for another Dave Young party, where reedmen Sam Parkins and Pepper Adams were playing. Cornetist Ruby Braff was there and Cary's entry is: "Ruby talks and talks and explains jazz continually. A very ambitious, probing mind—wants to learn writing. Has a drive which at times is not tempered."

He played alto horn at Buckley's on Sunday, the 4th, 4:30 to 8:30 p.m. with Doc Cheatham, Eddie Barefield and a drummer named as Magyar, and the same trio were at Brooklyn on the 11th. The previous day, also at Brooklyn, Cary had played trumpet with Barefield, Marty Napoleon on piano, and Jack Vogt, drums. It is suspected that when Cary writes "Brooklyn" he refers to Buckley's in Brooklyn, but this is not clear. Also, Cary mentions Frank Carey, who appears to have had a promoting role at many of the Buckley's/Brooklyn sessions. It is not known what instrument this "inept" musician plays, but probably it was double bass.

There was an afternoon recording session on January 15 for a "Parade of Pops" album, with Cary playing alto horn in a 20-piece orchestra, directed by Ray Martin. Two further sessions took place on the 20th and 21st. The Friday and Saturday between the sessions was spent in Washington, D.C., where he stayed with guitarist Charlie Byrd and visited Willis Conover and Squirrel Ashcraft. Though not mentioned, this would have been when he was asked to organise a band for a Washington jazz concert. Later he was advised there was a budget of $2700 and Willis Conover reported that the concert would be recorded by Mercury and there might be a European tour! (In due course Jack Tracy, the Mercury a&r man, decided that the standard of the recorded material did not justify an album release.)

Returning to New York he was able to play at Buckley's again on Sunday, January 18, with Doc Cheatham, Eddie Barefield, "not much of a trombone" Candy Ross, Carey and Magyar. Other Buckley's "meetings" were:

January 25: with Doc Cheatham, Benny Long, Eddie Barefield, Carey, Magyar

February 1: with Herman Autrey, trumpet, Sonny Russo, trombone, Joe Barufaldi, clarinet, Roy Burns, drums, Frank Carey

February 8: last afternoon—with Doc Cheatham, Eddie Bert, trombone, Joe Barufaldi, Carey and Magyar.

Cary visited the Celebrity Club on January 23 and was very impressed: "What a wonderful place—downstairs—large—everyone swinging—good show—band rough but very effective for this atmosphere. I'd love to play here."

During this period he was writing with and for Pee Wee Russell, organist Ethel Smith, Eddie Condon and his own rehearsal group, in addition to giving Saturday trumpet lessons to a Dave Levin. He even helped out "Aaron Sachs with arrangement for Machito" (the Cuban band).

On February 3 Cary started three weeks at the Eddie Condon club, sitting-in for pianist Gene Schroeder. He commented: "Band pretty rough. Cutty fine, Herb Hall unobtrusive, Rex [Stewart] unbelievably erratic, no tone or intonation, but at least inventive, Mousey [Alexander] not his cup of tea, RC [Dick Cary] very erratic with a piano that's ready for the city dump." This stint at Condon's ended February 23. Cary was the pianist on two recording sessions for Warner Bros. Records on February 26/27, which attempted to recreate some of Condon's early songs.

Cary worked at the Yorkville Casino on February 6, with Max Kaminsky and Jimmy McPartland, Vic Dickenson, Joe Barufaldi, Barry Galbraith, guitar, Al Hall, bass, and Cliff Leeman, drums. With no work at Buckley's, Frank Carey soon found other locations. On the 8th he is mentioned by Cary at the Sparrow's Nest, with Dick Vance on trumpet, Eddie Bert, Barufaldi, and Magyar, followed on subsequent Sundays by sessions at Max the Mayor's:

February 22: Herman Autrey, trumpet, Rick Nelson, trombone, Eddie Barefield, reeds, Frank Carey, Magyar.

February 28:   jingle session, including Mel Davis, trumpet, Frank Rehak, trombone.
March 1:   Buck Clayton, trumpet, Barefield, Carey, Tony ----, drums.

"The Thelonious Monk Orchestra at Town Hall" was an album recorded live by Riverside Records on February 28, 1959. This ten-piece group played a programme of Monk originals as arranged by Hall Overton. The week before the concert, on the 19th, Cary rehearsed "about an hour with Overton and the Monk band ... a piece called *Friday the 13th*, a big bunch of absolutely nothing."

It is not clear if it was by arrangement or by chance, but one day in January, Cary got into a bar-room conversation with John Hammond, with the forthcoming "Jazz Jubilee" charity concert ("A History of Jazz from Congo Square to Carnegie Hall") at the Sheraton Park Hotel in Washington, D.C., on behalf of the charity Friendship House, as one topic. Cary noted: "What an opinionated man. Thinks Hall Overton a bad composer because Hall disagreed with a thought of his once at Newport, a panel thing. He did make some good suggestions—Vic Dickenson, Buddy Tate, Buck Clayton, Jo Jones and Ray Bryant. He doesn't like anybody like Max Kaminsky, Lou McGarity, etc." But all these musicians were recruited by Cary for the Washington concert.

Perhaps because of Buddy Tate being hired, or because of Cary's visit to the Celebrity Club, Cary was booked to play with Tate's band at the Rockland Ballroom in Harlem, 11:00 p.m. to 2:00—"enjoyed it—guess I was the only ofay in joint."

There were rehearsals for Washington on March 9 and 14, the latter mainly for the benefit of singer Ernestine Anderson. Of the former, Cary said: "*Stompy Jones* sounded fine, then the Brass 5 played awhile. Bob Wilber got a loud ovation after doing my *In an Ellingtone*—first time that's happened." Then it was off to Washington the 15th, where Cary stayed with Squirrel Ashcraft, lawyer, pianist, jazz enthusiast, with a final rehearsal on the 16th in the Sheraton Park Hotel. "Jack Crystal helped me rounding up the cast. I got almost panicky. Haven't got this scared in years. 1500 people at 150 tables made a hell of a racket. Concert went on too long. Outside of my gang were Toshiko [trio], Ernestine Anderson, and the Newport Youth Band with Marshall Brown, who seems to antagonize a lot of the older musicians. We could have had a much better concert without Newport and Japan. Toshiko lost us almost half the house."

The members of "my gang" were "all star" by any reckoning. Cary lists: Max Kaminsky, Buck Clayton, Johnny Glasel, trumpets, Vic Dickenson, Frank Rehak, Lou McGarity, trombones, Pee Wee Russell, clarinet, Bob Wilber, Bud Freeman, Buddy Tate, Phil Woods, reeds, Ray Bryant or Willie "The Lion" Smith, piano, Billy Taylor Jr. or Keeter Betts, bass, Jo Jones, Cliff Leeman, Bertil Knox or Paul Barbarin, drums, Dick Cary, musical director. (Willie Smith and Paul Barbarin were actually advertised as guests. Charlie Byrd, guitar, and Harvey Phillips, tuba, were also listed in the press release.)

Cary also played with Buddy Tate on March 22, when the usual Tate band, plus Dickie Wells, trombone, Rudy Rutherford, reeds, and a second trumpet, played a Sunday gig 9.00 p.m. to 1:00, at the Manhattan Center. The previous day he had been at the Shorehaven Country Club with Charlie Shavers, Lou McGarity, Hank D'Amico, Jack Lesberg and Cliff Leeman.

1959 was a busy recording year, with February the most hectic month, containing seven sessions, followed by two in March:

February 16/17:   Bud Freeman dates for Dot Records.
February 23/24/25: Pee Wee Russell dates for Dot.
February 26/27:   Eddie Condon dates for Warner Bros.

Concerning the second Freeman session, Cary wrote: "Mary Mulligan pretty bad singer." [She] went completely to pieces and they sent her home. But [I] got the chance to do six tunes on trumpet with Bud, Jimmy [Jones] and Leonard [Gaskin]," Of Pee Wee Russell's "original tunes" album, he thought the second date "pretty bad," that the third date went "pretty well" and that overall it was a "pretty good album!"

Cary played piano on the Pee Wee Russell album and arranged the twelve titles, which were all original compositions by the clarinetist. Russell told sleeve-note writer George Simon, "I don't write very quickly. But Dick Cary—he always seems to be around when somebody wants him—he arranged the numbers as fast as I wrote them, and there you are." On a later reissue Cary was co-credited along with Russell for four of the titles, but in preparing the lead sheets for Bregman publishers, Cary wrote: "I'm on nine of the twelve tunes." Russell is quoted by his biographer, Bob Hilbert, as saying that writing the tunes did not present a problem, but getting them ready for a recording session was another matter.

About five years earlier Cary had provided the arrangements for a six-title session when Pee Wee Russell recorded for George Wein's Storyville label.

Cary's writing during 1959 was mainly for recording and jingles sessions or for the rehearsal groups. He also arranged for his "All Stars" at the Washington concert, for one of the Pat Boone television shows and for pianist/bandleader Nat Pierce. He mentions attending a Pierce rehearsal with four arrangements, but does not say if they were used.

Two March sessions were both by a quintet under Lou McGarity's name, held on the 19th and 20th, and giving Cary the opportunity, as he said, "to double on piano and harmon mute." These titles for Jubilee are further exemplary examples of Cary's skill on the two instruments, as well as McGarity's forthright trombone playing. Or as Cary put it: "Lou plays so well, so virile."

At the end of March Cary was employed to do some writing for the Pat Boone Show. On the 27th he met Mort Lindsey, arranger and conductor for Boone, Art Malvin, the vocal arranger, and Joe Delaney, manager of the Dukes of Dixieland—"a very capable manager, especially to get these little no-talent kids such fabulous coverage." He worked on the scores the next two days and attended a Dukes rehearsal on the 31st, meeting the musicians and Gene Bolen. On April 1 Pat Boone rehearsed and Cary noted "two real pros there—Boomie Richman and Phil Bodner," both saxophonists. After the television rehearsal and show, Cary realised that two of his arrangements had been cut. Then it was off to Baltimore with Jimmy McPartland, cornet, Ray Diehl, trombone, Joe Barufaldi, clarinet, Chubby Jackson, bass, and George Wettling, drums, for two or three days at an unspecified club.

He was back in New York on April 4, in time to play an evening gig with Ernie Caceres, and the next day he was with McPartland, Diehl, and Barufaldi again, this time at the Manadalay Club in Wantagh. "Rhythm sounded marvelous at times and we carried McPartland." The rhythm he referred to was John Drew, bass, and Mousey Alexander, drums.

Cary had an unusual job at the Monaco on April 18, 1959, 8:30 p.m. to 3.00, with "no break, one girl after another. Some sang very badly and didn't take clothes off. One tall blonde sat down in nude and played *Estrellita* on the fiddle in G-flat. Arms got slightly weary."

The following day he visited Virginia, probably for the last time. As he lamented, "What happened to Nikki? That nice gal with long soft brown hair and warm affection?"

There was a Sunday afternoon job at the El Dorado in New Haven on the 26th, playing alongside Don Goldie, trumpet, Miff Sines, trombone, Tony Parenti, clarinet, Freddie Moore, drums, and a local bassist. On the 29th he played trumpet ("my lip nil") in an Eddie Condon concert at the Villanova in Philadelphia, with Lou McGarity, Dick Wellstood, Jack Lesberg, and Cliff Leeman, and a "Sam," who presumably played clarinet. Another first was on May 1 when he had his "first time working in control booth with [Milt] Gabler, doing some double-tracking with Ethel Smith the organist." (Cary was to write arrangements for at least two of Ethel Smith's albums.) That evening and the following afternoon he played somewhere called R.P.I. with the unknown Sam, Ros Rudd, trombone, Al McManus, drums and Jim Andrews, piano.

Work during May and June can be summarised as:

May 8:	Princeton—with Max Kaminsky, Eff (sic) Resnick, Sam ?, Al Hall, Bobby Donaldson
May 9:	Ithaca College—with Jimmy McPartland, Leon & "gal singer."
May 18:	started week on trumpet at Eddie Condon's (subbing for Rex Stewart)
May 30:	Elm Tree Inn?, Amagansett—with Jack Fine, cornet, Ros Rudd, trombone
June 5:	Wes Nor—with Kaminsky, Vic Dickenson, Pee Wee Russell, Morey Feld
June 6:	Eddie Condon's—subbed on piano for Gene Schroeder
June 12:	Princeton—Kaminsky, Phil Olivella, Al Williams, piano, Al Hall, Jo Jones
June 13:	still at Princeton?—with Andy Fitzgerald, clarinet
June 19:	Wes Nor—with Kaminsky, Dickenson, Pee Wee Russell, George Wettling
June 25/26:	recording sessions with Ed Hall
June 26:	Wes Nor—with Kaminsky, Dickie Wells, trombone, Bob Wilber, Wettling
June 27:	Central Plaza—9:00 to 12:30 a.m.
July 2/3:	recording sessions with drummer Billy Gussak scheduled

Of the admirable recording by clarinetist Ed Hall, with Cary's piano playing some of his finest, he said, "Good date—Ed worked hard," and:

> *Edmond worked at Eddie Condon's Club for quite a few years and he's one of the nicest gentlemen I ever knew. On it is one of my favourite guitar players, Jimmy Raney.*

As from July 10, 1959, Cary started work at the Southward Inn at Orleans, Cape Cod. He calls it an easy job, 9:00 p.m. to 1:00 a.m. This engagement ended after two months, on September 7. There are no diary entries during this period, but it ties in with the recollections of pianist Dave McKenna, who told collector Gunnar Jacobsen that in the summer of 1959 he and Dick Cary were in Cape Cod together. McKenna was playing in the Teddy Charles trio and Cary with a band, and McKenna sat in with Cary a couple of times. He thought of Cary as a great musician, a good arranger and a nice guy. He also remembered that Cary had been a good wrestler. Later in the year McKenna began dating Cary's daughter, Judy.

As Cary wrote to Ken Gallacher: "It's a two month vacation—tennis, golf, swimming and even some baseball to occupy the day. Four hours of playing each night with a young six-piece group. I'm sure you haven't heard of any of them, only one with any talent, a trombone player named Roswell Rudd, who is a Vic Dickenson copier." [Rudd later moved into free-form jazz, working with leaders such as Charlie Haden and Thelonious Monk.]

Cary was credited as co-composer of *Funky Blues* with organist Ethel Smith on a Decca record date in September 1959. Three standard blues were recorded on August 19 with Miss Smith accompanied by a small band, so it is possible Cary plays the trumpet on these, if his Cape Cod booking permitted. He did arrange all or most of the titles on Ethel Smith's "Bouquet of Blues" album and *Funky Blues* was to be published by the Ethel Smith Music Corp. Cary commented that Milt Gabler supervised the Ethel Smith Decca albums, also saying: "I tried to make her swing, wrote every note out and she got good rhythm men, but her conception left a bit to be desired."

September is otherwise blank, except for recording sessions. On the 14th and 15th, he recorded again with Lou McGarity, this time on piano and alto horn in a septet for Argo, with Jack Tracy "at the controls," and on the 19th with Bob Wilber, "a nice date on Bechet tunes for Classic Editions." The five Wilber titles have Cary in fine form on trumpet, bright and clear.

On October 9, 1959, he saw the last game of the World Series at Eddie Condon's apartment with Johnny Mercer. "Mercer gave me list of 57 tunes to do for his daughter's Christmas party—a local Savannah, GA, band, Art Henry." Just what had to be done to these 57 tunes is not stated, but it seems to have taken Cary until mid-November to complete. The diary is then blank until the end of October. Cary recorded under his own name for Columbia on October 20, 23 and 30 and with Max Kaminsky for Westminster on October 29 and 30. Regarding the Kaminsky session he wrote: "I was too stiff—damn."

The omens for Cary's Columbia album were not auspicious. A cartoon on the sleeve of the album showing musicians with straw hats and banjos did not inspire confidence and neither did the titles, of which *Camptown Races* and *Waltzing Matilda* were typical, nor the band title, "The Dixieland Doodlers." One suspects that George Avakian should be blamed for the decision to use songs in the public domain. That Cary could make something of this material says much for his ability. The reviewer for *Down Beat* was not impressed and, in a critical notice, graded the performance only as "Competent."

Dick Sudhalter wrote: "Quietly, deftly, Cary subverted such thinking. Even saddled with a repertoire that included *Wait 'til the Sun Shines, Nellie,* and *There is a Tavern in the Town,* he produced an excellent, musically intense album, played by a band of first-rate jazzmen ... his arrangements are imaginative, swinging and, above all, humorous. (Kenny) Davern, who by his own admission had gone into the project expecting the worst album of his career, later judged Doodlers one of his best." In similar vein, Dick Wellstood's biographer, Edward Meyer, said: "...the combination of talented musicians and Cary's tight, swinging arrangements created an album with drive and sophistication."

Of the interesting Max Kaminsky album on the Westminster label, which has three compositions by Kaminsky-Cary, Cary said:

> *The gimmick on this was somebody wanted a Dixieland album with two clarinet players. We had Phil Olivella and Bob Wilber, pretty good ones. But it didn't come out as Dixieland as they thought it might. I did all the arrangements on the album and I want to just say one thing about a wonderful piano player on this named Dave McKenna, who almost became my son-in-law one-time.*

Also in October Cary found himself, as did Bobby Hackett and Ruby Braff, once again substituting for Muggsy Spanier, who had fallen off the wagon during a residency at The Roundtable.

Cary and Jimmy McPartland went to Valley Forge on October 28, where they played with a local band, and on the 31st he was with the Conrad Janis group at the Central Plaza. The band at the Old Lynne Country Club on November 6 and the Wes Nor in Westport on November 10 included Max Kaminsky, Ray Diehl and Bob Wilber, with Charlie Traeger, bass, and Cliff Leeman, drums, named for the second date. On the 11th he was in a recording studio again, with the John Glasel Brasstet. His diary entry is: "Marvelous date tonight at Golden Crest in Huntington—I pecked and pounded. One Duke, one Golson, *More Than You Know* and two of mine. Fine day." These five titles make one side of the album, issued on a Golden Crest subsidiary, "Jazz Unlimited."

Using Cary's arrangements, and two of his original compositions, *Time for One More* and *Vikki*, the Brasstet consisted of two trumpets, trombone, alto horn/piano, tuba, bass and drums.

> *John (Glasel) is a very fine trumpet player in New York. He used to do a lot of shows. He was doing "Bells Are Ringing," I think at the time. He did "West Side Story" and a lot of the very good shows. This is one of the rehearsal groups we had in my loft, after the big band. He'd come down after eleven and we'd rehearse the brass quintet and we'd have drums and bass with them, make them more interesting.*
>
> *The real, legitimate brass quintet is two trumpets, trombone, French horn and tuba, and we have the same thing, except that I played alto horn instead of the French horn. I wrote one side [of the LP] and on the other side there were several composers and they used a real French horn.*

Some of these Cary "Brass Quintets" arrangements were published for use in schools.

It is unfortunate that so much of Cary's best work was for small record companies with limited distribution. Any reissues now would be on the same small scale, but at least the music would be available for those who wished to hear and appreciate it.

* * * * * * *

There is no forewarning in Cary's diary for 1959 of plans being made to move to California; no preparations are mentioned. After the John Glasel recording date he writes of visiting Madison Square Garden and there is also a mysterious reference to going to "Columbia to see Morgan—sign my life away." That was on November 12, while on Saturday, the 14th, he does write the word "packing."

Thus, with no fanfare, Cary set out on a month-long drive from New York to Los Angeles. Commencing on Sunday, November 15, he drove Pee Wee Russell and Johnny Vine to Chester, where they played at a private club with Max Kaminsky. (Steve Gibson and the

Red Caps were the other group.) From there he drove to Lancaster, where he worked for a week at the Club Coronet, living in a "nice apartment" above the club. During this stay he "sent final batch of music to Art Henry in Savannah." Also, "John Dengler called—has nine record dates for me in December. Can't do it, so got Max [Kaminsky] on them." (These last are presumably the Marty Grosz sessions for Audio Fidelity.)

His last day at the Coronet was November 21, but he enjoyed the 22nd as a rest day, before setting off on the 23rd:

November 23:	Lancaster to Roanoke, Virginia
November 24:	Roanoke to Nashville, Tennessee
November 25:	Nashville to Pine Bluff, Arkansas
November 26:	Pine Bluff to Mt. Pleasant, Texas
November 27/28:	Mt. Pleasant to Abilene, Texas
November 29:	Abilene to Midland, Texas
November 30:	Midland to Las Cruces, New Mexico
December 1:	Las Cruces to Phoenix, Arizona

Cary spent the next two weeks in Phoenix, apparently working for Chief Jay Marago, or possibly drummer Don McGregor. He played with a small group, the jobs including three tunes in the lobby of the Westward Ho to open an Indian meeting (December 7), "his school in Globe—beautiful Baldwin grand" (December 8), "Short one in Junior High School" (December 9), "two schools—desolate settlement, then large modern gym in Casa Grande. Worked Riverside ballroom 9:00 to 1:00" (December 10), "Last school job in Mesa. Job in ballroom 10:45 to 2:00" (December 11), 9:00 to 1:00 at Desert Rose Motel with tenor, bass and drums (December 12).

He was on the road to Palm Springs on the 14th, and arrived in Hollywood on December 15th, where he immediately put his card into the union, Local 47 of the A.F.M. He stayed with his sister, Lois, but after just two days he found an apartment at 2254 North Cahuenga and moved in.

What made Cary decide that California was the place to be is unclear. All that is known is that he wanted to leave New York, about which he felt ambivalent. He knew it was the place in which to find work, but he disliked the traffic and the lack of green spaces. To *Jazz Forum* he said it was a combination of things, including the principle of the police card, which one had to have to work any place in New York which served liquor. He objected both to the two-dollar fee and to being fingerprinted.

Diary entries illustrate some of this ambivalence. On one

occasion, after a leisurely drive to town, he wrote: "Marvelous to be back." But he could also say: "I hate this city." Or: "Beautiful warm sunny day and how I'd like not to be in NYC." Eventually Cary chose the sprawl of Los Angeles. Perhaps, as Bob Wilber suggested, he had thoughts of arranging and composing for movies or television. Whatever the reasons, Dick Cary was now in California.

11. Interlude—Blackberry Brandy and Peppermint Schnapps

The main purpose of this book is to recount the story of Dick Cary's life, concentrating all the while on his music, to tell of the musicians with whom he was associated and the records he made, of his failures and successes in attempting to create quality music in the field of jazz and popular song. On the other hand, a musician's private life must have its influence upon his music. Reference has been made already to Cary's first marriage to Rose and to his long liaison with Virginia, and the resulting conflict between family and career, but it was addiction to alcohol which was a major factor in his life and which could so easily have ruined his talent.

It is unlikely that anyone reading this has not known the sense of relaxation and confidence which alcohol can give. In moderation alcohol can induce a feeling of euphoria, but to excess its medical effects include dizziness, vomiting, hangovers, memory loss and liver damage.

Problems with excessive drinking affected many a jazz musician during the first fifty years of the last century. As already mentioned, those who gathered around Eddie Condon were particularly noted for their hard drinking habits, having grown up during the era of Prohibition, making their living in the saloons and speakeasies whose existence depended upon the sale of strong drink. For the next generation, the bop era of Charlie Parker, Stan Getz, Wardell Gray and Art Pepper, hard drugs were to be the stimulant, with results which were even more tragic.

Starting in his early teenage years and throughout most of his life, Cary either embraced or fought the temptation of bottle and glass. It seemed not to matter what the contents were—whisky, bourbon, scotch, gin, rum, champagne, beer, brandy, chartreuse, Moscow mules, peppermint schnapps, blackberry brandy, vodka, Pernod, wine, or Bloody Mary's. He also dabbled with cannabis. All this excess had an effect upon his work, as indicated by his dismissal by Glen Gray, the drunk-driving convictions or the rare occasions he failed to make a gig, but generally in his circle such lapses were treated sympathetically. One of his concerns is contained in an April 1943 entry: "That's one of my horrors, being too loaded to play." But there is no evidence that his drinking materially affected either his playing or his writing. We just do not know if, for instance, his originals and arrangements for Bobby Hackett or Jimmy McPartland would have been even better if he had been a teetotaller.

No doubt there is a gene which can be blamed for indulgence in alcohol but there are other reasons why a jazzman of the 1930s and 1940s would drink. Working in clubs or saloons such as Nick's and Jimmy Ryan's, where booze was readily available, increased the temptation, as would the customers who liked to "buy a round for the boys in the band." Musicians had their own way of asking for a drink from, as Cary called them, the sponsors. Then there were the quiet nights, when customers were few, and a drink now and again took the edge off the boredom. Or the gigs where one was playing with inadequate musicians, and an alcoholic beverage would make the low musical level more tolerable.

In a February 16, 1947, entry, Cary gave one reason for being a toper: "Mine is the alcoholic escape and the lack of courage to put forward individual and anti-social, anti-average ideas, plus a terrible dissatisfaction with the routine and the trite." Confirmation of another was contained in an October 1958 observation, after he had taken his alto horn to a 25th anniversary party—"[It is] quite a sacrifice to go to these stuffy parties and perform without booze, so I drink, and there goes that wagon again! It can kill you but most people can't understand that. They crowd so many folks into such small areas."

Some claimed that drink helped to improve performance and certainly a glass or two helped to steady the nerves before an appearance in public, providing the Dutch courage to face an audience. There was peer pressure, too. In the circumstances described above it would take a strong personality to remain abstemious. Eventually, of course, chemistry would play its part and the glasses of whisky or gin became a necessity. It was a different era and it is astonishing that so many of these hard drinkers survived into their seventies.

Although Cary was well acquainted with members of Alcoholics Anonymous (Jimmy McPartland and Ruth Reinhardt were two), he did not accept that the A.A.'s precepts could help him as he wrestled with his addiction. He wrote: "The A.A. is an example—it's the admission of defeat. 'I am sick.' There is no other way—we can't help ourselves. 'I cannot drink!' and I almost brag to others in the club that there's no other way—I am sick. So if I do fall off [the wagon], my mind immediately tells me there is no hope, that any attempt to use will power will fail." This was a rather original take on the A.A.'s aims and beliefs and one that that organisation might find difficult to accept.

From time to time he would seek help from a doctor, but their assistance appears to have been restricted to prescribing pills, though one did suggest that he change his job!

* * * * * * *

From January 1940 onwards, Cary's diaries have many, many references to excessive drinking and the following examples, just a few of the entries, give an indication of the pernicious damage which alcohol can cause and of Cary's battle with it.

- 1941: Horrible hangover but drunk it off.
- 1942: Another pretty bad hangover. (He slept on train and went past stop—again.)
- 1942: Don't know how I made Nick's. Home at 2:00. Woke at 5:00 feeling as bad as I've ever felt ... my mind in awful state and dreadful nightmares.
- 1942: Another awful mental spell. Hour and half in clinic didn't help.

But he also wrote: "Just returned from St. Vincent's Clinic and taken ill for nervous spell, worst of three in last week. Doctor reassured me a lot and I passed rest of night easily, aided by M and M."

These problems with nerves, jitters and nightmares continued through 1943.

- 1943: Saw doctor—physically ok but "nerves shot to pieces." Change of job suggested!
- 1943: Worst hangover and jitters since last day after Christmas.
- 1943: Horrible morning—DT's or closest I've come.
- 1946: I must learn to drink moderately. Could make it a useful and enjoyable thing if done right.
- 1946: Drinking all day to get rid of hangover, but never did.
- 1946: I know my only hope is sobriety.
- 1946: Sobriety is wonderful.

But by 29 December 1946 he was in a confused mental state. At 1:00 a.m. he called Dr. Tabella, who told Cary to stop drinking and prescribed him sleeping capsules.

During 1947, 1948 and 1949 he continued to see-saw between being a drunk and a teetotaller. He could write, on February 14, 1948, that "I haven't even had a beer since attack of leg cramps," but just three days later, "I went off wagon. Several beers, then got a 5th." On March 16, 1948, he had "Scotch for breakfast" but on June 11 reported "This abstinence feels wonderful, down around 195-lbs, and feel very well."

A February 16, 1950, entry states: "Didn't sleep all night. Got into one of those states where I can't lie down and I'm dead tired to 'the staggering' stage, scared, anxious. When I lie down the mind wanders, no concentration is possible … can't sweat, nerves hold everything tense and bound up and there's no release but to wait and wait. Hours are like days. Virginia prescribed four donatols in a.m., drank some hot cocoa, and finally got a couple of nightmare filled hours. But staved off the lush and am scared enough to stop for awhile."

His entry the next day is: "This is finally the end of the alcoholic condition which started last weekend. They're getting longer and longer to shake off and I'm on wagon for a while now—I hope!" But these good intentions did not last for long. To quote two examples from 1951: on May 3 he noted: "This particular wagon about a week and a half old—feel wonderful," followed the next day by "left wagon late in evening."

He knew what he was doing, as he questioned on November 19, 1952: "I got fairly loaded with bourbon, brandy, pernod sponsors—stupid isn't it?" In 1953, on October 10, he says: "Ninth day on wagon—feel absolutely wonderful," but only four days later: "I went off wagon with vodka and brought two quarts of ale home." He tries again in November, on the 28th, "A long night without a drink. I'm back on wagon—for how long?" And the answer was six days.

In 1955 and 1956 he was fined for drunk-driving, but these two cases did not change his habits and he continued to veer between sobriety and intemperance, even when he considered what the future could be, as he did the evening of July 22, 1956, when he visited a number of bars in the evening and "saw several pretty hopeless drunks. Don't think I'll end up like that, but I am not too many steps away tonight." The next day was: "One of those days of torture, withdrawing from alcohol. Saw doctor who prescribed two medicines." The following month, on August 30, 1956, Jimmy McPartland drove himself and Cary to Detroit. During a break en route McPartland had spaghetti but Cary "had about 8 or 10 doubles."

His efforts to remain sober are exemplified during the first few weeks of 1957:

January 3: Wagon going strong
January 6: Toughest of all nights on wagon
January 27: I celebrated month on wagon with one bottle of beer.
January 30: I went out for a few dark beers and brought some home.
February 2: Few whiskies tonight—curses!

Towards the end of 1957, Cary's efforts to abstain became more frequent. Late in September he lasted a week before succumbing, but he quickly got back on the wagon. His November 22 entry is: "Five weeks on the wagon! Second longest since 16 years old. I once put in two months when at the Metropole with Jimmy McPartland." He lapsed again on December 7, after 7 weeks and one day, before trying once more a few days later.

He "finally saw" a doctor in November 1959, though no treatment is mentioned, and on two successive days in December 1960. On the latter occasions he had a cardiograph and was prescribed "pills, etc."

In October 1964, despite some shaky arithmetic, he could give himself a small cheer with the entry: "got my wagon derailed after about six weeks—34 days, whee!" But in 1965 he could congratulate himself on the fact that he: "was on wagon over 50 weeks, which is a good average." Unfortunately, this above average achievement was followed in March 1966 by the comment: "Alcohol is just marvelous! ... until the stomach protests later."

The struggle continued with, apparently, some success. References to alcohol become less frequent and in 1977 there were none. But in 1978, on a European tour, he started a week long binge. In Dusseldorf on 4 May 1978 he noted: "As I talked to Jake Porter tonight I was attracted by a large bottle of dark beer—so I'm off again after over a year." One week later he suffered "two hallucinations tonight" and his May 13 entry was: "God, this was a horrible nightmare!! Never again!" Later that year, in a November 4 letter to Bert Whyatt, he said: "I've had to quit entirely."

As references to alcohol become fewer and fewer in these last years one can surmise that Cary's European 'nightmare' in 1978 had a salutary affect on him. He continued to imbibe but without major problems. In the light of his struggle with the "demon drink" it is astonishing that his standard of creativity remained so high.

12. 9828 Wornom Ave., Sunland, CA (1960–1963)

Trees featured in Cary's reasons for moving to Los Angeles when he was interviewed by Floyd Levin and Scott Ellsworth. To Levin he said:
> *I got here December 15, 1959. I used to tell people I wanted to see a tree.*

While to Scott Ellsworth he gave his reason for moving as:
> *I think probably trees and grass. I wanted to see some of that before I got through. I wanted to play some golf instead of getting into traffic jams. New York got kind of hard to live [in].*

9828 Wornom Avenue, 2006
(Photograph by and courtesy of George Martinez)

He saw the New Year in doing a Sid Zaid date at the Naval Ordinance Training Station at China Lake "with Jerry Van, Paul Hebert, etc." The diary is then blank until early in April, though we can assume that such work as he had was limited.

By 1960, trumpeter Dick Cathcart was taking advantage of his work on the "Pete Kelly's Blues" movie and television show. One of his ventures was organising a band which played at the Flamingo Lounge in Las Vegas for four weeks, April 14 to May 11. The hours were 9:15 p.m. to 3:15 a.m. and "Dick was very nervous." The personnel was Cathcart, cornet, Al Jenkins, trombone, Bill Wood, clarinet, Fran Polifrani, tenor, Dick Cary, piano, Jud De Naut, bass, and Charlie Lodice, drums. "A pretty good band" was Al Jenkins' comment.

Cary filled in his time with writing, playing golf and seeing the Duke Ellington orchestra at the Riviera. A week after arriving he gambled for the first time—"After work my first crack at a table at Silver Slipper. Lost a saw at 21. Was ahead quite a while!"

The diary is blank again until June, by which time he has a number of individual bookings and becomes a member of AFM Local 47 on June 15th.

June 6:	Harding—with Harper, Bill Campbell (piano), Tom Toonan
June 9:	Roaring Twenties
June 10:	Elks, Lancaster—with Higgins, Stevens, Jerry Kipp
June 11:	La Jolla Country Club—with Bill Wood, clarinet, Sch]neider [Moe? trombone], C. Coat, Jud [de Naut, bass?], Tom Tedesco, banjo, Shanahan, drums?, and Polly.
June 12:	outdoor concert, Valley Junior College—with [Dick] Cathcart, [George] Van Eps, guitar, Jud [de Naut?], Moe [Schneider], etc.
June 16:	High School in Laguna—with Matty [Matlock, clarinet], Moe [Schneider], Stan W., [Wrightsman], piano, [Nick] Fatool, drums.
June 17:	Azuza High School—[Dick] Cathcart job
June 18:	Knickerbocker Hotel with Bob Crosby, mc, John Best, trumpet, Moe Schneider, Matty Matlock, Stan Wrightsman, George Van Eps, Walt Yoder, bass, Nick Fatool.
June 21:	Roaring Twenties—Cary on trumpet
June 22:	Gay Nineties—with Jack Coon, trumpet, Gene Bolen, clarinet, Rolly Furness, piano, Chas. Lodice, drums. "Fine duets with Jackie."
June 25:	opening of city dump, Palmdale—played Wurlitzer with [Bob] Higgins, trumpet, [Defebaugh], drums.
July 12:	transcribed four shows for Treasury dept—with Cathcart, Schneider, Don [perhaps

Bonnee], clarinet, Nick Fatool, Polly ?, Jud (har)?, and Connie, singer. *Mood Indigo* marvelous.

It was perhaps on July 2 that Cary began work at Basin Street with trumpeter Garner Clark. The clarinetist was Reul Lynch—"what a classy individual." But Cary was less complimentary about his leader—"Garner like a headless chicken and as effective!" He finished work at Basin Street on July 14 and, on trumpet, joined clarinetist Gus Bivona at the Beverly Cavern the following night. "Drums just awful" was what Cary wrote about the Garner band, while of Bivona's he said, "drummer terrible." When the job ended on August 4 Cary wrote: "So long to Walter, Danny, Stan, Pete and Gus." Earlier he had mentioned a rehearsal with Bivona, to which he contributed arrangements, commenting: "fine start for album." No details are known for this album.

But he did not leave the Beverly Cavern, as he now joined the Red Nichols Five Pennies at that establishment. At rehearsals he was already complaining—"No rhythm at all." By 2 a.m. on his first night, Cary "was wondering if I could stand any more of this silly Tick Tock Time in the Nursery. Christ!"

Veteran bandleader and cornetist Red Nichols underwent major surgery (hernia operation and colon removal) in May 1960. It was not until August, after a period of convalescence, that he reformed his Five Pennies, hiring Dick Cary as pianist but also planning to use his abilities as arranger and alto horn player. The new band, consisting of Nichols, cornet, Ed Anderson, trombone, Bill Wood, clarinet, Joe Rushton, bass-sax, Dick Cary, piano, Rollie Culver, drums, opened at the Beverly Cavern on Beverly Boulevard in Los Angeles on August 4, for two weeks. Cary was in the band for just ten weeks, the itinerary being:

August 4–19: Beverly Cavern, Los Angeles
August 20: appearance at annual Dixieland Jubilee, Los Angeles
August 22–September 2: Freddy's, Minneapolis ("lovely piano")
September 5–October 1: The Round Table, New York
October 4–9: Red Hell Inn, Delair, New Jersey
October 14: appearance on the Bell Telephone Hour, NBC-TV
October 17–22: Round Table, Toledo, Ohio

After the Toledo engagement the band returned to Los Angeles and Dick Cary was replaced. (The above itinerary is taken from Stan and Steve Hester's meticulous "Red Nichols—After the Intermission 1942-1965," though Cary also mentions a country club job in Jackson on September 3.)

Upon arriving in New York on September 4, he visited Hall Overton's loft apartment for a session which included Bob Brookmeyer and Jimmy Raney, etc., and the following night he sat-in at Eddie Condon's. He also played at the Central Plaza on the 9th, prior to The Round Table job, with Max Kaminsky, Cutty Cutshall, Tony Parenti and Mickey Sheen, drums.

Cary was again recruited by Jimmy McPartland for a recording session, on September 13 and 14, this time for the Design label. He arranged, played alto horn and, on one title, trumpet for this unusual session featuring television themes. Two days earlier, on September 10/11 he had recorded a selection of spirituals, under the leadership of Bobby Hackett, for Sesac transcriptions. These were later issued commercially and one obituarist wrote that Cary "contributed a series of gracile solos that marked him as a class musician." In the context of jazz, one wonders if that was a compliment.

His other activities while in New York included entertaining Judy, who was in town, taking her to one of the Bobby Hackett recording sessions. During two visits to the Yankee Stadium he saw the games from Joe Glaser's box. His diary says he played on an Ethel Smith session for Decca on the 29th, but the horn solos on *Lullaby of Birdland* and *Misty* which he mentions are missing on the issued record.

With Jimmy McPartland he was given a contract by the Edward B. Marks Music Corporation for another song book, "Jimmy McPartland's Sounds of Dixieland for Combo Orks, as arranged by Jimmy McPartland and Dick Cary." The 14 tunes included in the book consisted of five standards, five numbers by Nick La Rocca and four by McPartland and Cary—*Logan Square, Reminiscing, Red Hill* and *Keep Movin.*' However, only the last three titles were in the agreement which they signed in October 1960, and when *Logan Square* appeared on an Eddie Condon album it was credited to McPartland-Priestley. Cary's royalties on the first song book for the three years 1957/58/59 had totalled $555.52.

Apropos Dick Cary's great admiration for Willie "The Lion" Smith, he recalled that pianist's tour de force, *Fingerbuster*, saying, "I once played it while with Red Nichols."

Cary did not have a high opinion of Red Nichols and he was unhappy with the band from his very first rehearsals with them. His comments included: "Nichols becomes a hysterical, raving maniac with booze—what a sight—Mr. Hyde!" and "Got throroughly disgusted with what we play." On another occasion he wrote: "Almost enjoyed evening, First time I ever got a reaction on the banana and it has to be with this f. band." Towards the end of his employment he wrote that the band: "could use bass, drums and a trumpet player." Nichols always played the same choruses, spoke the same introductions, and was "intensely antagonistic at any rehearsal." He also criticised the limited repertoire, changing tempos and overlong medleys! Cary recalled that during the engagement at The Round Table in New York, an Eddie Condon party came into the club. In the party was singer Lee Wiley, a lady renowned for her short temper. Nichols had a habit of stabbing a finger at people and then he was rude to Lee Wiley, who just smiled and, surprisingly, stayed calm. As the party left the club, Wiley called to Nichols, "Stay as sweet as you are!"

An alternative view, from the late Phil Evans, jazz writer and researcher, who knew Nichols well, was that his sound was very distinctive. "I heard Red play countless times and he was very creative. Red was a very complex guy. I never saw the bad side of him, but I was certainly aware of it, but he did have a sense of moral judgement. I can well remember Red telling me about going to hire Cary and how complimentary Red was on Dick's coming into the band. It is sad that it ended with Red firing him. I was present the night (it happened). Red was clearly in the right. Red was on the stand ... as Dick came onto the bandstand with a drink in his hand, which he set down on the piano. Red told him that he had a rule of no drinks on the stand and to get the glass off ... it got heated, believe me, and I heard every word. Red very matter-of-factly said, 'You're fired!'"

Dick Cary's version is: "Nichols loaded tonight and we had blow off at bar." This was on October 6th and the following day—"Nichols up in afternoon to discuss our flare-up last night. I'll leave after week in L.A. We shook hands and agreed to stay amicable. So tonight was nice...."

It is unfortunate there was this clash, because private tapes show that Cary's inclusion on alto horn introduced a fresh conception to the Five Pennies sound, enlivening what often became formulaic Dixieland.

Among the bands Cary heard during his travels with Red

Nichols were, in Minneapolis, Donald Byrd and Pepper Adams, who "rehearsed yesterday at Herb's and sound marvelous—that Byrd!" In New York he heard the Horace Silver and Dizzy Gillespie groups at Birdland—"Horace quite a fellow," while Cootie Williams led the other band at The Round Table.

Cary celebrated his return to Los Angeles by enjoying a lot of golf and, on October 29, playing a good job at Victorville High School with Warner Spurrier, reeds, Haifer McKay and Milt Norman, guitar. "This has been a marvelous week, liberated from Nichols!"

During November, there were brass quintet rehearsals at trumpeter Dick Cathcart's home, with Betty and Barrett O'Hara on trombones or bass trombones, perhaps Phil Stephens on tuba or Pete Carpenter on trombone. (Betty O'Hara was an old New York friend, the former Mrs. Betty Peterson.) Otherwise Cary's work in November was limited to square or round dance recording sessions for Hi Hat Records (November 7 and 14); three or four shows with Buddy Lewis and Dianne Booth at Lancaster, playing trumpet, with Pete Beilmann, trombone, Phil Gomez, clarinet (November 18 and 19); and two recording sessions for Crown Records with Dick Cathcart, and including Matty Matlock, Eddie Miller, et al (November 23 and 28).

At the end of 1960, Cary began an occasional association with the singer Bob Crosby, brother of Bing. Crosby led his Bob Cats for a two week engagement (December 5–21) at the Starlight Room of the Riviera Hotel in Las Vegas, with Wild Bill Davison on cornet, Cutty Cutshall, trombone, Matty Matlock, clarinet, Eddie Miller, tenor, Cary, piano, Nappy Lamare, banjo, Jack Ryan, bass, and Cliff Leeman, drums. Cary drove to Las Vegas on December 2 and there he met Terry Lee Scott, "our singer (one leg)," visited Charlie Teagarden, and watched the Harry James band. The next three days were spent rehearsing, with the band opening on December 5 and Cary quitting on the 7th, complaining that the week was a nightmare—"job rotten, nothing to do—run-in with Crosby, an extremely dull, boorish fellow." He passed the 8th with Cutty Cutshall and Cliff Leeman, returning to Los Angeles on the 9th. A week later Eddie Miller saw him and handed over a cheque from Crosby, together with some "kind words." Perhaps it was this gesture which persuaded Cary to work for Crosby in the future.

He saw the year out with a "fine job at Bakersfield Jr. C.— Dick Cathcart, Moe Schneider, Ed Gilbert, bass, Nick Fatool, Stan Wrightsman, and two reeds" on December 17, and a Sid Zaid job at the Beverly Hilton on the 23rd. (Zaid is listed in the AFM handbook as a trumpeter and conductor, though he may have been active as a contractor.) He sat in with Gus Bivona's group at the Encore on the 28th and welcomed the New Year in with a quartet (Paul Hebert, piano, Dan Hall, drums, Bob Kimmick, ?) at the Annandale Country Club in Pasadena—"they gave us a steak and $33 in tips."

He had continued to play golf, and noted the foursome scores for one day—Nick Fatool, 73, Phil Gomez, 81, George Defebaugh, 87, Dick Cary, 86. During December tennis was featured more and he also played some softball. It is clear from his comments on the results just how competitive he was in such games. As a result his weight was down to about 203 pounds—"was over 225 at end of Nichols' tour." And a final note from 1960; when, in November, John F. Kennedy was elected President, Cary's comment was: "Thank God. Not for him but that Nixon isn't!!"

A January 1961 entry reads: "Unemployed—and for how long this time?" Jobs were scarce and those he did find were rarely satisfying. As he told Gudrun Endress:

When I was engaged for the first time in a restaurant on the West Coast, the host came to me upset and asked what kind of music we were playing. That was not Dixieland, he complained, as we did not play like the Firehouse Five.

Pianist Johnny Varro expressed his opinion to collector Gunnar Jacobsen that Cary changed when he moved to California. He admired Cary's playing and arranging, and they had had no problems when both were playing in New York. However, when Varro moved to Los Angeles twenty years later, about 1979, he felt that Cary was jealous. They played a few times together on the same bill but Dick was not the same as he had been in New York. They had some personality differences. Varro thought Cary was one of the most unkempt persons he had ever encountered.

The previous July, Betty Peterson had called Cary to say that she was in Los Angeles to stay. A meeting was arranged for him to meet "her intended, Barrett O'Hara, a bass trombonist," and the O'Haras became regular members of the rehearsal groups. On January 9, 1961, Cary and Barrett O'Hara were in a bar and "met nice lady, Jessie Bailey." All three went along to Gus Bivona's opening night at the Black Bull, where Cary sat-in on trumpet. (Clarinetist Bivona had a trio, with Russ Black, piano, John Lais, drums, and a bassist, "and a pretty good singer, Mike Douglas.") It transpired that the O'Haras were moving near Jessie Bailey in Sunland the following week.

Ms. Bailey (born July 23, 1915) was a singer-pianist who worked in bars or cocktail lounges. She studied piano and trombone at school and joined Ina Ray Hutton's all-female big band on trombone in 1935. Later she led a similar outfit, The Coquettes. Two husbands and three children later she is next mentioned on January 17, when Cary had "supper with Jessie and three children. Quiet evening of writing, TV and dozing on Jessie's shoulder. Guess I've got the bug—third stage in my life. Seems to occur at 15 year intervals, Rose at 15, Virginia at 30, Jessie at 44." On the 23rd he was at the union for a rehearsal by the Swinging Mothers, a group led by Jessie Bailey, with Fred Stulce as arranger and director, and the following day he and Jessie decided to get married. He was watching on TV when the Swinging Mothers appeared in the show "I've Got a Secret" on February 1, then he and Jessie drove to Las Vegas on March 5 and were married on the 6th.

Jessie Cary

Jessie Cary and Sean

As Cary had feared, jobs were in short supply for the start of 1961 and most of his playing was without pay, either sitting-in or rehearsing at Dick Cathcart's. He did sub for the pianist with Gus Bivona on January 13 and was offered the chair on a regular basis, starting on the 20th, but when he arrived the job was no longer available. And so it continued, with few gigs being listed:

January 28:   Professional Photographers Club—with Dick Cathcart, Eddie Miller, Walt Yoder, bass, Earl Smith, drums, "and the electric piano."
January 30:   Dick Dale's—on horns with Ken Cameron, Jim Brown, Walt Yoder

March 4: horrible non-union job with Jack Langlois
March 9/10/11: Bowling Alley, Prairie Ave—with Wild Bill Davison, Bob McCracken, clarinet, George Defebaugh, drums.

Wild Bill Davison too was trying to settle in Los Angeles and scuffling for work. On March 10 Cary reported: "Was doing fine until Davison objected to peck horn and I burned. This idiotic noise-maker is one of life's fakes, one who finds a con, a gimmick, and uses it at the expense of well-meaning people." That same day Cary, along with clarinetist Joe Darensbourgh and banjoist Nappy Lamare gave an audition in Pasadena. "One lady with a night club in Alaska liked us"—but the trio was not invited to Anchorage.

On March 16, Cary cleaned out his apartment, number 4, 2254 Cahuenga, and moved to 9828 Wornom Avenue, where he was to live for the remaining thirty-three years of his life. On the 31st he wrote: "No news—but pleased to be married. What a nice family."

Rex Stewart had also moved to the West Coast and on April 1 Cary played a job in Manhattan Beach with him. The group included George Washington on trombone, with violinist Stuff Smith sitting-in. Two days later Dick Cathcart telephoned to say there was a possible arranging job with Harry James. Cary called James' manager, Pee Wee Monte—"He doesn't know my work, so I must convince him some way ... deliver a few albums tomorrow so that Harry can judge. They wanted Matty Matlock but he's in hospital—and right away a vulture, namely me, is after his writing work. But goddam it, I haven't had anything out here yet!" Four albums were delivered to Monte but the band went on the road until the end of May and Matty Matlock was out of hospital weeks before it returned. (Matlock's arrangements for a Dixieland frontline playing with the James' big band were recorded for Verve in July the following year.)

There are no entries in the diary for the next five months and even after that they are brief or intermittent. It is known that he and Jessie played a date with Bill Alexander's band ("A Night in New Orleans") at the Apple Valley Inn on August 11. For the last two days of September there is mention of "Downey Bowl" and on October 1 a "Park concert" and there were a number of rehearsals with Kay Carlson's band and with trumpeter Art DePew's. But then things began to improve.

October 8: Kismet—with Art DePew
October 15: Kismet—with Art DePew
October 16: round dance recording session

October 20:	La Brea—with trombonist Bill Williams band
October 22:	Kismet—with Ruth Price
October 25	round dance recording session
November 1:	round dance recording session
November 4:	Lakeside Golf Club—Sid Zaid job, with Paul Hebert sextet
November 8:	Caine's Mutiny—piano in drummer Tom Riley's trio
November 11:	K of C—with Rex Stewart, George Washington, Leonard Bechet and drummer—$15.00
November 17:	UCLA—with Rex Stewart, George Washington, Gene Bolen, Hank Henry, Buddy Burns
November 18:	good job at naval flying base—played valve-trombone, trumpet and alto horn
November 22:	Wilton Hotel, 9:00 to 1:00 a.m., "colored dance, quite dull"—with Rex Stewart, George Washington, Hank Henry
December 2:	Mint Canyon: played for a wedding party—with Betty O'Hara and Bill Perkins
December 9:	lobby of Barb. Worth Hotel with Danny Thomas—band was 8-piece, including Bud Shank, alto, Red Callender, bass, Earl Smith, drums
December 11:	no location—sextet, with Bill Cooper, sax, Larry Bunker, drums, Kenny, Vi and Murray [Murray McEachern, trombone?]
December 15:	round dance date
December 16:	Thunderbird Hotel, El Segundo—with Murray [?] 9-pieces—Bud Shank, Lennie Mitchell, Kenny Jensen, reeds, Frank Albright, Red Callender, Dave Perlman, drums, Vi, Murray and me
December 17:	Irvine Coast Country Club, Corona Del Mar—with Murray group

On December 29, Cary went to the Chit Chat club in place of Jessie, who was not feeling well: "Played an hour—informed that I stunk, so went home at 10:15!"

Fortunately he did not face such criticism on New Year's Eve, when he played 9:30 p.m. to 1:30 a.m. at the Beverly Hilton Hotel with Bernie Halpert, violin, and George Russell, guitar. His comment was—"very hard work—nice view from the roof room."

Next came a month of work and business in New York, to where he flew on January 3, 1962. Marian McPartland was in Florida so he was able to stay in her apartment. Among the news he discovered that Nick Parito was now musical director for United Artists and that Max Kaminsky was at Condon's with Bob Wilber. On the 6th he saw trumpeter Roy Eldridge ("still very exciting") at the Sherwood Inn, with Milt Hinton, bass, and Gus Johnson, drums, in the group. There was a party in the basement bar afterwards and Cary played bass with Eldridge and a guitarist. The next day there was a "good evening at the Mandalay, with Jimmy McPartland, Cutty Cutshall, Paul Hubbell, clarinet, Bob Haggart and George Wettling, which was followed by a some "small work" for Ethel Smith and the first of a few brass quintet rehearsals with Johnny Glasel. Other participants included Lou Mucci, trumpet, Ephie Resnick, trombone, Bill Crow, bass and Harvey Phillips, tuba.

On the 9th he went to the Paramount to see Debbie Reynolds in the movie "Second Time Around"—"with Jessie getting about six to eight seconds as a marching trombonist."

It is not clear if he was at the Central Plaza as a spectator or a performer on January 12 and 13, but it was probably as a pianist, playing in Buck Clayton's group—"never heard Buck play like this." Kenny Davern was the clarinetist for both evenings, with "Big Chief" Moore, trombone, and Hap Gormley, drums, the first night and Cutty Cutshall and Panama Francis the second. Cutshall was also in the quintet which played the Carriage House at Simsbury on Sunday, January 14. Cliff Leeman was the drummer, and Ken was there, presumably Kenny Davern, while Cary had a "nice rebuilt upright to play on."

The next day, the 15th, he started two weeks at Eddie Condon's. He noted that "now there's dancing" and "band good"— Max Kaminsky, trumpet, Ephie Resnick, trombone, Bob Wilber, clarinet, Dan Mattucci, bass, and Buddy Lowell, drums. He took time off on October 19 to fly to Pittsburgh for a wonderful concert at Indiana University with Peanuts Hucko, Dave McKenna, Knobby Totah, bass, and Buzzy Drootin—"fine old hall and big Steinway."

Saturday night, the 20th, was rather dull at Condon's, with the rhythm lousy and the new bassist weak. Cary had lunch with his two daughters on the Sunday, but returning to work the following evening the band learned that Condon's was cutting out the bass. So, "band gave notice as well it should." They finished on January 27, with Cary saying "so long to a fine musical front line."

One of the main reasons for the New York visit was a proposed Dixie Twist album to include four originals and to be published by E.B. Marks. In connection with this planned album, two recording sessions were held January 22/23, with Jimmy McPartland, Harry DeVito, trombone, Bob Wilber, Dick Cary, George Barnes, Bill Crow and George Wettling. On the first day, seven of twelve titles were done, with the vocals to be dubbed in later, and on the second, three vocals and two instrumentals were made. Singer Byrdie Green was involved in this scheme, but as it appears that neither the music album nor the recordings were published, no other information is available.

An album made and released at this time was an Eddie Condon effort for Columbia's Epic label. Recorded on January 27, 1962, the personnel was Bobby Hackett, trumpet, Lou McGarity, trombone, Peanuts Hucko, clarinet, Cary, piano, Condon, guitar, Jack Lesberg or Knobby Totah, bass, and Buzzy Drootin, drums. This was a less successful session, with a repertoire of "foreign" and mainly unsuitable songs (*Dark Eyes, Swan Lake, Danny Boy*, etc.) and a long day (7 1/2 hours, 1:00 p.m. to 8:35) not helping the musicians one jot. Cary's entry: "Bobby and Lou got pretty beat now with this much strain, but they still sound marvelous. Peanuts really played *Hindustan*—one take."

The day after the Epic session Cary drove to Columbus, Ohio, with McPartland, Wettling, Dick Brady, clarinet, and Ronnie Reuben, tenor. They opened the following night, with a local bassist, for a week at Bernie Klein's—"terrible rhythm section, bad ensemble band." Cary mentions meeting trombonist Cutty Cutshall and saxist Deane Kincaide in town, but not as members of the McPartland band. Their engagement at Klein's ended on February 3 and the next day Cary flew back to Los Angeles.

Things were quiet on the return to Sunland. One evening he spent "at Stonewood to hear Jessie's trio"—his wife was playing with multi-instrumentalist Betty O'Hara and drummer Kay Carlson. She was working Monday and Tuesday nights at the Asbury and at the end of the month she started five afternoons a week, noon to 3:00, at the Rain Room of the Reseda Bowling Alley. These would have been solo piano gigs.

A February 26, 1962, entry states: "Third week without single job." Two rehearsals with Art DePew are mentioned, and he played horns, presumably as a sitter-in, at the Balboa Yacht Club, but it was not until the 28th that paid work started to come in:

February 28:   Rally for Senator Cuckel—with Warren Smith,

	trombone, John Tortolla, clarinet, Bill Campbell, piano, Nick Pelico, drums
March 2:	Casino Room, the Ambassador—with Jerry Vaughn and guitarist
March 3:	Santa Ana Jr. College—with Murray, vibes, Jerry King, "what a drummer," Glen De Weese and Paul Suter, piano
March 7:	Rainbow Country Club—with Jessie, Jerry King, Glen De Weese
March 17:	"nice night with Earl Smith, Ed Anderson, Jack Dulong & bass."
March 21:	Biltmore Bowl, hospital dance—with three horns and six rhythm, including Gordon Mitchell, trombone, Floyd Stone, reeds, Dixie Mitchell, guitar, Billy Hadnott, bass, Gene Washington, drums
March 23/24:	Jim's Roaring 20's, Downey Wonderbowl
March 27:	Downey Wonderbowl—glass company party, substituting for Jad Paul (presumably on piano, though Paul also played banjo and guitar)
March 28:	Downey Wonderbowl—another glass company party. "Jad quite a banjoist and guitarist."

From here Cary began working regularly at the Downey Wonderbowl on Fridays and Saturdays, possibly with just a trio. The only personnel mentioned is for May 11, when he gives Jad Paul and George Defebaugh. He writes that he may go to Lake Tahoe with Jad Paul.

During March he worked on an assignment for Leith Stevens, writing a prelude for a short (two-minute) film. No other details are known.

Rehearsals with his Brass Quartet and with the Kay Carlson and Art DePew big bands continued, as did his writing for them. On one afternoon Rex Stewart visited and they went over his, Rex's, *Israeli Suite*. There was another trio date at the Ambassador Hotel's Casino Room, with Jerry Vaughn and Tiny Timbrell, bass, on April 10, followed by a quintet job at the Santa Ana Country Club, when he noted: "My trumpet lip amazed me—I was way above staff." About this time Jessie had four nights a week at Joan Waldor's and, perhaps because of this, Cary started to play there on Sundays, as from April 22. His trio on that date had Glen De Weese and Herb Ellis on guitar.

On Sunday, May 6, he played a park concert, followed by his gig at Joan's, with Bill Cooper, bass, and Betty O'Hara. A week later, when his trio included Glen De Weese and Jad Paul, he refers to "many singers," no doubt meaning the tradition of allowing amateur singers to take the floor, an early, non-mechanical kind of karioke—and just as painful.

An entry for May 7 refers to a round dance date with Jerry Vaughn, Art Barduhn, Maury, and Tom Tedesco, banjo; presumably a recording date rather than an actual dance. On the 15th he saw "Dizzy Gillespie and his marvelous quintet at the Summit—Diz a genius."

There are no further diary entries for 1962, so it is not known if he went to Lake Tahoe, or for how long his bookings at Joan's or the Downey bowling alley continued. There was even mention of Lawrence Welk needing a fourth trumpet man. During July he worked Wednesday to Sunday with violinist Stuff Smith at Joani Presents on Lankershim Boulevard in North Hollywood, with Ira Westley on bass. To Ken Gallacher he wrote: "My job with Stuff was very nice but the saloon didn't advertise and we got through practically unnoticed."

He also told Gallacher: "Then I did rehearsal piano for a show for nine days at Ciro's on the Sunset Strip," returning there on August 24 for two more weeks—"This is easy work except that I detest the tuxedo."

Not so easy was his employment during September. In an October letter to Gallacher, Cary reported playing in a circus band, with Abe Lincoln in the trombone section: "Last week I got through 37 performances of the Ringling Brothers, Barnum and Bailey circus at the Los Angeles Sports Arena and was it a relief! That was the hardest playing I've ever done, with absolutely no pleasure involved! Am now doing two nights a week with Rex Stewart in a little beer joint in Cucamonga (60 miles from my house) for which they pay us $20 a night. Saturday was the best I've ever heard Rex play (since the old Ellington days, that is). We had a marvelous drummer, Buzz Daniels, who is first guy who has ever reminded me of Big Sid. Rex did everything, growled, played high, low, talked at 'em, but couldn't get a reaction."

Early in November 1962, Cary joined Ben Pollack's Dixieland band playing at the Knickerbocker Hotel. The pay was $115 a week for six nights, with Sundays off. He played trumpet and then piano with the Pic-A-Rib Boys, the first personnel being Cary, trumpet, Warren Smith, trombone, Gene Bolen, clarinet, Bill Campbell, piano,

Walt Yoder, bass, and Pollack, drums. The group was seen on the "Jazz Scene USA" television show. Cary left the band when, playing some typically tasteful piano, Pollack accused him of playing bop! He told Ken Gallacher: "God knows I wish I had the technique to be able to play with men like Donald Byrd and Dizzy." After his last night with the band, on February 8, 1963, Cary expressed "great relief." (But one wonders if his decision to take "off from the hotel job for Newporter Inn job with Murray McEachern" on the 6th played its part. For this gig he played with McEachern, trombone, Vi Winters, piano, Jerry King, fender bass, and Betty O'Hara, and with McEachern doubling on alto sax, plus Cary and O'Hara's versatility, variety was assured.)

On February 13, Cary signed at the unemployment office, but the single dates continued:

February 9: L.A. Athletic Club—trio gig
February 11: round dance recording session—with Jerry Vaughn
February 13/14/15: The Quail—subbing for pianist Tommy Todd with Pete Beilmann
February 16: La Canada Country Club—trio gig, incl. Gene Walsh, drums
February 17: Comet Lanes—with "all Welk guys"—probably country & western date
February 23: Catholic church on Nordhoff—played bass with Woody Standsburg, piano, Vince Perry, drums
March 1/2 : Bedouin, Huntington Park—with Buddy Ray, guitar
March 3: with Bob Lido, violin, and Neil Levang, guitar, Buddy Hayes, bass, & Kimmel
March 10: Comet Lanes—with Bob Lido
March 12: Palladium—rehearsal only? for Russ Klein, reeds—with Dick Cathcart, trumpet, Bob Havens, trombone, Don Bonnee, reeds, Cary, piano, Neil Levang, guitar, Buddy Hayes, bass, John Klein, drums
March 13: Helen O'Connell date for Navy recruiting show.
March 17: Comet Lanes—with Bob Lido
March 19: Plane to San Jose—with Lawrence Welk's jazz band. Also at concert were Sons of the Pioneers, Page Cavanaugh's septet ("good") et al.

March 23:	Disneyland Hotel—with Murray McEachern band, George Werth, Joe Cook, trumpets, Betty O'Hara, trombone?, Herbie Stewart, Don Raffell, reeds, Cary, piano, Ray Leatherwood, bass, Jerry King, drums. "Arrangements sounded fine—my best since California."
March 24:	Comet Lanes (?)—with Bob Lido, violin, and Buddy Hayes, bass
April 6:	Handlebar—with Wally Holmes, trumpet, Bus Bassey, reeds, Earl Smith, drums
April 7:	Comet Lanes (?)—with Bob Lido
April 8:	square dance date
April 12/13:	Handlebar

On April 20, Cary was in another band led by Murray McEachern, at the Bermuda Dunes in Palm Desert, where they played in a marquee. This was a 15-piece orchestra which included Conrad Gozzo, Ollie Mitchell, trumpets, Betty O'Hara, Vern Friley, trombones, Bud Shank, Bill Usselton, saxes, Don Bagley, bass, and Frank Capp, drums. "Mostly Basie arrangements. Murray led band but let Capp have his way a lot." O'Hara and Cary also played in a trio prior to the concert, as well as performing "for Sonny Burke and guests in club house, 1:30 to 3:00."

The Quail, the Handlebar and Comet Lanes were the main sources of employment for a few weeks. He was at the Handlebar on Fridays and Saturdays, with Paul Scott on clarinet, and the Comet on Sundays. The bowling alley job ended on May 19 and the Handlebar about the middle of July, the same time he realised: "I guess I'm not hired for the circus this season, so I'll do Quail Thursday, Friday and Saturday."

In fact, work at The Quail continued at least until the middle of August, when his 1963 entries end, but may have run on further into the year. Thursdays and Fridays at the club were generally quiet, with only Saturdays providing good business. One night in July he mentions a singer, ventriloquist and comics being present and on August 10 he wrote: "Quail better—a good old comic there." A week before, on the Friday, it was: "Quail dead. I get a terrible feeling of being completely degraded in this little San Fernando valley p.pot."

There were four other one-off jobs during the period, including a round dance date on May 22, a wedding party (with

Jessie in a quartet) and two hotel bookings, plus an 11-day engagement in San Diego, starting on May 18. During the first four days, which were reserved for rehearsals of the orchestra and show, Cary was able to commute to Los Angeles to fulfil his other commitments. The show ran between May 22 and May 26, but Cary gives no other information, except that Joe Hayes was the director and the "opening show went fair."

There was a small burst of jazz activity starting on June 22, when he played the El Caballero Country Club, on trumpet, with Pete Beilmann, trombone, Bob McCracken, clarinet, Stan Wrightsman, piano, and bass and drums. This was followed by a band concert the next afternoon at McArthur Park. On the 26th, Beilmann, McCracken, Wrightsman, Cary, with Eddie Shrivanek, banjo, and Joe Rushton, reeds, played briefly at the poolside of the Ambassador Hotel for a Wall Street Journal cocktail party—which seems rather a waste of good musicians. Cary and Wrightsman were also in a band on the 28th which played for the Rotary Club at the Sportsman Lodge, North Hollywood, together with Moe Schneider, trombone, Wayne Songer, clarinet, Ray Leatherwood, bass, and Nick Fatool, drums.

Uncertainty is the only certainty in a musician's life, as illustrated by the fact that early in April Jessie had no bookings and it may have been a month before she was in work again. Other domestic news was that Judy was married on June 22 to Dr. Alan Bernstein. In May the following year, Cary's first grandchild was born, Mathew Alan Bernstein. And Jessie celebrated her birthday on July 23.

During the summer, Cary was involved in a great deal of rehearsal activity. In addition to the Monday nights with Kay Carlson's band and occasional work with the Art Depew band, he also wrote for a "rock and roll big band," for which he presumably played as well. For July 14 he noted: "Kay's rehearsal band finally gets paid for a public performance." This was for a "Jazz at the Beach" concert at the Venice bandstand, featuring the Rex Stewart Sextet and the Kay Carlson 19-piece orchestra. Cary was the arranger, one of the soloists and composer of several of the numbers played.

Solo dates interspersed with the above included June 30 at the Vegas Club, Oxnard—"3 strippers and singer"; on July 2 a round dance date, with Stan Wrightsman, et al.; and on July 4, at Long Beach Yacht Club, "Jessie and I played with [bassist] Jess Flores' quintet."

Trombonist Pete Beilmann was involved with the Westchester Music School and he arranged for Cary to fill-in for a sick teacher, starting on Thursday, August 1. His schedule that day was for nineteen pupils, with just nine attending. The following Thursday the attendance had grown to eleven. His diary for 1963 ended on August 12, so how long he played the part of a school teacher is unknown.

No doubt the balance of 1963 was completed in much the same way as the first half and the year ended with a New Year's Eve visit to see Jessie, who was playing at a club called "Marsal's" in Southgate ("about half-a-dozen people in all night").

1964 now promised to bring with it longer travel and greater appreciation, as well as a reunion with old friends.

13. Down Under and Disneyland (1964–1968)

New Year's Day 1964 found Cary playing solo piano at a bar called Chum's, in Burbank across from the NBC Studios, and on the 7th he began work there on a regular basis—but not for long. His first-night comment was: "one singer after another—night goes fast." Because he "felt lousy" he sent in a substitute on January 15 and 16, and as a result the substitute was given the job, starting February 11!

In between these dates, on January 9, he "sidelined" on piano for an episode of the TV series "Temple Houston" and on the 26th he, Bob McCracken and Pete Beilmann played at a new apartment building, ending up by the pool. There was a church job with a quartet on February 1, followed by his last night at Chum's on the 8th, then the following:

February 12: The Ranch Club, Palm Springs—trumpet "with local trio"
February 14: (day) Disneyland—piano with the Disneyland band.
(night) Mint Canyon Community Hall—"a sheriff's posse dance" in quartet, including Tom Suthers, tenor, Vince Perry, drums.
February 15: Masonic Hall on Tujunga—in a trio
February 22: no location—hired by tenorist Don Raffell for trio job.

About this time, as he wrote to Ken Gallacher, he worked with the Pat Brady trio. "My last job has been with a trio, mainly accompanying all kinds of singers, pros, amateurs, hustlers, everyone sang. It made the nights go faster but the leader, a little Irish drummer named Pat Brady, was pretty unbearable."

There is a four months' gap in the Cary diary for 1964 between February and July, so we do not have his immediate views on the Australia/Japan tour in March, but the trip has been well documented.

International Talent Associates, Inc. had booked Eddie Condon for a tour of Australia, New Zealand and Japan during March and early April. Condon was to front a group which was well-accustomed to playing together, consisting as it did of Buck Clayton, trumpet, Vic Dickenson, trombone, Pee Wee Russell, clarinet, Bud Freeman, tenor, Dick Cary, piano, alto horn, Eddie Condon, guitar, Jack Lesberg, bass, Cliff Leeman, drums, and Jimmy Rushing, vocals. Lesberg, who for a time worked in Australia, had organised the band and his friend Kym Bonython had planned the Australian part of the tour. Condon was very ill, but made the tour regardless. Cary met the band in San Francisco, where they played two nights at Turk Murphy's club, Earthquake McGoon's.

> *We'd been on the plane for twenty-five hours and we were ready for the bar. Or at least the men's room. They stuck us in this [press] room; they start with the cameras and the first guy says to Eddie, "Eddie, since you grew up the guitar's changed quite a bit. What do you think of the guitar today? The electric guitar?" And Eddie looked at the guy and said, "I think they're dangerous!"*

Eddie Condon Far East tour, March 1964

Cary, a-h; Pee Wee Russell, cl.

(Photograph by Masao Ogawa. Courtesy: Dick Cary Archive)

Eddie Condon Far East tour, March 27, 1964

Condon, g; Cary, a-h.

(Photograph by Jyunichi Kawai. Courtesy: Dick Cary Archive)

The known itinerary is:

March 1 & 2:	Earthquake McGoon's
March 3:	flew to Sydney, arriving there March 5, a.m.
March 5:	flew to Adelaide
March 6–10:	concerts at the Regent Theatre, as part of the Adelaide Arts Festival; evening concerts on March 6, 7 & 10; midnight concerts on 9 & 10
March 11–12:	flew to Melbourne; evening concerts at Melbourne Festival Hall, plus morning telecast on March 11
March 13:	flew to Sydney—evening concert at the Sydney Stadium
March 14:	afternoon and evening concerts at the Sydney Stadium
March 15:	flew to Auckland, New Zealand—two evening concerts at each of the following venues:
March 16:	Town Hall, Auckland
March 17:	Embassy Theatre, Hamilton
March 18:	Town Hall, Wellington
March 19:	Town Hall, Dunedin
March 20:	Civic Theatre, Christchurch
March 21:	flew to Sydney
March 22:	band without Condon, Russell & Rushing flew to Melbourne to appear, afternoon and evening, at The Embers nightclub.
March 23:	flew to Sydney, then on to Tokyo, via Hong Kong
March 24 & 25:	concerts at Hibiya Public Hall, Hibiya Kokaido, Tokyo
March 26:	free day
March 27:	two evening concerts at Festival Hall, Osaka
March 28:	travel
March 29:	free day, unless a concert in Nagoya was a late booking
March 30:	Public Hall, Sapporo
March 31	travel
April 1:	two evening concerts in Kyoto Kaikan
April 2:	two evening concerts at Sankei Hall, Tokyo
April 3:	flew back to U.S.A.

Down Beat reported that upon its return the band was

scheduled to play two more dates at Earthquake McGoon's, but this did not happen. A more detailed account of the Condon tour can be found in "Ding! Ding!, a bio-discographical scrapbook on Vic Dickenson," by Manfred Selchow. Reference can also be made to "Pee Wee Russell: The Life of a Jazzman" by Robert Hilbert. There is no doubt that the tour was very successful, with enthusiastic audiences filling the halls and theatres. Some of the concerts were recorded by the New Zealand Broadcasting Corporation, which arranged the New Zealand tour, and by the Japanese Broadcasting System, resulting in both authorised and pirate record releases.

It is not clear when Cary began working with a Matty Matlock band which included Jackie Coon, cornet, mellophone, Eddie Miller, tenor, Ira Westley, bass, and Nick Fatool, drums. Cary called it "the first good band since being out here. Coon and I do a lot of two horn duets." Later he told Ken Gallacher: "The job with Matty came to an end in July. The manager turned out to be a crook, disappeared, left bad cheques, and shortly thereafter we were through."

When Cary resumed his diary entries on July 8, 1964, it was to report that he had started work at Disneyland for two weeks, later increased to five weeks, deputising for Ed Ericson who was in hospital. He lists the day's routine as:

10:45: march to flagpole
11:30: march to boat
12:00: lunch
 1:00: concert (one hour)
 2:30: Dixieland band (hour on, ½-hour off, hour on, till 5:00)
 5:30: retreat (and home about 7:15)

The full band consisted of 18-pieces, though only Ira Westley, tuba, and Cary, probably on alto horn, are names in jazz discographies. Later Cary mentions being one of the Regency Three playing in the Golden Horseshoe, doing five shows from 9:05 to 1:00. The bassist was Ward Irvin—"plays very well—strong—fine ear. He would have been a great friend of Brad Gowans', Joe Rushton's, etc. The more interesting square pegs in this rotten business—or this fascinating business."

Days at Disneyland permitted gigs to be worked in the evenings and at weekends, including:

July 12: (afternoon) Venice—with Rex Stewart, cornet, Moe Schneider, trombone, Barney Bigard, clarinet, Don Lodice, tenor, Cary, piano, Al Morgan, bass
(evening) Royal Lion—"job ends tonight."

July 18:   "worked in barefoot bar in Laguna with Art Lyons," (clarinet).
July 19:   MacArthur Park—"Jess and I played with Wilkins this afternoon."
July 26:   Venice—jazz band battle—Rex Stewart v Matty Matlock
July 28:   "Job with Jessie at Sir Sica's—crowded as hell"
July 31:   Terminal Island—with Bill Stumpp, trumpet, Jessie Cary, trombone, Art Lyons, clarinet, Cary, piano, Howard Pepe, "terrible bass," Earl Smith, drums.

The Venice engagement on July 26 was typical of the one-off jobs which jazzmen played at this time. It was a Jazz Band Battle, with Rex Stewart's group vying with Matty Matlock's. The personnels included Rex Stewart, cornet, Herbie Harper, trombone, Caughey Roberts, clarinet, Don Lodice, tenor, Johnny Guarnieri, piano, and Al Morgan, bass, opposing Jack Coon, trumpet, Matty Matlock, clarinet, Eddie Miller, tenor, Dick Cary, piano, Ray Leatherwood, bass, and Nick Fatool, drums, with clarinetist Barney Bigard as a guest. Hundreds of similar gigs, usually on a monthly basis, were arranged by such organisations as the New Orleans Jazz Club of California, the New Orleans Jazz Club of Southern California, the Society for the Preservation of Dixieland Jazz, the Southern California Hot Jazz Society and numerous others.

Rex Stewart, trumpet; Jackie Coon, flugelhorn; Bill Bacin; Cary, alto horn.
(Courtesy: Bill Bacin)

Listening to Johnny Guarnieri, Cary commented: "Guarnieri's imitation of Art Tatum was quite amazing. He's much like I am—neither of us has much of anything original to offer as jazz pianists and he's spent many more hours at it than I have. He hates it out here—has been at Plaza piano bar for about a year, I guess."

On July 29 Cary was prepared for a tough few days: "Started a back-breaking schedule. Up at 8 a.m., Disneyland, home at 7:15 p.m., work at night, bed by 3:00 or 3:30 a.m." The work at night was substituting on piano for Bobby Van Eps at the Roaring 20's in a band which included Brodie Schroff, trumpet, Pete Beilmann, trombone, Rick Fay, reeds, and Charlie Lodice, drums. He finished at Disneyland on August 9 and at the Roaring 20's on August 15. Of the latter job his thought was: "I try to look out at all these tourists with their inane requests and lack of attention with some degree of affection, but can't make it."

Apart from a round dance date on August 17, he enjoyed a restful two weeks up to the 23rd, when he was back at Disneyland for a band rehearsal for the premiere of the film "Mary Poppins" which took place on the 27th at Grauman's Chinese Theatre—"Band not good—we played mostly out on the sidewalk, 6:00 to 1:00 a.m., and watched the Cadillacs and Lincolns drive up and disgorge the money'd and the famous."

The afternoon of the 27th, Cary had played at the Ambassador Hotel with Jackie Coon, trumpet, Warren Smith, trombone, Bob McCracken, clarinet, Nappy Lamare, perhaps bass guitar, and Ray Bauduc, drums. Two days later he, Coon, Lamare and Bauduc were in a band with trombonist Abe Lincoln and clarinetist Pete Legare at Chavez Ravine, where Bob Hope opened a stars-versus-agents/union officials softball match. Movie actor Preston Foster joined the band on banjo.

Sunday, August 30, was a big band day. In the afternoon he was at McArthur Park in an orchestra which included six trumpets and two French horns, while in the evening it was a ten-piece unit, conducted by Dick Dale, playing at the Palladium for a Brunswick Company party. The ten men included Dick Cathcart, Bob Havens, Don Bonnee, Mahlon Clark, Buddy Hayes, "lousy electric bass," Neil Levang, guitar, and Johnny Klein, drums.

September 1964 began quietly until Sunday the 6th, when Cary played with the Herb Wilkins band at Hansen Dam Park in the afternoon. The programme included Cary's arrangement of *Caravan*. In the evening he played with Bob Higgins, trumpet, Warren Smith, trombone, Gene Bolen, clarinet, Bill Cooper ("damn him—he brought tuba, not bass fiddle") and Charles Lodice, drums, at a party in Woodland Hills. The following day he had a 10:00 p.m. start at the Statler Hotel, alongside Pete Beilmann, Bob McCracken, Stan Wrightsman, Ray Leatherwood, and Nick Fatool—"What a fine rhythm section; very pleasant job."

On the 8th he recorded a transcription with (or for?) Sonny Anderson with Kay Bell and the Straw Hatters of Dixieland, making the strange comment, "*Saints* in about one take." Then, on the 9th, he had a television "sideline" job: "Long, long day doing sideline on 'Rawhide' at CBS 9:30 to 4:00. I was on about an hour in all—silly song, dummy piano. Barbara Eden and the Cumquats sang and danced. At least the latter was real. Various cowboys came up with gems like 'for a finale she'll tap dance on twelve outstretched tongues.' English director said, 'When the fight starts you ladies scream and then bugger off.'"

Cary and Jessie travelled to Monterey on September 16, for Cary to appear at the jazz festival. Buck Clayton, Vic Dickenson, Pee Wee Russell and Bud Freeman were the frontline when, on the opening night, at the Country Fairgrounds, Friday the 18th, Russell nominally led the Newport All Stars at the Monterey Jazz Festival. They accompanied singer Joe Williams on a couple of tunes. Red Callender, bass, and Earl Palmer, drums, completed the personnel, and Gerry Mulligan, on baritone, sat-in. Cary's feature was, as so often, *Caravan*. "People seemed to like us and the next day the write-ups in the Monterey and Salinas papers said we saved the evening."

His comments on the other bands which played that first night were: "Miles Davis was on quite a while. He'd disappear quite often to the bar for a few doubles. Stops playing anywhere and sticks right forefinger in right ear. Art Farmer followed on flugelhorn—sameness of first two-and-half hours wasn't good." After the All Stars set on the 19th Cary watched the Horace Silver band and Duke Ellington's. He thought the Duke was "marvelous." On the 20th he saw Charlie Mingus and Thelonious Monk, before returning home on the 21st.

The 5th Annual Dixieland at Disneyland festival was held September 25/26 and Cary played trumpet in the Ben Pollack band, alongside Abe Lincoln, trombone, Bob McCracken, clarinet, Don Owens, piano, and Ira Westley, bass. "We play in the island on a large circular stage and there are dancers and stuntmen staging a brawl, then a fire and we're through after two numbers." He also refers to "show on island, then each band to different stands. This part was hard work and I felt for Ira and Don trying to pull Pollack along." The other five bands featured were Kid Ory with The Young Men from New Orleans, Firehouse Five Plus Two, Sweet Emma Barrett, Sharkey Bonano and the Louis Armstrong All Stars.

At the end of the month Cary accepted some substitute work at Disneyland, starting with two days on piano, September 30/October 1, at the Golden Horseshoe, five shows starting at 11:30 and ending at 5:15 p.m. Then from October 3 he began working Saturdays and Sundays on trumpet, 11:30 to 6:00.

At the same time (September 30) he started a job at the Ruben E. Lee, on Route 1 between Balboa and Newport Beach. The band was Jackie Coon, trumpet, Tommy Geckler, trombone, Bill Wood, clarinet, Ray Bauduc, drums, "and self on piano and horn. Nice place, built to look like a three-decker sternwheeler." This job, four nights a week, Wednesday to Saturday continued for six weeks. Cary was ill on November 11 and the following day; "I called to say I wasn't working tonight and heard good news. Coon tells me I'm fired. What a relief—I've been pardoned again."

Together with the Ruben E. Lee and the Disneyland work, Cary was continuing to write and play for the Kay Carlson rehearsal band on Monday evenings and he had also acquired two students for the piano, Judy Berger and Andy Zarchy, son of trumpeter Zeke Zarchy. "Judy OK, but Andy doesn't want to practice, except to improvise." Despite this comment, the lessons continued into the New Year.

In October, Cary learned of the death of another fine lead trumpet player, Conrad Gozzo, commenting: "He seemed to be gradually killing himself; drank continuously to hurt the liver, ate candy for his diabetes." (Cary appears to detect no irony in his mention of Gozzo's drinking habits.)

Other gigs played around this time were:

October 11:	Flintridge—"very nice outdoor affair 4:00 to 8:00—big band"
October 16:	Venetian Room of Ambassador Hotel: with Pete Beilmann, Bob McCracken, Stan Wrightsman, Bob Stone, bass, Ralph Collier, drums
October 25:	Statler Hotel—with same band, without Stone.
October 26/27:	"Pete's job 6:30 to 10:30."
November 13:	Embassy Room, Ambassador Hotel: Rex Stewart leading a big band, 15-piece including Cary, trumpet, Stewart, cornet, Jessie Cary, trombone, Eddie Miller, tenor,

>   Ira Westley, bass, Mickey Sheen, drums.
>   8:00 to 12:30 a.m.
> November 20:   La Salle High, Pasadena—with Bob Havens,
>   trombone, leader, McCracken, Eddie Miller,
>   Wrightsman, Westley, Earl Smith, drums.

Of the Rex Stewart date Cary wrote: "Some of Rex's 'head arrangements' came out very powerful ... Thing was a most formal 'Cotillon' ball." And of the Havens affair: "We never settled down to a real groove all night. Most everything was too fast and Stan battled Earl all the way."

Perhaps it was about this time that the following concert took place at The Lytton Center on Sunset Boulevard:

> "Budd Schulberg presents Contemporary Music and Poetry—
> Music produced and presented by Rex Stewart and Dick Cary."

The band consisted of eleven-pieces, featuring Stewart and Cary on trumpets, with mainly musicians from the Monday night rehearsal group, but with Jesse Price on drums.

Cary's spell at Disneyland ended on November 21 with five shows in the Golden Horseshoe. Then came some days of "resting," except for lessons for Amy and Andy Zarchy and the usual Monday night rehearsal, followed by a television sideline job for three days, December 2–4. This was for a series called "Bailey's of Balboa" and Cary was on set for 12 hours on two of the days and for 8 on the other. "Eight of us, plus four actors. Enjoyed this. Very little work. Enjoyed Paul Ford, Stirling Holloway and John Dehner. Paul is conductor of the Bailey's Landing 12-piece band." The payment for these three days was $156. Cary also refers to receiving a cheque for $34 for sideline work on a programme called, it seems, 'Roshes.' Jessie too did some sideline work and is "seen briefly, twice, in 'My Fair Lady.'"

> December 5:   Westchester—with Beilmann, Wrightsman,
>   Fatool, bass & accordion
> December 11:   Nicodell's—Greek Christmas party, 7:30 to
>   10:15. $45.00
> December 12:   "Fine job at night"—with 8-piece including
>   Gordon Mitchell, trombone, leader, Joe
>   Darensbourg, clarinet, Bill Mitchell, piano,
>   Johnny St. Cyr, guitar/banjo
> December 13:   morning: Wilmington Pier, for arrival of

      Israel boat—with Herb Wilkins band, including Jessie
      afternoon: Pasadena—with Zep Meissner, clarinet, Ed Anderson, trombone, Howard Koster, "and some broad who had tassels jiggling all over"
December 16: Round dance record date
December 18: Knollwood—with Gordon and Dixie Mitchell, guitar, Andy Blakeney, trumpet, Floyd Stone, reeds, Bill Mitchell, Johnny St. Cyr, Gene Washington, drums

  Pianist Bill Mitchell recalled playing the two gigs with Cary in Gordon Mitchell's Crown City Jazz Band. "He showed a sly and mordant sense of humor. Also referred to the San Fernando Valley, where he lived, as a 'cultural wasteland.' [The Crown City Jazz Band] was a 'laid-back,' fraternal outfit. Gordon would get remunerative casuals and use some of the old time greats (John St. Cyr, Andy Blakeney, Joe Darensbourg, Tudi Garland, Barney Bigard, George Orendorff, Dick Cary, etc). It was always a thrill for some of us lesser lights to play alongside them." Gordon Mitchell (1912–1981) was one of the founders of the Southern California Hot Jazz Society.

  The Christmas period is not documented but Cary spent the 1965 New Year holiday at the "Marine Air Force Base" in Yuma, Arizona, playing in a quintet, the personnel for which was: Jim Whitwood, trombone, Billy Miles, reeds, Frank Logar, drums, and, one assumes, Cary on trumpet and Kathy Donovan, piano. The job finished at 1:30 a.m. on January 1 and he drove home directly afterwards. "On the trip to Yuma, round trip almost exactly 550 miles, I was surprised to get almost 16 miles a gallon on the Olds."

  Jessie was working at lounges like the Oasis and the 55 Club, while Cary's number of pupils had grown to four, Judy Berger, Amy and Andy Zarchy, and now Kathy Donovan.

  Stan Kenton's Neophonic Orchestra opened at the New Music Center on January 4 and Cary asked himself: "Wonder if I can ever get something done by them?" Several weeks later he was still asking himself the same question, but it seems that this ambitious idea never got beyond the wishful stage. Even a year later, after hearing a Kenton album ("intricate writing"), he was still trying to decide.

January 9:   Westwood Village Exchange Club, Miramar—with Gordon Mitchell, Floyd Stone, soprano, tenor, Bill Mitchell, piano, Dixie Mitchell, guitar, Johnny St. Cyr, banjo, Tommy Johnson, tuba, Teddy Edwards, drums
January 11:   round dance record date, including Wayne Songer, reeds
January 15:   pizza joint in Garden Grove—with Bill Perkins, drums, Joe Bowers, bass, Dean Honey, clarinet
January 22:   same venue and group
January 29:   Oasis—Cary subbed for Jessie.
February 6:   Y.W.C.A.—with Gordon Mitchell, Joe Darensbourg, Bill Mitchell, Dixie Mitchell, Gene Washington, and "Jim"
February 12:   Disneyland 10:15 to 5:30—no details
February 13:   Lodge Hall, Tujunga Avenue—with Bill Perkins, Dean Honey
February 18:   Los Angeles Athletic Club—with Gene Walsh, guitar, and Clint----.

On February 19, Cary started work at the Beverly Cavern for a week, with Pepe, leader [probably Hal Peppie, trumpet], Art Lyons, clarinet, Warren Smith, trombone, and Lou Diamond, drums. "Art Lyons' boarder plays bass both nights for nil, but what a help. I enjoyed playing [but] the piano is frightful." And on the 27th he noted: "Well, it was a pleasant job, but like the very few good ones, this must end also. New manager next week, no licence."

For two Saturdays, February 20 and 27, Cary helped Barrett O'Hara by tutoring some of O'Hara's pupils, and he himself was still coaching the Zarchys and Judy Berger, as well as, now, Jimmy Baron, and the 14-year-old Mike Smitzer. Outside of music he was playing the occasional game of softball and, more frequently, golf. Some of his partners included Rex Stewart and Herbie Harper. On March 3 he exclaimed: "A phenomenal thing—birdie, birdie, par, birdie on first four holes! Ended up with 40 however" over nine holes.

The Monday night rehearsals continued, but on Tuesday, January 19, 1965, Cary organised his own rehearsal group—"Prepared food and rehearsal space in rear house and about 10:45 we got going, with Art DePew, trumpet, Bob Davis, alto, clarinet, Bob Havens, trombone, Ward Erwin, bass, Neil Levang, guitar, Charlie Lodice, drums. I had prepared *Jeannie, Nobody Knows, Deep River* and *Greensleeves*."

This was the first of Cary's band rehearsals, as opposed to those for the Brass Quintet and Brass Quartet, and they continued on an occasional basis. They would not become a regular weekly event yet awhile.

On Monday, March 1, 1965, the Kay Carlson rehearsal was enlivened by the presence, non-playing, of two great jazz musicians—"Benny Carter came with Rex Stewart and the two ladies. Stayed whole time—quite complimentary."

Also in the first week in March he played at Edwards Air Force Base with Doug Ingle, trumpet, Warren Smith, trombone, Gene Bolen, clarinet, and Roy Rootin, "one of worst drummers I've heard yet." On the Friday, March 5, they played for the Officers' Club dance, and the next day at the N.C.O.'s Club.

There is then an eight-week break in the 1965 diary, followed by entries for a few days in May which refer to two evenings of rehearsals, plus "debut of octet—Art DePew, trumpet, Hoyt Bohannon, trombone, Al Lasky, Mike Simpson, Dick Holgate, reeds, Cary, piano, Ward Erwin, bass, Charlie Lodice, drums. What a good group. Rex Stewart played *In a Mellotone* with us." This octet played Sunday afternoon, May 16, at La Canada High School and probably at St. Augustine's High School in San Diego on the 17th and another school in the Los Angeles area on the 18th. The octet personnel is built around the musicians who were rehearsing at Cary's home.

Cary ignored his diary for the rest of the year, but no major changes to his routine are known, except that he was willing to work with Bob Crosby. Sometime in the 1960s, trombonist Bob Havens worked at Disneyland with the Bob Cats and he told the author that Dick Cary did most of the trumpet work and that other regulars were Eddie Miller, tenor, and Ben Pollack, drums. A 1965 photograph of the Crosby orchestra shows 14-pieces, this time including Dick Cary at the piano. In September 1965 Cary was at Disneyland, playing trumpet in Bob Havens' band for a Benson Curtis radio broadcast. Others present included Matty Matlock, clarinet, Stan Wrightsman, piano, and Tudi Garland, bass. He also played on at least one of the monthly sessions which trumpeter Bob Higgins organised for patients at the Camarillo State Hospital.

Towards the end of 1965 Cary worked three sideline jobs, but there are no details for them, or for another at Columbia a little later.

His comment on the first month of 1966 was: "January was as dead a month as always. No word from [Johnny] Ukelele about Las Vegas and no reaction from Tony Bennett." Did he send an arrangement to Tony Bennett on spec. or was he asked to provide

Bob Crosby and his Orchestra at Disneyland
Dick Cary at the piano
(Courtesy: Dick Cary Archive)

1966. l-r: Cary, Nappy Lamare, Bob McCracken, Bob Higgins,
Nick Fatool, Moe Schneider
(Photograph by Ed Lawless. Courtesy of Bill Bacin)

one? So many questions! At least the Monday night rehearsals continued, there was an occasional rehearsal by an Art DePew big band, and he still had three of his pupils, Andy, Jimmy and Mike, joined at the end of February by "young Thom."

He did a Pabst beer jingle for Marty Berman—"Played horn. Berman contractor and bass sax, Bob Florence on piano, a banjo and drums"—on January 27, and on the 29th there was a job with drummer Vince Perry, a pianist, and a tenor (Irving Roth?). "I played bass, trumpet, horn." February continued the dearth of work:

February 12: afternoon—Woman's Club, Westchester—"played bass with Vince Perry, Irving Roth, Frank Morocco"
evening—Ambassador Hotel (a Zaid job)—3 brass, 3 saxes, 3 rhythm, including pianist Don Abney, "who sounded great. Old friend from years ago at Condon's"
February 13: Disneyland—10:30 to 5:30, piano in Strawhatter
February 18: Sepulveda Recreation Centre: with Bobby Esser, drums, Red Murphy, guitar, Al Jordan
February 19: church—piano with Vince Perry, Irv Roth and Paul Toenniges, bass

On March 1, he and Jessie drove to Palm Springs where Cary was to work with singer/comedian Phil Harris and his wife, Alice Faye. The rehearsal and show took place on the 2nd at the Chi Chi, with a band worth naming in full: John Best, Dick Cary, trumpets, Pete Beilmann, Moe Schneider, trombones, Wayne Songer, Matty Matlock, Eddie Miller, John Rotella, reeds, Stan Wrightsman, piano, Ray Leatherwood, bass, Nick Fatool, drums, and Joe Venuti, violin.

March 7: Governor's rally on Wilshire Boulevard—with Warren Smith, Nappy Lamare and Rollie Culver, 11:30 to 2:00
"The candidate even shook hands with us."
March 13/14: rehearsals with The Drake Sisters, but no subsequent show mentioned
March 17: "Esser called to talk about free record date— polkas for a Crown album"
March 25: recorded a jingle with "a gal singer—one hour—pleasant easy date." The band was Cary, trumpet, Phil Gray, trombone, Matty Matlock, clarinet, Ray Leatherwood, bass, Nick Fatool, drums

March 26:   Roaring '20s party at El Caballero, Tarzana—with Pete Beilmann. "Stan, Ray and Nick, the old rhythm section, were thoroughly subdued. We were denied use of (a) grand piano, (b) microphone, (c) food, (d) booze and (e) hospitality"

Cary's last gig in March was on the 29th when he played trumpet in a twelve-piece band at the Beverly Hilton, backing singer Anthony Newley and someone named as "Janet." He refers to Newley's "very pleasant and efficient pianist, conductor, writer, Ian Fraser." They rehearsed from 3:30 to 6:00, played dinner music at 8:00 and for the show at 9:00. "We played Janet, Rowan and Martin [comedians] and Tony Newley at 10:30."

Writing on April 1, Cary said: "These have been leanest three months of my professional life since Connecticut days." He then refers to "Mark McIntyre has given me a measure of optimism," which probably indicates that he is hoping for more jingle work. That same evening he and Jessie began working as a duo at Colbert's, Fridays and Saturdays, with Cary playing "two horns, bass and occasional piano." One Friday was an "awful long night," whereas another was "easy," with the added benefit of Matty Matlock as a sitter-in. A Saturday comment was: "To work at 8:30—loaded with singers of all kinds."

Prior to Cary's 1966 diary ending in the middle of April, there were typical one-off gigs:

April 10:   Shadow Hills church—played second trumpet in Betty O'Hara's trio at two performances
April 12:   round dance recording
April 16:   Oak Room—lunch and fashion show for cerebral palsy charity—with Betty O'Hara

They played three numbers and Cary "noodled" on piano behind models.

This was the start of a nineteen-month gap in his diary-keeping. Perhaps the job at Colbert's continued for a time and no doubt the rehearsals with Kay Carlson on Mondays and the "octet" on Wednesdays were a regular routine. (The octet at this time was built around Dick Collins, trumpet, Bob Havens, trombone, Matty Matlock, clarinet, and Eddie Miller, tenor.). In September 1966 he was invited to the three day Aspen Jazz Party, organised by Dick Gibson at the Hotel Jerome in Aspen, Colorado. The party was held over the weekend of September 16–18, with Buck Clayton, trumpet,

New Orleans Jazz Club session, Los Angeles, May 1966
Cary, tp; Eddie Miller, ts; Warren Smith, tb.
(Miller hit his head on Bill Bacin's garage door, hence the plaster.)
(Photograph by Don and Lura Larkin. Courtesy Bill Bacin)

1966. l-r: Cary, Matty Matlock, Eddie Miller, Warren Smith, Max Murray
(Photograph by Don and Lura Larkin. Courtesy of Bill Bacin)

Ed Hall, clarinet, Eddie Miller, tenor, Teddy Wilson, piano, George Van Eps, guitar, and Jack Lesberg, bass, among the other musicians.

It would appear that Cary's career changed little during the remainder of 1966 and for almost all of 1967, as the two known gigs indicate.

I played one night with Smokey Stover with Wild Bull (sic) and Abe Lincoln.

This refers to cornetist Wild Bill Davison's four-day engagement, June 21–24, 1967, at Norm Brown's Club in Long Beach, with Lincoln, trombone, and Stover, drums, when Davison was paid with a cheque that bounced.

Rex Stewart died suddenly on September 7, 1967, and the band which played at his funeral four days later included Cary on alto horn, Teddy Buckner, Norman Bowden, trumpets, Barney Bigard, Bob McCracken, Sammy Lee, reeds, Ira Westley, bass, and Edgar Hayes, organ.

Work had no doubt continued to be scarce because, when Cary resumes his diary in December 1967, it is to tell of a pet hate, being on the road. He started a nine-day tour as pianist with Bill Page and his orchestra on December 1. The little-known Page led a band of three brass, two reeds, four rhythm, three strings and an organ (Allan Stevenson), plus two bandboys and a technician. There were shows or dances in Minneapolis, Wauhegan, Dayton (Ohio), Greenville, Youngstown, and St. Joseph ("Directly to Silver Beach and Shadowland—first good sized audience and show went well, 8:00 to 10:30"), but one in Bloomington was cancelled. This trip ended December 9 with a second day in St. Joseph for afternoon and evening concerts at the local high school.

There were a few more dates with Bill Page once they returned to Los Angeles. On December 12 there was a poorly attended concert at a large auditorium in Bakersfield and on December 31/January 1 the band, eight-pieces ("mostly my library"), played the International Ballroom of the Beverly Hilton. January 6, 1968, a quintet played for Elks No. 99 and on the 12th a Page octet was back at the Beverly Hilton, in the Versailles Room—"extremely dull group."

Other December 1967 dates were:

December 15: Statler-Hilton—with drummer Lex Golden's octet, which included Moe Schneider, trombone, Bill Hood, reeds, Tom Wolfe, piano.

December 16: St. Sava Hall, San Gabriel—Cary led band, with Abe Lincoln, trombone, Jay St. John,

	clarinet, Stan Wrightsman, piano, Ray Leatherwood, bass, Nick Fatool, drums. "Brought vibes, trumpet and bedpan."
December 17:	unknown location—with Lincoln, St. John, Leatherwood, Jack Coon, trumpet, Morey Feld, drums

Drummer George Defebaugh obtained a job playing for a credit company's Christmas party at the Newporter Inn on December 21, commencing at 7:15. Cary, piano, and Lou Herwig, guitar, completed the trio. "The three of us played for dancing till 10:20, when a bad clarinet player and Al Jenkins arrived. Shortly after this a note was sent up to the stand saying, "Please! no more Dixieland." George was at a bit of a loss, since Dixieland is all he ever played. No one knew any of the current hits although we struggled through *Watermelon Man* and a couple of spurious twists. But having a few snorts on the job is something I haven't done in so long, 'twas a pleasure, although the band was so bad. It's refreshing to hear Al Jenkins' full trombone sound!"

On the 23rd Cary played at a surprise party for trombonist Moe Schneider before moving on to Donte's to hear the Benny Carter group—Carter, alto, Billy Byers, trombone, Jimmy Jones, piano, with bass and drums. He was reminded of Jones "working with us at Duane's in 1950s, Max Kaminsky, Bob Wilber, etc." "Benny Carter does everything in a self-conscious, exact way with absolutely no spark, and as a contrast Byers plays so much trombone it's almost a bore, though it is quite remarkable. I've never heard anyone get over the trombone quite that much. It reminds me of what Miff Mole used to tell me, that he played so many notes and couldn't help it!"

Cary reports that the "kids had a fine time" on Christmas Day. "Even old Scrooge enjoyed it!" However, on the 29th he commented, "Depressed and lonesome" and the main reason for that was Jessie's absence. Early in December, after visiting her sister in Chicago, she had travelled to New York to rehearse with the touring company of the musical "Cabaret." The rehearsals began on the 11th and, to quote Cary, "I think there could be nothing much more enjoyable than opening in New Haven on December 23rd with an exciting absolutely proven hit. I hope it snows opening night. What an atmosphere of a fine season and a fine sense of theatrical achievement. This in spite of fact that I can't stand that shitty music and those voices—ugh—has nothing to do with the aforementioned case. Jessie and I agreed it was better to get sick of crap than to have, say, a Harold Arlen score become boring and redundant."

He also noted: "I miss Jessie, although she wouldn't agree with my living room decor," but he was not to see her again until "Cabaret" arrived in Los Angeles in May, 1968.

"Marian McPartland will show my efforts to Tony Bennett's arranger," says an entry on January 19, 1968, and this is followed by the note: "Only three dates in January—whee!!" These would have been the three with Bill Page shown above. A few days later, on the 23rd and 24th he lists, mysteriously, "Warwick to work from 11:30 to 6:00 with Brad Plunkett on brass tone divider!" On the 27th he was at the Balboa Bay Club for a "pretty easy job" with drummer Bobby Esser, pianist Gene Garf and bassist (?) Bill Norman. The day after he was on trumpet with his usual friends for an afternoon concert at the Camarillo Hospital—Moe Schneider, trombone, Matty Matlock, clarinet, Stan Wrightsman, piano, Ray Leatherwood, bass, Ralph Collier, drums. On the 29th he had an interesting if frustrating day at the El Dorado in Palm Springs with Matlock and Wrightsman. "Molly Bee wasted 45-minutes when we should have been playing—got going at 8:15 for one set, then Bob Hope came on, followed by Jim Backus, Ray Bolger, etc."

Entries for the rest of 1968 are few, with May, July, August, and October through December completely blank. He notes that starting February 16 he will have lessons with Dr. Joseph Wagner on Fridays at 11 a.m. This tuition would continue into 1969.

Cary does mention that during February he played one Saturday at Disneyland and had one-off gigs with Sigi Rodman and Bobby Esser, for whom he was also writing arrangements.

The only session given for March is on the 27th, when in company with Ralph Harden, Abe Lincoln, Jay St. John, Ray Leatherwood, Bill Newman and a drummer, he played for disabled people in Burbank—another "very pleasant job." In April there was a round dance recording session and he also mentions a concert which Gordon Mitchell "put on with about 25 people at the Pasadena Playhouse—quite a good crowd." (This took place on April 1, 1968, An Historical Review of Classic New Orleans Style, under the auspices of the Southern California Hot Jazz Society, and included Barney Bigard, Joe Darensbourg, Alton Purnell, Ed Garland and John Lucas.) "Then there was the Saturday evening Abe Lincoln and I were professional guests of the 'Maestros.'" And on April 27 he was due to appear in Phoenix with Stan Wrightsman in a twelve-piece band fronted by Phil Harris.

Cary was signed up by Bill Bacin for the First Monterey

Monterey Dixieland Festival, May 11, 1968
Barney Bigard, c; Cary, a-h; Bob Havens, tb.   *(Courtesy: Bill Bacin)*

Dixieland Festival on May 10 and 11. He played trumpet, alto horn and piano with the Los Angeles All Star Band—Bob Havens, trombone, Barney Bigard, clarinet, Alton Purnell, piano, Ed Garland, bass, and Ben Pollack, drums. Trumpeter and singer Wingy Manone was the guest star.

Then on or about May 20, 1968, the touring company of "Cabaret" opened in Los Angeles, with Dick Cary as a member of the pit orchestra and his wife, Jessie, in the cast on stage. Cary remained with the show for its sixteen week run in Los Angeles and this is how he wrote about his September activities in his only diary entry for the last six months of the year. September 24: "'Cabaret' has run its 16 weeks and pushed on to Santa Fe with Jessie. I am again a bachelor, for probably well over a year. I played each and every performance—only fell off wagon twice, both at Sunday parties. Still with Dr. Wagner. Have had several Brass Quintet rehearsals—two of which have been a shambles due to a certain R. Maltbie [sic] sitting-in. [Although initially a trumpet player, Richard Maltby was best known as a bandleader and arranger.] On Sunday we had Uan Rasey and no interference and it was beautiful. Made my third Monday rehearsal (Kay Carlson) band meeting last night—third since show ended. First two were at old Ollie Mitchell studio which I hate.

But last night it was a Unitarian church on 8th Street near Vermont—excellent. Last Thursday/Friday I got two five-hour days at Disneyland, Burbank, playing Louis parts. Band on Friday was Matty Matlock [clarinet], Marvin Ash [piano], Don Kinch [trumpet], Roy Harte [drums], George Bruns [tuba] and vocalists Phil Harris and Scatman Crothers."

Another jazz party to which Cary was invited in 1968 and in subsequent years was that organised by Doctors Bill MacPherson and George Tyler for The Blue Angel Jazz Club. The first was held on December 28, 1968, at the University Club of Pasadena, with an all-star personnel, as the discography shows. Proceedings at all the parties were taped and Cary can be heard on several of the LPs which resulted.

During 1968, Cary philosophised about the state of the world (racial tensions, the Vietnam war, the Israel-Arab conflict) and about his own music and the music business. On February 4, he wrote down some of his frustrations: "Why does Herb Alpert make several hundred grand a year & Hall Overton has to spend his life teaching to be able to afford having a string quartet copied. A man can study music for 50 years—practise—learn to write—have a conscience which tears him up when he has to play shit—but he'll never in these 50 years make as much as a 'beetle' or a 'monkey' does in one year. How about a society which also makes it big for Mrs. Miller and Tiny Tim—makes Lombardo & Welk richer than Art Tatum & puts a Phineas Newborn in & out of Camarillo. Oh, we're in great shape; can't even put a little bitty country in Asia down on its knees."

"I had a strong inclination to write Harvey Phillips at the New Eng. Conservatory—to see if eventually I could get some type of job & compose—teach etc in an atmosphere of learning—instead of this one here. I love this home & Jessie but am so depressed and discouraged with my work—I can't stand much more of this. I know no contractors and no one wants what I write. Got to make some adjustment—& this addlepated idiot who walks in and out is either simple minded or plain stupid & hostile to any form of advancement or schedule or development. Got to move someday!!—HELP !!"

Dick Cary would have to wait until the 1970s before receiving wider appreciation as a jazz musician, but it was only with the rehearsal band that he was able to find fulfilment as an arranger.

Dick Cary hitting a home run? Studio City, March 2, 1968
"2 out—last of tenth—Jerry on third—ball went by short-stop and we won 12–11.
Double in 9th started 5 run rally to tie 11–11."

(Courtesy: Dick Cary Archive)

14. Blue Angels and the World's Greatest (1969–1972)

Despite his reservations about Richard Maltby's trumpet playing four months earlier, Dick Cary acted as contractor for him on New Year's Eve, putting together a 13-piece band to play at the Balboa Bay Club. He was also with Maltby on January 25 at the Elks in Santa Monica.

His few jobs at the start of 1969 also included:
January 6: round dance record date
January 18: Altadena Country Club—with a pianist, Ira Westley, bass, and, it seems, Doctor Bill MacPherson, drums
January 21: Mediterranean—with Betty O'Hara, Ira Westley. Cary on electric piano.
January 24: private party—with O'Hara & Westley. Cary on electric piano.

Cary's comment on this beginning to the year was: "Seems to me I'm gradually retiring [but] not because I want to."

During January and February he rehearsed a singer, or perhaps a dancer, called Jackie Britt, and accompanied her at auditions, including one for the show "Hair." Lessons with Wagner were continuing and on January 3 he noted: "We're on the Kennan Counterpoint book, two or three part inventions—nearing the fugue." A month later he had a "good lesson on the fugue," but the following week, "Got mad and frustrated at getting nowhere with fugue!"

There is an entry on Saturday, March 15, to list a date with George Defebaugh at the Antelope Country Club and that, to all intents and purposes, closes the 1969 diary.

In February 1969, Bill MacPherson and George Tyler, producers of the Blue Angel Jazz Club parties and records, travelled with Dick Cary to Sunnie's Rendezvous in Aspen, Colorado, to record his engagement there. Sunnie, pianist Ralph Sutton's wife, ran the club and her husband provided the music. Cary was booked for three nights, the 10th to the 12th, and was mainly featured on trumpet and alto horn, accompanied by Ralph Sutton, Al Hall, bass, and Cliff Leeman, drums, though he did play some piano solos. An Arbors CD contains a number of these recordings. Two weeks later, on the 24th, Cary and Jimmy McPartland were interviewed on the "We Call It Music" radio show.

One can be reasonably confident that 1969 and 1970 followed the pattern of previous years in Los Angeles, with the rehearsal bands a regular fixture on Mondays and Tuesdays, myriad single jobs for dances and weddings and cocktail parties and the occasional jazz club, mixed in with a square dance recording session or two and many a "rest" day.

Jessie was still travelling with the musical "Cabaret." It was due to close in Chicago on March 8 and the tour would continue around the country until its final night in Columbus, Ohio, on September 27.

Duke Ellington was born on April 29, 1899, and on his 70th birthday he was the honoured guest at a White House party. On May 13, 1969, the President, Richard Nixon, "signed" a letter to Dick Cary, sent via Louis Bellson, which said: "I want to thank you for contributing your arrangements for the Duke Ellington birthday celebration." No details of Cary's actual contribution have been traced and Cary is not mentioned in the notes to the Blue Note CD issue of the proceedings.

The 1969 Blue Angel Jazz Club party was held on November 1st, with Cary featured on trumpet and piano, playing with such Hollywood luminaries as John Best, trumpet, Bob Havens, Abe Lincoln, trombones, Matty Matlock, clarinet, Don Lodice, tenor, and Jack Sperling, drums.

During November and December 1969 Joe Marsala and his Reunion Band worked Tuesday nights at Donte's club. With Marsala on clarinet were his wife, Adele Girard, on harp, Gene Di Novi, piano, Dick Cary, piano, alto horn, Morty Corb or Art Shapiro, bass, Shelly Manne, drums and, as *Down Beat* put it, "changing others."

There is no diary for 1970, so again our knowledge is limited to those few engagements which received a mention in the musical press. About April 1970 he was a guest on the Scott Ellsworth radio show, "Scott's Place," and he appeared on the show again on June 11, 1971. Copies of the latter show, running to more than two hours of talk and records, exist.

On August 16, 1970, and then every Sunday, 9:15 p.m. to 1:45 a.m., a Dick Cary band opened at Bob Adler's 940 Club at 940 La Cienega. With him were Bob Havens, trombone, Matty Matlock, clarinet, Ray Sherman, piano, Ed Safranski, fender bass, Nick Fatool, drums, and numerous sitters-in. Over the months these included, among countless others, trombonist Herbie Harper, bassist Ray Leatherwood, saxist Deane Kincaide, and drummer Sonny Payne. Cary was impressed by the singing of Lucille Lane, the wife of Teddy Buckner's pianist, Ken Lane. Critic Leonard Feather gave the group a rave review in *The Melody Maker*. This was a long running engagement, with Cary still there in September 1971, when the band was Cary, Sherman and Fatool, with Herbie Harper, trombone, Deane Kincaide, clarinet, baritone, and Ray Leatherwood, bass.

In a September letter to Ken Gallacher, Cary writes that "the boss is particularly impressed at the type of customer we draw, so unlike his weekly mob" and that Bob Adler's sister is Polly Adler, "America's most famous madam, who wrote a nice book about her business, A House Is Not a Home." Cary also mentions: "I am involved with a studio called Maggio Brass World, headed by a former trumpet player named Carlton MacBeth. He's publishing brass quintets—trios—quartets of mine, aimed at schools."

Another date with Bob Crosby was on Saturday, September 26, the annual Dixieland night at Disneyland. The 16-piece orchestra included Zeke Zarchy, Matty Matlock, Deane Kincaide, Johnny Guarnieri, Nappy Lamare, Morty Corb and Nick Fatool. "Crosby's dialogue however is a catastrophe."

November 7, 1970, was the date for the Blue Angel Jazz Party, with Cary again present.

Leonard Feather, in his "Encyclopedia of Jazz," edited with Ira Gitler, reported that Cary "also led dance band featuring Abe Most in swing era re-creations. Led 9-piece band for jazz concerts in parks and schools from 1970." This was based on a questionnaire completed by Cary.

1971 began with a "foul job" at the Beverly Hills Hotel in a sextet which had Art Lyons on clarinet, though the back pains from which Cary was suffering at this time would not have helped. The Sunday jobs at Adler's continued, as did his participation in Kay Carlson's Monday night rehearsal band, plus his own Tuesday rehearsals. Then, on January 8 he began a series of Friday night jobs with Rich Lavelle at the Club Lido singles club. There was one other job in January, a TWA show at the Anaheim Convention Center, with a band including Cary on trumpet, Bob Enevoldsen, valve trombone, Matty Matlock, clarinet, Ray Sherman, piano, Ray Leatherwood, bass, Nick Fatool, drums, and Herb (presumably Herbie Harper, trombone, rather than Herbie Stewart, tenor). The

Dick Cary, 1966
(Photograph by Ed Lawless. Courtesy of Bill Bacin)

following day, a day of rest, he saw 'Catch 22,' "best war film ever made!"

During February there were two additional dates at the Club Lido, on Saturdays, and on the 17th, a recording session with Matty Matlock for Warner Brothers. The titles made do not appear to have been released. On February 24, he and Matlock played a party for the handicapped, alongside Abe Lincoln, trombone, Ray Leatherwood, Nick Fatool and others.

In Hollywood, inevitably, there was the possibility of work in the film studios, although the lucrative days were long gone when Johnny Green (M-G-M) and Ray Heindorf (Warners) and their peers had large orchestras under contract. Occasionally Cary would find such employment, playing either for the soundtrack or acting the part of a musician on screen. Sometime he would do both on the same film. One such epic from 1971 was set in the 1930s and featured Debbie Reynolds and Shelley Winters. He was in the Goldwyn studio on March 5 in a 12-piece band which included Joe Howard, trombone, Shelly Manne, drums, Frank Morocco, reeds.

I appeared and played in "What's the Matter With Helen?" and had the pleasure of meeting the music writer David Raksin, one of the few film writers I admire. This was a real dogass film and our scene was in a gambling boat. In that Debbie Reynolds film I was the trumpet player and also did the "sideline," which is appearing but not playing—merely "syncing" to the soundtrack. I did a lot of that for a while but actually did few of the soundtracks.

The film companies have to use musicians for sidelines now. Years ago it was silly. They used people that didn't know how to hold an instrument.

Cary remembered the film particularly because the make-up person, without asking, removed his small beard. After the filming he let his beard grow longer.

In addition to his regard for David Raksin's music, Cary had another reason to remember him:

When I was in the army one of the boys in the band at Camp Shanks had seen "Laura" and liked the music very much. He wrote to Hollywood asking where he could find the music for it. He received a personal letter from Raksin and he got a little score from one of the scenes. That impressed us very much.

Dates in March included:

March 8: Elks at Long Beach: with (one set) Roy Brewer, trombone, Barney Bigard, clarinet, Dee Woolem, Bob Snell, clarinet, Eddie Phyfe, drums.

March 13: church: with Gordon Mitchell, Herbie Harper, trombone, Barney Bigard, Joe Darensbourg, clarinets, Deane Kincaide, sax, Billy Hadnott, bass, Gene Washington, drums.

March 17: Regency restaurant, next to Downey Bowl: with Art DePew, trumpet, Bobby Pring, trombone, [Phil?] Stephens, tuba, Panama Francis, drums. "Frightful!"

March 20: Redondo Beach: with Herbie Harper trombone, Bill Wood, clarinet, Lee Countryman, piano, and Dick McKormick.

During April he still had the bookings at Adler's and at the Club Lido and there is mention of a Saturday evening at Masquer's on the 17th. May proved to be a busier month, starting on the 1st with a recording session for Bill Williams, with Matty Matlock, Herbie Harper, Deane Kincaide, Myerson [Charles Myerson, guitar?] and a rock rhythm section. "Lucille Lane sang *Baby Won't You Please Come Home* and *Melancholy*—first is a gem." This is another untraced session.

In May 1971, Cary had two trips which especially impressed him.

One trip was to the Texas jazz festival in Odessa, which is a six-day festival, the only one of its kind, I guess. There were nineteen of us, I think. There were about five from here [including] Peanuts Hucko, Kai Winding, Matty Matlock. From New York there was Lou McGarity, Carl Fontana, Johnny Mince, Teddy Wilson, Lou Stein, Cliff Leeman, Jack Lesberg, Milt Hinton, and then George Barnes and Bucky Pizzarelli, who were marvellous together, those two guitars.

His entry for the Odessa Jazz Party, organised by Dr. O.E. Fulcher at the Inn of the Golden West and held May 11–16, includes: "I worked hard to be invited next year and was. Did one lousy set on trumpet Saturday night, couple on alto horn, rest on piano. Did *But Not for Me* on Sunday matinee with George and Bucky and got the standard last-day standing ovation. Played bass with Teddy Wilson on last night. People were warm, all was so convenient and comfortable, really a very nice week!! and may it continue. So good to play with Cliff!!, Lou McG, Peanuts." (Other musicians present included Wild

Bill Davison, John Best, trumpets, Flip Phillips, tenor, Mousey Alexander, drums, and Ashley Alexander, a music teacher, trumpet and trombone.

A week earlier (May 3–6) it had been a different experience: *I played up in the woods for something they called the Ranchero Ride. The camps are right around Lake Cachuma, about twenty miles north of Santa Barbara. Kind of between Solvang and Santa Barbara. About five hundred mostly millionaires, I presume, bring their horses, gallop around the woods, put on shows, have calf roping and cutting and races. This goes on for a week. There was only one trouble ... it was quite cold and it rained almost every day and it was very windy. The only way to get warm was to stand around those big fires they have. We played during the day. I think we had one show called the Tiger Milk Show at six in the morning. Tiger Milk consists, I think, of bourbon and milk. By the time everyone goes to breakfast it seems like it's night.*

I [rode] some tired saddle horses in the daytime. Those are the only ones for general use. I rode a lot when I was in the army. I was up in Lake Placid for a while—we had some good horses there.

In his diary Cary refers to the Rancheros and playing "in our camp, Barrachos." (Each small camp had a musical group and the Barrachos always had a jazz band.) "Pee Wee Erwin in next camp—played with us." Others in the band included Bob Enevoldsen and Nick Fatool for the first two days, replaced by Herbie Harper and Bill Perkins for the last two. The bassist was Ray Leatherwood, on piano was Charlie LaVere, and on reeds, Deane Kincaide.

May 19, he played the Glendora Ballroom with Murray McEachern, followed on the 23rd by a film for Leonard Feather, with Bob Havens, Joe Darensbourg, Johnny Guarnieri, Ed Safranski and Panama Francis. (This was for a monthly jazz TV show for NBC, hosted by Billy Eckstine, scheduled for showing on the 29th.) The month ended with a job ("two parades") at Disneyland, while the first gig in June was on the 5th, at Windsor, with Bob Enevoldsen, Nick Fatool and bassist Alf Clausen. The Adler's session the following evening saw a full house of musicians including, in addition to the regulars, Nat Pierce, piano, Jake Hanna, drums, and Morty Corb, bass.

Eddie Miller was the leader for three Blue Angel Jazz Club recording sessions at Wally Heider's studio on June 14, 15 and 18, with Cary and Jack Coon on trumpets. Cary contributed a couple of arrangements, both unissued, including his original A *Portrait of Eddie*, which became the album title. As *Ballad for Eddie* it was played at the 1968 BAJC party and issued on a BAJC album. Subsequently it appeared under this title on albums by Jack Lesberg, with both Cary and Miller present, and by Rick Fay.

Other engagements during this time were:

June 26: Geffen Estate: "fine dinner and played till 2:00 a.m. with Barney Sorkin (unbelievably awful on alto), Bob Corwin on piano, Ed Grady on drums"

June 27: Greek Theatre: senior citizen day, with Joe Darensbourg, Nappy Lamare, Bill Campbell, Art Auton, drums?, Ira Nepus, trombone

July 4: Pier job at 4:15 p.m. with Herbie Harper, Ray Sherman, & Roger Nichols, bass

Louis Armstrong died in New York on July 6, 1971. Cary's entry for this day is simple but heartfelt: "News of death of Louis! All I can say is a deep 'thank you, Mr. A.,' for providing me with one of the most fabulous periods of my life."

Cary himself was feeling more content, writing in July: "With a couple of interesting trips this spring—an album—the Adler's thing continuing—only a brief booze illness—weather so nice—tennis every day—home better lately! The time races by and it's temporarily one of the most peaceful, happy times of my life. Jessie seems a little happier lately." It was perhaps about this time that Jessie was playing piano with Betty O'Hara, trumpet and valve-trombone, Betty Burke, drums, and a tenor player recalled as Ivy, at a club on San Fernando Road in Sun Valley. But it was not long before she resumed touring as a trombonist with the road company of "Cabaret."

The remainder of Cary's 1971 diary is blank, with the exception of the following:

July 17: Lionel Ames (no details)
July 18: Adler's
September 19: Pilgrimage Outdoor Theater, Cahuenga Blvd
September 29: Exchange Club, Burbank: for disabled people with Matty Matlock, Stan Wrightsman, Ray Leatherwood, Nick Fatool
October 1: Grove: with Bob Havens, Peanuts Hucko, Nappy Lamare, Nick Fatool
October 2: Chaminade: with Andrew Blakeney, Gordon

	Mitchell, Joe Darensbourg, Deane Kincaide, Don Abney, Ray Leatherwood, Nick Fatool, Dixie Mitchell, Max Murray, reeds, Ira Nepus, trombone
October 8/9:	Hollywood Park: "playing at the racetrack"
October 16:	Lionel Ames (no details)

The "free entrance Sunday afternoon event" at the Pilgrimage Outdoor Theater featured Dick Cary's Jazz Band, with Herbie Harper, trombone, Peanuts Hucko, clarinet, Dave Edwards, alto, Deane Kincaide, baritone, Ray Sherman, piano, Eddie Safranski, bass, Nick Fatool, drums, and Jessie Cary, vocals. Cary told Ken Gallacher: "I work quite a bit with various of the Lawrence Welk men—Havens, Dave Edwards and Peanuts Hucko. Edwards is a very fine alto player and this is the first time these two guys, who sit in the same row in the same band, ever heard each other really play."

The Sunday gig at Adler's continued into October at least, but the last mention of the Club Lido is in July. In a January 1972 letter to Ken Gallacher, Cary confirmed that "Bob Adler sold the place to a young man who prefers folk or rock music—our Sunday nights have ended." He also advised that the band had been doing occasional weekends at Hollywood Park, playing between the horse races, as well as for a political meeting by "our beloved" attorney general. In addition, in the last three months of 1971, the Adler band "worked on three films and a couple of TV pilots."

The rehearsals on Mondays, with Kay Carlson, and on Tuesdays with Cary's octet or brass quintet remain regular engagements in his diary. There are no entries for 1971 after October 16, but Cary did write to Ken Gallacher in January 1972 to say: "This week we start an album with our brass quintet plus two. The 'two' being Ed Safranski and Nick Fatool. This is under the direction of Carlton MacBeth. One side will be ten pieces from the book; second side will be new originals which we performed last week at two college recitals. MacBeth is sponsoring the album. Possibly the book-album tie-in will help school sales of both." (It is not known if the album was recorded or if it was released.)

During 1972 Jessie Cary was again on tour with the "Cabaret" company and, in the absence of a Cary diary, it is only from her generosity in making available Dick's letters to her that we know much of his activities during that year.

A major booking, though of uncertain duration, was with Bobby Hackett at the Theatrical Restaurant in Minneapolis, commencing late April or early May. Cary played alto horn, except "I play piano with Bobby about two numbers a set. We do four 45-minute sets, with 40 minutes between. The trio Bobby hired is young and very crude and they confuse Hackett considerably. Pretty hard to play with, but for Bobby, who's so weak and oversensitive to harmonies, it is really murder and he's merely going through the motions. It's a five minute walk to the joint and he has to get a cab home. He has a bad right leg and the diabetes makes it that much worse."

In May, Cary was booked for the Odessa Jazz Party, and from the end of June until the middle of August he led his small rehearsal band for a series of park concerts, usually on Sunday afternoons. On July 12 he writes of doing the rehearsal group's fifth concert at Garden Hill Park, "our best test yet. It was good acoustics on that cement half-shell with two rather hot mikes. I think Fred Cooper has become my favorite baritone player out here. Everyone played very well and Matty got a large response for *My Inspiration*. At nine we were supposed to quit but they kept yelling so the park director 'let' us do an encore." The full band was Jack Trott, trumpet, Betty O'Hara, trombone, Matty Matlock, clarinet, Fred Cooper, baritone, Cary, piano, Vince Terri, guitar, Ray Leatherwood, bass, and Nick Fatool, drums.

On the 13th "I go to some damn ballroom off the San Bernardino freeway to one of those useless [Art] DePew rehearsals." On the 14th he was at Terminal Island (location of a low-security prison) and on Sunday, the 16th, "another Sorkin night of unbelievable cacophony at the Beverly Wiltshire Hotel." He also reports that "Our Burbank concert went well, but only about 800 people there."

"Last Thursday [probably July 20] was my long day. Drove Bob Havens, John Setar, Matty Matlock and Bob Lawson to LeMoare Naval Airforce base, 200 miles each way. This was a 'Ron Bartlee production' starring Art DePew and his orchestra, featuring The Lancers. We arrived early to do a 4 p.m. show in the enlisted men's club, but no one knew about it ... Then to officers' club and supper and one of the loudest jobs I've ever been engulfed in. But I enjoyed The Lancers—they sing well, have good arrangements." Cary then details a few of the disadvantages of the return journey, with Matlock complaining he was cold, Lawson "blowing out the most atrocious cigar smoke" and Havens, when the reading lights could not be turned off, being the most helpful by saying 'they can get pretty hot and burn the wiring' or 'your battery will really get dragged down.' Finally got home and bed at 6:15 a.m."

Cary still wanted to learn more about composition and orchestration—"Earle Hagen's new course started tonight. I bowed out when I found it to be a class of forty. I am too old for classes—I want a personal teacher and will not even repeat that useless waste of time I did with Leith Stevens."

And there was another movie to mention—"I think there's a picture out now in which we play, called 'Pocket Money,' with Lee Marvin. I remember jamming real fast while some horses and cattle were romping across the screen, and wondering about the connection."

August 1972 was busier. "It's close to 100° weather lately and I'm at tennis every afternoon. Two sets of doubles today." (In September he records spending two full days at the L.A. Tennis Club watching some of the great tennis stars, including Pancho Gonzales, Ken Rosewall, Fred Stolle and Stan Smith.) "Ira gave me four pier jobs as leader and I got Ed Safranski, Betty O'Hara and Dave Howard, drums. Abe Most can't do one of his Woodland Hills Country Club Sundays in August, so I will sub for him on that. He always uses Ray Sherman, Ray Leatherwood and Nick Fatool."

Other odd dates given are:

July 23:	Whittier—park concert
July 29:	Pier date, 1:00 p.m. to 3:00
July 31(?):	round dance record session
August 9:	Pico Rivera park concert
August 20:	Verdugo Park concert by rehearsal band (last of season)

Another summary, in a September 6 letter, was: "There's been a few nice jobs lately, like with Abe Most's big band—another party at Cliff May's—this time I got Ray Sherman and made some double piano arrangements ... but it's been a week and a half now with nothing and it gets me terribly down." He also confesses that "Hot weather has made me very lazy this summer—have to force myself to write sometimes—although the nine piece library is over 150 now."

At Whittier "we played for almost nobody. They were having typical old picnic contests ... and as we were in the clubhouse, not many were willing to stray far from a possible trophy. So we had a nice-like rehearsal and left early." Of the Pico Rivera concert Cary says that Matty Matlock and Wayne Songer could not make this date as they were working the last night of a two week engagement with Ringling's circus. "It was the most meagre turnout of the summer, so it was like a pleasant outdoor rehearsal from 6:30 to 9:00." The band was Jack Trott, trumpet, Herbie Harper, Betty O'Hara, trombones, Abe Most, Don Raffell, reeds, Nick Terri, guitar, Ray Leatherwood, bass, Nick Fatool, drums.

A jazz organisation for which Cary played was the Poor Angel Jazz Club, started by Bob Tabor in 1972. At one meeting Floyd Levin introduced him to the famous pianist and composer Eubie Blake:

> *I was working with Betty O'Hara and Peanuts Hucko. I was shaking hands with him [Blake] and you [Levin] were going through this long introduction. You ended by saying: "You're going to like his playing." Eubie Blake looks up and says (very stern and gruff) "That remains to be seen." I thought that was wonderful.*

Hucko was one musician about whom Cary could be both complimentary and rude:

> *I've known Peanuts for fifty-two or fifty-three years and I could do without him. He's impossible, he really is. He used to play quite well, if you hear records he made back in the fifties when he was at Condon's and ABC. He had a lot of brilliance, but not anymore. He still gets by with it, but he dogs it a lot now. An awful lot of people won't work with him. It's something about him, I don't know what it is.*

In a letter dated September 6, 1972, Cary writes: "Tomorrow I start a four night sub for Billy Butterfield and that g.d. G.J.B. in the W. [The World's Greatest Jazz Band of Yank Lawson and Bob Haggart]. What a misnomer that's become! It's a terrible name and I think it's going to become more and more of an anchor. They aren't using stands anymore, so I've got about a dozen arrangements to memorize today and tomorrow—and I can't—can't—can't! Haggart had only one of their five albums to give me last night. The four [arrangements] I am studying in that are fairly reasonable, but the others I've never heard and to just look at a bunch of notes, well, it's got me down and I wish I'd never agreed to it."

He was far from complimentary about the band, which was appearing at Howard Rumsey's "Concerts by the Sea" club in Redondo Beach—"I was really amazed how terrible they sound—the only guy playing as if he meant it was Wilbur [sic]. The group sounds so unbelievably sterile, unenthusiastic and trite that I'd soon go nuts with the sameness." He was also annoyed that Butterfield said he would pay pro rata whereas Bob Haggart said the pay was "about $50 a night." "Now if BB is making only $300 a week I'll eat his alcohol soaked blue jacket. Haggart really carries on the Scottish tradition. I think he comes pretty close to the top of the list headed by Rudy Vallee.

"This was just after I wrote last and was wondering how I'd ever get through it. I shouldn't have been concerned. Spent most of the sets off the stand while they put on solos, duos, trios, quartets and quintets. Lawson, who runs the thing at night, seems to have no communication with Haggart, so he didn't even know I'd memorized all those damn arrangements. [He] called all the wrong ones, none of the ones I'd been given. But the second night I got, finally, to do a peck horn solo, one—count 'em—one, and got the best reception of the night and generally played much better and was complimented by members etc. Except Lawson who strode away after the last set and didn't talk to anyone. Bud calls him Clyde McCoy and says he's a 'jealous prick' among other phrases. I was glad someone said it—I tried to keep my yap shut. Rumsey's new place has the worst acoustics for a horn player I've ever encountered. Yank's phrase was "like playing in a casket"—the most astute thing—and the only thing he said in four days.

"Wilbur's [sic] turning originals out like mad and is featured all the time—but he only writes for himself. Poor Hubble feels like a poor relation—is the only one without any solo at all. So he got me to sketch out some chords on *Dear Old Southland*. I showed Wilbur [sic] some of our originals. Their next album (the 7th so far) is "gospel" tunes—then in the spring they might use something of mine.

"Haggart's latest efforts show a terrible paucity of ideas. I guess there won't be any more *What's New* or *My Inspiration*'s—the latest are very gimmicky and if it weren't for Vic's plunger—would have nothing. Wilbur's [still sic] things are reasonably musical, but lack something. Different ones asked if I was to replace Billy B., but Haggart's as taciturn as ever. His muttered comment the first night as we said goodnight was 'you know what you're doing,' but the second nite was much more exuberant."

Cary had a pier job on September 9, with Ray Sherman, Ray Leatherwood and Dave Howard, before going to play with the W.G.J.B, but then had no work for two weeks. On the 24th he began "a Sunday afternoon" thing at Canoga Park—"the old trombonist Joe Yukl got it," with Wayne Songer, clarinet, Ray Sherman, piano, Ed Safranski, bass, Gene Estes, drums, plus jobs on Terminal Island, at the Mulholland Tennis Club (with Sherman, Leatherwood, Fatool) and a private party with Matty Matlock and Leatherwood.

There were four of Joe Yukl's "Sunday afternoon things" in

Canoga Park, with Cary commenting: "Joe Yukl is 69 and plays tennis every a.m. The Knights of Columbus has marvelous, live acoustics, but I'm afraid this Sunday [October 15] will be our last—not enough attendance to pay the band. Hours are 1:30 to 6:00 and I feel sure this is too early of a Sunday." Cary played three dates at Hollywood Park (October 6, 7,and 14), being the leader on the last, with Betty O'Hara, Wayne Songer, Ray Leatherwood, Gene Estes and Tommy Wolfe, piano.

Other news which Cary mentions is that John Best, Ray Linn, Peanuts Hucko and Cliff Leeman are reported to be joining the Freddie Martin/Bob Crosby/Frankie Carle tour—"I hope it doesn't kill Cliff or Best. Just can't see how heavy drinkers their age can live in a bus for three months and play that material" ... that Nick Fatool "hasn't gone to Hawaii yet but is turning down drum jobs and teaching golf at some club" ... and that Abe Most "has become an occasional employer for me and his jobs are the best by far of any leader I've worked for out here. At first it was either quartets or large band doing 'old recreations.' Now we've added the sextet and the first is at Lakeside Country Club October 21."

The Abe Most big band played three half-hour shows on November 9 at Canoga High School, "where we're going to demonstrate the 'swinging years' to the adolescents. The strange part is that the first trumpet, first alto and drummer were all in the Artie Shaw band at the height of his notoriety—Frank Beach, Les Robinson and Nick Fatool—so we give a reasonable recreation." They played "three capacity assembly halls with some of the teachers jitterbugging and the kids loved the concerts. We opened with *Let's Dance* (I played lead!), then Nash did Tommy Dorsey's theme, then Shaw's *Beguine*, Glenn Miller's theme, then a Basie blues for closing." (Frank Beach was in the Artie Shaw Navy Band—and if Nick Fatool did make it to Hawaii it was not for long.)

Abe Most (1920–2002) was a highly accomplished clarinetist in the Benny Goodman tradition. After working with the big bands of Les Brown and Tommy Dorsey he became a studio musician. His brother Sam was also a well-regarded reed player. Dick Cary's attitude towards Abe Most was ambivalent. He worked with him on numerous occasions during the years in Los Angeles and appreciated his musical skills, but he had doubts about Most's abilities as a leader, although he did not enumerate these. One suspects it was the choice of repertoire which Cary disliked—he had strong objections to playing the "hits" (ie; *In the Mood*) which the public was always requesting.

It was in November that Jessie said she would be coming home for a time, but whether because "Cabaret" was appearing on the West Coast or the show was taking a break is not clear.

On November 15, 1972, Dick Cary's band (Cary, trumpet, alto horn, Betty O'Hara, trombone, trumpet, Wayne Songer, clarinet, sax, Nappy Lamare, guitar, Ed Safranski, bass, Nick Fatool, drums) played bon voyage to the Los Angeles Philharmonic orchestra when it departed from Los Angeles International Airport for a two week tour of Japan. Except for a four word note of an R.C.A. party at the Hyatt House on December 16, that completes the diary entries for 1972.

* * * * * * *

In his thoughts for the year Cary reflected on several subjects. He considered how many musicians develop a "poker face." "When jazz musicians are in such emotional contact every night—you can't fool your peers. They're all around you and if you're having a bad night—the peers will usually try not to show that they realize it; but you never know when some of them are listening. But there are the concentrators like Ray Sherman who don't hear you anyway.

"One thing that's very noticeable at a dance: if there's a group of old pros who hear each other and swing easily with a semblance of a flow—not an urgent collection of accents—but a graceful movement which doesn't stop and go and jerk and confuse.

"When one of these collections of 'jobbers' goes out under the aegis of a Zaid—Harmon—Surkin etc—it's an unbelievable mess and musicians aren't the only ones who feel it because it's so goddam obvious. People don't just give enough of a damn to do anything about it—but when they hear some class they know it and it's up to performers to try to improve gradually and attempt to chip away at the walls of shitty sounds perpetrated by the 'society' leaders. A few of the latter have hired a little class occasionally and been so much better off for it. But California is so far, far behind and the people have only a fraction of the taste which was almost recognizable back east, at least occasionally." [And, even more relevant today] "So what is honest food now? What is honest anything—when everything we do now is governed by the 'efficiency expert' influenced manner of conducting any business or service.

"And the loan companies and banks have simpering broads, crooning in their syrupy out-of-tune wailings about how the money-lenders love us all and are out to help us!! Whee—where is the end of 'con'? Does it have an end? I'll never know."

15. Slings and Arrows (1973–1974)

Cary is back in diary-writing mode as from January 1 for the year 1973, recording that he played a New Year party with Betty O'Hara, Phil Durant, drums, and Bob Bates, bass—"latter could have stayed at home."

January 13: Coral Tree Tennis Club, Santa Monica: played spinet in tent with Bob Havens, Peanuts Hucko, Dee Woolem, et al

January 15: Sir Sico's: indoor debut for Dick Cary's Nine—Jack Trott, Herbie Harper, Bob Enevoldsen, Wayne Songer, Abe Most, Ed Safranski, Nick Fatool, Frank ----

January 18: La Habra High School: two 45-minute concerts, with Peanuts Hucko, Harper, Ray Sherman, Safranski, Fatool

January 19: Sportsman's Lodge: 8:00–12:00—Cary, trumpet, bass; Jessie, piano, Vince Perry, drums

January 20: Sir Sico's: with quartet, mostly on bass.

January 27: Lakeside Country Club: Abe Most, Enevoldsen, Sherman, Leatherwood, Fatool

January 31: McCambridge Park—party for handicapped.

February 1: High School—Abe Most big band

February 10: Leukemia radio show, 5:00 to 8:00. Frank DeVol leader, 6 brass, 6 reeds

February 11: same, but 3:00 to 7:00. Steve Allen, m.c.

February 17: Century Hotel: as for January 27, plus Barney Kessel, guitar

February 21: folk singer recording session

February 23: rock black singer recording session—"sweetened a record"

February 24: Lakeside Country Club: with Abe Most. Cary has other references to McCambridge on the last Wednesday of March, April and May.

It is probable that the February 21 recording session was with singer/guitarist John Fahey, who had two titles from 1973 issued on his "Old Fashioned Love" album for Reprise. The accompanying band included Britt Woodman on trombone, Joe Darensbourg, clarinet, Allan Reuss, banjo, and Cary, piano and alto horn. (Cary also recorded a session with John Fahey in 1975, for the Tacoma label.) Cary wrote: "Strange record dates, United 1:00 to 4:00 and 5:00 to 8:00—folk singer, terrible material—two tunes in afternoon, one at night. Jack the trumpet player." The trumpeter on the two Reprise titles, as on the Tacoma session, is Jack Feierman.

An entry on March 2 indicates that he has no work at all, not even a rehearsal, but almost at once he is booked to play Sundays at the Nave Pierson Winery ("with terrible bassist and bad drummer!"), commencing on the 4th. And so it continues:

March 5:	Sheraton University, 8:00 to 12:00
March 11:	Nave Pierson Winery, 1:00 to 4:00, Century Hotel—with Abe Most, 6:00 to 10:00
March 13:	Century Hotel 6:00 to 11:00—sextet with Abe Most and Bob Enevoldsen
March 16:	Sportsmen Lodge, 7:30 to 11:15—with Roy Brewer, Joe Darensbourg, Bill Campbell, Nick Fatool
March 18:	Nave Pierson Winery
March 23:	college in Pomona—with Brewer, Darensbourg, Campbell
March 24:	Burbank Mall, noon to 3:00—with Betty O'Hara, Herbie Harper, Abe Most, Cary, electric piano, Ray Leatherwood, Nick Fatool
March 25:	Nave Pierson Winery (last day)

Of the March 11 engagement with Abe Most, Cary wrote: "West side room, dance, dinner, and a show with singers and an interminable comic. One of those rotten situations where you get trapped immediately behind the performer and you're constantly blinded by a spot[light] and you must stay awake and appear to enjoy all the bad jokes. You wonder when that cramp in your calf will really grab."

For four days (March 29 to April 1) Cary worked at Sir Sico's, including afternoon and evening on the Saturday, and he mentions clarinetist Del Simmons for the first day. There is one other mention of Sir Sico's, on April 5.

The Abe Most big band worked at the Lakeside Country Club on April 7, with singer Frankie Avalon as the star guest. Cary thought the band was "pretty bad." The following day Abe Most suffered a heart attack and the diary notes that he is to have a by-pass.

On April 9 and 10, Cary was at the Biltmore Hotel in Santa Barbara, playing with the J. Newton Perry band, with wife Marilyn. His comment was: "band of amateurs!" For the 13th there is an enigmatic entry stating: "Western Rec. 6000 Sunset. Carl Fartina." And on the 14th he was back at the Lakeside Country Club, with Peanuts Hucko substituting for Abe Most in a septet including Bob Enevoldsen, Ray Sherman, Ray Leatherwood, Nick Fatool and Barney Kessel on guitar. Cary drove singer Irene Kral to and from San Diego for an April 29 concert held at the Catamaran Hotel, where he did one set with his "Nine."

Not mentioned in the diary is an April 1973 concert for which Cary led a nine-piece band as part of a Music of the Swing Era concert at Mission Beach. With Cary on trumpet were Ray Linn, trumpet, Herbie Harper, Lloyd Ulyate, trombones, Peanuts Hucko, clarinet, Bob Lawson, baritone, Ray Sherman, piano, Ray Leatherwood, bass, Nick Fatool, drums. Bill Bacin reported that "Dick also supplied comic relief when his peck horn gurgled water instead of music on a solo. He stopped the band to empty all valves and slides. Peanuts said, 'He played in the rain last night,' as the audience laughed at this allusion to the horn's nickname, the raincatcher. Cary also informed the crowd of Condon's nickname for it, the musical bed-pan! As usual, Cary played impeccably the rest of the set. Dick also furnished many of the day's arrangements." There is also a report that in the spring of 1973 clarinetist Johnny Lane had a booking at the Sky Room of Breakers Hotel in Long Beach, with Cary, trumpet and Nick Fatool, drums in the personnel.

There was what Cary calls "Abe's Prom" on May 5, when Abe Most's big band without Abe played at Busch Gardens, with Liza Morrow as the vocalist. The diary comment is: "Outdoors, windy, cold, no piano, no audience. Found piano in warehouse."

Cary was back at "Concerts by the Sea" in Redondo Beach on May 6, when clarinetist Joe Darensbourg "started Sunday and Monday thing. We have a terrible or non-existent rhythm group—awful drummer Rich Parnell, [Bill] Campbell on the raggy piano and Nappy [Lamare] holding a fender bass." Abe Lincoln was the trombonist, with Cary on trumpet. The same band, but with Nick Fatool on drums, played at the Burbank Elks on Saturday, May 12. The last "Concerts by the Sea" session mentioned is on June 24, though Cary did not attend every one which was held. At least twice he put in a sub and there was no session on May 28, when Stan Kenton was playing the club.

Clarinetist Mac McReynolds organised big bands in the Los

Angeles area and Cary was with him on Terminal Island May 17: "This was the night McReynolds conned so many into coming to play for nothing."

Piano problems are a fact of life for jazz pianists and Cary was faced with another on May 19 at a ballroom he calls "Proud Bird," where he was with "a Carole Wax band." The instrument had "about a dozen notes missing and a feeling of goo all through it, sticky mushy goo. So I sat there and listened!"

With Max Murray, sax, Bill Campbell, piano, and Ed Safranski, bass, Cary played the Long Beach Elks on May 20, while on the 26th, at the Palladium, trombonist Bob Havens was featured on three of Cary's arrangements with the Lawrence Welk orchestra. Havens reported that Welk said, "I'm in love with your arrangements, Bob."

The Lakeside Country Club takes centre stage for a few days, starting on May 30 with a session including Abe Most, Ray Leatherwood, Nick Fatool and Tom Wolfe, piano. On June 1 Cary was in the "surprise band" for actor Andy Griffith's birthday party, "arranged by his manager, Dick Linke, prexy of Lakeside." Then after a Westwood Country Club date with Abe Most on June 2, and the two Darensbourg sessions at Redondo Beach, Cary worked at Lakeside between June 6 and 9 rehearsing and playing for an amateur show and dance.

The 1973 summer season of park dates began on June 17 when the "Nine" played in Farnsworth Park, Altadena, with the usual miscellaneous dates in-between:

June 18:   Annex Studios—recording a jingle
June 21:   Terminal Island (no details)
June 22/23:   Little Rock: with the Nine (no details)
June 24:   Redondo Beach: Joe Darensbourg session
June 25:   recording date with Barney Bigard

On June 26, it was off to White Sulphur Springs in Virginia to play at the Greenbriar Hotel. "Perry" organised the band which was hired by the Society of Corporate Secretaries for five days. The nine-pieces included an old friend, Ed Anderson on trombone, plus J. Newton [Perry?] and others unnamed. The schedule was not arduous:

June 26:   Cary played a large grand piano in the ballroom
June 27:   no work today
June 28:   "Played cocktails outside tonight in sun and heat, then gala night in ballroom"

June 29: "Played a noon hour and in evening"
June 30: "Banquet at night—not much playing"

Cary writes that it took him 14 hours to get from White Springs to Los Angeles. He arrived to find that Jessie had left to go to New York.

Then it was back to the one-off gigs:

July 4: Smith Park, 1:00 to 4:00: presumably the Nine
July 7: Valley Hunt Club 2:30 to 6:00: with J. Newton. Temple Israel, Loomis 8:00 to 12:00 (enjoyable piano gig with Ray Leatherwood on bass)
July 8: Chinese funeral: two hours in midday heat!
July 10: Barney Bigard recording session

The Barney Bigard sessions were for RCA. Cary played piano on the first, and trumpet and alto horn on the second, as well as providing the arrangements and three originals, *Wampum* (with Bigard), *Slings and Arrows* and *Florence Off Ramp*. The overdubbing to which Cary refers took place on August 23:

I played piano on all the ballads which were done on the first date with a guitar, which is almost unnoticeable. Then Ray Sherman played the second date for all the brite tunes. Later, Barney and I overdubbed and I helped the engineer edit the thing. 32 hours altogether of editing. Since then I've met engineers who could have done it in two hours. Barney plays three clarinets on Mood Indigo. *This was his first experience overdubbing. Florence is an off ramp on our Santa Ana freeway—an exit which Nick Fatool missed on one of my park concerts and was about an hour late.*

To resume:

July 13: Terminal Island: with big band
July 14: Valley Hunt Club, 6:00 to 10:00: with J. Newton
July 15: Norwalk Park: with the Nine
July 17: Turf Club, Hollywood Park: with leader Neal Hefti (Enevoldsen, Abe Most, Leatherwood, Fatool, Frank Morocco, reeds) "Silly ass party for charity, donkey races, etc."
July 18: Alhambra, 500 N. Palm: 7:30 to 9:00—piano.
July 19: Rec. Western 2:00 to 4:00: alto horn (no other details). Starlight Bowl, 8:00 to 10:00: with good band

July 21: Los Angeles Country Club: with J. Newton
July 22: Woodland Hills (afternoon): sextet including Terry Harrington, tenor, Betty O'Hara, Ed Safranski. Montebello (evening): presumably the Nine. ("One of best outdoor shells yet")
July 27: Business man's banquet, 8:00 to 12:00: with Abe Lincoln, Ray Sherman, Ray Leatherwood, Nick Fatool—"They talked and ate, so why do they hire us anyway?"
August 1: Garden Hill, 7;30 to 9:00: (no details—probably solo piano)
August 3: made test record of *Satchmo* and *Gabriel*, written and sung by Buddy Carroll, with Bill Court. "Overdub one trumpet chorus—I imitated Mr. A. as best as I could."
August 8: Santa Barbara: with J. Newton
August 12: McArthur Park: "Large parade of Dixielanders from Bob Crosby's big one to Nick Pelico's and Joe Darensbourg's. I provided band for Barney Bigard."
August 14: round dance record date

Also on the 14th Cary was in a large band rehearsal for a booking the following day by Colonial Caterers at the Marriott Hotel. The personnel included Bob Enevoldsen, trombone, John Setar and Terry Harrington, saxes. He played with Bob Reid at the Santa Barbara Country Club on the 18th and 10:00 p.m. to midnight at the Beverly Hills Hilton on the 22nd, in an octet which included Bob Havens, trombone, Rick Fay, reeds, and Nick Fatool, drums. The following night, the 23rd, he worked a Riverview job, 7:30 to 9:30 with clarinetist Johnny Lane.

He was with Bob Havens again on Saturday, August 25, when they flew to Knoxville—"Played at Browns-Falcons game, 15-minutes before game and 20-minutes between halves!" The air tickets and the hotel bill must have made this a very expensive gig.

Dee Woolem and J. Newton remain uncertain figures but were probably booking agents. On September 2, Cary refers to a job on Catalina Island at a "ridiculous hotel Newton owns. Ballroom great, band pretty silly." And there were four Woolem dates included in the following September and October listings:

September 8: Jack McClure's house, Orange County: with Stan Wrightsman, Ray Leatherwood,

September 9: Nick Fatool (McClure was a guitarist)
Orange Jazz Club: Dee Woolem job, with Abe Most, Nick Fatool, et al.
September 15: Uplands: Dee Woolem job, with Cary, piano, Bob Havens, guest
September 17: square dance recording session
September 21: Terminal Island: with big band
September 22: Hollywood Park: with Max Murray, etc

At the end of September Cary refers to Peanuts Hucko taking an arrangement of *Do You Know What It Means to Miss New Orleans* on tour with him and playing it on the (Merv?) Griffin Show on September 27. The editing of the Barney Bigard album for M-G-M was finally completed early in October, and on October 9, he received his first call from the Lawrence Welk Agency, to work with Cliff May, Charles LaVere—"lousy party, dumb guests, loaded!" In November, Cary attended a Lawrence Welk rehearsal—at the time Welk had a long-running and extremely popular television show—where he discussed an album to feature trombonist Bob Havens. On November 26, the Monday night rehearsal band played "four things for Havens-Welk album—not satisfactory." Some further action on this took place in 1974, but it still proved to be another false trail.

October 13: Lakeside Country Club: with Abe Most, Bob Enevoldsen, Ray Sherman, Ray Leatherwood, Nick Fatool
October 14: a pier in Wilmington: with Joe Darensbourg at 6 a.m. Dee Woolem job, 11:00 to 3:30.
October 19: Hollywood Park: with Joe Darensbourg, Nick Fatool, et al.
October 20: Disneyland Hotel: large ballroom, with Joe Lister (3 horns, 3 rhythm, fiddle)
October 21: Buena Park: Dee Woolem job
October 27: McGuire's: with Abe Most, Marvin Ash, piano, Ray Leatherwood, Nick Fatool
October 31: Riverview House, San Pedro: Johnny Lane job
November 3: Fullerton Elks: Ed Leach big band, 9:00 to 1:00
November 10: Lakeside Country Club: Abe Most 15-piece band, including Jack Trott, Dick Cary, trumpets, Herbie Harper, Bob Enevoldsen, trombones, Les Robinson, Jerome Richardson, Roger Neumann, Terry Harrington, reeds,

	Ray Sherman, piano, Ray Leatherwood, bass, Nick Fatool, drums. "Much gabbing, not enough playing. Should be so much better."
November 17:	Elks, Thousand Oaks: piano, with Ray Linn, trumpet, Terry Harrington, tenor, Nick Fatool, drums
November 21:	Mayflower Ballroom: Ernie Barrell's orchestra—2 brass, 3 saxes, 3 rhythm, including Cary on piano
November 23:	Mayflower Ballroom: 8:30 to 12:30. Ed Anderson drove

There are no diary entries for December, but he was booked to lead a band Saturday night, December 1, and four Sundays at a Cannery in Newport Beach, plus New Year's Eve. He had hired Abe Most, Ray Sherman, Ed Safranski, Nick Fatool and "Hub" ("my Adler's band"), though the band for December 31 was very different, with bassist Ray Leatherwood the only familiar name. Nevertheless, one can safely assume that 1974 was welcomed in to the strains of *Auld Lang Syne*.

In November Cary had been upset upon receiving a flyer about the clarinetist Mac McReynolds and his orchestra—"I've become a sideman in my own goddam band!" This would have referred to an event at El Camino College on January 5, 1974, when the 18-piece band contained many familiar names from the Monday night rehearsal band. The group rehearsed in the afternoon and played a show with singer Helen Forrest as guest in the evening. The brass section was particularly strong, with Zeke Zarchy, Jack Trott, Betty O'Hara, Dick Cary, trumpets, Herbie Harper, Bob Enevoldsen, Bob Havens, Dan Barrett, trombones. The instrumentals played were hits from the bands of Artie Shaw, Glenn Miller and Benny Goodman, plus *Showboat Shuffle*, *Rockin' in Rhythm*, *Cotton Tail*, and *Come Sunday* from the Duke Ellington library.

Two days later, on the 7th, Cary was in the Paramount Studios for just over seven hours, helping to record the soundtrack for "The Great Gatsby," starring Robert Redford and Mia Farrow, which had been filmed in England towards the end of 1973. The music was "supervised and conducted" by Nelson Riddle.

> *I was just one of three trumpet players (John Best and Shorty Sherock). It was a very rainy day and I almost didn't get through the highway lakes, but did make it and was there from 9 a.m. to 7 p.m. I thought the score was terrible. Not one*

jazz band piece all day and we had some fine guys, like Nick Fatool, Ray Sherman, Jess Stacey (sic), Mahlon Clark, etc.

In his diary Cary reports that he worked 9:30 to 5:30 (hour for lunch) and that the full orchestra was: Best, Sherock, Cary, trumpets, Tom Shepard, Tom Johnson, Pete Lofthouse, trombones, Mahlon Clark, Harry Klee, Justin Gordon, reeds, Ray Sherman, piano, Nappy Lamare, banjo, guitar, Allan Reuss, guitar, Morty Corb, bass, Nick Fatool, drums, plus four violins. (Jess Stacy was present to record a solo.)

Bassist Eddie Safranski (b. 1918) became well-known as a result of his work for Stan Kenton in the mid-1940s. After Ray Leatherwood he was the bassist who worked most frequently with Dick Cary during the early 1970s, so his death must have been a shock. This is the diary entry for January 9, 1974: "Tonight, after his job, Eddie Safranski died returning home. Ed had a great spirit! Ed was not Bertrand Russell, neither was he Joe McCarthy or Richard Nixon. He was on the plus side somewhere in the great middle. In his case, like millions of others, Catholicism did him a tremendous disservice. Eddie played as hard as he could and money had become a very unnerving influence." [Safranski's date of death is shown elsewhere as January 10, indicating he was returning home after midnight.]

On January 10, Cary worked at 12:30 and 7:45 for Don Wagner, apparently on piano—"Wagner is a hustler," running 'Heavenly Cosmetics' and recruiting salesmen. Next day Cary was at an AFM union meeting to discuss "the upcoming school series, starting Wednesday, with my Dixieland nine men, Ruben Leon our narrator."

Peanuts Hucko replaced clarinetist Buddy DeFranco as leader of the Glenn Miller "ghost band" on January 17. He led the band for several months until he had to withdraw because of exhaustion. Of the clarinet role in the Miller revival band, Hucko told reporter Alan Stevens (*The Melody Maker*, October 18, 1975): "I played some Goodman things, some Shaw things, some arrangements that Dick Cary had done for me, and I put clarinet solos into some of the Miller charts."

After the schools concert on the 16th, his next gig was a "terrible job" at the Calabasas Country Club on the 19th which included the presentation of golf prizes, a slide show and other distractions. "One couple shone through—the guy didn't believe in requests and liked Duke and Fats." Two days later—"Bell Sound 7:00–8:00, a Jack Daniels travelogue for Phil Harris" with Bob Enevoldsen, valve trombone, Maury Harris, trumpet, Al Hendrickson, banjo, Tom Johnson, tuba, Jack Sperling, drums, and Dick Cary, alto horn.

At this point Cary entered the stock market again, buying 75 shares in Warner Communication—"I got in at 15 3/4." The next day the price rose to 16 3/4, "So in one day I'm ahead $75."

One story in a letter to Jessie concerned January 23: "Last Saturday I did a two piano job with Don Abney and it was quite a night. We were hired 8:00 to 12:00 by Larry Gelbart, who produces the 'M*A*S*H' show. His wife had a birthday party—she was a pro singer named Pat Marshall. (I had not heard of her.) A lot of TV people were there—Dom DeLuise—George Segal—Leonard Stern—writers—actors—producers. Don Abney paced himself for the 4 hrs quite well—but then the party went on and on. Pete Rugolo sat down for me for a while so I got out the horn and pulled up a chair. By this time Pat was singing and then Mel Brooks and wife Anne Bancroft arrived with some others and we went till 3. But Don (being a diabetic) was hopeless by 1:30 and I took over and Pat sang the last hour and a half; impressions of all the girl singers, etc. Quite an audience for one's living room. Several people asked me if I was accompanying these days—they were aware of Abney being with Pearl Bailey. I've always enjoyed accompanying and who knows." (Cary was invited back to the Gelbarts' in September.)

He was back with Mac McReynolds on Saturday, January 26, playing at the Balboa Pavilion. Again the personnel was mainly from the rehearsal band, with Don Beamsley, piano, Ray Leatherwood, bass, and Nick Fatool as the rhythm section. In the saxophone section was altoist Warne Marsh. Next, on the 28th and 29th came a round dance recording session, followed by a rehearsal at the ABC Studios for Lawrence Welk, doing "three tunes for Bob Havens album. Very good reaction." Cary shows Havens, trombone, George Thow, trumpet, George Cates, Louie Norman and a sax section.

During February Cary mentions two dates with clarinetist Johnny Lane, at the Monarch Room on Long Beach on the 3rd, with Al Jenkins, trombone, Bill Campbell, piano, Bill French, drums ("My lip needs whatever I can do.") and on the 14th at San Pedro, Riverview Home for the sick and indigent.

Lane combined a day job with all manner of musical work in the evenings and at weekends:

About Johnny Lane; I worked quite a few small jobs with him. Such a pleasant old man, with great memories of Jimmie Noone and the Chicago days.

Drummer Bill French worked often with Johnny Lane and recalled: "I was lucky enough to have worked a handful of gigs with him [Cary] and one I remember was with Betty O'Hara and a piano player and Johnny Lane. A strange job it was—the grand opening of some auto dealer in Long Beach. There couldn't have been more than 30 people who wandered into the place. Of course that dealer lost his shirt. Other gigs with Dick were at senior citizen centers, a couple at the Long Beach Veterans Hospital and sundry other places. I never could understand how Lane could talk Dick into doing such rinky-dink gigs. Had to be the money, which was never all that great."

In a later letter French modified his opinion, "In Cary's case I think he just plain loved to play. Either that or he needed the money. Anyway, it was a kick playing along with a musician of his ilk. Despite all my inefficiencies he was always considerate."

On this subject of loving to play, Barry Martyn's view was: "Dick would generally turn up at jazz parties and would always play. I never saw him anxious to get up. He wasn't one of those guys who played three numbers and then got up and wanted a drink. And he could play whatever number you called. He had a very, very extensive repertoire. Dick was basically a jazz fan."

Joe Darensbourg had organised a promising band for February 4 to play on Pier 195 in Wilmington "to attract customers to ocean steamer"—Cary, trumpet, Abe Lincoln, trombone, Darensbourg, clarinet, Bill Campbell, piano, Nappy Lamare, banjo, Nick Fatool, drums—though the 7:30 a.m. start was perhaps a dampener.

A round/square dance recording session on the 5th was followed on the 6th by a rehearsal for two nights on the Queen Mary the following Saturday and Monday. Booked by the Scott Allen Agency, the leader was Manny Glass. An 11-piece band played in the Queen Salon on Saturday, February 9, 9:00 to 1:00 a.m. with Cary noting that "Devon [D'Vaughn] Pershing is a good keyboard player—Lou Malin is a loud drummer and rushes." The band increased to 15-pieces on Monday the 11th, in the Grand Salon from 8:00 p.m. It played some of Cary's arrangements and included in its ranks Bob Enevoldsen, Randy Aldcroft, trombones, Dave Edwards and Art Pepper, reeds.

Between the Queen Mary dates, on the 10th, Cary travelled to Sacramento for a guest appearance at the McClellan "O" Club, "for jazz club reps." as he put it, playing four sets, one on trumpet, one on piano and the last two on alto horn. The mainly local musicians included Rex Allen on trombone and drums, and Bob Ringwald, piano and banjo.

There was a rehearsal at Warner Brothers on February 16, conducted by Frank DeVol, in preparation for a marathon radio appeal for a leukemia charity starting at 5:00 that afternoon. His diary entry includes: "Ray Leatherwood, Don Raffell and I were only ones to do the 25 hours." The big band played 5:00 to 9:00 on the Saturday and 2:00 to 5:00 on the Sunday, with Ray Linn and Cary, trumpets, Britt Woodman, Lloyd Ulyate, trombones, Les Robinson, Jerome Richardson, Don Raffell, reeds, Ray Sherman, piano, Ray Leatherwood, bass, and Alvin Stoller, drums, among the personnel. The proceedings contained "the weirdest assortment of singers, including Rudy Vallee."

He gave another "history of jazz" presentation on February 26, at Garfield High School—"Kids were very responsive." With Ruben Leon narrating, the band was Cary, Betty O'Hara, trumpets, Herbie Harper, Bob Enevoldsen, trombones, Abe Most, Terry Harrington, reeds, Don Abney, piano, Herb Mickman, bass, Gene Estes, drums. As Cary wrote to his wife: "Yesterday morning we did our 3rd high school concert (at Garfield in E. L.A.) and someone named Kathie Maine of CBS News showed up with camera and sound—so we were on CBS News at 6:55 and 11:25 last nite. The kids love these shows and for the first time we stayed after and the music students came up to consult with the members. I've got Betty on trumpet and the female students think it's just great to see a girl in the band—and scream and applaud when she is introduced.

"I wonder if these programs will spread over the country—they should. Anyway my "NINE" now has a few more things to do and it all helps—especially for our own experience together."

He played for a handicap party on February 27; then there is a gap until Saturday, March 2, when he was with Murray Korda at the Beverly Hilton; piano 4:00 to 5:30; small group at 6:15 and dance starting at 9:15. The 10-piece band was Graham Young, Cary, trumpets; Herbie Harper, trombone; Abe Most, Bus Bussey, ---- Popilardo, reeds, Sherman, piano, Lamare, guitar, Leatherwood, bass, Fatool, drums. "At rehearsal we played for old Nick Lucas." (Lucas had contributed vocals to "The Great Gatsby" movie.)

On March 6 Cary noted that "today is 13th anniversary," but Jessie was at the other side of the country, in Washington, where, we later discover: "she's been living with Jean Puchard for quite a while. They both work solo piano jobs, Jean at the Hilton and JB at the Gaslight."

The next day Abe Most got "a sudden job to play for an Andy Griffith party at a joint called 'King's Four in Hand' on Beverly

Boulevard. They did a new pilot and had a party. On the 13th we're doing the fourth in the hi-school series of five—the one tomorrow is at Van Nuys—where I did the first one 4 weeks ago. We'll have 6 reeds—6 brass—6 rhythm (2 percussionists have been added). Don Abney's on piano. Feather will be there & this one little fact has Abe in a terrible dither. I keep telling Abe—'We're playing for the kids.' Anyway I get to do *Come Sunday* because I said Leonard would like it."

Entries in the diary become even less frequent from this point. "So here it is Wednesday afternoon and I have absolutely nothing to do till Saturday night [March 16] when I meet Nick again and we play with Les Robinson, Trott and Leatherwood out around 1000 Oaks. Then Sunday I'm pianoing again with Gordon Mitchell at Van Nuys airport in a hangar." The following Saturday he was at Balboa, presumably in the Pavilion,

Letters to Jessie fill in one or two dates, plus Cary's growing annoyance with Lawrence Welk and the proposed album featuring trombonist Bob Havens. "That goddam Welk still hasn't named Havens' first recording session—he put one on [his TV] show and Dave Edwards told me Bob made a couple of clams and it worries Welk. He thinks maybe the arrangements are causing it. He wants to hear them again, so I go down again next Tuesday. This will be my seventh trip into Hollywood just for these four lousy things which I've had done since November." In April Cary could write: "And still we haven't done Havens' first date—although he did one song on the April 6th show and Bob started the first phrase of *Blue and Brokenhearted* with two clams. He's told me how nervous he gets recording and is seeing a hypnotist. But having the thing drag out like this at the whim of a silly boor like L. Welk is inexcusable! One thing surprised me. After Bob finished, Welk got through dancing with some little girl in the audience and said it was a 'Dick Cary arrangement.' I've had no calls about it—mostly I suppose because I don't know anyone who watches it." (In 2006 Havens recorded the Cary arrangements, and others, for a private CD issue.)

Other unfulfilled plans included calls from Adler's about Cary resuming the Sunday night sessions and calls from Don Abney about writing for Ernestine Anderson ("one of my favorite singers and there are hardly any"), who was to sing with the Louis Bellson band, which was doing a week at Disneyland. Cary had written three charts for her before he discovered that she was not to appear with Bellson after all.

A Monday rehearsal is all that is entered by Cary during the next three weeks, but to Jessie he mentions a cast party at Paramount on April 9, with Nick Fatool on drums—"I think it is a party for 'Day of the Locust.'" On the 13th there was a round dance recording session—"Then nothing till the 20th"—which was when he and Ray Leatherwood drove to San Diego to play a dance for John Best and Abe Most. He played the Queen Mary again on April 23 when the rehearsal band performed 8:00 to midnight, and there was a job with J. Newton in Santa Barbara on the 29th.

The jobs which Cary does list are well-spaced:

May 5: "Sell out concert in San Diego—played a lot of crap." 15-piece band, including John Best, Uan Rasey, Cary, trumpets, Harper, Ulyate, Joe Howard, trombones, Abe Most, Les Robinson, Don Raffell, Willie Schwartz, Bob Lawson, reeds, Sherman, Lamare, Leatherwood, Fatool.

May 24–27: appeared for four days at the Sacramento Jazz Jubilee

May 29: McCambridge 7:30 to 9:30: with Matty Matlock, Betty O'Hara, et al.

June 1: "on truck for Noni Bernardi": with Betty O'Hara, Henry Cuesta, clarinet, Nappy Lamare, Dave Howard, Ira Westley

June 5: Airport Marina: with Bob Thomas.

June 22: Calabasas wedding on electric piano

August 24: Malibu beach party: 8:00 to 12;00, with Al Hendrickson, guitar, Leatherwood, bass. Jerry McKenzie, drums

August 25: Verdugo Park, 1:00 to 3:00: Trott, Cary, trumpets, Harper, O'Hara, trombones, Tommy Newsom, Harrington, reeds; Sherman, piano, Hendrickson, guitar, Fatool, drums.

August 29: "Played [trumpet] at Arabian horse auction, Klee Ranch, Santa Inez, 4:00 to 8:30. "Dave Bourne drove wife, Pat, Gene Washington and me. Lip got weak."

August 30: square dance recording date

August 31: Balboa Pavilion—14 piece band, Mac McReynolds, based on rehearsal group.

September 1: Larry Gelbart's, party for his wife, Patricia Marshall. Two pianos, with Ray Sherman. Guests included Mel Brooks, Carl Reiner, Marty Feldman ("talked to me all evening") and Jackie Cooper ("drummed").

>"Pat Marshall enjoyed herself and we played medley from "Good News," 1947 film she did."

September 25: McCambridge: with Betty O'Hara, Ray Leatherwood, Bill Perkins, drums

October 20: Skillet's: with Ray Leatherwood & guitarist.

Earlier in the year Cary commented to Jessie about spring in Sunland—"This place is as green and beautiful this month of April as I've ever seen it. Everything came out, iris, lilies, etc. etc. It's about 50 at night and 75 in afternoon and most of the days have been very windy but very clear"—and about the capitalist system—"The present existence of writing—tennis—and an occasional job, forces more introspection, more about living and the way people cope with this insane society of monumental crooks running a government; enormous, wealthy, dark-suited men controlling lives of so many people, forcing certain kinds of thinking on all the sheep who go through the daily routines of traffic jams and 9 to 5 jobs. Gee—am I lucky to sit back and see it all from a sideline seat!!"

It was in August 1974 that Cary received, from Washington, the "Dear John" letter which he had no doubt been expecting and fearing. Jessie's letter stressed the respect and admiration she had for him and how she hoped that they could separate in a reasonable and civil manner. After three weeks of joyless reflection Cary replied in a similar vein and their marriage gradually came to an amicable close. He emphasised that her room would always be available to her. However, when she did return to Los Angeles in early February of 1975, she chose to stay with Judy, though visiting her husband regularly. On March 5 Cary wrote: "JB's been over every day. She returns tonight to her 'new love,' in Chicago." Their divorce followed shortly afterwards. His feelings are clear in the sentence: "She is not to return and I am alone for maybe the rest of my life."

With the separation from Jessie now permanent, it is perhaps not surprising that Cary lost interest in his diary for the last three months of 1974, but as the New Year started we know that he was playing with the Abe Most big band. We know because on January 1, 1975 he resumed writing down his activities. And at least 1975 would broaden his horizons, present him with new challenges and start to gain him wider appreciation among the world's jazz fraternity.

16. Interlude—
Hi Hat and Merry-Go-Round

Towards the end of his first year in Los Angeles, Dick Cary began to write for and play on records produced by Merl Olds, whose Hi Hat label specialised in music for square and round dances. The company released 45 rpm single records, and operated from Flores Street, Los Angeles, and then Inola Street, San Dimas. It also used a post office box number, P.O. Box 69833, Los Angeles.

Cary was associated with Olds between 1960 and the late 1980s. In addition to preparing the music and playing, he also contracted some of the sessions and was leader on a large number of them. A modest attempt has been made in the discography to list the Hi Hat releases under Cary's name, together with information from his diaries, but it has not been possible to directly match the known issues with the personnels which Cary gives. It is assumed that Cary sometimes played on records which were released by other leaders, such as Joe Leahy, Jerry Vaughn and Gene Garf. There were also a number of releases on a Hi Hat subsidiary, Merry-Go-Round.

Each record was accompanied by a sheet giving the dance steps for each side, but the musical content varied—and not just in quality. Issues might contain a different tune on each side or they could have the same instrumental on both sides, but with cues or calls inserted on one of them.

On the Dick Cary records which have been auditioned the music varies between straight (waltzes) and corny, or pleasant Dixieland. *Swingin'* is a feature for a capable clarinetist (perhaps Wayne Songer) with banjo, bass guitar and drums; *Lazy Swing* is another clarinet feature, with bass guitar and drums; *Beale Street Blues* is acceptable; while *Road Runner Two-Step* has good interplay between trombone and clarinet, backed by vibes, banjo, bass and drums. An ensemble *Muscrat* (sic) *Ramble* appears to have no piano behind the tedious bass guitar, which suggests that Cary is the good trumpet player.

No composer credits are given. This is just as well when, for example, *Swinging Sal* is actually *My Gal Sal*, *Tuxedo Blues* is *Ballin' the Jack*, and *Peachie Keen* is really *Georgia on My Mind*.

Musicians known to have played on some of these recordings,

in addition to Wayne Songer, include Stan Wrightsman, piano, Ray Leatherwood, bass, Art Barduhn, trumpet, Dick Collins, trumpet, Gene Estes, drums, vibes, and many lesser known players, shown in the discography.

The work for Olds involved not only straightforward composing, arranging and playing for the records, but also writing and overdubbing, or overlaying, music onto previously recorded material, as one of Cary's entries explains:

> Just to give you an idea how much overlaying is done out here. We [Cary and Wayne Songer] have made an awful lot of 45s (singles) for a Merl Olds who produces these things for square and round dance clubs. Recently a fine reed player, Wayne Songer, and I "sweetened" nine records for him, overdubbing almost 50 parts, which I had to write. This took us almost three hours and the engineer had it all edited in another three hours. That was a very remarkable engineer.

Musically the recordings for Merl Olds, judged on those heard, add little to the Dick Cary oeuvre and presumably Cary persevered with this work because each year it provided an occasional if modest boost to his income.

17. Europe Beckons (1975—1976)

The New Year's Day gig with Abe Most was at the Balboa Pavilion. It appears that Most undercut Mac McReynolds for the job and that Cary was not sympathetic towards Most—"He's an amazing contradiction. He makes nothing of quite a technical ability. Most amazing is, he seems impervious to reaction of musicians and listeners alike."

Cary had a "pleasant evening" with Johnny Lane and Bill French at San Pedro on January 3, and on the 12th he and Betty O'Hara played with Bob Thomas (clarinet?) at the Statler Hilton. Between January 14 and February 8 he played five nights at a bar called Tweetie's, the opening personnel being Ray Linn (trumpet) and Bruce Paulson (piano). For January 18 Cary comments: "Ray took his band into Beverly Hilton, so I got Nick, Ray L, Ray S., Herbie H. and Artie Lyons and we had a marvelous night. Full house of very appreciative people. What a fine evening."

During the Tweetie's engagement he did the monthly gig for the handicapped at McCambridge, with Betty O'Hara, Ira Westley and Gene Estes, and on February 2 he participated in a "strange album" with Dave Bourne. "We did seven tunes from 7:00 to 11:00 p.m." This recording session, and a second on March 2, was for Dave Bourne's 'Arcane' label, twelve titles by the Dawn of the Century Ragtime Orchestra, featuring early orchestral ragtime compositions. For the March date Cary's note was: "Rough—no rests—old music."

Reminiscing about Cary, Dave Bourne said: "I used Dick Cary quite often along with Betty O'Hara for Dixieland casuals. Dick would start the evening on trumpet with Betty on valve trombone. Before too long he would break out the alto horn and have Betty switch to trumpet. Betty was a wonderful horn player on any instrument so it never made any difference to me what they played. She and Cary worked together like hand in glove, the sound always mellow and pleasant. It was refreshing to work with players who never let egos interfere with their music. No loud and fast crap here, just wonderful, interesting melodies intertwining one another.

"I first met Cary while I was playing tenor horn in the Southern California Hot Jazz Society Marching band (later known as The Resurrection Brass Band) in the 1960s, '70s and '80s. It was a twenty piece band that marched in twos. Dick and I followed the trombones in the second rank. Behind us on clarinet was often Barney Bigard and Joe Darensbourg.

"When I asked him to record an album for my Dawn of the Century Ragtime Orchestra, he refused to let me send him the charts beforehand and wouldn't do any wood-shedding before the session. The charts were stock arrangements of ragtime, all published between 1895 and 1910. He pissed and moaned throughout all of the sessions, griping that even a New York studio player would never be able to cut this stuff. He spent half the time cutting out repeats and giving his part to the clarinet player. The parts were very demanding but my previous trumpet player Jack Langlois (who was murdered by a business partner) never had any problem with them. Dick was used to the usual jazz form of playing the chart down one time, laying out until it was solo time, then one chorus at the end. He wasn't ready (chop wise) to play Sousa march style with everybody playing all four parts with repeats and no rests.

"Cary was a hard case and was pretty grumpy and sarcastic most of the time. He never cared much about money and never had any to speak of. He drove an elderly Cadillac with the paint peeling off. It was always difficult to get him to dress up for a gig. He always wore his shirt out and would never wear a tie unless he was hog-tied.

"In all the time we worked together he only paid me one compliment. We were playing *Do You Know What it Means to Miss New Orleans* and after the ensemble opening he leaned over and said, 'You're the only West Coast piano player I've ever heard play those chords right!' From Cary, that was high praise."

On February 10 Cary played at Sir Sica's with Don Beamsley, piano, Ira Westley, bass, and Jerry McKenzie, drums, and on the 13th he 'rehearsed' (presumably accompanied on piano) singers Andy Russell, Helen Forrest and Johnny Desmond, prior to a performance at the Palladium on the 14th. Apparently the conductor was Abe Most, leading Zeke Zarchy, Graham Young, Manny Klein, Dick Cary, trumpets, Herbie Harper, Lloyd Ulyate, Joe Howard, Ken Shroyer, trombones, Les Robinson, Willie Schwartz, Don Raffell, Babe Russin, Don Lawson, reeds, Ray Sherman, piano, Al Hendrickson, guitar, Ray Leatherwood, bass, Nick Fatool, drums.

"A Joan Tratner has sent me three lyrics—bad poetry—but I've done a melody for *Quiet Sea*. Could I possibly make myself write a song which might have a chance of selling?? I wonder—it's all out there and I should get some of it." More wishful thinking?

And so the mixture of bookings continued:

February 15:   Skytrails Restaurant, Van Nuys Airport: with Abe Lincoln, Bill Wood, Lee Countryman, Ray Leatherwood, Nick Fatool
February 16:   Jazz Inc., Moose Lodge, Santa Ana: with John Best, trumpet, Charlie Romero, clarinet, Frank Amos, drums
February 21:   Bullocks: with Matty Matlock, Nappy Lamare, Nick Fatool
February 24:   Sir Sica's: with Ray Linn, Wayne Songer, Ira Westley, et al.
February 26:   McCambridge Park: with Betty O'Hara, Bill Perkins, Ray Leatherwood
February 28:   Miramar: with Jack Feierman, trumpet, Joe Darensbourg, Herbie Harper, Cary, piano, Nappy Lamare, Ray Leatherwood, and no drummer
March 1:   round dance record date
March 2:   the second recording session for Dave Bourne's Arcane label
March 8:   Bachelor's Ball at Beverly Hilton, 8:15 out front, 9:30 in ballroom. 10-piece band, Murray Korda in front, with Graham Young, Herbie Harper, Bill Byrne, Wayne Songer, Terry Harrington, Beamsley, Lamare, Leatherwood, Fatool

Cary writes: "I've agreed to start Golden West Ballroom, three nights per for three weeks—starts 12th on piano." This booking would have occupied him until the end of March, but his diary does not confirm this as it is blank between the middle of March and September 27. It is safe to assume that the dates above are indicative of those he played during these lost months. He fails to mention his regular appearance at the Sacramento Dixieland Jubilee, two sessions each day May 23–25, during which he was scheduled to play the 23rd with the Smogsville Society Orchestra and the Jazz Minors, the 24th with Jazzberry Jam and the Queen City Jazz Band, and the 25th with the Capitol City Jazz Band and the SPDJ Stars (the Society for the Preservation of Dixieland Jazz, led by trumpeter Johnny Lucas).

In Germany in 1975 Dick Cary told *Jazz Podium* writer, Gudrun Endress, a little of his life is Los Angeles:

> I am writing a lot, mostly for myself, and compose for college bands, a mixture of chamber music and jazz. That is profitable for the time being. There are numerous rehearsal bands with whom I practice two or three times during the week. There are hardly any places where you can really play jazz.
>
> I am a member of a nine-piece band and a sixteen-piece orchestra. We play in parks, at festivals, in dance-halls, mostly in the summer. Besides that I play tennis and golf. It is not easy to be successful as a composer unless you have a name like Aaron Copland, to name one. However, what Leonard Feather wrote about me, that I was writing a symphony, is not true. I write music arrangements for saxophone sections, quintets for woodwinds, etc. Right before we left for this tour my publisher called me [about] pieces he had ordered. That forced me to work those even here in Europe.

The tour referred to came at the end of 1975, when cornetist Jimmy McPartland, at the age of 68, decided he would make a return visit to Europe. McPartland had married a young Englishwoman (born Margaret Turner in 1918, but using the stage name of Marian Page) during his military service in Europe. She was to become a celebrated pianist in her own right, using her married name of Marian McPartland, despite a subsequent divorce.

McPartland asked Dick Cary to be his companion for the tour. As *Jazz Podium* reported, Cary carried the burden of the tour. "He organised the travel, rehearsed the different bands they appeared with and showed a youthful energy that was appreciated by musicians and audiences alike." Cary said:

> This is Jimmy's tour. He asked me to help him organise his European trip. He knew that for some time I had planned to tour Europe and for that reason he was pretty certain I would agree.

Both McPartland and Cary wished to visit Britain, partly because Bud Freeman was living there at the time, but Cary had to wait another two years before he reached the U.K. He flew to New York, via Dallas and Nashville, on September 28, visiting the new Eddie Condon's and Jimmy Ryan's while he was there, before catching the flight to Copenhagen on the 30th.

Sweden, Germany, Italy and Holland were on the 1975 itinerary. The duo were in Gothenburg, Sweden, between October 1st and 3rd, when they played two dates with the Carnegie Jazzband to enthusiastic young audiences at the students' union and at a place called Volrat Tham. "They received a short but very positive review in *Orkester Journalen* of November 1975."

Next came a tour with the Barrelhouse Jazz Band of Frankfurt, Germany. The first concert, on October 5, was arranged by the Hannover Jazz Club. (Cary mentions they were at the Storyville Club in Braunschweige "after the three days in Gothenburg," but perhaps they were just visiting.) The official dates with the Barrelhouse Jazz Band, split by one in Vienna with the Printers Jazz Band and one with the Barrelhouse Jazz Band of Vienna (a different band to that from Frankfurt), and three in Italy with the Milan College Jazz Society, led by guitarist, Lino Patruno, were:

October 5:	Hannover (Aegi Theater), Germany
October 6:	rest day
October 7:	Frankfurt am Main (Volksbildungsheim)
October 8:	Pforzheim (beer joint—"piano terrible")
October 9:	Mainz (Eltzer Hof) (beautiful hall but piano needed tuning)
October 10:	Erkelenz ("high school with grand, grand Bechstein")
October 11:	Bergisch-Gladbach
October 12:	Bergkamen (beer joint "McPartland didn't make this one")
October 13	flight to Vienna
October 14:	Vienna (Club Jazzland) (with the Printers Jazz Band)
October 15:	Vienna (Club Jazzland) (with the Barrelhouse Jazz Band of Vienna)
October 16:	Genoa (Louisiana Jazz Club), Italy with the Milan College Jazz
October 17:	Lecco (Teatro Sociale), Italy—Society band
October 18:	Milan, Italy (recording session) (ditto)
October 19:	Milano Jazz Club (ditto)
October 20:	flight to Stuttgart
October 21/22:	Stuttgart (Dixieland Hall), Germany
October 23:	Munich
October 24/25:	Munich (Lowenbraukeller)

Clarinetist Reimer Von Essen is the leader of the Barrelhouse Jazz Band from Germany and he remembers the tour with some

At Jazzland, Vienna, 1975 *(Photograph courtesy of Axel Melhardt)*

affection: "In 1974 and 1975 we took part in the traditional Jazz Festival in Nice and at some occasion [it was 1974] Jimmy McPartland sat in, which was nice. So the idea came up to invite him for a tour with us. The organisation was taken over by our manager, Dieter Nentwig, and he informed us that McPartland was going to bring "his musical director." We had no idea what that meant but, a few days before the tour, McPartland told Dieter on the phone that he would bring along Dick Cary—which was a thrill because his name to us was bigger than McPartland's. So when the two arrived we asked what "musical director" meant and Jimmy informed us that Dick would rehearse with us and arrange the programme. So it happened.

"The first rehearsal (probably in our rehearsal cellar) showed us that Dick played trumpet (we knew of only piano then) and he played the parts that Jimmy would play (who meanwhile rested in the hotel). The whole rehearsal was kicks. Dick was nice, pedagogic and easygoing, so we soon had a programme for the tour. Of course, we wanted him to play, so we arranged for some numbers where he would play his alto horn, but also some numbers on piano, at our insistence. Later, he would also play F-trumpet.

"So we started the tour and Jimmy would prefer to be taken in a private car, whereas Dick liked to go with us in the band bus. He was very interested in learning about the sights we would pass, about history, about our views on jazz, and so the touring was a thrill.

"As far as I remember, Dick would never drink, but Jimmy did. The tour started somewhere in the Rhineland and on some gigs we used a pianist from there. Jimmy would act the star and as the tour went on played less and less, [due to an] illness of some sort. But we insisted on his appearing. Dick played throughout and now on trumpet also. The highlight was the concert at the Volksbildungsheim in Frankfurt. [One title from this concert, *St. James Infirmary*, was included on an album for Intercord.]

"On an off day Dick accepted my invitation to show him the second-century Roman ruins north of Frankfurt called SAALBURG and he was so taken by what he saw that he wrote a melody *On the Saalburg*, which we later found to be a melody he had recorded as a solo many years earlier. [It was a paraphrase of Cary's chorus from the Eddie Condon recording of *How Come You Do Me Like You Do?*] He also wrote us a number about New Orleans. Months after the tour we found out that Jimmy had promised him a share of the fee but never paid!"

No doubt von Essen was told this by Dick Cary, who was embittered by the fact that he received no payment for the tour. He had seen McPartland's contract with Dieter Nentwig and the trumpeter was to receive $2,400 for three weeks (six concerts a week, each not to exceed two hours; any additional concert $100). He was to record one side of an album with the Barrelhouse band for $250, plus three tunes in Austria for $150. Then there were plans for $1000 for one week in Holland. This still rankled years later:

> My first trip to Europe was taking care of him, for which he paid me not a dime. I was pretty mad about this for awhile but don't care much anymore. McPartland always tried to screw people. In the army he dealt on the black market.

Cary had mixed feelings about the Barrelhouse Jazzband—"This band has a wide variety of records from way back that they've copied. Some numbers are absolutely atrocious, some a bit nostalgic, some silly, but they ... have much energy. It's a unit but no individual talent as soloists." Further comments included: "These boys in Barrelhouse are most cordial indeed!" and, on October 12, "A poignant farewell to the Barrelhouse Band."

with members of the Barrelhouse Jazz Band October 5, 1975 Jimmy McPartland, tp; Hans-Georg Klaver, d; Dick Cary, a-h; Reimer von Essen, cl

(Photograph by Roland Kauder. Courtesy: Reimer von Essen)

Mike Gehrke talking to Dick Cary, October 5, 1975.

(Photograph courtesy of Friedrich Hackenberg)

He was very impressed with the Printers Jazz Band with which they played at the Jazzland in Vienna on October 14: "Tonight was first time I've really gotten going in Europe. I did first set without Jimmy—played *Mellotone*, Duke's *Squeeze Me* and *Perdido* and really enjoyed it. Then McP the last two sets [and] back to the mud flats." "What a group ... the bass player is better than anyone I work with in California. Robert [Goodenough] is from San Francisco originally. Alto [Peter Kölbl] very strong man, aggressive. Guitar leader [Gerd

Bienert] good rhythm, fine drummer [Erich Metzger], and Humbert [Augustynowicz] the pianist is quite good. He's in the steel game. They only play once a month at club—don't travel as band but try for weekly rehearsals."

Of the trip itself he wrote: "It's a new sensation being in Germany, a sort of frantic confusion. I'm continually straining my ears to understand a constant din of voices and I need sleep. But they absolutely admire the bringers of the American art form." "Each band has been so different, but all very cordial and very complimentary!! If I could sleep more and eat less I would enjoy it all."

Guitarist Lino Patruno, leader of the Milan College Jazz Society, had similar memories of Dick Cary, having played with him in 1975 and 1977: "I remember Dick as a serious man and of few words. He lived in a hotel facing my house and he rang the bell about 9 in the morning. We sat at the piano and he played up to 1 p.m. Then we were ready for lunch. In the afternoon, around 3 p.m., he played the piano up to the time we had to go places. He didn't care about dressing elegant, but always with taste. On stage he was always very professional and serious and interested in the music each musician played."

Commenting on the Milan College Jazz Society band Cary wrote: "This band doesn't swing like Tuesday in Vienna but the horn players are much better, except for [Peter Kölbl]. The clarinet tries to get a good sound and likes Bob Wilber and Peanuts Hucko. The trombone is an m.d., not bad; good baritone; and rhythm isn't bad either." On October 19 he said: ."... farewell to a group of gentlemen. I will write a tune, *The Hippocratic Brass Section (and the patient reeds)*. A very nice evening indeed."

Of the recordings made on October 18 with Lino Patruno, for Carosello, Cary said: "All in all not a bad session ... McPartland has composed two things so far ... the second is *Where Are You, Guiseppe?* or *Caprice Milano*. This starts with the first phrase of *Caprice Viennois* by Kreisler and then goes smoothly into *O Sole Mio* or some such deathless phrase ... I must admit *Caprice* came out well." The final title was *Caprice in Milan for Giuseppe (Joe) Venuti*.

It was during this tour that Cary was interviewed by Gudrun Endress for the German magazine, *Jazz Podium*, published in Stuttgart, where Cary and McPartland played on October 21 and 22. Ms. Endress was later to become the magazine's editor. Cary commented in 1990, "Several years back I was in an advanced state of silliness over G.E."

At the time Cary recorded that a reporter from a jazz magazine called to interview Jimmy McPartland—"Not a chance I said, how about tomorrow? I said I had the rest of the afternoon … she wouldn't come up so I went to the restaurant and we had coffee and a cigarette and talked into the cassette. She is Gudrun Endress and the first beautiful woman I've seen in Germany—or almost anywhere. I was captivated and talked my goddam ass off. Probably saying much I shouldn't, but with little sleep, a hectic trip, cigarettes, too much coffee all day, your mouth flaps like mad and the mind darts about."

In Stuttgart Cary and McPartland played with the Darktown Jazz Band. On October 21 "we started at 8:30 and I played all four sets tonight. Werner [Lener] piano very good. Wolfgang [Trattner] has some lip. We did a duet, trumpet and alto horn, on *Honeysuckle Rose* that went great." The following day they recorded three titles for the Intercord label, including "a quartet on *Baby Won't You Please Come Home* on alto trumpet which came out well in one take."

> I have worked with this band, but for such a short time that I did not become really acquainted with them. They are very enthusiastic. In the U.S. you don't find this enthusiasm anymore. The last time I went into Eddie Condon's or Jimmy Ryan's in New York I had the impression the musicians would soon fall asleep while playing.
>
> I have heard quite a few good drummers and this one [Elmar Wippler] belongs to them. He has tremendous drive. When I heard Werner [Lener]—that is the pianist—I was very impressed. His playing would fit many different bands. He reminded me a lot of Roger Kellaway. Werner plays very fluently and has many good melodic ideas.

Of the Stuttgart stay Cary wrote: "They treat me so well I feel guilty, because no one but a Tatum could be worth all this," but it was a different story on the 23rd when he arrived by train in Munich. "After sleep to jazz club. No one greeted me. No one spoke to me and I got on a crowded bandstand with no mood for our four B-flat tunes. It was dull, fast ones accelerate and slow ones retard. No one during evening introduced me to anyone, except the trumpet player's quite amiable wife. We did our two sets and got out!"

The 24th and 25th were spent in an enormous beer hall sitting 3,000. Cary and McPartland were with two of the bands, the Hot Dogs ("the strongest and loudest of them all!!") and the Feetwarmers—though McPartland did not play on the last night.

From Germany, Cary and McPartland moved on to Holland where they were featured with Ted Easton and his band at "The New Orleans Jazzclub" in the seaside resort of Scheveningen, near The Hague. Drummer Ted Easton (nee Theo van Est, 1932–1990) founded the club in 1968 in the Palace building. The Palace was demolished in 1978, but throughout the 1970s Easton booked many jazz stars from the U.S.A and Europe as guests to play with his band. Wild Bill Davison, Ralph Sutton, Max Kaminsky, Vic Dickenson, Bob Wilber, Buddy Tate, Cootie Williams, Bobby Hackett, Peanuts Hucko, Billy Butterfield and Bud Freeman were just a few of those to appear.

Cary recorded a delightful LP for the Riff label ("The Amazing Dick Cary") with Easton on October 27th and 30th, and on the 28th was the pianist for a Nat Gonella session. Veteran British trumpeter and singer Gonella had reached the Dutch hit parade in 1970 with a recording of *Oh Monah*, with the Easton band, and he continued to be in demand. The resulting LP, on the CNR label, was entitled Wishing You a Swinging Christmas. Cary and Easton co-composed one song on the album, titled *At Christmas*.

"The Amazing Dick Cary," which was reissued by Jazzology on CD, also featured Ralph Sutton on piano and Bob Wilber, on one track, on soprano. Cary commented:

The Riff album contained a mixture of dates which I had not expected, some from a Sutton date and Wilber only overdubbed—I didn't see him that time. Mandy is Ralph [Sutton], so he's on piano and I'm playing lousy trumpet. Same on Somebody Stole My Gal *and* Sin [to Tell a Lie]. Sleigh Ride *and* Save It Pretty Mama, *I play all the parts, except bass [and drums].* New Kind of Love *is Ralph's date. What's New is just me and bass [and drums] again and Wilber inserted his part three days after I had left—and not inserted very well at all.*
Easton also has an

Germany 1975, on the bass.
(Photograph by Dieter Nentwig)

> *album—I overdubbed all the melodies while [Bobby] Hackett was noodling. I spend every spare minute when I'm with Ted Easton in a small studio in Leiden and he has an enormous amount of unpublished tapes. I always enjoyed my stays in Scheveningen by the ocean. Ted was the only guy in Europe to put me in a decent hotel. He's quite a guy!*
>
> *I must have recorded enough for about nine or ten albums. Some are piano tracks with bass [and undoubtedly, drums]—for some future guest soloist to join us. I did one with Hackett, shortly after Bobby's death. Hope Ted sends them along as he puts them out. He has stacks and stacks of material from a lot of artists.*

The reference to Hackett refers to playing accompaniment to a pre-recorded tape by the trumpeter, who was at the club in 1973. The fate of all these recordings is unknown.

On October 30th and 31st Cary and McPartland recorded an album of tunes associated with Bix Beiderbecke. Of this Bix tribute Cary wrote:

> *Later that week we did the McPartland thing and he didn't show up the first night. We got him to overdub the next day and I added piano because Ted didn't use me in the club.*
>
> *In the Dark is [Ralph] Sutton, In a Mist is my rather faltering rendition. I never did perform the latter or even bother to remember it very accurately, so I was following the music. I am sure there are many purists who would be absolutely horrified at this, but I will not keep it a dark secret. Let the world know. I'm getting too old to give a damn. I think I overdubbed piano in* Davenport Blues. *I'm sure I did, because I don't think I did it with Sutton.*
>
> *The Bix album was recorded in the club—which is an easy place to play—all the rest in that home in Leiden.*
>
> *[Ralph] Sutton did a week, I followed him, overlapping a Monday, and [Bob] Wilber followed me, but I didn't get to see Bob at all. The Sutton date, which is the first night I worked for Ted, my very first time [October 27] in Holland. It was a small, crowded living room—terribly close to work in—all muffled and Ted's banjo player (from who a lot of the finances flow) was fortissimo all through. It's terribly hard to record in a small living room. I was amazed at Ralph's seeming serenity—and I wish he'd had a little booze that evening because I'm sure he would have turned the plucker down at least during the piano solos.*

Cary was correct when he spoke of the amount of recording with Ted Easton. His diary suggests that he recorded on six of the ten days he was in Scheveningen and that he was satisfied with his fees. "He laid $900 on me, two albums plus $100 for piano with Nat's Christmas songs." This was followed, on the day of the flight home, by "$800 for last two albums—which is now a total of $1700, plus the 900 marks in Germany, about $2050 so far."

His views on the Easton band were that it was: "very rough, unbalanced and has arrangements also, so what need is there for me. Fritz Kaatee, the clarinet, alto, tenor and baritone, a damn good hot alto player and good big band sound on baritone. He's a real pro." He also says of one set that "they played their large Dutch asses off." And of Easton's 'second band' he remarks: "What energy! Sat in a little. Just a few people ... such courteous people. If they knew what a slob I really am—or am I? Europe gives me some self-esteem which all humans should have but which American society has done its damndest to stifle in its musicians."

The Chris Barber band played at the club on October 31— "Chris Barber surprised me—has a wide variety and they play well and very energetically, as all Europeans ... I talked to Chris like mad until about 4 a.m."

He played at Ted Easton's club on November 1/2, did a full day of recording on the 3rd, plus further recording and an evening session at the club on the 4th, before flying back to Los Angeles on November 5. There is a small mystery here in that a notebook detailing the European tour gives November 5 as the day he was to catch his flight to L.A., but his diary for November 18 states that this was his first day home since the end of September. Was the November 18 date an error or did he stop-over in New York and appear with Jimmy and Marian McPartland at the Plaza Hotel? He does write on his first day home, "There was some depression and loneliness today, but it will be easier tomorrow, with some sleep and no alcohol."

The diary gives little detail for the rest of the year, except for a handicap party in November with a trio and a job in Santa Clara on December 28 which probably did not materialise. In January 1976 he received a "Dinah Shore re-run check," indicating work on the singer's show during 1975.

Pianist Stan Wrightsman (b.1910) died on December 17th, causing Cary to write:

> *He'd been living in Palm Springs since he'd had bad lung trouble for years. His activities had been limited—only a few*

times a year with Phil Harris, who he tried to keep reasonably sober. Stan was one of the most gracious gentlemen I've known in this business. Someone whom I call a no-bullshit man.

The early hours of New Year's Day, 1976, found him ending the last night of a two week engagement with the World's Greatest Jazz Band in Spark's at the Nugget in Las Vegas—"Enjoyed piano. We did three shows a night. Tennis every day. The poker players didn't even glance up from their desperate holdings." The band was Yank Lawson, trumpet, George Masso, trombone, Joe Muranyi, clarinet, Dick Hafer, tenor, Cary, piano, Bob Haggart, bass, Cliff Leeman, drums. He played a quartet job at Sir Sico's on January 2, followed by two late night sets with the Lawson-Haggart band at the Coconut Grove on Saturday, January 3.

He then notes that there were no more dates for January. This meant that he played a lot of tennis. Not surprisingly, on January 23, he created a big scene when he foot-faulted his opponent! But there were one or two jobs:

January 14: Balboa Marriott: on trumpet with Esser for Mercedes Benz
January 17: Sir Sico's: with Del Simmons, piano
January 24: Glendora, Pasadena: played piano with Catron [Johnny Catron, drums?], Ed Mihelich on bass
January 28: McCambridge Park
January 30: Valley College, Fulton: with Abe Most Octet Small audience, fine large grand piano
February 6: "guest" at Cliff May's
February 7: Skytrails: with Herbie Harper, Joe Darensbourg, ----Small, Jack Lesberg, Nick Fatool, Marge Murphy, vocal (Bob Tabor job)
February 13: gave Dixieland music lesson to Janet Anderson's four sons
February 19/20: Warner Bros. recording with Fred Carlin
February 21: Papa Choux: afternoon ("some man marrying for the fourth time"): with Joe Yukl, leading Wayne Songer, Ray Sherman, Ray Leatherwood, Norm Jeffries, drums, Balboa: evening: big band
February 25: McCambridge Park: with Betty O'Hara and Perkins (Bill Perkins, drums?)
February 27: Andersons' lesson

The weekend of March 6 and 7 he was back with the Lawson-Haggart band, playing on the Saturday at El Camino and the Sunday at a gymnasium at Mount San Antonio, San Bernardino. The personnel was Yank Lawson, trumpet, George Masso, trombone, Phil Bodner, clarinet, Tommy Newsom, tenor, Cary, piano, Bob Haggart, bass, Jerry McKenzie, drums. (Haggart, who asked Cary to select the tenor saxist and drummer, had requested a change to Cary's first choice of Dick Hafer.)

After another lesson for the Andersons on March 10 Cary flew to Pine Bluff for a jazz weekend on March 13/14. He played with Ralph Sutton, piano, Jack Lesberg, bass, and Gus Johnson, drums, for a wedding reception in Pine Bluff, then emceed a concert at the Arts Center the next day.

And the one-off dates continued:
March 22:   recorded in septet, 8 tunes for Glenn Shipley
March 24:   round dance recording—overdubbing session
March 26:   Andersons' lesson
March 31:   McCambridge Park
April 10:   trumpet with Abe Most 16-piece big band
April 17:   round dance recording—more overdubbing

Cary commented on the Abe Most date, which included such names as Zeke Zarchy, trumpet, Bob Enevoldsen, trombone, Les Robinson, Dick Hafer, Chuck Gentry, reeds, and the usual rhythm section of Sherman, Leatherwood, Fatool: "A potentially good big band was completely and shamefully wasted and ruined." He also mentions the addition of "a young egotist who insulted a guitar." A week later he noted: "So pleased to stay home Saturday night. I'd rather play but not *Proud Mary* or *Sweet Caroline*—or with Herman Zaid or the rest of the garbage heads."

The Tuesday rehearsal band continued, as did the lessons for the Anderson brothers. They were scheduled to play *High Society* and *Basin Street Blues* on a television show on April 2.

On April 25, 1976, Cary flew to Santa Clara to appear at the local jazz society meeting—"This is another TRAD club and makes TRAD mean inept and stupid ... I feel like I did nothing today but people were very agreeable." At the end of April he wrote: "Another month gone forever and I stay the same, trying to write and not having enough incentive to do anything but stay still while the time passes inexorably."

At 9:45 on the morning of May 1 he, in company with Herbie Harper, Joe Darensbourg, Nappy Lamare and Nick Fatool, "played a private jet into Burbank—some wealthy asshole, chairman of AMWAY, whatever the hell that is!" In the evening there was a casual at Vanowen and Corbin in Reseda with Al Jenkins, trombone, Bill Wood, clarinet, Lee Countryman, piano, Walt Yoder, bass, and George Defebaugh, drums—"fairly pleasant evening, Al Jenkins only one playing however. Defebaugh worse than he used to be, Yoder has no sound, Countryman says nil, and Bill Wood older and less inventive."

There was a recording date for Terry Maretti on May 6; then he was on what he called a "Mexico cruise" from May 8 to 15, in a more-than-promising band—Cary, trumpet, Bob Enevoldsen, trombone, Abe Most, clarinet, John Bunch, piano, Remo Palmieri, guitar, Milt Hinton, bass, Jake Hanna, drums—which was underused. There were only two days on which they played two shows, and he and Enevoldsen were sitting-in with the Mexican band on board.

Then it was back, as Cary noted, to television, tennis, writing and his dogs, "the good Lady Albert and Sean."

The Andersons were still taking lessons—"They improve a little each time," but Cary would not say this about Abe Most. On May 22 at the Lakeside he complained: "Tonight he ... brought some one-chorus 'stocks,' something that resembled a high-school band rehearsing. Finally ... he starts on my library. After *One Morning in May*, Arnold Ross was heard to say, 'Now, that couldn't hurt anybody.'" The following night he played at the Pilgrimage with Gordon Mitchell, saying that the "jazz club band has been rehearsing."

For the weekend of May 28–31, he participated in the Sacramento Dixieland Jubilee. One set was by the Dick Cary All Stars, with Al Smith, trumpet, Dick Cary, alto horn, Abe Lincoln, trombone, Abe Most, clarinet, Pud Brown, tenor, Jack Gumbiner, piano, and Nick Fatool, drums. Elsewhere he played with the Capitol Jazz Band ("good"), the Queen City Jazz Band ("pretty bad") and with the Wingy Manone All-Stars. "I was on piano with Abe Lincoln, Joe Darensbourg, Nick Fatool, Wingy Manone—latter saw Phil Harris, got him up on stage—they said 'shit' for half-an-hour. We played two songs—awful. Then Peanuts Hucko and Billy Butterfield came out and saved some of evening. Billy really did *Black and Blue*." His comments on the final day are: "In early afternoon played only good set of the weekend, with Peanuts and Ray Leatherwood at Chinese Temple. At night Butterfield's alcohol level was too high and we stumbled through a set—saved somewhat by an eager Peanuts."

(The afternoon set was with the Louise Tobin All Stars, while the evening was with Butterfield's All Stars. Other sets during the weekend were with the Rose City Jazz Band, the Fulton Street Jazz Band, and the Johnny Guarnieri All Stars.)

At the end of May Cary wrote: "A pretty good month with a variety and a little money. Now I have a blank June to cope with."

Bobby Hackett died on June 7, 1976, and Cary wrote: "Strange little man—very big little man in many ways. Unaware of so much in the world and yet so aware of some things. One of the most timid souls ... but had such an artistry, a very symmetrical artistry, that we wonder what this little figure would have been without his music."

Cary reported that June was the "slowest month I've had since I started to sustain myself with only music. Two weddings, a small overdub for Olds. Andersons over twice. So I made little more than 200 bucks in the whole month." But he also lists:

June 6:	(afternoon) Busch Gardens
June 25:	Corbin
June 26:	Abe Most
July 1:	"A new month and some work and I finally attain the distinguished age of 60"
July 3:	Hawthorne Eagles: Johnny Lane gig
July 4:	Norwalk: (afternoon) with nine piece (from rehearsal band)
July 7:	La Mirada, Gardenhill
July 10:	Lafayette Hotel, Long Beach: Mac McReynolds big band
July 15:	Barnsdall Park: (evening) Abe Most big band, including Arnold Ross, piano, Al Hendrickson, guitar. "Howard Lucraft drivelled, crowd apathetic."
July 16:	Andersons' lesson
July 17:	Braille Institute: (morning) Abe Most, Al Hendrickson, Nick Fatool
July 18:	Hilton Inn: 2:00–6:00 and 10.00–12.30, with Bill Hill, piano: Peanuts Hucko, clarinet, Red Norvo, vibes, Tom Newsom, tenor, John Kitzmeller, bass, Jack Sperling, drums. "Bobby Gordon did last set on clarinet—did a marvelous Pee Wee chorus on *Indiana*"
July 22:	Barnsdall Park: an Abe Most nonet, including Jack Trott, Herbie Harper, Bob Enevoldsen, Nick Fatool, Ray Leatherwood, Charlie Myerson, guitar

July 24: private party, "on back porch, 7:30 to midnight, very pleasant quartet": Myerson, guitar, Leatherwood, bass, Fatool, drums
July 25: Ambassador College, Pasadena: Abe Most 16-piece big band—"Best concert since I've lived here. Programme included: *Jumpin' Punkins, The Mooche, Blue Skies, Clarinet a la King, Maid with the Flaxen Hair, Benny Rides Again, How Hot It Was!, Midriff, Ambassador, Mission Bay, Moon Mist, Cottontail* (mainly Cary arrangements and one or two originals)
July 29: Mystic Studios on Selma: a job for Howard Lucraft, cues for piano, trumpet, organ
July 30: Andersons' lesson
August 1: Valley Hospital: with Gordon Mitchell, 2:00 to 4:00
August 7: private party: 7:30 to midnight. Cary, piano

Concerning this private party on Wilshire Terrace, Cary wrote: "Apartment full of people—I played and felt quite alone for four hours. Then an MD joined me about midnight and was quite pleasant. It takes but one person to save an evening for me, to make at least one connection between the 'piano player' and the people who regard [him] as a servant or a prop. It wasn't too bad."

August 14: Timbres: played third trumpet with Catron.
August 15: Monterey Park, 7:30 to 9:30: nonet, with Trott, Harper, O'Hara, Dave Edwards, reeds, Leatherwood, Fatool, and Charlie W.
August 21: Timbres
August 22: San Diego: with Bill Hill band: Kai Winding, trombone, Mahlon Clark, clarinet, Tommy Newsom, tenor, Jack Lesberg, bass, Jack Sperling, drums, John Collins, guitar. ("Second hour unbelievably dull. John Best arrived at 4:00.")
August 28: Timbres
August 29: McArthur Park: septet (Trott, Hafer, Harrington, Sherman, Leatherwood, Fatool. (Went on 80 minutes late, trombones had to leave)
September 11/12: Harry's N.Y. Bar & Grill, Newport Beach: Johnny Lane job

At Harry's New York Bar & Grill on the 11th, with Johnny Lane on clarinet and Andy Blakeney on trumpet, there was a banjoist, and "some complete ass with a bass and amplifier who set a new record—not one correct note in four hours, even accidentally."

The weekend of September 18/19 Cary appeared in the Los Angeles Jazz Festival, which Floyd Levin and Barry Martyn organised. On the 18th he was part of Joe Venuti's Trio (Red Callender, bass, Nick Fatool, drums) and on the next night he was in the "All-Stars" on piano, alongside Teddy Buckner, trumpet, Trummy Young, trombone, Barney Bigard, clarinet, Red Callender, bass, and Cozy Cole, drums, playing "Memories of Satchmo." Cary's solo feature was *Echo of Spring*.

Barry Martyn has a particular reason to remember the band rehearsal: "Floyd and I put on the 'Los Angeles Jazz Festival,' three days, September 17, 18, 19. John Lee Hooker was supposed to be the headliner on the 17th and he didn't turn up, which was a drag.

"The All-Stars were set to rehearse on the Saturday afternoon (the 18th), down in what we called our office, which was Floyd's basement of his factory, dirty, dusty old place. But it was great for our purposes. You could make as much noise, playing music, and nobody would complain.

"Early on the Saturday morning I had a phone call from Cozy Cole to say he couldn't get out of Columbus, Ohio, until later than he had intended. Therefore, would I do him a big favour and play with the All-Stars in his place? You can imagine what that meant to me. I said, 'Sure, I'll be tickled pink.' Thanks for getting busy, Cozy!

"So, I was the drummer with that band [for the rehearsal]. Dick, as I remember, was the one that actually took over the rehearsal. Trummy was pretty astute, Barney was quiet, Teddy you could barely understand and Red wasn't a table thumper, but Dick said 'Let's get this straight, we'll have to do this here, do that there.' So Dick, as a bandleader, was pretty good. And that Sunday night was a huge success."

Cary worked as a pianist for Bob Crosby on September 24, driving to San Diego with Nick Fatool and Les Robinson. He does not comment on the music but complains that "Boob" Crosby "took 12 bucks out of $75 which John Best had assured me would be taxless." The following day he flew to Eugene, Oregon, where he played piano, trumpet and alto horn for the jazz club during the afternoon of the 26th. And these single engagements continued:

September 29:   McCambridge Park: Betty O'Hara, Ray Leatherwood "and singers."

September 30: King Arthur, 1;00–4:00: Bill Tole rehearsal—terrible music
October 2: Andersons' lesson. No work this Saturday night.
October 9: Timbres: with Catron—"I like piano better than third trumpet."
October 11: Disneyland Hotel, 9:30 to 1:00: with Bill Tole band
October 16: Timbres, 9:00 to 1:00: "third trumpet with Catron's band—hard!"
October 18: Sir Sico's 7:30: with Barry Martyn
October 20: McCambridge Park
October 22/23: with Bob Esser
October 24: Woodland: with Jack Weaver
October 30: Masonic Hall, 9;00 to 1:00: Abe Most, with Cary, trumpet, Bob Enevoldsen, Ray Sherman, Ray Leatherwood, Gene Estes ("fine job")
October 31: Andersons' lesson
November 2: round dance record date
November 12: Andersons' lesson

Other than the weekly rehearsal night and an occasional brass quintet rehearsal, Cary's date book contained a lot of blanks. He was in a Van Alexander orchestra (5 brass, 5 reeds, strings, and 3 rhythm) which accompanied a show featuring an Irish singer and The Modernaires at the Riviera Hotel in Palm Springs on November 22. Abe Most, alto, and Nick Fatool, drums were among the personnel. On the 26th, after a lesson for the Anderson brothers, he subbed in the Art DePew band for a Notre Dame rally at the Regency Hyatt, and he played a party with clarinetist Art Lyons on December 4.

Thereafter there are just three entries in the diary, including two dates with the Lawson-Haggart band on December 18 and 19 in Phoenix, Arizona. He flew to Phoenix on the 18th, played the two jobs, then caught a late flight on the 19th back to Los Angeles. He had recruited Eddie Miller, tenor, and Gene Estes, drums, to complete the line-up.

The reason for his haste in leaving Phoenix is clear from the final entry for December 1976 in his diary. On the 21st he records that he caught the 8 p.m. Pan American flight to Australia.

18. Brisbane, The Red Lion and The Revolution Club (1976–1977)

Just received a letter from Australia saying I was one of seven pianists being considered for a large jazz convention, December 26th to January 1st. Was there with a Condon band about ten years ago and always wanted a return visit. I am going to Brisbane in December (20th) and stay on for dates in January. I know Sutton couldn't go, Wilson wouldn't "float around" etc, and since I asked to play the other instruments, I guess that swung it.

I landed at Brisbane and there's a little band out in the rain. And they always did this, they herded you into a television room right away. You didn't even have a chance to get to the can. They started asking me questions and I made the front page of the paper the next day. It said, in a big block down the side of the paper, "'DIXIELAND' DONE OUT OF BUSINESS" [The Brisbane Courier Mail].

I had told them what I thought. I said, "It's a terrible thing. You can't get a job. That word [Dixieland] signifies several things. You can't read, you don't play very well and you're unreliable."

Dr. Mileham Hayes, president of the convention, wrote that he was going to fix me up with an Australian, Wimbledon and Forest Hills tennis champion all rolled into one. Dr. Hayes knew I was very keen on tennis—in fact, I play every day when I'm home—but I thought he was just cooking up a joke. When I got to Brisbane I found that his brother-in-law was Ashley Cooper, a great tennis champion, and he took me over to Ashley's house every day for a lesson. That was the big part of the convention for me—it's like studying with Art Tatum!

Leaving Los Angeles on December 21, Cary arrived in Sydney around noon on the 23rd. He was met by pianist Adrian Ford who guided him to the flight for Brisbane, where he landed an hour later in the fog. Mileham Hayes rescued him from the press and took him home, where he was installed in a guest house.

The Australian Jazz Convention of 1976, held in Brisbane, was the 31st of these annual events, when jazz musicians from all over the country assembled for a week of music-making. Collector Bill Haesler wrote about Dick Cary: "My first meeting with Dick Cary was in the men's toilet of the Festival Hall in Melbourne in 1964, during a warm-up rehearsal when he toured Australia with the Eddie Condon All Stars. Unusual but memorable. Dick in 1976 had mellowed but still retained the charm that endeared him to us 14 (sic) years ago. In 1964 he was amazed that Australians had ever heard of him. At the Convention in 1976, he modestly accepted the fact that he was a jazz celebrity in this country. He mixed and played throughout the Convention week with whoever involved him. Unlike some previous overseas Jazz Convention guests, he was always available, Hawaiian shirt, shorts, smile and instrument case. I find it difficult to talk jazz to celebrated jazz people as I am afraid I will bore them with the usual questions everyone asks. So Dick and I swapped dirty jokes. I remember most of his and I hope he remembers some of mine. Jazz Convention memories can be vague but I will never forget the annual midnight blow on New Year's Eve with Dick Cary trying to outblow everyone on stage for the traditional *Auld Lang Syne* and the usual New Orleans marching style music. He came to our Convention as a guest and from day one was part of it. Dick Cary is without a doubt one of the greatest jazz people."

During his short stay in Australia Cary recorded for E.M.I. with Mileham Hayes' World's Hottest Jazz Band, in two sessions, December 27th and 28th, at the University of Queensland auditorium. The band, so-called because it was "recorded in the hottest state of Australia during a heatwave," included such Australian luminaries as Bob Barnard, Frank Johnson, trumpets, Ade Monsbourgh, reeds (instead of his usual valve-trombone), and Len Barnard, drums, as well as Mileham Hayes himself, who played clarinet. In addition, sets from the Convention which included Cary were subsequently released on audio cassettes, a CD and a video.

The main concerts were held in the Schonell Theatre, with Cary being heavily featured with Bob Barnard, of whom he wrote: "a hell of a trumpet player—strong—shows Louis, Bobby, Billy influences." He also played one concert with the Brisbane Jazz Club Big Band. His programme appears to have been as follows, with the starred* performances listed in the catalogue for Audio Alchemy cassettes:

    December 26 afternoon: piano set?
    December 26 evening: Dick Cary and his Convention Hotshots*
    December 27 afternoon: Convention Guests: Barnard, Cary, Monsbourgh*
    December 27 evening: Dick Cary and Bob Barnard with Mileham Hayes, clarinet, leader,

	Ade Monsbourgh, reeds,
	Ken Herron, trombone,
	Len Barnard, drums*
December 28 evening:	Brisbane Jazz Club Big Band with Cary and Barnard*
December 29 afternoon:	Dick Cary and Friends*
December 30 evening:	Graeme Bell featuring Dick Cary (Ken trombone, Ed Gaston "a good bass," et al.)*
December 31 afternoon:	Ade, Bob, Dick, Ed, Bob, Ken ("at the university—good set—best one of the week")*
December 31 evening:	Dick Cary

Australia recording session, Brisbane, December 1976.
l-r: Cary; Ed Gaston, b; Len Barnard, d; Lachie Thomson, cl; Bob Barnard, tp; Neville Stribling, bar; Ade Monsbourgh, ts; Ken Herron, tb; Frank Johnson, tp; Mileham Hayes, cl. *(Courtesy: Mike Sutcliffe)*

After the Convention, Cary enjoyed a five day holiday with the Hayes family, spending time on the beach and also taping "a long interview" with Mileham Hayes. Then, on January 6, 1977, he flew back to Los Angeles, via Sydney and Honolulu. Cary's main grouse about his time in Brisbane was the weather—"God! It's hot and humid ... If the temperature were a bit lower I'd be buzzing about more, but it's too damn oppressive."

Work was slow during January—"Phone very silent." Other than three Monday night rehearsals, a brass quintet session at Zeke Zarchy's, and a lot of tennis, he mentions only "Buckley's at 10:30" on the 9th and a McCambridge Park 'handicap' dance with Betty O'Hara and Ray Leatherwood on the 19th. He was scheduled to work with Eddie Miller in San Diego on the 28th, but does not confirm that he did.

On February 1, 1977 he was off to Europe again, flying to Milan via Chicago and Frankfurt, where his engagements were:

February 3: Canelli, Italy (Gazebo club)
(with the Milan College Jazz Society band)
February 4: Milan, Biblo's club (ditto)
February 5: Hilton, private party 1 set (plus Biblo's ?) (ditto)
February 6: Milan,Teatro Uomo (ditto)
February 8: Mannheim, University, Germany
(with the Chicagoans)
February 9: Pforzheim, Schlobkeller (ditto)
February 11: Ludwigsburg, Bahnhotel (ditto)
February 12: Pforzheim, Reuchlinhaus (ditto)
February 13: Pforzheim ("lovely hall in museum") (ditto)
February 14: Munich, Schwabinger Podium
(with Allotria Jazzband)
February 15: same venue? ("easy night—did 3 piano solos")
February 18: Vienna, Jazzland (with Barrelhouse Jazz Band)
February 19: Vienna, Jazzland (with Axel's Dream Band)
February 20: Vienna, Jazzland (with Printers Jazzband)
February 22: Stuttgart—TV studio (for video taping?)
February 23 Pforzheim, Schlobkeller (with The Chicagoans)
February 24 Stuttgart, Dixieland Hall
(with Darktown Jazzband)

Cary's comments on this part of his trip are as one might guess. Of his nights with Lino Patruno's Milan College Jazz Society he wrote: "Pianos so far are atrocious" and, on the 4th, "Tonight our audience was slightly less than enthusiastic, but there really isn't a hell of a lot to be excited about. Numbers are too long, go the rounds every time." And on the 19th—"Thank God, no banjo tonight."

Recordings were made with The Chicagoans on February 23rd, then with the Old Merry Tale Jazzband on March 4, 5 and 6. Jost Münster, the trombonist-leader of the latter band remembered: "We did not tour with him, we just spent some time together during his stay in Germany. He joined us for one concert (sic) in Hamburg. But I had plenty of time to talk with him as he was a guest in my home. He was extremely sympathetic, played on a very high level, piano as well as tenor horn. I was fascinated by his knowledge of so many things, especially the history of jazz. He knew all the famous jazz musicians.

"He was particularly proud about his cooperation with Louis Armstrong and that the famous concert in Boston was a 'milestone' in the history of jazz for us young musicians in Germany. He told me that he composed *Swing Down to New Orleans* especially for Louis, hoping Louis would use it [as his signature tune], but Louis preferred *Sleepytime Down South*. I think, if I remember right, Dick admired Bobby Hackett as a friend and as musician the most." Cary recalled playing with the Old Merry Tale, saying:

Lino Patruno and Dick Cary, Italy in the 1970s.
(Photograph courtesy of Lino Patruno)

> Their big jazz hall, the Fabrik, was burned down just before I arrived and we worked in a tent on an adjoining lot. Their album isn't half bad and there are two tunes which don't bother me too much, Crazy Rhythm *and* Please.

Cary flew to Scheveningen in Holland on February 25, where he worked at Ted Easton's club that night and the following night, and played a concert on the Sunday afternoon, the 27th. The next three days, February 28, March 1/2, he worked in the recording studio in Easton's home in Leiden. Over the first two days he recorded 22 titles with bass and drums, some as trio items, others—"as tracks for future soloists like Buddy Tate and [Roy Williams] the trombone with the Alex Welsh band—very good on records I've heard." On the third day he added "some random trumpet and horns on songs from Monday and Tuesday," as well as dubbing some alto horn onto an unissued album which Bobby Hackett recorded in 1973.

After the three days in Hamburg, already mentioned, Cary flew to London on Sunday, March 6, for his first British tour, organised by the agent, Robert Masters. His itinerary was:

March 7: The Red Lion Hotel, Hatfield
March 8: Bristol gig was cancelled: sat-in with Alex Welsh at Wembley.
March 9: College of Further Education, Derby (with Tony Bracegirdle, trombone)
March 10: Great Harwood Football Club, near Burnley (with John Barnes & Doug Whaley Quartet)
March 11: Grasshoppers Club, Preston (with John Barnes, Roy Williams & Ribble Valley Jazzmen)
March 12: train to Glasgow—stayed with Ken Gallacher
March 13: Black Bull, Milngavie, Glasgow ("one of best days")
March 14: train to London (visited 100 Club—"poor band") and Ronnie Scott's ("impressed by Cedar Walton, Billy Higgins, Sam Jones")
March 15: Chapter Arts Centre, Canton, Cardiff
March 16: Concorde, Southampton (with Teddy Layton, tenor, & rhythm)
March 17: London's Seven Dials, Covent Garden (Bruce Turner & Keith Ingham Trio)
March 18: Pizza Express, Dean Street, London
March 19: Day off ("saw Googie Withers/John McCullum in 'Circle' at Haymarket Theatre")
March 20: Adur Hotel, Hove (Benny Simkins band)
March 21: flight to Los Angeles

I wish my one and only tour of the U.K. had been under a different management. Some of the nights were very difficult and some of the amateur groups really were atrocious, although individually the men were most gracious to me. The pianos generally were the worst anywhere. In Cardiff some kids kept me up till 6 a.m.—no heat in their flat and I caught a really lousy cold, then arrived in Southampton the following night in pouring rain—no cabs, no hotel reservations, so I drank my way through the remainder of the dates.

That agent I had is an absolute ass. But in spite of this I'm very glad I did come at least once, because I met some marvellous people. My stay in Glasgow was the best of all due to a very kind man and his family, Ken Gallacher, a sports writer who I had been corresponding with for many years. He got some nice guys to play with at a very charming inn. [We] even had a rehearsal. I stayed at his house and [found] him and his very marvellous and sensitive wife two of my favourite people. It was places like Derby, Southampton and Wales, plus that frightful hotel in London that was not so pleasant. I'd never been to London and seemed to be completely ignored there, which is not the case in Europe, where the entertaining sometimes gets too much. But I want to see London again, with someone.

My second night in England [March 8] Bristol had been cancelled and I spent the whole evening sitting-in with the Alex Welsh group. I'd heard the band on records and I've long admired [them], so it was a great thrill to play with Alex and the boys. I've enjoyed playing with the groups in the clubs where I've appeared. Then Roy and John [Roy Williams, trombone, John Barnes, reeds] each worked with me around a couple of towns near Manchester. I found John to be one of the most agreeable persons I have ever run into, on any trip.

I spent five weeks on the Continent. Over there it's mainly six- or seven-piece bands. They play ferociously and stick very much to Dixieland. Since I've been in Britain I've had a chance to play more varied music and this has been a pleasure.

I had a very good friend, pianist Stan Wrightsman. After many years you get fed up with the same old tunes and Stan would refer to them as "the mud-flats." We'd get to the job and he'd say, "Let's play as few mud-flats as we can tonight." On the Continent there were plenty of mud-flats. Over here, not so many.

Some of these tours are really very tedious. There is so much time wasted in sleazy hotel rooms, airports, etc. and I have a lot of trouble in just doing nothing but hang around. For instance, in England I was only expected to do two sets, and these not very long, and I always prefer to play a lot more, especially when I travel so far just for this reason. Another problem is that we find the repertoire very limited and almost always the same all over Europe, and filled with certain harmonies we're not used to. But I must say that the "amateurs" in Europe play so much better than our amateurs. In England I was lucky to get some pros, like Roy Williams, John Barnes and two or three good pianists. But I must say that the average night club piano in England, the instruments themselves, are the worst anywhere, but they're terrible in

> *California also. I know I shouldn't generalise this way after but one U.K. tour.*

Ken Gallacher, whose hospitality was so appreciated by Cary, was a Scottish sports journalist and jazz enthusiast who, in 1964, had contributed a major article about Cary to the British magazine, *Jazz Journal*.

Cary's first gig on his British tour, March 7 at The Red Lion in Hatfield, Hertfordshire, just north of London, indicated that he was not being treated as a "Dixielander." His accompaniment included three musicians associated with Alex Welsh, Al Gay on clarinet, soprano, tenor, Roger Nobes on vibes and Brian Lemon on piano. They were backed by Kenny Baldock, bass, and Stan Burke, drums. Band numbers for the second set, for example, were far from "mud-flats": *Sunday, Please, Dearly Beloved, China Boy*, a ballad medley, and *Perdido*. Cary played four piano solos during the evening, the two compositions he nearly always featured, *Echo of Spring*, by Willie "The Lion" Smith, and *Love Stream*, by Phineas Newborn, plus a blues and *Runnin' Wild*.

The Pizza Express band bookings were arranged by jazz expert Dave Bennett, then working for the club. Pianist Pat Hawes recalled: "It was Dave Bennett who set it up. 'Would I like to do a session with Dick Cary?' I didn't even know until I got there who else was going to be involved. I knew [drummer] Lennie Hastings well enough. Bill Skeat [tenor, clarinet] I'd never played with, nor his brother [Len, the bassist], but it was all very casual. So far as I can remember Cary didn't have a great deal to say. It was just another gig to him."

Cary himself had a particular reason for remembering the Pizza Express in Dean Street:

> *I did one night there and the agent told me it was a house record, but only because the boss wasn't there to enforce the fire-law limit. He was most hospitable. I had a terrible cold and he presented me with a beautiful bottle of brandy. Places like the P.E. are so small and crowded. Brandy is a very valuable ingredient, especially chased by good, rich-dark ale.*

The comments on brandy and drinking do not match with his telling Alan Stevens that he was drinking only ginger-ale!

> *Like everyone else who worked with Condon, I did my share of heavy drinking, but I saw the light and gradually kicked the habit.*

at the Pizza Express, London, March 18, 1977
l-r: Bill Skeat, cl; Lennie Hastings, d; Len Skeat, b; Cary, p.
(Photograph courtesy of Pat Hawes)

    For the Covent Garden Community Centre engagement Cary's accompaniment ("pretty good quartet") was by the brilliant alto saxophonist, Bruce Turner and "fine pianist" Keith Ingham, Ron Rubin, bass, Derek Hogg, drums, while the date in Hove was with the Benny Simkins band, which included such good mainstream musicians as Roy Bower, trumpet, Mike Collier, trombone, Randy Colville, clarinet, Pete Simkins, piano, and the leader on tenor. Cary noted: "Piano one of worst in entire trip. Place jammed—people very nice." He was interviewed on local radio in Burnley and Brighton.

    So Cary's first visit to Britain came to a close. Socially it was like the curate's egg, but musically it was an undoubted success. As Cary said to Alan Stevens:

> *It's taken me a long time to get here. I guess I'm finally in the land of my ancestors and I hope I'll be back again soon.*

    The next main event in 1977 was to be the Sacramento Dixieland Jubilee at the end of May, but in the meantime there were the occasional engagements, mixed in with the regular rehearsal band dates, movie shows and tennis matches:

March 26: Valley Presbyterian Hospital: pleasant evening with Gordon & Elaine Mitchell (piano), Joe Darensbourg, clarinet.
March 27: Abe Most band—"Of course we ended with *In the Mood*—what else is there?"
April 2: party 2:00–5:00: with Steve Ferand, Charles Myerson, Ray Leatherwood, Nick Fatool.
April 7: lesson for Anderson brothers
April 20: McCambridge Park

On Saturday, April 23, 1977, he was a member of Nappy Lamare's New Orleans Dixieland Jazz Band, which was one of three featured in a concert at the Wilshire Ebell Theater. The other bands were led by Buddy Burns and Bob Allen. Advance publicity gave the personnel as: Cary, trumpet, Abe Lincoln, trombone, Eddie Miller, tenor, Don Owens, piano, Nappy Lamare, banjo, Phil Stephens, bass, and Nick Fatool, drums, but Cary lists Lincoln, Max Murray, reeds, Lee Countryman, piano, Lamare, Gene Estes, drums, and "Chief," presumably on bass. Bassist Bob Allen was leading a quartet which included Mike Baird, clarinet, Alton Purnell, piano, and Sylvester Rice, drums, and he recalls that: "While Mike and I were selecting our tunes, Mike suggested *Sweet Georgia Brown*. Just then Dick Cary walked by and said, 'You can't play that, that's Joe's tune.' Immediately Mike and I smiled and Mike said, 'Let's play it then!'" Cary's verdict was: "we were by far the best of the three groups. Poor house."

Joe Darensbourg, who was on the bill with the Buddy Burns band, played clarinet on the recording of *Sweet Georgia Brown* which was featured at all the Harlem Globetrotters' basketball games.

April 24: Dick McCormick Dixieland group, with "Ray, Ray, Bob, Art."
April 29: Lesson for Anderson brothers
April 30: "usual Saturday—no work"
May 6: Sun Spot: with Ira Westley, bass, Dave Howard, drums
May 7: Sun Spot: with Westley and a.n.other—"played mostly background noises while the different ones sang."
May 13: lesson for Anderson brothers
May 16: Bob ("Boob") Crosby at Universal NBC 7; small band: Cary, John Best, trumpets, Eddie Miller, tenor, Ray Sherman, Ray Leatherwood, Nick Fatool, et al.

May 21: Lakeside Country Club: "terrible show"
May 22: Harry's Bar: with Johnny Lane, clarinet, Bill Wells, piano, Bill Stumpp, bass sax, Cary, horns
May 25: Warner Bros., 9:00–10:00: Fred Carlin; presumably as a visitor

Right after the Warner Bros. visit on the 25th Cary headed north to Sacramento, where he was to play with the One O'Clock Jazz Band in "A Spring Jazz Concert":

> *Bill Borcher, who runs [the Sacramento Jubilee], is a teacher at a comparatively small college, River College, just east of Sacramento. He's arranged for me and Abe Most to do a concert with the school stage band the Wednesday [May 25] evening before the big weekend. I've sent up the music for them to rehearse, then we do one rehearsal the afternoon of the concert. We are planning on "period" pieces which I think should not be forgotten. Duke's* Creole Rhapsody, Moon Mist, *Strayhorn's* Midriff, *and Sauter's two great pieces for Goodman,* Benny Rides Again *and* Clarinet a la King, *plus some originals of mine. I hope it will lead to more of this kind of work.*

Cary felt that the River College concert went well, though he was not so sure about the Sacramento party, as he called it. The Jubilee ran from May 27 to the 29th, but on the 26th Cary says he did one set at the Enterprise with a group including Pee Wee Erwin, trumpet, Abe Most, clarinet, Dutch Deutsch, reeds, Wilda Baughn, piano, and Ray Leatherwood, bass. He did a lengthy interview with Dorothy Melinsky, but the article did not materialise.

The 1977 Jubilee attendance was 6,200, a minute audience for the weekend in comparison with the multitudes who attended in the years ahead, but even then Cary wrote:

> *Sacramento is less fun each year as it gets so crowded. This year I played mostly piano with Haggart-Lawson-Fatool-Eddie Miller-Peanuts [Hucko] and George Masso. They stuck a banjo in with us and it's almost impossible to rectify these miscastings.*

In addition to the Lawson-Haggart group he sat-in with numerous other groups, including Bob Crosby's, Bob Ringwald's, Pete Daily's (with Al Jenkins, Don Owens, Nappy Lamare), and Pee Wee Erwin's (with George Masso, Abe Most).

After the Sacramento festival the World's Greatest Jazz Band played for one night only, three sets, Monday, May 30th, at Earthquake McGoon's, Turk Murphy's club in San Francisco. The personnel was Yank Lawson, Billy Butterfield, trumpets, George Masso, trombone, Peanuts Hucko, clarinet, Eddie Miller, tenor, Dick Cary, piano, Bob Haggart, bass, Nick Fatool, drums. The cover for the evening was $4.00, rather than the normal $2.00.

It was back to Los Angeles on the last day of May, where he took the opportunity "to watch WGJB start a Gershwin album with Roger Kellaway on piano—didn't fit band and some of members felt this keenly."

The usual pattern re-started June 3 with a lesson for the Anderson brothers, followed the next day playing trumpet with a small group, in a tent. The personnel included Art Lyons, clarinet, and "a horrible chordavox player." On Sunday the 5th he played at Harry's Bar with Johnny Lane, plus Bill Stumpp, trumpet, and a banjoist. Five days pass, until June 11, when he worked a four-hour gig on piano for drummer Bob Esser, with Dick Hafer at the Officers Club on Terminal Island. After a four day break, on the 16th, Abe Most had a job at the Lakeside Country Club, using the old reliables, Cary on piano, Ray Leatherwood, bass, and Nick Fatool, drums. "Very easy job ... but rhythm is not like it used to be, between Nick's boredom, lack of energy and booze, and Ray's working too hard, and Abe's choice of material, it's a shame."

His criticism of the audiences continued the next two days, when the clarinetist led a band at the Palace Ballroom—"Band was fine for three sets, the fourth was a fiasco. If one played *In the Mood* and *Moonlight Serenade* every set, these clods would be in paradise." He mentions some of the musicians, including Jack Trott and Les Robinson ("drunk and spoilt things") and that he had written an arrangement of *Yours* for vocalist Lucy Ann Polk.

On June 19 he drove to San Diego for an afternoon session featuring Pee Wee Erwin on trumpet, plus Peanuts Hucko and four local musicians. Next he travelled to San Francisco to play again with Erwin, alongside Abe Lincoln, Peanuts Hucko, Eddie Miller, Ray Leatherwood and Nick Fatool, on the 22nd, at both the Mark Hopkins and the Fairmont hotels for the A.M.A.

The afternoon of Thursday, June 25, a band played at William Wyler's birthday party in Beverly Hills—Cary, trumpet, Bob Enevoldsen, valve-trombone, Abe Most, clarinet, Nick Fatool, drums, a bassist, and Joe Moreno on electric Wurlitzer. Among the guests were Bette Davis, Myrna Loy and Paul Henreid. Cary complained that Wyler "never even acknowledged our presence" and that Miss Davis "didn't recognise *A Woman's Intuition*."

> And so the days passed:
> June 26: Santa Fe Springs, 4:00 to 6:00—"good job" on trumpet, with Bob Enevoldsen, Herbie Harper, Peanuts Hucko, Eddie Miller, Ray, Charles McKenzie.
> June 28: Dr. Lasell's, 7:30 to 11:30—with "Chas, Ray, Jerry."
> June 29: lesson for Anderson brothers
> July 2: Long Beach University, wedding 1:30 to 5:30—piano, with Mahlon Clark, clarinet, Ray Leatherwood, bass, Jack Sperling, drums.
> July 4: Los Nietos, 1:00 to 2:00—with Bob Enevoldsen, Peanuts Hucko, & rhythm.
> Granada Hill Recreation Center, 4:00 to 6:00—with Vernon Brown, trombone, Nick Fatool, drums, et al.
> July 6: Gardenhill, 8:00 to 9:30—with Abe Most nonet, including Jack Trott, Betty O'Hara, Dick Hafer and Gene Estes.

Of this last date Cary wrote that "new sound system made us sound awful," which led him to wonder how people like the Dorseys could be leaders for so many years without ending up in a psychiatric hospital.

Further work with the WGJB followed;

I had two tours, one in July and one in August, with the WGJB. It sounds best with Nick Fatool, but I get the feeling Haggart is losing interest and their albums are getting to sound like MUZAK (or department store noodling).

In company with Peanuts Hucko, Cary flew to Jackson Hole, Wyoming, via Salt Lake City, on July 7. "Sometimes with no one else around, I can get along fine with Peanuts. But in a group he can be so abrasive." With Cary on piano and Hucko on clarinet, the World's Greatest Jazz Band was completed by Yank Lawson, trumpet, George Masso, trombone, Eddie Miller, tenor, Bob Haggart, bass, and Gus Johnson, drums. The dates played were:

> July 7: Jackson Hole
> July 8: Snow Bird
> July 9: Vale

July 10:   Denver (Zeno's—afternoon and evening)
July 11 to 14:   Chicago (four shopping centers); Barrett Deems joined on drums
July 15/16:   Harbor Spring (played in tent, then a club show)
July 17:   Flight to Los Angeles

Collector Jim Gordon saw the band on July 12 at the Riverhope shopping centre and on the 14th at the Hawthorn shopping centre. These were evening shows, with the temperature over a hundred.

On July 18 Cary was part of a small band which recorded a jingle for Toys"R"Us and on the 22nd there was another lesson for the Andersons, and it was back to single gigs again:

July 23:   Las Posas: piano with Abe Most sextet (Enevoldsen, Fatool, etc.)
July 24:   Norwalk, 2:00 to 3:30: 9-piece including Trott, Enevoldsen, Betty O'Hara, Dick Hafer Terry Harrington;
            Bowl in Burbank: with Gordon & Elaine Mitchell, Joe Darensbourg, Chuck Conklin, Dan [perhaps Barrett], trombone, Marge Murphy, et al.
July 30:   Odyssey
July 31:   San Diego: concert with Cary, trumpet, Bob Havens, trombone, Sam Most, reeds, Johnny Guarnieri, piano, plus three local musicians
August 5:   lesson for Andersons
August 11: Galleria, Glendale: "job with DePew on horrible electric keyboard," Bob Enevoldsen, Mahlon Clark, Wayne Songer, Rollie Bundock, Gene Estes

Elvis Presley died August 16, 1977. Cary's diary entry was typically forthright. "A lady on TV says EP revolutionised our music. She is so right. The tragic part of making this creature a national hero is no one speaks the truth in print. When he first appeared, people were horrified and revolted. But years of brainwashing make a monster a hero. To my ear his singing was an absolute abomination, his features were as nauseating as his stage movements. Perhaps he was as much of an influence on 'Rock & Roll'—if so, all the more tragic. I cannot see a more rotten, decadent period of 'music' than the last twenty years in this country!"

Another August death, on the 19th, which caused a very different reaction, was that of Groucho Marx: "Heard on TV tonight about the death of one of my favorite people of all time, GROUCHO. Virginia and I used to be convinced that Mr. Marx should have been President."

On August 19, in company with Eddie Miller, Abe Most, and Nick Fatool, he travelled to Monterey in readiness for a job with the World's Greatest Jazz Band of Yank Lawson and Bob Haggart in Carmel on the 20th. Bucky Pizzarelli was added on guitar, but Cary does not mention the name of the trombonist. The band then moved on to San Francisco where it was featured at Earthquake McGoon's on August 21 and 22.

After the tours were over, Cary commented:

I don't have any more to do with the WGJB for two reasons. One, I cannot stand the fat, wealthy slob who owns the band—Barker Hickox, who is one of our many millionaires who should not be a millionaire. I think this group has gone and will continue to go down hill. I do really believe that Lawson is the largest liability Haggart ever had, except of course, for B. Hickox.

Cary's views on The World's Greatest Jazz Band were understandable. The excitement of the early years had faded and the later recordings by the group were gentle concept albums. When the band was formed at the end of 1968, Bob Haggart's arrangements of popular tunes of the day, in addition to jazz standards, were a highly original feature. It is said that the written arrangements were put aside in favour of "head" charts because the band members disliked wearing their spectacles in public!

Then it was back into the old routine:

August 28: McArthur Park, 4:30 to 5:20: including Barney Bigard, Eddie Miller, Herbie Harper, Betty O'Hara, Wayne Songer, Nick Fatool

September 1: King's 4 in Hand: with "Nick, Morty, Abe" (Nick Fatool, Abe Most)—"I played Abe's Wurlitzer and enjoyed some tunes quite a bit."

September 5: Museum of Science & Industry, 2:00 to 4:00: with Abe Most big band

September 7: round dance date

September 9: Long Beach Convention Center, 12:00 to 2:00: piano, with Jack Trott, Bob Enevoldsen, Betty O'Hara, Abe Most, Frank Morocco, clarinet, Dick Hafer, tenor, Ray Leatherwood,

	Nick Fatool. "Morocco sounded great on *All the Things You Are*, Hafer same on *Lester Leaps In*."
September 10:	Chaminole: with Ed Lafata—"horrible, piano bad."
September 17:	job in Bel Air
September 21:	McCambridge Park
September 24:	Sportsman's Lodge, fashion show: with Nick Fatool & lady pianist.
October 1:	Bob Tabor job: trumpet with Rex Allen, trombone, Wayne Songer, clarinet, Walt Yoder, bass, "bad drums," Marge Murphy, vocal.
October 15:	Elks: Johnny Lane job, trumpet with Al Jenkins, trombone, Bill Campbell, piano, "a miserable drummer, but I enjoyed it; my old 'don't-expect-anything' theory."
October 16:	Jazz Club, Disneyland, Bill Hill job: personnel included Betty and Barrett O'Hara, Charles Myerson and Nick Fatool—"good band, no mikes, no music, and an idiot to lead us."
October 19:	McCambridge Park: with Bob Enevoldsen and Ray Leatherwood
October 22:	Cerritos Regional County Park: Jack Trott, trumpet, Bob Enevoldsen, Bob Havens, trombones, Henry Cuesta, clarinet, Eddie Miller, tenor, Charles Myerson, guitar, Ray Leatherwood, bass, Nick Fatool, drums. Cary, piano. "Turned out well."
October 26:	Concert "at the Bank": with Wayne Songer, Ray Sherman, Ray Leatherwood, Nick Fatool, and "HN."
October 27:	San Diego: concert with Bob Crosby

The Anderson brothers were still visiting for occasional lessons and there was plenty of tennis on the days that he was "resting."

Towards the end of 1977, with a German tour looming, Cary wrote:

Life is uneventful in L.A. Tennis each morning, then I write every day for my rehearsal band which meets Monday night, almost every week. There's no place to sit-in, no place which requires the services of the likes of me. So I do occasional recording and country club dances, at which the level of music is absolutely abominable, due mostly to the crap everyone plays at these affairs.

Fatool and I just did a fashion show today [September 24] at noon, accompanying a lady piano thumper who, as Nick put it, "plays like the lady next door."

After two earlier rehearsals at Wornom Avenue, a recording session took place on October 28 for Harry Lim's Famous Door label. The leader was bassist Jack Lesberg and with him were Dick Cary, trumpet and arranger, Bob Enevoldsen, valve-trombone, Eddie Miller, tenor, Ray Sherman, piano, and Nick Fatool, drums. Cary's *Ballad for Eddie* was one of the tunes recorded. Cary commented:

What happened is almost beyond belief! We had two three-hour sessions scheduled for the same day. Now, having some pretty fair pros like this, we got a lot done in the morning, went to lunch, then had three more hours from 2 to 5. By three o'clock we had completed at least one or more versions of each song and were eagerly looking forward to using the other two hours to correct and improve. To my horror and complete disbelief Harry Lim informs us that we're through—because he had no more room on his second reel of tape and didn't want to stand the expense of a third reel. We were all shocked! On the first two tunes there had been a faulty line on the brass microphone, the tempo of Henry Lee was slow and sluggish and various other things that could have been so much better. I should have bought Mr. Lim another reel myself, but we stood around so stunned that no one did anything and the session broke up.

Nick was miserable about his playing on some cuts; Ray Sherman desperately wanted to re-do a couple of things, etc. I will never understand why an album which will be around for years can be ruined by the miserliness of an idiot producer.

Eddie M. is such a modest and mild mannered man that he will never speak up and I often wonder about that phrase which was thrown at me as a child—about "the meek inheriting the earth." It must be some earth in a future life, certainly not this one.

Cary's reservations were not reflected in the reviews of the Lesberg album. Writing in *Jazz Journal* Sinclair Traill wrote that, "Everyone plays with vigour and intelligence and if to my ears Dick

Cary takes top honours it is by the narrowest margin imaginable. He blows throughout with admirable restraint, fine control, and everything he does ... is in perfect taste."

Two days later, on October 30, Cary caught a flight to Germany, to spend most of November guesting with local bands. Known dates for this tour are:

October 31:   Lindau, concert (with The Chicagoans)
November 1:   day off
November 2:   Stuttgart, Dixieland Hall (with The Chicagoans)
November 3:   Gaufelden, Gruner Baum
              (Green Tree, with The Chicagoans)
November 4:   Ludwigsburg—afternoon, department store
              2;00 to 5:00 evening—Bahnhotel
              (with The Chicagoans—"good job tonight")
November 5:   Tübingen University
November 6:   Pforzheim, Revolution Club
              (with The Chicagoans)
November 7:   day off
November 8/9/10:   Munich, Schwabinger Podium
              (with Barrelhouse Jazzband)
November 11: day off
November 12: Ludwigsburg, Jazzkeller
              (with Barrelhouse Jazzband)
November 13: Vienna, Jazzland: (with Red Hot Pods)
November 14: day off
November 15: Vienna, Jazzland: (with Printers Jazz Band)
November 16: Vienna, Jazzland (with Barrelhouse Jazzband)
November 17/18:   off
November 19: Nuremberg: played in cellar
November 20/21:   off
November 22: Lindau, town auditorium: "nice Steinway
              and I played theme from *The Bad and the
              Beautiful, Echo of Spring & Love Stream.*"
November 23: Stuttgart, Dixieland Hall.
November 24: Pforzheim
November 25: Plane to Los Angeles

Titles from the November 6 Pforzheim session, with saxophonist Klaus Bader's Chicagoans, were issued by WSO Records as "Jazz Night at Revolution Club." British singer Beryl Bryden, who had sat in during Cary's Pizza Express engagement, was featured on several titles. Cary's diary entry was: "Awful place to play. It was recorded and was our very worst night by far." On the 12th he and the Barrelhouse band appeared on television—"Show seemed to be one tune by band, talk, *That's a Plenty* to close." He enjoyed the night with the Printers Jazz Band—"they swing not chug." And while in Stuttgart he met Gudrun Endress again—"She looks so good!"

During one rest day he was played a batch of old records and one trumpet player in particular impressed him: "Realized what a bitch Jabbo Smith was for the 20s, speed, range—my god!"

Klaus Bader commented: "I did several tours with Dick. Once we had the first concert of a tour in Lindau, at Lake Constance. Dick took a flight from Los Angeles to Stuttgart and it was not possible to pick him up at the airport. I let him know to take a taxi the 150 miles to Lindau—'I'll pay for it and you could get to the concert on time.' He arrived ten minutes before the concert began, had no bags, nothing to wear, not even underwear and came in his pantoffles as he left his home, like you would go out to get some milk or cigarettes. He had only one bag and the only thing in it was his trumpet and his peck horn." Cary writes of a problem with the plane. He left home at 5:30 a.m. on the Sunday and arrived at 8:40 p.m. on the Monday—"No clothes or peck horn (sic), but I made it."

However, Cary was becoming disenchanted:

I am goddam sick of being used by these people. One guy in Pforzheim has put out two albums already for which I was paid a ridiculously low fee and they don't even have the decency to send me either album. For a while I found it all very charming to tour about, correct chords, fix up fake books, teach them songs, play in smoky cellars with no air and large, rude, beer-filled bodies, but the charm wore off. For instance, in Milano, Italy, I did several arrangements for one band, but when I enquired about the fee a very marked coldness and turning away was almost a little frightening.

Of one band he wrote: "... a very different evening with a horrible band, sounding like a typical San Francisco type of rotten out-of-tune banjo-infested chug-chug band with horrible harmonies. I found it so hard to sit there and try to look pleasant. When Teddy Wilson came in for the last set I was embarrassed to death."

His comments on his February tour had been similar— "Quite a month in Europe, good and bad moments. Most of the playing alright but it's the lack of sleep and not knowing much what to do in between" and "So much dead time, so many wrong chords, bad pianos, but usually by night and if my hosts are agreeable, and most are, I think I can do it yearly, although I may not be worth it to any agent. We'll have to find out."

Jim Turner has pointed out that whenever Cary complained about fees he was doing so as a matter of principle. The money involved was of lesser importance. "Dick told me that he had, many years earlier, received a tip on American Express stock and that the huge increase in the value of these shares was the basis of his financial well-being. It is not true that he was miserly with money. He had a healthy respect for saving it, however, as do many people of his generation whose upbringing was dominated by the hardships of the Great Depression."

Once more it was back to lessons for the Andersons, tennis matches, the Monday night rehearsal band and the occasional gig:

December 2: Knox: piano with Abe Most, Morty Corb, bass, Nick Fatool

December 3: no location: with trio—"I filled in all 3 horn & piano—job not bad at all."

December 10: KCOP Channel 13, 8:00 p.m. to 3:00 a.m: trumpet with band in variety show, apparently. Rex Allen, trombone, Bob Bailey, piano, Ray Leatherwood, bass, Jack Sperling, drums, Connie Haines, King Sisters, vocals. "We didn't work very hard—only swung with Scatman Crothers."

December 11: Senator Room, San Francisco: Bob Ringwald sextet, including Wayne Songer, Eddie Miller, "Ray and Gene."

On December 13 Cary records: "Our CETA job starts this week 200 per, so until January we meet at union four afternoons a week." This appears to refer to preparations for musical performances to be given in schools during 1978. He refers to nine afternoons spent at the union hall between December 14 and 29. (CETA is the California Educational Theater Association.)

The remaining jobs for 1977 were at the Hotel del Coronado on December 16, with a vocal group and a band which included Ray Linn, Shorty Sherock, trumpets, Bob Havens, trombone, and Eddie Miller, tenor; a Christmas party at McCambridge Park with Betty O'Hara and Ray Leatherwood on the 21st; a recording session with Pud Brown on the 27th; and a New Year's Eve show at the Lakeside Country Club.

Pud Brown, who played clarinet and tenor, had lived in Los Angeles for several years, but by 1977 was established in New Orleans. In December he travelled to Los Angeles and recorded a session for his 'New Orleans Jazz' label and an excellent album resulted. The personnel was Dick Cary, trumpet, Bob Havens, trombone, Pud Brown, clarinet, tenor, Eddie Miller, clarinet, tenor, Bill Campbell, piano, Nappy Lamare, guitar, Monty Budwig, bass, Shelly Manne, drums. In addition to three seldom heard standards, there were seven originals, two of them by Cary, *Swing Down in New Orleans*, with a vocal by Lamare, and *Bayou Lafourche*.

> *Pud's album suffered from bad editing. He took it back to New Orleans and did it in his living room, so he informed me, to my horror. There is no distribution, only mail and selling one by one in New Orleans.*

Despite this, Cary could write:

> *You will find the Pud Brown much better than the Lesberg. We did it at Capitol.*

The season of goodwill did not extend to Cary's view of the December 31 show at the Lakeside Country Club. The headliner was Andy Griffith, plus a ventriloquist, and the band was led by Abe Most, with Zeke Zarchy, Uan Rasey, Cary, trumpets, Ed Anderson, Betty & Barrett O'Hara, trombones, Les Robinson, Dick Holgate, Bus Bussey, James Snodgrass, Bob? Lawson, reeds, Ray Sherman, piano, Ray Leatherwood, bass, Nick Fatool, drums. An accomplished personnel, but Cary was unhappy about the repertoire.

Perhaps 1978 would see an improvement.

Pud Brown

19. Tours, Festivals and Disc Troubles (1978–1980)

Cary's routine for 1978 was much as it had been during the previous year, except that he could write at the end of January: "Since I returned from Europe work has poured in, at least for me, compared to previous years. I get $300 a week now, leading the hi-school 'Dixielanders,' telethons, recording, casuals, etc, and a good rehearsal every Monday."

Between January 3, when at Pacoima Junior High, and April 19, at Bethune Junior, Cary was playing four days a week for one, sometimes two, 1-hour 'lessons' per school. On January 24 he became leader for these school concerts. His only mention of other musicians is a reference to the "Gordon Mitchell group" for the January 3 appearance, and to driving to one school with Nappy Lamare.

Interspersed with the school dates were the usual variety of gigs:

January 5/6: recording at Capitol Studios with Mickey Finn
January 7: Ed Anderson's, 3:30: no details
January 11: recording for B.B. King album

Cary on trumpet, with Bob Enevoldsen, Abe Most and Eddie Miller, over-dubbed one title for an ABC album by blues-singer B.B. King. It was not unusual for such musicians to be asked to add a different sound, a touch of "Dixieland," to flavour the odd title by a popular singer. Cary called it "a very enjoyable hour."

January 18: McCambridge Park: handicap party with Betty O'Hara, Eddie Miller
January 29: (a.m.) KTLA arthritis telethon, with Rex Allen, trombone, Bob Bailey, piano, Ray Leatherwood, bass, Gene Estes, drums
(p.m.) Rowan Inn: trumpet, with Herbie Harper, Wayne Songer, Ray Sherman, Ray Leatherwood, Nick Fatool
February 2: Town & Country: with John Best, trumpet leading Carl Fontana, trombone, Abe Most, clarinet, Eddie Miller, tenor, Ray Sherman, piano, Cary, piano, Leatherwood, bass, Fatool, drums. "What a sloppy, inane 'bow-tie' job."

February 4: tent job in Venice: with Abe Most, Ray Sherman, Al Hendrickson, guitar, Morty Corb, bass, Fatool, drums, and "S.H."
February 5: Lobster House, Marina del Rey: with George Probert, reeds, Dan Barrett, trombone, Al Weber, drums. Cary also "played drums and enjoyed it."
February 16: Cliff May job (no details).
February 25: (a.m.) Valley Hospital: with Betty O'Hara, Herbie Harper, Abe Most, Wayne Songer, Ray Sherman, Ray Leatherwood, Nick Fatool and Bob(?).
(afternoon) wedding at LACC

During these entries there are cryptic notes regarding "Connie Haines—5," "Rex Music Center" and "Joe Marino, Black Bank," but their significance is not known. An Andersons' lesson is noted for March 3, and for March 4 Cary lists a Bob Tabor job at Skytrail—"a catastrophe! [Walt] Yoder didn't play one beat anywhere near Nick [Fatool], who ended up stoned. Mike Silverman ... on trumpet—the only asset a strong lip. Wayne tried, Dan Barrett tried, Peanuts, Louise [Tobin, Hucko's wife]—but no time!!"

March 17: Terminal Isle, enlisted men's club: Johnny Lane job, incl. Jerry McKenzie, drums. "Piano half-tone flat."
April 1: Los Robles Ballroom, Thousand Oaks: with Abe Most band, including Les Robinson, alto, Ray and Nick.
April 3: Convention dinner, Bonaventure Hotel: trumpet with Abe [Most?], Eddie Miller, Ray Sherman, Ray Leatherwood, Nick Fatool
April 8: after Anderson lesson, the Elks Lodge: piano & horns with Art Lyons, clarinet, Davis, drums, vocal, Rod Allen, leader, vocal.
April 15: noon recording with Chuck Conklin
Marriott Hotel, 9:00 to 1:00: with John Best big band. "Lip gave out."
April 16: Jazz Forum, 3:30: 15-piece band including Zarchy, Trott, Cary, trumpets, Betty & Barrett O'Hara, Bob Havens, trombones, Abe Most, clarinet.

Cary flew to Canada on April 20, 1978, for six days in Toronto, commencing at the DJ Tavern on his first night there. He worked for three nights, had two rest days and on the 25th appeared on a television show with the Climax Jazz Band, presumably his accompanying group throughout. Back in Los Angeles, he played trumpet with Bob Enevoldsen, Abe Most, and the usual rhythm section (Sherman, Leatherwood, Fatool) for a tax assessors' dinner at the Beverly Wilshire.

After a day of tennis and a movie he joined a tour organised by Barry Martyn and Floyd Levin, commencing April 28 at the Variety Arts Playhouse in Hollywood. The tour was called "Night in New Orleans," an all-star concert package which Martyn and Levin promoted for several years. Cary's subsequent dates for this American-European tour are slightly at odds with those given by Floyd Levin. To quote Cary first:

April 29:	Queen Elizabeth Hall, Vancouver
April 30:	Anchorage, Alaska
May 1:	travel
May 2:	Edmonton, Canada
May 3:	flight to Dusseldorf, Germany
May 4:	Amsterdam, Holland
May 5:	Munich—solo piano at Kleine-Rondel
May 6:	Vienna (Jazzland, with Trevor Richards + Blind John Davis guest)
May 7:	Belgano, Italy
May 8:	Laruno, Italy
May 9:	Zurich, Switzerland
May 10:	Frankfurt, Germany
May 11:	Kamen, Germany
May 12:	Groningen, Holland
May 13:	Flight home

Floyd Levin recalled: "We left Los Angeles on April 29 for Vancouver, April 30 Vancouver to Anchorage, May 1 Anchorage to Edmonton, May 2 day off, May 3 Edmonton to Dusseldorf—Amsterdam, Vienna, Turin, Zurich, Kamen. Tour ended in Groningen, Holland. We bussed to Amsterdam for flight back to L.A. Dick got very car sick going over the Alps! Dick played with the Benny Carter Quartet (Carter, alto, Cary, piano, Red Callender, bass, Cozy Cole, drums) and then with Barney Bigard, clarinet, Callender, bass, Cole, drums." (Cary said the auditorium in Edmonton "was one of the best anywhere.")

"The big band was fronted by Jake Porter in our tribute to Louis Armstrong during the 1978 tour. They played *Sleepy Time*

Down South, Glad When You're Dead, Sweethearts on Parade and *Mahogany Hall.*" Barry Martyn recalls Porter as "very big locally. He was a black trumpet player of enormous popularity and girth. And he could get up there. If you wanted something played an octave above, no trouble to him."

For the band's personnel Martyn suggested that it might have been: Andrew Blakeney, Jake Porter, trumpets, Gene Connors, trombone, Harold Dejan, Peter Mueller, alto, Sam Lee, Floyd Turnham, tenors, Dick Cary, piano, Red Callender, bass, Martyn, drums. Of the arrangements used, Martyn said: "I could write small band arrangements, but nothing as big as this. So I went to Dick. He wrote out these arrangements. He took the old records and first copied them note for note, then altered a few things and left room for soloists. They were beautifully penned. I said, 'How much will it cost?' He said, 'You can't put money on this. I love doing this.' I remember he would not take any money for it. It must have taken him hours, although he was very fast. He sketched out a couple of things while I was sitting there with him. I've still got them."

Cary failed to mention the Louis Armstrong tribute when commenting on the tour, so it is unlikely that he was in the big band. He writes only of working with Benny Carter, Barney Bigard and that he played the four nights prior to May 3 with "that bit of nonsense," the Louisiana Shakers, consisting of Sammy Lee, tenor, Duke Burrell, piano, and Teddy Williams, drums?. Their numbers were *Tenderly, Rosetta* and Lee's feature *Hi Ho Silver,* "where he roams about the audience honking." Cary's instrument is not mentioned.

> *The tour in Europe was a nightmare, for every reason possible—the way it was managed, the method we travelled, the hotels, the "music" itself, except possibly for Bigard and Carter. But all Carter played, and every goddam night, was* Honeysuckle Rose *and* Misty.

Throughout the 1970s, at least, Benny Carter featured *Misty* seemingly on every possible occasion, more so than Cary played *Echo of Spring* and *Love Stream*!

Later, in 1985, these Dick Cary transcriptions were used by trumpeter Chris Clifton, a Louis Armstrong devotee, at a Jazzology recording session. The five tunes, recorded by a nine-piece band, which included Barry Martyn on drums, were: *You Rascal You, Dinah, Sweethearts on Parade, Someday You'll Be Sorry,* and *Mahogany Hall Stomp.*

German collector Manfred Selchow was at the Amsterdam concert. The main thing he remembered about the Benny Carter set was Carter threatening to walk off stage unless the audience stopped setting off flashlights in his face. He was impressed that when a youth band played *Blue Moon* in the interval, Cary sat with them at the piano, decided the key and then played with the youngsters.

Cary's first date after this "horrible nightmare" was May 17 at McCambridge Park, followed May 20 by a sextet date at Rosemont Pavilion—"10:30 to 12:30, book of childish arrangements." On the 24th he travelled to Sacramento, presumably to the River College, where the band was terrible but the concert went fine. Then it was the jazz jubilee—"I am deeply hurt by the schedule. No concerts on Friday and no sets with either Ralph Sutton or Vic Dickenson." He "played a few with Johnny Mince and Bill Allred" on the 25th and on the Friday, the 26th, he was invited to play with Tom King and Mudville's Finest, plus a late night set with the Rosie O'Grady band. On Saturday afternoon he had two sets with Red Norvo and two evening sets with Manny Klein, trumpet, Urbie Green, trombone, Johnny Guarnieri, piano, Red Callender, bass, and Ray Price. For Sunday he had "12:45 to 3:40 with my group—Urbie Green, Johnny Mince, clarinet, Norma Teagarden, piano, Ray Price," and two sets with Wild Bill Davison, Urbie Green, Abe Most, Red Callender and a drummer, as well as sets with Mudville's Finest and with the Tom King band.

When Cary returned from Europe he had been happy to spend a day at home with his two dogs, Sean and Albert, but two weeks later Albert, "my dear little friend," died.

He had outlined his plans in a letter, but did he avoid that "dance music" entirely?

I decided to have a good summer at home, just writing and playing tennis every morning and not playing any jobs which require the typical Hollywood repertoire of atrocious dance music. I'm really only happy when I'm writing.

June 2: Glendale City College: with Doug Davis, Rod, Bob Enevoldsen, Art Lyons ("pleasant night even though Doug and Rod play a lot of the current crap.")

June 3: Sorrentino's Riverside: "it's a show-biz singles thing," probably with singer Connie Haines. Band led by Neal Hefti, including Rex Allen and Gene Estes.

June 4: afternoon, Cal Tech dining room: in a trio at wedding; evening, Riviera Country Club: with Doug Davis
June 9: lesson for Andersons (also June 24, July 8)
June 11: Sambi's of Tokyo: piano with Bob Broomfield, trumpet, bass. Bob Enevoldsen, Bob Thomas, clarinet, Derek, drums.

Matty Matlock, clarinetist and arranger, born 1907, died June 14, 1978. On June 18, a "Matty's Day" was held at the Pacifica Hotel, where Cary played trumpet with the "Bob Cats," including Abe Lincoln, Eddie Miller, Abe Most, Peanuts Hucko, Ray Sherman, Ray Leatherwood and Nick Fatool. The following day Matlock's funeral service was held and Cary played with Lincoln, Hucko, Miller, Nappy Lamare, Phil Stephens, bass, and Fatool.

June 18: Sambi's, Downey: with quartet including Bob Thomas
June 24: Canoga Park—Italian wedding at a Moose Hall, with Doug Davis, Rod, and Art Lyons.
June 25: Sambi's, Downey: piano with Ed Anderson, Bob Thomas, Jerry McKenzie.
July 2: afternoon, Magnolia(?); evening, Sambi's, Downey: with Vernon Brown, trombone, Wayne Songer, Eddie Miller, Nick Fatool, Ray and Chas.
July 3: with Jack Stacy.
July 4: Los Nietos, 5:00 to 6:30: with Bob Enevoldsen, Betty O'Hara, Eddie Miller, Dick Holgate, Nappy Lamare. Nick Fatool, Ray and Chas.
July 9: afternoon, Drelinger; evening, Sambi's.
July 13: Century Plaza:—3 trumpets, 2 trombones, 3 tenors, baritone, piano, bass, drums
July 16: afternoon, Northridge Park: with Abe Most; evening, Sambi's
July 22: Glendora Country Club: with Frank Jordan
July 23: Sambi's
July 26: round dance record session
July 30: with Bob Ringwald band; then no entries until...
August 25: House party at Toluca Lake: with Rex Allen, trombone, Gene Estes, drums
August 27: afternoon, N. Hollywood Park: with Betty O'Hara,

	Abe Most, Eddie Miller, Al Hendrickson, guitar, Nick Fatool, Ray; evening: Sambi's
August 29:	with Art DePew
August 30:	round dance record session
September 9:	McArthur Park: with Betty O'Hara, Wayne Songer, Nappy Lamare, Ray Leatherwood, Gene Estes, Bob and Chas. M.

Elks Club, Burbank, CA, September 16, 1978
Cary, tp; Doc Cenardo?, d; Joe Darensbourg, cl; Nappy Lamare, bj; Eddie Miller, ts.
(Photograph courtesy of Peter Vacher)

He flew to Monterey on the evening of the 9th, though he does not give details of his appearance at the jazz festival that weekend, nor for events during the rest of September and early October. It is known that he played trumpet with old friends Joe Darensbourg, Eddie Miller, Nappy Lamare and pianist Bill Campbell in a band which appeared at the Elks Club in Burbank on September 16, 1978, and he was scheduled to appear as a guest of the South Bay Traditional Jazz Society on Sunday the 24th.

October 7:	Pike's: with Ken Greco
October 8:	Sambi's
October 10:	Fedmart 11:00 to 1:00: with Betty O'Hara, Wayne Songer, Nick Fatool, Ray and Chas.

October 15: afternoon, City Hall: with Russ Reinberg, Ray Leatherwood, Nick Fatool; evening, Sambi's
October 17: Fedmart, H. Beach: with Betty O'Hara, Wayne Songer, Charlie Myerson, Herb Mickman, Nick Fatool

There are no further diary entries for 1978, except for the first two weeks of December, but elsewhere Cary wrote of his November plans:

This Saturday [November 4] I am doing a local concert with Nick Fatool, Ray Sherman, etc, which will be OK, although our guest star is a screwball overbearing monstrosity called Ricky "Cougar" Nelson, who really should be captured, caged and shown only at either of the Disney places. [Nelson was a trombonist.]

Bob Wilber's coming to California soon with Pee Wee [Erwin] and we'll do a concert in San Diego at the Yacht Club, along with Fatool, Bob Havens and Ray Leatherwood.

The concert with Erwin was part of A Thanksgiving Jazz Festival on November 25, 1978, followed by his last few entries for the year:

December 1: Farrand—with Abe Most, Ray Leatherwood, Nick Fatool. "Very pleasant, Steinway just lovely."
December 2: Telethon, Channel 13: Rehearsal, then show 8:00 to 3:00—Rex Allen, Bob Bailey, Ray Leatherwood, Jack Sperling.
December 7: Rotary Club, Knollwood, Balboa—with Doug Davis and Rod
December 10: Valley Hilton—with Doug Davis
December 15: quartet job for Sid Lasalle—including Gene Estes

During 1978 Cary also added another rehearsal group:

[I] have a new rehearsal group which is somewhat unusual: my two alto horns on top, two valve-trombonists (Bob Enevoldsen and Betty O'Hara), then two excellent baritone saxes and, underneath it all, either tuba or bass trombone. The rhythm is guitar, bass, drums. Both valve-trombones double on baritone horns. It's a rich texture and it can really move and is not heavy as might be expected. In ten weeks since we started all this, I am up to just over 60 pieces. I

believe in the old songwriter's law, if you write enough tunes, you may get a good one.

As January 1979 passed there were the usual rehearsals, plus tennis, a lesson for the Anderson brothers and two arrangements for Bob Havens, interspersed with:

January 14:	Eagle Rock High School—no details
January 26:	Canoga Park Elks: with Doug Davis
January 27:	Porter Valley Country Club—wedding: with Doug Davis
January 28:	band for George Ball: John Best, Abe Lincoln, Eddie Miller, Ray Sherman, Ray Leatherwood, Nick Fatool, Cary, horns
February 3:	Bob Tabor job: Wayne Songer leading Dan Barrett, Nick Fatool, et al.
February 10:	10 a.m: recording for Tom Jones: Bob Havens, Abe Most, John Fresco, tenor
	9 p.m. to 1 a.m.: Lobster House with Doug Davis

We occasionally are called to overdub on singers' albums, like the B.B. King. Did a similar thing on a Tom Jones album last month, with Abe Most and Bob Havens. It's strange to be the only "Dixieland" trumpet player in a place like this. The word "Dixieland" has cost me thousands of dollars here and in New York. Calls for recording come only when that sort of thing is required. I did one with Abe Most a couple of years ago for two young rock geniuses. I asked them what style they'd like and they said they didn't know, but would make a few takes and see what happened. So I tried my best Armstrong imitation. They came running out and said it was just what they wanted. So I said, "Something like Louis Armstrong, you mean?" and the two young chaps looked at each other and exclaimed, "Oh, that's the name!" Abe and I almost slid off our chairs.

Cary's interest in other forms of music continued.
I am studying orchestrating with a fine man, Albert Harris. Besides, there's a new 82-piece symphony in L.A.—48 strings, 10 woodwinds, 4 horns, 8 brass, etc, and some of our best jazz players in it. When they asked me to do something, I was terrified, since it's been 25 years since I wrote things for the Paul Whiteman radio orchestra in New York. But I did a piece and decided to continue thinking along these lines and

go to an experienced man each week. This new orchestra is called "The Orchestra," which is almost as silly a title as the W.G.J.B. of Haggart's. But there's a lot of money behind it. For instance, each rehearsal at 20th Century Fox costs over five grand.

"The Orchestra" has forced me to do what I always really cared about; someday getting a bigger work performed and perhaps recorded. I hope I have time left and I sometimes realize that travel is not the way for me to prolong my life. I wish we realized the values and possibilities of this existence when we were somewhat younger.

February 15: first mention of taking a lesson from Albert Harris
February 18: Proud Bird Aviation, 4:00 to 5:00: with Betty O'Hara, Tommy Newsom, Peanuts Hucko, Herb Mickman, Jack Sperling Sportsman, 7 p.m: with Abe Most, Morty Corb, Gene Estes, Frank Scott, piano
February 24: UOP Campus, Stockton: for Bill Renwick— with Mudville's Finest, Doc Renwick, drums, leader
February 28: McCambridge Park (and March 28)

One photograph reports him playing a Jazz Forum session at the Proud Bird on February 18, 1979. The band is Betty O'Hara, Cary, trumpets, Peanuts Hucko, Tommy Newsom, Don Beamsley, piano, Herb Mickman, and Jack Sperling.

March 4: Roadway, Eugene, Oregon: "four sets, one on piano."
March 6: Pico—Japanese paper company: trumpet ("lip felt good") with quintet, including Bob Enevoldsen.
March 12: wake for Jim Frissell: with Betty O'Hara, Ray Sherman, Nick Fatool, ("Betty and I got some good duets going"); to Jerry Van Dyke's: with Bob Enevoldsen, Monty Budwig, bass.
March 16: McCaddan: "Jimmy Zito was my competitor. Steve Martin and Bernadette Peters sang a duet, Carl Reiner coached them."
March 17: Blue Moon Saloon, 3:00 to 7:30: in sextet. Mary Ann McCall sang.

The weekend of March 30/31/April 1, he played in Claremont at Griswold's Spring Jazzfest. He and Ray Leatherwood were "special guest stars." Cary appeared with the Night Blooming Jazzmen, the Bull Moose Party Band, High Sierra Jazz Band, Angel City Jazz Band and the Jack Taylor orchestra—"Ray Leatherwood and I did three tunes with high school band." This was followed on April 4 by "a completely ridiculous 'They Shoot Horses, Don't They' put together and 'starred' in by Kathy Lee Crosby." The band was Billy Berry, trumpet, Tommy Newsom, tenor, Cary, piano, Gene Estes, drums, and a bassist.

April 15: Jazz Forum: with Abe Most
April 21: 2:00 to 6:00: Joe Yukl job (quartet?)
           evening, Donte's: sextet job
April 22: 5:00 to 7:00: Disneyland Hotel rehearsal;
           8:00 to 10:00: Johnny Lane job

On April 23 Cary started a seven day booking, probably with banjoist Mickey Finn, at Disneyland—"a week was long enough!" The personnel included 'Cougar' Nelson, trombone, David Poe, reeds, Freda 'Fred' Finn, piano, Dick Gomez, drums, and Betty O'Hara. Four days after finishing at Disneyland, on May 3, he was in the Sunset Studio at 7:00 p.m. with Jack Elliott [orchestrator], Sol Gubin [drums], and a Roy Brown. He wrote: "Cornet on *What'll I Do*—best I ever was recorded." This recording has not been traced.

May 4: a Mickey Gravine job, with Abe Most, Morty
        Corb, Frank Capp, drums, Tom Tedesco,
        guitar, and John Knapp.
May 5: El Caballero, 7:00–11:00: with Jack Stacy,
        reeds, Hank Speakerman, John Jensen, piano.

For some time after this, Cary's diary entries are imprecise, with references such as "Santa Barbara" (May 9), "Rancheros" (May 10), "Mickey Gravine, Abe" (May 11), and "D.D. 9-1 Canoga Elks—Osborne, De Soto" (May 12). The last is presumably a Doug Davis date. On the 13th he played at Jack Murphy's, another gig with Johnny Lane, and on the 18th he refers to Oregon at 9, Neskowin Lodge—"a horrendous group—piano, banjo and the boss Les Roach, terrible reed player. But I enjoyed night and restaurant after." Two days later he lists the Jazz Club at Elks, Portland, Oregon—"four nights of this at two hours a night." Then it was Sacramento Dixieland Jubilee time again,

May 25–28, though Cary has no observations on this festival.
And so these hints at jobs continue:

May 30: McCambridge Park
June 2: UCLA Faculty Center: 8:00 to 12:00, with Doug Davis
June 3: Roman Inn, 4:30.
June 9: Jonathan Club: 8:00 to 12:00 with Doug Davis
June 10: Proud Bird: 3:30, with Abe Most
June 12: Castaway: 7:00, with John Best
June 13: Gaffey [?], 2:00 to 4:00
June 16: Moose: piano with Curt Williams, banjo, Bill Perkins, drums
June 17: Burton Chace: 2:00 to 4:00, with "Abe, Tom, Betty, Bob, Chas, Gene, Ray"
June 20: Disneyland "nightmare"
June 21: Century Plaza: 7:00 to 11:00, with Zeke [Zarchy]
June 29: Leonard Moss, 4:00 to 8:00
June 30: V.F.W. (Veterans of Foreign Wars), Pomona: 9:00 to 1:00, with Curt [Williams].
July 4: Los Nietos, Santa Fe Springs: 3:00 to 4:30, with Eno, Eddie M, Bill R, DH, Chas, Jerry, Ray.
July 14: George Fields

Then, for a spot of variety, a week at Disneyland, July 15–21, with Bob Crosby, though he provides no details for the engagement.

July 22: Toluca Tennis Club: 7:30 with Ed Anderson
July 28: Malibu: 3:00 to 5:00. 8:15, private party?
July 29: 4:00 to 6:00, with Art Drellinger (reeds). 8:00, Al Hendrickson party
August 4: 4:30, no details
August 5: Canoga Park: for Knights of St. Columbus 4:00 to 5:00, with Ray Sherman, piano, Morty Corb, bass, Nick Fatool, drums.

The diary is blank between August 7 and 11, but a press cutting shows that Dick Carey (sic) and his (six-piece) band played a concert in McArthur Park on August 10.

August 12: Ambassador Hotel: 2:30, with Abe Most
August 19: McArthur Park: with Betty O'Hara, Bob Enevoldsen, Wayne Songer, "Tom, Chas.,

	Ed Gaston," Gene Estes
August 21:	Glendale Savings: 6:00 to 9:00, with Abe Most
August 25:	7:30 with Dick McCormick—Bob Enevoldsen, Eddie [Miller], [Bill] Campbell, Morty [Corb].
August 26:	Bunny Donin
September 25:	Heider's: 1:00 to 6:30, with Jack Elliott. (Wally Heider recording?); Bonaventure Hotel: 7:00 to 9:00, with Abe Most septet
September 27:	Blue Seagull: 4:30, with Howard Lucraft. Queen Mary: 12:30 to 8:00, [Manny] Klein, [Al] Jenkins, Abe Most, "Ray, Jerry, Chas."
October 7:	Little Bavaria, San Diego: 2:00 to 6:00, with John Best, Betty O'Hara, Ray Leatherwood, Nick Fatool, Benn Gas [?]—"Best job so far in San Diego. Betty and I did our art and it was approved."

On the same day that Dick Cary was playing on the Queen Mary, the Modern Brass Quintet appeared in concert at Barnsdall Park in Hollywood and their programme was scheduled to include music by Richard Cary.

In October 1979, this writer, in company with Bert Whyatt, visited Dick Cary at his Sunland home. Travelling to the sparser north side of Los Angeles, we were welcomed by Dick on the afternoon of October 11, spending four hours talking about jazz and allied activities. He confirmed that he was interested mainly with his daily tennis workout and with writing for his Monday night rehearsal band. Tapes of this band indicated that it had a beautifully unique sound of its own. As noted at the time, "Our schedule was now in ruins, as was Dick Cary's. He had planned to watch the World Series from the start of the television coverage!"

Within the house there was a general atmosphere of untidiness, the lack of a female presence. To

Dick Cary in the greenery of 9828 Wornom Avenue, 1979
(Photo by and courtesy of Bert Whyatt)

be able to sit on a dilapidated armchair one had to walk through a gangway formed by piles of manuscript paper, stacked twelve or fifteen inches high. Bert Whyatt recalled that he asked to use the bathroom and had to go through the kitchen and was somewhat appalled by the state of everything. "Both rooms were distinctly unkempt—very much the bachelor thing."

On October 15 there was a round dance recording session for Merl Olds and on the 21st Cary appeared at the Ojai festival. His alto horn feature on *Singing the Blues*, recorded at the concert, was included in a collection on the Town Hall label.

He rode with Betty O'Hara, Ray Leatherwood and Bill Reichenbach to Bakersfield for an Abe Most date on October 27. There was a rehearsal at 5:00 p.m. but despite this, Cary thought it was a "rotten band. [Johnny] Rotella, lead alto. Dick Hafer only one who played well."

November 1–3:	George Ball, 7:00 to 11:00, red vest, with Wayne Songer, Ray Sherman. "Easy, nice job."
November 17:	Biltmore Bowl, with Abe Most
December 1:	Knox: with Eddie Miller, Ray [Leatherwood?], Nick Fatool
December 7:	job with Jake Porter
December 8:	Canoga Park: 8:30 to 12:30, bow tie, red vest. Doug Davis job, with Art Lyons, clarinet

Thus 1979 came to a close, with a "terrible" evening, musically speaking, at the Lakeside Country Club, where he saw the New Year in with Betty O'Hara, John Setar, reeds, John Heard, bass, Chiz Harris, drums, Tom Denver [?] and unnamed saxophonist and guitarist.

1980 really got underway with a weekly rehearsal on January 2, followed by a Poor Angel Jazz Club meeting at which the band was Cary, trumpet, Betty O'Hara, trombone, Peanuts Hucko, clarinet, Johnny Varro, piano, Billy Hadnott, bass, Nick Fatool, drums, and Tom Newsom, tenor. Bud Freeman, who was staying in Los Angeles at this time, and pianist/composer Eubie Blake were the guests for dinner at the Pickwick.

Bill French had memories too: "When Bud Freeman was staying with me (late 1979 and into April 1980), we went out to Cary's home for an afternoon. Bud took along his horn and he and Dick had a ball just noodlin' around (Dick on piano of course), not to mention reminiscing about their days in New York. You can imagine what a kick that was for me. Bud and I attended one of those Monday rehearsal band meetings (Bud refused to take his horn!) as Cary put the band through its paces with his intricate arrangements. Most interesting."

On January 15 Cary refers to "Good Time Girls"—"new TV show about girls during World War II. Looks like a hit, only because I never saw anything worse." He then refers to "Nick, Abe, Ray, Ray," which infers that he, Abe Most, Ray Sherman, Ray Leatherwood and Nick Fatool provided some of the music for this new TV show.

A week later he was contacted by Pete Carpenter to write "two 1940s type dogs for his new television show" and on January 28 he went "to former Magnolia Theater, now a recording place, to watch Mike Post and Pete Carpenter conduct some noises for 'Tenspeed and Brown Shoes,' a silly piece of crap on CH7. Finally about 12:30 they did my two efforts, ballroom scene M31 and M31A. I felt completely humiliated and thoroughly demoralized and I went home in a terrible state."

It was in February that Cary first mentions back pains, disc problems, which were to bedevil him in the future. On March 26 he re-visits his doctor—"Back very bad—to Dr. Stitt out of desperation," and on the 28th—"Wrote on back all day!" Six months later he writes: "That Valium may have damaged my memory—I still can't remember names that would immediately come to mind."

But he fulfilled his gigs:

February 22:   Century Plaza: 4:30, with Buddy Rogers and the L.A. Pops
February 24:   Plane to [Oregon?]
February 25:   Carlo Spiga, piano with local pops.
February 27:   Universal Studios: 9 a.m.
March 13:   Jingle for Greig McRitchie, with Eddie Rosa clarinet, Watrous [Bill Watrous, trombone?], Mike Lacy, et al.
March 15–17:   Disneyland: with Fred Finn ("Mickey Finn has 3 days for Betty and me in March")
March 21:   Central Juvenile Hall: 3:00 to 5:00, the Rehearsal band, 10-piece, incl. Abe Most, Enevoldsen, Hafer, Holgate, Trott, et al.
March 29:   Elks, Van Nuys: Gus Erhmann job, 9:00 to 1:00.
March 30:   Canoga Park—Knights of St. Columbus: 4:00 to 6:00, with Abe Lincoln, Wayne Songer, Eddie Miller, Johnny Varro, Ray Leatherwood, Nick Fatool.

There are no diary entries for April and May; Cary does not even mention the fact that he was at the Sacramento festival, held May 23-26. On June 2 he records travelling by plane to Los Angeles and then recording with Pee Wee Erwin, but this appears to be a late entry. The sleeve note to the Qualtro music album gives the recording dates as May 26-27, 1980, stating: "All five of the West Coast men (Cary, Eddie Miller, Bob Havens, Ray Leatherwood, Nick Fatool) had just returned from the annual Memorial Day jazz weekend in Sacramento and were all warmed up and ready to go. Pee Wee and Kenny [Davern] arrived from the annual Odessa, Texas, jazz party...."

The album on Qualtro Music, part of a series to document the playing of veteran Pee Wee Erwin, includes a trumpet and piano duet by Erwin and Cary.

In 1980 Pee Wee Erwin came out here to do an album with us. I was in a wheelchair at the time, full of valium and booze, an out-patient from the veteran's hospital where they finally fixed my back. This is not a bad album.

Drummer Bill French recalled that Cary "loved to play tennis but had to quit because of a bad back. He had to spend a little time in the hospital and I visited him there a couple of times." (In fact Cary had a few more years of tennis to come.)

Cary neglected his diary for the next three months, resuming again in September, when he could write: "This book pretty blank and so is this year but, thank God, I can walk and whack a tennis sphere each a.m."

He had two engagements on September 6, the first at 12:30 at the Marina del Rey, for a birthday party on a boat, performing with George Probert, reeds, Charles Myerson, guitar, Ray Leatherwood, followed by a 9 p.m. job with reedman Roger Neumann at the Rose Marie Ballroom. After September 13, which has the enigmatic entry "Cotron: 9:00 to 1:00," there is a two week gap until the 27th, which refers to "Knott's wagon camp," apparently a festival featuring Al Hirt, the Dukes of Dixieland, Joe Darensbourg, the Night Blooming Jazzmen, Bob Crosby and trumpeter Ray Linn. "They put us all together at 12:40—a mess!" Linn's band included Dave Frishberg piano, Gary Foster, reeds, Jim or Ted Hughart, bass, Dick Berk, drums, and another saxophonist. Cary presumably played alto horn.

September 28:   Delbert Hill: 2:00 to 4:00, with Bob Enevoldsen —"never got one horn solo."
Money Tree, Toluca Lake: 7:30, with

Composed by Dick Cary, 1975 for Barrelhouse Jazzband:

October 3:	Doug Davis, singer Ruth Olay, and a bassist. Lakeside Country Club: Abe Most job, with Frank Marocco, clarinet, Gene Estes, drums. "Best night in many moons—marvelous time. Yamaha—best piano in twenty years out here and in tune!"
October 4:	St. Martin's Church: 6:30, with Ray Linn band, incl. Bob Wrightmire, Frank Scott, Glenn Corbett, and Ed Mihelich, bass.

The October 3 engagement raises an interesting point. In the AFM Local 47 Directory Frank Marocco (also known as Frank Morocco) is shown as an orchestrator as well as a pianist, organist and clarinetist. If Cary did list the full personnel for the evening, and as he indicates that he was pianist for the date, presumably Marocco played clarinet, giving the interesting and unusual line-up for such a gig of two clarinets, piano and drums (perhaps doubling on vibes).

At the end of October 1980, Cary flew the Atlantic again for a two-week European tour as part of a show, "Music of Eddie Condon and Benny Goodman," organised by clarinetist Peter Bühr, leader of the Flat Foot Stompers in Germany. On October 20, he caught a flight to Frankfurt, arriving on the 21st, and on the 22nd he played his first engagement, with The Chicagoans, at the Garkeller in Pforzheim. His diary gives no bookings until his last job on November 1, recording all afternoon on the 2nd and the flight home on the 3rd. Concerts were given in about ten cities, including one at the Casino in Lucerne in Switzerland on October 25, when Cary and Wild Bill Davison featured with the Bühr band. The guests for the show itself, in addition to Cary and Davison, were Peanuts Hucko, clarinet, Ralph Sutton, piano, Jack Lesberg, bass, Gus Johnson, drums, and Carrie Smith, vocals. Peter Bühr recalled Dick Cary as "a very close friend. He was with me several times to play with the Flat Foot Stompers. Always, when he was in Europe and he had some off-days he would come into the Stuttgart area to play with us, and we always had a ball with him, because he was so wonderful a musician and he had a wonderful sense of humour. Very important for us, we learnt a lot from him."

It was in Pforzheim on November 1st and 2nd that he and The Chicagoans, led by Klaus Bader, recorded for the WSO label. Of the eleven titles released, two were Cary originals, *Swing Down in New Orleans*, with a Cary vocal, and *Ellen*. On November 3, Cary caught his flight back to Los Angeles.

With few entries during November and December, the last weeks of 1980 gradually slipped away:

November 7: jingle recording session
November 8: McGuire's: 9:00 to 1:00, with Doug Davis
November 15: Cornwallis High School: with Doug Davis
December 14: with Doug Davis
December 18: San Diego: scheduled to play with Ray Linn, John Best, Abe Lincoln, Abe Most, Eddie Miller, Ray Leatherwood, Nick Fatool
December 30: Skytrails: 7:00 to 10:00, with trumpeter John Jensen
December 31: Bel Air Country Club: with Frank Marocco (Doug Davis job)

The band for the New Year's Eve dance included clarinetist Gus Bivona, plus "a bad drummer, a rotten saxophone, nice young guitar." Thus the year ended in typical fashion, with Cary playing a gig with the best and the worst of Los Angeles musicians.

20. Louis Tributes, Harry James, Banjos and Tubas (1981–1984)

The first week in January found Cary involved with a show called "Turn to Right," starring actor Buddy Ebsen—"how does the kindergarten get so enmeshed in the music business?" The show's run was for four nights, ending January 7, with Cary noting that on that last night he "didn't even play." That same evening he worked for Del Summers at Montelioni's in a trio.

On January 9 and 10, he again worked for Summers, this time at Sica's. On the 15th, there was a Merl Olds round dance recording session, and on the 17th, he was scheduled to work with Doug Davis at the Elks, Canoga. On Sunday the 25th, he was in a tribute to Hoagy Carmichael at the Mark Taper Forum, organised by trumpeter Dick Sudhalter. Also in the band were Dave Frishberg, piano, Dick Berk, drums, Howard Alden, guitar, Putter Smith, bass, Bob Reitmeier, reeds. Later that night Cary was again at Sica's.

January 26:	Brookside: "fine night for Ken Greco," with Abe Most, Tommy Newsom, Gene Estes
February 6:	Bel Air Country Club: with Abe Most, Frank Marocco, Gene Estes, and a guitarist
February 11:	quartet gig
February 13:	4:00 p.m. Metro Media, stage 4: Abe and Sam Most, Jackie Coon, trumpet, Ray Leatherwood, Nick Fatool evening: Sica's
February 14:	Anaheim: a Valentine's Day Massacre party, with Tom King, trumpet, Betty O'Hara, Eddie Miller, Dick Hafer
February 19/20:	Sica's
March 22:	Valley Hospital: with Wild Bill Davison, Peanuts Hucko, Nick Fatool.
March 28:	Lakewood Golf Club: Abe Most nonet.
March 31:	Warner's #1 stage: 2:00 to 5:45, Barry De Vorgon. "Large orch. I sat in back with peck horn and in front were Tom Johnson, tuba? Tom Shepard, bass trombone, Lloyd Ulyate

	and Barrett O'Hara, trombones, Malcolm McNab and Chuck Findley, trumpets."
April 2/3:	Sica's.
April 4:	job for Tabor, 9:00: with Betty O'Hara, Peanuts Hucko, Eddie Miller, Johnny Varro, Ray Leatherwood, Nick Fatool.
April 10:	Gary Burghoff, 3 shows: with Jack Feierman, trumpet, Herbie Harper, Ernie McDaniel, bass, John Rodby, piano, John Bambridge, reeds.
April 11:	Sica's
April 15:	Marriott Grand Ballroom, for Norman Panto: "chordavox—nightmare! painful guitar, Italian sax, Panto's son on drums. A Western Airline 'Go Dodgers' night and you can't get any stupider than that. NO MORE!"
April 17/18	Sica's
April 21:	Abe Most
April 24:	possible job in San Diego

On Sunday, April 26, Cary flew United to New York and then Swissair to Zurich, arriving on Monday morning. He does not document this short tour but the main purpose was to appear at the Bern Jazz Festival, playing alto horn with The Tremble Kids, a Swiss trad group, and piano with the All Stars (Billy Butterfield, trumpet, Trummy Young, trombone, Kenny Davern, clarinet, Flip Phillips, tenor, Jim Galloway, soprano, George Duvivier, bass, Barrett Deems, drums).

He arrived back in Los Angeles on May 17, followed by a short break and then a flight to Sacramento on the 21st. He took his Monday night band to the Festival, including Dick Cathcart, Bob Enevoldsen, the O'Haras, Abe Most and Ray Leatherwood.

Cary wrote:

It wasn't a big band I brought up, but only eleven people, which is the rehearsal group I've had for about six years. We were miscast up there, since I think about 85% of that enormous crowd prefers the tubas and banjos. Some musicians in London told me they refer to bands of that type as "the dog and frying pan." The dog is the way those players sound and the frying pan is obviously the banjo. The Sacramento Jubilee is based on this style; amateur bands, over 70 in all, from all over the world. Even though I picked a repertoire I thought was appropriate, we still offended some of the "DAGS," which really need to be offended. I am very proud of this rehearsal band and although I've been content so far to keep it only as a rehearsal group, there are requests to appear starting to come in. I'm afraid we will have to come out pretty soon. Already three concerts for the summer, but no "trad" type concerts.

For the 1981 Festival, which ran May 22–25, the attendance had grown to 22,000.

May 30th there was a 9:00 to 1:00 engagement for the U.S. Air Force, with no further entries until two rehearsals for recording sessions which took place on June 16 and 22. Despite the problems with the Jack Lesberg recording session, Cary had agreed to work with Harry Lim again, acting as leader, arranger and instrumentalist (trumpet and alto horn) on an album for Famous Door called "California Doings." The personnel here was Bob Havens, trombone, Tommy Newsom, Dick Hafer, tenors, Ross Tompkins, piano, John Heard, bass, Nick Fatool, drums. This excellent record contains one Cary original, *What's That You're Playing?*, a re-working of *Honeysuckle Rose*. Cary's comment was: "Could have been better! H. Lim is a pain in the ass."

This was done in a studio and Tommy Newsom agreed with me that playing jazz in a dead studio is almost impossible.

June 18:	private party?: piano, with Howard Alden, Ray Leatherwood, Nick Fatool.
July 9:	music center: septet with Bob Enevoldsen, Gene Estes, et al.
July 25:	Malibu, 3:00 to 5:00—sextet. Russ R. (Reinberg?) in evening, at 8:00.
July 26:	Santa Fe, 4:00 to 5:30: septet, including Ray Leatherwood, Nick Fatool, and, it would seem, Bob Enevoldsen on clarinet.
August 9:	McArthur Park, 3:30: octet, incl. Enevoldsen, Abe Most, Leatherwood, Fatool. evening: for George Ball, 7:30 to 9:30: sextet incl. Betty O'Hara, Wayne Songer, Ray Sherman, Leatherwood.
August 12:	Sica's: 12:00 to 1:00—septet incl. Enevoldsen, Most, Leatherwood, Fatool.
August 19:	Maxime: 7:30 to 12:30—with Bob Havens,

	Ray Sherman, Nappy Lamare, Leatherwood, Fatool.
August 20:	Maxime: 7:00 to 12:00.
August 29:	Cliff May job, 8:00: octet incl. Betty O'Hara, Bob Havens, Dick Hafer, Eddie Miller, Leatherwood, Fatool.
August 30:	Sherry Chase—no details
September 12:	Sherry Chase: with sextet, including Bob Enevoldsen
September 20:	Hacienda, Jazz Forum: rehearsal band, incl. the O'Haras, Abe Most, Bob Enevoldsen,

The "Maxime" referred to was the French clarinetist Maxim Saury. Cary recorded on trumpet under his leadership, together with regular friends Bob Havens, Ray Sherman, Nappy Lamare, Ray Leatherwood and Nick Fatool, playing a bunch of old warhorses. Ten titles were issued on the French Black and Blue label and later three titles were added for a Honey CD. Cary gave the record short shrift:
The album was slapped together and very boring.

That same month collector Charlie Crump, on holiday from the U.K., saw the Abe Most Big Band in concert at a religious college. The band included Betty O'Hara and Dick Cary, the latter on alto horn.

Cary flew to Gatwick with Freddy Laker's airline on September 11 for two months' work in Britain, arranged by trumpeter Keith Smith (1940–2004). Smith had organised a tour which he called the Wonderful World of Louis Armstrong, playing 27 dates between October 1 and 31, covering the length and breadth of the country. Each of the musicians booked by Smith had been a member of the Louis Armstrong All Stars at some time—"Big Chief" Russell Moore, trombone and vocals, Peanuts Hucko, clarinet, Dick Cary, piano, Arvell Shaw, bass and vocals, Barrett Deems, drums.

Smith had asked Cary to write some arrangements ("tops and tails") for the show and to come to the U.K. early to discuss them. During September, Smith was to tour with his own band, with trombonist George Chisholm as the guest star, but when Chisholm went into hospital, Cary was asked to replace him.

The Red Norvo Trio (Norvo, vibes, Tal Farlow, guitar, and, from England, Peter Ind, bass) was booked for a British tour (September 4–October 6) and the trio was slotted into Smith's band itinerary towards the end of September.

Cary had his usual misgivings about the trip: "This will be a

Remo Palmieri, Red Norvo and Dick Cary. England, c. September 1981.

small adventure, back in vaudeville again, back with the animated penguins. I am giving up tennis, 'Mash,' Dick Cavett, hot sun, freeway battling, my rehearsal band, all for a tired old vaudeville act of some guys who as young men hung on to Louis' coattails briefly. Louis had few associates who ranked anywhere near him. Teagarden the closest and probably led among the ofays. Hines had a large niche, Bigard, Ed Hall, Sid Catlett, but few others."

The Keith Smith band itinerary was:

September 13:	Tewkesbury
September 14:	Swansea
September 15–17:	rest days
September 18:	Thetford
September 19:	King's Lynn
September 20:	Mold, Wales
September 21:	BBC recording (Birmingham)
September 22:	rest day
September 23:	Rotherham
September 24:	BBC Radio 2
September 25:	Portsmouth (TV show)
September 26:	uncertain
September 27:	Manchester

Smith's band at this time included Mickey Cooke on trombone, Ron Drake, clarinet and tenor, Jim Douglas, guitar, and Ron Hetherington, drums, and "Paul" on fender bass, with Al Gay, clarinet and tenor, joining at Thetford, on the 18th. Of Ron Drake Cary commented: "very tall, nice guy, who is fast and fluent, one of best I've heard in any band like this ... I enjoyed our quartet on *Honeysuckle Rose*." Al Gay was "someone I can converse with, is older, smarter, better musician, actually the only professional. He toured with the W.G.J.B. and was dubbed 'soprano de Bergerac,'" while Jim Douglas was "the Scot with lovely speech, very pleasant man." He referred to Mickey Cooke as "the more impish member, whose lip is strong, arm is quick."

During the stay in Britain Cary made six radio and television appearances:

September 18:   Anglia Television, appearance with pianist Graeme Bell, Brian Prudence, bass, Tony Allen, drums—("very pleasant time")
September 24:   BBC Radio 2, with Keith Smith
September 25:   Southern Television, Portsmouth, with Ron Rubin, bass, Tony Allen, drums
September 27:   BBC Radio in London, with Keith Smith; Roy Hudd as presenter
September 30:   Pete Murray Show (London). Peter Sellers & David Frost also guests
September 30:   BBC, Pebble Mill, Birmingham

The shows on the 30th featured the Armstrong tribute band. "When Pete Murray got to me, the first question was, 'Does Keith Smith play like Louis Armstrong?' My reaction of silence and raised eyebrows caused him to quickly amend, 'Is that a dangerous question?' I said, 'Yes, it is ... let's get on to the next question.' He didn't stay too long with me."

Cary's last night with the Smith band was on September 27, and the following day he went with Smith to meet the rest of the Armstrong alumni at Heathrow. They rehearsed on the 29th, in readiness for their first concert on October 1, the start of a tour which took them across England and Wales—London to Cardiff, Bath to Manchester, Sheffield to Bournemouth—plus an appearance at the Cork Jazz Festival in Ireland. The tour played to packed audiences, with a similar programme each night; a collection of tunes associated with Louis, plus features for the individual

Wonderful World of Louis Armstrong, Keith Smith's tour, October 1981
l-r, standing: Sandy Saunders (road manager), Peanuts Hucko, Keith Smith, Barrett Deems. seated: Dick Cary, Russell "Big Chief" Moore, Arvell Shaw
(Photograph courtesy of Peter Vacher and Keith Smith)

musicians. Peanuts Hucko played *Stealin' Apples*, Arvell Shaw *Summertime* and Cary *Echo of Spring* and *Love Stream*, as he had with Smith's own band.

Trombonist "Big Chief" Russell Moore fell ill just before the tour ended. He was taken into hospital in Oxford during the last three day of the tour and Mickey Cooke deputised for him.

The full itinerary for the October tour was:

1. Reading	11. Manchester	21. Chichester
2. Maidstone	12. Cardiff	22. Uttoxeter
3. London club	13. Charnock Richard	23. Eastbourne
4. Bournemouth	14. Stevenage	24. Birmingham
5. rest day	15. Grays	25. Sheffield
6. Camberley	16. Street	26. Cork Festival
7. rest day	17. Bletchley	27. rest day
8. Lincoln	18. Bath	28. Warwick
9. Barnstaple	19. rest day	29. Oxford
10. Swindon	20. Sunset Jazz Club	30. Telford
	31. Bury St. Edmunds	

Overall the standard of the pianos which Cary was expected to play seems to have been fairly high. For every "lousy upright" (Oxford) and "old Bechstein in its declining years" (Cork), there were more remarks about "a beautiful concert Steinway" (Manchester), "fine new Yamaha baby grand" (Rotherham), "a fine hall with a Boesendorfer with the nine extra bass notes" (Mold), "a fairly good German grand" (King's Lynn) and "a large beautiful Steinway on which I wandered from 6:00 to 7:30" (Warwick).

Cary also saw two plays while in London, Deborah Kerr and Ian Carmichael in Peter Ustinov's "Overhead," and Donald Sinden in Noel Coward's "marvelous" "Present Laughter." He enjoyed the latter so much that he went twice.

Smith admired Cary as a musician but recalled him as a loner. He did not care about his appearance and even after arrangements had been made to hire a dress suit and white shirts, he would appear on stage in Hawaiian shirt and brown sandals!

Referring to Cary's frugality, Jim Turner has confirmed that he was careful, as were many people who recalled the Depression years. It would seem that Cary's major expenses were his cigars and his manuscript paper.

Cary arrived home in Sunland at 6:30 on November 2 and underlined his original misgivings by writing: "I never so happy to be done with something in my life!!!!!" A later thought was, "When ffff is required most of the time, it must be because there's a terrible lack of quality."

Writing arrangements for a round/square dance recording session, plus a great deal of tennis, was keeping him occupied, but on November 13 he worked in a quartet with Bob Enevoldsen which played the Sherman Clay piano store (7:30, three short sets). The following day he was in a sextet which worked 9:00 to 1:00 at a Unitarian Church—"pleasant job and church folks seemed to like us," the "us" including Eddie Miller, Bob Stava, drums, Chas Myerson, guitar, Valda Hammick and Ed Slanson(?). At the end of that week, the 21st, he was with Elaine Mitchell at Sterling's.

The round dance recording sessions were scheduled for November 23/24, then no more entries until Christmas Eve, a gig at the Music Center (Joe Casparoff, Joe Braden ?), with Betty O'Hara, Abe Most, Bob Enevoldsen, Ray Leatherwood, and Chas. Myerson, followed by New Year's Eve at the Lakeside Country Club in a 13-piece big band led by Abe Most, with singer Herb Jeffries as the headliner. The band featured Zeke Zarchy, Dick Cathcart, trumpets, Ed Anderson, Hoyt Bohannon, trombones, Les Robinson, Eddie

Miller, Dick Holgate, John Bambridge, reeds, Putter Smith, bass, Jack Whitaker, Gene Estes, drums.

Elsewhere Cary encapsulated his views of popular swing hits and of certain types of business men when he wrote: "Why do defenceless trumpet players have to play *In the Mood* for 52 years, just to get paid union scale, for some ... slobs to conduct their alcoholic business meetings at Lakeside Country Club...."

On January 2 he watched a W.C. Fields television festival— "I thought who of all our great funny people really lasts the longest, holds up through decades, and Will C. Fields has it over all of them. The Laurel and Hardy fans and some Marx Brothers fans might disagree, but the last two belong to a certain era and Fields is undying. And so is Groucho, without his marvelous brothers." He was also driven to comment on "that monumental bore" "Close Encounters of a Third Kind," after watching it on television—"I hope the first and second were more interesting!"

Two telephone calls during January 1982 were out of the usual. One was from Peanuts Hucko about a European trip in March and the other was from Pee Wee Monte, Harry James' manager, offering six nights work later in the month. Cary gives only three dates with James in January, but there are others in February, March and April:

January 23: Camino College, El Camino
January 25: Pavilion Room, Hilton Hotel, Las Vegas
January 26: party for Danny Kaye
February 3: Burlingame, 7:00 p.m.: birthday party for a heart doctor. "Beautiful country club."
February 24: Biltmore Bowl, 9:00: "Grammy" dance.
March 3:   MGM Hotel, Las Vegas

For the Danny Kaye party, "Ralph Carmichael wrote an overture which we rehearsed. Then they used it to introduce Kris Kristofferson, who is probably the world's most boring singer of tired western material."

Trumpeter Harry James, one of the last surviving leaders from the big band era, was born March 15, 1916, and died on July 5, 1983. In 1982 Cary wrote:

> *Since January [1982] I have been playing piano with Harry James, but only in California. Only west coast jobs and not too many of these. Now they're off for two months all over the U.S. and I can't do that anymore. Airline prices and hotel rates have ruined the big bands or rather, merely put in the*

finishing touches, and very few remain. Most leaders now assemble groups who are residents of the area where they are appearing.

Did about four months with Harry James, [who] was pretty loaded every job. I don't know if he was aware of the cancer, but he seemed more like a zombie, merely going through the motions. But then, I can't imagine how a man can go 43 years with the same old tunes which were hits and he was obliged to perform them over and over and over. Playing piano with these groups is something one can easily do in his sleep.

Cary mentions only two members of the Harry James orchestra, the first altoist Quinn Davis and the drummer Les Demerle.

Between the various James engagements he played trumpet on January 25, with Bob Enevoldsen, Peanuts Hucko, Johnny Varro, John Oliver, guitar, Morty Corb and Jack Sperling, for the television series, "Hart to Hart," and on February 5 he was on piano for an unlisted gig, alongside Bob Havens, Eddie Miller and Ray Leatherwood.

In April 1982, Cary wrote:
I have just returned from another one—the third Armstrong tour in a year and I think I am going to give up playing Hello Dolly. *I suppose these European promoters will milk the last drop out of the Armstrong name, but I've had enough!! Any traveling from now on will be on my own, group travel is terrible, mostly buses and the feeling that I'm on some kind of cub-scout expedition.*

We did the last week in March in Ronnie Scott's. Before that we did two weeks all over Germany, Italy, Holland, Belgium—it was bus, bus, bus—very tedious and it sounded like a vaudeville show. Right at our opening set I had a strong feeling about being in the wrong place! We had a rather tired, banal and boring vaudeville act. It really ceases to be jazz when a group plays exactly the same program every bloody concert and, in the case of Hucko, the same solos. I've had all I can stand of this vaudeville nonsense.

I enjoyed the one week in London and went to the theatre six times. One was a Shaw play, "Arms and the Man," and this was the best.

In addition to Peanuts Hucko and Dick Cary, the personnel for this particular Louis tribute band was Jimmy Maxwell, trumpet, Trummy Young, trombone, Jack Lesberg, bass, and Danny D'Imperio on drums. The tour was arranged by promoter George Wein.

The itinerary for the continental section as given by Cary was:
March 10: flight to Europe
March 11/12: no entries
March 13/14: Hamburg
March 15: Hamburg to Bologna
March 16: concert in Civitanova
March 17: Jazz Club Gerhilla, Pforzheim
March 18: rest day
March 19: Dixieland Hall, with Flat Foot Stompers
March 20: Concert—Stadtsaal
March 21: Concert—Audimax
March 22: Amsterdam—Concert Muziekcentrum
March 23: Concert in Brussels
March 24: rest day
March 25: Nick Vollebrecht's Jazz Cafe

The band played at Ronnie Scott's Club in London between Friday, March 26, and Thursday, April 1, 1982. Chris Barber's band was also on the bill for the two concerts in Hamburg.

On March 20, Cary recorded with Peter Bühr's Flat Foot Stompers. As Bühr recalled: "In March 1982 he [Cary] came for a short visit ... That was when we recorded with Dick on piano and Trummy Young, *Way Down Yonder in New Orleans*. That was only recording where Trummy was singing scat."

Arriving home on April 2, Cary noted: "It really is a marvelous thing to achieve by your sixties a shack amid all kind of leaves."

During April, Cary was originally scheduled to play nine dates with Harry James, but he made only five, April 17 to 21 inclusive. No details are given, except for the notation "Pasadena" against the last two days. He also wrote:

I have (possibly) a chance to interest the Boston Pops in a piece and it's quite an incentive.

But second thoughts prevailed:

The piece I was advised to do for the "Pops," something called Sgt. Pee Wee, is just too long a job for a speculative venture of this kind. The time, the money for copying, etc, doesn't seem worth the chance that it could be rejected. If I knew John

Williams [conductor of the Boston Pops orchestra] better, I might send him a tape of a performance, but he's a busy man and I don't really want to spend the time.

Sgt. Pee Wee was eventually recorded in 1997 by Dick Cary's Tuesday Night Friends, directed by Dick Hamilton, and appeared on a Klavier CD. The title refers not to clarinetist Pee Wee Russell, but to Pee Wee Marquette, who was doorman at the famous New York jazz club, Birdland. Cary told many stories about the small but pompous Marquette. In the CD notes it says: "Tommy Newsom once observed that, if this piece had been written by Stravinsky, it might well have come to fame as a masterpiece!"

Other dates following the All-Stars tour included:

April 13: Gingerbread House: horns with Bob Enevoldsen, Tommy Newsom, John Hammond, Dick Berk, Jim Hughart

May 1: Tabor, 9:00: Ray Linn, Betty O'Hara, Bill Wood, Clyde Amsler, reeds, Ray Leatherwood, Gene Estes

May 6: San Diego: piano job for Dick McCormick

On May 7 there was a Noni Bernardi fund raiser at the Empire Room. The 14-piece band, led by trombonist Bill Tole, included Abe Most, Babe Russin, Don Raffell, Jack Trott, Betty and Barrett O'Hara, Dick Holgate, Ray Sherman, Roland Bundock, Gene Estes. Cary's comment: "We did Bunny over again (Abe left) and we did a cheap watered-down rendition of Dorsey, Miller and Basie—awful, under Tole's baton—what redundancy."

There was another date at the Gingerbread House on May 13, then nothing mentioned until the Sacramento Dixieland Jubilee which ran May 28 to 31.

It is surprising perhaps that Cary appeared for so many years at the Sacramento Dixieland Jubilee when the emphasis there was on amateur and semi-professional bands playing music which did not interest him. In one rant he referred to: "the morons at Sacramento who have to hear *That's a Plenty* and stupid tuba and banjo players and resent the few pros who try to pull jazz out of the slime...." But he continued to attend.

There is just one job shown for June 1982, at the Hyatt Regency, playing trumpet with Gus, Bob Enevoldsen, Eddie Miller, Ray Sherman, Ray Leatherwood and Nick Fatool. He also notes "various singers." Gus is presumably clarinetist Gus Bivona.

On July 11 the Dick Cary Jazz Band (ten pieces, including Enevoldsen, Chas Myerson, Jerry McKenzie, the O'Haras, Tom, Dick, Fred and Ray) appeared at the John Anson Ford County Cultural Arts Theatre. Similar one-offs continued:

July 14:	City Hall: with Chuck Conklin band
July 15:	Ginger House
July 17:	Variety Arts Theatre: with Del Kasher, rehearsal and show
July 18:	Hacienda Hotel: for Jazz Forum, 2:00 p.m. Eddie Miller and Nappy Lamare day
July 19:	job for Sid Lasalle, 7:00
July 20/21:	trumpet at Shill's

Dick Cary and his Jazz Masters appeared at the Ojai Festival August 14/15. The personnel, which was drawn from the weekly rehearsal band, was Dick Cathcart, trumpet, Betty O'Hara, Barrett O'Hara, Bob Enevoldsen, trombones, Abe Most, clarinet, Tommy Newsom, Fred Cooper, reeds, Charlie Myerson, guitar, Ray Leatherwood, bass, Jerry McKenzie, drums. Betty vocals on *Old Folks* and *Skylark*. Cary played trumpet, alto horn, piano.

The only other engagement noted, prior to Cary catching a flight to Edinburgh on August 28, was on the 18th, when he worked a job with Joe Dixon, 12:00 to 1:00, with Betty O'Hara, Howard Alden, Ray Leatherwood, and Gene Estes.

The Edinburgh Jazz Festival was the major jazz event to be held in Britain and in 1982 it opened on August 29th. Among the overseas guests scheduled to appear were Teddy Wilson, Benny Waters, Jim Galloway and—Dick Cary. In later years solo or small group tours followed on from festival appearances, but for this year Cary was invited to Scotland for just four days, Monday, August 30 to Thursday, September 2. He played with the other guests (there was a "Pianorama" on the first afternoon) and with the best British mainstream musicians, several of whom were veterans of the Alex Welsh band. In the course of the twelve sets he played, Cary worked with, among others, Roy Williams and Roy Crimmins, trombones, Al Gay and John Barnes, reeds, Jim Douglas and Paul Sealey, guitars and Dave Green, bass.

> *The Edinburgh party was the first time I met Humphrey Lyttelton. It was a hectic week. One place I played with Roy Williams was a small theatre—no one came at all. It wasn't listed I guess. Another two concerts in a hotel—the rhythm*

section was absolutely useless, piano drunk, bass knowing no tunes. So bad that the English tenor player (I won't name him) stopped right in the middle of Singing the Blues, *turned, and walked away. But I found most of the Edinburgh musicians very pleasant personally, especially Mike Hart, the director [of the Edinburgh Festival], who I see at Sacramento each year.*

Mike Hart's comment on Cary was, "A hell of a nice guy."

Dick Cary, with Edinburgh Festival director Mike Hart on the right. Edinburgh, Scotland, summer 1982.

(Photograph by Bill Clarke. Courtesy: Dick Cary Archive)

From his return to Los Angeles on September 3 through to the end of December there are no diary entries, except for a few notes on another European trip starting on October 12 and ending with his arrival back in L.A. on October 31. Cary was part of a tour organised by Rems-Murr Jazztage, sometimes shown as featuring the Lawson-Haggart Jazz Band or even the "The World's Greatest Jazz Band." The personnel was Yank Lawson, trumpet, George Masso, trombone, Johnny Mince, clarinet, Al Klink, tenor, Dick Cary, piano, Bob Haggart, bass, Charly Antolini, drums, and Carrie Smith, vocals. On October 17, members of this group recorded with the Flat Foot Stompers and two titles were released on the Timeless label. Cary refers, on the 23rd, to "final concert for Peter. Four towns this week—

Waibling, Schorndorf, Anenwold, Leonberg. Tonight the Dixieland Hall with Haggart...." To quote Peter Bühr, leader of the Stompers: "Dick Cary played alto horn with the Flat Foot Stompers. He pointed out the soloists and wrote the endings for the tunes."

Cary also played some dates with Klaus Bader's Chicagoans during the October 1982 tour. Bader remembers that when his daughter, Laura, was born on the 15th, "Dick was with me in the hospital. We had a concert in Karlsruhe that evening and we were a little late." *Laura* was one of the tunes which Cary recorded with The Chicagoans about this time for Bader's own label, BAD.

Diary entries for 1983 and 1984 are infrequent. Adding a few other known engagements, 1983 can be summarised as follows:

January 2:	Valley Jazz Club, 3:45: with Betty O'Hara, Abe Most, Ray Leatherwood, Jerry McKenzie, and Ashley (Alexander?).
January 15:	Medford, Oregon (no details)
January 16:	Ashland, Oregon (guest of South Oregon Traditional Jazz Society at Ashland Hill Hotel)
March 4:	Rodeway Inn: guest with the Jazz Minors, again for the S.O.T.J.S.
March 30:	*Swing Down in New Orleans*, words & music by Cary, was copyrighted.
April 16:	Lincoln Junior High School auditorium, Santa Monica: Cary guesting with the 7-piece Dixielanders, incl. Betty O'Hara, Eddie Miller, Dick Hafer and Ashley Alexander (double bell euphonium)
June 26:	Paradise: the 3rd Annual Great Northern Dixieland Jazz Festival
July 31:	Malibu Festival

He was at the Sacramento Dixieland Jubilee which was held May 27–30, and on June 27 he noted "have dates with H. James, one with Ray Leatherwood," though it is doubtful that those with James, who died the following month, took place.

A report in the Chico News and Review (June 30, 1983) of the Paradise festival held the previous Sunday said of Cary's playing with the Hangover Jazz Co., "His solo on *My Blue Heaven* was a model of perfection...." Cary was quoted as saying: "There is a very precious commodity called 'swing'; most groups tend to play too fast." While the Malibu Surfside News for July 28, 1983, reported that this year would be the fifth for Dick Cary's 9-piece jazz band at the Malibu Festival, which would play on Sunday noon to 2:00.

In October, Cary summarised life in Los Angeles in 1983 in a letter:

> *My existence is pretty much the same. Try to write about half the day, get out on the tennis court every afternoon at 4 p.m. to clear out my pores and my head. This Sunday [October 23] I journey to Eugene, Oregon, to a jazz club as the guest for their monthly meeting. I don't see how this can last, now that the air fare is higher than my salary for one afternoon.*
>
> *I have my ten-piece band at my house each Tuesday evening and it is more practical to get three or four things ready for them every week. That library now numbers over 1000 things. Years ago in New York City, the guys in the Brill Building, which housed most of the pop music publishers, often commented about how many tunes a good song writer would turn out to get one hit and I guess I've been operating on that theory. I keep thinking I am near an album but keep wanting to get it better.*
>
> *Last week I was asked to be an adviser for a proposed stage show about Louis Armstrong, our impressionist George Kirby to be Louis. I always hated impressions of certain people, especially Louis, but I must admit Kirby's is almost palatable. But I am horrified to find that they intend to pre-record something that is supposed to represent the first small group with Jack Teagarden, Barney Bigard, Sid Catlett. They tell me a lot of musicals now use pre-recorded stuff but it does not seem like very good theatre. But then, I dislike almost all American "musicals," although I have been mixed up in several, both on the stage and in the pit.*
>
> *The musician I went to see is one I have some respect for, a guy named Allyn Ferguson. I've heard some lovely ballads he arranged for one of the London Symphonies. He must [go] to London at the end of October to work on a T.V. mini-series and will be there about three months, so wants to get a lot of the prerecording in immediately. I don't see how we can possibly get it done in the next week and there are problems with the book and, of course, the backing. I'm sorry Allyn has to leave. I'd feel a lot more comfortable with him as a sort of shield from the average Hollywood musical mentality.* [Ferguson was scheduled to fly to London on October 29.] *We won't do any recording till he returns and by that time the book may be pretty well along.*

This project was not mentioned again, so presumably the book or, more likely the backing, were not "well along."

    Details of a few more engagements complete 1983:
November 5: Canyon Country Club, Palm Springs: 7:30 to 11:30 with Ray Leatherwood; "Ray Sherman impeccable as ever."
November 25/26: San Diego: with John Best, Bob Havens, Abe Most, Eddie Miller, Ray Sherman, Ray Leatherwood, Nick Fatool
December 3: Tucson: rehearsal in afternoon, dinner & show at 8:00, with Phil Harris, Forrest Tucker, George Gobel, etc. Band included Bob Havens, Stan Keyes, the Simmons.
December 31: Canyon Country Club: with Mac McReynolds band.

    Similarly, details for 1984 are rather sparse. On January 4 he was a member of the "Bob Crosby All Stars" which spent twelve hours at A&M Music on La Brea taping a video. Also in the show were trumpeter Al Hirt, pianist Judy Carmichael, trumpeter Teddy Buckner's band, and singers Irma Thomas, Scatman Crothers, Jim and Martha Hession. The musicians mentioned by Cary are Dick Cathcart, Bob Havens, Peanuts Hucko, Eddie Miller, Ray Sherman, Ray Leatherwood, and Gene Estes. "No jazz really. I made my debut as a whistler in *Big Noise from Winnetka*."

    In March, the 2nd to the 4th, he worked at the Double Tree Inn in Monterey, presumably as a solo pianist, and shortly afterwards he was in a Wild Bill Davison band playing piano and alto horn, at an unnamed jazz festival. Also in the band were Chuck Hedges and probably Red Callender and Barrett Deems. On April 10 he was scheduled to play with Bob Enevoldsen, Ray Leatherwood and Gene Estes. Dick Holgate had telephoned on April 7 to tell Cary that he was "artist of the day" on KLON. The Sacramento Dixieland Jubilee was held May 25–28, and on June 30 he was due to fly to Phoenix with Eddie Miller and Bob Haggart for a Bob Crosby engagement.

    For the Los Angeles Classic Jazz Festival on Labor Day weekend (August 30–September 2, 1984), Cary was shown as All Star Band Co-ordinator. Bass player Bob Allen said: "I know that Dick did the selection and placing of the all star musicians for the first two Los Angeles Classic Jazz Festivals. Then when Chuck Conklin got the hang of it he started doing it himself. Dick was a little miffed about Chuck's lack of gratitude. So were many others." During the festival Cary led his rehearsal band at the Airport Marriott Hotel on August 31.

1984 ended with a job on the Queen Mary, 8:30 to 1:30, seeing in the New Year with trumpeter Joe Graves and the Harry James Orchestra.

* * * * * * *

With few engagements listed for 1983 perhaps one could surmise that it was in this year that he composed *White April* and *Pale September*. To quote the notes to Klavier KD-77024, "These two selections are not, as is often assumed, musical descriptions of beautiful, wintry landscapes. Rather, the titles refer to the paucity of penciled-in gigs on Dick Cary's monthly calendar! In September, he had only a few jobs and his calendar was 'pale'! In April, none—white!"

Cary still gave occasional piano lessons and trumpeter Zeke Zarchy's son was one of his pupils:

> Andy Zarchy was a pupil of mine for two or three years. He is now Andrew Fielding, living in Monterey. He has composed quite a few piano pieces and was influenced mostly by Johnny Guarnieri in these.

But his favourite pupil was Jim Turner (born Pasadena, December 16, 1951):

> There's a brilliant young man, Jim Turner, a pianist, who I will leave everything to. He was my recording engineer until he moved to Indiana to work for the Boesendorfer piano, handling the duplicator, a new expression for "player piano." He has recently amazed me by making stride piano solos of my works for ten piece band. He had no music, took them off by ear. He plans eventually to do a whole album. Outside of Dick Hyman I think he's the only one I'm aware of now who can still do justice to the James P. Johnson pieces and has two albums out so far, which includes some of James P's.

Jim Turner remembered: "I first met Dick [about 1983] when I asked him to give me piano lessons—and he did. I tape-recorded some of them, especially when he demonstrated something for me. Later, he loaned me a cassette of some of his Tuesday rehearsal night music he thought I might enjoy. I liked it and he invited me to visit on a Tuesday night. I did and went back again and again.

"After a few weeks, I noticed that Dick struggled with his tape-recorder during the rehearsals and I offered to operate it for him so he could concentrate on the music. He seemed immensely appreciative of this. So, for a period of years, I went every Tuesday night.

"Soon, he wouldn't take any more money for my piano lessons [which] became—more and more—sessions during which I would take him the arrangements I had written for the Great Pacific Jazz Band and he would correct them and fix them up. This went on for years. He subbed a lot in that band, both before and after my departure from it. He subbed for Bob Havens, playing alto horn, for Zeke Zarchy, playing trumpet, for me on piano.

"In about 1985, I took a day job in Indiana and, very sadly for me, that was the end of that. My friendship with Dick remained very strong, however, and we spoke on the phone frequently—maybe weekly, on average—and our phone conversations tended to be long, highlighted by his monologues on his remarkable experiences in jazz. I saw him each time I visited California, which was several times a year. Sometimes, I would also see him at a jazz festival somewhere. He was one of my best friends. Our son is named after him."

In 2003 Jim Turner joined the Jim Cullum band in San Antonio, staying until July 2011. And he did become Dick Cary's executor.

21. We never did play *In the Mood* (1985–1990)

Cary reported that he "got through January without a job," though the Tuesday rehearsals continued unabated. There was one on February 4, which was a Monday—"Changed night just for Cathcart and he didn't come!" The first job in 1985 was the weekend of February 9/10, his fourth appearance for the Sacramento Traditional Jazz Society, when he played at the Marina both days and the Elks on the Sunday. On February 15 he noted "Loyola—Bruce 8:30."

He started 1985 with mixed feelings!
> I am not traveling much lately. The dollar has gotten too high for one thing and I can't compose when "on the road." At present it is just writing and playing tennis and working very few evening jobs and I rather miss it. But I refuse to play this inane dance music and there is little else around here.
> On February 16th we did our best one so far at California Tech in Pasadena. They made me a tape but it was pretty badly balanced, so I am going to finally get us recorded in a studio, though it won't have the energy we got at Cal Tech, before a very nice audience of about a thousand.
> There is a young man in Hollywood called Dick Hamilton who is probably the finest musician I have ever met. Built his own studio, plays flute, trumpet, piano, trombone, all extremely well. [He] is one of the most creative arrangers and composers, and as good a recording engineer as I've met, so we'll get together and probably do one at his place. Although I'd really prefer natural acoustics, like in a church or one of our large lodge halls.

Either Cary is providing fewer details of his engagements or, more likely, he is not getting the work, as the following list indicates:
March 23:   Ahbay, 6:30: with Ray [Leatherwood], Gene [Estes].
April 6:   7:30 to 11:30: with Diane Sassen
April 10:   noon, Ahbay

April 12:   Palladium: with Helen. rehearsal 4:30, show 8:00
April 13:   Riverside, 7:00 to 11:00

For the weekend of April 20/21, 1985, bassist Bob Finch formed a band he called The Chicago Six for a festival at the Belly Up Tavern in Solano Beach near San Diego. The front man was clarinetist Bill Reinhardt, famous as owner of the Jazz, Ltd. club in Chicago. Dick Cary played trumpet and Johnny Varro was the pianist.

April 27:   Unitary Church, 7:30 to 10:30: with Betty [O'Hara], Dave [Koonse].
May 12:   no location, 6:30 to 10:30: with Abe Most, Ray Sherman, Ray Leatherwood, Dick Shaw [reeds?].
May 23:   Sidney L., 6:30: with Eddie Miller, Dave Koonse, Herb Mickman.

The 1985 Sacramento Jubilee was held May 24–27 and Cary has noted down the names of Abe and Sam Most, Gene Estes, John K. and Bob. One of the sets was reviewed by Floyd Levin: "Abe and Sam Most deviated further from the Dixieland mode than any other featured band ... the two reed virtuosos worked beautifully with the strongest rhythm section we heard. Dick Cary's piano and Gene Estes' drums created the pulse that subtly propelled the brothers Most."

There are three single gigs for June, cursorily entered:
June 8:   Joe Darensbourg—Russ Bisset
June 22:   Disneyland—8:00—H.J.
June 27:   Del Mar

Followed on June 30 by an engagement at Disneyland with Bob Crosby. The 30th was spent rehearsing, with the band performing between July 1 and 6. Its personnel was: John Best, Dick Cathcart, Dick Cary, trumpets, Bill Tole, Bob Havens, Chauncey Welsch, trombones, Skeets Herfurt, Peanuts Hucko, Dick Hafer, Fred Cooper, Dick Holgate, reeds, Frank Scott, piano, Dave Stone, bass, Alvin Stoller, drums, plus singer Kay Starr.

July 19:   no location: 8:30 to 12:30: with Dick Cathcart, Ray Leatherwood, Gene Estes
July 27:   Malibu, noon: with Abe Most, Betty O'Hara, Gene Estes, and probably Tommy Newsom, Dick, John and Bob B.
August 10: Barnsdall Park, 4:00 to 5:00: with Betty O'Hara, Dick Hamilton, Dave Koonse

August 11: Warner Center, 5:30 to 7:30: [Johnny] Varro after Abe.
August 16: Hilton Lodge, Lake Arrowhead: Mac McReynolds band: Bobby Williams on piano; presumably Cary on trumpet.
August 17: Sunset Hills Country Club, 6:30 to 10:30: with Dave Bourne

Surprisingly Cary does not mention the Conneaut Lake Jazz Party in his diary, merely showing that he was in Pennsylvania, leaving L.A. on August 22 and returning August 25. This was his first appearance at the party, which was held August 23–25. He played alto horn on two sets with an Ed Polcer group (Polcer, trumpet, Bob Havens, trombone, Mahlon Clark, clarinet, Bud Freeman, tenor, Dick Hyman, piano, Marty Grosz, guitar, Bob Haggart, bass, and Hal Smith, drums) and two with a Bob Havens band (similar personnel, but Billy Butterfield, trumpet, Eddie Miller, tenor, Dave McKenna, piano, and Jake Hanna, drums).

Conneaut Lake Jazz Party 1985
l-r: Eddie Miller, Dick Hyman, Marty Grosz, Ed Polcer, Bob Haggart, Maxine Sullivan, Jake Hanna, Bob Reitmeier, Bud Freeman, Scott Hamilton, x , Dan Barrett, Betty O'Hara, x . Dick Cary, Joe Wilder, Gene Estes, Billy Butterfield

Joe Boughton, organiser of the party, said: "I will always remember the meeting when Dick arrived at the front door of the Hotel Conneaut. Bud Freeman was waiting for him 'cause it was a surprise ... Bud was lined up late and was not in our advertisements. They embraced for a long interlude and were always the best of friends."

Away from Conneaut Lake, Boughton recalled another occasion: "Best Cary I ever heard was at Los Angeles Labor Day Hot and Sweet many years ago, when he was playing solo piano in the little room in the basement where they did small group things."

The Los Angeles Times writer, Charles Champlin, reviewing the 1985 Los Angeles Classic Jazz Festival in the September 5 issue, referred to one set—perhaps at Baxter Hall—by guitarists George Van Eps and Dave Koonse, with Dick Cary, piano and alto horn, saying: "Not often is any music more melodically beautiful."

September 5: Baxter Hall: with Dick Cathcart, Dick Hafer, Dave Koonse, Gene Estes, Paul G.
September 13: Unitarian Church
September 14: Sheridan Town House, 6:00 to 10:00: with Betty O'Hara, Dave Koonse, Herb Mickman
September 16: Sage & Sound, 7:30 to 12:30—McReynolds

Galen "Mac" McReynolds was a clarinet player and his wife, Margaret Jean, was the singer with the band. Of the above date Cary wrote: "Band did my arrangements very well and even the clarinets were pretty well in tune ... wish Mary (sic) Jean could get some personality in her singing. Dick Hamilton's comment: very boring." This presumably was the date for the LP, which McReynolds produced for his own label, though Cary does mention another date with McReynolds (November 25) when he comments "Album went well." The album shows the orchestra to be a well-organised, proficient unit, though not particularly distinguished. Best known musicians present, in addition to Cary as pianist and arranger, were Dick Hafer on tenor and Arnold Fishkin on bass. Cary is featured on alto horn on *Poor Butterfly*, but is otherwise anonymous.

Cary mentioned in a letter (1986) the connection with an air museum at Chino, California:

> During the last year I've been writing quite a few things for a 15-piece band which works mostly up around the Riverside area, about 75 miles east of Los Angeles. The group is called Mac McReynolds and his Planes of Fame Orchestra. They are sponsored by a large airplane museum which has air-shows featuring World War II planes in flying condition, including a Jap Zero which set them back about half a million. The band

is not bad at all and has been attracting some good players from my area, since there is so damn little to do in this San Fernando Valley, which I still refer to as the cultural cesspool of the U.S.A.

Dick Cary with Mac McReynolds' Planes of Fame orchestra, c.1986
(Courtesy: Dick Cary Archive)

September 21: Canoga Park Bowl: a Tabor job, trumpet with John Allred, trombone, Eddie Miller, Gene Bolen, clarinet, Ray Sherman, Ray Leatherwood, Nick Fatool
September 27: Telcar, 12:00 to 3:00 (no details)
October 2: 6:30: Jim Turner
October 5: Mac McReynolds, Planes of Fame, 8:00
October 19: Las Vegas, 12:00: James [possibly Harry James "ghost" band at the Sherman Hotel?]
October 20: no location: Bob Ringwald, 6;00 to 10:00
October 25: Whittier Elks
October 27: no location: Bob Ringwald, 6:00 to 10:30
November 17: San B[ernardino?], 7:00 to 11:00: Mac McReynolds' rehearsal
November 24: no location: Mac McReynolds

November 25:	no location: Mac McReynolds recording date? "Album went well."
December 6:	Knox: with Eddie Miller, Herb Mickman, Nick Fatool
December 7:	L.B. Convention Center, 8:00 to 12:00: Mac McReynolds band, incl. Zeke Zarchy, Dick Hafer, Gene Estes.
December 14:	no location: Dave Bourne
December 31:	Red Lion in Ontario, with Mac McReynolds' Planes of Fame Orchestra. incl. Dick Cathcart

The January 1, 1986, entry, which perhaps overlooks the Bobby Hackett band at the Henry Hudson Hotel, is: "So far this is first band which uses mostly my scribblings. Tonight the rhythm was frightful and MacR picked out all the garbage."

January 4:	Marriott Hotel: Wild Bill Davison (born January 5, 1906) 80th birthday party. Cary played with Dick Cathcart, Bob [Havens], Mahlon Clark, Eddie Miller, Ray Leatherwood, Gene Estes.
January 6:	Air Tel, 6:00 to 10:00: "Rotten piano. Ray slowed down, Mahlon and Eddie steaming, Higgins blissfully unaware of changes."
January 10:	no location: with Mac McReynolds
January 31:	Loyola, 8:00: Bruce—Dick Rolph—"On a rainy Friday night it is a monumental pain in the ass to have to drive to a lousy job in Loyola and play an amateur show."

Old colleagues Bob Havens and Dick Hafer were on hand when Cary recorded four titles on February 4, 1986, for trumpeter Jackie Coon's album on the Sea Breeze label. The personnel for this eight-piece band, with arrangements by Cary, who also played trumpet, alto trumpet and alto horn, appears to have been drawn from the Tuesday rehearsal band, including Holgate, Hafer and Havens ("3 Dicks and a Bob"). He was peeved with Coon because he "chooses to do the first date with Johnny Varro" on piano.

I did part of one album for Jackie Coon which got "album of the week" in The New York Times. The producer, Wally Holmes, had a hell of a time finding a label.

Although he makes no mention of it in his diary, with most of February blank, during the month he had a cancerous growth ("wide resection melanoma") removed from his left calf. He reacted in typical Cary fashion; his first entry for March, on the 4th, indicates he was playing tennis.

The next entries are at the end of March. He travelled to Palm Springs on March 26 to be ready for an afternoon rehearsal with the Abe Most band and Phil Harris on the 27th. The show at the Riviera followed that evening—"band sounded a hell of a lot better than last Saturday." Then nothing more until the end of April, when Chuck Conklin, trumpet, leader of the new Angel City Jazz Band, started Sunday and Monday nights at the Gammon Room of the Marriott Hotel, 9:00 to 1:30—"The drummer is ridiculous, Dolph Morris [bass] not in shape, Bill on clarinet and Betty [O'Hara]." One photograph shows a personnel of Chuck Conklin, trumpet, Betty O'Hara, trombone, Bill Wood, clarinet, Dick Cary, piano, alto horn, Paul Gormley, bass, and Jerry McKenzie. This was reported to be a nine-month gig, though the Monday booking seems optimistic and was probably soon cut. How long Cary worked with the band is not known.

Cary was back in Palm Springs on Saturday, May 3, playing for a C.P.A. party at the Hilton Riviera, 8:00 to 12:00, with Mac McReynolds. He mentions Zeke Zarchy, Larry Koonse and Rollie Bundock, bass, among the personnel, commenting: "rhythm celebrating the Kentucky Derby." The next day his entry is "Marriott—Dave Stone" (the Chuck Conklin engagement) and on the 5th it is: "Brad Dechter—Paramount 2—Stage M—studio date—"We copied Conrad Janis record!! I entered a few Armstrong phrases on *Muskrat Ramble*." He gives a 12-piece group, including himself, Virgil Evans, Jack Trott, trumpets, Herbie Harper, trombone, Bob Hardaway, Dave Edwards, Roger Neumann, reeds, Ray Sherman, piano, Monte Budwig, bass, a guitarist/banjoist, a drummer, and Les Benedict, uncertain. Presumably this was for a film or television soundtrack.

On the Saturday, the 24th of May, he worked a Fred Meister job at the Long Beach Hyatt, playing piano from 7:00 p.m. and with the band at 9:00. The 10-piece personnel was drawn from the Tuesday rehearsal band, apparently including Betty O'Hara, Herbie Harper, Dick Hafer, Tommy Newsom and Bob Summers, reeds. Perhaps this was the dance to which Cary referred in a 1986 letter:

I made the mistake of playing a dance with my rehearsal band in May and every time we played any original music, everyone quickly got off the dance floor like a flock of good obedient sheep. Never again! We have one concert at Cal Tech, in Pasadena, in October, but outside of a concert like this, the band belongs only in my back room.

And possibly it was also the dance which Betty O'Hara recalled: "He didn't take the rehearsal band out to play in public very often, but one time he agreed to play a dance. Someone asked if he'd play *In the Mood*. Being a special hate of his, he shouted 'No!' and turned away to play something more palatable. 'But we want to dance' was the plaintive call. It was ignored. Finally a group of men stood in a circle in front of the stand and sang in unison the intro for *In the Mood*. It didn't do them any good. We never did play it!!"

This Long Beach job meant that he did not play at the 1986 Sacramento Dixieland Jubilee until the Sunday (May 25), when he mentions a set with Peanuts Hucko, Peter Appleyard, vibes, Bob Haggart and Gene Estes, and one with Jerry Murphy, plus sets on the Holiday Inn top floor. On the Monday he sat-in with a Bobby Levine group and singer Maxine Sullivan at the Turntable Tent, and played at the Marriott Hotel at night.

Bob Crosby and his Orchestra, Disneyland, uncertain date, including Dick Cary at piano, Bob Haggart, bass, Eddie Miller, Peanuts Hucko, saxes, Dick Cathcart, trumpet, Bob Havens, trombone.   *(Courtesy: Dick Cary Archive)*

June 2:	Marriott Hotel, 9:00: no details
June 3:	Hilton Hotel, 8:30 to 12:30: with Mac McReynolds, Dick Cathcart, Bob Havens, Ed Bennett, bass, Gene Estes
June 4:	Disneyland: "best band Boob'll (sic) have in years ... and I can run for cover when that— Kay Starr is on." Personnel was John Best, Dick Cathcart, trumpets, Bob Havens, trombone, Eddie Miller, Les Robinson, reeds, Cary, piano, Bob Haggart, bass, Gene Estes, drums
June 7:	Claremont: with Mac McReynolds small group. [may have been cancelled]
June 11:	Donte's: with Betty O'Hara, Dave Koonse, Herb Mickman, Gene Estes
June 21:	"Dizzyland," ie; Disneyland, 7:00 to 11:00: with Harry James band. "same old stand— new faces"

On July 12 Cary "played a few sets of doubles and wrote a new thing for the next rehearsal a week from Tuesday."

There was no rehearsal on the coming Tuesday because:
> *Tomorrow, early a.m., [July 13] I am flying to Sacramento with Abe Most, getting a rental car and spending a week teaching at a new "jazz camp": boys from 12 to 22, two teachers on each instrument—most of them in the education game, very few so-called "pros." We'll be located by a lake about 50 miles east of Sacramento. Arise at 7 a.m., live by a schedule. I am really looking forward to getting away and dealing with young minds.*

He was back in Los Angeles in time on the 20th for an octet job at the George Izay Park with Abe Most, Betty O'Hara, Bob Havens, Dick Hafer, Dave Koonse, Herb Mickman and Gene Estes. Then, on August 9, he refers to "Last day at Dizzyland," suggesting perhaps a week at Disneyland. This is followed by a note on August 14 that he left for Oregon, perhaps for another jazz society meeting. On August 16, The Pussyfoot Stompers, with Dick Cary, played for a wedding anniversary at The Red Lion Inn in Springfield.

Cary travelled south to La Jolla on Saturday, September 13, noting "$500 for one night of a Yamaha." It appears that he, Bob

Haggart and Nick Fatool played for a rehearsal at 3:00 p.m. ("all those singers") and then for a show in the evening. He gives no details except to say that he played second trumpet to Warren Vache, Jr, on some of Haggart's arrangements and to opine that "Vache [is a] hell of a cornet player!"

At the end of September, on the 25th, he worked with singer Martha Tilton, rescoring some of her hits from the Benny Goodman days, in preparation for her Australian tour in December 1986. The following day he worked for "Russ," with Dave Koonse, Gene Estes and Paul Gormley, 12:30 to 2:00, "for senior citizens who act much nicer as an audience than do young or middle-aged people." Earlier in the month he would have played at the Los Angeles Classic Jazz Festival.

It is not until February 1987 that the "white" pages started to turn "pale" when, on the 3rd, he was involved in a strange-sounding session. "1:00 p.m. near Saticoy—Ray Sherman, Bob Havens, Mahlon Clark, Ira Westley, Dick [?] Shanahan, drums, for some gimmick in St. Louis—'mechanical birds and whiskyland'—4 derangements, then they really started in, song after song, but we got them in one or two takes. Then this guy had us sing Cab Calloway's most famous, *Minnie the Moocher.*"

February 12:   Sepulveda, Veteran's Hospital, 11:00 a.m. to 1:00 p.m.: with Abe Most

February 15:   Hacienda, 4:00 to 5:00: with Abe Most, Bob Enevoldsen, Sam Most, Chauncey Welsch (trombone—"the militant non-smoker!"), Dave Koonse, Gene Estes, "and Ray Sherman on a beat-up upright. They seemed to like the little B.G. show."

February 20:   Loyola, 8:00: with Betty O'Hara and "Dick the drumming clergyman!"

February 21:   Beverly Wilshire: with Abe Most big band for award dinner

The next music entry is for the weekend of May 1–3, when Cary spent three nights on trumpet with Bob Finch's Chicago Six in Cathedral City. They played in the Lexington Hotel on Friday ("impossible drummer"), and perhaps again on the Saturday. Sunday was spent at the Cathedral Canyon Country Club, in the dining room from 1:30 and in the Royce Room from 4:30, with Phil Harris joining them.

Jazz festivals and parties were the highlights of 1987:

I'm doing that Conneaut Lake thing again in August and have

one this weekend in Palm Springs for three days [May 1–3]. This has even made me practise! [In May] we do Sacramento again. I have done every year and I am to be the Emperor this year which amazes me since I thought a lot of them knew my views about the quality of all those, over 100, amateur bands they hire. But I'm leading the "alumni" band (Cathcart, Miller, Van Eps, Fatool) and I have also gotten "liltin'" Martha Tilton to appear with us. I just rehearsed with her—what a pleasant little lady and just my age, 70.

Also she will do our Los Angeles Festival in September in a Goodman segment with a large group Abe [Most] and I will put together. There's a rash of Benny Goodman memorial concerts this year and it has kept me busy writing my combination of Fletcher Henderson and Eddie Sauter.

Martha Tilton was the vocalist with Benny Goodman between 1937 and 1939, and on many recording sessions and special occasions thereafter. The musicians Cary refers to were Dick Cathcart, trumpet, Eddie Miller, tenor, George Van Eps, guitar, and Nick Fatool, drums. Fletcher Henderson (1897–1952) and Eddie Sauter (1914–1981) were the two major arrangers for Benny Goodman (1909–1986).

To summarise:
May 17: City of Industry: with Estes, Mickman, Juiez, and "my first time with [trumpeter] Jack Sheldon."
May 22–25: Sacramento Dixieland Jubilee
June 22: Red Lion, Sacramento: benefit for pianist Merle Koch, with Abe Most, Bob Havens, Eddie Miller, Ray Sherman, Herb Mickman, Nick Fatool.
July 10–17: Sacramento music camp for boys, with Abe Most and Bob Havens.

At the opening ceremony for the Sacramento Jubilee on May 22, when Cary was crowned "Emperor," he led the "All Time Favorites"—Dick Cathcart, Rex Allen, Abe Most, Eddie Miller, George Van Eps, Ray Leatherwood, and Nick Fatool.

The 1987 Conneaut Lake jazz party (August 28–30) had Cary playing alto horn in a group led by trumpeter Ed Polcer and trumpet in trombonist Dan Barrett's band. He also played piano in a set with singer Polly Podewell, which included Bud Freeman, tenor, Howard Alden, guitar, Monty Budwig, bass, and Mel Lewis, drums.

The Los Angeles Times reported that two Sunday night concerts on September 6 by the Abe Most 17-piece band were a feature of the

Conneaut Lake Jazz Party 1987
l-r, standing: Ed Polcer, Bud Freeman, Johnny Mince, Marty Grosz, Dick Hyman, x , Bob Reitmeier, Joe Wilder, Bob Haggart, John Bunch, Scott Hamilton, Ray Sherman, x , Gene Estes, x , x , Dick Cary, Dan Barrett, Harry DeVito. sitting: Polly Podewell, Howard Alden. *(Courtesy: Dick Cary Archive)*

1987 Los Angeles Classic Jazz Festival. Playing "A Tribute to Benny Goodman," the personnel included Dick Cary, trumpet and arranger, Dick Cathcart, Les Robinson, alto, Sam Most, flute, Abe Most, clarinet, Jack Sperling, drums, and Martha Tilton, vocals.

There may have been a round dance recording session early in October, but otherwise October and November are blank. On December 9 Cary played tennis, but the next day he went into Verdugo Hills Hospital for a cancer operation. His post-op comment is that he found it "hard to move" and that the hospital had "the worst food I've ever eaten anywhere!!"

He left hospital on December 16, 1987, and played a few dates to see the year out:

December 18: Knox: with Betty O'Hara, Eddie Miller, Ray Leatherwood, Nick Fatool

December 19: "Chasers, 7:30 and on & on & on": with Betty O'Hara, Mahlon Clark, Dave Koonse, Gene Estes, Buddy Cl.(?), and Martha Tilton.
December 24: The Palace Kasparoff, 8:00 to 3:00: "got tired. Fun but terrible player piano."
December 27: Knox, 6:00 to 10:00: with Dave Koonse, Dave Stone.

New Year's Eve was spent at home—"the year changed very quietly and unnoticed"—and it appears that the first months of 1988 continued in that mood until May arrived. Cary did not maintain a diary during 1988 and what is known of his activities comes mainly from letters.

Three recent trips have interrupted my fairly serene Sunland life. In May it was a week in Stockholm with Doc Cheatham— night clubs, recordings and a large concert, all concerning Mr. Louis Armstrong. I hadn't seen Doc in about 46 years. One evening I told him I thought he sang a bit like Noel Coward. He amazes me, how active he is at 83!

The whole week was in honour of Louis Armstrong, ending with a concert [May 9] at the 60-year old China Teatern Theatre. Mr. Hägglöf informed me later that they lost $10,000. Next year they do Ellington. I told him I had some Duke music in my library and he wanted a list. When I got home I found a total of 41 titles. But I think the trouble next year will be this: doing Duke Ellington with amateurs will not be quite the same.

Not much to report about two days (May 6/7) in Garfella outside Stockholm, done at the home of the producer, Gösta Hägglöf, a rather unusual character. About 6 foot 3, unmarried and extremely obdurate in his musical views; one of those who really don't care for much past 1930. The musicians were sort of semi-amateurs. A few were quite interesting [including] a trumpeter named Bent Persson.

Ten numbers by Doc Cheatham (1905–1997) and his Swedish Jazz All Stars, featuring Dick Cary, and recorded on May 6/7, were issued on a Kenneth LP, titled "A tribute to Louis Armstrong: 'The Deccas.'" Songs for a Billie Holiday tribute were also recorded.

When I got back home the back problem got very bad and I finally had a disc removed. Was barely able to get through

Dick Cary, Doc Cheatham, Jack Bradley in Sweden, May 1988
(Courtesy: Dick Cary Archive)

our annual "labor day" local festival [the L.A.], but now I am walking four miles every day and starting to feel fine again. That's three operations in two years and it removed about 35-lbs from the frame. I'll try to stay that way. Then there was the Sacramento festival, 15th for me, all of them, and this year I think the attendance was over 300,000. An enormous tribute to amateurism.

This was no doubt the year that Betty O'Hara recalled: "A favorite story of his was at a Sacramento Jubilee, the year that Dick was confined to a wheelchair, due to a back injury. Dick was talking to some sanctimonious person at his hotel. Nick Fatool, that wonderful drummer, was staying on the floor above Dick. Dick was saying how glad he was he got through the festival and the guy said, "Yes, thanks to the man upstairs." And Dick replied,"Oh, yes, Nick was a big help!!"

Another reference to his medical treatment is in a Klavier CD note: "Dick Cary was in the hospital for two weeks straight in 1989 [sic]; he was unable to move except for turning in bed. Shortly after he got home, Cary called a Tuesday night rehearsal and the musicians were amazed that he had written 10 or 12 new pieces in the hospital." One of the pieces, recorded for Klavier, was called, in typical Cary manner, *Between Prone and Supine*!

> *The following week [June 2–5] to Connecticut for my 50th college (Wesleyan) reunion and a memorable week of old faces and over celebrating. Then a tour of my youthful haunts, seeing people I had no idea were still around and some pretty good drinking every day, which I don't do at home. But it was all worth it. I spent two afternoons with Jack O'Brien, a guy who influenced me greatly while in college. He was a fascinating man and pianist. [He] was a close friend of Dave Tough and lived in Europe a couple of years in the 1920s. He's 82 now and never stopped talking for both days. He quit playing years ago and doesn't even have a piano in his home.*
>
> *I have met quite a few [surgeons] in the last two years. In fact tomorrow [November 14] I go to a cancer specialist; we must watch out for any signs of melanoma, which one can never be certain of its not returning somewhere, sometime. (Melanoma, commonly skin cancer, is a malignant tumour.)*
>
> *But I have recuperated now, back to writing, tennis and rehearsing on Tuesday nights. A much more healthy and satisfying routine. After 40 years of looking I found another alto horn in Stockholm.*

Of Sacramento, Cary also wrote:
> *I took my group to Sacramento a few years ago and it was a complete waste of effort. I really believe that about 85% of the audience just has to hear banjos and tubas. It is very similar to Disneyland. Years before they didn't want anything beyond 1930, now they've advanced to* In the Mood *and* The Modernaires. *Sacramento, with its tremendous attendance records, has had an effect all over this country—a frightening development.*
>
> *Some of us feel we've been relegated to a very small corner, surrounded on three sides by synthesizers, horrible singers, banjos and tubas and, worst of all, those strident guitars. So we go on, enjoying our Tuesday nights and actually paying little attention to public tastes. I love something Noel Coward wrote in his diaries: "The infection of American vulgarity will someday subdue the world." Some*

of our children cough up over $500 for a seat at a Bruce Springsteen concert?! Whither???

Cary was still arranging jingles, as his following comments show. They also continue his blasts against the lack of appreciation for his rehearsal band.

There's a guy in San Francisco, Gary Remal, who used to get me to arrange jingles for radio and TV. I have never met him—we did all this by phone. He seemed most pleased at everything I did. He wanted to get the sound of the 1930s recordings and I didn't mind doing them and it paid quite well. So the last time I did one of these I had our Tuesday night group record it, to hear what it sounded like, and made the fatal mistake of sending a cassette to Mr. Remal. Anyway, I got paid for the work but will never hear from Mr. R. again. On the phone he told me it had no "sparkle or sheen" and I realized what he meant: our playing it well and in tune merely annoyed him. It didn't sound like 1927 and now "sparkle and sheen," aside from sounding like a vaudeville act, has a special meaning for us.

One little man here named Bob Tabor, who puts on "jazz" dinners about every two months, just hates my band. At our only Sacramento appearance, he'd show up only to be seen "walking out" on us. Just after Andre Previn came back to Los Angeles to conduct our local symphony, he scheduled a work by Benjamin Britten. About a third of the house walked out. These people certainly "know what they like."

It's so interesting to find out, after 68 years of struggling with music, to try to attain a small measure of proficiency, that what you're doing is really only a general source of annoyance and indifference. This, however, doesn't deter me in the slightest. If I can please nine musicians I respect each week, that's reward enough.

Cary continued to play occasional dates with banjo and piano player Bob Ringwald, leading The Great Pacific Jazz Band, and he was probably with them at the Beef 'n' Barrel in Van Nuys on October 8, 1988.

Towards the end of 1988, Cary's only entries on his 1989 calendar were the festivals at Ojai and Sacramento during May and he did not keep a diary for 1989. Just one date is known in January. Bob Ringwald continued to find work for his Great Pacific Jazz

Band and it appeared at the New 450 Steakhouse, Northridge on January 15, 1989. Dick Cary was named as "guest."

Then early in 1989 the booking for the Swedish concert came through.
> *I am going over for the Ellington week. I'm quite disappointed about the Ellington plans. [Gösta Hägglöf] is using none of my music. (I had given him a list of 41 titles in my various libraries.) So all the amateur groups are preparing their own pieces, mostly a lot of pre-1930 lesser Ellington. My part seems to be only* Caravan *on the alto horn and a couple of pianos solos. I find that the main reason for going is to help the producer get a Hoagy Carmichael album done, arrangements, piano, etc.*

But it was a different story afterwards!
> *My second Stockholm visit was infinitely better. [The] Ellington concert [April 16] was a very good show—well rehearsed, excellent dancers, three reed players, very impressive. Also did a Hoagy Carmichael album [April 13/14] for the producer, [who] has his own home studio and is most contemptuous of any modern methods which might help. [In 1990] they are honoring Hoagy Carmichael but I've had no word.*

Gösta Hägglöf, who issued the recordings on his Kenneth label, recalled some of the background to the Hoagy Carmichael dates: "Dick wrote several of the arrangements for the sessions, sometimes while the rest of the musicians were drinking coffee or eating. He was very observant if he traced something wrong, no matter how small the error, and had a very diplomatic way of saying it. All the musicians were very impressed by the way he acted, played and arranged. He also wrote several great arrangements especially for my 10-piece band, 'The Royal Blue Melodians,' some of which will appear on CD later [Kenneth CKS 3414].

"The concerts in which Dick performed were recorded too. There he did some other songs. Especially I remember his blowing horn on the Irving Berlin concert in *The Song Is Ended* in a small group."

Included in Cary's regular annual engagements for 1989 would have been the Sacramento Festival in May and the Sacramento Traditional Jazz Society Jazz Camp (STJSJC) for boys in July.

The 8th Annual Conneaut Lake Jazz Party, organised by Joe

Boughton, was held August 25–27, 1989, with seventeen of the best mainstream musicians. Cary played only two sets, on the Friday and Saturday, with Randy Reinhardt, cornet, Bob Reitmeier, clarinet, Ken Peplowski, clarinet, tenor, John Sheridan, piano, Bucky Pizzarelli, guitar, Isla Eckinger, bass, and either Hal Smith or Gene Estes, drums. Also at the party was Cary's old colleague, trombonist Bob Havens.

Conneaut Lake Jazz Party 1989
l-r, back row: Bucky Pizzarelli, Isla Eckinger, John Sheridan, Bob Reitmeier, Dick Cary, Bobby Gordon, Bob Havens, Greg Cohen, Gene Estes.
middle row: Ken Peplowski, Joe Wilder, Nancy Nelson, x , Keith Ingham, Hal Smith. front row: Marty Grosz, Randy Reinhardt, Peter Ecklund.
(Courtesy: Dick Cary Archive)

In a letter to Jim Turner dated November 6, 1989, Cary wrote: "Last Monday I did a movie date on alto horn—a film about the civil war called 'Glory.' There was a 120 piece orchestra at M-G-M ... it was extremely easy and us horn players only worked about a half hour out of five hours—but get paid for the five." In an obituary note in *Overture* (August 1994) Jerry Kessler wrote: "I first encountered Dick on a session at M-G-M. He told me of the peck horn seminar he'd given in Europe and invited me to come hear him play at the Barn in Northridge."

Cary also told Jim Turner that he worked at the '450' on November 12, which is his last known engagement in 1989.

He kept no diary for 1990 but the routine was very much the same:
> *The Tuesday night rehearsals are going well, getting excellent recordings and making cassettes. By now I have five different books, with over 200 pieces in each. I am writing all the time. There is little else to do. There are festival weekends, Sacramento [May], Los Angeles [September], more springing up in California, due to the success of the enormous Sacramento one, which I've attended all 17 years.*

At the Sacramento Jubilee one of Cary's sets, playing piano, was with the Betty O'Hara/Abe Most All Stars, with John Allred, trombone, O'Hara, cornet and valve-trombone, Most, clarinet, Mary Osborne, guitar, Eugene Wright, bass, and Gene Estes, drums. No banjo or tuba here.

As a faculty member of the STJSJC he would have been at the boys camp in July, and he was present at the Los Angeles Classic Jazz Festival in August 1990. There were also the occasional gigs with Bob Ringwald's band:
> *Almost all the jazz [radio] shows have gone off [the air], due to that pop slop. Also the few jazz clubs that existed around my area are either going out of business or changing to what is called by some, "fusion." Nobody knows what this means, but it seems to sell better than jazz. I worked with a guy, Bob Ringwald [piano, banjo], who has a famous daughter in films named Molly. [He] has Bob Havens, a great trombone player, [and] a large library of Louis Armstrong things which Zeke Zarchy performs—and they've cut us down to one Sunday a month. Thank God for my Tuesday night band.*

Warren Vache, Sr., who had talked with Cary at Nick's in the early 1940s, recalled: "Many years later, Floyd Levin took me to a nightclub on the outskirts of Los Angeles, where a band called something like The Great Pacific Jazz Band was playing. During intermission I had a wonderful time talking to Dick Cary, who was playing cornet, and Zeke Zarchy who, when he found out I had friends named Pee Wee Erwin and Chris Griffin, became an instant buddy. We had a grand reunion."

It *was* The Great Pacific Jazz Band and Cary continued playing gigs, on piano, with the band until shortly before his death.

In the fall of 1990 there came a belated form of recognition when the Jazz Forum Society in Los Angeles honoured Dick Cary as their Jazzman of the Year, featuring him at their meeting at the Viscount Hotel on September 16, 1990. An excellent interview with him, by Al Rieman and Chuck Conklin, was published in the programme for that session.

A local jazz club gave me a day, September 16, naming me as "Musician of the Year." I brought in a band for the Sunday afternoon, received several awards and Mayor Bradley officially pronounced it "DICK CARY DAY" in Los Angeles. I think at least 80 or 90 people in the whole city were aware of this. There was no mention in any paper, even the musicians' magazine ignored it and one of the plaques was from them.

But it was really gratifying and I even got a plaque from my home town, Hartford, Connecticut, also one from Sacramento.

I've been a genius at avoiding any notoriety. In some ways I'm even thankful for this. Life is more peaceful, my time is my own, it avoids a lot of stress, which I think can lead to a shorter life. If it sounds like complaining, it really isn't. I'm just sad that there's no place for us to play any more and hardly any record people who care for anything but rock, rap, heavy metal and all the rest of that shit. But it is the way things are and not very much to do about it.

The final part of the resolution which proclaimed "Dick Cary Day" read as follows:
NOW, THEREFORE, BE IT RESOLVED that Mayor Tom Bradley and the City Council of Los Angeles, by the adoption of this resolution, hereby commend RICHARD "DICK" CARY for his many outstanding achievements in the world of music, his promotion of better world understanding and appreciation through the medium of Jazz music, wish him continued success and well being for the future.

BE IT FURTHER RESOLVED that the Mayor of Los Angeles joined by the Los Angeles City Council hereby proclaim September 16, 1990 "DICK CARY DAY" in Los Angeles.

The resolution was signed by the Mayor and by Councilman Ernani (Noni) Bernardi. Before going into politics Noni Bernardi had been well-known as a big band saxophonist, playing with Joe Haymes, Tommy Dorsey, Benny Goodman, Bob Crosby and others.

The Jazz Forum programme for September reported that The Great Pacific Jazz Band, with Cary on piano and sometimes horn, was working Sunday nights at My Brother's Place in Reseda. Cary also starred at the November meeting of Jazz Forum on trumpet, alongside Dick Cathcart, Bob Enevoldsen, Tommy Newsom, John Hammond, piano, David Stone, and Gene Estes.

With nothing but a few Christmas parties at which to play, Cary wrote, looking back at the last month of 1990: "December in California for R.C. is the worst month, but I guess if my music was a big hit I'd be traveling, smoking, losing sleep, etc.—all that goes with it and life would be shorter. I think I'd rather do it with my few friends, stay in one rather comfy little house with a nice dog."

Cary resumed his diary writing duties in 1991, not as systematically as in earlier years, but sufficient to show that though jobs were few and far between, with occasional flurries of activity, he was content in his routine.

A Tuesday Night rehearsal, May 26, 1992 *(Photo by Derek Coller)*

22. Interlude: The Rehearsal Bands

The story of the Dick Cary rehearsal band in New York is outlined in Chapters 9 and 10, with Cary's own recollections and those of Bob Wilber. When the Bobby Hackett sextet disbanded in 1958, Dick Cary, Bob Wilber and Dick Hafer started a rehearsal band, meeting in Cary's loft on Monday evenings. During the year the rehearsals lasted, many of New York's best musicians attended, usually in a ten or eleven piece band and including Hall Overton, piano; Buzzy Drootin, drums, Johnny Glasel, trumpet.

Cary also told *Jazz Podium*'s Gudrun Endress:

In Manhattan I had many contacts with Jimmy Raney [guitar], Zoot Sims [tenor] and Bob Brookmeyer [trombone]. Another genius is Clare Fischer, with whom I played in the big band.

These rehearsals were in addition to jam sessions held at the Sixth Avenue loft, when musicians Buck Clayton, Vic Dickenson, Bud Freeman, Pee Wee Russell and others would be present. Another observation is that Cary spoke of having a rehearsal band during his Connecticut days, but no details are known for this.

It is reasonable to assume that the New York rehearsals led to the recordings which Cary made for Stere-o-craft (with a reed section of Al Cohn, Bob Wilber and Ernie Caceres); for Jazz Unlimited by the Johnny Glasel Brasstet; and for Golden Crest, the "Dixieland Goes Progressive" album, which included Glasel, Wilber, Urbie Green and Hall Overton. Three unique groups, each infused with Cary's individual approach.

Cary's diary confirms that he was part of drummer Kay Carlson's rehearsal band in L.A. at least from February 26, 1961. On March 26, he noted: "Rehearsal of Kay's band—played second trumpet. My *Prologue and Theme* got a nice hand from the gals. Jessie played *Jesseme, Rum Red* and *Dance of the Termites*."

In a 1971 interview, on the Scott Ellsworth radio show, Cary explained how he became involved in the Los Angeles band:

I had rehearsal bands in New York so I started one here. We've been doing every Monday night. It was strange how it started. It was originally an all girl band that my wife played with and it became increasingly difficult to get girls, so they started integrating the band. I'd come down and play a saxophone part or a trombone part or trumpet part or whatever they needed. Gradually all the girls dropped out and now it's an all-male band. But we still have Kay Carlson, whose band it was originally. She's the drummer and does all the calling for me, which is a terrible chore. I couldn't do that.

It's just for musicians. There's seventeen of us and we get together every Monday night from eight to eleven. [We play] a variety of things. I try to do anything at all. Nobody's looking over my shoulder and telling me what to do. That's the nice part of this.

Twenty years later, in 1991, by which time the rehearsals were being held on Tuesday nights, he said to Floyd Levin:

After that we went over to a garage near here, a guy named Dick Holgate, who was a very fine baritone player. We rehearsed there for several years with a sixteen piece band with [clarinetist] Abe Most. The first ten years I did over 900 arrangements for the 19-piece band, then with the Abe Most band probably four or five hundred. That lasted about six or seven years. There were literally hundreds of rehearsal groups [in Los Angeles]. There's more here than in New York because the music here is so deadly. They're awful good musicians and they want to do something different.

One time there was a group out here called the Phillips-Madison Tuba Consortium. It was Harvey Phillips, a great tuba player who used to play in my rehearsal band in New York. He was head of the music department at Indiana [University] for several years. He and Rick Madison had a group of three tubas and three euphoniums and four rhythm. They played in Donte's [a Los Angeles club]. I liked the group but I thought, "This thing of mine with Abe Most is turning into a social event. People come and drink and talk all the time." So I put together a group patterned after this Phillips-Madison group. I knew I couldn't get three good tuba players, so I used Ernie Tack [bass-trombone] and two baritone saxophone players. For the euphoniums I had my peck horn and Betty O'Hara and Bob Enevoldsen doubling on baritone horns and valve-trombones. So we had three uppers and three lowers.

Later on I added Dick Cathcart [cornet] and made a whole different kind of sound out of it. Now [1991] we have the two trumpets and the regular trombone, four brass. I have five different libraries for this band.

I enjoy writing so much—I'm miserable if I'm not doing it—and that I can do something that seems to satisfy these guys who I have great respect for. My God, they all read better than I do. For instance, Terry Harrington is one of the best tenor players I ever heard anywhere. He played originally with me in the 1960s. We did a lot of park dates then. Just to write, it's very therapeutic, if that's the word. I don't drink anymore like I used to. I don't do other things like I used to, so what is there left to do?

These quotations by Dick Cary are an outline history of his rehearsal band, though it is his diaries which pinpoint various changes more accurately. Other details of the band's library, the musicians and the recordings are shown in an appendix and/or the discography. It was probably in 1983 that the rehearsals moved from Monday to Tuesday nights on a regular basis, and subsequently gave rise to the name for the band, Dick Cary and his Tuesday Night Friends. This title was coined by trumpeter/enthusiast Chuck Conklin, when he engaged the band for The Jazz Forum club in Los Angeles. Cary told critic Leonard Feather that he was very busy as an arranger and composer in the 1960s and that his rehearsal bands included a brass quintet, a reed octet and a woodwind quintet.

Recalling those days, Bob Enevoldsen (who Cary called "superbone") said: "I don't think Dick ever wrote scores to his arrangements and compositions—he just wrote the parts. He watched TV while writing. He slept on his couch with his dog. One night somebody poured a cup of coffee and found a carrot floating in it. There were times when mushrooms were found growing out of the floor. I guess this best describes a genius, which of course he was."

As Cary indicates, drummer Kay Carlson was the driving force behind the rehearsal band when he arrived on the scene and she was still running it towards the end of 1971. (A diary entry on April 5, 1962, shows the gradual change from an all-woman band, with Cary praising the rehearsal and noting "9 guys, 7 gals.") On July 14, 1963, he reports that "Kay's rehearsal band finally gets paid for a public performance—at Venice Beach." An 18-piece band was featured, and included Mick McMahon, Jack Trott, Jack Hohman, Ralph Osbourne, trumpets, Herb Harper, Gale Martin, Jessie Cary, Don----, trombones, Herb Stewart (Steward?), Roz McDougald, Vernon----, Bob----, reeds, Terry Trotter, piano, Herb Ellis, guitar, Ray Leatherwood, bass, John Bambridge, tuba, Kay Carlson, drums. Cary does not say which instrument he played, but the programme included several of his originals, including *Tequila, San Diego, Hi Life* and *Sgt. Pee Wee.*

During 1962 and 1963, Cary and Jessie (on trombone) were also playing with trumpeter Art Depew's rehearsal band. At one session Cary lists Herb Harper, trombone, and Frank DeVito, drums, and that "Joe Dolney has fine arrangement of *Donkey Serenade.*"

There is no diary for 1972 but as Ms. Carlson is not mentioned from January of 1973, it is reasonable to assume that the organising passed to Cary sometime in 1972. However, this chronology is complicated by the fact that Cary did arrange occasional small group rehearsals. His first such was on Tuesday, January 19, 1965, the day following a "good rehearsal" at Kay's: "Prepared food and rehearsal space in rear house and about 10:45 we got going, with Art DePew, trumpet, Bob Havens, trombone, Bob Davis, clarinet, alto, Neil Levang, guitar, Ward Erwin, bass, Chas. Lodice, drums."

For the Kay Carlson rehearsals the only reference to a location is "Santa Monica" Boulevard, but during 1971, if not earlier, the rehearsals were held in a Unitarian Church, location unknown. By early 1973 they were taking place "at Ray L's new place." This was a warehouse where Ray Leatherwood stored items for his aircraft parts business.

During 1972 and into the early months of 1973 Cary held a number of rehearsals with a group he called The Nine. There was, of course, a fluctuating personnel, but Jack Trott, Bob Enevoldsen, Herbie Harper, Abe Most, Wayne Songer, Chas Myerson, Ray Leatherwood, and Nick Fatool were typical members. When the group played its first indoor booking on January 15, 1973, Ed Safranski was on bass.

On Sunday, June 17, 1973, when The Nine played an open-air park date, the personnel was Trott, Enevoldsen, Harper, Songer, Myerson, Fatool, Eddie Miller and Terry Harrington. The following month Cary noted: "Very gratified with the NINE lately, not as much my contribution, but the fact that there are such competent players around and they are a bit wistful about a pleasant youth spent in bands and nightclubs, etc. The occasional flashes each night of performing something well, at least we thought so once in a while. So where can we do it now—I can provide a few frames with as large windows as possible."

In addition to the regular attendees, other musicians would visit on an occasional basis, either to play or to listen. At a 1963 rehearsal Zeke Zarchy and a Teddy Edwards (the tenor player?) were there. Herbie Stewart, tenor, and Willie Smith (the altoist?) played in February 1965, and the following month Rex Stewart and Benny Carter were present to hear the band and were "quite complimentary." In 1966 Buddy Arnold, tenor, and Ralph Pena, bass, visited, while during 1973 reedman Lew Tabackin and guitarist Joe Pass attended. In October 1977, Cary held a sextet rehearsal which included Jack Lesberg on bass, and Bud Freeman visited on two Mondays in January 1980, when the band played three of his compositions.

In January 1975, Cary began rehearsing "my newest group, a WW8." This was in Dick Holgate's garage. These gatherings of eight woodwinds and rhythm lasted a few months, the reedmen including John Setar, Wayne Songer, Dick Hafer, Roger Neumann, Dick Holgate and Herman Riley, with Ira Westley, bass, and Earl Smith or Jerry McKenzie, drums. On one occasion clarinetist Mac McReynolds was present.

On February 3, 1976, Leatherwood telephoned Cary to tell him that the warehouse had burned—everything lost—no insurance. "There goes a lot of work from the '60s." A week later Cary collected the charred library, no doubt salvaging what he could. But this disaster had little impact upon the rehearsal band. At least by March 1 the meetings were continuing at Dick Holgate's. (Perhaps Kay Carlson was still involved with the band's organisation, for Cary telephoned her with the bad news.)

For a while, early in his Los Angeles stay, Cary had rehearsed with a Brass Quartet—on March 8, 1962 he remarked, "BR4—had ten new ones—*Sgt. Pee Wee* was the best." Some years later a Brass Quintet, or the BR5 as Cary called it, was active from 1976, usually convening at Zeke Zarchy's house. One session on March 1, 1979, had Zeke Zarchy, Jack Trott, Cary, Betty O'Hara and Ernie Tack, while two weeks later the personnel was Zarchy, Cary, Betty O'Hara, Tack and trombonist Alan Kaplan. Then, in 1978, as noted in Chapter 19, he mentions a rehearsal group consisting of two alto horns, two valve trombonists, two baritone saxes, plus a rhythm section.

In a March 14, 1979, letter he wrote:

The names of my present Monday night band are: Bob Enevoldsen and Betty O'Hara on valve trombones and baritone horns, Dick Holgate and various other baritone sax players, like Bill Perkins, etc.—we rehearse in the Holgate garage—Charlie Myerson, a very, very talented unknown guitar player, Ray Leatherwood, one of my favorite bass players, various drummers but mostly Jerry McKenzie or Gene Estes, and on bass trombone, Betty's husband, Barrett,

> *and sometimes Bill Reichenbach, one of the most talented young players I ever knew, also a composer, also plays lead trombone with the Toshiko-Tabackin orchestra. It's a marvelous small group of very agreeable people.*

Six months later, in a letter dated September 28, 1979, Cary expressed similar feelings about the rehearsal band:

> *I play when someone agreeable calls and write every day for my own groups. I am glad I have become an amateur in my own way. Our Monday night band is a very exceptional group. I have never said this before in my 63 years, but I mean it now ... It's a great pleasure for us and every Monday night I come home and listen to the tapes and realize it is such a privilege to have such men performing my own scribblings.*

Cary's views of the rehearsals varied from week to week. His diary entry for January 2, 1980 (the rehearsal was on a Wednesday because of the New Year holiday) reads: "Not our best tonight. New etude for clarinet disappointing. Tonight as I listen to tapes I feel a large enveloping confusion. We plodded tonight—the notes didn't seem to like each other. I've got to write better jazz—flow better—lighten up—float!!!" The band for the evening, if the interpretation of the Christian names is correct, was: Betty and Barrett O'Hara, Bruce Paulson, Ray Leatherwood, Chas. Myerson, Jerry McKenzie, Abe Most, Tom Newsom and Dick Holgate.

Just five days later he would write: "Marvelous night. What a thing to assemble people of this caliber and have it really jell on an occasional Monday—I can ask for no more, unless I had the goddam incentive to spend my time writing for a large orchestra, but it's too damn precarious. Such a chunk of your life for maybe one performance. Our society is not conducive for this activity anymore." The personnel was similar, with Bill Reichenbach for Paulson and Gene Estes for McKenzie. Cary made a similar comment two years later, when he refers to one of the best of all rehearsals, with Jerry McKenzie back and all regulars, except for Jackie Coon on trumpet. "What a satisfaction to have men like these come to my back room each week!!!"

Not every reaction was positive. One musician remarked about the CD issues: "I can't imagine they would want to issue those rehearsal-band tracks, which are little more than reading/playing exercises." This is a view with which the writer has some sympathy, if one wishes the swing to be less under-stated, the whole more jazz-orientated. But the rehearsal band was always going to be more

Dave Koonse, guitar; Cary, keyboard, Jack Trott, trumpet. May 26, 1992. The T-shirt on the wall states, "Cary Me Back To Dick C.Land" and "Jazz Man of the Year." *(Photo by Derek Coller)*

Tuesday Night Friends rehearsal, May 26, 1992. Cary, with chin in left hand, playing with his right. *(Photo by and courtesy of Bert Whyatt)*

Tenor player Tommy Newsom, a key member of the Tuesday Night Friends. May 26, 1992.

(Photo by Derek Coller)

Claude Thornhill than Count Basie, as the lovely writing and playing in the recorded examples of the Tuesday Night Friends reveal.

As shown in other chapters, the rehearsal band made a number of public appearances, including those at the Sacramento Dixieland Jubilee, at Cal Tech and park dates, but generally Cary was disappointed by the reaction. It was that *In the Mood* problem again. As H.L. Mencken said, "Nobody ever went broke underestimating the taste of the American public."

Finally, to indicate the continuity within the personnel of the Tuesday Night Friends, the musicians attending on May 26, 1992 were: Jack Trott, trumpet, Dick Hamilton, trombone, Ernie Tack, bass-trombone, Terry Harrington, tenor, Tommy Newsom, clarinet, soprano, tenor, Fred Cooper, baritone, Dick Cary, electric-piano, Dave Koonse, guitar, and Herb Mickman, bass. No drummer showed! Nearly sixteen years later, and many years after the death of Dick Cary, four of those same musicians, plus two other of the band's veterans (Setar and O'Hara) were present in January 2008, during a rehearsal at Dick Hamilton's house which featured Hamilton on trumpet, alto horn and piano, leading Kathy Ryan, trumpet, Dave Ryan, trombone, Rick Blanc, bass-trombone, John Setar, clarinet, Phil Feather, soprano, tenor, Terry Harrington, tenor, Charlie Orena, baritone, flute, Steve Bethers, guitar, Herb Mickman, bass, Jerry White, drums. Also present were Barrett O'Hara, Jack Trott, Ernie Tack and Jim Turner.

More details can be found in the discography and in the notes to the CDs, Arbors ARCD19132 and ARCD19253 and Klavier KD-77024.

23. Final Notes (1991–1994)

Cary began 1991 by venting some of his feelings on the popular music scene! "This is my 75th year, three-quarters of a century. I see no hope for 'pop' music—it's silly, monotonous, monstrous, disgusting slop, performed by young freaks on less than a kindergarten level. The Ringwald Sunday job [at My Brother's Place, presumably] ended recently, so as of now there is nothing till March. I must force myself to practice and write better things. They've been rather stupid lately!"

The gaps between jobs continued:
January 23:   singing lesson for Bill Hayes
January 27:   San Fernando Elks, 2:30: for Diz Mullins, flugelhorn. Sextet plus singers, including Morty Corb, Jerry McKenzie
February 8:   Escondi's: piano with Bob Finch's Chicago Six
February 9:   Rancho Bernardo: piano in quartet, with Bobby Gordon, clarinet
February 10: El Segundo: with Diz
February 15: probably a party in Pasadena
February 23/24:   weekend in Pismo Beach: trumpet with The Chicago Six, "which includes Bobby Gordon, a pupil of Joe Marsala"
March 23:   "terribly dull job for awards to television technicians": with Abe and Sam Most and old drummer
March 24:   Beverly's Club: one set with The Chicago Six, one with Wally Holmes, Jackson Stock, Herb Mickman, Jerry McKenzie

One event Cary which had been anticipating, with its opportunity to meet old friends, was the Grand Toronto Jazz Party, hosted by Gordon Fancy, and held April 12–14, 1991. Cary refers to "Don Valley—Radisson." Among the friends he met were Bob Haggart, Doc Cheatham, Ken Peplowski, Ed Hubble, Yank Lawson, Marty Grosz and Barbara Lea. As a result of this meeting, Miss Lea asked

Cary to help her record additional titles to expand her Willard Robison album into a CD. This was to become Cary's last recording session.

He mentions working with Buster Brown, Higgins and Betty at Simi Valley on April 21. One assumes this might be Bob Higgins on trumpet. Then no entry until a rehearsal with the Bob Ringwald band on May 2, in readiness no doubt for the gig on May 5 for the Knights of Columbus at the Valley Club.

The 1991 Sacramento Dixieland Jubilee was held May 31–June 3 and Cary mentions sets with Abe Most, Gene Estes and Jack Sperling, on the Friday; one with The Chicago Six, plus Abe Most and one with his own group, at the Crest Theatre and the Holiday Inn on Saturday; two shows on Sunday—"finally a good big Kawai at big Expo in evening"; and a set with Bob Ringwald at the Crest Theatre on Monday.

Cary's complaints against the Sacramento Jubilee continued. This was his 18th year as a participant and though his diary does not show it, he took the rehearsal band to the 1991 edition.

> Most agreed it [the rehearsal band] was the best thing that dumb festival ever had. Sacramento and all the rest, full of horrible amateur bands who work cheap and put a lot of pros out of work. The JAZZ BAND has completely disappeared from the L.A. vicinity.
>
> Due to the success of the Sacramento festival others are springing up all over and I think 1991 will find me doing about eight or nine of them, including one week in Sun Valley, Idaho, which I'm looking forward to—will include daily workouts with the tennis pro.

Perhaps he meant the Sun Valley festival when, on July 22, he refers to three sets with Bob Enevoldsen, Tommy Newsom, John Hammond, John Kurnik, Putter Smith, and Gene Estes.

The Sacramento camp was held August 4–10, while the 8th annual Los Angeles Classic Jazz Festival was held at the L.A. Airport Marriott and Hilton Hotels between August 30 and September 2. Dick Cary's Tuesday Night Band was scheduled to play a programme which included some Duke Ellington compositions (*Jumpin' Pumkins, Little African Flower*), and some early jazz pieces (*Davenport Blues, Ostrich Walk* and *Wa Da Da*). Among other appearances, Cary played with Bob Ringwald's band at the Cafe Rouge.

Critic Len Shaw wrote in the *West Coast Rag*: "A high point of the Los Angeles Classic Jazz Festival over Labor Day weekend for this reporter was the two sets by Dick Cary's Tuesday Night Band... [who] presented a collection of intricate and fresh arrangements of familiar tunes reminiscent of the classic big bands."

But Cary still wrote:

The boob who now runs our L.A. festival will not hire someone who, as he puts it, "plays too good."

Thereafter the gaps become even wider:

September 9:	Mateo (?)
September 10–15:	Sisters, Oregon ("No more of these cheap, amateur excursions!!")
September 29:	Orange County: 3 easy sets with Zeke Zarchy, Don Nelson, ss, Betty O'Hara, Ray Templin, drums, Jack Wadsworth, reeds.
October 15:	Sun Valley, Idaho
October 26:	Riverside: with Bob Ringwald; Art Depew, Bob Havens, Don Nelson, ss, Jack Arnold, drums, Ludwin ? ("no piano, no mikes.")
November 27:	State Theatre concert
November 28:	restaurant

On December 26 Cary flew to Tampa, Florida, to take part in a concert at the Tampa Bay State Theatre on December 27 and to record for Arbors. The concert featured Cary with Rick Fay, reeds, Chuck Hedges, clarinet, Bill Sharp, cornet, Mike Vreeland, piano & bass, John Lamb, bass, Eddie Graham, drums, and Jerry Lee Briley, singer.

The recording sessions were held in Orlando on December 29 and 30, for reedman Rick Fay "and friends." Cary was the pianist and he also played alto horn on one title. Released on an Arbors CD, the tunes included Cary's *Ballad for Eddie*, his arrangement of Bix Beiderbecke's *In the Dark* and his piano solo *Echo of Spring*. Cary expressed particular admiration for the trumpeter on the session, Jon-Erik Kellso.

Dan Barrett, trombonist on the recording, said: "Mat Domber flew Dick and I to Florida in 1991, when we recorded a CD called *Rolling On*, under the name of the late Rick Fay. I remember Dick on the date as being the quintessential sideman: quiet and attentive

Arbors recording session, Orlando, Florida, December 30, 1991
l-r: Rick Fay, Dick Cary, Paul Scavarda, Chuck Hedges, Jon-Erik Kellso, Joe Ascione, Dan Barrett, Lou Mauro, Mat Domber, Howard Alden.
(Photograph by John Callahan)

and playing great. I was more or less in charge of the proceedings and Dick would do as I asked, no muss, no fuss. Then, when I seemed stumped for an idea to give a given song a little "twist," Dick would politely offer a musical idea that would usually turn out to be the bon mot.

"I recall that he was having back problems that day and while the rest of us were listening to recently-finished takes, Dick would be in the studio, laying on the floor on his back, over by the piano. He was rather reserved the times I encountered him, but would occasionally exhibit a quirky and funny sense of humour that manifested itself not so much in jokes, but more in observances made on the spot—humorous comments about the topic at hand."

Arbor's owner, Mat Domber, said: "On the occasion of the Rick Fay CD, we invited Dick to Florida, first for a concert in St. Petersburg, we played tennis, and then drove him to Orlando for the record date. Dick and I spent many enjoyable hours on the telephone. He seldom spoke less than an hour at a time and I am sorry that I wasn't able to record these anecdote filled conversations."

One suspects that many of Cary's friends have similar regrets, but a happy outcome of these contacts was that Mat Domber later released two CDs of music recorded by the Dick Cary rehearsal band.

Cary flew home on the last day of 1991, but failed to keep a diary for 1992. This was the year when another illness hit him, though it was to be some months before there was an accurate diagnosis.

At present I am going through a malady which has the symptoms of something called "myasthenia gravis." Have been to three m.d.'s so far and all tests show nothing wrong, but I know there is, and am consulting a fourth in May. The main symptom is an almost crippling fatigue.

Bill and Renee Cary, with Dick Cary at the piano.
Orlando, Florida, December 30, 1991.
(Courtesy: Dick Cary Archive)

Myasthenia gravis is a slow, progressive disease, a peculiar form of paralysis, which gets worse with fatigue or use of the affected muscles. It is "a disorder of the neuromuscular junction." Most often it affects the eye, facial and shoulder girdle muscles and it was the last which caused Cary such distress. In 1993 he was prescribed mestinon and prednisone for the condition.

On the afternoon of May 17, 1992, The Great Pacific Jazz Band, promoted by the Jazz Forum Society, played at the Viscount Hotel, near Los Angeles airport. The personnel, led by Bob Ringwald on banjo, was: Art DePew, trumpet; Bob Havens, trombone, John Bambridge, reeds, Jack Wadsworth, bass sax, Dick Cary, piano, and Jack Arnold, drums. Bert Whyatt and the writer were at the session and it was clear that Cary was not well. He played with one hand while resting his chin in the other. He confirmed that the

Above: Great Pacific Jazz Band, Viscount Hotel, Los Angeles, May 17, 1992 Bob Ringwald, banjo, John Bambridge, clarinet, Art DePew, trumpet, Bob Havens, trombone.
(Photo by Derek Coller)

Left: Great Pacific Jazz Band, Viscount Hotel, Los Angeles, May 17, 1992 Dick Cary, piano, Bob Ringwald, banjo.
(Photo by Derek Coller)

doctors were still unable to diagnose the reason for his weariness and his difficulty in holding up his head.

One doctor at least earned Cary's respect, hence a composition dedicated to Doctor Salkin, "a physician who tended to Cary's health during his last years." This quote is from Jim Turner, who played the tune as a piano solo on his Klavier CD.

Nine days later, on a Tuesday evening, Whyatt and I arrived at Cary's home in Sunland at around 8:45 p.m. From then until 11 p.m. we sat listening to the band's rehearsal. When it was over we sat conversing with our host until the early hours. In view of his health problems perhaps we should have left earlier, but I am not convinced that he wanted us to leave even when we did finally depart. Despite his poor health he was determined not to give way.

Jim Turner clarified the description of the room in which the rehearsal was held. "It was not a garage. It was a room which looks as if it might have once been a garage, but that is not correct. It was a room, one might say a den, which was originally a bedroom, which was added on by a friend of Jessie's. Later, Dick Cary broke out the wall between the two adjoining bedrooms. When I say 'broke out' I don't mean he hired a carpenter or professional contractor to do it. He took an axe to it himself, leaving plenty of hazardous rough edges, which contributed to the garage-like appearance."

Then, as the year progressed:

The goddam melanoma cancer reappeared in my left leg. I've had three chemotherapy sessions and am finally recovering somewhat.

It hasn't stopped the rehearsal band and we did two concerts at the local Labor Day festival [ie; The Los Angeles Classic Jazz Festival].

On September 28, 1992, what is believed to be Cary's last recording session took place. He arranged and played piano on five songs, written by Willard Robison and sung by Barbara Lea. These enabled a 1976 LP by Miss Lea to be released as an Audiophile compact disc. With Cary were Dave Koonse, guitar, and Putter Smith, bass, both associated with the Tuesday night band. This connection was completed by the fact that the session took place in Dick Hamilton's recording studio. As Barbara Lea wrote of Cary: "That's why I contacted him to expand the Willard Robison CD. He really understood the Robison style, which most musicians love to distort. These recordings were done in a studio that one of the musicians had in his basement."

In 1993, Cary resumed writing his occasional diary, making entries in a small notebook. He began by saying that "January was a transition month. Have seen a Dr. Keesey at UCLA ($350 per hour) who says the other m.d. bums are full of shit—that I have myasthenia gravis and I am to take prednisone and mestinon." On February 5, he saw a Dr. Spitzer, reporting, "I can drive without an eye patch" and by the 14th could write, "God! I feel better!!! How wonderful to see!!!!!" Then on the 20th, his spirits were boosted by an outing with Jim Turner, taking in a jazz concert at Claremont College and visiting "a joint to hear Alan Broadbent, Putter Smith and Mintz, drums—I haven't had a night like this in many months."

It was during February 1993 that Gösta Hägglöf asked him to arrange three Cole Porter songs—and later, four by Irving Berlin—for the Swedish band, The Royal Blue Melodians. He was also asked by someone called Kasparoff to arrange 17 titles for Cassie Miller, but in April he wrote: "Wonder what happened to the great vocal album for Kasparoff." And, of course, he was still writing material for the Tuesday Night Band.

The first gig of the year to be mentioned was on March 5, when he was hired by Tom Haralambos to play for his mother's birthday party at the Hunt Club with Betty O'Hara and Dave Koonse, but the good news was not to last. On April 16, apparently under a local anasthetic, "Bautiste took out malignant golf ball in left leg," but he was at the Tuesday rehearsal on April 20. Then in May he was in an Adventist hospital for a five day stay. Other than complaining about the worst food he ever didn't eat, he does not give the reason for his stay, but no doubt it was for chemo-therapy treatment. In his diary he noted: "and now we skip some sick days and suddenly it's Thursday afternoon, May 20."

Nevertheless there was a band rehearsal on May 18, plus a mention that "Last week did a jingle ... got Dick Hamilton, Bob Enevoldsen, Jack Trott, Betty O'Hara, Jerry McKenzie, Putter Smith and a loud ---- banjo: 3 hours for a 30-second spot. I must practice for Sacramento week after next."

The Tuesday Night band made another appearance at both the Sacramento Festival in May and then at the Los Angeles Festival in September. The latter was Cary's last public performance with the rehearsal band.

Fourteen titles by Cary's Tuesday Night Friends, selected from the hundred or more recorded during the rehearsals, between June and August 1993, were chosen for release on the Arbors label. Cary died before the CD was issued but, as Betty O'Hara put it, "although he didn't live to see the finished recording, he did hear the mastered version."

After a gap of more than two weeks Cary wrote on June 12: "As usual I neglect the book. A lot has happened, mostly bad. Two chemo stays—after second I was really sagging." Then three months go by, to September 13, when he writes: "I'm beat from chemotherapy last week and I must do Banu's arrangement."

"Banu" was the singer Banu Gibson, who had telephoned Cary in June to ask for a special score, though Miss Gibson remembered the dates a little differently: "Pianist Jim Turner saw one of our symphony concerts at Evansville, Illinois, on October 10,

1992, and recommended we should ask Dick Cary to do an arrangement for us. We subsequently got a repeat booking with the St. Louis Symphony for October 16–17, 1993. Since we had played with the St. Louis Symphony two times before, we needed new material. This was a perfect time to get in touch with Dick Cary and see if he wanted to write something for us. At David Boeddinghaus, my pianist and musical director's urging I agreed I should call Dick, [who] consented to take on the assignment. When we spoke I found we both had a love of Vincent Youmans' song *More Than You Know*, especially the verse. Most of my arrangements include my band but I wanted this one to be just with the orchestra.

"I found out later that Dick was nervous about writing for strings again and asked Tommy Newsom to be his sounding board. I do know that after the performance I sent him a tape of the song that someone made for me from the audience. He played it for his Tuesday night gang, apparently to favorable reviews.

"I performed the song again at the Hollywood Bowl on August 12, 13 and 14, 1994, with John Mauceri and the Hollywood Bowl Symphony Orchestra."

Cary's remembrance was:

On the bright side, I had a wonderful experience recently. Last August a lady named Banu Gibson asked me to do a background on More Than You Know *for St. Louis Symphony. I accepted, but then started worrying. The biggest orchestra I ever wrote for was the Paul Whiteman radio orchestra, in the fifties, which was about half the size of the average symphony. So I got some advice and did the thing, scared to death. She performed it last week and I was amazed at the favorable reaction and they want more like it. A new career at 77!*

In his diary, on September 14, he noted: "Struggled with Gibson arrangement. I don't know what the hell I'm doing," but things felt better on the 24th when "Barrett O'Hara examined my symphony score—was most encouraging."

This Banu Gibson success cheered him to the extent that he could write:

I have made a small recovery, although through all this I continued to write for Tuesday nights.

During October some Christmas party dates began to come in, at least three of them (November 27, December 3 and 9) were scheduled for the Hunt Club at 520 South Orange Grove. The other parties, probably private affairs, were to be held on December 3, 4, 18 and 19, though Cary does not confirm that he attended them all. Among the musicians involved were Tommy Newsom, Betty O'Hara, Putter Smith, Gene Estes and "Buddy," a clarinetist.

Betty O'Hara, seconded by bassist Putter Smith, remembered: "I think one of the last gigs we did together was last Christmas season (1993). We were to play at the rather exclusive Hunt Club in Pasadena. A new doorman said to Dick, who was not a great dresser, as he was about to enter the club through the front door, the way we had for years, 'The musicians go through the rear entrance.' Dick elbowed his way past saying, 'We don't go in the back door!'"

There are few details in Cary's notebook for 1994. On January 28 he records that he watched the "Ladies finals from Melbourne" and that his "BACK is lousy!" followed by a ten-day gap until February 7, when he states: "Spitzer 4 p.m." This appointment with his doctor is the final entry.

It was the cancer, a metastasis malignant melanoma, rather than myasthenia gravis, which killed Dick Cary. He died at 00:50 in the Glendale Adventist Medical Center in Glendale, Los Angeles, on April 6, 1994, and was buried in Forest Lawn Cemetery in Glendale.

24. Tributes and Memories

Tributes to Dick Cary appeared worldwide, with newspaper and magazine obituaries recording the high spots of his career. There were words of insight and truth and humour included therein, with the majority of them coming from his fellow musicians. The following are a few of those words.

"Highly respected by jazz and big band luminaries, Cary was better known by musicians than by the public."
(Myrna Oliver, *Los Angeles Times*, April 8, 1994)

"In the often hell-for-leather New York jazz world, Cary contributed a supreme gift of lyricism, both in his playing and arranging. Secondly, he was a marvellously empathetic accompanist, especially of singers. His skills—on piano, alto horn and as arranger/conductor—are displayed extensively and to perfection on two excellent (but neglected) records by the singer Barbara Lea, *Nobody Else But Me* and *Lea in Love* (1956–57)"
(Richard Baker, letter to *The Independent*, April 1994)

"Dick's love of traditional jazz and his colorful participation in the making of jazz history, came to life on Tuesday nights at his rehearsals. Dick's beautiful compositions are an exciting blend of tradition and modern inventiveness.
"No matter how late the band would play, I never wanted to stop. I am very fortunate to have known this gentle musical giant."
(saxophonist John Bambridge, *Overture* May 1994)

"Each Tuesday was a lesson in sight reading and improvisation. Dick would write or redo up to four original arrangements each week. He could compose while watching tennis, baseball or old movies. A great arranger, trumpet player—a real genius. He was in his glory when, during a gig, he could relate a story about the upcoming tune or an anecdote involved in events he was involved with."
(clarinetist Abe Most, *Overture*, May 1994)

"It was my great privilege to know him and play his music.

The scope of the music was vast, from *Ostrich Walk* (1913) up to orchestrated Clifford Brown and Zoot Sims solos. My favorites are Dick's Prokofiev sounding pieces; the 'Weird' ones. He said Eddie Sauter was one of his preferred writers.

"Dick was a true character; appearing cynical but really very kind and generous. He was hell to all who employed him; he wore it like a badge of honor. He was a rebel of the '30s, enemy of the bosses.

"I can't imagine anyone giving more of themselves than Dick Cary gave to music. He produced music through his last two years of catastrophe. When all others would have given up he continued to write and rehearse. There was a period when he had to hold his head up with his hand and he continued. He was creative. His writing will endure, and endure, and endure."

(bassist Putter Smith, *Overture*, May 1994)

* * * * * * *

In the years since Dick Cary died, the Tuesday Night Friends continue to meet for their weekly rehearsal, playing the arrangements upon which Dick Cary lavished so much time and care. From time to time they make a public appearance, as the following sample reviews show:

In his report on the L.A. Classic Jazz Festival of September 1994, reporter Charles Champlin said: "The late player-arranger Dick Cary's Tuesday Night rehearsal band reassembled in a double-session tribute to him, with Dick Hamilton as leader (doubling on piano and trumpet, as Cary often did). Cary, who died in April, left a great legacy of exciting and demanding charts, including many originals. The group, with trombonist Betty O'Hara and tenor saxman Dick Hafer chief among the soloists, did them and Cary full justice."

Or as Floyd Levin wrote in *Jazz News*: "Dick Cary's Tuesday Night Band played its first night club engagement on March 24, 1998, at the Moonlight Supper Club in Sherman Oaks. The 11-piece band included Jack Trott, trumpet, Les Benedict, trombone, Ernie Tack, bass trombone, Abe Most, clarinet, Tommy Newsom, Roger Neumann, tenor, Fred Cooper, baritone, Dick Hamilton, piano, alto horn, trumpet, Dave Koonse, guitar, Herb Mickman, bass, Jerry White, drums."

Levin reported that Betty O'Hara was missing, "hospitalized with a serious ailment just a few days before ..." and continued:

"Dick Cary's death four years ago left a vast void that will never be filled. Despite Dick's absence, his image dominated every moment."

Jim Turner recalled: "On the day he died, the woman who rented his pool house went into the main house and found Dick's handwritten will. My brother went to get it and it proved to be valid. Dick had told me he intended to turn everything over to me, but I never really gave it much thought until it actually happened.

"I had visited him in California only a few days before he died, but I was in Indiana when it happened. I immediately flew back and took care of his final affairs. I organized a memorial party and a small ceremony at his gravesite. He had a lot of good friends who pitched in and helped immensely with all these activities.

"Sandi (Jim's wife) and I have tried to carry out his wishes. We sorted and microfilmed almost all of the music in the house. We have produced two CDs of his music so far. We kept the rehearsal band going weekly at the house from 1994 to 2003, when we moved to Texas. [Jim Turner became the pianist with the Jim Cullum band in San Antonio.] It now carries on at Dick Hamilton's home-studio.

"Sandi and I fixed up the house and lived there from 1997 to 2003. We still own it and it is leased to a good tenant and watched over by friends George and Bonnie Martinez. About half of the poolhouse is occupied by the Dick Cary music and memorabilia. The tenant occupies the other half as an office. Sandi and I dream of retiring there someday when our Texas adventure is over.

"Dick was a great genius of music. His musicians—I say "his" because some of them played with and under him almost constantly for decades—loved him. He loved them."

Or as Jim Turner put it on another occasion:

"Meanwhile, the Dick Cary library is still at the old Cary residence in Sunland. That residence consists of a house and guest house. The house has been leased to a tenant; the Cary library (music, manuscripts, letters, catalogs, recordings, photos, etc) is in the guest house watched over by Dick Hamilton of the 'Tuesday Night Friends' group."

And, as Betty O'Hara said, "Dick Hamilton is the perfect person to carry on the band and I think Dick Cary would be pleased." The late Betty O'Hara (1926?–2000), a remarkable musician herself, was a long-time associate of Dick Cary. For the Local 47 AFM union paper, *The Overture*, she wrote, in part: "Dick was my friend, mentor and musical inspiration for over forty years. His marvelous jazz on piano and distinctive sound on the alto horn are well known.

"He was a wonderful composer/arranger, and had one of the best rehearsal bands ever, in the Tuesday Night Friends. As a writer he was under-sung and under-paid a lot of the time but, mainly, he wrote for the pure joy of it. He admired Eddie Sauter and, even more, Duke Ellington and Billy Strayhorn. He could interpret the Ellington style better than anyone, and was the constant source of the correct chords to so many great tunes.

"The Tuesday night after Dick left us, the rehearsal band met at his house to play his music and remember. Christy, who lives there, let us in the music room, but somehow the security alarm was activated. The police arrived while we were playing and were met by Tony, who also lives on the property. When asked, 'What's going on here?' Tony said, 'I don't know—they just broke in and started rehearsing!!!'

"Dick Cary would love that!"

For this book, she provided the following memoir:

My first memory of Dick Cary was in 1947. I was then married to "Tweet" Peterson, a trumpet player Dick had worked with in Albany, New York. Dick was sitting in his tiny living room in Middletown, Connecticut, listening to and scoring a baseball game and, at the same time, writing an arrangement of some tune for somebody. At the end of his life, it was almost the same: the living room in Sunland was bigger, the medium was television, the game was tennis, but he was still writing at the same time. By this time he was writing almost exclusively for his rehearsal band, "The Tuesday Night Friends," as it was named by Chuck Conklin, when he hired the band for a concert for the "Jazz Forum," a Los Angeles jazz club.

During the ten years I lived in Connecticut, Dick joined Local 802 in New York, and was there most of the time, playing at Condon's and elsewhere, while he waited out his time to be a member of 802. He occasionally came to Connecticut to play jazz concerts and to play with a band I was with, the Al Gentile big band. He wrote some arrangements for Al and they were always the highlight of a gig.

When I left Conn. in 1955, I didn't see Dick until he came to Chicago with a show called "Joy Ride." I was living a hundred miles from there, so I saw the show. It featured a jazz band on stage. We had continued to write each other and he always wrote very interesting letters. For example, he once (in a moment of weakness) gave me a birthday card and wrote on it, "May you have as many more as you need."

We both moved to California around the same time. He married a friend of ours (I had by then married trombone player Barrett O'Hara) and we had rented a house three doors from where he and Jessie, also a trombone player, lived. This led to his writing the first of a series of libraries for different numbers of players. This was the quartet, Dick playing trumpet and alto horn, me playing trumpet and valve trombone, Jessie on trombone, and Barrett on bass trombone. As with all his libraries, most of the music was original material, with a few great arrangements of tunes he liked thrown in. I first met Dick Cathcart in a rehearsal of Dick's quintet book.

Then there was the big band that he wrote for, for a number of years. That finally ended when most of the book burned in a fire at bass player Ray Leatherwood's airplane parts place, where we did the weekly rehearsals. Dick said he didn't care; that the band was too big, anyway!!

This led to the present band, with Dick playing trumpet and piano, me on trumpet (and sometimes valve trombone), Dick Hamilton on trombone, Barrett or Ernie Tack on bass trombone, Fred Cooper on baritone sax, Tommy Newsom on tenor and soprano saxophones, Terry Harrington on tenor and clarinet, Abe Most on clarinet, Gene Estes, drums, Herb Mickman, bass, and Dave Koonse, guitar.

Then there was the "Lower Book" made up of Dick on alto trumpet and alto horn, me and Bob Enevoldsen on valve trombones and euphoniums, Fred and Tommy on baritone saxophones and the same rhythm section. He had a smaller version of the band he used for park concerts and I played a lot of other gigs with him, also.

He was a marvelous accompanist and I loved to sing when he played the piano. He had known Willard Robison in New York and he taught me *Old Folks* and *Pigeon-Toed Joe*. He greatly admired Lee Wiley and I learned from Dick, *A Woman's Intuition*. He had a lot of Ellington tunes in his books and I always felt he understood Ellington's mind as well as anyone.

His last few years were tough, his having contracted myasthenia gravis and melanoma. He had several operations and kept writing such pieces as *The Gurneyman*. He never lost his sense of humor or his rage at the world, either.

* * * * * * *

When Banu Gibson sang *More Than You Know* at the Hollywood Bowl on August 12, 13 and 14, 1994, with John Mauceri and the Hollywood Bowl Symphony Orchestra she ended her tribute to Dick Cary by saying: "I was hoping that Dick would get a chance to hear

Dick Cary during England tour with Keith Smith, 1981.

(Photograph by Denis Williams. Courtesy: Dick Cary Archive)

his arrangement here at the Bowl, but unfortunately Dick passed away this April. Although the musician is gone, his music lives on."

In the years which have passed since then, Dick Cary's music has lived on, thanks to the work of Jim Turner, Dick Hamilton and all the members of the Tuesday Night Friends, aided by CDs issued on the Klavier and Arbors labels.

Apropos Betty O'Hara's remark about Cary understanding Duke Ellington's mind, how interesting it could have been if Cary had become Billy Strayhorn's replacement when he, Duke's closest ally, died in 1967.

Cary wrote a piece called *Oh, Really*. His explanation to Jim Turner for this title was that a friend introduced Dick to Duke Ellington one night and, in doing so, said, "Dick is a composer, too." To which Ellington raised one eyebrow and said, "Oh, really."

Someday Cary may receive the full recognition which is his due, and his compositions, arrangements and recordings are available should this time come. New listeners to any of this material will soon realise that they are listening to a consummate musician and a man of unswerving integrity. Many of his contemporaries spent their later years revisiting the past, but that was not Cary's way, hence his scorn for the Louis Armstrong tributes into which he was sometimes tempted to stray. His dedication to his music was always undeniable, even when the music scene around him was descending into electronic cacophony.

The world of jazz and of popular music in general will be a far better place when musicians heed the example of Richard Durant Cary.

The Appendices

Appendix One

CARY'S VIEWS

Dick Cary reflecting on audiences, Dixieland, likes, dislikes, and musicians.

The following comments are extracts from the interview and blindfold test in *Jazz Podium*, as noted, from letters to the author, the dates for which are shown, and other sources.

* * * * * * *

I admire greatly a fine healthy ego in an artist if it almost matches his talent. But some of our really great players like Dave McKenna, Pepper Adams, Eddie Miller, Jack Teagarden—and the list is fairly long—have talent which is way ahead of the ego. These are the fine players, ones who get the musicians to extend their ears. For instance, Art Tatum was the kindest, most encouraging guy to be around. Of course, he had no one to envy, which must be a remarkable position to be in.

Musicians don't fool other musicians at all, only the public, most of whom don't seem to want the best until they go to a symphony concert and even then some only want to hear Mozart for the rest of their lives and Bartók dies almost a pauper. Why do people want new TV shows, new movies, new stage productions, but only want to dance to *In the Mood* or scream for *The Saints* like crazed parrots?

After awhile we take all this in our stride and what I've been doing is not really criticizing or complaining but stating the case for my colleagues. I got in a lot of scenes doing this in my younger years, but by the age of 62 I figure, why lie and nod my head. There must be ways of discussing all this in a reasonable way and attempt a very small amount of educating some of the more reasonable "dags" [Australian for jazz fans] who often exhibit too few windows and skylights in their preferences.

I know a very charming young man in Frankfurt, a school teacher who has a jazz band. A very bright guy. We had long talks and I tried to understand why he only liked George Lewis and Kid Ory. Maybe there's an answer in what some composer here said, that quite a few great writers of literature were almost tone deaf and had no liking or appreciation of any music whatsoever. It's all very fascinating, trying to judge people's range of hearing sounds. One of the worst beliefs is that one is born with a certain kind of ear and can never develop it. It has a great deal to do with concentration and the great American businessman has more important things to think about than music, so he remembers a song or a band from a happy day at age 19 and wants to stick with that. I agree with the guy who said, "Nostalgia is a dangerous thing to wallow in."

I wish we realized the values and possibilities of this existence when we were somewhat younger. Most people have no idea what a religion an art such as music can be—and although some jazz players may be very undisciplined—they must have some natural honesty—if they're good jazz creators. There are a lot of bluffs who use music as an act—never doing anything new or different—safely remaining in a small framework and using a personality and appearance plus their meagre knowledge. That's fine; but when most musicians listen to music, records, etc, they don't listen to the likes of Braff, Davison, McPartland and so many others who are completely sterile and have merely an act or haven't changed a whit in their entire career.
(March 14, 1979)

Our movies, TV, pop music, are all aimed at the huge lowest denominator.
(July 7, 1990)

No matter what I hear any idiot scream, it is not bad to be intelligent and it is not bad to have a conscience and it is not foul to be a liberal. A human with a locked-in mind, no humor, no curiosity, is close to being a plant, and a very undesirable and predatory plant quite often!
(diary entry, November 1970)

The great music public is no longer interested in us elderly relics—we can hardly find anyone to publish anything we do, the reply coming back, "We're no longer interested in acoustic instruments." (July 12, 1986)

On Songwriting

I remember my days in New York City, around the Brill Building, the home of most of the songwriters and publishers, the general idea was to write as many tunes as possible; maybe one out of a hundred might be a hit.
(March 15, 1989)

I have several books of early Ellington songs, some unbelievably terrible. Also, several years ago, someone got hold of a lot of early, college days of Cole Porter scribblings and published them in a collection of "non hits" and some of them were pretty awful. (March 15, 1989)

On Fame

I sometimes think I am kind of lucky. I think I might not have the kind of mentality to stand being a star—whatever that is! But I don't envy anybody who's always in the limelight wherever he goes. (Levin)

Having known [Bob] Wilber and Dick Hyman and others since their middle teens—I appreciate the practise they put in, which I don't do for two reasons. One, I tried various instruments and second, the very consuming urge to scribble, which by now has become very rewarding, to have musicians of such calibre come to my back room every Tuesday night and appear to be enjoying themselves fully.   *(March 15, 1989)*

I never really looked at [my career] that way. Only tried to get as much pleasure out of playing with, accompanying the fine group I got to be with.
(March 15, 1989)

I think I liked the word "redoubtable" which Hugh Rainey applied to me. Of course I had to see what the dictionary said—"formidable, especially as an opponent." Our local Leonard Feather has used "protean" [readily changing form or appearance; inconstant]. One of my favourite words was found in a Belgian paper when an article called me "duisenpoodle" which later I was told, is like a centipede. All these make everything worthwhile.
(August 11, 1987)

On Imagined Failings

1953: "Someday I may start hustling. Hardly know how yet—really a difficult thing to learn."

1955: "Altogether, things seem as promising as ever in my life ... Now if I could learn to play piano!!"

1955: "Often rather deep loneliness. Became 39 and wonder if by 40 anything will happen. When will the first good record be?" [The Hackett, McPartland, Condon, Glasel, Cary recordings were just a short time away....]

1958: "A good trumpet exercise is Clifford Brown's two choruses on *Kiss and Run*. How can some of those guys move so fast! Make Hackett sound like a backward child."

1958: "Practised a piece by [guitarist] Jimmy Raney—boy, do I need a faster ear!"

1958: "Feeling most sterile possible. No decision or incentive to compose—or really just a terrible laziness. Hope this terrible period passes."

1964: It does no harm to repeat his note on Johnny Guarnieri, that "neither of us has much of anything original to offer as jazz pianists," a statement which is both true, when considered in the light of a jazz genius, and false in all other respects.

1976: "Wonder when I'll ever figure out what to do, where to aim, etc??"

1980: practised: "felt great. But each time I sit down I play differently. After Phineas it's best, after McKenna likewise. Brad Gowans said sometimes I was the best and sometimes the worst."

1982: "Me, I never figured out a set chorus and play it on every song."

(all diary entries)

On Ragtime

Those who are able to really improvise will not get much fun out of rags. I personally was not too excited by rags. A stride piano piece swings, an original rag swings never. To me rags are very sterile music. That music fits perfectly for amateurs. *(Jazz Podium, February 1978)*

... and Dixieland

I have no use for the point of view of the "Dixieland" ragtime fans, most of whom are so extremely narrow about all the better music, or real music. The California point of view is as narrow as anything I've run into.

(April 30, 1987)

When I was in New York with Condon I wasn't aware of this mass of tin-eared TRAD lovers. Eddie liked show tunes, good songs and good players, which is really almost opposite to the California jazz club point of view. Beside that, these people at these clubs never listen anyway, they talk continually, especially when anyone is playing. *(April 30, 1987)*

Eddie Condon always tried to get the best guys he could and we all deplored the word "Dixieland." *(July 7, 1990)*

That word [Dixieland] has cost me a fortune in my career. Any music contractor here and in New York City associates that word with people who don't play well, can't read, and are generally unreliable. I was saddled with it as a pianist in New York and as a trumpet player out here.

(February 20, 1985)

There are so many people out here on the West Coast who preferred Turk Murphy and also the Lu Watters band. In our society we learn to nod agreeably and keep our "traps shut." *(July 7, 1990)*

I wish so much that there wasn't this narrow, blinkers-on approach. California is full of these so-called jazz fans. Many of them think that jazz ended with Kid Ory and Turk Murphy and George Lewis. Between these people and the rock fans there is no longer any audience around here for so many talented people. Even Eddie Miller very seldom worked locally.

(November 14, 1988)

And Old Jazz and New Jazz

People like Eubie Blake, Joe Darensbourg or the Legends of Jazz are not in the same class [as Fats Waller, Art Tatum, etc], but they create a unique atmosphere. I like these colleagues very much and know them very well. One time Louis took us to San Francisco to hear Kid Ory and we felt the same atmosphere. It was wonderful to see him, although he did not have top class musicians in his band. *(Jazz Podium, June 1976)*

There are so many people now who think they must point toward Coltrane, who was pretty fantastic and toward Ornette Coleman who's fantastically ridiculous. There are some contemporary "jazz" records which sound like a barnyard full of demented guinea-hens. All of this stuff the musicians understand but keep conveniently quiet because it is easier than being accused of being senile, or moldy. Sometimes the existing "entertainment" business makes me feel like I'm living in a huge kindergarten.

(July 7, 1990)

On Popular Music

A very scary part to me is, how many young people in these sixties will continue to like horrendously bad guitar and saxophone playing and such sick, illiterate, foul-mouthings which the vapid, stringy-haired idiots scream in front of those electronic monstrosities. Just because a few kids have come through with talent is no excuse at all. This is the excuse that's used by everyone from the Down Beat critic to the brain-washed housewife. But some of the young people now had better not have glowing memories of their protesting years and carry along this crap all their lives.

Many people did it to 1920s jazz. I do honestly think that there was just a slightly higher degree of instrumental proficiency in a music which produced Art Tatum, Jack Teagarden, Benny Goodman, Fletcher Henderson, Barney Bigard, Johnny Hodges, etc....

We have saxophone players now who are setting records for the fastest arpeggios in the fewest bars and also the loudest grunts and tortured squeals. Anything goes, turn up the knob. Take a pen and splash the canvas of manuscript.

(diary entries, March 27, 1968)

* * * * * * *

Ernestine Anderson
I worked with a very promising girl thirty years ago in New York called Ernestine Anderson who completely dropped out of sight for many years, but has made some records with Ray Brown in recent years. She had a lovely musical sound which should have been developed. *(April 30, 1987)*

Whitney Balliett (writer for *The New Yorker* magazine)
Some of that crap in *The New Yorker* is just-oh-so-precious! Beside, Whitney Bellyache (as Condon referred to him) just didn't have the ear to appreciate Eddie Sauter. *(August 11, 1987)*

Bix Beiderbecke
I myself saw Bix only once, in a theatre in Connecticut, when he was with Paul Whiteman, when I was about sixteen. Otherwise I only know him from records. I wrote out his solos note by note. The reason that he became so famous is that there is no other musician playing the cornet the way he does. We will never know what would have become of Bix if he was still with us today. Personally I do not find anything unusual about his compositions *Davenport Blues* or *In a Mist*, although quite a few people will not like to hear this. *(Jazz Podium, June 1976)*

Bix was not so special when playing in an orchestra but when he started to improvise you got the feeling you had entered another room which you only left when he stopped blowing. To create such effects it needs tremendous talent. I transcribed Bix's choruses from records and realised that his harmonic knowledge was not on the level we have today and that, for example, Bobby Hackett has. Bobby always had changes and harmony-changes perfect, because he hated it if something was not absolutely perfect. Bix did not have that insight. In his time the musicians were not so slavish about the changes and chords. When you strictly analyse Beiderbecke's playing you come to the result that a lot was incorrect. But that was part of his individuality to push the notes out, to attack. I don't know how he did that and to this day nobody has. *(Jazz Podium, Feb 1978)*

Ruby Braff
To me, for instance, Braff's playing is exactly like him, energetic, nervous, derivative completely, with a tone quality resembling at times an ailing goat, and the ego that little man has is awesome. *(March 14, 1979)*

Eddie Condon
Eddie Condon was a very interesting man. You never heard him play a solo. Reason for that was originally he started out on the plectrum banjo and when he changed to the guitar he tuned the first four strings like a banjo, C-G-B-D. This unusual instrument he called his "porkchop." I did numerous tours with him. He worked so hard it was difficult to follow him. His sessions were like parties. *(Jazz Podium, June 1976)*

Condon was one of my best friends; he did a lot for me. He was never down and he was always funny. His judgement and opinion were accepted by all and I liked his way of Dixieland interpretation the best. He always had the best rhythm sections, with drummers like Dave Tough, Cliff Leeman and George Wettling or the great bassman Walter Page, and he tried to gather the best hornmen. *(Jazz Podium, June 1976)*

I really didn't want to go into Nick's (1941) because I thought Davison made about the worst noise I'd ever heard. [Later] I somewhat revised my feeling about him. He's hard working, still is, a terrible musician by some standards, but all these guys are specialists and must be judged this way.
(letter to Ken Gallacher, August 20, 1962)

Roy Eldridge
Just as I loved Louis, I loved Roy Eldridge, although he, contrary to Louis, embellished his phrases. To me Roy was the most exciting trumpeter of the '30s and I was lucky to play with him now and then. At that time he was enormous and my absolute favourite. This break-neck style of his was not the one of Louis Armstrong, but they are two different conceptions.
(Jazz Podium February 1978)

Duke Ellington
When I was 13 or 14 years old, *Creole Rhapsody* was my favourite record. I rated it above all and thought it was the greatest thing I had ever heard. I once took it off the record to perform it in a concert, but it is problematic to play such Ellington pieces. There are no musicians who sound like Harry Carney, Johnny Hodges or Barney Bigard. That was the wonder of the Ellington band that all its members were unique. Ellington's pieces became second nature to the musicians so that they did not stick to the notes. I heard the orchestra many times, standing or sitting close to the musicians and never experienced Johnny Hodges, say, playing an arrangement twice the same way. *(Jazz Podium, June 1976)*

Pee Wee Erwin
About Pee Wee Erwin, a most pleasant guy. He had, about thirty years before, an almost losing battle with booze but had pulled out of it. A really nice gentleman. *(June 1988)*

Carl Fontana
Fontana amazed me in Texas. He's an amazing trombone player. He and McGarity are very exciting when they play together and they did that quite a bit in Texas. But McGarity I have known for many years and he's one of my favourite guys. *(Ellsworth)*

Bud Freeman
Bud [was] one of a kind, an absolute original and I admire that especially, having been lucky enough to work with several. *(November 14, 1990)*

When we lived in the Village not far from each other we became good friends. Unfortunately he considered himself a great golfer but, honestly, he was dreadful. When we toured with Eddie Condon in New Zealand, a nice Englishman showed us a golf course and Bud was ready to demonstrate his remarkable talent. He hit the ball and it crashed into a tree. In his excitement he had not realized this and told us what an unbelievable stroke he had played. As he could not see the ball he thought it was on the green. We let him boast for a while before we suggested a search under the tree. From that moment on he did not speak to me for the next two days.
(Jazz Podium June 1976)

Eddie Condon called this band [Bud Freeman's Summa Cum Laude Orchestra] "summa cum loaded." *(Jazz Podium February 1978)*

Bud Freeman told me, "If you live long enough you'll get to be a curiosity and work all the time." (Ken Gallacher letter, February 1978)

Bobby Hackett
Bobby Hackett was an extra-ordinary personality. [His] was a natural talent. Most people, like myself, have to work very hard at their vocation. Zoot Sims and Dave McKenna also belong to these privileged people. Music was with them in the cradle. It was always clear that they would play jazz and they needed no special education. The chorus that Bobby blew in 1938 on *Embraceable You* was a composition in itself. David Rowles arranged it for strings, Harry James played it with his brass section and other musicians picked it up. However, Hackett played such things spontaneously, they came out of him naturally. I still play Hackett's chorus on *Embraceable You* in concerts. In the army my bed neighbour was a trumpeter, a member of the Philadelphia Symphony. I gave him the written music of Bobby's improvisation on *Ja Da*. He tried to play these two choruses, but what he blew sounded dreadful. *(Jazz Podium June 1976)*

Al Haig
Heard Al Haig, a sailor [at a Harry Lim session]; he's good but monotonously like Teddy Wilson, etc, without much expression." *(diary, February 15, 1943)*

Scott Hamilton
He's a talented young man. I played a few festivals where he was and I admire his taste. *(July 7, 1990)*

Johnny Hodges
Sometimes he did not blow at all and made the most bored face. In my whole life I have never met another human being who looked so bored into the audience. His long facial line appeared even longer and thus his nickname, the rabbit, was absolutely right. He was a fantastic musician. He had

enormous control of his instrument. Duke gave freedom to him and Hodges could always do what he wanted. At any rate, the Ellington orchestra is the greatest and best jazz band I have every heard. *(Jazz Podium, June 1976)*

Max Kaminsky
Eddie Condon rated Max Kaminsky's lead very highly. Maxie himself, however, had not the slightest idea about changes and many musicians thought he played wrong notes. Yet his sound was always wonderful. He had an enormous feeling for the rhythm, reason why drummers scrambled to play with him. In his youth he naturally adored Louis Armstrong but did not sound a bit like his idol. Reason for his powerful tone comes from the fact that he worked many, many years in orchestras [Tommy Dorsey, Artie Shaw, etc]. *(Jazz Podium, February 1978)*

Cliff Leeman
I love George Wettling and know what a fine drummer he is, but there is such a different feel from Cliff Leeman. I can play with one and not the other. Cliff is a painter, he doesn't play vertically, he moves like waves, always shading, listening. Buzzy Drootin is a little Cliff. I guess Dave Tough was like that, but I never got to know Dave much.
(letter to Ken Gallacher, October 10, 1962)

Art Lyons
Art Lyons has worked with me a lot—happens to be one of the best clarinet players in L A and drives a cab to make a living. *(undated 1976)*

Don Marino
An old friend of mine from Boston named Don Marino was on drums [with the Lou McGarity Quintet]. I think this was one of the very few dates he did in New York. He was a good drummer, too. He used to run, when I was in the army, a lot of jazz concerts in Boston. *(Ellsworth)*

Dave McKenna
This guy is one of the best jazz piano-naturals I've ever heard. Tremendous rhythmical force. Doesn't read much, but just a natural. Not a copy of anyone either, which is getting rarer than ever these days.
(letter to Ken Gallacher, October 18, 1959)

It is similar with Dave McKenna, a piano colleague. Music is flowing out of him. You cannot define that. It is a natural talent. The best example is Louis Armstrong and I am very proud that I was allowed to play with him.
(Jazz Podium June 1976)

Found his cassette made at Father's, which flows strongly. Mr McKenna seems equally at home in all 12 keys. Why doesn't his name appear in jazz magazines? What dead-ears surround us!! *(diary entry, late 1993)*

Phineas Newborn
He's given me more pleasure than any other piano player currently. *(1971)*

I think he's just unbelievable. I used to hear him in New York quite a bit, when he had his own quartet, I think he was really in shape then. Unfortunately he hasn't worked too much since he's lived out here (Los Angeles) and it hasn't done him any good. I used to drag everybody I could to listen to this kid because he's unbelievable. His left hand is just faster than anybody's right hand that I know and he plays things in octaves that Bud Powell used to play with one hand. *(Ellsworth)*

Tommy Newsom
Tommy Newson is the conductor of the "Tonite Show" band in the absence of [Doc] Severinsen.

Tom plays all the reed instruments very well and is a fine writer—makes guest appearances on stage bands, concert bands, symphonies. Last winter [1981] the Boston Pops did a TV show featuring Buddy Rich and Newsom orchestrated his "West Side Story" medley for the full symphony. I've never heard an ovation on that show comparable to the one Rich received and the writing was excellent. *(April 20, 1982)*

[Note: It was Bill Reddie who arranged the original version of the "West Side Story medley" for the Buddy Rich Orchestra.]

Pee Wee Russell
Pee Wee was one of the nicest people I ever knew in my life. He didn't appear that way in a club. I think a lot of people thought he was sort of a clown and they approached him that way and he had a habit of saying, when he saw somebody bearing down on him, "Whatever it is, no." Which I found out later he got from a W.C. Fields film. He had his bad times, when he was broke and drinking a lot, but he straightened out and before he died he made some money. He did some very interesting paintings. *(Ellsworth)*

Pee Wee Russell was the most sensitive man I ever met.
(Jazz Podium, June 1976)

Willie "The Lion" Smith
Willie "The Lion" Smith I also adored. He was a fascinating man. I knew all his solos. Sometimes I played like him, but I did not have the time to practice. Of the three great piano players of that time, Fats Waller, James P Johnson and Willie, he was the most interesting. They were all outstanding, but he had the best musical ideas. Art Tatum learned a lot from these people. *(Jazz Podium, June 1976)*

Bob Sommers

Last night at my rehearsal I had a guest on trumpet, a Bob Sommers, who I am adding on for a fall concert. He brought a cassette of his recent album of Clifford Brown—I couldn't believe the speed this young man has.

(March 15, 1989)

Wayne Songer

Wayne Songer played with me ('60s and '70s)—we did a lot of park concerts, also recorded with me for a local dance (square and round) record company. A very fine man—did all the Jack Benny shows—occasionally picked to do bit parts because of his unusual face and a deep resonant voice.

(March 1, 1991)

Rex Stewart

He told me he was very discouraged about his waning strength. I reminded him of all his great performances with Duke Ellington and I tried to put his mind at ease with the fact that he had achieved what others could only dream of. In his time with the Duke he was able to play fast and powerful phrases and had a wide spectrum of sound. He was a master cornet player, the cornet being an instrument even harder to play than a trumpet. Moreover he had arrived at his own very individual style. Later he became an excellent critic, writing remarkable reviews for the Los Angeles Times and articles for Playboy and Esquire. *(Jazz Podium, February 1978)*

Jack Teagarden

Jack Teagarden was totally uncomplicated and he moved very slowly. He was very shy and always had a key with him to tune a piano. He had more fans than any other trombonist because he was a wonderful but reserved human being, often taken advantage of. Such shy people, when disappointed, start to drink and life grows hard and bitter for them. Jack's brother, Charlie, was the same with Jimmy Dorsey's band. If you have to play in nightclubs night after night you begin drinking in kind of self-defense. We had to work hard night after night, while the people who came to talk and drink with us did that only once or twice a week, to make a night of it. *(Jazz Podium, June 1976)*

Joe Venuti

Once Joe did recordings with a sound engineer he disliked. This was when there was no microphone cable between the recording studio and the sound booth, which were separated by two large doors. The engineer had to walk through these two doors each time he needed to give instructions. When he gave the sign to record the musicians raised their instruments and only pretended to play. The sound man ran through the doors to let the guys know there was something wrong and he would try to fix it. At once Venuti and his men started playing properly. The engineer ran back to his booth and the musicians again only mimed. Not hearing anything the engineer ran back again—and again, to the amusement of the musicians. *(Jazz Podium June 1976)*

Lee Wiley

I forgot to say about Lee Wiley, that to my ear and almost every colleague in New York, she was the best (by miles!) singer of all. Her diction, her intonation, phrasing were so natural. One of our best film composers, Victor Young, shared this feeling and I've been spoiled for any other singers by that great lady. *(April 30, 1987)*

No one affected me ever like she did and I was lucky to work with her, mostly in the '40s and some in the '50s. *(August 11, 1987)*

Johnny Windhurst

At age 15 or 16 [he] used to journey from the Bronx to Greenwich Village and if his mother noticed his bed hadn't been used [she] would call either Condon or me and know he was in safe hands. Johnny could never learn how to read music at all, but naturally had a very nice sound on the trumpet. He started trying to copy Hackett. When he realized sometime later that his ear wasn't quite as accurate as Bobby's, he switched to Louis Armstrong. Johnny hung about with Condon so much he was sometimes referred to as Eddie's chauffeur. We all found him a very bright, pleasant, talented young man, but one who floundered a bit and never really found much of a career, which was too bad. *(April 20, 1982)*

Appendix Two

AT REHEARSAL

Musicians' Biographies (The Tuesday Night Friends)

RANDY ALDCROFT—Baritone Horn
With Terry Gibbs for 15 years and the Dinah Shore Show for 5 years. Extended stints with Frank Sinatra and Natalie Cole among others, and active in classical music ensembles.

JOHN BAMBRIDGE—Reeds
For 37 years, lead alto saxophonist with Ray Conniff and appeared on every recording Conniff made. From 1970 to 1992, a member of the NBC Orchestra on the Tonight Show. Also occasionally with the Los Angeles Philharmonic Orchestra. Recorded with Doc Severinsen and Louis Bellson.

LEE CALLETT—Reeds
Worked with Doc Severinsen's Ex-Tonight Show Orchestra, the Clayton-Hamilton Hollywood Bowl Jazz Orchestra and Roger Neumann's Rather Large Band. Saxophonist with the Los Angeles Philharmonic Orchestra.

DICK CATHCART—Trumpet
Best known for his "ghost playing" of Pete Kelly in the radio show, film and TV shows, Pete Kelly's Blues. Worked with Alvino Rey, Ray McKinley, Bob Crosby, Ben Pollack. Recorded with Billy May, Matty Matlock and many others. Recorded (1958), under own name, a tribute to Bix Beiderbecke for Warner Brothers. Guest star at many jazz festivals. Born 1924, died 1993.

BUDDY CLARK—Bass
Worked with Bud Freeman, Tex Beneke, Les Brown, Peggy Lee, Red Norvo and Gerry Mulligan. Part of the original Supersax band, working with Med Flory in transcribing Charlie Parker solos in the early '70s. Born 1929.

MAHLON CLARK—Clarinet
Clarinetist in the Benny Goodman tradition who worked with Lawrence Welk for many years. Active studio musician whose credits included Madonna, Elvis Presley, Frank Sinatra and Ella Fitzgerald, as well as the Will Bradley and Ray McKinley bands. Born 1923, died 2007.

FRED COOPER—Reeds
A distinctive voice on the baritone. 27 years with Les Brown's Band of Renown. Innumerable Hollywood credits. A close collaborator with Dick Cary for many years.

BOB ENEVOLDSEN—Trombone
Described as the perfect utility jazz player. Although best-known as a valve trombonist, Enevoldsen was a talented tenorman and also played string bass. Moved to Los Angeles in 1951 and became a busy studio musician. With the Bobby Troup trio 1954–55 and appeared on West Coast jazz dates headed by Gerry Mulligan, Shorty Rogers, Shelly Manne and Marty Paich among many others. Worked on Steve Allen's television series, 1962–64. Enevoldsen recorded as a leader, including for Nocturne, Tampa and Liberty. Born 1920, died 2005.

GENE ESTES—Drums
Credits with Jack Teagarden, Tex Beneke, Bob Crosby, Harry James, etc. Worked in all major film, TV and recording studios. Also played vibes in his own Gene Estes Quartet. Recorded on many CDs for Arbors, including as leader. Born 1931, died 1996.

JACK FEIERMAN—Trumpet
Trumpet player and conductor. Recorded extensively with Count Basie and also with John Fahey and Lincoln Mayorca, among others.

DICK FORREST—Trumpet
Worked in orchestras led by Billy Butterfield, Tony Pastor, Louie Bellson, Woody Herman and many more.

DICK HAFER—Reeds
Worked with Charlie Barnet 1949, Claude Thornhill 1950, Woody Herman 1951–55, Benny Goodman, Bobby Hackett and Charles Mingus, among others. In 1994 released "Prez Impressions" (a tribute to Lester Young). Born 1927.

DICK HAMILTON—Leader, Trumpet, Alto Horn, Trombone, Piano
Accomplished studio musician. Composes, produces, arranges and performs on countless albums, soundtracks and commercials. Originally played trombone with Dick Cary's rehearsal band as early as 1966. He is the current leader of Dick Cary's Tuesday Night Friends.

TERRY HARRINGTON—Reeds
A first-call studio musician in Los Angeles for many years. Repeatedly recognized for excellence by the National Academy of Recording Arts & Sciences. Dick Cary wrote volumes of music for Harrington.

BOB HAVENS—Trombone
One of Dixieland's great trombonists. Worked and recorded with Pete Fountain and Al Hirt in New Orleans. Then 23 years with the Lawrence Welk Orchestra as featured jazz artist. Currently a guest star at numerous

worldwide jazz festivals. Has a vast discography. Born 1930.

DICK HOLGATE—Baritone Saxophone
Recorded with Russ Garcia and Roger Neumann.

DAVE KOONSE—Guitar
Versatile musician whose collaborators have included Benny Goodman, Harry James, George Shearing, Red Norvo and many other greats. Recorded two Dobre albums with his son Larry, also a guitarist. Own CD on Jazz Compass JC1016 ("What's in the Box," 2007).

RAY LEATHERWOOD—Bass
Worked and recorded with Bob Chester, 1939–41, Les Brown 1947–51, Tommy Dorsey, Rosemary Clooney, Eddie Miller, Rosy McHargue, Jack Teagarden, Billy May, Abe Most and many others. Was bassist on Julie London's "Cry Me a River." Born 1914, died 1996.

DAVID LIBMAN—Drums
Graduate of the Juilliard School of Music in New York. A versatile musician, equally at home in jazz and rock music. Has worked with pianist Adam Makowicz.

JERRY McKENZIE—Drums
Three years with Stan Kenton. Worked with Dexter Gordon, Count Basie, Gerald Wilson and Les Brown. Arranged for Herb Jeffries and Johnny Desmond.

HERB MICKMAN—Bass
Also an accomplished pianist and conductor. Formerly music director for Sarah Vaughan. Credits include the Newport Youth Band, Tommy Dorsey and Woody Herman and many others. Has taught at UCLA.

ABE MOST—Clarinet
A distinguished career in the best big-bands, including Tommy Dorsey, Ray Anthony and Les Brown. Recreated the jazz of Benny Goodman, Artie Shaw, Woody Herman and Barney Bigard for the acclaimed Time/Life recording series. Toured with World's Greatest Jazz Band 1985. Recorded several albums as small group leader. Born 1920, died 2002.

ROGER NEUMANN—Reeds
An experienced tenor player with credits including Woody Herman, Bob Crosby and Anita O'Day. As an arranger worked for Buddy Rich, Count Basie, Ray Brown and the Beach Boys. Leads his own "Rather Large Band."

TOMMY NEWSOM—Clarinet, Soprano, Tenor and Baritone Saxophones

For 17 years, assistant conductor and lead saxophonist of the NBC Orchestra on the Tonight Show. Spent 4 years with the Airmen of Note and was in the Benny Goodman orchestra which toured Russia. A regular participant with Dick Cary since the mid-1970s. Jazz recordings range from a 1960 Riverside LP by Tommy Gwaltney's Kansas City Nine to a 2005 CD of his arrangements by the DIVA big band. Was leader on "Friendly Fire" and, with Ken Peplowski, "The Feeling of Jazz" on Arbors ARCD19251 & ARCD19195 respectively. Also on Dick Cary's "California Doings" album. Born 1929, died 2007.

BARRETT O'HARA—Bass Trombone
Ten years as staff trombonist on radio and TV station WGN, Chicago. Original bass trombone with Dick Cary's Tuesday Night Friends. Film and TV studio musician and supervisor of music preparation for TV shows. Born Kankakee, IL, 1920, died in Los Angeles, October 13, 2010.

BETTY O'HARA—Trombone, Baritone Horn, Double-Belled Euphonium
One of the world's great female brass instrumentalists. Mainly self-taught. Did not play while two children were growing up. Two tours (Japan, Brazil) with Billy Vaughn orchestra. Co-led the all-woman quintet The Jazzbirds and a featured soloist in the all-female big-band Maiden Voyage. Travelled worldwide as a guest-star at jazz festivals. Of her own career, briefly, she wrote:
"I came up through the girl band days of World War II, moved to Connecticut, played trumpet in the Hartford Symphony for five years. Came to California in 1960, married bass trombonist Barrett O'Hara. Besides playing (1994) in the Maiden Voyage band, I co-lead, with Stacy Rowles, trumpet playing daughter of pianist Jimmy Rowles, a female quintet called The Jazzbirds, playing cornet, valve trombone, double bell euphonium, singing and writing originals and arrangements of standards."

On her 1985 album for Magnagraphic (reissued on Delmark DD-482) she plays trumpet, flugelhorn, trombone, valve trombone, euphonium and piccolo trumpet. Born in Dittus on May 24, 1925, she died in Los Angeles, on April 18, 2000.

HARVEY PHILLIPS—Tuba and Bass
Friend and collaborator with Dick Cary. Appearances on record include with Gil Evans, Stan Getz, Dizzy Gillespie, Jimmy McPartland, John Lewis, George Williams and Wes Montgomery; from Pee Wee Erwin's Dixieland Eight to the Sauter-Finegan Orchestra. Retired Professor Emeritus at the Indiana University School of Music. Born 1929, died 2010.

JOHN SETAR—Reeds
Started with bands of Jess Stacy, Buddy Morrow, Freddy Martin and Jerry Gray. Prominent studio musician in Los Angeles, including two years with

Steve Allen. At home in many styles of jazz and klezmer music. Recorded three albums with Bill Tole. Born 1924.

PUTTER SMITH—Bass
Jazz recording credits include Alan Broadbent, Karrin Allyson, Mose Allison, Warne Marsh, Dick Sudhalter, and Betty O'Hara among many others. Also recorded with Bill Perkins and Mark Masters, plus two excellent albums as a leader, 1977 for VeeJay and 1994 for GAM. Also teacher and actor (gay killer in Diamonds are Forever). Brother of Carson Smith. Born 1941.

BOB SUMMERS—Trumpet
Berklee College of Music. Recorded with Maynard Ferguson, Count Basie, Bill Perkins, and Bill Holman, as well as several sessions with Tom Talbert. Two albums under his own name for Discovery. In 1994, world tour with the Horace Silver Brass Ensemble.

ERNIE TACK—Bass Trombone
Worked with the Harry James for several years and with Charlie Barnet. Recording credits include Sy Zentner, Gil Fuller, Supersax, and Doc Severinsen. Stalwart with the NBC Orchestra on the Tonight Show for 20 years. Like John Bambridge, a regular member of Ray Conniff's Orchestra for 37 years.

JACK TROTT—Trumpet
Veteran of the bands of Harry James, Skinny Ennis and Roger Neumann. Many film-soundtrack credits and a long-standing member of the Dick Cary rehearsal band.

JERRY WHITE—Drums
Touring credits include Rosemary Clooney, Helen O'Connell, Margaret Whiting and Rose Marie. Recorded with The Mills Brothers and Kay Starr. A regular band member with Ray Conniff since 1989, he recorded 5 albums with Conniff.

ZEKE ZARCHY—Trumpet
One of the great lead trumpet players, Zarchy played with almost every major Swing orchestra since Benny Goodman, including Bob Crosby, Artie Shaw, Joe Haymes and Paul Weston. The first man chosen by Glenn Miller for what was to become his famous Army Air Force Band. His travels have included many tours to Europe, South America and Australia along with thirty-two trips to Japan. Played Louis Armstrong solos with the Great Pacific Jazz Band. Born 1915. Died 2009.

These biographical notes are based upon those listed by Jim Turner on the Dick Cary website and in the insert to the "Catching Up" CD on Klavier KD-77024.

Appendix Three

BANDLEADERS AND SINGERS FOR WHOM DICK CARY MADE ARRANGEMENTS

The numbers quoted in brackets are an indication of the number of arrangements which Cary wrote for the band or singer. Cary was not punctilious in listing these details, so the following can only be a guide to his work in this field.

1939
Emery Deutsch orchestra (3)

1940
Bill Tasillo (large & small band) (17+)
George Fenton orchestra (2)
Al Scully band (?)
Dick Cary band (4+)
Joe De Fazio orchestra (15)
   (incl: Bar Fly)
Art Mooney band (19)

1941
----- Barnet Orchestra (1+)
   ("has been playing Bar Fly
   quite a while now")
Tommy Di Carlo orchestra (13)
   (incl: Bar Fly and Tabs)
Charles Margulis orchestra (11)
Joe Napoleon (singer) (3)
Saxie Dowell orchestra (1)
Al Johns orchestra (25)
Charley Paley orchestra (3)
Jimmy Pratt orchestra (3)
Mario ----- National Guard Band (2)

1942
Enoch Light orchestra (11)
Bobby Day orchestra (21)
   (incl: Bar Fly)
Lee Castle orchestra (4)
Joe Marsala orchestra (4)
Ray McKinley orchestra (1)
Frank Orchard orchestra (2)

1942/1943
Charles Peterson orchestra (40)

1943
Carmen Cavallaro orchestra (5)
Will Osborne orchestra (1)
Jules Maudlin orchestra (3)
Jim Grenada orchestra (10)
Benny Goodman orchestra (9)
New Yorker Ice Show (4)

1945
Billy Butterfield (NBC small band) (6+)
Eddie Condon band (?)
Tommy Di Carlo orchestra (1)
Sam Alessi orchestra (5)

1946
Billy Butterfield orchestra (24)
Hank D'Amico (4)
Eddie Stone orchestra (1)
Lesniak Polish Band (2)
Warren Stephen (1)
Al Gentile orchestra (20+)
Russ Shurer orchestra (15)
Joe D'Agostino orchestra (10)
Paul Lauderman orchestra (8)
Murray Godfrey orchestra (9)
Paul Bond (2)
Allan Wylie (2)
Hank D'Amico (4)

1947
Jean Goldkette orchestra (8)

1948
Benny Goodman orchestra (1)
Morey Feld (3)
Quinn Sisters (2)
Woody Herman orchestra (1?)
Ilick Krakowska (3)

1949
Gene Krupa orchestra (1)
Hank D'Amico/Paul Whiteman (1?)
Eddie Condon Floor Show (23)
Peanuts Hucko (3)
Pete Pelizzi (2)
Ethel Smith (trio) (4)
Ruth Brown/Count Basie orchestra (1)

1950
Jack Palmer orchestra (?)
Betty O'Neil (singer) (5)
Hot Lips Page (1)
Stu McKay Quintet (1)
WPIX studio band (16+)

1951
Stu McKay Quintet (8)
Art Mooney orchestra (6)
Don Costa orchestra (1)

1952
Irene Manning (singer) (2)
Peanuts Hucko (3)
Lee Castle (4)
Jimmy McPartland band (4)
Harry Lookofsky - soloist (8)

1953
Harry Lookofsky - soloist (7)
Ernie Stewart orchestra (3)

1954
Tommy Dorsey orchestra (4+)
Ernie Burnett (2)
Al Gentile orchestra (3)
Guy Lombardo orchestra (2)
Betty Peterson (O'Hara) (singer) (2)
Marian McPartland/Paul Whiteman (1)

1955
Al Gentile orchestra (12+)
Tony Pastor orchestra (6)
Woody Herman orchestra (1)
Sonny Calella (singer) (2)

Sol Yaged (2)
Paul Whiteman orchestra (1)

1956
Tommy Dorsey orchestra (4)
Art DePew orchestra (2)
Stan Rubin band (3)
Bobby Hackett sextet (20+)

1958
Rex Stewart band (9)
Lee Castle band (2)

1959
Pat Boone TV Show (?)
Nat Pierce orchestra (4)
Washington concert band (3+)

1960
Ethel Smith (trio) (9)
Red Nichols sextet (1)
Gus Bivona orchestra (5)

1961
Rex Stewart band (5)
Swinging Mothers orchestra (1)
Art DePew orchestra (1)
Murray (McEachern?) band (7)
Kay Carlson rehearsal band
    (many from 1961 onwards)

1962
Jacques LaFarge (1)
Chalprin (?) (2)
Leith Stevens (short film prelude)

1963 onwards
Kay Carlson rehearsal band
    and Dick Cary Octet

1966
Ron Bartlee trio (6)
Art DePew orchestra (?)

1967
Lex Golden Octet (1)
Bill Page orchestra (1+)

1968
Bob Esser orchestra (30)
Carol Love (singer) (1)

1973
Bob Havens (11)
Peanuts Hucko (1)

1974
Buddy Carroll (singer) (1)
Joe Venuti (requested arr's)

1976
Gary Foster orchestra (1)
Bob Esser orchestra (8)
Abe Most orchestra (1)
Don Waldrup (4 tuba concert) (1)

1977
Lucy Ann Polk (singer) (1)
Bill Hill orchestra (5)
River College Youth Band (4)

1978
River College Youth Band (2)

1979
George West (?) (2)

1980
"Tenspeed & Brown Shoes" TV (2)
Musky Ruffo band (2)

1982
Klaus Bader band (2)

1986
Mac McReynolds Planes of Fame
  orchestra (many)

1987
Abe Most orchestra (1)

1993
Cassie Miller (singer) (17)
The Royal Blue Melodians (7)
Banu Gibson (singer) (1)

Appendix Four

ORIGINAL COMPOSITIONS RECORDED AND/OR PUBLISHED

(Dick Cary's ASCAP number was 2776800)

This is a partial listing of Dick Cary compositions, based upon known recordings and Cary's own notes. Co-composers are shown, as are the recording artist and the year of recording. Publishers are named in brief where known, with the full names listed at the end, together with a few notes on royalty payments.

The titles Cary composed for the rehearsal band and which were recorded by the Tuesday Night Friends or by Jim Turner are included in this list. However, no attempt has been made to list the hundreds of other compositions which Cary wrote for that band.

Title	Co-composer	Publisher	Recorded
Agora		Cary	
Albatross, The	Jimmy McPartland	Marks	Jimmy McPartland 1957, Bobby Hackett 1957, Eddie Condon 1958
And the Sky Was Blue	Joan Tratner	Cary	
Another January		Cary	Dick Cary 1993
April Mood	Bud Freeman	Beatrice	Bud Freeman 1957
Are You Here	Pee Wee Russell	Vernon	Pee Wee Russell 1959
As I Have Indicated		Maggio	
At Christmas	Ted Easton		Ted Easton 1975
Ballad		Maggio	
Ballad for Eddie			Jack Lesberg 1977, Rick Fay 1991
Bayou Lafourche			Pud Brown 1977
B-e-t-t-y O'H-a-r-a		Cary	Dick Cary 1997
Between Prone and Supine		Cary	Dick Cary 1997
Black Shadow		Cary	Dick Cary 1993
Blue Echo	Rex Stewart		Rex Stewart 1958
Bud		Cary	Dick Cary 1993
But Why	Pee Wee Russell	Vernon	Pee Wee Russell 1959
Cary Me Back to Old Kaminsky	Max Kaminsky	Crestwood	Max Kaminsky 1954
Catching Up		Cary	Dick Cary 1997
Chang Mai	Max Kaminsky		Max Kaminsky 1959
Chase, The (Tidal Wave)		Maggio	
Cross Eyed Penguin		Beatrice	Dick Cary 1958
Cutie Pie	Pee Wee Russell	Vernon	Pee Wee Russell 1959
Danzon d'Amor	Rex Stewart		Rex Stewart 1958
Darts		Cary	
December Song		Cary	Dick Cary 1997
Dialogue		Maggio	
Ding		Cary	Dick Cary 1993
Dixieland Mambo	Lee Castle		Lee Castle 1954
Doctor Salkin		Cary	Jim Turner 1994

444

Duisenpoot		Cary	Jim Turner 1994
Eddie and the Milkman	Eddie Condon /Jack Lazar		Eddie Condon 1958
Ellen			Dick Cary 1980
Far East Mood	Max Kaminsky		Max Kaminsky 1959
Florence Off Ramp			Barney Bigard 1973
Forty-Seventh Street		Cary	Jim Turner 1994
Fritz		Cary	Dick Cary 1993
Fugue		Cary	Dick Cary 1993
Funky Blues	Ethel Smith	Ethel Smith	Ethel Smith 1959
Gal Has a Way, A	Bud Freeman	Embassy	
Gentlemen's Blues	Bud Freeman		Bud Freeman 1959 (note 1)
Georgia Sketches	Rex Stewart		Rex Stewart 1958
Ginger Brown	Bud Freeman	Tee Pee Music	Bud Freeman 1957, Eddie Condon 1956/58
Go, Go, Go	Max Kaminsky	Crestwood	Max Kaminsky 1953
Going No Place			1960
Gramercy Park		Cary	Dick Cary 1997
Gwenders		Cary	Jim Turner 1994
Handle With Cary			Bobby Hackett 1957
Hanid	Bud Freeman		Bud Freeman 1957
Henry		Cary	Dick Cary 1993
Henry Hudson		Ardmore	Bobby Hackett 1957
Holiday Hop			Bobby Hackett b/cast 1957
Idyl		Cary	Jim Turner 1994
In an Ellingtone		Cary	
Jazz on the Campus	Max Kaminsky	Crestwood	Max Kaminsky 1954
Junket to Plunkett's, A	Bud Freeman	Embassy	
Just One Minute	Max Kaminsky		Max Kaminsky 1959
Keep Movin'	Jimmy McPartland	Marks	
Kreik		Cary	Dick Cary 1993
Lackadaisy Lazy	Jimmy McPartland	Marks	Jimmy McPartland 1957
Last Mile		Beatrice	Dick Cary 1958
Late Sunday		Cary	Dick Cary 1997
Little Eddie's Song		Cary	Dick Cary 2000
Logan Square	Jimmy McPartland	Marks	(note 2)
M and M		Cary	Dick Cary 1993
Mpingo		Maggio	
Missy	Pee Wee Russell	Vernon	Pee Wee Russell 1959
Montevideo	Bud Freeman	Embassy	Tommy Dorsey 1954
Mood in Blue	Lee Castle		Lee Castle 1954 (note 3)
My Kind of Gal (w/m)			Rex Stewart 1958
Newport News	Bud Freeman	Woodward	Bud Freeman 1957, Eddie Condon 1958
Night Life			Harry Lookofsky b/cast 1952
Oh No!	Pee Wee Russell	Vernon	Pee Wee Russell 1959
On the Saalburg			Dick Cary 1975 unissued

Title	Composer/Artist	Publisher	Recording
Oofy		Cary	Dick Cary 1997
Pee Wee's Song	Pee Wee Russell	Vernon	Pee Wee Russell 1959
Pong		Cary	Dick Cary 1993
Portrait of Eddie, A (see Ballad for Eddie)			
Pretty Ditty	Rex Stewart		Rex Stewart 1958
Quiet Sea	Joan Tratner	Cary	
Red Hill	Jimmy McPartland	Marks	
Reminiscing	Jimmy McPartland	Marks	
Reverend's in Town, The	Bud Freeman	Tee Pee	Dick Cary 1957, Bud Freeman 1957
Rialto		Cary	Jim Turner 1994, Dick Cary 1997
Russian Roulette		Maggio	
Samat Joy Blues	Max Kaminsky	Crestwood	Max Kaminsky 1953
Saucy, Sassy, Saucy, Sassy Sue	Al Trace/Laura Adams	Playhouse	Dick Cary 1979
Sea of Cortez		Cary	Jim Turner 1994, Dick Cary 1997
September Etude		Cary	Dick Cary 1997
Seven Card Stud		Cary	Jim Turner 1994
Sgt. Pee Wee		Cary	Dick Cary 1997
Sleepwalkers, The		Cary	Dick Cary 2000
Slings and Arrows			Barney Bigard 1977
Soul Bass		Maggio	
Spinning (Spinney)			Bobby Hackett b/cast 1957
Swing Down in New Orleans (w/m)			Pud Brown 1977, Chuck Conklin 1978, Doc Cheatham 1988, etc
Tent Blues		Cary	Dick Cary 2000
Third Street Blues	Jimmy McPartland	Marks	Jimmy McPartland 1957, Eddie Condon 1958
This Is It	Pee Wee Russell	Vernon	Pee Wee Russell 1959
Thursday Blues		Cary	Dick Cary 1993
Time Carries On	Eddie Condon		Eddie Condon 1949 (note 4)
Time for One More		Chamber	John Glasel 1959
Time Is Right, The	Bud Freeman	Embassy	Tommy Dorsey 1954
Touché		Beatrice	Dick Cary 1958
Tuxford		Cary	Dick Cary 1993
Twelve/Eight		Maggio	
Two Channel Blues	Bud Freeman	Beatrice	Bud Freeman 1958 (note 5)
Vallen's Waltz		Cary	Dick Cary 1993
Vikki		Chamber	John Glasel 1959
Waltz for Judy		Cary	Jim Turner 1994
Wampum	Barney Bigard		Barney Bigard 1973
Warm for June		Cary	Dick Cary 2000
Way, The	Bud Freeman	Beatrice	Bud Freeman 1957
We're Through	Bud Freeman		Bud Freeman 1959 (note 6)

Whatever Turns You On		Maggio	
What's That You're Playing			Dick Cary 1981
Whistle Stop	Jimmy McPartland	Marks	Jimmy McPartland 1957
White April		Cary	Dick Cary 1997
Windmill on a Hill	Johnny DeVries	Cary	
8th Avenue Rag		Cary	Dick Cary 1993

Notes:
1: *Gentlemen's Blues* also credited to Jimmy Jones, Leonard Gaskin & George Wettling.
2: *Logan Square* is credited to McPartland-Cary for the E.B. Marks book, but the Eddie Condon recording shows the composers as [Jimmy] McPartland—[Bill] Priestley.
3: *Mood in Blue* also credited to Virginia Canyon.
4: *Time Carries On* label credits Condon as composer and Cary as arranger.
5: *Two Channel Blues* also credited to Al Hall & George Wettling.
6: *We're Through* also credited to Arnie Freeman.

Publishers
Ardmore: Ardmore Music Corporation (1957)
Beatrice: Beatrice Music Corporation (1958)
Cary: The Dick Cary Music Library
Chamber: Chamber Music Library (1961)
Crestwood: Crestwood Music Publications (1953/1955)
Ethel Smith: Ethel Smith Music Corporation (1959)
Maggio: Maggio Music Press (1972)
Marks: Edward B. Marks Music Corporation
Playhouse: Playhouse Music Company (1979)
Tee Pee: Tee Pee Music Company (Teddy Powell) (1957)
Vernon: Vernon Music Corporation (1958/1959)
Woodward: Woodward Music, Inc. (1959)
It is not known if Cornucopia Publishing, the Dick Cary / Rex Stewart enterprise, published any music.

Instrumentals and Songs Presumed Lost:

instrumentals
Bar Fly	Compo Beach	Don't Answer	Home and Country
Humphrey's House	Indubitable, The	Larson E. Whipsnade	Mars Rock
Moby	Now's the Time	Out Tate	Red Run
Spence de Fence	Swiss Kriss (with Bobby Hackett)		Tabs
Up the Podium	Who Was It Last Night		

lyrics by Ralph Besse
Why Did You Take My Love   You Made Me Cry

lyric by Dick Cary?
When Loves Comes Along

lyrics by Johnny DeVries
Franklin and Winnie and Joe
Rockabye Baby on the Be-Bop
Streetcar Named Desire
Whatever Happened to the Big Bands

Peanut Brittle Time
Sacre Coeur de Moonlight
Sweet Daddy

Richard Cory

lyric by Arnie Freeman
Don't Be Ridiculous, Nicholas

lyric by Nellie Mae Leonard and Ruth Simpson
Bridge in the Mist

lyrics by Joan Tratner (contract signed with Janco Music Inc)
Dark Night   You—You Are My Living Soul

Dick Cary's Music

In his Klavier notes, Jim Turner refers to the sheer quantity of Cary's writing: "He wrote over 3,200 arrangements for jazz bands.

"Here are the staggering statistics about the original manuscripts at Cary's home in Sunland, California, when he died in April, 1994."

      19   Folios of arrangements, ranging in size from 25 to 800 selections
      81   Cartons of music with about 1,500 sheets of music each
  1,856   Original compositions known
  3,211   Total arrangements cataloged to date (1999)
120,000   Estimated number of sheets of music manuscript, mostly believed to have been created since 1960. That equals 9 pages of music for every day of Dick Cary's life since 1960.
       0   Number of computers used

"And that is not all the music Dick Cary wrote! Those who knew him before he moved to California in 1959 say Cary may have written just as much music in New York as he did in California."

One can understand why Cary complained about the rising cost of music manuscript paper!

Refer also to website—www.dickcary.com

                                 *   *   *   *   *   *   *

Royalty Payments

Among Dick Cary's papers were a few relating to royalty payments. These are listed below for general interest.

October 11, 1955:   Crestwood Music Publications, period ending June 30, 1955: Go, Go, Go Ford Motors Film Commercial, Royalty $500.00. Cary share: $125.00.

June 30, 1958:	Ardmore Music Corp. royalty period ending June 30, 1958: "Mechanical Income" (50%) $13.31.
1958:	Tee Pee Music Co. royalty statement for Ginger Brown period July 1, 1957 thru December 31, 1957: $135.62 — 25% = $33.90. period January 1, 1958 thru June 30, 1958: $133.61— 25% = $33.40.
January 6, 1959:	Woodward Music Inc. Royalty Statement, period ending June 30, 1958: M-G-M Records (Eddie Condon), Newport News, copies sold 887. $4.28 to Bud Freeman, $4.28 to Dick Cary.
June 30, 1959:	Eddie and the Milkman (Eddie Condon), copies sold 887. Royalty due $8.87; one-third to Eddie Condon, Jack Lazar, Richard Cary—$2.85.
January 1, 1960:	from Edward B. Marks, 3 years royalties (1957/58/59) for Jimmy McPartland's Dixieland Series originals and three Chorale Preludes, $555.52
December 6, 1996:	ASCAP statement of Foreign Incoming Distribution for Wampum (Britain 1995)—$4.62
June 1996:	Vernon Music Corporation royalty statement January to June 1996:

Missy	$3.12
This Is It	$2.76 (Germany)
Oh No!	$34.71 (Canada, Germany, Scandinavia)

The original agreement for Oh No! was signed with Bregman, Vocco & Conn, Inc.

Appendix Five

A SURVEY OF DICK CARY'S RECORDINGS

Readers may find it helpful to read these notes in conjunction with the Discography.

The Dick Cary discography contains many recordings of little or no interest in the Cary oeuvre. For example, in the album by the Dawn of the Century Ragtime Orchestra (Arcane, 1975), which is an interesting look back at pre-jazz roots, he is just one of two trumpeters in the ensemble. He fulfils the same role in an excellent LP by Eddie Miller (Blue Angel Jazz Club, 1971). Then there are various single releases, such Mike Riley (M-G-M, 1949), Eddie Condon (Atlantic, 1949), Wingy Manone (Atlantic, 1953), Jeff Stoughton (Preview, 1953), Bob Wilber (Cub, 1958), and Chuck Conklin (Angel City, 1978) which are of limited merit, as too are the many releases on the round-dance label, Hi Hat. Not every record listed has been auditioned, but it is not anticipated that those unheard will demand inclusion in this review.

Of the LPs and CDs discussed below availability will be a problem. Some will be obtainable on CD, but many will have to be sought through specialist dealers in used records; via record dealers on the Internet; or from your local friendly collector.

Now for a look at what the writer considers to be the more significant recordings of the Dick Cary career.

Dick Cary acquits himself well as pianist on his first recording session in July 1942, which was with Joe Marsala for Decca. Four early jazz standards are given a relaxed interpretation by seven seasoned musicians. Similarly, with Marsala in February 1944, Cary has creditable solos on *Four or Five Times* and *Wolverine Blues*, plays a sympathetic opening chorus on *Blues in C*, and helps to push along the ensembles on *Weary Blues*.

The two issued piano titles (with drums accompaniment) from March 1944 are indicative of things to come. Cary thoughtfully selects two Rodgers and Hart songs, showing a good left-hand on *I Thought About You* and swinging hard on *You Took Advantage of Me*.

1944 recordings with Muggy Spanier and 1945 with Wild Bill Davison are not outstanding, but he plays powerful trumpet on two of the Eddie Condon Blue Network broadcasts, as well as receiving credit for writing various backgrounds. It is not until 1946 that we first hear his work on alto-horn—*Thou Swell*, by the Billy Butterfield orchestra.

The Louis Armstrong Town Hall concert of May 1947 is one of the great jazz concerts, in which Cary was proud to have participated. He makes his contribution on piano, though he was very much the junior member of the band. On *I Can't Give You Anything But Love,* Louis, unable to remember his name, calls, "Take it, piano!" He was in the same junior position with the Armstrong All-Stars later in the year. Listen to the All-Stars records for the work of Armstrong and Teagarden, but do not expect too much of Mr. Cary.

Of no great distinction are the Dixieland recordings for Columbia by Jimmy Dorsey and his so-called Original Dorseyland Jazz Band, though Cary's arrangements of these "good-old-good-ones" contain some deft touches. For example, the clarinet/piano closing to *Tin Roof Blues* and the two trombone effect on *When You Wore a Tulip* and other titles.

It is interesting to hear Cary's version of be-bop piano on *Ornithology*, playing with Charlie Parker at a Jerry Jerome concert in March 1952, and he is in fine form on a $5^{1}/2$-minute *I Never Knew* from a Jerry Jerome jam session—to quote notator Ross Firestone, "It's good to hear those flowing choruses by Dick Cary."

Other recordings from the 1950s show seasoned professionals playing a variety of material, generally speaking to a high standard, but not requiring any detailed mention of Dick Cary's playing. Albums by Walt Gifford (Delmar, 1954), Jimmy McPartland/Dizzy Gillespie (M-G-M, 1952), Rex Stewart (Felsted, 1958) and Bob Wilber (Classic Editions, 1959) come into this category, as do such items as broadcast excerpts by Eddie Condon and George Wettling on Storyville (1952).

The Lee Castle recordings for Davis in 1954 and 1957, featuring the leader's forthright trumpet playing, include two Castle-Cary originals, and some good arranging touches by Cary. It sounds like Cary's scoring on *Fair Jennie's Lament* and the long, nearly $4^{1}/2$ minutes, *Mood in Blue* is just that, a slow blues-y original, with a good theme, well-arranged and containing an excellent Cary piano solo.

Also in 1954, November, Jack Teagarden made three sessions for Period which rate among the best of his later recordings. Teagarden, clarinetists Ed Hall and up-and-coming Kenny Davern, and lesser-known trumpeter Fred Greenleaf are each in splendid form, but Cary has no problem maintaining the standard set, particularly by Big Tea and Ed Hall. He plays piano on one date, trumpet on a second and arranged all three. On piano his work behind the ensemble and soloists on *High Society*, as well as his backing Teagarden's vocal on *Mis'ry and the Blues* should be noted. On trumpet the high points include his muted work on *Blue Funk* and his playing, both muted and open, on *Meet Me Where They Play the Blues*.

Davenport Blues gets a special mention, being well-scored and showcasing Cary's strong, melodic trumpet playing. The *Down Beat* review said: "Cary's piano and trumpet work is solid, at times imaginative."

In 1954 two Bud Freeman-Dick Cary originals were recorded by the Tommy Dorsey orchestra and issued on Columbia, *The Time Is Right* and *Rhumba Montevideo*. This is a rare opportunity to hear Cary's arrangements played by a regular working big band, making one regret that he never became a staff arranger for such a unit.

During the 1950s Cary was a regular with veterans Bud Freeman, Max Kaminsky, Jimmy McPartland and Pee Wee Russell. He played with Bud Freeman for sessions on five different record labels, though he was not always featured, as mentioned in Chapter 7 in connection with the quartet titles for Capitol in 1953. Similarly, the only surprise with the band sides for Victor in March and April 1957 is that Cary the pianist is ignored. He is heard only on alto-horn, in unison with Freeman, on the theme for a Gerry Mulligan-style *The Reverend's in Town*. Again, on the four Harmony titles, also recorded in April, it is not until the final *Odd Aardvark* that he is heard, playing a tidy piano introduction.

Any merit in the Bud Freeman Dot sessions of February 1959 is hidden by poor balance and sound, plus an unsatisfactory singer on four of the titles. The quartet session of June 1957 for Stere-o-Craft does at least allow one to hear Cary as a tasteful and satisfying pianist.

Cary's association with clarinetist Pee Wee Russell included writing the arrangements for a March 1954 session organised by pianist and promoter George Wein and to be issued under Russell's name on Wein's own label, Storyville. At the time the Wein band was playing at the Basin Street club in New York, with Al Drootin on clarinet. Cary's deft voicings and outlines are evident on all six titles, including the Russell original, a good blues, *Missy*.

Five years later Russell had an album on the Dot label which featured twelve of his original compositions. Cary makes little impact as pianist, but does as the arranger, adapting Russell's collection of melodious themes (attractive riff tunes, catchy rhythm numbers, ballad, blues) for a band, which also included Buck Clayton, Vic Dickenson and Bud Freeman. Although all the tunes are shown on the record as Russell compositions, at least five were copyrighted at the time as by Russell-Cary. Subsequently on a few others they are shown as joint composers, including the well-known *Pee Wee's Blues*, a favourite of such clarinetists as Kenny Davern, Bobby Gordon and Joe Muranyi.

Max Kaminsky, a most impressive small-band trumpeter, had record dates for M-G-M in 1953 and Victor in 1954 and both the resulting albums were worthy additions to the Kaminsky and Cary discographies. Apart from a piano solo on *Royal Garden Blues*, Cary's main contribution to the M-G-M sessions are his pleasing arrangements (note *I've Got the World on a String*). Much the same can be said of "Jazz on the Campus Ltd," Kaminsky's album for Victor. Cary shows his Teddy Wilson roots on this album, puts some neat alto-horn interjections into *Shim-Me-Sha-Wabble* and is scintillating on piano throughout *If I Had My Way*. There are a total of four worthy Kaminsky-Cary originals, including the cheerful *Go, Go, Go* which Kaminsky sold to Ford Motors. (Eddie Condon said the title *Carey Me Back to Old Kaminsky* "can be forgiven as long as Dick Carey (sic) doesn't stop making arrangements.")

In 1953 Cary arranged 8 titles for Jimmy McPartland's "Shades of Bix" 10-inch album, followed by a further four in 1956 when the album was expanded to 12-inch. This is an excellent tribute to the famed cornetist, with all the musicians involved playing well, confidently led by the Bix-influenced McPartland. Cary's charts capture the spirit of the original records, but the version of *In a Mist*, nearly five minutes long, is special, adding bassoon and oboe to create a sound picture from the Bix original. Refer to Chapter 8 for more background on this album. The *Down Beat* reviewer's summary of the music was: "Good taste is the tonic all the way through—the solos, Dick Cary's arrangements...."

Twenty-two years later a "Salute to Bix" album by Jimmy McPartland, with Dick Cary and the Ted Easton Jazz Band, recorded in Holland, was issued on the Riff label. This is another enjoyable set, with Cary impressive on alto-horn, as well as taking a good solo on muted trumpet on *I'm Coming Virginia*. Also on the LP is *In a Mist*, a piano solo reading by Cary.

Very different, quite modern in approach, is an album of television theme tunes recorded by Jimmy and Marian McPartland for Design in September 1960.

McPartland's album for Camden, in May 1959, contains ten old warhorses, played fortissimo and hell-for-leather, and full of energy. Cary contributes alto-horn to two numbers and can be heard beavering away on piano in the background on three others, and no doubt he contributed the useful variations to the stock arrangements. Digby Fairweather in "Rough Guide to Jazz" called this "another superb Dixieland session with Dick Cary arrangements."

Less frantic are the two good but underrated McPartland sessions for Epic in February and March 1957, with Cary, on piano and alto-horn, and Tyree Glenn on trombone in particularly fine form. The piano solos on *Third Street*

Blues and *Original Dixieland One Step* rate special attention, while Dick Sudhalter has pointed out that Cary's solo on *Sugar Foot Strut* reflected his admiration for modernists like Horace Silver. There are also four McPartland-Cary originals which, as Sudhalter suggests, are good enough to have become standards in an earlier jazz age.

Background to "The Music Man" recordings will be found at the end of Chapter 10, making the reader aware that this is one of the classic Cary albums, for which his arrangements have been rightly praised. "A supreme example of Cary's talents as an arranger," was Digby Fairweather's opinion. Recorded in December 1957 and January 1958, as Jimmy McPartland's All Stars, they feature many of the best musicians then playing in New York.

The Eddie Condon session of November 1953 had Cary playing both trumpet and piano on an exciting *Jam Session Blues/Ole Miss*, which Condon had instructed the band to make as respectable as possible! Cary trades fours with Gene Schroeder on piano and plays two excellent trumpet solos.

Cary seemed to save many of his best alto-horn performances for Eddie Condon groups. From the April 1955 session of Beiderbecke-related songs both *Royal Garden Blues* and *I'll Be a Friend With Pleasure* are recommended as examples. Better, however, are the June 1954 titles from the "Jammin' at Condon's" album, which feature the "house ensemble" (Davison, Cutshall, Ed Hall) with a second front-line (Butterfield, McGarity, Hucko), plus two guests (Cary, Freeman). It is on the justly popular *How Come You Do Me Like You Do* that he makes his famous clinker, after which Condon threatens to send him to Lake Placid! Cary is soloing rather well on this 13-minute stroll until he reaches the end of his break.

The sextet which Bobby Hackett led at the Henry Hudson Hotel during 1956 and 1957 was one of the highlights of Dick Cary's career. His work on alto-horn and piano is featured, as are his arrangements and originals. *Henry Hudson* and *Handle With Cary* are fine examples of the latter. *Caravan* is a feature for his alto-horn and was to become a fixture in his repertoire. *In a Little Spanish Town*, with its *Salt Peanuts* references, illustrates the humorous side of his arranging skill. These factors, combined with a steady engagement, Hackett's willingness to use any arrangements which Cary offered and the versatility of the musicians, contributed to the band's success. Cary seldom enjoyed such artistic freedom and despite the musicians' reservations, the Capitol session is a first-rate example of the band's excellence.

The three albums taken from the AFRS transcriptions of the "Bandstand U.S.A." broadcasts (later to be consolidated into a 2-CD set on Lonehill Jazz) offer a broader view of the sextet's repertoire, including the opportunity to hear the personnel with reedmen Bob Wilber and Dick Hafer. Unfortunately the sound quality of these recordings is not up to the standard of those on Capitol, but they should be heard, as a reminder of this unique band and Cary's major part in it. More information about Bobby Hackett's sextet, including Cary's arrangements and original compositions, can be found in Chapter 9.

A long way from hot jazz are the four December 1957 titles for Capitol by Hackett and Cary, with strings and voices, but they do show two great melodic horn players combining beautifully.

Two other recordings which Cary made with Bobby Hackett were originally for transcriptions, Muzak in 1958 and Sesac in 1960. Of the Muzak Cary commented, "what we refer to as wallpaper for stores, markets, dental offices, etc." This is music "under wraps," but with Hackett, Cary, on piano, and Bill Bauer, guitar, there have to be moments of interest. Cary is on alto-horn for the Sesac LP, a pleasant enough programme of spirituals.

On the titles which Cary recorded with Barbara Lea for Prestige in 1956 and 1957, the spotlight is on Miss Lea's singing and on the trumpet playing of Johnny Windhurst, but Cary provides sympathetic moments of both piano and alto-horn accompaniments, as well as the suitable arrangements. Lea and Cary's mutual appreciation is shown by her request, 35 years later, that Cary play and arrange five titles for a 1992 session for Audiophile.

The *Georgia Sketches* suite which Rex Stewart wrote with Dick Cary for the Fletcher Henderson revival band to play at the Great South Bay Jazz Festival is in three movements, the opening two of which are short. The first, *Motion*, is perhaps more Ellington than Henderson, while the third, *The Earth Is Good*, lasts 13 minutes, has several changes of tempo and is mainly a series of solos. Cary has 16 bars on alto-horn but is rather distant. Allowing for the criticism that the band went on stage much later than planned, affording extra time for alcoholic intake, this is still impressive playing by the band as a unit and by most of the featured soloists.

Ed Hall was the essential "hot" clarinet player, one of the finest in the history of jazz, and the six titles he recorded in 1959 under his own name for Rae-Cox are among his best. Dick Cary is the pianist in Hall's quintet and is inspired to some of his finest piano playing on record.

The two albums which Cary recorded with trombonist Lou McGarity are both worth hearing as examples of prime music-making in the jazz idiom. The Quintet titles take precedence, allowing the musicians more space, with Cary contributing a number of pertinent muted trumpet interpolations to McGarity's features. Cary's presence is not so obvious on the Big Eight titles, though his arrangements are neat (cf: *Under a Blanket of Blue*). He plays muted trumpet to Doc Severinsen's open on *Blue Lou* and alto-horn in a duet with McGarity on *Blue Skies*.

Similar in sound, harking back to the Miles Davis "Birth of the Cool" band on Capitol, and onwards to the Tuesday Night Friends of the 1990s, were Dick Cary's "Dixieland Goes Progressive" album of June 1957 and the Johnny Glasel Brasstet of November 1959. Cary is little heard with Glasel, but his two originals and his arranging show his forward-looking intentions. The chart for *It Don't Mean a Thing* is the one he used with Bobby Hackett.

"Dixieland Goes Progressive" is also an experiment in which he applies advanced writing to six standard Dixieland numbers. Refer to Chapter 9 for comments from Gerry Mulligan and Cary himself. Listening to these titles it is not difficult to appreciate Cary's versatility, writing such arrangements in the afternoon, then dropping into Condon's club that same evening to play *Muskrat Ramble* for the umpteenth time. This album was recorded on June 11, 1957; four weeks later Bob Brookmeyer made his "Traditionalism Revisited" LP for World Pacific. Gil Evans' famous "New Bottle, Old Wine" album, also for World Pacific, on a similar theme but with a large band, was not recorded until the following year.

On June 20, 1957, Cary recorded again under his own name, playing trumpet, alto-trumpet, alto-horn and piano with a versatile all-star reed section—Bob Wilber, Al Cohn and Ernie Caceres—of which Cary makes full use. His arranging skills are applied to three of his own compositions, his and Bud Freeman's *The Reverend's Back in Town*, and four standards, including a dramatic *More Than You Know*. Good trumpet playing here. This "Hot & Cool" album is long overdue for reissue, both for its orchestrations and for the ability of all the musicians involved.

Of Joe Marsala's June 28, 1957, session on Hi-Life, Cary commented that he "...sweat several towels full—but enjoyed date." He clearly works hard, mostly on piano, with *Singin' the Blues* and *Sweet Georgia Brown* standing out on this admirable small group recording.

Eddie Condon recorded four albums with Cary in 1958 and 1959, for M-G-M, World Pacific, Dot and Warner Brothers. The M-G-M is straightforward Condon, though with a newer repertoire. Cary is on alto-horn, best heard on *St. Louis Blues*. For Pacific Jazz in May 1958 he also played alto-horn on four titles, one of which remained unissued for nearly fifty years. He takes a good solo, plus two breaks, on *Reisenweber Rag*, and trades fours with Cutty Cutshall on *Skeleton Jangle*. He is little heard on the Dot album, but does manage four piano solos on the 1959 Warner Brothers release, which was a celebration of the 20th anniversary of the "first jazz album ever recorded," George Avakian's 78rpm album on Decca, "Chicago Jazz." These are not typical Condon-type solos and he is unfazed by the fast tempo of *I've Found a New Baby* and reflective on *Someday Sweetheart*. His effort on *Oh Baby* is closer to the more modern sounds of the time.

It was disappointing that when Cary was asked to make an album for a major company, in this case Columbia, in October 1959, he should be saddled with non-copyright songs, and a banjo. It is difficult to believe that Cary would have chosen to use such Stephen Foster-type material, especially as it precluded the use of any of his originals. In the circumstances the musicians, and the leader, do the best that they can. Cary's trumpet playing is sound and his arrangements have some clever touches, with *I Dream of Jeannie With the Light Brown Hair* notable.

Cary's main contribution to the Westminster album by Max Kaminsky are his arrangements. Those for *Henderson Stomp*, *Far East Mood*, *Bye Bye Blackbird* and *Just a Minute* are noteworthy. The two-clarinet work on *Eccentric* echoes the 1953 M-G-M recording by Kaminsky. Cary plays piano, alto-horn and trumpet on the sessions, splitting trumpet choruses (Cary is muted) with Kaminsky on *Far East Mood* and piano choruses with Dave McKenna on *Eccentric Rag*. Much of Cary's playing is lost in the ensembles, though that does not detract from another excellent record.

The first studio recording made by Dick Cary after his arrival in Los Angeles in 1960 was with The Kings of Dixieland for an album aimed at the then popular "Dixieland" market, with short playing times and banjo and tuba on four titles He is not well featured, but of his two alto-horn outings one is a chase with trombonist Moe Schneider, and on piano he provides a pertinent introduction to Matty Matlock's interesting original *Kingfish Blues*, as well as backing Matlock's clarinet solo.

In a like manner to Dick Cary's Columbia 1959 album, the 1962 recording by Eddie Condon for the Columbia subsidiary, Epic, is also hampered by unsuitable tunes such as *Dark Eyes*, *Swan Lake* and *Londonderry Air*. Regardless, Cary receives a cry of approval for his piano solo on *Dark Eyes* and his opening to the theme from *Swan Lake* is well conceived. In fact Cary is in fine form throughout the session. Writer Max Harrison, in the notes to the Mosaic set, is lukewarm about the album, ending "there is little to be said about this music." That is unfair to the musicians and he could have added that most of the songs get a much better treatment than they deserved. Musician Ron Hockett takes a differing view of the chosen tunes, pointing out that they "swing like crazy and the guys are playing QUITE seriously ... Dick (on peck horn) and Lou McGarity trade fours beautifully on *Meadowlands* after their very nice duet intro."

Eddie Condon's tour of Australasia in the spring of 1964 produced some "unofficial" records, plus the interesting CD on Chiaroscuro, recorded in Tokyo. This has the band's frontline, Buck Clayton, Vic Dickenson, Pee Wee Russell and Bud Freeman, demonstrating a satisfying consistency. In his notes Dan Morgenstern praises the rhythm section and comments: "Dick's piano interludes on *Savoy* and *Manhattan* are especially tasty, and his peck horn outings give the band an added color...." The horn outings include a worthy band version of Cary's feature number, *Caravan*, and Cary trading fours with Dickenson—and having fun—on *I Can't Believe*.

Although the Condon concert programmes listed in the discography look similar, variations do occur. For example, assuming it has not been edited, the Chiaroscuro version of *When You're Smiling* lasts for just 2:31 minutes, but that on the private tape of the March 14 concert in Australia lasts twice as long, with Cary, on piano, taking an excellent solo and digging in behind Pee Wee Russell. (Condon, quoted in the Australian press, said his success was due to his group of "well-seasoned players. I only call the tune and take the praise. It's really cheating.")

In 1968, 1969 and 1970 Cary was heard in relaxed mood on several tracks included on albums issued from the annual jazz parties of the Blue Angel Jazz Club. On alto-horn there is his feature *Caravan*, and on trumpet he is heard best soloing during Matty Matlock's unusual arrangement of *Ida Sweet as Apple Cider*. On piano he takes a reflective solo on *Black and Blue* and a good one at faster tempo on *Wolverine Blues*. His arrangements for a medium-size band, *Blues My Naughty Sweetie Gave to Me* and *Save It, Pretty Mama*, are interesting and worth hearing.

Also on the Blue Angel Jazz Club label, recorded in 1971, is a top rate album featuring tenor sax star Eddie Miller. Dick Cary is in the two-trumpet team, alongside Jack Coon but, as with The Dawn of the Century Ragtime Orchestra album from 1975, these are strictly band appearances. (Though one suspects that perhaps Cary plays the second trumpet solo on *I'm Gonna Stomp Mr. Henry Lee*).

Arbors ARCD 19284 was recorded at Sunnie's Rendezvous in Aspen, Colorado, in 1969, a club run by Ralph Sutton's wife, Sunnie. It is an opportunity to hear Cary featured on trumpet and alto-horn with his friend Ralph Sutton, but Cary is not at his most confident and it is Sutton who is the star of the CD.

As well as Cary's own session for Famous Door, other small band recording sessions made in Hollywood during the 1970s and early 1980s included those with Barney Bigard, for RCA, Jack Lesberg, also for Famous Door, Pud Brown for Brown's own label, Maxim Saury for the French company, Black and Blue, and Pee Wee Erwin for Qualtro music. Regular colleagues such as Bob Havens, Eddie Miller, Ray Sherman and Nick Fatool play with him on various of these records.

"Easy on the Ears," the Bigard LP (1973) is, naturally, a feature for the leader's clarinet playing, with Cary contributing two originals as well as satisfying cameos on trumpet, alto-horn and piano. *Florence Off Ramp* is perhaps the better of his compositions, but his alto-horn playing is impressive on *Slings and Arrows*, aided by a fine rhythm section. *Wampum* is a joint Bigard-Cary tune which has much in common with Sidney Bechet's *Egyptian Fantasy*.

For the Jack Lesberg Sextet (1977) session, Cary provides several trumpet solos, mainly muted. His arrangements are loose, with that for *Stomp Mr. Henry Lee* providing a fresh take on the Condon-Teagarden original and it is good to hear his *Ballad for Eddie* tribute, played by tenor saxophonist Eddie Miller himself.

Pud Brown's album of December 1977 on his own "New Orleans Jazz" label, has eight veterans of the Los Angeles jazz scene in a relaxed session which includes seven originals by members of the group, plus three standards which should be heard more often. This is excellent listening. Less interesting is the Maxine Saury session of 1981, perhaps because the French clarinetist, a traditionalist, does not gel with the rest of the band. Cary's best alto-horn outing is on *Sweet Georgia Brown*, while *Together* provides a good opportunity to hear his forceful trumpet lead.

More enjoyable is the Pee Wee Erwin session from 1980, despite the fact that Cary as pianist has limited opportunities to shine. He takes acceptable solos on *Farewell Blues* and *It Don't Mean a Thing*, and there is a tasteful three-minute trumpet/piano duet on *Monday Date* by Erwin and Cary which one wishes had lasted longer.

Cary considered that his own session for Famous Door in June 1981 could have been better. There are some nice arranging touches, but there is a kind of West Coast "cool" about the eight songs, with seven of them lasting between 5 and 7 minutes. One suspects that Sy Oliver's *Dream of You* is perhaps closest to Cary's aims, with its sympathetic arrangement and good solos from the frontline.

The recordings which Cary made in Europe during the 1970s and 1980s are a mixed bag, with those made in Holland for Ted Easton amongst the best. Mention has already been made of the "Salute to Bix" album with Jimmy McPartland, while the LP titled "The Amazing Dick Cary" from October 1975 is also to be recommended. The recording balance for the four titles with the

Easton band does not favour Cary's trumpet playing, though he solos well on alto-trumpet on *Somebody Stole My Gal*, but there are four other titles by just trios or quartets. Three contain fine alto-horn solos (*What's New?, Sleighride in July, You Brought a New Kind of Love to Me*) and the fourth, *Save It, Pretty Mama*, illustrates Easton's enthusiasm for multi-tracking, utilising Cary's versatility on trumpet, alto-horn and piano. "Rough Guide to Jazz" (Digby Fairweather) says: "Cary plays beautifully, including a faultless interpretation of Burke and Van Heusen's seldom heard *Sleighride in July*..."

The all-vocal Nat Gonella LP, October 1975, with Cary on piano, plus the Easton band, is a Christmas album, with the inherent drawbacks that implies. Cary thought that the duet which he and Nat did on the Mel Torme composition, *The Christmas Song*, was "quite a version," but it is not really that. However, the pleasant Cary-Easton song, *At Christmas*, has a good piano contribution.

It is a unfortunate that so much Cary material recorded by the late Ted Easton remains unissued. As the discography shows, there are many titles which include Ralph Sutton, and nothing from the 1977 dates was released.

One of the better bands that Cary worked with was the Milan College Jazz Society, led by guitarist Lino Patruno, during the 1975 tour with Jimmy McPartland. The recordings for Carosello afford the opportunity to hear him on F-trumpet (*New Orleans, Caprice in Milan* ...) and soloing well on piano in a duet with McPartland *(Davenport Blues)*.

The bands in Germany were of variable quality and of the five which recorded with Cary, three used a banjo, leading to Cary's heartfelt cry, "Thank God, no banjo tonight." Only four titles with the Flat Foot Stompers, three by the Darktown Jazz Band (including a nice alto-trumpet, with rhythm, feature on *Baby, Won't You Please Come Home?*), and one by the Barrelhouse Jazzband (F-trumpet on *St. James Infirmary Blues*) were released. The Polydor double-album by the Old Merry Tale Jazzband in 1977 can be noted for Cary's alto-horn on Jelly Roll Morton's *Get the Bucket, Shine* and *Lonesome Road*, as well as the two alto-horn features, with rhythm only, *Please* and *Crazy Rhythm*. In addition, there is the *Echo of Spring* piano solo and a version of Cary's song, *Swing Down in New Orleans*.

Cary is on four albums issued by The Chicagoans, a group led by reedman Klaus Bader, two being made in 1977. One was taped at the Revolutionary Club and Cary was critical of this engagement ("awful place to play ... was our worst night by far"), yet his playing gives no indication of this. Despite a noisy audience and a not always sympathetic drummer, he plays a good piano accompaniment to singer Beryl Bryden on *Please Don't Talk About Me When I'm Gone*, plus satisfactory trumpet and alto-horn contributions

(*Margie*, for instance) elsewhere. The other 1977 session, for AGM, also has *Echo of Spring*, and more good work on piano on *Ain't Misbehavin,'* plus an alto saxophone/piano duet on *Misty*.

The 1982 LP on BAD has less to commend it, but the WSO from 1980 has another version of *Swing Down in New Orleans*, also with a Cary vocal; *Can't We Be Friends?* with a worthwhile piano solo; and an alto-horn, with rhythm, feature on Cary's pleasant theme, *Ellen*.

From his 1981 British tour with Keith Smith only three titles were released, on Smith's own labels. Two of them were piano solos, another version of *Echo of Spring*, plus a short sketch on Phineas Newborn's *Love Stream*.

While one may have reservations about many of the musicians with whom Cary worked and recorded during his European tours, these additions to his discography do give the chance to hear him in a variety of settings.

Similarly, his appearance at the week-long Australian Jazz Convention of 1976, to judge by the two broadcast sets and the album by The World's Hottest Jazz Band this writer has heard, saw him enthusiastically taking part in typical manner in these loosely organised proceedings. The World's Hottest LP includes the piano solo *Phineas Newborn Jr.'s Waltz*, showing his continuing admiration for the work of Mr. Newborn, plus a piano outing on Willie "The Lion" Smith's *Fingerbuster*, with musical interjections by the band.

Singing the Blues from the Ojai Jazz Festival of 1979, on Town Hall label, is an excellent feature for Dick Cary, accompanied by a rhythm section. This is a recommended example of his dexterity on the alto-horn.

A disappointment is the album recorded in 1985 by Mac McReynolds Planes of Fame Orchestra, a big band with which Cary worked and arranged for a time. Other than the "E flat peck horn" solo on *Poor Butterfly*, Cary is little heard on this undistinguished LP. The following year he had few opportunities on four titles with Jackie Coon (*Sea Breeze*, 1986). There is also a late 1960s album for Maximus, "Have a Good Time With Big George Bruns," which can be safely ignored.

When Gösta Hägglöf booked Dick Cary for concerts in Stockholm in 1988, with Doc Cheatham, and in 1989, he also recorded him for his "Kenneth" label. The 1988 album was a tribute to Louis Armstrong, with Doc Cheatham's trumpet playing and confidential vocals featured, though Cary takes a number of suitable piano solos. Of *Save It, Pretty Mama*, an established favourite of Cary's, Hägglöf writes: "Note that piano introduction!" In addition, this number, arranged by Cary, has an attractive solo, and one can pinpoint *I'm in the Mood for Love* as another worthy of mention. Listening to these it is difficult to understand how such an accomplished pianist could underestimate his own abilities. (Refer to "Imagined failings" in Appendix 1.)

From the 1988 sessions there came another version of the Cary song, *Swing Down in New Orleans*, but this time with the vocal by Doc Cheatham.

It was nearly twenty years before the 1989 recording of a tribute to Hoagy Carmichael was released, on a CD. This was under Cary's name, affording examples of his exemplary playing, in his seventies, on his three main instruments. Particularly worth hearing are *One Morning in May*, where he solos on alto-horn and piano, *Ev'ntide*, where he and Bent Persson split trumpet choruses, and *What Kind o' Man Is You*, with his melodic muted-trumpet work. Another little-heard but melodious Carmichael song is *Kinda Lonesome*, which has Cary on trumpet, first stating the theme muted and closing it open. Add to which there is a delightful and extended piano solo, with rhythm, on *Little Old Lady*.

Cary's piano playing (note writer Floyd Levin refers to him as "an astute and intuitive accompanist") is also featured in the 1991 recording by Rick Fay and Friends for Arbors records. Perhaps it was a pity that he chose to record another version of *Echo of Spring* rather than something new to add to his too short a listing of recorded piano solos, but on the plus side his band arrangement of Bix Beiderbecke's *In the Dark*, though less complex, evokes memories of the classic *In a Mist*, in the 1956 Jimmy McPartland album, "Shades of Bix." Elsewhere on the CD his piano playing is heard to advantage on such titles as *Can't We Be Friends* and *Possum Jump*.

The story of Dick Cary's rehearsal bands, including the views of participants and critics, is set out in Chapter 22. The three issued CDs, recorded between 1993 and 2000, all have the same high level of music making and can be recommended as such. The record selected as one of the "important ten," listed on the following page, has been chosen solely on the basis that Cary is present as the pianist.

Important Ten

A newcomer to jazz wishing to hear a representative sampling of Dick Cary's music-making should endeavour to hear the following albums/CDs, details of which will be found in the discography. Layout is: band title / (year of recording) / original issue / latest known CD issue / album title.

Bobby Hackett and his Jazz Band (1957) Capitol T857 Mosaic MD5-210
Gotham Jazz Scene

Eddie Condon and his Band (1954) Columbia CL616 Mosaic MD5-152
Jammin' at Condon's

Jimmy McPartland and his Band (1957/58) Epic LN3463 Mosaic MD8-206
'The Music Man' Goes Dixieland

Johnny Glasel Brasstet (1959) Jazz Unlimited JA1002

Ed Hall and his Orchestra (1959) Rae-Cox LP1120 IAJRC CD-1020
Rumpus on Rampart Street

Lou McGarity Quintet (1959) Jubilee JLP1108 Lonehill LHJ10321
Some Like It Hot

Dick Cary (1957) Golden Crest CR3024
Dixieland Goes Progressive

Dick Cary (1957) Stere-o-craft RTN106
Hot & Cool

Dick Cary (1975) Riff 659.014 Progressive PCD-7125
The Amazing Dick Cary

Dick Cary Tuesday Night Friends (1993) Arbors ARCD19132
...Playing Dick Cary Originals

Appendix Six

DICK CARY—OTHER SOURCES
(excluding those named in the text)

1. School Days and The Wesleyan Serenaders

Bill was a musician of sorts…	Renee Cary, Bill's widow, e-mail, April 20, 2004
It is in a nice area on a nice quiet street…	Albert and Sara Tangarone, e-mail, September 12, 2005
Details from the 1920 Census…	Provided by Peter Hanley, e-mail August 25, 2005
Details from the 1930 Census…	Provided by Peter Hanley, e-mail August 26, 2005
Durant. That was my mother's maiden name…	Levin
There's a theory among a lot of parents…	*ibid*
She didn't approve of jazz at all…	*ibid*
I can remember the first time…	*ibid*
My mother would have me give…	*ibid*
I played in the Hartford Symphony…	*ibid*
There were three enormous high schools…	*ibid*
I didn't graduate high school…	*ibid*
There were so few people of artistic…	*ibid*
Lois Cary died on July 15, 1930…	this and other family details from Renee Cary, e-mail April 20, 2004
If my mother had lived…	Levin
His father wanted him to study mathematics…	*The South Bay Beat*, October 1978
When I was fourteen my mother died…	interview with Ken Gallacher, *Jazz Journal*, September 1964
because it had been a constant struggle…	Ellsworth
I still have the fiddle…	interview with Ken Gallacher, *Jazz Journal*, September 1964
I got a lot from Fats Waller…	Levin and Ellsworth
Art Tatum influenced everybody…	Ellsworth
When I went to college there was…	Levin
He was a big fan of Willie "The Lion" Smith…	*ibid*
I had the band after the first year…	*ibid*
I found I could make five dollars…	Ellsworth
We had a dance orchestra called the…	Levin
The Camel Caravan was Benny Goodman's…	*ibid*
It had an introduction…	*ibid*
A non-vocal version of Exactly Like You…	David Jessup, e-mail January 18, 2004
Another thing that happened in New York…	Levin
Allan Reuss, the guitar player…	*ibid*
I spent a whole week in New York…	*ibid*
We were going to stay in New York…	*ibid*

I went back to school…	*ibid*
We had a pretty good band…	Ellsworth
Cary "graduated with the class of 1938…	Jeffrey Makala, archivist, Wesleyan University, e-mail December 9, 2003
It has also been reported…	*The South Bay Beat*, October 1978
I came perilously close to working for…	Levin
It [the Carter band] was good…	*ibid*
It was just a band to play a show…	Ellsworth
These places were all run by hoods…	*ibid*
After five we'd go out and play in…	Levin
There were some wonderful black places…	*ibid*
I was fooling around with a lot…	*ibid*
I practiced trombone years ago…	*ibid*
I left Albany with Art Mooney…	Ellsworth
After Albany I got a job…	Levin
That lasted a while and then I went…	*ibid*
We had a place up in West 85th Street…	*ibid*
Enough for a three-handed pinochle…	Ellsworth
These guys did a lot of smuggling at that time…	Levin
Finally this best friend of mine got a job…	*ibid*
Right next door to us lived (the film stars)…	Levin
We played there the whole summer…	*ibid*
After I got through with Westport…	*ibid*
I was broke until I was in my forties…	*ibid*
We would go to the union…	*ibid*
On 52nd Street there were two blocks…	*ibid*
I would go up to Harlem quite often…	*ibid*
[Willie "The Lion" Smith was] fascinating…	*Jazz Podium*, June 1976

2. Nick's, Eddie Condon and Uncle Sam

For the next eight years…	Eddie Condon, "We Called It Music"
I was only getting an occasional gig…	Interview with Ken Gallacher, *Jazz Journal*, September 1964
When we were young…	Levin
At that time Art Hodes had…	*ibid*
When I met him he [Pee Wee Russell]…	*Jazz Podium*, June 1976
When I first went into Nick's…	Levin
The best band in that two years…	letter, March 1, 1991
Brad Gowans was a marvellous, talented guy…	letter, November 14, 1990
He got in the habit of playing fours…	Levin
Brad Gowans could play like Harry Shields…	*ibid*
When he was at Nick's we had…	letter, November 14, 1990
I [came to know] Eddie very well…	Ellsworth
The two years I was there we had…	Levin
Wild Bill Davison's contract at Nick's…	Hal Willard, "The Wildest One"
I was broke until I was in my…	Levin

About 1942 George Avakian gave me…	Leonard Feather questionnaire
As an autographed Nick's table card…	Art Pilkington
One gig away from Nick's took place…	Bob Hilbert, "Pee Wee Russell"
The sets lasted only twenty minutes…	to Alan Stevens, *Crescendo*, October 1977
On a visit to Nick's in Greenwich Village…	letter from Warren Vache Sr., October 4, 2003
Wild Bill and I were supposed to go on tour…	Levin
I finally got to write for Benny Goodman…	*ibid*
Goodman wasn't too happy then…	*ibid*
Sauter was always my favourite…	Ellsworth
I wrote arrangements for Goodman…	interview with Gudrun Endress, *Jazz Podium*, June 1976
On the telephone he is very charming…	*ibid*
There is one arrangement by Cary in Yale…	e-mail from David Jessup, January 14, 2004
Cary was inducted into the U.S. Army…	Hal Willard, "The Wildest One"
Davison went to Fort Dix…	letter, March 1, 1991
…on the embarkation piers in New York…	interview with Alan Stevens, *Crescendo International*, October 1977
I played trumpet in the 28 piece band…	interview with Ken Gallacher, *Jazz Journal*, September 1964
It went through two world wars…	Ellsworth
It's an old rhythm instrument…	Levin & letter, November 14, 1990
I was at Camp Shanks…	Levin
Although I was in the army…	interview with Ken Gallacher, *Jazz Journal*, September 1964
Shanks, being the largest embarkation…	letter, March 1, 1991
Billy Butterfield was at ABC…	Levin & letter, November 14, 1990
I was doing all the things…	Levin & letter, November 1, 1978
The Eddie Condon Blue Network broadcasts…	for fuller details refer to: 'The Eddie Condon "Town Hall Broadcasts" 1944-45', by C.K. Bozy White (self-published)
In 1945 the army sent me…	letters, November 1, 1978 / November 14, 1990
I was living in Middletown…	Levin

3. Billy Butterfield, amusement parks and Polish hop

I was in the service…	Levin
I suppose it cost me…	John Chilton, "Stomp Off, Let's Go"
Butterfield began auditioning…	*Down Beat*, April 22, 1946
Urbie Green's brother…	letter, February 20, 1990
Stegmeyer hired…	*ibid*
On June 14…	*Down Beat*, May 20, 1946
The fact that they…	letter, February 20, 1990
The situation was this…	letter, November 14, 1988

Billy liked something I did…	letter, February 20, 1990
"This Believing World"…	*ibid*
We did quite a few…	letter, November 14, 1988
Stegmeyer was a fine arranger…	letter, February 20, 1990
Several months later…	*ibid* and letter, July 7, 1990
I only made a $110…	Levin
Avalon Ballroom…	*International Musician*, August 1946
I didn't play with very many big bands	Ellsworth
"… is a good pianist, but …"	to Max Jones, *The Melody Maker*, June 21, 1975
This is just a temporary thing…	*Down Beat*, December 3, 1947
Matarese's Circle Bar…	*Down Beat*, March 26, 1947

4. With Louis Armstrong and the All-Stars – and Jean Goldkette

In 1947 Louis Armstrong's career…	letter, January 18, 1991
We don't have to rehearse…	*Storyville* No. 160
Dick Cary knew everything…	Max Jones & John Chilton, "Louis"
However, trombonist Geoff Cole, well-versed…	conversation with author, June 19, 2005
This was the first time I met Louis…	Ellsworth
Dick cary was a dear friend…	letter, November 12, 1991
The *Down Beat* review…	*Down Beat*, June 4, 1947
Critic Max Harrison, reviewing…	"The Essential Jazz Records"
Louis was in bad shape…	Levin
Jean Goldkette was due to open…	*Down Beat*, June 18, 1947
Jean Goldkette was a real gentleman…	*Jazz Podium*, February 1978
Goldkette came to New York…	*ibid* and Levin
The following August…	to Ken Gallacher, *Jazz Journal*, September 1964
That little ofay who played…	Levin
I never picked my own bands…	Sinclair Traill, "Just Jazz"
Louis Armstrong gave Billy Berg's…	*Down Beat*, August 27, 1947
We opened at Billy Berg's…	to Ken Gallacher, *Jazz Journal*, September 1964
Critic Ralph Gleason wrote…	*Down Beat*, September 24, 1947
Another *Down Beat* critic, George Hoefer…	*Down Beat*, December 3, 1947
Armstrong's appearances during 1947…	*Down Beat*, October 22, 1947
Cheering customers jammed…	*Down Beat*, December 17, 1947
Greenbach lost money…	*Down Beat*, January 28, 1948
…his poetic introduction…	letter, December 1, 2004
Cary told Swedish promoter…	letter, September 28, 1995
He couldn't accompany crap…	telephone, June 23, 2004
There was not a harsh word…	*The New Yorker*, date uncertain
One joke which Louis played…	to author, May 26,1992
I spent the best time of my life…	*Jazz Podium*, June 1976
Armstrong did have one complaint…	letter, January 30, 1992
They had a big argument…	Levin

That's when I met my second wife…	ibid
Whatever the stories about Joe Glaser…	letter, June 1988
There was one thing…	Levin
I shared a room with Jack…	ibid
We had two pianos on stage…	ibid
They had specifically asked…	letter, June 1988
Before they went to Europe…	ibid

5. Composition and Condon

So I went back to Connecticut…	Levin
I wanted to stay In New York…	to Alan Stevens, *Crescendo*, October 1977
He (Volpe) had a thing called…	Levin
Then I had a year with a man…	ibid
I studied the Schillinger system…	ibid
I sat in a lot with the band…	James Shacter, "Loose Shoes"
I'd sometimes see Ralph…	ibid
I accidently had the first jazz concert…	"Eddie Condon's Scrapbook of Jazz"
After the war we had our next TV…	Ernie Anderson letter, October 24, 1985
There was a total of 49 known…	as listed by C.K. Bozy White, *IAJRC Journal*, January 1986
At that time all the guests…	letter to Bert Whyatt, November 4, 1978
I did all the arrangements…	Levin
What happened was: Muggsy Spanier…	letter, March 15, 1989
Also, Mr. A. TATUM was there…	ibid
I went to quite a few Benny Goodman…	Levin
There were two people I declined…	ibid
I liked these guys very much…	letter April 30, 1987
I only travelled with two bands…	Levin
I played quite a bit with Parenti…	letter, February 20, 1990
We had no bass and the rhythm…	letter, July 7, 1990
Cary, better known as a pianist…	*Down Beat*, November 18, 1949

6. Jimmy Dorsey, Jingles and Television

I did all the arrangements…	Levin
But I had a great time with Jimmy…	letter, April 30, 1987
I did a lot of miles with Jimmy…	Ellsworth
Jimmy came over to our table…	letter, April 30, 1987
I had the last band in Billy Rose's…	Max Kaminsky, "My Life in Jazz"
An all-star video band…	*Down Beat*, January 12, 1951
Those guys loved doing jingles…	notes for Arbors ARCD19168
After a jingles session we sometimes…	Jerome speaking on Arbors ARCD19168

About Jerome, I did a lot…	letter, November 14, 1990
We were busy all the time…	Levin
I figure I had over 120 originals…	*ibid*
Mr. Cary was at one time a member…	letter, Lynne Enman, ASCAP, June 1, 2004
A battle of music between…	Manfred Selchow, "Profoundly Blue"
We did that in '50s, New York City…	letter, April 17, 1992
I remember these concerts vividly…	letter, November 14, 1990
Wild Bill Davison was rehearsing…	*Down Beat*, March 21, 1952
When I lived in New York…	Levin
Harry was the only concert violinist…	Manfred Selchow, "Profoundly Blue"
It is known that Harry Lookofsky…	refer to discography
The Whiteman Collection at…	e-mail, Sylvia Kennick Brown, Williams University
One day somebody said, "You…	Levin
One long date during 1952…	Manfred Selchow, "Ding! Ding!"
I do remember the Hot-Cool nite…	*ibid*
McPartland's first move was to hire Dick…	Leonard Feather, sleeve notes, MCA 2-4110 ("Shades of Bix" album)

7. We'll Send You To Lake Placid

We recorded this in the big Columbia…	Ellsworth
In his autobiography, Kaminsky wrote…	Max Kaminsky, "My Life In Jazz"
I made a very large clam…	Ellsworth
He was well known as a very thorough musician…	e-mail, Conrad Janis, June 7, 2004
I liked to play golf and tennis…	Levin

8. Joy Ride

This was the third in the series…	*ibid*
One night Bud was at Tommy's home…	letter February 20, 1990
Another was called "A Junket…	letter, April 30, 1987
Bud and I had become single…	Ellsworth
(Charlie Shavers) wrote…	*ibid*
I said, "Bix you should…	sleeve notes, MCA 2-4110 ("Shades of Bix" album)
They wanted me to take…	Ellsworth
Lasting the greater part of…	"The Essential Jazz Records"
"Joy Ride", Conrad Janis memoir…	e-mail, June 7, 2004
and then we went to Chicago…	Levin
The Critic's Choice…	*Down Beat*, August 8, 1956
Readers Poll…	*Down Beat*, December 26, 1956

9. Bobby Hackett at the Henry Hudson

I did all the arranging for the Henry Hudson…	letter, July 7, 1990
(Hackett) gave me a small amount…	letter, May 1976
We (Hackett and Cary) both were…	ibid
Capitol wouldn't even consider…	to Ken Gallacher, *Jazz Journal*, September, 1964
I'll give it five stars … I liked that…	*Down Beat*, August 7, 1958
Incidentally, that place in Toronto…	letter, 1976 (undated)
I left Hackett in Toronto…	ibid
Around New Year's Ernie left…	letter, April 4, 1973
The Caceres brothers roomed together…	ibid and April 13, 2004
It was a very unique band…	letter, April 4, 1973
I would arrive at the hotel…	letter, May 1976
This was an experimental group…	Ellsworth
the tutelary spirit here, as on so many…	R. Sudhalter notes to Mosaic MD8-206
That's loaded with humor, isn't it?	*Down Beat*, November 14, 1957
Sometimes there'd be five horns…	interview, the We Call It Music radio show
On the whole I found Dick Cary's set…	*Down Beat* Jazz Reviews, Volume 2, 1957
He was an absolute artist, through…	Levin
This all seems like sort of a wild dream…	letter, May 1976
It led to Wilber, Hafer and I…	letter, May 1976
I had a loft right in the middle…	Levin
It was in the early '60s, I believe…	letter, April 13, 2004
McPartland, like Condon and others…	R. Sudhalter notes to Mosaic MD8-206
Shy, even reclusive, Cary…	ibid
The choice of Dick Cary to arrange…	*Down Beat* Jazz Record Reviews, Volume 2, 1957
My Fair Lady had an album…	Ellsworth
Cary's scores are full of…	R. Sudhalter notes to Mosaic MD8-206
Cary was one of the greatest…	to Ken Gallacher, *Jazz Journal*, October 2003

10. Georgia Sketches

As an example of the genius…	letter, April 30, 1987
The title, explained Stewart…	N. Hentoff notes to United Artists UAL4009
Rex and I laboured over…	Ellsworth
Originally that was a suite…	*Jazz Podium*, February 1976
The Henderson reunion didn't come on…	Walter C. Allen, "Hendersonia"
The New York Times critic, John Wilson…	letter, October 19, 1983
contributed a series of gracile solos…	uncredited, *The Daily Telegraph*, May 5, 1994

470

Edmond worked at Eddie Condon's club...	Ellsworth
The real, legitimate brass quintet...	*ibid*
I don't write very quickly...	Pee Wee Russell to George Simon, notes to Dot DLP3253
The gimmick on this was...	interview, the "We Call It Music" radio show
McKenna thought of Cary...	Dave McKenna to Gunnar Jacobsen, October 23, 2003
Quietly, deftly, Cary subverted such thinking...	R. Sudhalter notes to Mosaic MD8-206
the combination of talented musicians...	Edward Meyer, "Giant Strides"

12. 9828 Wornom Avenue, Sunland, CA

Red Nichols and his Five Pennies...	Much of this information is courtesy of Stan and Steve Hester, authors of "Red Nichols—After the Intermission"
I once played it while with Red Nichols...	to Gudrun Endress, *Jazz Podium*, June 1976
Cary did not have a high opinion...	to author, May 1992
I heard Red play countless times...	Phil Evans letter, February 2, 1993
Red was on the stand...as Dick...	Phil Evans letter to Stan Hester, August 15, 1993
Pianist Johnny Varro expressed his opinion...	Johnny Varro to Gunnar Jacobsen, October 25, 2003
"even found himself playing in Barnum and..."	to Ken Gallacher, *Jazz Journal*, September 1964
When I was engaged for the first time...	to Gudrun Endress, *Jazz Podium*, June 1976
I had rehearsal bands in New York...	Ellsworth
It's just for musicians...	*ibid*
After that we went over to a garage... et seq	Levin
I don't think Dick ever wrote scores...	letter, June 2005
I didn't play too much: I spent most of my time...	to Alan Stevens, *Crescendo International*, October 1977
I don't think Dick ever...	letter, June 2005
with violinist Stuff Smith at Joani...	*Down Beat*, July 19, 1962
He told Ken Gallacher these were happy jobs...	*Jazz Journal*, September 1964
When the group appeared on the "Jazz Scene...	Mark Cantor e-mail, February 9, 2003
Cary left the band when...	to Ken Gallacher, *Jazz Journal*, September 1964
About Johnny Lane; he moved to California...	letter, November 14, 1990

13. Down Under and Disneyland

We'd been on the plane for twenty-five hours...	Levin

A major event occurred early in 1964…	Manfred Selchow, "Ding! Ding!" & Bob Hilbert, "Pee Wee Russell"
This was a Jazz Band Battle…	Bill Bacin auction list #17
I played one night with Smokey Stover…	letter, March 14, 1979 (Refer also to Hal Willard, "The Wildest One")
In 1968 trumpeter Dick Cathcart was…	letter, c. November 4, 1991
I got a group together with Dick Cary…	Joe Darenbsourg, "Telling It Like It Is"
He showed a sly and mordant sense of humor…	letter, Bill Mitchell, August 23, 1998
"Florence" is an off ramp on our Santa Ana…	letter, November 1, 1978
One trip was to the Texas jazz festival…	Ellsworth
I played up in the woods for something…	*ibid*
I appeared and played in…	letter, April 30, 1987
When I was in the army, one of the boys…	Ellsworth
I was working with Betty O'Hara and Peanuts…	Levin
I was lucky enough to have worked…	letter, May 3, 1994
In Cary's case I think he just plain…	letter, November 10, 1997
Dick would generally turn up…	letter, June 23, 2004

15. Slings and Arrows

Dick also supplied comic relief…	Bill Bacin, *The Jazzologist*, Vol. 11, Nos: 4,5,6
I played piano on all the ballads…	letter, November 1, 1978
I was just one of the trumpet players…	letter, October 19, 1983
Dick, playing trumpet, worked with us…	e-mail, June 28, 2004

17. Europe Beckons

I used Dick Cary quite often along with…	e-mail, October 6, 2006
I am writing a lot…	*Jazz Podium*, June 1976
I am a member of a nine-piece…	*ibid*
He organised the travel, rehearsed…	*ibid*
This is Jimmy's tour. He asked me…	*ibid*
The duo were in Gothenburg…	Bo Scherman quoting Lennart Blomberg, *Orkester Journalen*, November 1975
They received a short but very positive…	e-mail, August 5, 2005
Sweden, Germany, Holland and Italy…	e-mail, Dieter Nentwig, September 2, 2004
In 1974 and 1975 we took part…	letter, July 4, 2994
My first trip to Europe was taking…	letter, November 14, 1988
McPartland always tried to…	to author, May 26, 1992
I remember Dick as a serious man…	e-mail, June 26, 2005
The Riff album contained…	letter, March 14, 1979
Mandy is Ralph…	letter, September 28, 1979
Easton also has an album…	letter, March 14, 1979

I must have recorded enough…	letter, September 28, 1979
Later that week we did…	*ibid*
In The Dark is [Ralph] Sutton…	*ibid*
The Bix album was recorded…	*ibid*
[Ralph] Sutton did a week…	*ibid*
I have worked with this band…	*Jazz Podium*, February 1978
I have heard quite a few good…	*ibid*
He'd been living in Palm Springs…	letter, undated, 1976
Floyd and I put on the 'Los Angeles…	interview tape, June 23, 2004

18. Brisbane, The Red Lion and The Revolution Club

Just received a letter from…	letter, May 1976
I am going to Brisbane in December…	letter undated, 1976
My first meeting with Dick Cary…	unknown Australian magazine
I landed at Brisbane…	Levin
I'm not aware of any outside engagements…	e-mail, October 8, 2003
Dr. Mileham Hayes, president of the Convention..	Alan Stevens, *Crescendo International*, October 1977
German tour details…	provided by e-mail, Dieter Nentwig, September 2, 2004, and Wolfram Knauer, *Jazzinstitut Darmstadt*, June 16, 2005
We did not tour with him…	letter, Jost Munster, November 5, 2004
Their big jazz hall, the Fabrik…	letter, September 12, 1978
I wish my one and only tour…	letter, November 1, 1978
That agent I had is an absolute…	*ibid*
My second night in England…	*ibid*
I'd heard the band on records and I'd long…	Alan Stevens, *Crescendo International*, October 1977
I spent five weeks on the Continent…	*ibid*
Some of these tours are really very tedious…	letter to Bert Whyatt, December 13, 1978
It was Dave Bennett who set it up…	Pat Hawes, August 7, 2003
I did one night there and the agent…	letter, November 1, 1978
Like everyone else who worked with Condon…	Alan Stevens, *Crescendo International*, October 1977
It's taken me a long time to get here…	*ibid*
Bill Borcher, who runs [the Sacramento…	letter, May 12, 1977
Sacramento is less fun each year…	letter, September 24, 1977
I had two tours, one in July…	*ibid*
I don't have anymore to do with the WGJB…	letter, November 1, 1978
Life is uneventful in L.A.…	letter, September 24, 1977
Fatool and I just did a fashion show…	*ibid*
What happened is almost beyond belief!…	letter, September 12, 1978
I did several tours with Dick…	e-mail, July 25, 2005
I am goddam sick of being used…	letter, September 12, 1978

Jim Turner has pointed out…	telecon, September 27, 2005
Pud's album suffered from bad editing…	letter, March 14, 1979
You will find the Pud Brown much better…	letter, September 28, 1979

19. Tours, Festivals and Disc Troubles

Then again in 1978, the last of April…	letter, September 24, 1977
We left Los Angeles on April 29…	e-mails, June 29/July 2, 2004
Barry Martyn recalled Porter as…	cassette, June 23, 2004
I could write small band arrangements…	*ibid*
The tour in Europe was a nightmare…	letter, November 1, 1978
German collector Manfred Selchow…	telecon, December 12, 2003
I decided to have a good summer…	letter, July 12, 1978
I'd like to interest someone in an album…	letter, November 1, 1978
Collector Charlie Crump recalled seeing…	telecon, May 14, 2004
Just to give you an idea how much…	letters, November 1, 1978/ March 14, 1979
This Saturday [November 4] I am doing	letter, November 1, 1978
We occasionally are called to overdub…	letter, March 14, 1979
I am studying orchestrating with…	*ibid*
Both rooms were distinctly unkempt…	letter, June 21, 2004
When Bud Freeman was staying…	letters, May 3, 1994/ November 10, 1997
In 1980 Pee Wee Erwin came out here…	letter, April 20, 1982
Cary loved to play tennis but…	letter, November 10, 1997
a very close friend. He was with me…	letter, July 29, 2003

20. Louis Tributes, Harry James, Banjos and Tubas

It wasn't a big band I brought up…	letter, April 20, 1982
This was done in a studio and…	letter, February 20, 1985
The album was slapped together…	letter, October 19, 1983
Smith had asked Cary to write…	telecon, February 6, 2002/ February 9, 2004
Sometime in 1981 bassist Bob Finch…	*The Mississippi Rag*, January 1994
I have just returned from another one…	letters, April 20, 1982/ October 19, 1983
In March 1982 he [Cary] came for…	letter, July 29, 2003
I have (possibly) a chance to interest…	letter, April 20, 1982
The piece I was advised to do…	letter, October 29, 1983
The Edinburgh party was the first time…	letter, February 20, 1985
A hell of a nice guy!…	telecon, August 31, 2005
Dick Cary played alto-horn with…	letter, July 29, 2003
My existence is pretty much the same…	letter, October 29, 1983
I have my ten-piece band…	letter, April 20, 1982
Last week I was asked to do…	letter, October 29, 1983
and we won't do any recording till…	*ibid*

I know that Dick did the selections…	e-mail, August 2, 2005
Andy Zarchy was a pupil of mine…	letter, March 1, 1991
There's a brilliant young man…	letter, July 7, 1990
I first met Dick when I asked him…	e-mail, May 6, 2005

21. We Never Did Play *In the Mood*

I am not traveling much lately…	letter, February 20, 1985
On February 16th we did our best one…	*ibid*
There is a young man in Hollywood…	*ibid*
Abe and Sam Most deviated further from…	*Jazz Journal*, September 1985
I will always remember the meeting…	e-mail, October 9, 2003
Best Cary I ever heard…	*ibid*
I did part of one album for Jackie Coon…	letter, June 1988
I made the mistake of playing a dance…	letter, July 12, 1986
I'm doing the Conneaut Lake thing…	letter, April 30, 1987
[In May] we do the Sacramento thing…	*ibid*
Also she will do our Los Angeles…	*ibid*
There's a rash of Benny Goodman memorial…	letter, August 11, 1987
Three recent trips have interrupted…	letter, June 1988
The whole week was in honor…	letter, November 14, 1988
Not much to report about two days…	*ibid*
Then there was the Sacramento…	letter, June 1988
A favorite story of his was…	letter, November 14, 1988
The following week to Connecticut…	letter, June 1988
Then a tour of my youthful haunts…	letter, November 14, 1988
When I got back home the back problem…	*ibid*
I have met quite a few…	*ibid*
But I have recuperated now…	letter, June 1988
I took my group to Sacramento…	*ibid*
Sacramento, with its tremendous attendance…	*ibid*
Some of us feel we've been relegated…	*ibid*
There's a guy in San Francisco…	letter, November 14, 1988
One little man here named Bob Tabor…	*ibid*
It's so interesting to find out…	*ibid*
I am going over for the Ellington week…	letter, March 15, 1989
My second Stockholm visit was…	letters, February 20/July 7, 1990
Dick wrote several of the arrangements…	June 22, 1994
Dick Cary was in the hospital…	notes to Klavier KD-77024
The Tuesday night rehearsals are going…	letter, November 14, 1990
Almost all the jazz [radio] shows…	*ibid*
Many years later, Floyd Levin took me…	letter, October 4, 2003
A local jazz club gave me…	letter, November 14, 1990
But it was really satisfying…	letter, March 1, 1991
I've been a genius at avoiding…	letter, November 14, 1990

23. Final Notes

nothing but a few Christmas dates…	*ibid*
Most agreed -- it was the best thing…	letter, April 17, 1992
Due to the success of the Sacramento…	letter, March 1, 1991
A high point of the Los Angeles…	*West Coast Rag*, October 1991
The boob who now runs our L A…	letter, April 17, 1992
Matt Domber flew Dick and I…	e-mail, September 28, 2005
On the occasion of the Rick Fay CD…	e-mail, November 3, 2003
At present I am going through a malady…	letter, April 17, 1992
The goddam melanoma cancer…	letter, November 9, 1993
That's why I contacted him to expand…	e-mail, November 3, 2003
Although he didn't live to see the finished…	letter, July 10, 1994
Pianist Jim Turner saw one of our…	e-mail, February 9, 2004
On the bright side, I had a wonderful…	letter, November 9, 1993
I have made a small recovery…	*ibid*
I think one of the last gigs…	Betty O'Hara letter, July 10, 1994 & Putter Smith, Overture, May 1994

24. Tributes and Memories

The late player-arranger Dick Cary's Tuesday…	*Los Angeles Times*, September 5, 1994
Dick Cary's Tuesday Night Band played…	*Jazz News*, May-June 1998
On the day he died, the woman who…	e-mail, May 6, 2005
Meanwhile, the Dick Cary library is still at…	e-mail, September 15, 2003
Dick Hamilton is the perfect gentleman…	letter, July 10, 1994
I came up through the girl band days…	letter, November 14, 1994
Dick was my friend, mentor and musical…	*Overture*, May 1994
Dick Cary, as remembered by Betty O'Hara…	letter, November 14, 1994

The Discography

THE DICK CARY DISCOGRAPHY

Acknowledgements to the following for their help
in compiling this discography:

Nils Gunnar Anderby
Dr. Michael Arie
Gerard Bielderman
Len Bickley
Joe Boughton
Dave Bourne
Bill Brown
Mark Cantor
Charlie Crump
Bill Emery
Milt Gabler
Pete Goulding
Ron Hockett
Gösta Hägglöf
Ron Hockett
George Hulme
Gunnar Jacobsen
Tom Lane
Jack Mitchell
Brian Peerless
Ed Polic
Erik Raben
Michel Ruppli
Norman Saks
Manfred Selchow
Tony Shoppee
Dan Simms
Mike Sutcliffe
Jim Turner
Bob Weir
Bert Whyatt
Bob Wilber
Eric Woodward

Specials thanks to Charlie Crump and Brian Peerless for help with rare records.
With sincere apologies to anyone who may have been inadvertently overlooked.

Reference works which have been consulted include **Jazz Records 1942-1968** by Jorgen G. Jepsen, **The Jazz Discography** by Tom Lord, **Pee Wee Speaks** by Robert Hilbert, with David Niven, **Muggsy Spanier, The Lonesome Road** by Bert Whyatt, **Ding! Ding!** and **Profoundly Blue**, bio-discographical scrapbooks on, respectively, **Vic Dickenson** and **Ed Hall**, by Manfred Selchow, **Boy From New Orleans** by Hans Westerberg and **All of Me**, by Jos Willems, the Louis Armstrong discographies.

The main aim in this discography has been to show all material which has been released on commercial recordings. Details of a radio broadcast will be shown if one or more of the titles have found their way onto a record, whether or not it is a pirate release. Radio transcriptions are included where details are known.

Allowing for space limitations, I have not adhered strictly to discographical principles. Only original 78 rpm releases are shown. Refer to Jepsen/Raben or Lord if further details of 78rpm releases are needed. Where an artist's recordings have been widely reissued on LP and CD only representative releases are shown. For instance, the Louis Armstrong sessions with Cary have appeared on all manner of labels worldwide. Some private recording tapes have been included as a matter of interest but no attempt has been made to list every Dick Cary engagement which has been captured on cassette tape. To take one example, there are several hundred cassettes of the Tuesday Night Friends rehearsals which, theoretically, could have been examined and included.

Standard layout and abbreviations have been used, including:

a-h	alto-horn	cl	clarinet	p	piano
arr	arranger	co	cornet	ss	soprano saxophone
as	alto saxophone	d	drums	tb	trombone
b	string bass	e-g	electric guitar	tp	trumpet
bar	baritone saxophone	fl	flute	ts	tenor saxophone
b-cl	bass clarinet	fr	french horn	tu	tuba
bj	banjo	g	guitar	vtb	valve trombone
cel	celest	org	organ	vl	violin
				vo	vocalist

Abbreviations for the types of record issues are:
- (78)   78 rpm recording, 10" or 12"
- (45)   45 rpm recording, 7"
- (EP)   45 rpm recording, extended play, 7"
- (LP)   33⅓ rpm recordings, microgroove long-play, 10" or 12"
- (AC)   audio cassette tape
- (VC)   video cassette tape
- (DVD) digital video disc
- (Tx)   33⅓ rpm transcription, 12" or 16", produced for use by radio stations
- (FST) film soundtrack

JOE MARSALA and His CHOSEN SEVEN (Max Kaminsky, tp; George Brunis, tb; Joe Marsala, cl, as-1; Dick Cary, p, arr; Carmen Mastren, g; Haig Stephens, b; Zutty Singleton, d):
New York City — July 6, 1942

71001-A	Chimes Blues	(78) Decca 27074
71002-A/B	Sweet Mama	(78) Decca 27074
71003-A	Walkin' the Dog -1	(78) Odeon 286186
71004-A	Lazy Daddy	(78) Odeon 286186

Other issues: all titles, except 71002-B, on (LP) Decca DL5262, Brunswick (E) LA8545, and (CD) Classics 763. Odeon 286186 was an Argentinian release. Cary believes he scored 71001/71002. Marsala plays both cl & as on 71003.

BRAD GOWANS (Wild Bill Davison, co; Brad Gowans, v-tb; Dick Cary, p; Bob Casey, b; Tony Spargo, d):
Nola's Studios, New York City — October 22, 1943

Sign-Off Blues — private recording for Kathryn Dunham

JOE MARSALA and His Band (Billy Butterfield, tp; Lou McGarity, tb; Joe Marsala, cl; Dick Cary, p; Eddie Condon, g; Bob Casey, b; George Wettling, d):
World Studios, New York City — February 29, 1944

N1776-1	Panama	(LP) Jazzology J106
N1776-2	Panama	(Tx) World JS-25
N1777-1	Four or Five Times (false start)	(LP) Jazzology J106
N1777-2	Four or Five Times	(Tx) World JS-23
N1778-1	Jazzin' Babies Blues	(LP) Jazzology J106
N1778-2	Jazzin' Babies Blues	(Tx) World JS-23
N1779-1	Weary Blues	(Tx) World JS-23
N1780-1	Wabash Blues	(LP) Jazzology J106
N1780-2	Wabash Blues	(LP) Jazzology J106
N1780-3	Wabash Blues	(Tx) World JS-25
N1781-1	High Society (incomplete)	(LP) Jazzology J106
N1781-2	High Society (false start)	(LP) Jazzology J106
N1781-3	High Society (false start)	(LP) Jazzology J106
N1781-4	High Society	(Tx) World JS-25
N1782-1	Wolverine Blues (incomplete)	(LP) Jazzology J106
N1782-2	Wolverine Blues (false start)	(LP) Jazzology J106
N1782-3	Wolverine Blues	(Tx) World JS-23
N1783-1	Blues in C (incomplete)	(LP) Jazzology J106
N1783-2	Blues in C	(Tx) World JS-25

Other issues: every take on (LP) Jazzology J106. N1777-2 on (LP) IAJRC 36. Recorded for World Transcriptions and released on 16″, 33 1/3 rpm discs in the Jam Session series.

DICK CARY (piano solos; George Wettling, d):
New York City — March 4, 1944

BW9	'S Wonderful	Black and White unissued
BW10	I Thought About You	(78) Black and White 28
BW11	'T'ain't Ungood Blues	Black and White unissued
BW12	You Took Advantage of Me	(78) Black and White 28

Other issues: BW10/12 on (CD) Pickwick PJFD15002, Classics 909

MUGGSY SPANIER and His Ragtimers (Muggsy Spanier, co; Miff Mole, tb; Pee Wee Russell, cl; Dick Cary, p; Eddie Condon, g; Bob Casey, b; Joe Grauso, d):
WOR Studios, New York City — April 15, 1944

A4762-1	Angry	(LP) Commodore XFL15777
A4762-2	Angry	(78) Commodore 616
A4762-TK1	Angry	(LP) Mosaic MR23-128
A4763-1	Weary Blues	(78) Commodore 625
A4763-TK1	Weary Blues	(LP) Commodore XFL15777
A4764-1	Snag It	(LP) Commodore XFL15777
A4764-2	Snag It	(78) Commodore 616
A4764-TK1	Snag It	(LP) Mosaic MR23-128
A4765-1	Alice Blue Gown	(LP) Commodore XFL15777
A4765-2	Alice Blue Gown	(LP) Mosaic MR23-128
A4765-3	Alice Blue Gown	(78) Commodore 625

All eleven takes appear on (LP) Mosaic MR23-128. Other issues have appeared on (LP) on the Mainstream, Stateside, Fontana, London, Jazztone and Deja Vu labels; and on (CD) on Commodore CCD7009, Membran 221990 and Neatwork RP2027.

(Muggsy Spanier, co; Pee Wee Russell, cl; Ernie Caceres, bar; Dick Cary, p; Eddie Condon, g; Sid Weiss, b; Joe Grauso, d):
WOR Studios, New York City — April 22, 1944

A4766-1	Sweet Lorraine	(78) Commodore 1517
A4766-TK1	Sweet Lorraine	(LP) Commodore XFL15777
A4767-1	Oh, Lady Be Good	(78) Commodore 629
A4767-2	Oh, Lady Be Good	(LP) Commodore XFL15777
A4767-TK1	Oh, Lady Be Good	(LP) Mosaic MR23-128
A4768-1	Sugar	(78) Commodore 629
A4768-TK1	Sugar	(LP) Commodore XFL15777
A4769-1	September in the Rain	(78) Commodore 1517
A4769-2	September in the Rain	(LP) Mosaic MR23-128

All nine takes appear on (LP) Mosaic MR23-128. Other issues include: on (LP) as for the labels listed for the April 15, 1944 session. CD issues include Neatwork RP2027, Membran 221990. Commodore 1517 was a 12″ 78 rpm record.

(as last, except Bob Casey, b; for Weiss): **World Studios, New York City — April 26, 1944**

N2156	Sugar	(Tx) World JS31
N2157	Oh, Lady Be Good	(Tx) World JS31
N2158	Sweet Lorraine	(Tx) World JS30
N2159	September in the Rain	(Tx) World JS30
N2160	I Wish I Could Shimmy Like My Sister Kate	(Tx) World JS30

Recorded for World Transcriptions and released on 16″ 33 1/3 rpm discs in the Jam Session series.

The Eddie Condon broadcasts on the Blue Network of the American Broadcasting Company, first from a studio in the Town Hall and then the Ritz Theatre, ran weekly between May 21, 1944 and April 7, 1945. They were recorded by the Armed Forces Radio Service and edited recordings were sent to U.S. armed forces broadcasting stations on 16″ transcriptions. The AFRS transcriptions were subsequently used for commercial releases and the whole series was released on CD by Jazzology Records.

Dick Cary was present at many of these broadcasts, writing backgrounds where required, including those for singers Red McKenzie and Lee Wiley. As a general rule Eddie Condon acknowledges Cary's work and these titles are shown at the end of the discography in an "arrangements only" section.

A bigger problem concerns Cary's participation in the broadcasts as a trumpeter. Some discographies show him as playing on all the titles which he arranged and in many of the "Impromptu Ensembles" which closed each show. However this is all conjecture, both as to instrumentation and to Cary's presence. If indeed he is present his playing is as part of a section and is insignificant. For that reason only the titles on which he solos are being listed:

For full details of the Eddie Condon broadcasts on the Blue Network refer to the notes to the Jazzology CD releases and to the self-published booklet by Bozy White, "The Eddie Condon 'Town Hall Broadcasts' 1944-45."

EDDIE CONDON'S JAZZ CONCERT (Max Kaminsky, Dick Cary, tp; Lou McGarity, tb; Pee Wee Russell, Joe Marsala, cl; Ernie Caceres, bar; Jess Stacy, p; Sid Weiss, b; George Wettling, d):
broadcast, Ritz Theatre, New York City — October 28, 1944
Impromptu Ensemble   (Tx) AFRS CONDON 33

Other issues: (LP) IAJRC 38, Jazzology JCE-1012, (CD) Jazzology JCD-1012

EDDIE CONDON'S JAZZ CONCERT (Muggsy Spanier, co; Billy Butterfield, Dick Cary, tp; Lou McGarity, tb; Pee Wee Russell, cl; Ernie Caceres, bar; Jess Stacy, Gene Schroeder, p; Bob Casey, b; George Wettling, d):
broadcast, Ritz Theatre, New York City — November 4, 1944
Impromptu Ensemble   (Tx) AFRS CONDON 23
Cary, Stacy and Schroeder are announced.

Other issues include: (Tx) AFRS CONDON 36, (LP) Rarities 44, Jazum 63, Tono TJ6004, Jazzology JCE-1013 and (CD) Jazzology JCD-1013
Refer to "Recorded Arrangements" section for notes on Cary's contributions to these broadcasts.

Between November 1945 and February 1946 Cary mentions five transcription dates.
These would seem to be with the 320th ARMY BAND. He mentions "peck horn on solos" for January 26th. November 29: "played only one, on 4th violin— *Whispering.*" January 9: no details. January 26: *Satanic/Take Me in Your Arms/High Society.* February 1: *Thou Swell/ Funny to Me/Nobody Knows.* February 8: *Mournin' Blues/Ugly Child/Riverboat [Shuffle].*

WILD BILL DAVISON and His Commodores (Wild Bill Davison, co; Lou McGarity, tb; Pee Wee Russell, cl; Dick Cary, p; Eddie Condon, g; Bob Casey, b; Danny Alvin, d):
WOR Studios, New York City — January 19, 1945
A4844-1	Jazz Me Blues	(78) Commodore 623
A4844-TK1	Jazz Me Blues	(LP) Mosaic MR23-128
A4845-1	Little Girl	(78) Commodore 635
A4845-TK1	Little Girl	(LP) Mosaic MR23-128
A4846-1	Squeeze Me	(78) Commodore 623
A4846-2	Squeeze Me	(78) Mosaic MR23-128

Other issues include: all takes on (LP) Mosaic MR23-128. all takes -1 on (LP) Commodore FL20.013, London(E) HMC 5012, (CD) Commodore CMD14052

Note: the original pianist on the session was George Zack and he plays on A4843, *A Ghost of a Chance*. Cary, who was in the studio as a visitor, replaced Zack, who was, in Cary's words, "pretty fractured when he arrived." In his diary Cary wrote: "Zack very drunk, so I made last three sides, *Jazz Me, Little Girl, Boy in Boat.*" (*Boy in the Boat* was an earlier title for *Squeeze Me*.) Cary is listed on the label of Commodore 623 as present on *Jazz Me Blues*, yet surprisingly Milt Gabler, owner of the Commodore label, later aurally identified Zack on both *A Ghost of a Chance* and *Jazz Me Blues*. However, in addition to Cary's comments, the *Jazz Me* solo sounds like Cary, not Zack.

BILLY BUTTERFIELD and His Orchestra (Billy Butterfield, Fern Caron, Archie Johnson, Bob Peck, tp; Dick Cary, a-h; Jack Green, Marshall Hawk, tb; Lennie Hambro, as; Bill Stegmeyer, as, cl; Bill Cervantes, Bob Levine, ts; Bob Horner, bar; Mickey Crane, p; Barry Galbraith, g; Bob Haggart, b; Morey Feld, d; Allan Wylie, vo):

WMCA Studios, New York City — April 29, 1946

940-3D	More Than You Know		(78) Capitol 815
941-3D	Whatta Ya Gonna Do?	vAW	(78) Capitol 265
942-3L	Billy the Kid		(78) Capitol 265

The unissued master 939, *Along With Me* vAW, is by a small group, without Cary.

Other issues: 940 on (LP) Capitol H201; 942 on (LP) Capitol H424, Capitol (E) LC6684, and on (CD) Jazz Band EBCD 2147-2. *More Than You Know* on (Tx) Capitol B-244 may be from a different session.

(unlisted personnel, but including Butterfield, tp, vo; Bill Stegmeyer, as, cl; Lenny Hambro, as; Bob Levine, ts; Bob Horner, bar; Mickey Crane, p; Dan Perri, g; George Ryan, b; Bob Dickenson, d; Patricia O'Connor, vo):

New York City — May 16, 1946

943-	It's There for the Taking If You Take It		
		vBB&band	Capitol unissued
944-	Hey, Now	vPOC	Capitol unissued

masters 945 Butterscotch/946 Butterball from this session are by a small group, without Cary.

(Butterfield, Johnson, Peck, tp; Cary, a-h, arr; Green, Hawk, tb; Earl Pearson, as; Stegmeyer, as, cl, arr; Cervantes, Levine, ts; Norman Elvin, bar; Crane, p; Cliff Wiley, g; Ryan, b; Dickenson, d; Patricia O'Connor, vo):

WMCA Studios, New York City — June 12, 1946

(a)	Thou Swell	aDC	(Tx) Capitol
(b)	Jeepers Creepers		(Tx) Capitol
(c)	My Heart Stood Still		(Tx) Capitol B-242

Cary also mentions that two other of his arrangements were played at a transcription rehearsal the previous day: *Wrap Your Troubles in Dreams* and *April in Paris*.
Cary, a-h; solos on (a) and (b). (c) appears to be from this period.

Other issues: (a), (b) on (CD) Jasmine JASMCD2606, (c) on (CD) Jazz Band EBCD 2147-2 and Hep CD49. Originally on Capitol Transcriptions B241/2 or B311/3.

(same personnel): *New York City — June 12, 1946*

949-1R	Rumors Are Flying	vPOC, aBS	(78) Capitol 282
950-6R	The Sharp Scarf		(78) Capitol 282
951-4D	Wild Oats		(78) Capitol 15186

Other issues: 951 on (LP) Capitol H424, Capitol(E) LC6684 and (CD) Jazz Band EBCD2147-2. Masters 947/948 not by Butterfield.

LOUIS ARMSTRONG (Louis Armstrong, tp, vo; Dick Cary, p; Bob Haggart, b; Sid Catlett, d):

concert, Town Hall, New York City — May 17, 1947

(a)	Cornet Chop Suey		(LP) Pumpkin 109
(b)	Our Monday Date	vLA	(LP) Pumpkin 109
(c)	Dear Old Southland (Armstrong/Cary duet)		(LP) Pumpkin 109
(d)	Big Butter and Egg Man	vLA	(LP) Pumpkin 109

(add Bobby Hackett, co; Jack Teagarden, tb, vo; Peanuts Hucko, cl):

(e)	Tiger Rag		(LP) RCA Jazz Tribune PM45374
(f)	Struttin' With Some Barbecue		(LP) RCA Jazz Tribune PM45374
(g)	Sweethearts on Parade	vLA	(LP) RCA Jazz Tribune PM45374
(h)	Saint Louis Blues		(LP) RCA Jazz Tribune PM45374
(i)	Pennies From Heaven	vLA	(78) Victor 40-4005
(j)	On the Sunny Side of the Street	vLA	(LP) RCA Jazz Tribune PM45374
(k)	I Can't Give You Anything But Love	vLA	(LP) RCA Jazz Tribune PM45374
(l)	Back o' Town Blues	vLA,JT	(78) Victor 40-4006
(m)	Ain't Misbehavin'	vLA	(78) Victor 40-4005
(n)	Rockin' Chair	vLA,JT	(78) Victor 40-4004
(o)	Muskrat Ramble		(LP) RCA Jazz Tribune PM45374

(same, except George Wettling, d; for Catlett):

(p)	Save It, Pretty Mama	vLA	(78) Victor 40-4004
(q)	St. James Infirmary (Teagarden & rhythm only) vJT		(78) Victor 40-4006
(r)	Royal Garden Blues		(LP) RCA Jazz Tribune PM45374
(s)	Do You Know What It Means to Miss New Orleans	vLA	(LP) RCA Jazz Tribune PM45374
(t)	Jack-Armstrong Blues	vJT,LA	(LP) RCA Jazz Tribune PM45374

On (l) an unknown member of the band sings the line, "Don't mistreat your woman."
The Victor 78 rpm record releases were allocated matrix numbers D8-VC-73 to 78 inclusive.

Other issues include: all titles on (LP) (French) RCA Jazz Tribune PM45374; (CD) RCA Victor 09026 68682 2, Fresh Sound FSR CD701, Definitive DRCD11291. (i) (l) (m) (n) (p) (q) on (CD) Properbox 24. Many, many other issues worldwide. For more details on all the Louis Armstrong sessions listed here, refer to "Boy From New Orleans," a Louis Armstrong Discography by Hans Westerberg, 1981, or to "All of Me: the complete discography of Louis Armstrong" by Jos Willems, 2006.

LOUIS ARMSTRONG (Louis Armstrong, tp, vo; Bobby Hackett, co; Jack Teagarden, tb, vo; Peanuts Hucko, cl; Ernie Caceres, bar; Dick Cary, p; Jack Lesberg, b; George Wettling, d):

concert, Winter Garden Theatre, New York City — June 19, 1947

(a)	Way Down Yonder in New Orleans		(78) Jazz Society(F) AA531

(b)	Basin Street Blues	vLA,JT	(LP) Ariston(It) 12004
(c)	Muskrat Ramble		(LP) Ariston(It) 12004
(d)	Dear Old Southland (Armstrong/Cary duet)		(78) Jazz Society(F) AA575
(e)	Do You Know What It Means to Miss New Orleans	vLA	(LP) Ariston(It) 12004
(f)	Someday (You'll Be Sorry)	vLA	(78) Jazz Society(F) AA551
(g)	Tiger Rag		(LP) Ariston(It) 12004

Not broadcast and probably unrecorded titles from the second half of the concert are reported to have been: *Swing That Music/Exactly Like You/I Cover the Waterfront/Coquette/ Rockin' Chair/Jack-Armstrong Blues*. The concert began at midnight.

Other issues include: all titles on (LP) Fanfare 21-121, (CD) Storyville STCD8242, Jazz Band EBCD2174-2, Definitive DRCD11291. Various titles issued on many labels, including Fox, Everest, Bulldog, Trip, Ember, SagaPan, Metronome, etc.

LOUIS ARMSTRONG and His ALL STARS (Louis Armstrong, tp, vo; Jack Teagarden, tb, vo; Barney Bigard, cl; Dick Cary, p; Arvell Shaw, b; Sid Catlett, d):

Chicago — October 16, 1947

D7VB1082-1	A Song Was Born	vLA,JT	(78) Victor 20-3064
D7VB1083-1	Please Stop Playing Those Blues, Boy	vLA,JT	(78) Victor 20-2648
D7VB1084-1	Before Long	vLA	(78) Victor 20-3064
D7VB1085-1	Lovely Weather We're Having	vLA	(78) Victor 20-2648

Other issues include: 1082/1083,1085 on (LP) RCA Victor UPM6044; 1084 on RCA RD7706; all titles on (CD) Definitive DRCD11225, OLP 223016, Quadromania 222484-444. D7VB1082 on (CD) Metronome METCD2023; 1083/1084/1085 on (CD) Properbox 24; 1083 on (CD) Properbox 80. The Victor Studio was at 445 Lake Shore Drive.

LOUIS ARMSTRONG and The ALL STARS (same personnel; Velma Middleton, vo):

concert, Symphony Hall, Boston — November 30, 1947

80352/3	Muskrat Ramble		(78) Decca 9-28095
80354	Black and Blue	vLA	(78) Decca 9-28096
80355	Black and Blue		unissued
80356/7	Royal Garden Blues		(78) Decca 9-28096
80358	Lover (Teagarden & rhythm only)		(78) Decca 9-28097
80359/60	Stars Fell on Alabama	vJT	(78) Decca 9-28101
80361/2	I Cried For You	vVM	(78) Decca 9-28099/9-28100
80363	Since I Fell for You	vVM	(78) Decca 9-28098
80364	Since I Fell for You		unissued
80365/6	Tea for Two		(78) Decca 9-28100/9-28099
80367/8	Body and Soul		(78) Decca 9-28099/9-28104
80369/70	Steak Face		(78) Decca 9-28108
80371	Mahogany Hall Stomp		(78) Decca 9-28098
80372/3	On the Sunny Side of the Street	vLA	(78) Decca 9-28105/9-28106
80374	High Society		(78) Decca 9-28107
80375	Baby Won't You Please Come Home	vJT	(78) Decca 9-28107
80376/7	That's My Desire	vLA,VM	(78) Decca 9-28106
80378	C Jam Blues		(78) Decca 9-28102
80379/80	How High the Moon		(78) Decca 9-28104/9-28103

80381	Boff Boff		unissued
80382	Boff Boff		(78) Decca 9-28102
80383	Mahogany Hall Stomp		unissued

Armstrong does not play on *C Jam Blues* or *That's My Desire*. Armstrong and Bigard do not play on *Lover*. Jos Willems notes that "The recordings issued by Decca are the same, without cuts, as the original acetates with the exception of Dick Cary's piano solo on *Royal Garden Blues* and Barney Bigard's final notes in *Tea for Two* were edited out."
An edited version of *Muskrat Ramble*, in which the piano, bass, clarinet and trumpet solos were omitted, was included in the "Satchmo: A Musical Autobiography" LP series, on Decca DL8606, DL4230, DL74230 and Brunswick (E) LAT8213.

Other issues include: (LP) Decca DL8037/DL8038, Brunswick (E) LAT8017/LAT8018, Ace of Hearts AH73/AH74, Coral CP48/CP49, (CD) Definitive DRCD11291, Giants of Jazz CD53011(excluding 80363 & 80379/80), Properbox 24 (various) and many others.

DAVE GARROWAY SHOW (Muggsy Spanier, co; with full orchestra, perhaps including Dick Cary, p): *broadcast, Chicago — October 1948*

	Relaxin' at the Touro		(CD) Jazzology Press Book CD2

Cary was working with the Muggsy Spanier band at the Blue Note in Chicago, commencing October 11. On a Sunday, possibly the 17th, Spanier was a featured guest on the Garroway radio show. Cary said, "I ... went along, I guess, to play piano and rehearse the band."

> **The Eddie Condon Floor Show television series** ran from September 7, 1948 to November 23, 1948 on Station WPIX, channel 11, New York City, and from January 1, 1949 to September 24, 1949 on station WNBC, channel 4, NYC.
>
> Dick Cary played on a number of these telecasts and some titles have been issued commercially. Set out below are those telecasts from which records have been released. Personnel details are subject to scrutiny, as not all musicians are announced and tapes, where they exist, are often of poor quality.
>
> No definite information is on hand to identify any "backgrounds" which Dick Cary contributed. Eddie Condon plays on some titles, but his main duty was as compere.

EDDIE CONDON'S FLOOR SHOW (Wild Bill Davison, co; Brad Gowans, v-tb; Pee Wee Russell, cl; Dick Cary, p; Jack Lesberg, b; George Wettling, d; Johnny Mercer, Thelma Carpenter, vo; Teddy Hale, vo, dancer): *telecast, WPIX, New York City — November 16, 1948*

(a)	Jelly Roll	vJM		(CD) LJR08
(b)	Happy Birthday to You			unissued
(c)	Just One of Those Things			unissued
(d)	I Told Ya I Love Ya	vHRA		unissued
(e)	Big Fine Mama	vTH		unissued
(f)	I'm Confessin'			unissued
(g)	Come Rain or Come Shine	vTC		unissued
(h)	Down Among the Sheltering Palms		vJM	unissued
(i)	Blues	vJM		unissued

(c) is by Sidney Bechet, ss; with Cary, Lesberg & Wettling.

(d) is by Henry 'Red' Allen, tp, vo; with Cary, Lesberg & Wettling. Band plays a few chords. (f) is a Wild Bill Davison feature. (g) is by Thelma Carpenter, with Cary, Lesberg & Wettling. LJR08 is an Italian Jazz Institute release, which lists Cutty Cutshall as trombonist, though Cary's diary gives Gowans, as well as dancer Pearl Primus and pianist Mary Lou Williams on the show.

EDDIE CONDON'S FLOOR SHOW (Louis Armstrong, tp, vo; Jack Teagarden, tb, vo; Peanuts Hucko, cl; Dick Cary, p; Arvell Shaw, b; Sid Catlett, d; Velma Middleton, voc):

telecast, WPIX, New York City — November 23, 1948

(a)	Lover		unissued
(b)	(tap dance by Teddy Hale)		unissued
(c)	Mop Mop		unissued
(d)	Rockin' Chair	vLA, JT	unissued
(e)	King Porter Stomp		(78) Jazz Society AA530
(f)	A Song Is Born	vLA, JT	unissued
(g)	Muskrat Ramble		unissued
(h)	Don't Worry About Me	vVM	unissued
(i)	Small Fry	vLA	unissued
(j)	Where the Blues Were Born in New Orleans	vLA	(LP) Palm Club PALM23

Other issues include: (e),(i) on (LP) Windmill WMD215, Saga PAN6931; (e) on (CD) Laserlight 15700. All under Louis Armstrong's name.

EDDIE CONDON'S FLOOR SHOW (Lee Wiley, vo; Dick Cary, org; Bob Casey, b):

telecast, WNBC-TV, New York City — January 29, 1949

(a)	Someone to Watch Over Me	(CD) Yadeon 503

(unknown, but including Flip Phillips, ts; Dick Cary, p):

(b)	Perdido	unissued

JIMMY ATKINS (vo, with Bob Haggart and his Orchestra: Dick Cary, tp; Buddy Morrow, tb; Johnny Mince, cl; Art Drellinger, ts; Buddy Weed, p; unknown, g; Bob Haggart, b, arr; unknown, d):

New York City — February 24, 1949

14780-	Tennessee Saturday Night	Decca unissued
14781-	All Right Louie, Drop That Gun	Decca unissued

EDDIE CONDON'S FLOOR SHOW (Wild Bill Davison, co; Cutty Cutshall, tb; Peanuts Hucko, cl; Dick Cary, p; Jack Lesberg, b; Buddy Rich, d; Rosemary Clooney, vo; Peter Nugent, dancer):

telecast, WNBC-TV, New York City — March 12, 1949

(a)	Just One of Those Things	(LP) Queen-disc Q029

(Sidney Bechet, ss; Cary, p; Lesberg, b; Rich, d):

(b)	I Know That You Know	unissued
(c)	Call of the Wild	unissued

(Rosemary Clooney, vo; Cary, p; Lesberg, b; Rich, d):

(d)	There'll Be Some Changes Made	unissued

(as for (a), plus Sidney Bechet, ss):

(e)	Jam Session	unissued

This telecast also includes *As Time Goes By* by pianist Teddy Wilson, *Running Wild* by Peanuts Hucko, with Teddy Wilson, and a version of *Old Man River* by the Kingdom Choir.

EDDIE CONDON'S FLOOR SHOW (Jimmy McPartland, tp; Cutty Cutshall, tb; Peanuts Hucko, cl; Dick Cary, p, arr; Eddie Condon, g; Jack Lesberg, b; Buddy Rich, d; Helen Ward, vo; Baby Lawrence, tap-dancer): *telecast, WNBC-TV, New York City — March 26, 1949*

    (a)   Thou Swell   unissued

(Sidney Bechet, ss; with p; b; d – as for (a):

    (b)   September Song   (LP) Queen-disc Q-029
    (c)   Just You, Just Me (Baby Lawrence feature)   unissued

(as for (a), with Muggsy Spanier, co; replacing McPartland):

    (d)   Relaxin' at the Touro   (Tx) Voice of America 45

(as for (a), with Bechet, ss):

    (e)   Dixieland Band   vHW aDC   (LP) Queen-disc Q-031

(Hucko, cl; with p; b; d):

    (f)   My Funny Valentine   vHW   (LP) Queen-disc Q-030

(everybody, with Dick Cary, tp; Cliff Jackson, p):

    (g)   Jam Session   (LP) Queen-disc Q-029

Other issues: (d) on (LP) Queen-disc Q-031.
(g) shown on Queen as *Argonne Stomp/Ole Miss.* Broadcast also includes a piano solo, *Squeeze Me,* by Cliff Jackson.

EDDIE CONDON'S FLOOR SHOW (Bobby Hackett, co; Cutty Cutshall, tb; Ernie Caceres, cl; Dick Cary, p, org; Eddie Condon, g; Jack Lesberg, b; J.C. Heard, d, or Buddy Rich d, vo; Helen Ward, vo; Steve Condos, dancer): *telecast, WNBC, New York City — April 16, 1949*

    (a)   George Gershwin medley: (LP) Queen-disc Q-030
                              Fascinating Rhythm   (band)
                              I've Got a Crush on You   vHW   (co, p, b, d)
                              'Swonderful   (cl, p, b, d)
                              They Can't Take That Away From Me   (tb, p, b, d)
                              The Man I Love   (p, b, d)
                              Embraceable You   (co, org duet)
                              I Got Rhythm   vBR   (band)

(Sidney Bechet, ss; with p; b; d):

    (b)   Summertime   (LP) Queen-disc Q-029

(as for (a), plus Hot Lips Page, tp):

    (c)   Sweet and Lowdown   unissued

(Hackett, co; p; b; Buddy Rich, d):

    (d)   But Not for Me   vHW   (LP) Queen-disc Q-03l

(as for (a)):

    (e)   Lady Be Good   unissued

(add Sidney Bechet, ss):

    (f)   Jam Session   unissued

EDDIE CONDON'S FLOOR SHOW (Bobby Hackett, co; Cutty Cutshall, tb; Dick Cary, a-h, arr; Peanuts Hucko, cl; Ernie Caceres, bar; Joe Bushkin, p; Jack Lesberg, b; Buddy Rich, d, vo; Thelma Carpenter, vo): *telecast, WNBC-TV, New York City — May 21, 1949*

    (a)   Fats Waller medley: (LP) Queen-disc Q-031
                              I've Got a Feeling I'm Falling   (bar, p, b, d)
                              Keeping Out of Mischief Now   vTC aDC (band)
                              Handful of Keys   (cl, p, b, d)
                              Squeeze Me   aDC   (band)

	The Joint Is Jumpin'	vBR (band)	
(b)	Ain't Misbehavin'	vTC aDC	(LP) Queen-disc Q-03l

(add Sidney Bechet, ss):
(c)	Black and Blue (ss feature)	(LP) Queen-disc Q-029
(d)	Honeysuckle Rose	(LP) Queen-disc Q-029

(d) Cary plays alto-horn and may also play trumpet in final ensemble.

EDDIE CONDON'S NBC TELEVISION ORCHESTRA (Bobby Hackett, co; Will Bradley, tb; Dick Cary, a-h, arr; Peanuts Hucko, cl, ts; Ernie Caceres, bar; Joe Bushkin, p; Eddie Condon, g; Jack Lesberg, b; Sid Catlett, d; Ruth Brown, vo):   ***New York City — May 25, 1949***

A236	Seems Like Old Times		(78) Atlantic 661
A237	Time Carries On		(78) Atlantic 661
A238	It's Raining	vRB	(78) Atlantic 879*
A239	So Long	vRB	(78) Atlantic 879*

* issued under RUTH BROWN's name.
A237 composer credit (Condon—arr. Dick Cary), though Cary claimed he was composer.
Other issues include: A236/237 also on (CD) Classics 1177
A238 also on (LP) Route 66 KIX16, (CD) Rhino 8122 7748-2
A239 also on (EP) Atlantic EP505, and (LP) Atlantic LP8004, Atco SD7009, Official 6053

EDDIE CONDON'S FLOOR SHOW (Billy Butterfield, tp; Cutty Cutshall, tb; Dick Cary, a -h; Peanuts Hucko, cl; Ernie Caceres, bar; Joe Bushkin, p; Jack Lesberg, b; Sid Catlett, d; June Christy, Johnny Desmond, vo; Walter Long, dancer):
telecast, WNBC-TV, New York City — May 28, 1949

(a)	Everything Happens to Me	vJC	(LP) Queen-disc Q-030
(b)	My Old Flame		(LP) Queen-disc Q-031
(c)	Oh, Look at Me Now	vJC, JD	(LP) Queen-disc Q-030
(d)	Ole Miss		unissued
(e)	Skyscraper Blues	vJD	unissued

(b) is a Billy Butterfield feature and could be a Cary chart. (c) labelled as Look at Me Now.

EDDIE CONDON'S FLOOR SHOW (Hot Lips Page, tp, vo; Cutty Cutshall, tb; Dick Cary, a-h; Peanuts Hucko, cl; Ernie Caceres, bar; Joe Bushkin, p; Jack Lesberg, b; Sid Catlett, d):
telecast, WNBC-TV, New York City — June 4, 1949

(a)	Happy Feet		unissued

(add Sidney Bechet, ss):
(b)	High Society	(ss feature)	(LP) Queen-disc Q-029
(c)	The Blues		unissued

For (b) Queen-disc lists Ralph Sutton, piano. Other titles from this telecast are believed to feature Page and Sutton. (Eddie Condon in hospital on June 4 and did not return to the show until June 25.)

EDDIE CONDON'S FLOOR SHOW (unknown tp; unknown tb; Peanuts Hucko, cl; Ernie Caceres, bar; Dick Cary, p, tp; Count Basie, org; Jack Lesberg, b; Sid Catlett, d; Ray Malone, dancer):
telecast, WNBC-TV, New York City — June 18, 1949

(a)	Blues In E-Flat	unissued

(omit Basie; Lee Wiley, vo):

(b) Rodgers & Hart medley:
    It Never Entered My Mind   vLW   (CD) Yadeon 503
    A Ship Without a Sail   vLW   (CD) Yadeon 503
    You Took Advantage of Me   vLW   (CD) Yadeon 503

EDDIE CONDON'S FLOOR SHOW (Bobby Hackett, co; Cutty Cutshall, tb; Dick Cary, a-h; Peanuts Hucko, cl; Ernie Caceres, bar; Joe Bushkin, p; Jack Lesberg, b; Buddy Rich or Sid Catlett, d): *telecast, WNBC-TV, New York City — June 25, 1949*
(a)   In the Groove   unissued
(same, plus Sidney Bechet, ss):
(b)   Sweet Georgia Brown   (ss feature)   (LP) Queen-disc Q-029
(as for (a), except Bushkin, p, tp*, vo):
(c)   I'm Gonna Sit Right Down and
    Write Myself a Letter *   vJB   (LP) Queen-disc Q-030
(d)   Seems Like Old Times   (LP) Queen-disc Q-031
(as for (a), plus Bechet, ss):
(e)   Ole Miss   unissued

PHIL NAPOLEON'S MEMPHIS FIVE (Phil Napoleon, tp; Andy Russo, tb; Phil Olivella, cl; Dick Cary, p; Jack Fay, b; Tony Spargo, d):
broadcast, Nick's, New York City — September 20, 1949
Cary's diary indicates the broadcast was recorded for the Armed Forces Radio Service (AFRS). No other details.

MIKE RILEY and his Orchestra (Al Alston, tp; Mike Riley, tb, vo; Peanuts Hucko, cl; Ben Parrish, ts; Dick Cary, p, arr; Miles, ?; Buzzy Drootin, d):
WOR Studio 3, New York City — October 13, 1949
49-S-352-2   I've Been Floatin' Down the
    Old Green River   vMR&band   (78) M-G-M 10569
49-S-353-3   The Music Goes 'round
    and Around   vMR&band   (78) M-G-M 10569
49-S-354-   Do-Wak-A-Do   ( ) M-G-M unissued
49-S-355-   Ellen   ( ) M-G-M unissued

All arrangements by Cary. Banjo and tuba were featured. Files quoted by Ruppli indicate nine musicians. Above names given by Dick Cary. [10:45 to 14:15]

JIMMY DORSEY and his Original Dorseyland Jazz Band (Charlie Teagarden, tp, vo; Cutty Cutshall, tb; Jimmy Dorsey, cl, cl&as-1; Frank Maynes, ts; Dick Cary, p, celeste-2, arr; Carl Kress, g; Bill Lolatte, b; Ray Bauduc, d; Claire Hogan, vo):
New York City — November 1, 1949
CO41829-1   Johnson Rag   vCH&band   (78) Columbia 38649
CO41832-1   Struttin' With Some Barbecue   (78) Columbia 38655
CO41843-1   Charley, My Boy   vCH,CT -1   (78) Columbia 38649
CO41844-1   Chimes Blues   -2   (78) Columbia 38655
CO41845-1   South Rampart Street Parade   (78) Columbia 38657
CO41846-1   Tin Roof Blues   (78) Columbia 38657
CO41848-1   Jazz Me Blues   (78) Columbia 38654
CO41848-2   Jazz Me Blues   (CD) Mosaic MD8-206
Masters CO41830, 41831 and 41847 are by other artists

Other issues include: CO41832/44/45/46/48-1 on (LP) Columbia CL6095, CL608. CO41829/43 on (LP) Columbia CL6114. All titles, except CO41848-2 on (LP) Ajazz 418, (CD) Definitive DRCD11205, Collectables COL-CD-7519. All titles on (CD) Mosaic MD8-206.

(same personnel, with Maynes, cl-1, ts; unknown glockenspiel-1):
New York City — November 2, 1949

CO41852-1	Muskrat Ramble		(78) Columbia 38656
CO41853-1	Panama		(78) Columbia 38654
CO41854-1	High Society	-1	(78) Columbia 38656

Other issues include: all titles on (LP) Columbia CL6095, CL608, Ajazz 418 and (CD) Definitive DRCD11205, Collectables COL-CD-7519, Mosaic MD8-206. Lord reports 41854-2 on Japanese Columbia M513.

(same personnel; Kenny Martin, vo):
New York City — January 17, 1950

CO42650-1	Rag Mop	vCH&band	(78) Columbia 38710
CO42651-1	That's a Plenty		(78) Columbia 38710
CO42652-1	When You Wore a Tulip	vKM	(78) Columbia 38731
CO42653-1	Clap Hands, Here Comes Charlie	vCH,CT	(78) Columbia 38731

Other issues include: CO42651 on (LP) Columbia CL608. All titles on (LP) Columbia CL6114 and (CD) Definitive DRCD11205, Collectables COL-CD-7519, Mosaic MD8-206.

JIMMY DORSEY and his Original Dorseyland Jazz Band (same personnel):
New York City — March 7, 1950

CO 42952-1	It's a Long Way to Tipperary	vCH	(78) Columbia 38879
CO 42953-1	Let a Smile Be Your Umbrella	vCH	(78) Columbia 38968
CO 42954-1	When You're Smiling		(78) Columbia (Argentina) 20230
CO 42954-2	When You're Smiling		(EP) Columbia B1950
CO 42955-1	Levee Blues vCT		(EP) Columbia B1950

Other issues: 42952/54-2/55 on (LP) Columbia CL608; 42953/54-2 on (LP) Columbia CL6114. All five takes on (CD) Mosaic MD8-206. 42954-2/55 on (LP) Ajazz 418. All titles, except 42954-1 on (CD) Definitive DRCD11205, Collectables COL-CD-7519.

JIMMY DORSEY and his Orchestra (Charlie Teagarden, Shorty Sherock, Dick Hoffman, Dick Murphy, tp; Frank Rehak, Bob Hackman, Dick Bellerose, tb; Jimmy Dorsey, cl-1, as-2, cl&as-3; Ben Fussell, Nick Palotti, as; Frank Maynes, Phil Cenicola, ts; Mimi La Rocca, bar; Dick Cary, p; Carl Kress, g; Bill Lolatte, b; Ray Bauduc, d; Claire Hogan, Terry Shand, vo; Howard Gibeling, arr):
New York City — March 17, 1950

CO 42999-1	Kiss Me	vCH	(78) Columbia 38774
CO 43000-1	You Don't Have to Be a Baby to Cry	vTS, aHG -1	(78) Columbia 38879
CO 43001-1	Sweet Georgia Brown	aHG -2	(78) Columbia 38774
CO 43002-1	In a Little Spanish Town	aHG -3	(78) Columbia 38968

Some sources quote the recording date as May 17, but Cary gives March 17. The Dorsey band was in St. Paul on May 17.

Other issues: all titles on (LP) Ajazz 427; 42999/43001 on (7˝ 33rpm) Columbia 1-594.

JERRY JEROME (?) (Dick Cary, horn, p, cel; Jerry Jerome, b-cl; Bernie Kaufman, cl, fl; Nick Parito, acc; Don Costa, g, arr; Jack Zimmerman, b; Terry Snyder, d; unknown vo):
WMGM Studios, New York City — July 31, 1950
    Lost in the Stars   aDCosta
    3 other titles   aDCosta
No other details.

DON COSTA / NANCY REED (tp; 2 cl; 2 b-cl; 2 fl; oboe; 15 strings; 4 rhythm; vibes: Cary played horn — probably alto-horn, Reed played vibes and presumably sang; Costa, arr, conductor):
New York City — November 6, 1951
No other details

TOM ELDREDGE (vo: with Dick Cary, a-h?, p, cel, b-cl, arr; Jerry Jerome, reeds; Nick Parito, acc; Jack Zimmerman, b; Mel Zelnick, d; Don Costa, arr. & g?):
Fulton Studios, New York City — November 8, 1951
    You'd Be So Nice to Come Home To aDCosta
    an original   aDCosta
    Easy to Love   aDCary
    Skylark   aDCary
No other details.

UNKNOWN (vo; with Dick Cary, a-h, p, arr; tp; fl; 5 strings; g; b; d; Don Costa, Nick Parito, arr; Jerry Jerome, conductor): *RCA Studios, New York City — November 26, 1951*
    Basketball Song aDCary
    3 others
The singer's Christian name was Hal.

SONNY CALELLA (vo; with Dick Cary, horn; 3 reeds; 5 strings; Lou Stein, p; Nick Parito, acc; Don Arnone, g; Jack Zimmerman, b; Mel Zelnick, d; vocal choir; Don Costa, arr, conductor):
New York City — January 2, 1952
 K8160 The King   King 15158
 K8161 Cindy Lou   King 15158

DAN BROWN (vo; with same personnel):   *same session*
    Symphony   King unissued?
    Night Riders in the Sky King unissued?

Cary refers to playing "horn," which could mean trumpet or alto-horn. Eli Oberstein was the producer.

WETTLING'S STUYVESANT STOMPERS (Hot Lips Page, tp, vo; Wild Bill Davison, co; Lou McGarity, tb; Peanuts Hucko, cl; Dick Cary, p; George Wettling, d):
"Dr. Jazz" broadcast, Stuyvesant Casino, New York City — January 4, 1952
 (a) (I Would Do) Anything For You vHLP (LP) IAJRC 36

(Pee Wee Russell, cl; replaces Hucko):   *same date*
 (b) How Come You Do Me Like You Do vHLP (CD) Storyville STCD6046
 (c) You're Driving Me Crazy   (LP) IAJRC 36

(Peanuts Hucko, cl; replaces Russell):   *same date*
    (d)   Keepin' Out of Mischief Now   unissued
    (e)   Royal Garden Blues (incomplete/voice over)   unissued

The Casino was at 140 Second Avenue, Ninth Street. Cary not present on other titles from this broadcast. Other issues: (a) (c) also on (CD) Storyville STCD6046.

EDDIE CONDON'S BAND (with Dick Cary, tp, a-h; Lou McGarity, tb; as guests):
                                Eddie Condon's, New York City — January 15, 1952
        Cary reported that the Voice of America recorded several sets

EDDIE CONDON'S BAND (Dick Cary, tp; Cutty Cutshall, tb; Ed Hall, cl; Gene Schroeder, p; Eddie Condon, g; Bob Casey, b; Buzzy Drootin, d):
                "Dr. Jazz" broadcast, Eddie Condon's, New York City — March 17, 1952
    (a)   The Lady Is a Tramp   (CD) Storyville STCD6061
    (b)   It's Been So Long   (CD) Storyville STCD6061
    (c)   Danny Boy   (CD) Storyville STCD6061
    (d)   It All Depends on You   (CD) Storyville STCD6061
    (e)   Bill Bailey (incomplete/voice over) (CD) LJR08

STCD6061 notes listed Ralph Sutton, who plays a piano solo and a duet with Ed Hall on the broadcast, as pianist with the band. LJR08 is an Italian Jazz Institute release. The voice-over on (e) obscures Cary's trumpet solo.

JERRY JEROME ALL STAR JAZZ CONCERT (Henry 'Red' Allen, tp, vo; 'Big Chief' Russell Moore, tb; Jerry Jerome, ts; Dick Cary, p; Ed Safranski, b; Don Lamond, d):
                    concert, Loew's King Theatre, Brooklyn, New York — March 24, 1952
    (a)   Fidgety Feet   (Tx) Voice of America No. 38
    (b)   St. James Infirmary vRA   (Tx) Voice of America No. 38
(Jerome, ts; Cary, p; Safranski, b; Lamond, d):
    (c)   When I Grow Too Old to Dream (Tx) Voice of America No. 38
(Cary, p; Safranski, b):
    (d)   Finger Buster   (Tx) Voice of America No. 38

JERRY JEROME ALL STAR JAZZ CONCERT (Bill Harris, tb; Buddy DeFranco, cl; Charlie Parker, as; Dick Cary, p; Eddie Safranski, b; Don Lamond, d; Jerry Jerome, producer):
                    concert, Loew's Valencia Theatre, Jamaica, New York — March 25, 1952
                    Ornithology   (Tx) Voice of America No.

Other issues include: (LP) Bird Box(It) LP-1, Blue Parrot AR-701, Scam JPG-1 and (CD) Philology(It) W80.2, Royal Jazz(Dan) RJD-505, Verve(Jap) DCI-3005.
On Rare Live Recordings RLR88634 the piano solo is edited out.

DON COSTA (Dick Cary, horn, b-cl; Sid ----, cl, fl; Dominic(?) Cortese, acc; Don Costa, g, arr; Jack Zimmerman, b; Phil Kraus, d; Sonny Calella, vo):
                                                            New York City — May 12, 1952
    4 songs, all with Sonny Calella vocals. Perhaps as audition records?

DON COSTA (large band, incl. Red Solomon, Doc Severinsen, tp; Dick Cary, tp, a-h; 2 tb; 5 reeds; 8 strings; rhythm section; unknown, vo; Don Costa, arr, conductor):
                                            Fulton Studios, New York City — June 20, 1952
    4 songs, all vocals.

DON COSTA (Doc Severinsen, Bernie Glow, Dick Cary, a.n.other, tp; Bobby Byrne, a.n. other, tb; Charles Kennedy, George Greene, Sid Jacowsky, 2 others, woodwinds; a.n.other, p; Al Casamenti, Alan Hanlon, Art Ryerson, Don Arnone, Sam Herman, g; Jack Zimmerman, b; Don Lamond, d; vocal quintet; Don Costa, arr, conductor):
Fulton Studios, New York City — August 14, 1952
    no other details

UNKNOWN (Dick Cary, horn, piano, organ, celeste, arr; Lester Merkin, fl, piccolo, b-cl; Jerry Jerome, reeds; Allan Hanlon, g): *New York City — August 21, 1952*
    "recorded background music for two children's stories"

JIMMY McPARTLAND and the HOT JAZZ STARS (Jimmy McPartland, co; Vic Dickenson, tb; Ed Hall, cl; Dick Cary, p; Jack Lesberg, b; George Wettling d):
"Birdland," New York City — November 24, 1952

52-S-505-A	Muskrat Ramble	(78) M-G-M 30744
52-S-506-A	Battle of Blues	(78) M-G-M 30745
52-S-507-A	Indiana	(78) M-G-M 30743
52-S-508-B	How High the Moon	(78) M-G-M 30742

52-S-507 as Edmond Hall and the Hot Jazz Stars.

Other issues: 505/506 on (EP) M-G-M X4115; 507/508 on (EP) M-G-M X4114; 507 on (LP) Verve 845 149-1, (CD) 845 149-2, (AC) 845 149-4. All on (LP) M-G-M E194, E3286 and M-G-M(E) D115.

DIZZY GILLESPIE and the COOL JAZZ STARS (Jimmy McPartland, co; Dizzy Gillespie, Don Elliott, Dick Cary, tp; Buddy DeFranco, cl; Ray Abrams, ts; Ronnie Ball, p; Al McKibbon, b; Max Roach, d): *same date*

52-S-510	A Battle of Blues	(78) M-G-M 3074

Other issues: on (EP) M-G-M X4115, M-G-M(E) EP681; (LP) M-G-M E194, E3286, E3611and M-G-M (E) D115. Album title: Hot versus Cool.

DON COSTA (Dick Cary, tp, cel; Sid Jacowsky, George Greene, reeds; Nick Parito, acc; Don Arnone, Sam Herman, g; Jack Zimmerman, b; Frank Ippolito, d; Phil Kraus, a.n.other, marimbas; Costa, arr, conductor; Nancy Reed, vo; vocal trio (Costa, Zimmerman, Cary)):
Fulton Studios, New York City — January 7, 1953
no other details, but perhaps for Emerald.

JIMMY McPARTLAND and his Jazz Band (Jimmy McPartland, tp; Lou McGarity, tb; Peanuts Hucko, cl; Ernie Caceres, bar; Dick Cary, p, arr; Carl Kress, g; Jack Lesberg, b; George Wettling, d): *New York City — March 10, 1953*

84144	Clarinet Marmalade	(LP) Brunswick BL58049
84145	Singin' the Blues	(LP) Brunswick BL58049

Other issues: both titles on (LP) Vogue(E) LRA10006. 84145 on (LP) Brunswick BL54018, MCA2-4110, and (CD) J&M J&MCD8007. 84144 lasts 3:15 and includes a piano solo. Another version of *Clarinet Marmalade* (84504, May 14, 1953), lasting 3:00, without a piano solo, was used for the 12″ albums.
The Decca files show a version of *Singin' the Blues* (master 88869) recorded on February 6, 1955, but this appears to be a shortened version of 84144 listed above, with 1:08 deleted

from the opening (the standard introduction and most of the clarinet solo). This version was released on (LP) Decca DL-8250 and Swaggie S1279.
Cary gives "Pythian Temple" as the studio for the April and May recordings, which no doubt applies to this session also.

KEN HOPKINS (?) (Dick Cary, p, a-h; string section; Don Arnone, g; Jack Zimmerman, b, arr; Ken Hopkins, arr; Mrs. Hopkins, Sonny Calella, vo):
Huntington, Long Island — March 12, 1953
    2 titles   vMH, aKH
    2 titles   vSC, aJZ

MARY CARUSO (vo: with 2 tb; f-h; 6 woodwinds; Dick Cary, p, cel; 2 g; Jack Zimmerman, b; a.n.other, d; vo group; Don Costa, arr, conductor):   *New York City — March 13, 1953*
no other detail

MAX KAMINSKY and his Orchestra (Max Kaminsky, tp; Cutty Cutshall, tb; Peanuts Hucko, cl, ts-2; Ernie Caceres, bar, cl-3; Dick Cary, p, a-h-1, celeste-1, arr; Al Casamenti, g; Bob Haggart, b; Jo Jones, d):   *New York City — March 17, 1953*

53-S-159	Royal Garden Blues		(LP) M-G-M E261
53-S-160	Squeeze Me	-1	(LP) M-G-M E261
53-S-161	Go Go Go -3 (Kaminsky-Cary)	vMK&band	(LP) M-G-M E261
53-S-162	When the Saints Go Marching In	vMK&band	(LP) M-G-M E261

Ernie Caceres not heard on *Royal Garden Blues*.

(same personnel, except Jack Lesberg, b):   *New York City — March 18, 1953*

53-S-163	Original Dixieland One-Step		(LP) M-G-M E261
53-S-164	Samat Joy Blues (Kaminsky-Cary)		(LP) M-G-M E261
53-S-165	Eccentric Rag	-2, -3	(LP) M-G-M E261
53-S-166	I've Got the World on a String		(LP) M-G-M E261

Other issues include: 53-S-159 to 162 on (EP) M-G-M X4156, M-G-M(E) EP656; 53-S-163 to 166 on (EP) M-G-M X4157, M-G-M(E) EP600. 53-S-159 & 164 on (LP) MK1001. 53-S-163 on (LP) Verve(Eu) 845 149-1, (CD) 845 149-2, (AC) 845 149-4. All titles on (double LP) Verve(Eu) 2683-051 (163 & 166 on 2352 055; other 6 titles on 2352 056) and on (CD) OLP 224003.
MK 1001 was a compilation album sold by Kaminsky at Jimmy Ryan's.

JIMMY McPARTLAND and his Jazz Band (Jimmy McPartland, tp; Cutty Cutshall, tb; Bill Stegmeyer, cl; Ernie Caceres, bar; Dick Cary, p, arr; George Barnes, g; Sandy Block, b; George Wettling, d):   *New York City — April 7, 1953*

84272	Davenport Blues	(LP) Brunswick BL58049
84273	Since My Best Gal Turned Me Down	(LP) Brunswick BL58049
84274	Singin' the Blues	unissued

Cary said: "I played horn and piano." Perhaps he played horn on the unissued title?
Other issues: both titles on (LP) Brunswick BL54018, MCA 2-4110, Vogue(E) LRA10006 and (CD) J&M J&MCD8007.

(same personnel, except Paul Ricci, bar; for Caceres):   *New York City — April 9, 1953*

84297	Ostrich Walk	(LP) Brunswick BL58049

84298	Louisiana		(LP) Brunswick BL58049

Other issues: all titles on (LP) Brunswick BL54018, MCA2-4110, Vogue(E) LRA10006; and (CD) J&M J&MCD800

(same personnel): **New York City — May 14, 1953**

84501	I'm Coming Virginia	(LP) Brunswick BL58049
84502	Riverboat Shuffle	(LP) Brunswick BL58049
84503	Singin' the Blues	unissued
84504	Clarinet Marmalade	(LP) MCA 2-4110

Other issues: 84501/02/04 on (LP) Brunswick BL54018, MCA 2-4110, and (CD) J&M J&MCD8007. 84501/84502 on (LP) Vogue(E) LRA10006. This 3:00 version of *Clarinet Marmalade* (84504) was used for the 12″ albums: it follows same routine, with no piano solo and differing solos.

JEFF STOUGHTON and his Jazzband (Max Kaminsky, tp, vo; Jeff Stoughton, tb; Dick Cary, a-h, cel-3; Charlie Harmon, cl-1, ts-2; Paul Jouard, p; Slam Stewart, b; George Wettling, d):
WOR Studios, New York City — June 5, 1953

(a)	Black and Blue	-1,-2	(78) Preview P-100
(b)	Saints Come Marching In	vMK&band -1,-3	(78) Preview P-101
(c)	Basin Street Blues	-1,-3	(78) Preview P-102
(d)	Won't You Come Home Bill Bailey	-1 vMK	(78) Preview P-103

Note that each side is given a different release number. Cary is omitted from the personnel given on label, although his diary lists the session, mentioning "—and occasional celeste."

BUDDY GRECO, vocal with orchestra conducted by Don Costa: (3 tb; f-horn; 5 woodwinds; Dick Cary, p, celeste; unnamed, g; Ed Safranski, b; Phil Kraus, vb (& d?); vocal quartet; Don Costa, arr): **New York City — June 11, 1953**

84696	Ain't No In-Between	(78) Coral 61265
84697	What Word Is Sweeter Than Sweetheart?	(78) Coral 61190
84698	Don't Say Goodbye	(78) Coral 61038
84699	How Do You Think I Feel?	(78) Coral 61038

Bob Thiele was the producer. "The Decca Labels" shows Greco on piano.

JILL WHITNEY, vocal with orchestra conducted by Don Costa: (Jack Hanson, tp; unnamed, organ; Dick Cary, a-h, p, celeste; Bucky [Pizzarelli?], g, bj; Jerry Bruno, b, tu; Sid ----, d; Dominic(?) Cortese, a.n.other, acc): **Fulton Studios, New York City — August 1, 1953**

84986	On the Carousel	unissued
84987	The Tennessee Wig Walk	(78) Coral 61055
84988	That Old River Line	(78) Coral 61055
84989	Ragamuffin Doll	(78) Coral 61082

"The Decca Labels" has 84986 listed as "unknown." As Cary lists, by name, the four titles recorded, it is assumed that 84986 is the Jill Whitney title as shown.

WINGY MANONE and his Band (Wingy Manone, tp, vo; Cutty Cutshall, tb; Peanuts Hucko, cl; Dick Cary, tp, arr; Carmen Mastren, g; Jack Zimmerman, b; Cliff Leeman, d; The Town Criers, vo):
Engineering Society Hall, New York City — August 4, 1953

A1100	Vaya Con Dios	vWM,TTC	(78) Atlantic 15001
A1101	The Song From Moulin Rouge		
	(Where Is Your Heart)	vWM,TTC	(78) Atlantic 15001
A1102	Rose of San Antonio		unissued
A1103	Little Liza Jane		unissued

Cary says: "No piano – played trumpet all way."

HARRY RANCH (6 brass; 5 reeds; p; b; d: vo; personnel includes Stan Fishelson, tp; Jeff Stoughton, tb; Mrs. Harry Ranch, as; Dick Cary, tp or p; Bob Peterson, b):
New York City — October 1, 1953

    Don't
    Still Feel the Same
    Ding Dong Daddy
    Red Wing

No release details known.

EDDIE CONDON'S ALL-STARS (Wild Bill Davison, co; Dick Cary, tp; Cutty Cutshall, tb; Ed Hall, Peanuts Hucko, cl; Gene Schroeder, p; Eddie Condon, g; Walter Page, b; Cliff Leeman, d):
New York City — November 24, 1953

CO50398	Medley: Emaline	(Cutshall feature)	(LP) Columbia CL547
	Don't Worry 'Bout Me	(Hall feature)	
	I Can't Give You Anything But Love	(Davison feature))	

(same personnel, plus Lou McGarity, tb; George Wettling, d; Cary, tp, p):   *same date*

CO50399	Jam Session Blues/Ole Miss	(LP) Columbia CL547

Album notes state that Cary and Hucko supported "the harmony of the tempo-change pop tune medley." Other issues: all titles on (LP) CBS 53348, Philips BBL7013, 7023, Mosaic MQ-7-152; and (CD) Mosaic MCD-5-152, Collectables COLL-CD-7525, Classics 1354
Album title: Jam Session Coast To Coast

BUD FREEMAN and his Group (Bud Freeman, ts; Dick Cary, p, arr; George Barnes, g; Jack Lesberg, b; Don Lamond, d):   **New York City — December 4, 1953**

20256-3	Margo's Seal	(LP) Capitol H625
20257-7	I Guess I'll Have to Change My Plans	(LP) Capitol H625
20258-9	I Could Write a Book	(LP) Capitol H625
20259-1	Blues for Tenor	(LP) Capitol H625

(same personnel):   **New York City — December 11, 1953**

20271-10	Sweet Georgia Brown	(LP) Capitol H625
20272-3	Three Little Words	(LP) Capitol H625
20273-13	Blue Moon	(LP) Capitol H625
20274-8	Indian Summer	(LP) Capitol H625

Original title for *Blues for Tenor* was *Dorsey Brother Blues*.
Other issues for all 8 titles: on (LP) Capitol(E) LC6706, Affinity AFF64; on (CD) Mosaic 12-170, OLP 223997. 20274 also on (LP) Capitol T794. 20257/58/71/72/73/74 on (LP) Regal REG2074.
Album title: Bud Freeman

On December 15, 1953, Cary was at the M-G-M Studios to record a Pabst Blue Ribbon beer transcription. He wrote: "Some band." It included Andy Ferretti, Yank Lawson, Chris Griffin, trumpets; Cutty Cutshall, Bobby Byrne, Jack Satterfield, Will Bradley, trombones; Bill Stegmeyer, Paul Ricci in the reeds; Bob Haggart, bass; Don Lamond, drums. Bill Gale was the leader.

MARTY WILSON (?) (singer & male vocal quartet; Dick Cary, p, organ; a.n.other, p; Don Arnone, Dan Cortesi, a.n.other, g; Jerry Bruno, b; Don Lamond, d; Ben Bennett, arr):
New York City — December 20, 1953
    4 unknown titles for Columbia

JERRY JEROME (Jerome, ts; Phil Kraus, vb; Dick Cary, p; Allen Hanlon, g; Tommy Abruzzo, b):
New York City — February 15, 1954
    I Never Knew (That Roses Grew)   (CD) Arbors ARCD19168

PEE WEE RUSSELL and the Mahogany All Stars (Doc Cheatham, tp; Dick Cary, tp, arr; Vic Dickenson, tb; Pee Wee Russell, cl; George Wein, p; John Field, b; Buzzy Drootin, d; Al Bandini, vo):
Mastertone Studios, New York City — March 4, 1954

(a)	Lulu's Back in Town	(EP) Storyville EP408
(b)	We're in the Money	(EP) Storyville EP407
(c)	Gabriel Found His Horn vAB	(EP) Storyville EP407
(d)	Sweet and Slow	(EP) Storyville EP408
(e)	Sugar	(EP) Storyville EP408
(f)	Missy	(EP) Storyville EP407

Cary arranged all titles. He said: "I brought trumpet and played ensemble and background." *Missy* named for Pee Wee Russell's dog. The George Wein band, with Al Drootin on clarinet, was playing at Basin Street in New York.

Other issues: all titles on (LP) Storyville LP308, STLP 909, Jazztone J1257; (CD) Black Lion BLCD760909. (e),(f) on (CD) DA Music 874714-2.

LEE CASTLE'S JAZZTETTE (Lee Castle, tp, arr; Lou McGarity, tb; Peanuts Hucko, cl; Dick Cary, p, a-h*, arr; Bob Haggart, b; George Wettling, d):
Mastertone Studios, New York City — March 22, 1954

DA281	Alabama Blues		(LP) Jay-Dee LP-4
	Trombone Jitters		(LP) Jay-Dee LP-4
	On the Banks of the Wabash	aLC	(LP) Jay-Dee LP-4
DA284	Stars and Stripes Forever *	aLC	(LP) Jay-Dee LP-4

Mastertone Studios were located at 709 8th Avenue. Joe Davis, session producer and label owner, referred to a person playing French horn on *Stars and Stripes Forever*! Cary said he arranged all four titles.

Other issues: DA281/284 on (45) Jay-Dee 666; all titles on (45) Jay-Dee EP203, (LP) Davis JD-105, Harlequin HQ2003.

WALT GIFFORD'S NEW YORKERS (Johnny Windhurst, tp; Ed Hubble, tb; Bob Mitchell, cl; Dick Cary, p, arr; Paul Smith, g; Walt Gifford, d):
Rudy van Gelder Studio, Hackensack, NJ — May 16, 1954

(a)	I Can't Believe That You're in Love With Me	(LP) Delmar DL-206
(b)	Louisiana	(LP) Delmar DL-206

(c)	Struttin' With Some Barbecue	(LP) Delmar DL-206
(d)	It All Depends on You	(LP) Delmar DL-206
(e)	California, Here I Come	(LP) Delmar DL-206
(f)	Fidgety Feet	(LP) Delmar DL-206
(g)	Ida	unissued — acetate exists
(h)	Hindustan	unissued — acetate exists

All titles recorded in one take, except 3 takes for (a), 2 for (c) and 4 for (e).

Other issues: all DL-206 titles also on (LP) Esquire 32-197 and (AC) Jazz Connoisseur Cassette JCC126. (Delmar later became Delmark Records.)

Jepsen correctly gives the recording date and the unissued titles, but incorrectly lists John Field on bass. Joe Boughton, joint organiser of the session, confirms the presence of Paul Smith, brother-in-law of Eddie Condon and father-in-law of Bob Mitchell, as a late replacement, on guitar, for the scheduled bassist.

Sleeve note says that Gifford added "arranger Dick Cary on piano 'to keep us from falling through the ropes.'" Album title: Walt Gifford's New Yorkers.

MAX KAMINSKY and his Dixieland Bashers (Max Kaminsky, tp, vo; Ray Diehl, tb; Hank D'Amico, cl; Dick Cary, p, ah-1, cel-2; Don Arnone, g; Jack Zimmerman, b; Cliff Leeman, d):

New York City — May 24, 1954

E4VB 4305-1	Shim-Me-Sha-Wabble -1	(LP) Victor LJM3003
E4VB 4306-1	I Wish I Could Shimmy Like My Sister Kate vMK -1	(LP) Victor LJM3003
E4VB 4307-1	Whiffenpoof Song -2	(LP) Victor LJM3003
E4VB 4308-1	Jazz on the Campus (Carey [sic] — Kaminsky)	(LP) Victor LJM3003

(same personnel):   *New York City — May 25, 1954*

E4VB 4309-1	If I Had My Way	(LP) Victor LJM3003
E4VB 4310-1	Carey Me Back to Old Kaminsky (Carey [sic]-Kaminsky)	(LP) Victor LJM3003
E4VB 4311-1	Ugly Chile vMK	(LP) Victor LJM 3003
E4VB 4312-1	Satanic Blues	(LP) Victor LJM3003

Cliff Leeman arrived late and is not on *If I Had My Way* (and *Carey Me Back* also). Personnel is from RCA data sheet and confirmed by Cary. Some listings have shown Jack Lesberg on bass. Album title: Jazz on the Campus Ltd.

Other issues include: all 8 titles on (CD) Victor 74321 36408-2, OLP (Membran) 224003. 4305/6/9/10/11 on (CD) Vintage Music Productions VMP0311.

EDDIE CONDON and His All-Stars (Wild Bill Davison, co; Billy Butterfield, tp; Dick Cary, a-h; Lou McGarity, Cutty Cutshall, tb; Ed Hall, Peanuts Hucko, cl; Bud Freeman, ts; Gene Schroeder, p; Eddie Condon, g; Al Hall, b; Cliff Leeman, d):

New York City — June 24, 1954

CO51636	Blues My Naughty Sweetie Gave to Me	(LP) Columbia CL616
CO51637	How Come You Do Me Like You Do	(LP) Columbia CL616
CO51638	Medley: When My Sugar Walks Down the Street / I Can't Believe That You're in Love With Me	(LP) Columbia CL616

Other issues: all titles on (LP) Philips B 0744 L, Mosaic MQ-7-152, (CD) Classics 1464, OLP (Membran) 223217 (#22), Collectables COLL-CD-7526, Mosaic NCD-5-152
Album title: Jammin' At Condon's

LEE CASTLE'S JAZZTETTE (Lee Castle, tp, arr; Lou McGarity, tb; Peanuts Hucko, cl; Dick Cary, p, a-h, arr; Bob Haggart, b, wh*; George Wettling, d):
Mastertone Studios, New York City — October 21, 1954

(a)	Birmingham Special	(LP) Jay-Dee LP-4
(b)	Dixieland Mambo	
	(Lee Castle-Dick Carey [sic])	(LP) Jay-Dee LP-4
(c)	Mood in Blue	
	(Castle-Carey [sic] & Canyon) *	(LP) Jay-Dee LP-4
(d)	When the Saints Go Marching In aLC	(LP) Jay-Dee LP-4

Other issues: all titles on (EP) Jay-Dee EP204; (LP) Davis JD-105, Harlequin HQ2003.
Mood In Blue, composed by Lee Castle, Dick Cary and Virginia Canyon, was originally to be called *Virginia's Blues*

JERRY JEROME and His Orchestra (Louis Mucci, a.n.other, tp; Art Drellinger, Jerry Jerome, reeds; Dick Cary, p, arr; Don Arnone, g; Milt Hinton, b; Jimmy Crawford, d):
Fulton Studios, New York City — November 3, 1954

54-S-556-2/-3	Christopher Columbus	(78) M-G-M 12216
54-S-557-2	Goofus	(78) M-G-M 12216
54-S-558-3	Let Me Call You Sweetheart	unissued
54-S-559-6	Sleepy Time Gal	(78) M-G-M 11890

JACK TEAGARDEN & Friends (Fred Greenleaf, tp; Teagarden, tb, vo; Kenny Davern, cl; Norma Teagarden, p; Kass Malone, b; Ray Bauduc, d; Dick Cary, arr):
Esoteric Studios, New York City — November 12, 1954

(a)	Riverboat Shuffle	(LP) Period SLP-1110
(b)	Mis'ry and The Blues vJT	(LP) Period SLP-1106
(c)	King Porter Stomp	(LP) Period SLP-1110
(d)	Milenberg Joys	(LP) Period SLP-1110

Cary wrote: "I wasn't officially hired for this one, but I played on *Mis'ry*." It is possible there are two trumpets in the ensemble. Other issues: see over page

(Jimmy McPartland, co; Jack Teagarden, tb, vo; Ed Hall, cl; Dick Cary, p, arr; Walter Page, b; Jo Jones, d):
Esoteric Studios, New York City — November 13, 1954

(e)	Original Dixieland One Step	(LP) Period SPL-1110
(f)	Eccentric	(LP) Period SPL-1110
(g)	Bad Actin' Woman vJT	(LP) Period SPL-1106
(h)	High Society	(LP) Period SPL-1110

This was an afternoon session, starting at 2:30. Other issues: see over page

(Dick Cary, tp, arr; Teagarden, tb, vo; Ed Hall, cl; Leonard Feather, p; Carl Kress, g; Walter Page, b; Ray Bauduc, d):
Esoteric Studios, New York City — November 13, 1954

(i)	Meet Me Where They Play the Blues vJT	(LP) Period SLP-1106

(j)	Davenport Blues		(LP) Period SLP-1106
(k)	Blue Funk		(LP) Period SLP-1106
(l)	Music to Love By	vJT	(LP) Period SLP-1106

This was an evening session, starting at 6:00 p.m. Cary indicates that a fifth title was recorded – he mentions "my tune and a tune we made up like *Ja Da*." This last comment presumably refers to *Blue Funk*, credited to (Teagarden), leaving the Cary tune unissued. Other issues, many, including: all titles on (LP) Bethlehem BCP 6040 & BCP-32 (except (d) & (k)), Jazztone J-1222, LondonE LTZ-N 15077 (except (d) & (k)), Polydor(Eu) 545 104, (CD) Quadromania 222484-444, Giants of Jazz (It) CD-53123, OLP (Membran) 222981(#16). (d),(i) on (CD) Living Era AJS2005.(i),(j) on Collectables COL-CD-0870.

It appears that *Bad Actin' Woman* and *Milenberg Joys* were edited when the two 10″ Period LPs were transferred to a 12-inch album. The full version of *Bad Actin' Woman* lasts 5:18; the edited version 3:57. *Milenberg Joys* lasts 4:19 against 3:17.
Album titles: Jack Teagarden — Jazz Great / Meet Me Where They Play the Blues

BUD FREEMAN (Freeman, ts; Dick Cary and others?): **New York City — March 22, 1955**
        You're on My Mind
        Guada lajara (Guadalajara ?)
Cary: "made two sides at ARS with Bud." Possibly audition recordings.

ED HALL (Dick Cary, tp, a-h; Lou McGarity, tb; Ed Hall, cl; Eddie Barefield, bar; Gene Schroeder, p, arr; Don Arnone, g; Walter Page, b; George Wettling, d; string section; Sunny Calella, vo; one male-1, one female-2, vo): **Esoteric Studios, New York City — April 1, 1955**

(a)	You Promised to Write	vSC	unissued
(b)	Rose in her Window	vSC	unissued
(c)	Adam and Evie	-2	unissued
(d)	One World	-1	unissued

Apparently recorded for Ed Hall's private use.

EDDIE CONDON and His All-Stars (Bobby Hackett, co; Cutty Cutshall, tb; Dick Cary, a-h, arr; Ed Hall, cl; Gene Schroeder, p; Eddie Condon, g; Walter Page, b; George Wettling, d):
New York City — April 20, 1955

CO53225	Singin' the Blues	(LP) Columbia CL719
CO53226	From Monday On	(LP) Columbia CL719
CO53227	I'm Comin' Virginia	(LP) Columbia CL719
CO53228	I'll Be a Friend With Pleasure	(LP) Columbia CL719
CO53229	Royal Garden Blues	(LP) Columbia CL719

Other issues: All titles on (LP) Mosaic MQ-7-152, (CD) Mosaic MCD-5-152, OLP (Membran) 223217, Starlite CDS51039, Collectables COLL-CD-7525, Classics 1464, Avid AMSC988.
Album title: Bixieland.

On May 12, 1955 the **AL GENTILE** orchestra taped 4 or 5 titles at the New Brunswick teachers' college. Cary and Betty O'Hara were in the band. Presumably these were audition records. The titles included: *Everything I Have Is Yours* / *I've Got the World on a String* vBOH / and *Darts*.

MARION EVANS (Dick Cary, p; 2 bj; Jerry Bruno, tu; Phil Kraus, d; singers; Marion Evans, presumably conductor & arranger):   ***New York City — June 24, 1955***

    shown in Dick Cary diary — no other details, except that Cary refers to playing "whorehouse piano."

BARBARA LEA (vocal, with Johnny Windhurst, tp; Dick Cary, a-h, arr; Dick Hyman, p; Al Hall, b; Osie Johnson, d):   ***Hackensack, NJ — October 18, 1956***

983	Baltimore Oriole	(LP) Prestige P-7065
984	I Had Myself a True Love	(LP) Prestige P-7065
985	Nobody Else But Me	(LP) Prestige P-7065

Thursday's Child (986) from this date is without Cary. Dick Hyman used pseudonym of Richard Lowman for this session, held in the Rudy Van Gelder Recording Studio. Other issues: all titles on (LP) Prestige DIW 9004, Esquire 32-043 and (CD) Fantasy OJCCD-1713-2

BARBARA LEA (vocal, with Windhurst, tp; Cary, p arr, a-h-1; Al Casamenti, g, Al Hall, b; Osie Johnson, d):   ***Hackensack, NJ — October 19, 1956***

987	My Honey's Lovin' Arms -1	(LP) Prestige P-7065
988	I've Got a Pocketful of Dreams	(LP) Prestige P-7065
989	Where Have You Been?	(LP) Prestige P-7065
990	I'm Comin' Virginia	(LP) Prestige P-7065
991	Honey in the Honeycomb	(LP) Prestige P-7065
992	Gee Baby, Ain't I Good to You (Windhurst out)	(LP) Prestige P-7065
993	I Feel At Home With You	(LP) Prestige P-7065
994	Blue Skies -1	(LP) Prestige P-7065

An alternative take for 993 has been reported on (CD) Fantasy OJCCD-1713-2.

Other issues: all titles on (LP) Prestige DIW9004, Esquire 32-043 and (CD) Fantasy OJCCD-1713-2. (g) on (45) Prestige 45-101. (b) & (e) on (AC) Jazz Connoisseur Cassette JCC126. (Cary noted: "double date in NJ.") Album title: Nobody Else But Me.

DON COSTA, His Orchestra & Chorus (Don Costa, conductor arranger; strings; harp; acc; Dick Cary, p; g; b; d; voices):   ***First Sound Studios, New York City — October 24, 1956***

565	Around the World	(45) ABC-Paramount 45-9770
566	Everybody Loves Pierre *	(45) ABC-Paramount 45-9770
567	C'est Ca!	(45) ABC-Paramount 45-9783

(add brass section — including Dick Cary, tp):

568	By the Fireside	(45) ABC-Paramount 45-9783

* "out-of-tune" piano on this track, a Costa original. Cary plays celeste on 567 or 568. 565/566 contain voices; 567/568 a vocal group.

LEE CASTLE'S JAZZTETTE (Lee Castle, tp, arr; Lou McGarity, tb; Bob Wilber, cl; Dick Cary, p; Bob Haggart, b; George Wettling, d): ***Mastertone Studios, New York City — January 10, 1957***

	Save It Pretty Mama	(LP) Davis JD-105
	Feeling Sentimental	(LP) Davis JD-105
	My Wild Irish Rose aLC	(LP) Davis JD-105
	Fair Jennie's Lament	(LP) Davis JD-105

Other issue: all titles on (LP) Harlequin HQ2003
Album title: Dixieland Heaven

JIMMY McPARTLAND and his Dixieland Band (Jimmy McPartland, tp; Tyree Glenn, tb; Ernie Caceres, cl; Dick Cary, p, cel-1, a-h-2, arr; Al Casamenti, g; Bill Crow, b; George Wettling, d):

New York City — February 26, 1957

CO 57470-5	Ballin' the Jack	(LP) Epic LN3371
CO 57471-2	Lackadaisy Lazy (J McPartland-D Cary)	(LP) Epic LN3371
CO 57472-4	Blues My Naughty Sweetie Gave to Me -2	(LP) Epic LN3371
CO 57473-2	The Basin Street Stomp	(LP) Epic LN3371

Other issue: all titles on (CD) Mosaic MD8-206

(same personnel, except Peanuts Hucko, cl; and Cliff Leeman, d; replace Caceres and Wettling):

New York City — March 5, 1957

CO 57510-5/6	The Albatross J McPartland-D Cary	-2	(LP) Epic LN3371
CO 57511-11	Third Street Blues (J McPartland-D Cary)	-2	(LP) Epic LN3371
CO 57512-4	Shim-Me-Sha-Wabble (LP) Epic LN3371		
CO 57513-2	Whistle Stop (J McPartland-D Cary)	-2	(LP) Epic LN3371
CO 57514-3	Oh, Didn't He Ramble	-1	(LP) Epic LN3371
CO 57515-7	Original Dixieland One-Step	-2	(LP) Epic LN3371
CO 57516-2	There'll Be Some Changes Made	-2	(LP) Epic LN3371
CO 57517-1	Sugar Foot Strut		(LP) Epic LN3371

master 57510 consists of two takes spliced together. Two sessions, 3 pm to 6 & 11 pm-2 am.

Other issues: all titles on (LP) Fontana Z4005, (CD) Mosaic MD8-206
Album title: Jimmy McPartland's Dixieland.

BUD FREEMAN's Summa Cum Laude Orchestra (Jimmy McPartland, tp; Pee Wee Russell, cl; Bud Freeman, ts; Dick Cary, p; Al Casamenti, g; Milt Hinton, b; George Wettling, d):

New York City — March 7, 1957

H2JB2160	Liza	(LP) Victor LPM1508
H2JB2161	China Boy	(LP) Victor LPM1508
H2JB2162	Sugar	(LP) Victor LPM1508
H2JB2163	Nobody's Sweetheart	(LP) Victor LPM1508

Other issues: all titles on (CD) Mosaic MCD-1002.
Album title: Chicago/Austin High School Jazz In Hi-Fi.

> The broadcasts by the Bobby Hackett band which follow were made on Saturdays from the Voyager Room of the Henry Hudson Hotel in the Mutual network's "Bandstand USA" series. Many were included on AFRTS (Armed Forces Radio and Television Service) transcriptions, from which commercial issues were taken. Refer additional note after January 25, 1958 broadcast.

BOBBY HACKETT and his Jazz Band (Bobby Hackett, co; Dick Cary, a-h-1, p-2, arr; Tommy Gwaltney, cl-3, vbs-4; Ernie Caceres, cl-5, bar-6; John Dengler, tu; Nat Ray, d):

broadcast, Henry Hudson Hotel, New York City — March 16, 1957

(a)	It Don't Mean a Thing	-1,-2,-3,-6	(Tx) AFRTS Bandstand USA
(b)	Sugar	-2,-3,-6	(Tx) AFRTS Bandstand USA

(c)	Muskrat Ramble	-1,-2,-3,-6	(Tx) AFRTS Bandstand USA
(d)	Creole Love Call (incomplete) -2,-3,-5,-6		(Tx) AFRTS Bandstand USA

Other issues: (a),(b),(c) on (LP) Alamac QSR2443, on (CD) LonehillJazz LHJ10271, and on (AC) Jazz Connoisseur Cassettes JCC52

(same personnel):   **broadcast, Henry Hudson Hotel, New York City — March 23, 1957**

(a)	Handle With Cary (Cary)	-1,-2,-3,-6	(Tx) AFRTS Bandstand USA
(b)	Basin Street Blues	-2,-3,-6	(Tx) AFRTS Bandstand USA

Other issues: both titles on (LP) Alamac QSR2443, on (CD) LonehillJazz LHJ10271, and on (AC) Jazz Connoisseur Cassettes JCC52

BOBBY HACKETT and his Jazz Band (Bobby Hackett, co; Dick Cary, a-h; Tommy Gwaltney, cl-1, vbs-2; Ernie Caceres, cl-3, bar-4; Mickey Crane, p; Milt Hinton, b; John Dengler, tu; Nat Ray, d):   ***New York City — March 27, 1957***

21451-5	Caravan	-2,-3	(LP) Capitol T857
21452-13	Lazy Mood	-1,-2,-4	(LP) Capitol T857
21453-8	The Continental	-2,-4	(LP) Capitol T857

Other issues: all titles on (CD) Dormouse DM1 CDX03, Mosaic MD5-210

(same personnel and instrumentation as March 16, 1957):
   broadcast, Henry Hudson Hotel, New York City — March 30, 1957

(a)	Spinning (Cary)	-1,-2,-3,-6	(Tx) AFRTS Bandstand USA
(b)	Tin Roof Blues	-2,-3,-6	(Tx) AFRTS Bandstand USA
(c)	Just One of Those Things	-2,-4,-5	(Tx) AFRTS Bandstand USA
(d)	I Got It Bad and That Ain't Good (incomplete)	-2,-4,-6	(Tx) AFRTS Bandstand USA

Hackett & Dengler out on (c). Correct title for (a) is Spinney. Other issues: (a),(b),(c) on (LP) Alamac QSR2443, on (CD) LonehillJazz LHJ10271, and on (AC) Jazz Connoisseur Cassettes JCC52. (b) also on (AC) Jazz Connoisseur Cassettes JCC55.

BUD FREEMAN'S Summa Cum Laude Orchestra (Billy Butterfield, tp; Tyree Glenn, tb; Russell, cl; Bud Freeman, ts; Dick Cary, p, a-h; Casamenti, g; Al Hall, b; Wettling, d):
   New York City — April 3, 1957

H2JB3214	Chicago	(LP) Victor LPM1508
H2JB3215	At Sundown	(LP) Victor LPM1508
H2JB3216	Sunday	(LP) Victor LPM1644

(Glenn, Russell out; Cary a-h only):   ***same date***

H2JB3217	The Reverend's in Town	(Freeman-Cary)	(LP) Victor LPM1644

Other issues: all titles on (CD) Mosaic MCD-1002. Album titles: LPM1508 Chicago/Austin High School In Hi-Fi; LPM1644 Bread, Butter and Jam in Hi-Fi.

BOBBY HACKETT and his Jazz Band (same personnel as March 27, 1957, except Al Hall, b; replaces Hinton):   ***New York City — April 4, 1957***

21454-10	In a Little Spanish Town	-1,-4	(LP) Capitol T857
21455-3	Tin Roof Blues	-1,-4	(LP) Capitol T857

21456-11	Albatross (Cary-McPartland) -1,-4 *		(LP) Capitol T857
21457-4	It Don't Mean a Thing		(CD) Mosaic MD5-210
21463-6	Cornet Chop Suey	-1,-4	(LP) Capitol T857

* Hackett calls out, "Come on, Nat."

Other issues: Capitol T857 titles on (CD) Dormouse DMI CDX03, Mosaic MD5-210.

(same personnel, except Milt Hinton, b; replaces Hall):   **New York City — April 10, 1957**

21480	Henry Hudson (Richard Cary)	-1,-4	(LP) Capitol T857
21481	Wolverine Blues	-1,-3,-4	(LP) Capitol T857
21482	Rose Room	-2,-3	(LP) Capitol T857
21483	At the Jazz Band Ball	-1,-4	(LP) Capitol T857

Other issues: all titles on (CD) Dormouse DM1 CDX03, Mosaic MD5-210
Album title: Gotham Jazz Scene

BARBARA LEA (vocal, with Dick Cary, p, arr; Al Casamenti, g; Al Hall, b):
Bell Sound Studio, 247 W. 46, New York City — April 19, 1957

1204	Will I Find My Love Today?	(LP) Prestige P-7100
1205	Aren't You Glad You're You?	unissued
1206	Autumn Leaves	(LP) Prestige P-7100
1207	Ain't Misbehavin'	(LP) Prestige P-7100

Dick Cary confirmed *Aren't You Glad You're You* for this session.

Other issues: all titles (LP) Esquire 32-063 and (CD) Prestige OJCCD-1742-2

BUD FREEMAN All Stars* / GEORGE WETTLING All Stars# (Max Kaminsky, tp; Cutty Cutshall, tb; Pee Wee Russell, cl; Bud Freeman, ts; Dick Cary, p; Eddie Condon, g; Leonard Gaskin, b; George Wettling, d):   **New York City — April 22, 1957**

CO 57831-1	Ginger Brown	*	(LP) Harmony HL7046
CO 57832-2	Runnin' Wild	#	(LP) Harmony HL7080
CO 57833-1	Dinah	*	(LP) Harmony HL7046
CO 57834-2	Odd Aardvark	#	(CD) Mosaic MD8-206
CO 57834-3	Odd Aardvark	#	(CD) Harmony HL7080

Other issues: all titles on (CD) Mosaic MD8-206.
Cary notes that Odd Aardvark, a Wettling composition, was also called *John Ringling North went south and brought Mae West back east*. *Ginger Brown* credited to Bud Freeman, but Cary also received royalty payments for this tune.

BARBARA LEA (vocal, with Dick Cary, a-h, arr; Ernie Caceres, cl, bar-1; Garvin Bushell, oboe, bassoon-2; Jimmy Lyon, p, cel-3; Jimmy Raney, g; Beverly Peer, b; Osie Johnson, d):
New York City — April 24, 1957

1214	Sleep Peaceful, Mr. Used-To-Be	-3	(LP) Prestige P-7100
1215	I'm Old Fashioned		unissued
1216	The Very Thought of You	-2	(LP) Prestige P-7100
1217	I've Got My Eyes on You	-1	(LP) Prestige P-7100

Cary confirmed *I'm Old Fashioned* for this session.

Other issues: all titles on (LP) Esquire 32-063 and (CD) Prestige OJCCD-1742-2

BARBARA LEA (vocal, with Johnny Windhurst, tp; Ernie Caceres, cl, bar-1; Dick Cary, p, a-h-2, arr; Al Casamenti, g; Al Hall, b; Osie Johnson, d): **New York City — April 26, 1957**
(a)	We Could Make Such Beautiful Music Together	-1,-2	(LP) Prestige P-7100
(b)	Am I in Love?	-2	(LP) Prestige P-7100
(c)	Mountain Greenery		(LP) Prestige P-7100
(d)	More Than You Know		(LP) Prestige P-7100

Master numbers for this session, reported in Lord, were 1225 through 1228.

Other issues: all titles on (LP) Esquire 32-063 an (CD) Prestige OJCCD-1742-2

BARBARA LEA (vocal, with Johnny Windhurst, tp; Dick Cary, a-h, arr; Jimmy Lyon, p; Jimmy Raney, g; Beverly Peer, b): **Bell Sound Studio, New York City — May 1, 1957**
(a)	You'd Be So Nice to Come Home To	(LP) Prestige P-7100

(same, except Adele Girard, harp; replaces Windhurst): **same date**
(b)	True Love	(LP) Prestige P-7100

Cary also lists *Guess I'll Go Back Home This Summer* and *Ev'ry Time We Say Goodbye,* presumably unissued. Master numbers for this session, reported in Lord, were 1235 to 1239.

Other issues: both titles on (LP) Esquire 32-063 and (CD) Prestige OJCCD-1742-2.

DICK TODD (vocal, with Dick Cary, tp, a-tp, a-h, p; Joe Marsala, cl; Al Casamenti, g; Al Hall, b; Buzzy Drootin, d): **New York City — June 8, 1957**

an unissued session for Stere-O-Craft, mentioned in Dick Cary's diary

THE DICK CARY GROUP (Johnny Glasel, tp; Dick Cary, tp, a-h, arr; Urbie Green, tb; Bob Wilber, cl-1, ts; Hall Overton, p; Sal Salvador, g; Jack Zimmerman, b; Bill Stanley, tu; Jerry Segal, d): **Huntington, Long Island, NY — June 11, 1957**
(a)	Mahogany Hall Stomp		(LP) Golden Crest CR3024
(b)	Muskrat Ramble	-1	(LP) Golden Crest CR3024
(c)	That's a Plenty	-1	(LP) Golden Crest CR3024
(d)	St. James Infirmary		(LP) Golden Crest CR3024
(e)	Darktown Strutters Ball	-1	(LP) Golden Crest CR3024
(f)	Milenberg Joys	-1	(LP) Golden Crest CR3024

Other titles on album by John Plonsky, without Cary. Album title: Dixieland Goes Progressive.

DICK CARY (Cary, tp-1, a-tp-2, a-h-3, p-4, arr; Al Cohn, ts, cl; Bob Wilber, cl, b-cl; Ernie Caceres, cl, bs; Al Casamenti, g; Al Hall, b; Buzzy Drootin, d): **New York City — June 20, 1957**
(a)	Touché (Cary)	-1	(LP) Stere-o-Craft RTN-106
(b)	Crosseyed Penguin (Cary)	-1	(LP) Stere-o-Craft RTN-106
(c)	Roseroom (sic)	-2?,-3	(LP) Stere-o-Craft RTN-106
(d)	Lady in a Lavender Mist	-3,-4	(LP) Stere-o-Craft RTN-106
(e)	You Do Something to Me	-2,-3	(LP) Stere-o-Craft RTN-106
(f)	More Than You Know	-1	(LP) Stere-o-Craft RTN-106
(g)	The Reverend's Back in Town (Cary-Freeman)	-3	(LP) Stere-o-Craft RTN-106
(h)	Last Mile (Cary)	-1,-4	(LP) Stere-o-Craft RTN-106

This was an afternoon session, starting at 1 p.m. — 8 titles in 3 1/2 hours.

Other issues: all titles on (LP) Bell BLP44, Bell SBLP44, and (reel-to-reel) Hi-Life THL-44.
(a),(e) on (45) Stere-o-Craft SS103. The label credits Cary with the Duke Ellington composition, *Lady of the Lavender Mist*. Album title: Dick Cary: Hot and Cool.

Soloists for these titles, identified by Bob Wilber, are:
Touché: DC, tp; EC, bar; AC, ts; BW, b-cl, cl. 2 cl & b-cl in ensembles.
Crosseyed Penguin: DC, tp; EC, cl; AC, ts; BW, cl. 2 cl & b-cl in ensemble.
Rose Room: DC, a-tp?; EC, bar; AC, ts; BW, cl.
Lady in a Lavender Mist: EC, cl; BW, cl. 2 cl & ts in ensemble.
You Do Something to Me: DC, a-tp; BW, b-cl; AC, ts; EC, cl; b-cl in ensemble.
More Than You Know: DC, tp; BW, cl; EC, bar.
The Reverend's Back in Town: DC, a-h; AC, ts; EC, bar; BW, cl. b-cl in ensemble.
Last Mile: AC, ts; EC, bar; BW, b-cl. b-cl in ensemble.

THE BUD FREEMAN GROUP (Freeman, ts; Dick Cary, p; Al Hall, b; George Wettling, d):
New York City — June 20, 1957

(a)	Rosalie	(LP) Stere-o-Craft RTN103
(b)	April Mood (Cary-Freeman)	(LP) Stere-o-Craft RTN103
(c)	Why Shouldn't I?	(LP) Stere-o-Craft RTN103
(d)	'Swonderful	(LP) Stere-o-Craft RTN103
(e)	Hanid (Cary-Freeman)	(LP) Stere-o-Craft RTN103
(f)	Three Little Words	(LP) Stere-o-Craft RTN103
(g)	Two Channel Blues (Freeman-Cary-Wettling-Hall)	(LP) Stere-o-Craft RTN103
(h)	I'll Get By	(LP) Stere-o-Craft RTN103
(i)	You Do Something to Me	(LP) Stere-o-Craft RTN103
(j)	The Way (Cary-Freeman)	(LP) Stere-o-Craft RTN103
(k)	Sweet Sue	(LP) Stere-o-Craft RTN103
(l)	Crazy Rhythm	(LP) Stere-o-Craft RTN103
(m)	Newport News (Cary-Freeman)	(tape, 7 1/2 ips) Stere-o-Craft TN103

Cary shows this session following on from his own date — "Then Bud's quartet 5-7." But as the quartet recorded a total of 13 titles, the "5-7" must have a meaning other than time.

Other issues: (g) on (LP) Stere-o-Craft RCN500. (c),(d),(e),(f),(i),(k),(l),(m) on (tape, 7 1/2 ips) Stere-o-Craft TN103. Album title: The Bud Freeman Group.

JOE MARSALA and his Chicago Jazz (Rex Stewart, co; Joe Marsala, cl; Adele Girard, harp; Dick Cary, p, tp-1; Carmen Mastren, g; Pat Merola, b; Johnny Blowers, b):
New York City — June 28, 1957

(a)	Wolverine Blues	-1	(LP) Stere-O-Craft RTN102
(b)	Mandy	-1	(LP) Stere-O-Craft RTN102
(c)	Night Train		(LP) Stere-O-Craft RTN102
(d)	Singin' the Blues		(LP) Stere-O-Craft RTN102
(e)	Sweet Georgia Brown		(LP) Stere-O-Craft RTN102
(f)	I Cried for You	(see note)	(LP) Stere-O-Craft RTN102
(g)	Viva Rex		(LP) Stere-O-Craft RTN102
(h)	Chicago		(LP) Stere-O-Craft RTN102

(d) omit Stewart. (f) omit Girard. (g) omit Marsala, Girard. (h) omit Girard. No composer credits given, so not known if Cary contributed to *Viva Rex*.

(f) a query hangs over *I Cried For You*, one which clarinetist Bobby Gordon, who was one of Joe Marsala's pupils, told to drummer/writer Sonny McGown. Jack Gordon, Bobby's father, was the producer of the Marsala session and also of a George Wettling session, with Herman Autrey, tp; Vic Dickenson, tb; Herb Hall, cl; Gene Schroeder, p; Leonard Gaskin, b; for Stere-O-Craft in April 1957. Bobby Gordon was present at the Wettling session and remembers Joe Marsala dropping in. He stated that *I Cried For You* was recorded on that day, with Marsala using Gordon's clarinet. Aurally this seems likely, as the harmonising behind Marsala appears to be by clarinet and trombone. If so, this number is not a Dick Cary item. However if, as Cary stated, 8 titles were recorded, then one unknown title was unissued.

Other issues: all titles on (LP) Hi-Life 65

BOBBY HACKETT and his Jazz Band (Hackett, co; Dick Cary, a-h-1, p-2; Tommy Gwaltney, cl-3,vbs-4; Ernie Caceres, cl-5, bar-6; John Dengler, tu; Buzzy Drootin, d):

Newport Jazz Festival, Newport, RI — July 5, 1957

(a)	Royal Garden Blues	-1,-2,-3,-6	(Tx) Voice of America J107
(b)	Handle With Cary (Cary)	-1,-2,-4,-6	(Tx) Voice of America J107
(c)	Caravan	-1,-2,-4,-5	(Tx) Voice of America J107
(d)	Lady of the Lavender Mist	-1,-2,-4,-5	(Tx) Voice of America J107
(e)	Off Minor	-2,-4	(Tx) Voice of America J107
(f)	Fidgety Feet	-1,-2,3,-6	(Tx) Voice of America J107
(g)	My Funny Valentine	-2,-4	unissued?

Bobby Hackett does not play on (e) and (g).

Other issues: the J107 titles are on (CD) Vipers Nest VN162.

BOBBY HACKETT (with orchestra directed by Dan Terry: Bobby Hackett, co; Dick Cary, a-h, a-tp; strings, incl. 4 cellos; Dick Hyman, harpsichord; guitar; bass; drums; vocal choir):

New York City — December 19, 1957

21815-	Ev'rything I Love	(LP) Capitol T1002
21816-	Wonderful One	(LP) Capitol T1002
21817-	Don't Take Your Love From Me	(LP) Capitol T1002
21818-	Street of Dreams	(LP) Capitol T1002

Other issues include: 21816/818 on (LP) Pickwick PC/SPC3012, Sears SPC410; all titles on (CD) Mosaic MD5-210

JIMMY McPARTLAND'S ALL STARS (Jimmy McPartland, co; Max Kaminsky, Johnny Glasel, tp; Tyree Glenn, Vernon Brown, Al Gusikoff, Cutty Cutshall, tb; Peanuts Hucko, cl; George Berg, tenor, bassoon; Dick Cary, p, F-tp-1, cel-2, arr; Billy Bauer, g; Bob Haggart, b; Bill Bell, tu; Cliff Leeman, d; unknown male chorus -1): *New York City — December 19, 1957*

CO59268-6	Seventy-Six Trombones -2	(LP) Epic LN3463
CO59269-8/9	Marian the Librarian -1	(LP) Epic LN3463

59269 has two takes spliced together. (In his diary Cary gives Marian McPartland as pianist for this session.)

BOBBY HACKETT and his Jazz Band (Hackett, co; Dick Cary, p-1, a-h-2, arr; Bob Wilber, cl-3, ts-4, vbs-5; Dick Hafer, ts-6, bar-7, cl-8; John Dengler, tu; Buzzy Drootin, d):

broadcast, Henry Hudson Hotel, New York City — December 21, 1957

(a)	It Don't Mean a Thing	-1,-2-3,-7	(Tx) AFRTS Bandstand USA 20
(b)	Spain	-1,-5	(Tx) AFRTS Bandstand USA 20
(c)	Swing 39	-1,-4,-6	(Tx) AFRTS Bandstand USA 20
(d)	Guess I'll Go Back Home This Summer		
		-1,-3,-5,-7	(Tx) AFRTS Bandstand USA 20
(e)	Jingle Bells		unissued?
(f)	Caravan (incomplete)		unissued?

Hackett & Hafer out on (b).

Other issues: (a),(b),(c) on (LP) Shoestring SS108 and (d) on (LP) Shoestring SS113. (a),(b),(c),(d) on (CD) LonehillJazz LHJ10271.

(same personnel): **broadcast, Henry Hudson Hotel, New York City — December 28, 1957**

(a)	Lullaby in Rhythm	-1,-2,-3,-5,-8	(Tx) AFRTS Bandstand USA 21
(b)	New Orleans	-1,-5,-6	unissued?
(c)	Holiday Hop (Cary)	-1,-2,-3,-6,-7	(Tx) AFRTS Bandstand USA 21
(d)	I'm Beginning To See The Light		
		-1,-2,-3,-7	(Tx) AFRTS Bandstand USA 21
(e)	Cornet Chop Suey (incomplete)		
		-1,-2,-3,-5,-6	(Tx) AFRTS Bandstand USA 21
(f)	'Swonderful	-1,-2,-5,-6	unissued?
(g)	It's All In Your Mind (incomplete)		
		-2,-3,-6	unissued?

Other issues: (a),(c),(d),(e) on (LP) Shoestring SS113 and on (CD) LonehillJazz LHJ10271.

JIMMY McPARTLAND'S ALL STARS (McPartland, co; Kaminsky, Glasel, Dick Cary, tp, a-h-1, F-tp-2, arr; Cutshall, Lou McGarity, Frank Rehak, tb; Sol Yaged, cl; Bud Freeman, ts; Marian McPartland, p; Sal Salvador, g; Bill Crow, b; Bill Stanley, tu; George Wettling, d; Cary, arr):

New York City — January 2, 1958

CO59279-6/7	Till There Was You	-1	(LP) Epic LN3463
CO59280-6	It's You	-2	(LP) Epic LN3463
CO59281-2/5	Iowa Stubborn		(LP) Epic LN3463
CO59282-	Lida Rose/Will I Ever Tell You		unissued

59279/59281 both have two takes spliced together.

(same co/tp; Cutshall, McGarity, Al Gusikoff, tb; Pee Wee Russell, Bob Wilber, cl; Freeman, ts; same rhythm, except Eddie Condon, g; for Salvador): **New York City — January 3, 1958**

CO60300-3	Gary, Indiana	-1	(LP) Epic LN3463
CO60301-5	The Wells Fargo Wagon	-3	(LP) Epic LN3463

In his diary Cary says *Goodnight My Someone* was recorded on this date by Barbara Lea, with Marian McPartland and Bill Crow. -3 Cary plays doctored piano. For other issues, see below.

BOBBY HACKETT and his Jazz Band (personnel as for December 21, 1957):
broadcast, Henry Hudson Hotel, New York City — January 4, 1958

(a)	Fidgety Feet	-1,-3,-6	(Tx) AFRTS Bandstand USA
(b)	Old Folks		(Tx) AFRTS Bandstand USA

(c)	Cottontail	-1,-4,-6,-8?	(Tx) AFRTS Bandstand USA
(d)	The Reverend's in Town (Freeman-Cary)		unissued?
(e)	Sweet and Lovely		unissued?

Other issues: (a),(c) on LP Shoestring SS108, and on (CD) LonehillJazz LHJ10271.

(same personnel): **broadcast, Henry Hudson Hotel, New York City — January 11, 1958**

(a)	It Don't Mean A Thing	-1,-2,-4,-7	(Tx) AFRTS Bandstand USA 23
(b)	Ill Wind	-1,-3	(Tx) AFRTS Bandstand USA 23
(c)	Swiss Criss (Hackett-Cary)	-1,-2,-4,-6,-7	(Tx) AFRTS Bandstand USA 23
(d)	Lady of the Lavender Mist	-1,-2,-3,-5,-8	(Tx) AFRTS Bandstand USA 23
(e)	Cancel the Flowers		unissued?
(f)	Tenderly		unissued?

Hackett & Hafer out on (b).

Other issues: (a) on (LP) Shoestring SS108. (b),(c),(d) on (LP) Shoestring SS113: and on (CD) Lonehill Jazz LHJ10271, (d) shown as *The Lady With the Lavender Hair* on both issues.

JIMMY McPARTLAND'S ALL STARS (McPartland, co, vo; Cary, tp, a-h-1, F-tp-2, arr; Charlie Shavers, tp; Cutshall, tb; Peanuts Hucko, cl; Freeman, Coleman Hawkins, ts; Gene Schroeder, p; Condon, g; Milt Hinton, b; Cliff Leeman, d; Cary, arr):

New York City — January 16, 1958

CO60360-4	Goodnight My Someone	-2	(LP) Epic LN3463
CO60361-7	The Sadder-But-Wiser Girl for Me	vJM	(LP) Epic LN3463
CO60362-2/6	Ya Got Trouble	vJM	(LP) Epic LN3463
CO59282-13	Lida Rose/Will I Ever Tell You	-1	(LP) Epic LN3463

60362 has two takes spliced together. Take details for all titles as listed in the Mosaic set.

Other issues: Epic LN3463 on (LP) Fontana Z4060 and (CD) Mosaic MD8-206.
Album title: "The Music Man" Goes Dixieland.

BOBBY HACKETT and his Jazz Band (same personnel was January 11, 1958):

broadcast, Henry Hudson Hotel, New York City — January 18, 1958

(a)	Morning Air	-1,-2,-3,-7,-8	(Tx) AFRTS Bandstand USA 24
(b)	The Seal	-2,-4,-6	(Tx) AFRTS Bandstand USA 24
(c)	Lazy Mood (incomplete)		(Tx) AFRTS Bandstand USA 24
(d)	You Asked for It		unissued?
(e)	The Cross Eyed Penguin (Cary)		unissued?

Hackett out on (b).

Other issues: (a),(b) on (LP) Shoestring SS113: and on (CD) LonehillJazz LHJ10271.

(same personnel): **broadcast, Henry Hudson Hotel, New York City — January 25, 1958**

(a)	Handle With Cary (Cary)	-1,-2,-3,-5,-6,-7	(Tx) AFRTS Bandstand USA 25
(b)	Guess I'll Go Back Home This Summer	-2,-5,-7,-8	(Tx) AFRTS Bandstand USA 25
(c)	Zig Zag	-2,-4,-6	(Tx) AFRTS Bandstand USA 25
(d)	Spain (incomplete)		(Tx) AFRTS Bandstand USA 25
(e)	The Voyager		unissued?
(f)	Royal Garden Blues (incomplete)		unissued?

Other issues: (a) on (LP) Shoestring SS108: (b),(c) on (LP) Shoestring SS113: on (CD) LonehillJazz LHJ10271.

There are a number of untraced "Bandstand USA" transcriptions by the Bobby Hackett sextet at the Henry Hudson Hotel which will include Dick Cary in the personnel. There are 10 broadcasts known for Mondays between April 13 and June 22, plus one on December 7, 1957. Tapes of these broadcasts exist. Refer for details to the forthcoming Bobby Hackett Discography by George Hulme and Bert Whyatt, and to the article in the Fall 1992 issue of the IAJRC Journal. The last title on almost every broadcast is obscured by conversation between Guy Wallace and a guest critic such as Leonard Feather or Bill Coss.

REX STEWART (Stewart, co, vo; George Stevenson, tb; Haywood Henry, cl; George Kelly, ts; Dick Cary, p; Leonard Gaskin, b; Art Trappier, d):
Victor Studios, New York City — January 27, 1958
My Kind of Gal (Cary) vRS   (LP) Felsted FAJ 7001

Willie "The Lion" Smith is the pianist on the other titles from this session. Cary is probably arranger for *My Kind of Gal.*

(Stewart, co; Hilton Jefferson, cl, as; Garvin Bushell, cl, bassoon -1; Dick Cary, tp, p, arr; Everett Barksdale, g; Joe Benjamin, b; Mickey Sheen, d):
Victor Studios, New York City — January 31, 1958
(a)	Pretty Ditty (Stewart, Cary)		(LP) Felsted FAJ 7001
(b)	Danzon d'Amor (Stewart, Cary)		(LP) Felsted FAJ 7001
(c)	Blue Echo (Stewart, Cary)	-1	(LP) Felsted FAJ 7001

Cary plays trumpet in the ensembles. Piano only evident on (c). He lists *Mauve,* but not *Blue Echo,* so presumably a retitling prior to release. All FAJ7001 titles on (CD) Solar 4569908.

EDDIE CONDON and His Boys (Rex Stewart, co; Billy Butterfield, tp; Dick Cary, a-h; Cutty Cutshall, tb; Herb Hall, cl; Bud Freeman, ts; Gene Schroeder, p; Eddie Condon, g; Leonard Gaskin, b; George Wettling, d):
New York City — February 11, 1958
(a)	The Lady's in Love With You	(LP) M-G-M E3651
(b)	Third Street Blues (McPartland-Cary)	(LP) M-G-M E3651
(c)	Wherever There's Love	(LP) M-G-M E3651
(d)	Ginger Brown (Freeman-Cary)	(LP) M-G-M E3651
(e)	Newport News (Freeman-Cary)	(LP) M-G-M E3651
(f)	Ya Got Trouble	(LP) Verve 2352 055

(same personnel, plus Stewart, vo):
New York City — February 12, 1958
(g)	Eddie and the Milkman (Cary-Condon)		(LP) M-G-M E3651
(h)	The Albatross (McPartland-Cary)		(LP) M-G-M E3651
(i)	St. Louis Blues		(LP) M-G-M E3651
(j)	Ain't Misbehavin'		(LP) M-G-M E3651
(k)	Everybody's Movin	vRS	(LP) M-G-M E3651
(l)	Blue Lou		(LP) M-G-M E3651

It is possible that Butterfield and Stewart are out on (a), Butterfield and Cary are out on (g) and (k), Stewart & Cary are out on (c), and Stewart out on (d) and (j). Cary may play trumpet in one or more of the final ensembles on the February 12 date.
Note writer Jack Lazare also claimed some credit for "putting together" *Eddie and the*

Milkman. The label credits (Cary-Condon) but Cary said it was "by Jack Lazare and I," and all three, Cary, Condon & Lazare, shared the large royalties!

Other issues: E3561 also on (LP) MGM C768, Metro 2356.133, Verve 2352 055 (in a 2-LP set, 2683 051). Album title: Eddie Condon Is Uptown Now!

BOBBY HACKETT and his Orchestra (Hackett, co; Dick Cary, p, a-h-1; Bill Bauer, g; George Duvivier, b; Buzzy Drootin, d): *Capitol Studios, New York City — March 20, 1958*

(a)	Mary Lou	(LP) Muzak X-1082
(b)	Cuddle Up a Little Closer	(LP) Muzak X-1082
(c)	I'll Never Say 'Never Again' Again	(LP) Muzak X-1082
(d)	The One I Love Belongs to Somebody Else	(LP) Muzak X-1082
(e)	Skylark	(LP) Muzak X-1082
(f)	When My Sugar Walks Down the Street	(LP) Muzak X-1082
(g)	Toot, Toot, Tootsie! (Goodbye)	(LP) Muzak X-1082
(h)	Did You Ever See a Dream Walking?	(LP) Muzak X-1082
(i)	Smiles -1	(LP) Muzak X-1082
(j)	I Let a Song Go Out of My Heart	(LP) Muzak X-1082

There are three other Hackett titles known on Muzak — *Singin' the Blues/Stars Fell on Alabama/I Can't Believe That You're in Love With Me*, with no issue number available — with the same instrumentation, plus a vibes player. Cary says ten titles were made on March 20, 1958, though he has also said "we did seventeen tunes and all but one in one take"! However, these three titles were probably made at a separate session in which Cary did not participate.

Other issues: (c) (d) on (Tx) Muzak M2332; (e)(f)(g)(h)(i)(j) on (Tx) Muzak M2333.

MAX KAMINSKY and his Band (Kaminsky, tp; Dick Cary, a-h; Joe Barufaldi, cl; Charlie Queener, p; John Giuffrida, b; Charles Smith, d):
broadcast, Duane Hotel, New York City — c. April 1958
no details   (Tx) AFRS "Bandstand USA"

EDDIE CONDON ALL STARS (Rex Stewart, co; Cutty Cutshall, tb; Dick Cary, a-h; Herb Hall, cl; Bud Freeman, ts; Gene Schroeder, p; Eddie Condon, g; Leonard Gaskin, b; George Wettling, d):
New York City — May 22, 1958

Bluin' the Blues	(LP) World Pacific WP1292
Ostrich Walk	(LP) World Pacific WP1292
Reisenweber Rag	(LP) World Pacific WP1292
Skeleton Jangle	(CD) Mighty Quinn MQP1105

Cary is not present on the other 8 titles recorded for this album, but he was involved in some or all of the arranging. *Skeleton Jangle* and *Nasty Blues* sound like Cary arrangements. Other issues: WP1292 titles on (LP) World Pacific 9268, Sunset 5242, VogueE LAE12249, and on (CD) Mighty Quinn MQP1105. *Reisenweber Rag* as *Original Dixieland One Step* on Vogue LAE12249. *Skeleton Jangle* as *Skeleton Jungle* on Mighty Quinn MQP1105.

ART FORD'S JAZZ PARTY (Jimmy McPartland, co, vo; Tyree Glenn, tb, vb-1; Bob Wilber, cl, ts-2; Bud Freeman, ts; Dick Cary, p, tp-4, a-h-3; Chuck Wayne, g; Vinnie Burke, b; Harry Leon, d; Abbey Lincoln, vo): *telecast, WNTA, Newark, NJ — May 29, 1958*

>
> Basin Street Blues
> Royal Garden Blues
> All of Me   vAL
> Crazy Rhythm   -2
> Three Little Words (Freeman feature)
> Don't Blame Me   vAL
> I Can't Believe That You're in Love With Me   -3 (Cary a-h feature)
> St. James Infirmary   vJM
> NBC Chimes Blues   -3
> Bugle Call Rag   -3,-4
> Basin Street Blues (theme)

Only three Billie Holiday titles, without Dick Cary, have been commercially released from this telecast/broadcast.

Dick Cary's participation as a trumpet player on the next two sessions is another discographical mystery. His diary entry confirms that he was present 9 a.m. to 12.30 p.m. on June 10, but was probably only a visitor on the 11th, 9 a.m. to 10 a.m., and then again towards the end of the session. Rex Stewart and Billy Butterfield were the main horn soloists, making it difficult to be sure on which of the full-band titles Cary plays. His presence is peripheral; he does not play lead and appears not to solo. (The sleeve notes offer no guidance.) For that reason all titles are listed, with aural identifications for the frontlines and, perversely, including those titles which clearly do not involve Cary.
This album contains 23 titles divided into 7 medleys with fluctuating personnels.

The medleys are: Side 1, track 1: (a),(b),(c),(d); Side 1, track 2: (e),(f),(g),(h);
Side 1, track 3: (i),(j),(k),(l). Side 2, track 1: (m),(n); Side 2, track 2: (o),(p),(q);
Side 2, track 3: (r),(s),(t),(u); Side 2, track 4: (v),(w):

EDDIE CONDON and his Band (Rex Stewart, co; Billy Butterfield, tp; Cutty Cutshall, tb; Herb Hall, Peanuts Hucko, cl; Bud Freeman, ts; Gene Schroeder, p; Eddie Condon, g; Leonard Gaskin, b; George Wettling, d):

Capitol Studios, 46th Street, New York City — June 10/11, 1958

(a)	Copenhagen	(LP) Dot 3141
(b)	Riverboat Shuffle	(LP) Dot 3141
(c)	Sugar Foot Stomp	(LP) Dot 3141
(d)	Fidgety Feet	(LP) Dot 3141

(Billy Butterfield, tp; Cutshall, tb; Peanuts Hucko, cl; Freeman, ts; same rhythm section).

(e)	Little White Lies	(Butterfield & rhythm) -1	(LP) Dot 3141
(f)	Louisiana	(Cutshall & rhythm)	(LP) Dot 3141
(g)	Dinah	(Freeman & rhythm)	(LP) Dot 3141
(h)	Indiana	(Hucko & rhythm) -2	(LP) Dot 3141

-1 band in backing role. -2 band at close.

(Stewart, co; Cutshall, tb; Hall, cl; same rhythm section):
(i)	Original Dixieland One Step	(LP) Dot 3141

(Butterfield, Cary, tp; Cutshall, tb; Hucko, cl; Freeman, ts; same rhythm section):
(j)	I've Found a New Baby	(LP) Dot 3141

(Stewart, co; replaces Butterfield):
   (k)   China Boy   (LP) Dot 3141

(Stewart, Butterfield, Cary, Cutshall, Hucko, Hall, same rhythm section):
   (l)   South Rampart Street Parade   (LP) Dot 3141

(Butterfield, tp; Hucko, cl; Freeman, ts; same rhythm section):
   (m)   At the Jazz Band Ball   (LP) Dot 3141

(Stewart, co; Butterfield, tp; Cutshall, tb; Hall, cl; same rhythm section):
   (n)   That's a Plenty   (LP) Dot 3141
   (o)   Now That You're Gone (Cutshall & rhythm)   (LP) Dot 3141
   (p)   Willow Weep for Me (Hall & rhythm)   (LP) Dot 3141
   (q)   Blue Again (Stewart & rhythm) -3   (LP) Dot 3141
-3 band at close.

(Stewart, co; Cutshall, tb; Hucko, cl; same rhythm section):
   (r)   Sugar   (LP) Dot 3141

(Butterfield, tp; Cutshall, tb; Hucko, cl; Freeman, ts; same rhythm section):
   (s)   Liza   (LP) Dot 3141

(same, except Stewart, co; added; Hall, cl; replaces Hucko):
   (t)   There'll Be Some Changes Made   (LP) Dot 3141

(full personnel, without Cary?):
   (u)   Nobody's Sweetheart   (LP) Dot 3141

(same, except Freeman out):
   (v)   Clarinet Marmalade   (LP) Dot 3141
   (w)   High Society   (LP) Dot 3141

Cary no doubt contributed the little arrangement touches. Clarinetist Ron Hockett suggests, for example, the 4-bar transition by the horns on (i); the ensemble background on the bridge on (j); and the parts for (l). He believes Cary is present only on (b),(d),(i),(j),(k),(l), though others suspect three horns in other ensembles. Hockett also advises that tracks (r),(s),(t),(u) are from a different take on the mono release. Brian Peerless who, along with Bert Whyatt and Charlie Crump, also helped clarify these personnels, spotted that at the end of (u) *Nobody's Sweetheart*, Condon says: "Bud, you remind me so much of Arny." This remark is faint, but seems to have been included only on the stereo issue. A shout by Condon of "Whoa" at the end of (n) is heard only on the sampler LP on Rediffusion 0100174.
Album title: Dixieland Dance Party.

Other issues: all titles on (LP) Dot DLP25141, London LZ-D15158, SAH-D 6014, Rediffusion ZS162. (m),(n),(v),(w) on (LP) Rediffusion 0100174.

REX STEWART leads the Fletcher Henderson Alumni (Rex Stewart, co; Allan Smith, Joe Thomas, Paul Webster, Taft Jordan, tp; Benny Morton, Dickie Wells, Leon 'Jim' Comegys, tb; Dick Cary, alto-horn; Hilton Jefferson, Garvin Bushell, cl, as; Buddy Tate, Bob Wilber, ts; Haywood Henry, bar; Red Richards, p; Chauncey Westbrook, g; Bill Pemberton, b; Mousie

Alexander, d; 'Big' Miller, vo):
Great South Bay Jazz Festival, New York — August 1, 1958

    Wrapping It Up   (LP) United Artists UAL4009
    D Natural Blues   (LP) United Artists UAL4009
    medley: These Foolish Things/Willow Weep
      for Me/Over the Rainbow   (LP) United Artists UAL4009
    Hello Little Girl vBM   (LP) United Artists UAL4009
    Georgia Sketches (Stewart-Cary)   (LP) United Artists UAL4009
      1st movement: Motion
      2nd movement: Tiempo Espagnole
      3rd movement: The Earth Is Good

Other titles played at the concert included: *Down South Camp Meeting, Whatcha Call 'Em Blues* and *Blues* (vocal by Debbie Morris).
The Festival was held at the Timber Grove Club, Great River, near East Islip, Long Island.

Other issues: all titles on (LP): United Artists UAL4083 (mono), UAS5009 & UAS5083 (stereo). Album title: Henderson Homecoming.

LOU ANN SIMMS (vo; with Dick Cary, tp?; Phil Bodner, reeds; 4 strings; rhythm section; Dave Terry, leader):   **Pathe Studios, New York City — August 13, 1958**
    listed in Dick Cary's diary — no other details given.

Unknown Leader (Dick Cary, tp?; Bob Wilber, reeds; Leroy -----; Parke Hill, g; John Drew, b; Bob Smith, Barbara Lea, vo):   **United Studios, New York City — August 15, 1958**
    listed in Dick Cary's diary — no other details available, except that the date
    was for Bob Weil and that the vocalists had two songs each.

RALPH BURNS and his Orchestra (Clark Terry, f-h; Frank Rehak, Bill Byers, ---- Welch, Bob ----, tb; Dick Cary, a-h; unknown, p; g; b; d; Ray Charles Singers)
    Olmstead Studios, New York City — September 5, 1958
    listed in Dick Cary's diary — no other details available

THE COMMANDERS (big band, led by Jimmy Sedlar, tp; incl. Frank Rehak, Effie Resnick, tb; Charles Harmon, reeds; Bill Stanley, b; Dick Cary, p):
    Columbia Studios, New York City — October 18, 1958
    listed in Dick Cary's diary — no other details available — not recorded for Columbia.

RAY MARTIN and his Orchestra (Bernie Glow, Nick Travis, Red Solomon, Ernie Royal, Mel Davis, tp; Frank Rehak, Urbie Green, Bill Byers, Al Godlis, a.n. other, tb; Klein, fr-h; Dick Cary, a-h; Dick Hyman, p; George Barnes, g; a.n. other, b; Terry Snyder, d):
    Victor Studios, New York City — November 17, 1958

(similar, with Joe Wilder, tp):   **Victor Studios, New York City — November 21, 1958**

(similar):   **Victor Studios, New York City — December 1, 1958**
    listed in Dick Cary's diary — no other details available, except for comment,
    "Loud band for stereo" ("Sounds of Brass") and, on last date, "had two solos
    taken away by producer."

DAVE ALLEN (with Nick Travis, Dick Cary, tp; string quartet; Norman Paris, p; Milt ---, g; Osie Johnson, d; Dave Terry, arr, ldr): *Victor Studios, New York City — December 22, 1958*
    listed in Dick Cary's diary — no details except that it was a Warner Bros. date

BOB WILBER'S JAZZ QUARTET (Bob Wilber, cl; Dick Cary, p; Barry Galbraith, g; Bill Crow, bass; Cliff Leeman, d): *Bellsound Studios, New York City — December 26, 1958*

58-OR-41	Petite Fleur	(45) Cub K9021
58-OR-42	Atlas No.1	(45) Cub K9021
58-OR-47	unknown title (ballad)	unissued
58-OR-48	unknown title (jump tune)	unissued

The above master numbers are as quoted in The M-G-M Discography by Michel Ruppli, stating the titles were purchased by M-G-M from Bill Randall. (Cub was an M-G-M subsidiary, originally called Orbit.) No master numbers are shown on the Canadian issue, M-G-M K9021. The Jepsen and Lord Discographies list two titles on Kapp K-459 adjacent to those on Cub K9021, but these are by a sextet without Cary. Cary's diary indicates that *Petite Fleur* and three Wilber originals were recorded. 58-OR-40 and 43 through 46 are by vocal groups and 58-OR-49 was not used.

RAY MARTIN and his Orchestra (4 tp; 4 tb; Al Godlis, Dick Cary, a-h; 6 reeds; Harvey Phillips, tu; 3 d; Ray Martin, arr): *Webster Hall, New York City — January 15, 1959*

(same instrumentation): *Webster Hall, New York City — January 20/21, 1959*
    three sessions, as given in Dick Cary's diary, for album "Parade of Pops"

BUD FREEMAN and his Orchestra (Dick Cary, tp; Cutty Cutshall, tb; Pee Wee Russell, cl; Bud Freeman, ts; Dick Wellstood, p; Leonard Gaskin, b; George Wettling, d; Mary Mulligan, vo):
Victor Studios, New York City — February 16, 1959

(a)	A Foggy Day	vMM	(LP) Dot DLP25254
(b)	I Got It Bad and That Ain't Good	vMM	(LP) Dot DLP25254
(c)	They're Playing Our Song	vMM	(LP) Dot DLP25254
(d)	Try a Little Tenderness	vMM	(LP) Dot DLP25254

These vocals shown as "conducted by Eddie Condon." Personnel, including Condon, listed by Dick Cary. Due to the poor balance on these sides Pee Wee Russell's contribution, other than (a), is hard to detect. Cary's comment: "Mary Mulligan pretty bad singer. Got four tunes done." Other issues: as next session.

(Dick Cary, tp; Bud Freeman, p; Jimmy Jones, p; Leonard Gaskin, b; with George Wettling, d; added on *): *Victor Studios, New York City — February 17, 1959*

(e)	The Birth of the Blues	(LP) Dot DLP25254
(f)	Mimi *	(LP) Dot DLP25254
(g)	I Guess I'll Have To Change My Plan *	(LP) Dot DLP25254
(h)	The Very Thought of You	(LP) Dot DLP25254
(i)	Gentlemen's Blues * (Freeman, Cary, Jones, Wettling Gaskin)	(LP) Dot DLP25254
(j)	We're Through (B. Freeman, A. Freeman, Cary)	(LP) Dot DLP25254

Cary also lists as present Jimmy McPartland, co; Pee Wee Russell, cl; Eddie Condon, g. Presumably they left the studio when: "Mary Mulligan went completely to pieces and they sent her home. But [I] got a chance to do six tunes on trumpet with Bud, Jimmy and

Leonard. Sunny Lester seemed very happy." George Simon's notes state that Ms. Mulligan went to hospital with a bad case of laryngitis.

Other issues: all titles on (LP) Dot DLP3254; (i) also on (LP) Dot DLP25878, Rediffusion 0100174. Album title: Midnight Session.

PEE WEE RUSSELL (Buck Clayton, tp; Vic Dickenson, tb; Pee Wee Russell, cl; Bud Freeman, ts; Dick Cary, p, arr; Eddie Condon, g; Bill Takas, b; George Wettling, d):
Victor Studios, New York City — February 23/24/25, 1959

[a]	Pee Wee's Blues	(LP) Dot DLP 3253
[b]	What's the Pitch	(LP) Dot DLP 3253
[c]	Dreamin' and Schemin'	(LP) Dot DLP 3253
[d]	Cutie Pie	(LP) Dot DLP 3253
[e]	Oh No	(LP) Dot DLP 3253
[f]	Pee Wee's Song	(LP) Dot DLP 3253
[g]	Oh Yes	(LP) Dot DLP 3253
[h]	Missy	(LP) Dot DLP 3253
[i]	Are You Here?	(LP) Dot DLP 3253
[j]	Write Me a Love Song Baby	(LP) Dot DLP 3253
[k]	This Is It	(LP) Dot DLP 3253
[l]	But Why?	(LP) Dot DLP 3253

Other issues: all titles on (LP) Dot 25253, MCA 2-4150, Impulse IA-9359/2, and (CD) Lonehill LHJ 10347. [a] on (LP) Dot DLP25878.

The dates for this session are usually given as February 23/24, but Cary refers to a third Pee Wee date on the 25th.
All titles are credited to Russell as sole composer. However, on other versions of some of these songs the composer credit is to Russell and Cary. This applies to nine of the above titles, all except [b],[c],and [j]. Cary also wrote on January 24: "Pee Wee and I wrote *Oh Yes,* sequel to *Oh No.*" Album title: Pee Wee Russell Plays.

EDDIE CONDON and his Chicagoans (Max Kaminsky, tp; Cutty Cutshall, tb; Pee Wee Russell, cl; Bud Freeman, ts; Dick Cary, p; Eddie Condon, g; Leonard Gaskin, b; George Wettling, d):
Bell Sound Studios, New York City — February 26, 1959

B50230	There'll Be Some Changes Made	(LP) Warner Bros. WS 1315
B50231	I've Found a New Baby	(LP) Warner Bros. WS1315
B50232	Oh Baby	(LP) Warner Bros. WS1315
B50233	Love Is Just Around the Corner	(LP) Warner Bros.WS1315

(same personnel, except Al Hall, b; for Gaskin): *New York City — February 27, 1959*

B50234	Nobody's Sweetheart	(LP) Warner Bros.WS1315
B50235	Chicago	(LP) Warner Bros.WS1315
B50236	Shim-Me-Sha-Wabble	(LP) Warner Bros.WS1315
B50237	Someday Sweetheart	(LP) Warner Bros.WS1315
B50238	Friars Point Shuffle	(LP) Warner Bros.WS1315
B50239	Liza	(LP) Warner Bros.WS1315

Other issues: all titles on (LP) Warner Bros. 68011 and (CD) Atlantic 7/90461.2

Matrix numbers as listed in Jepsen1942-80. *Liza* is the Eddie Condon composition.
Album title: That Toddlin' Town (Chicago Jazz Revisited).

DICK CARY and Orchestra (Max Kaminsky, Buck Clayton, Johnny Glasel, tp; Vic Dickenson, Frank Rehak, Lou McGarity, tb; Pee Wee Russell, Bob Wilber, cl; Phil Woods, as; Bud Freeman, Buddy Tate, ts; Ray Bryant, p; Keeter Betts or Billy Taylor, Jr., b; Jo Jones, d):
concert, Sheraton Park Hotel, Washington, D.C., — March 16, 1959

This concert was recorded for Mercury Records, but it was decided by a&r man Jack Tracy that there was insufficient satisfactory material for an album. Titles played at rehearsal and arranged by Cary included *Stompy Jones* and *In an Ellingtone*. Drummers Bertil Knox and Cliff Leeman, and guitarist Charlie Byrd were also present. Further details can be found in Chapter 10.

LOU McGARITY Quintet (Lou McGarity, tb; Dick Cary, tp, p, arr; George Barnes, g; Jack Lesberg, b; Don Marino, d):
New York City — March 19/20, 1959

(a)	Some Like It Hot	(LP) Jubilee JLP1108
(b)	By the Beautiful Sea	(LP) Jubilee JLP1108
(c)	Stairway to the Stars	(LP) Jubilee JLP1108
(d)	Sweet Sue—Just You	(LP) Jubilee JLP1108
(e)	Down Among the Sheltering Palms	(LP) Jubilee JLP1108
(f)	I Wanna Be Loved by You	(LP) Jubilee JLP1108
(g)	La Cumparsita	(LP) Jubilee JLP1108
(h)	I'm Thru With Love	(LP) Jubilee JLP1108
(i)	Runnin' Wild	(LP) Jubilee JLP1108
(j)	Sugar Blues	(LP) Jubilee JLP1108
(k)	Sweet Georgia Brown	(LP) Jubilee JLP1108
(l)	Some Like It Hot	(LP) Jubilee JLP1108

Cary plays piano on all titles, plus trumpet on all titles, except (a),(e), and (l). (a) runs for 2:56 minutes, (l) for 57 seconds.

Other issues: all titles on (CD) J&M CD8008, Lonehill LHJ10321, and (a) to (i) on (AC) Holmia HM20. Album title: Some Like It Hot

ETHEL SMITH

In his diary Cary refers to sessions with organist Ethel Smith on May 5, 6 & 8, 1959, but no such sessions are given in Michel Ruppli's Decca masters listings. Cary does refer to being in the Decca Studios, 2:00 to 5:00, on May 1 – "first time working in control booth with [Milt] Gabler—Ethel double-tracking."

JIMMY McPARTLAND and His Dixielanders (McPartland, tp, vo; Charlie Shavers, tp, vo; Cutty Cutshall, tb; Bob Wilber, cl; Ernie Caceres, bar, cl-1; Dick Cary, p, a-h-2; George Barnes, g; Harvey Phillips, tu; Joe Burriesce, b; George Wettling, d):
New York City — May 26, 1959

K3JB3690	Muskrat Ramble		(LP) Camden CAL549
K3JB3691	Darktown Strutters Ball	-2	(LP) Camden CAL549
K3JB3692	High Society	-1	(LP) Camden CAL549

(same personnel): *New York City — May 27, 1959*

K3JB3693	Fidgety Feet	-2	(LP) Camden CAL549

K3JB3694	Original Dixieland One Step	(LP) Camden CAL549
K3JB3695	That's a Plenty	(LP) Camden CAL549
K3JB3696	Way Down Yonder in New Orleans vJM	(LP) Camden CAL549
K3JB3697	Farewell Blues	(LP) Camden CAL549
K3JB3698	South Rampart Street Parade	(LP) Camden CAL549
K3JB3699	When the Saints Go Marching In vJM,CS	(LP) Camden CAL549

Arrangements probably by Dick Cary. Album title: The Happy Dixieland Jazz.

ED HALL and his Orchestra (Ed Hall, Herb Hall, Omer Simeon, cl; Dick Cary, p; Jimmy Raney, g; Al Hall, b; Jimmy Crawford, d; Eddie Wilcox, arr):

Nola Studios, New York City — June 25, 1959

(a)	Lover	(LP) Rae-Cox LP1120
(b)	Sweetheart *	(LP) Mount Vernon Music MVS124
(c)	Hallelujah!	(LP) Rae-Cox LP1120
(d)	Neighbours	(LP) Rae-Cox LP1120
(e)	Dawn on the Desert	(LP) Rae-Cox LP1120

* (b) is a spliced version of (a) Lover.

(omit Herb Hall, Omer Simeon): *Nola Studios, New York City — June 26, 1959*

(f)	Flyin' High	(LP) Rae-Cox LP1120
(g)	Rumpus on Rampart Street	(LP) Rae-Cox LP1120
(h)	Swingin'	(LP) Rae-Cox LP1120
(i)	Rose in Her Window	(LP) Rae-Cox LP1120
(j)	African Tempo	(LP) Rae-Cox LP1120
(k)	African Fu-Fu	(LP) Rae-Cox LP1120

Other issues: all titles except (a) on (LP) Mount Vernon Music MVS124/MVM124; (a),(k) on (LP) Top Rank TR5019, (a),(f),(g),(h),(k) on (EP) Top Rank TEP144; all titles except (b) on (CD) IAJRC CD-1020, Avid Jazz AMSC1019. (j) labelled as *American Tempo* on LP1120 sleeve and on MVS124/MVM124 sleeve and label, and on Avid Jazz AMSC1019. Album title: Rumpus On Rampart Street.

GOOD TIME CHARLIE (Goes To College) (Cutty Cutshall, tb; Dick Cary, p, arr; Ed Safranski, b; Billy Gussak, d, leader): *New York City — July 2/3, 1959*

"honky tonk" album of college songs.

It is not known if this album was released. Cary refers to a "tricked-up piano" and "a pretty good rhythm section," so a guitarist could also be present.

ETHEL SMITH At The Organ (Smith, hammond organ; unidentified tp (Dick Cary?); tb; cl, as-1; g; b; d): *New York City — August 19, 1959*

107969	Basin Street Blues	(LP) Decca DL8955
107994	Livery Stable Blues	(LP) Decca DL8955
107995	St. Louis Blues (Part 2) -1 aDC	(LP) Decca DL8955

Cary probably arranged all three titles. This session is repeated, with other Ethel Smith sessions, in the separate listing of recorded Cary arrangements.

LOU McGARITY Big Eight (Doc Severinsen, tp; Lou McGarity, tb, vo; Bob Wilber, cl-1, b-cl-2, ts-3; Dick Cary, tp-4, a-h-5, cel-6; p, arr; George Barnes, g; Jack Lesberg, b; Don Marino, d):

Bell Sound Studios, New York City — September 14/15, 1959

9738	Blue Skies	-1,-5	(LP) Argo LP654

9739	Born to Be Blue	-1,-6	(LP) Argo LP654
9740	Blue Lou	-3,-4	(LP) Argo LP654
9741	Blue Champagne	-1,-6	(LP) Argo LP654
9742	Under a Blanket of Blue	-3	(LP) Argo LP654
9743	Blue Turning Grey Over You	-1	(LP) Argo LP654
9744	Blue Moon	#	(LP) Argo LP654
9745	Blue Again	-5	(LP) Argo LP654
9746	Blue and Broken Hearted	-1,-4	(LP) Argo LP654
9747	Black and Blue	-1?,-4	(LP) Argo LP654
9748	Blue Prelude	-2	(LP) Argo LP654
9749	I Get the Blues When It Rains	vLM -1	(LP) Argo LP654

#Severinsen & Wilber out. Cary plays piano on all tracks, plus tp, a-h & cel as indicated. The notes confirm Cary's muted trumpet playing on 9746/9747, but perhaps he solos on trumpet on 9740 & 9743 also. Notes give a-h behind tp solo on 9742. Album title: Blue Lou.
Other issues: all titles on (CD) J&M CD8008, Lonehill LHJ10321, and (AC) Holmia HM20.

BOB WILBER SEPTET (Dick Cary, tp, a-h -4; Vic Dickenson, tb; Bob Wilber, cl-1, bs-cl-2, ts-3; Dick Wellstood, p; Barry Galbraith, g; Leonard Gaskin, b; Bobby Donaldson, d):
New York City — September 19, 1959

Ghost of the Blues	-3	(LP) Classic Editions CJ5
When the Sun Sets Down South	-1,-3	(LP) Classic Editions CJ5
Polka Dot Stomp	-1	(LP) Classic Editions CJ5
Little Creole Lullaby	-2,-4	(LP) Classic Editions CJ5
Blackstick	-1	(LP) Classic Editions CJ5

Cary not on other tracks on this album.

Other issues: all titles on (CD) Classic Jazz CJ5, Classic Jazz 70005.
Album title: Spreadin' Joy

DICK CARY and his Dixieland Doodlers (Dick Cary, tp; Harry DeVito, tb; Kenny Davern, cl; Leroy Parkins, cl, ts, bsx; Dick Wellstood, p; Lee Blair, bj; Harvey Phillips, tu; Tommy Potter, b; Cliff Leeman, d):
New York City — October 19, 1959

CO63697-11	Nobody Knows the Trouble I've Seen	(LP) Columbia CL1425
CO63698-7	Billy Boy	(LP) Columbia CL1425
CO63699-6	Swanee River	(LP) Columbia CL1425

Other issues: all titles on (CD) Mosaic MD8-206

(same personnel, except Phil Cadway, tu; for Phillips): *New York City — October 23, 1959*

CO63700	Waltzing Matilda	(LP) Columbia CL1425
CO63701	In the Good Old Summertime	(LP) Columbia CL1425
CO63702	Camptown Races	(LP) Columbia CL1425
CO63703	I've Been Working on the Railroad	(LP) Columbia CL1425
CO63704	Shreveport Stomps	unissued — master no longer exists

Other issues: all titles, except *Shreveport Stomps,* on (CD) Mosaic MD8-206.

MAX KAMINSKY (Kaminsky, tp; Cutty Cutshall, tb; Dick Cary, tp-1, a-h-2, p-5, arr; Phil Olivella, cl-4, bar-3; Bob Wilber, cl; Dave McKenna, p; Barry Galbraith, g; Tommy Potter, b; Osie Johnson, d):
Victor Studios, New York City — October 29/30, 1959

(a)	Henderson Stomp	-1,-4	(LP) Westminster WP6125

(b)	The Preacher	-2,-3	(LP) Westminster WP6125
(c)	The Song Is Ended	-1,-2,-3,-4	(LP) Westminster WP6125
(d)	I Ain't Gonna Give You None of My Jelly Roll	-2,-3	(LP) Westminster WP6125
(e)	Far East Mood (Kaminsky-Cary)	-1,-4	(LP) Westminster WP6125
(f)	Bye Bye Blackbird	-2,-3,-4	(LP) Westminster WP6125
(g)	Just One Minute (Kaminsky-Cary)	-2,-3	(LP) Westminster WP6125
(h)	Eccentric Rag	-2,-4,-5	(LP) Westminster WP6125
(i)	What's The Use	-2,-3	(LP) Westminster WP6125
(j)	Chang Mai (Kaminsky-Cary)	-2,-3	(LP) Westminster WP6125

(e) Cary plays muted trumpet behind Kaminsky. (h) Cary & McKenna trade piano choruses on this track. Cary listed the personnel in his diary. Most of the piano work, for example on *Chang Mai,* is clearly by McKenna, though he told Gunnar Jacobsen that he did not participate in the recording because "Max and I never got along!"

Other issues: all titles on (LP) Westminster S15060. Album title: Ambassador of Jazz

DICK CARY and his Dixieland Doodlers (same personnel as October 23, 1959):

New York City — October 30, 1959

CO63705	Mack the Knife		(LP) Columbia CL1425
CO63706	There Is a Tavern in the Town		(LP) Columbia CL1425
CO63707	I Dream of Jeannie With the Light Brown Hair	-1	(LP) Columbia CL1425
CO63708-4	Swing Low Sweet Chariot		(LP) Columbia CL1425
CO63709	Wait 'Til the Sun Shines, Nellie		(LP) Columbia CL1425

-1 Cadway also plays bass & Blair omitted.

Note: this Columbia session of October 30 was recorded before the Max Kaminsky session of the same date, but there is no available information to be able to allocate the Kaminsky titles to specific dates.

Other issues: all titles on (CD) Mosaic MD8-206.
Album title: Dick Cary and the Dixieland Doodlers.

THE JOHN GLASEL BRASSTET (John Glasel, Louis Mucci, tp; William Elton, tb; Dick Cary, a-h, p-1, arr, all titles; Harvey Phillips, tu; John Drew, b; Ed Shaughnessy, d):

Huntington, Long Island, NY — November 11, 1959

(a)	Time for One More (Cary)	(LP) Jazz Unlimited JA1002
(b)	Stablemates	(LP) Jazz Unlimited JA1002
(c)	It Don't Mean a Thing	(LP) Jazz Unlimited JA1002
(d)	More Than You Know	(LP) Jazz Unlimited JA1002
(e)	Vikki (Cary) -1	(LP) Jazz Unlimited JA1002

(Cary not on other tracks on this album.)
All titles on (CD) Fresh Sound FSRCD 2247.

DICK CATHCART (Dick Cathcart, tp; Moe Schneider, tb; Don [Bonnee?], cl; Dick Cary, p; Jud [de Naut?], b; Nick Fatool, d; Polly [   ], Connie [   ], vo):

Los Angeles — July 12, 1960

four shows, including: Mood Indigo   (Tx) Treasury Department

THE BOBBY HACKETT QUARTET (sic) (Bobby Hackett, tp, arr; Dick Cary, a-h; Bob Wilber, cl-1, ts-2; Dave McKenna, p; Jimmy Raney or Jim Hall, guitar; Joe Williams, b; Jake Hanna, d):
Columbia Studios, New York City — September 10/11 1960

(a)	David and Goliath	-1	(Tx) Sesac N4101
(b)	Swing Low, Sweet Chariot	-1	(Tx) Sesac N4101
(c)	I'm Climbing Up the Mountain	-2	(Tx) Sesac N4101
(d)	Nobody Knows the Trouble I've Seen	-2,-3	(Tx) Sesac N4101
(e)	When the Saints Go Marching In	-2	(Tx) Sesec N4101
(f)	Heaven's Full of Joy	-1,-2	(Tx) Sesac N4101
(g)	Golden Gate	-1,-2	(Tx) Sesac N4102
(h)	Way Up There	-2	(Tx) Sesac N4102
(i)	Balm in Gilead	-2	(Tx) Sesac N4102
(j)	Steal Away	-1	(Tx) Sesac N4102
(k)	Better Be Ready	-2	(Tx) Sesac N4102
(l)	Bye and Bye	-1,-3	(Tx) Sesac N4102

-3 there is a celeste on these titles, possibly played by Cary.
Cary quotes "Jim" for September 10, presumably meaning Jim Hall. He also states that nine titles were recorded on the 11th. Hackett listed as arranger for all titles, except (a) and (c).

Other issues: (LP) Jazz Vault JV108, Jazz Club (Belgian) N4101/2, Ronco 4c/ EGS5006. N4101/4102 are numbers for each side; the issue is one disc. Album title: The Spirit Swings Me.

JIMMY and MARIAN McPARTLAND (Jimmy McPartland, co; Dick Cary, tp-1, a-h, arr; Urbie Green, tb; Andy Fitzgerald, cl, fl-2; Marian McPartland, p; Ben Tucker, b; Mousey Alexander, d):
Mastertone Studios, New York City — September 13/14, 1960

(a)	Thanks For Dropping In		(LP) Design DLP-144
(b)	Londonderry Air		(LP) Design DLP-144
(c)	Mystery March	-2	(LP) Design DLP-144
(d)	Peter Gunn	-2	(LP) Design DLP-144
(e)	Peter Gunn	(alternative take)	(CD) Simitar 5614
(f)	Mr. Lucky		(LP) Design DLP-144
(g)	I-M-4-U	-1	(LP) Design DLP-144
(h)	Sentimental Journey		(LP) Design DLP-144
(i)	Bat Masterson	-2	(LP) Design DLP-144

Design sleeve shows "Arrangements—Aul Hedd"; Marian on label, Marion on sleeve; Urbie Green listed as 'Manhattan Red.' On Simitar 5614 (a) shown as *Thanks For Dropping By*, and (b) shown as *Danny Boy*. (b),(f) are piano features, with band in background.
Design album is titled "Jimmy and Marion (sic) McPartland Play TV Themes"; the Simitar as "Thanks For Dropping By."

Other issues: all titles on (CD) Simitar 5614; (c) on (LP) Allegro ALL737 and (AC) Alphorn ALH-124; (g) also on (AC) Alphorn ALH-124. as I'm For You. To complicate matters, Alphorn released two versions of ALH-124, with only one tune, by Teddy Wilson, the same.

RED NICHOLS and his Five Pennies (Red Nichols, co; Ed Anderson, tb; Bill Wood, cl; Joe Rushton, bsx; Dick Cary, p, a-h-1; Rollie Culver, d):
NBC TV rehearsal, New York City — October 12, 1960

medley: I Know That You Know/
    I Want to Be Happy -1   (LP) Broadway Intermission BR-130

KINGS OF DIXIELAND (Dick Cathcart, tp; Elmer 'Moe' Schneider, tb; Matty Matlock, cl, arr; Eddie Miller, ts; Dick Cary, p, a-h-1; George Van Eps, g; Red Callender, b; Nick Fatool, d):
Los Angeles — November 23, 1960

(a)	Bicycle Built for Two		(LP) Crown CLP5200
(b)	Meet Me in St. Louis, Louis	-1	(LP) Crown CLP5200
(c)	Dark Eyes		(LP) Crown CLP5200
(d)	On the Banks of the Wabash		(LP) Crown CLP5200
(e)	Merry Widow Waltz		(LP) Crown CLP5200

(same personnel, except Nappy Lamare, bj; for Van Eps; Callender, tu):
Los Angeles — November 28, 1960

(f)	The Stars and Stripes	-1	(LP) Crown CLP5200
(g)	You Tell Me Your Dreams		(LP) Crown CLP5200
(h)	East Side, West Side		(LP) Crown CLP5200
(i)	And the Band Played On		(LP) Crown CLP5200

(same personnel, but Fatool out, and Lamare on g; Callender, on b).

(j)	Kingfish Blues	(LP) Crown CLP5200

Sleeve notes state: "George Van Eps on one date and Nappy Lamare on the other." Cary quotes George Van Eps for November 23, though he does give "same band" for the 28th! For the second date he notes: "Matty ended with a very nice blues." But *Kingfish Blues* has Callender on bass, with probably guitar and no drums.

Other issues: all titles on (LP) Crown CST464 (as The Dixieland Scramblers). (j) on Bright Orange X-BO-728 (Volume 3) and (CD) Hermes HRM7004. (a),(g),(e),(h) on (CD) Hermes HRM7004. All other titles issued on various Bright Orange albums, with untraced release numbers.

> Lord lists Cary on a number of Kings of Dixieland recordings from this period, but CLP5200 is the only one mentioned by Cary.

BYRDIE GREEN (?) (Jimmy McPartland, co; Harry DeVito, tb; Bob Wilber, cl; Dick Cary, p; George Barnes, g; Bill Crow, b; George Wettling, d): *New York City — January 22/23, 1962*
> twelve titles recorded for a twist album; two instrumentals and ten with vocals to be dubbed in later.

EDDIE CONDON and the Dixieland All-Stars (Bobby Hackett, co; Lou McGarity, tb; Peanuts Hucko, cl; Dick Cary, p, a-h-1; Eddie Condon, g; Jack Lesberg, b; Buzzy Drootin, d):
30th Street Studios, New York City — January 27, 1962

C069040-8	Midnight in Moscow		(LP) Epic BA17024
C069041-5	Meadowlands	-1	(LP) Epic BA17024
C069042-6	Dark Eyes		(LP) Epic BA17024
C069043-1	theme from "Swan Lake"		(LP) Epic BA17024
C069044-8	Londonderry Air		(LP) Epic BA17024
C069045-10	La Vie en Rose		(LP) Epic BA17024
C069046-4	Loch Lomond		(LP) Epic BA17024

(same personnel, except Knobby Totah, b; for Lesberg): *same date*

C069047-1	Hindustan	(LP) Epic BA17024

```
CO69048-3    The Sheik of Araby                        (LP) Epic BA17024
CO69049-10   Japanese Sandman           -1,-2          (LP) Epic BA17024
```
-2 Drootin out; Hucko plays tambourine.

Other issues: all titles on (LP) Epic LA16024 (mono), Mosaic MQ 7-152; on (CD) Mosaic MCD 5-152, Collectables COL-CD-7527. (Epic BA17024 is stereo).
Album title: Midnight in Moscow.

BEN POLLACK and His Pic-A-Rib Boys (Dick Cary, tp, a-h-1; Warren Smith, tb; Gene Bolen, cl; Bill Campbell, p; Walt Yoder, b; Ben Pollack, d):

telecast, "Jazz Scene U.S.A.," Los Angeles — probably December 1962

```
        At the Jazz Band Ball              videotape exists
        Wolverine Blues
        Tin Roof Blues
        Royal Garden Blues        -1
```
Personnel and year are announced. Cary plays tp on all titles.

HELEN O'CONNELL (vocal, with Dick Cary, Fred Mitchell, Jerry King, d; Paul Suter, p; Barney Kessel, g):   *Universal Studios, Los Angeles — March 13, 1963*
  for Navy Recruiting show; "Helen did about 10 songs -
  we played about 10." — no other details

EDDIE CONDON ALL STARS (Buck Clayton, tp; Vic Dickenson, tb; Pee Wee Russell, cl; Bud Freeman, ts; Dick Cary, p, a-h-1; Eddie Condon, g; Jack Lesberg, b; Cliff Leeman, d; Jimmy Rushing, vo):

ABC broadcast, concert Sydney Stadium, Melbourne, Australia — March 14, 1964

```
(a)     Caravan                   -1
(b)     Dinah (BF & rhythm)
(c)     St. Louis Blues
(d)     Sugar                     (PWR with DC-1 & rhythm)   (LP) IAJRC 28
(e)     Stompin' at the Savoy     (BC & rhythm)
(f)     I Can't Get Started       (BC & rhythm))
(g)     Am I Blue?                vJR
(h)     When You're Smiling       vJR
(i)     medley: Goin' to Chicago vJR / Outskirts of Town vJR / See See Rider vJR
                / St. Louis Blues        vJR
(j)     Sent for You Yesterday    vJR
(k)     That's a Plenty (fades)
```

(same personnel):
TBS broadcast, concert Hibiya Kohkaidoh, Tokyo, Japan — March 24, 1964

```
(a)     Muskrat Ramble                          (LP) Chiaroscuro(J) UPS2069/70
(b)     Do You Know What It Means to Miss New Orleans
                                                (LP) Chiaroscuro(J) UPS2069/70
(c)     Please Don't Talk About Me When I'm Gone (VD & rhythm) -1
                                                (LP) Chiaroscuro(J) UPS2069/70
(d)     St. Louis Blues                         (LP) Chiaroscuro(J) UPS2069/70
(e)     I Can't Get Started (BC & rhythm)       (LP) Chiaroscuro(J) UPS2069/70
(f)     I Can't Believe That You're in Love With Me  (LP) Chiaroscuro CR154
(g)     Pee Wee's Blues (PWR & rhythm)          (LP) Chiaroscuro CR154
```

(h)	Stompin' at the Savoy	(BC & rhythm)	(LP) Chiaroscuro CR154
(i)	Rose Room	-1	(LP) Chiaroscuro CR154
(j)	Manhattan	(VD & rhythm)	(LP) Chiaroscuro CR154
(k)	Caravan	-1	(CD) Chiaroscuro CRD154
(l)	Basin Street Blues		(CD) Chiaroscuro CRD154
(m)	Three Little Words	(BF & rhythm)	(LP) Chiaroscuro CR154
(n)	I Would Do Anything for You		(LP) Chiaroscuro CR154
(o)	All of Me	vJR	(LP) Chiaroscuro CR154
(p)	Am I Blue	vJR	(LP) Chiaroscuro CR154
(q)	When You're Smiling	vJR	(LP) Chiaroscuro CR154
(r)	blues medley: Goin' to Chicago vJR / Every Day vJR / See See Rider vJR / St. Louis Blues vJR		(CD) Chiaroscuro CRD154
(s)	Royal Garden Blues		(LP) Chiaroscuro CR154

TBS = Tokyo Broadcasting Service. CRD154 does not show *St. Louis Blues*.

Other issues: all CR154 titles on (CD) Chiaroscuro CRD154. All titles on (LP) Chiaroscuro(J) UPS2069/70 & ULS1684/85. titles (f) to (j), (m) to (q) & (s) on (AC) Jazz Connoisseur Cassettes JCC117

(same personnel):   ***concert, Festival Hall, Osaka, Japan — March 27, 1964***

(a)	Muskrat Ramble		(LP) blank label
(b)	St. Louis Blues		(LP) blank label
(c)	Basin Street Blues		(LP) blank label
(d)	Caravan	-1	(LP) blank label
(e)	Pee Wee Blues	(PWR & rhythm)	(LP) blank label
(f)	Stompin' at the Savoy	(BC & rhythm)	(LP) blank label
(g)	All of Me vJR		(LP) blank label
(h)	Am I Blue vJR		(LP) blank label
(i)	When You're Smiling	vJR	(LP) blank label
(j)	medley: Goin' to Chicago vJR / I'm Gonna Move to the Outskirts of Town vJR / See See Rider vJR / St. Louis Blues vJR		(LP) blank label
(k)	Sent for You Yesterday	vJR	(LP) blank label

BIG GEORGE BRUNS (Dick Cary, tp; George Bruns, tb; Dick Anderson, cl; Marvin Ash, org; Allan Reuss, g; Jess Bourgeois, b; Irv Cottler, d; (Miss) Lou Norris, vo):

Ron Roy Studio, Los Angeles — probably late-1960s

Happy Rag		(LP) Maximus R-2584
You're Gonna Be Sorry	vLN	(LP) Maximus R-2584
Inky the Crow		(LP) Maximus R-2584
Please Come Back Big Daddy	vLN	(LP) Maximus R-2584
Have a Good Time	vLN	(LP) Maximus R-2584
Ah, See the Moon	vband	(LP) Maximus R-2584
When You're Smiling		(LP) Maximus R-2584
Where Has the Melody Gone?	vLN	(LP) Maximus R-2584
Wabash Blues		(LP) Maximus R-2584
Mama's Gone, Goodbye		(LP) Maximus R-2584
Uptown, Downtown Man	vLN	(LP) Maximus R-2584
Herbie	vband	(LP) Maximus R-2584

Album title: Have a Good Time With Big George Bruns.

BLUE ANGEL JAZZ CLUB   *University Club of Pasadena, CA — December 28, 1968*
(Abe Lincoln, tb; Dick Cary, a-h; Wayne Songer, reeds; Roger Kellaway, p; Chuck Berghofer, b; John Guerin, d):

1.	unknown	BAJC unissued
2.	Honeysuckle Rose	BAJC unissued
3.	S'Posin'	BAJC unissued
4.	When You're Smiling	BAJC unissued
5.	Keeping Out of Mischief Now	BAJC unissued
6.	Perdido	BAJC unissued

Dick Cary's Big Band (Dick Cary, Jack Coon, Ray Linn, tp; Elmer 'Moe' Schneider, tb; Betty O'Hara, mel, v-tb; Matty Matlock, cl; Wayne Songer, as, bar; Jack Chaney, ts; Stan Wrightsman, p; Chuck Berghofer, b; Ira Westley, tu; Gene Estes, d):

17.	Shiny Stockings (MM feature)	BAJC unissued
18.	Old Folks (BO'H feature)	BAJC unissued
19.	Weatherbird (DC & SW feature)	BAJC unissued
20.	Stardust (WS feature)	BAJC unissued
21.	Bess, You Is My Woman Now (BO'H feature)	BAJC unissued
22.	Ballad for Eddie (Cary) aDC	(LP) BAJC 503
23.	Wang Wang Blues	BAJC unissued

22 by O'Hara, v-tb; Cary, p; possibly Westley, b; Estes, d; with horns in background..

(Dick Cary, Ray Linn, tp; Abe Lincoln, tb; Joe Venuti, vl; Stan Wrightsman, p; Gene Estes, vb; Ward Erwin, b; Jack Sperling, d):

40.	Muskrat Ramble	BAJC unissued

Ray Linn Big Band (Ray Linn, tp; Dick Cary, tp, a-h; 'Moe' Schneider, tb; Wayne Songer, cl, as-1, bar; Matty Matlock, cl; Jack Chaney, ts; Stan Wrightsman, p; Nappy Lamare, g, bj-2; Chuck Berghofer, b; John Guerin, d):

41.	I Can't Get Started		BAJC unissued
42.	Dixieland Shuffle		BAJC unissued
43.	My Inspiration (MM feature)		BAJC unissued
44.	medley: Solitude/In a Sentimental Mood		BAJC unissued
45.	Love Lies (MS feature)		BAJC unissued
46.	Fidgety Feet	-1,-2	(LP) BAJC 502

Clancy Hayes' Levee Loiterers (vo, bj; with Jackie Coon, tp-1, mel; Dick Cary, a-h; Stan Wrightsman, p; Ward Erwin, b; Gene Estes, d):

47.	Basin Street Blues	-1	(LP) BAJC 513
48.	Willie the Weeper	-1	(LP) BAJC 502
49.	Lights Out		BAJC unissued

Other issues: 47/48 also on (AC) Jazz Connoisseur Cassettes JCC124

Ray Linn Jazzband (Ray Linn, tp; Moe Schneider, tb; Matty Matlock, cl; Jack Chaney, ts; Dick Cary, p; Ward Erwin, b).

55.	Panama	BAJC unissued

(add Nappy Lamare, g; Jack Sperling, d).
	56.	Do You Know What It Means to Miss New Orleans	BAJC unissued
	57.	Wolverine Blues	(LP) BAJC 502
	58.	South Rampart Street Parade	BAJC unissued

The Dick Cary Big Band (Ray Linn, tp; Dick Cary, a-h, arr; Betty O'Hara, v-tb; Moe Schneider, tb; Matty Matlock, cl; Wayne Songer, as-1, bar, cl; Jack Chaney, ts; Stan Wrightsman, p; Nappy Lamare, g; Ward Erwin, b; Jack Sperling, d):

66.	Satanic Blues		BAJC unissued
67.	Save It Pretty Mama	-1 aDC	(LP) BAJC 503
68.	Blues My Naughty Sweetie Gave to Me	-1 aDC	(LP) BAJC 503
69.	Lazy Mood		BAJC unissued
70.	Caravan	-1	(LP) BAJC 513

(Dick Cary, a-h; Matty Matlock, cl; Stan Wrightsman, p; George Van Eps, g; Ira Westley, tu; Jack Sperling, d):

81.	Singing the Blues		BAJC unissued
83.	Oh, Baby		BAJC unissued

80. is *Moonglow*, by Wrightsman & rhythm section, on (LP) BAJC 502. 82. is *Do You Know What It Means to Miss New Orleans* by Matlock & rhythm section on (LP) BAJC 503.

The Blue Angel Jazz Party recordings are now owned by Storyville Records of Denmark. It is not known if the numbers shown above are matrix numbers allocated by Blue Angel or reference numbers used by Storyville. Neither the ledger listing held by Storyville nor the Blue Angel Jazz Club sleeve notes are faultless, hence the variations which may be found.

RALPH SUTTON and DICK CARY (Dick Cary, trumpet -1, alto-horn -2; Ralph Sutton, piano; Al Hall, bass; Cliff Leeman, drums):

Sunnie's Rendezvous, Aspen, CO — February 10-12, 1969

(a)	I Can't Believe That You're in Love With Me	-2	(CD) Arbors ARCD 19284
(b)	'Swonderful	-1	(CD) Arbors ARCD 19284
(c)	Everything Happens to Me	-1	(CD) Arbors ARCD 19284
(d)	Save It, Pretty Mama	-1	(CD) Arbors ARCD 19284
(e)	Honky Tonk Train (omit Cary)		(CD) Arbors ARCD 19284
(f)	Someday Sweetheart	-1	(CD) Arbors ARCD 19284
(g)	I Found a New Baby (omit Cary)		(CD) Arbors ARCD 19284
(h)	Louisiana	-1	(CD) Arbors ARCD 19284
(i)	A Hundred Years From Today	-1, -2	(CD) Arbors ARCD 19284
(j)	Echo of Spring (omit Cary)		(CD) Arbors ARCD 19284
(k)	In a Sentimental Mood	-2	(CD) Arbors ARCD 19284
(l)	Undecided	-1	(CD) Arbors ARCD 19284
(m)	Sweet Georgia Brown	-2	(CD) Arbors ARCD 19284

These recordings were originally made for The Blue Angel Jazz Club. The Arbors catalogue stated that this was to be a double-CD and listed the following titles as part of this issue:
Out of Nowhere

You're Driving Me Crazy
Street of Dreams
Shine

Label owner Mat Domber advised: "We originally planned to issue a double CD but when we reviewed the audio quality on the various tracks we decided to eliminate some that we felt were not up to our standards. The catalog was printed before this decision was made."

Other titles taped were:

(Cary, Sutton, Hall, Leeman): **February , 1969**

    Keepin' Out of Mischief Now   BAJC unissued
    Blue Lou   BAJC unissued
    Sunday   BAJC unissued
    If I Had You   BAJC unissued
    Blues My Naughty Sweetie Gave to Me   BAJC unissued
    St. Louis Blues   BAJC unissued
    Do You Know What It Means to
        Miss New Orleans   BAJC unissued
    Sunny Side of the Street   BAJC unissued
    'Deed I Do   BAJC unissued
    Ain't Misbehavin'   BAJC unissued
    Love Lies   BAJC unissued

DICK CARY (p; Hall, b; Leeman, d):
    Sunnie's Rendezvous, Aspen, CO — February 10, 1969
    The Bad and the Beautiful   BAJC unissued
    Spring Is Here   BAJC unissued
    Laura   BAJC unissued
    All the Things You Are   BAJC unissued
    Cottontail   BAJC unissued

RALPH SUTTON and DICK CARY (Cary, tp, a-h; Sutton, p; Hall, b; Leeman, d):
    Sunnie's Rendezvous, Aspen, CO — February 11, 1969
    Them There Eyes   BAJC unissued

(same):   ***Sunnie's Rendezvous, Aspen, CO — February 12, 1969***
    Undecided   BAJC unissued
    All the Things You Are   BAJC unissued
    Sweet Georgia Brown   BAJC unissued
    Old Folks   BAJC unissued
    Do You Know What It Means to
        Miss New Orleans   BAJC unissued
    Fine and Dandy   BAJC unissued
    How High the Moon   BAJC unissued
    Ain't Misbehavin'   BAJC unissued
    Dancing on the Ceiling   BAJC unissued
    Struttin' With Some Barbecue   BAJC unissued

(same): **Sunnie's Rendezvous, Aspen CO — February 13, 1969**
    Keepin' Out of Mischief Now   BAJC unissued
    You Can Depend on Me   BAJC unissued
    Ol' Pigeon-Toed Joe   BAJC unissued
    Sharecropper's Blues   BAJC unissued

DICK CARY (p; Hall, b; Leeman, d):   *same date*
    Old Fashioned Love   BAJC unissued
    I Would Do Anything for You   BAJC unissued
    Monday Date   BAJC unissued

BLUE ANGEL JAZZ CLUB   *University Club of Pasadena, CA — November 1, 1969*
(Dick Cary, tp; Bob Havens, tb; Matty Matlock, cl; Wayne Songer, sax; Don Lodice, ts; Johnny Guarnieri, p; Nappy Lamare, g; Ray Leatherwood, b; Jack Sperling, d):
  (a)   Jazz Me Blues   BAJC unissued
  (b)   My Melancholy Baby   BAJC unissued
  (c)   Wolverine Blues   vCH   BAJC 505
  (d)   St. James Infirmary   BAJC unissued

Personnel as listed in BAJC/Storyville files, but (c) is by Clancy Hayes, vo, bj; with Cary; Havens; Matlock; Marvin Ash, p; Leatherwood; Sperling.
Other issues: (c) also on (AC) Jazz Connoisseur Cassette JCC 124.

(John Best, tp; Bob Havens, tb; Matty Matlock, cl; Don Lodice, ts; Dick Cary, p; Nappy Lamare, g; Artie Shapiro, b; Jack Sperling d):
  (a)   Who's Sorry Now   BAJC unissued
  (b)   Black and Blue   (LP) BAJC 505
  (c)   Struttin' With Some Barbecue   BAJC unissued
  (d)   Oh! Baby   BAJC unissued

Matty Matlock and the Paducah Patrol (Dick Cary, John Best, tp; Bob Havens, Abe Lincoln, tb; Matty Matlock, cl, arr; Wayne Songer, cl, as, bar, Don Lodice, ts; Johnny Guarnieri, p; Nappy Lamare, g, vo; Ray Leatherwood, b; Jack Sperling, d):
  (a)   Love Is Just Around the Corner   BAJC unissued
  (b)   Smokey Mary   aMM   (LP) BAJC 505
  (c)   Ida, Sweet as Apple Cider   aMM   (LP) BAJC 505
  (d)   Boogie Woogie Maxixe   aMM   (LP) BAJC 506
  (e)   Milk Cow Blues vNL   (LP) BAJC 505

(c) and (d) are shown in the Storyville files with takes 1 and 2, though the significance of this in a jazz party context is unknown. The files show John Finlay in the trumpet section, but he is not given in the sleeve notes.

Lyn Keith (vocal, with Dick Cary, tp; Bob Havens, tb; Don Lodice, ts; Johnny Guarnieri, p; Artie Shapiro, b; Panama Francis, d):
  (a)   Hello Young Lovers   BAJC unissued
  (b)   Somebody Loves Me   BAJC unissued
  (c)   Here's That Rainy Day   BAJC unissued
  (d)   There'll Be Some Changes Made   BAJC unissued

John Best Big Band (John Best, tp; Bob Havens, tb; Matty Matlock, cl; Don Lodice, ts; Dick Cary, p; Nappy Lamare, g; Clancy Hayes, vo, g, bj; Ray Leatherwood, b; Panama Francis, d):
(a)	Please Don't Talk About Me When I'm Gone	BAJC unissued
(b)	I Gotta Right to Sing the Blues	BAJC unissued
(c)	Rose of Washington Square	BAJC unissued
(d)	Ballin' the Jack	BAJC unissued
(e)	What's New/Darn That Dream	BAJC unissued
(f)	Viper's Drag	BAJC unissued

JAZZ PARTY AT PASADENA 1970 (Peanuts Hucko, cl; Dick Cary, p; Eddie Safranksi, b; Nick Fatool. d): *University Club of Pasadena, CA — November 7, 1970*
(a)	When You're Smiling	( )	BAJC unissued
(b)	Do You Know What It Means to Miss New Orleans	( )	BAJC unissued
(c)	Indiana	( )	BAJC unissued

(Dick Cary, tp; Bob Havens, tb; Matty Matlock, cl; Ray Sherman, p; Eddie Safranski, b; Nick Fatool, d):
(a)	Just You, Just Me	(7:35)	BAJC unissued
(b)	Just Friends	(3:53)	(LP) BAJC 508
(c)	E Flat Blues	( )	BAJC unissued

(b) feature for Matty Matlock.

(Flip Phillips, ts; Peanuts Hucko, cl; Red Norvo, vb; Dick Cary, p; Gene Cherico, b; Joe Porcaro, d):
(a)	Three Little Words	(8:10)	BAJC unissued
(b)	On the Alamo	(8:58)	(LP) BAJC 508
(c)	Runnin' Wild	(8:30)	BAJC unissued

Other issue: (b) on (AC) Jazz Connoisseur Cassette JCC112.

Double Front Line (John Best, Dick Cary, tp; Bob Havens, Murray McEachern, tb; Matty Matlock, Peanuts Hucko, cl; Ray Sherman, p; Eddie Safranski, b; Nick Fatool, d):
(a)	Who's Sorry Now	(5:26)	BAJC unissued
(b)	Someday You'll Be Sorry	(6:20)	BAJC unissued
(c)	I Can't Get Started	(6:18)	BAJC unissued

(Peanuts Hucko, cl; Dick Cary, p; George Van Eps, g; Ray Leatherwood, b; Nick Fatool, d):
(a)	I'm Gonna Sit Right Down	(5:52)	BAJC unissued
(b)	Just a Closer Walk With Thee	( )	BAJC unissued
(c)	Stealin' Apples	( )	BAJC unissued

MATTY MATLOCK (Dick Cary, tp; Herbie Harper, tb; Matty Matlock, cl; possibly Deane Kincaide, reeds; Ray Sherman, p; Ray Leatherwood, b; Nick Fatool, d):
Los Angeles — February 17, 1971

no known titles   Warner Bros.

listed in the Cary diaries. Presumed to be an unissued recording session.

BILL WILLIAMS (Dick Cary, tp?; Herb [Harper, tb?]; Matty Matlock, cl; Deane [Kincaide, reeds?]; Charlie Myerson, g; "& rock rhythm section"; Lucille Lane, vo):
Sound City Studios, Los Angeles — May 1, 1971

        Baby Won't You Please Come Home vLL
        Melancholy [Baby?] vLL
        2 other titles
Bill Williams may be the trombonist.

DICK CARY   **Los Angeles — June 10, 1971**
    interview with Scott Ellsworth on "Scott's Place" radio show.
    Cassette tapes have circulated.

EDDIE MILLER (Dick Cary, Jack Coon, tp, a-h; Bob Enevoldsen, vtb, cl; Peanuts Hucko, Matty Matlock, cl; Eddie Miller, ts, vo; Deane Kincaide, bar, cl; Stan Wrightsman, p; Nappy Lamare, g; Ray Leatherwood, b; Nick Fatool, d):

        Hollywood Recording Studio, Hollywood, June 14, 15, 18, 1971

(a)	I've Got a Crush on You	(3:27)	(LP) BAJC 509
(b)	Rose of the Rio Grande	(2:45)	(LP) BAJC 509
(c)	A Letter to Three Wives	(3:34)	(LP) BAJC 509
(d)	Black Zephyr	(2:37)	(LP) BAJC 509
(e)	Street of Dreams	(3:00)	(LP) BAJC 509
(f)	Tishomingo Blues	(5:47)	(LP) BAJC 509
(g)	I'm Gonna Stomp Mr. Henry Lee	(3:16)	(LP) BAJC 509
(h)	It's Easy to Remember	(3:50)	(LP) BAJC 509
(i)	Riverboat Shuffle	(3:20)	(LP) BAJC 509
(j)	Louise, Louise vEM	(3:29)	(LP) BAJC 509
(k)	Rose of Washington Square	(3:25)	(LP) BAJC 509
(l)	Lazy Mood	(3:04)	(LP) BAJC 509
(m)	A Portrait of Eddie (Cary)	(2:27)	BAJC unissued
(n)	The Hour of Parting	(3:25)	BAJC unissued

June 14 session: Matty Matlock and Nappy Lamare were not present.
June 15 session: Matlock ("very shaky, not well") and Lamare played.
June 18 session: Matlock not present (in hospital).
Sleeve notes show Hucko as present on all titles, except (g) and (k).
(i) clarinet trio on Riverboat Shuffle is Bob Enevoldsen, Peanuts Hucko and Deane Kincaide.
(a) arranged by Stan Wrightsman; (b),(f),(g),(h),(i),(l) by Matty Matlock; (c) by Mickey Ingalls; (d),(e),(j) by Deane Kincaide. Billy May listed as "conductor, chief rewrite man, cheerleader."
A Portrait of Eddie also known as *Ballad for Eddie*.

Other issues: BAJC 509 titles also on (AC) Jazz Connoisseur Cassettes JCC103. (f) on (AC) Jazz Connoisseur Cassettes JCC104 (sampler). Album title: A Portrait of Eddie.

    In January 1972 Cary was scheduled to record an album for Carlton MacBeth, head of Maggio Brass World publications, with a brass quintet, plus two (Ed Safranski, b; Nick Fatool, d). The album would be released at the same time as a book of music. It is not known if this happened.

    Also unconfirmed is a claim that Cary and Dick Hamilton were booked for a recording session so that the producer could have two alto-horns in the orchestra.

JOHN FAHEY and his Orchestra (Jack Feierman, tp; Britt Woodman, tb; Joe Darensbourg, ss-1, cl; Johnny Rotella, as; Dick Cary, p; Allan Reuss, g; Ira Westley, bb; unknown, d):

United Studios, Hollywood, February 21, 1973

(a)	Old Fashioned Love		(LP) Tacoma C-1043
(b)	Boodle Am Shake	vBB-1	(LP) Tacoma C-1043
(c)	Keep Your Lamp Trimmed and Burning	-2	(LP) Tacoma C-1043

-1 add Bobby Bruce, vl, vo; Fahey also on jug. -2 Feierman out.
This session fits with Cary's entry for this date. He refers to a folk singer and recording two tunes in the afternoon (1:00 to 4:00) and one in the evening (5:00 to 8:00), with "Jack on trumpet."

Other issues: Tacoma C-1043 also on (CD) Shanachie 99001

UNKNOWN (Dick Cary, tp?; unknown tb; Abe Most, cl):   *Los Angeles — February 23, 1973*
"...sweetened a black rock singer's record"

CARL FARTINA (?)   *Western Recording Studios, Los Angeles — April 13, 1973*
mentioned in Cary's diary — no other details. Perhaps for Merl Olds?

BARNEY BIGARD and his Jazz Greats (Barney Bigard, cl; Dick Cary, p; Dave Koonse, g; Eddie Safranski, b; Nick Fatool, d):
Remote Recording Studio, Los Angeles — June 25, 1973

(a)	Off Shore	-1	(LP) RCA APL1-1744
(b)	Satchmo's Dream		(LP) RCA APL1-1744
(c)	Mood Indigo	-2	(LP) RCA APL1-1744
(d)	Memoir de Bayou		(LP) RCA APL1-1744
(e)	Easy on the Ears	-3	(LP) RCA APL1-1744

-1 Cary also on trumpet by re-recording. -2 Ensemble clarinet trio by Bigard re-recording. -3 Cary also on alto-horn by re-recording. Other issues: all on (LP) RCA(F) FLX1 7119. The overdubbing session was held on August 23, 1973.

(Dick Cary, tp-4, a-h-5; Barney Bigard, cl; Ray Sherman, p; Eddie Safranski, b; Nick Fatool, d):
Remote Recording Studio, Los Angeles — July 10, 1973

(a)	Tea for Two	-5	(LP) RCA APL1-1744
(b)	Clarinet Gumbo	-4	(LP) RCA APL1-1744
(c)	Struttin' With Some Barbecue	-5	(LP) RCA APL1-1744
(d)	Wampum (Bigard-Cary)	-4	(LP) RCA APL1-1744
(e)	Florence Off Ramp (Cary)	-5	(LP) RCA APL1-1744
(f)	Slings and Arrows (Cary)	-5	(LP) RCA APL1-1744

Other issues: all on (LP) RCA(F) FLX1 7119. Album title: Easy on the Ears.

JOHN FAHEY and his Orchestra (Jack Feierman, tp; Britt Woodman, tb; Joe Darensbourg, ss-1, cl; Johnny Rotella, as; Dick Cary, p, a-h; Allan Reuss, bj; John Fahey, Peter Jameson, g; Joel Druckman, b; unknown mandolin, possibly Chris Darrow-1):   *Los Angeles — 1973*

(a)	New Orleans Shuffle		(LP) Reprise MS2145
(b)	After the Ball	-1	(LP) Reprise MS2145

JAZZ PARTY AT PASADENA 1974   *Pasadena, CA — November 30, 1974*
Time-Life Big Band (Dick Cary, John Best, Zeke Zarchy, tp; Lloyd Ulyate, Joe Howard, Herbie

Harper, tb; Abe Most, cl; Willie Schwartz, Les Robinson, as; Wayne Songer, bar; Ray Sherman, p; Ray Leatherwood or Gene Cherico, b; Nick Fatool or Jerry McKenzie, d):

(a)	Mission to Moscow	(2:45)	BAJC unissued
(b)	Begin the Beguine	(3:10)	BAJC unissued
(c)	Let's Dance	(2:45)	BAJC unissued
(d)	Moonlight Serenade	(3:35)	BAJC unissued
(e)	The Kid From Red Bank	(3:35)	BAJC unissued
(f)	Night and Day	(3:40)	BAJC unissued
(g)	Two O'Clock Jump	(5:45)	BAJC unissued

Dick Cary Big Band (John Best, Dick Cary, tp; Joe Howard, Lloyd Ulyate, tb; Abe Most, Willie Schwartz, cl; Babe Russin, as; Don Raffell, ts; Ray Sherman, p; others unknown):

(a)	Front Page Rag	(3:00)	BAJC unissued
(b)	Body and Soul	(3:35)	BAJC unissued
(c)	Wrappin' It Up (DR&DC)	(3:00)	BAJC unissued
(d)	Song of India	( )	BAJC unissued
(e)	Little Rock Getaway	( )	BAJC unissued
(f)	Clarinet a la King	( )	BAJC unissued
(g)	Love Walked In	( )	BAJC unissued
(h)	Benny Rides Again	( )	BAJC unissued

(Dick Cary, a-h; Sam Most, fl; Joe Pass, g; Gene Cherico, b; Jerry McKenzie, d; Mavis Davis, vo):

(a)	Here's That Rainy Day	(12:15)	BAJC unissued
(b)	Just Friends vMD	( )	BAJC unissued

(Big band as above, plus Ray Leatherwood, b; Jerry McKenzie, d):

(a)	In the Mood	(3:40)	BAJC unissued
(b)	Wrap Your Troubles in Dreams	(3:30)	BAJC unissued
(c)	Skater's Waltz	( )	BAJC unissued
(d)	Honky Tonk Train Blues	(3:10)	BAJC unissued
(e)	Bess, You Is My Woman	(4:00)	BAJC unissued
(f)	That Old Black Magic	(2:00)	BAJC unissued
(g)	South Rampart Street Parade	( )	BAJC unissued

DAWN OF THE CENTURY RAGTIME ORCHESTRA (Dick Cary, tp; Bill Stumpp, co; Dave Kennedy, tb; Mike Baird, cl; John Jewett, fl; Dick Zimmerman, p; Art Levin, sous; Roy Roten, d; Prof. David E. Bourne, cond):

Artists Recording Studio, Los Angeles — February 2, 1975 & March 2, 1975

(a)	Here Comes the Band	(LP) Arcane AR-603
(b)	Danny's Dream	(LP) Arcane AR-603
(c)	Meet Me in St. Louis (medley waltz)	(LP) Arcana AR-603
(d)	Rastus on Parade	(LP) Arcane AR-603
(e)	El Corrupto's Favorite	(LP) Arcane AR-603
(f)	The Pride of Smokey Row	(LP) Arcane AR-603
(g)	Pass Dat Possum	(LP) Arcane AR-603
(h)	Red Pepper	(LP) Arcane AR-603
(i)	Mammy's Little Coal Black Rose	(LP) Arcane AR-603
(j)	Silver Swan	(LP) Arcane AR-603
(k)	Russian Rag	(LP) Arcane AR-603
(l)	Kerry Mills Ragtime Dance	(LP) Arcane AR-603

JIMMY McPARTLAND & DICK CARY with the BARRELHOUSE JAZZ BAND
(Jimmy McPartland, co,vo; Dick Cary, F-tp; Horst Schwarz, tp; Reimer von Essen, cl; Frank Selten, ts; Norbert Kemper, p; Bernd K Otto, bj; Eberhard Jirzig, b; Hans-Georg Klauer, d):
Volksbildungsheim, Frankfurt am Main, Germany — October 7, 1975

(a)	St. James Infirmary Blues vJM	(LP) Intercord INT 155.030
(b)	By the Salzburg (Cary)	unissued

(b) is based on a paraphrase on *How Come You Do Me Like You Do* & Cary's chorus on Condon's record. Title as given by Dick Cary, though Reimer von Essen called it *On The Saalburg*. Other issue: (a) also on (AC) Intercord INT 455.030

(same):   *concert, school, Erkelenz, Germany — October 10, 1975*
mentioned in Dick Cary's diary; no doubt unissued.

DICK CARY with LINO PATRUNO and the MILAN COLLEGE JAZZ SOCIETY (Giorgio Alberti, co, f-h*; Dick Cary, F-tp, a-h; Gianni Acocella, tb; Bruno Longhi, cl; Carlo Bagnoli, bsx; Renato Barzago, p; Lino Patruno, g; Marco Ratti, b; Remi Ettore, d):
Milan, Italy — October 18, 1975

(a)	Beale Street Blues	(take -2)	(LP) Carasello CLE21029
(b)	New Orleans *	(take -2)	(LP) Carasello CLE21029
(c)	Riverboat Shuffle		(LP) Carasello CLE21029
(d)	Original Dixieland One-Step	-1	unissued

-1 Giancarlo Cinti, b; replaces Ratti.
Other issues: (b) also on (CD) Carasello CDCGG 21006, 300 556-2.

JIMMY McPARTLAND & DICK CARY with LINO PATRUNO and the MILAN COLLEGE JAZZ SOCIETY (Jimmy McPartland, co, speech; Dick Cary, p; Lino Patruno, g; Marco Ratti, b; Remi Ettore, d):   *Milan, Italy — October 18, 1975*
   (a)   Davenport Blues (take -2)   (LP) Carasello CLE21029
guitar over-dubbed on this title on October 27, 1975.

(McPartland, co, speech-4; Dick Cary, a-h, Ftp-1; Acocella, tb; Longhi, cl; Paolo Tomelleri, ts; Patruno, g; Ratti, b; Ettore, d):   *same date*
   (b)   Caprice in Milan for Guiseppe
                 (Joe) Venuti   (take -2) -1,-4   (LP) Carasello CLE21029

(add Barzago, p):
   (c)   I Can't Give You Anything
                 But Love, Baby!   vJM   (LP) Carasello CLE21029

(add Alberti, co; Bagnoli, bar, ss-3; Longhi also ss-3):

(d)	Original Dixieland One Step		(LP) Carasello CLE21029
(e)	Singin' the Blues	-3	(LP) Carasello CLE21006
(f)	Nobody's Sweetheart	(take -2) -1	(LP) Carasello CLE21029

(e) soprano saxophones recorded on October 27, 1975.

Other issues: (a),(b),(d),(f) on (CD) Carasello CDCGG 21006, 300 556-2. (c) on (CD) Carasello 300 674-2. (e) on (CD) Carasello 300 556-2. (a),(e) on (CD) Musica Jazz 2MJP 1085. Carasello CLE21029 Album title: Singin' the Blues.

DARKTOWN JAZZ BAND (Jimmy McPartland, co, vo; Wolfgang Trattner, tp; Dick Cary, a-h; Dieter Riempp, tb; Siegfried Seyffer, cl; Werner Lener, p; Ludwig Stimmler, b; Elmar Wippler, d):
Stuttgart, Germany — October 22, 1975

(a)	At the Jazz Band Ball	-1	(LP) Intercord INT 155.057
(b)	Baby Won't You Please Come Home	-2	(LP) Intercord INT 155.057
(c)	I Gotta Right to Sing the Blues	vJM	(LP) Intercord INT 155.057

-1 omit Trattner. -2 Cary, a-tp; with rhythm section only.

DICK CARY with Ted Easton's Jazzband (Dick Cary, tp, a-tp-1; George Kaatee, tb; Frits Kaatee, cl; Ralph Sutton, p; Pim Hogervorst, bj; Hans Eekhoff, sou; Ted Easton, d):
J.P.S. Studios, Leiden, Holland — October 27, 1975

(a)	Sunday	(LP) Riff 659.014
(b)	Somebody Stole My Gal -1	(LP) Riff 659.014
(c)	It's a Sin to Tell a Lie	(LP) Riff 659.014
(d)	Truckin'	unissued
(e)	Stumblin'	unissued
(f)	Imagination	unissued
(g)	Ugly Child	unissued
(h)	If I Had You	unissued
(i)	Come Back Sweet Papa	unissued

(Cary, a-h; Sutton, p; Jacques Kingma, b; Easton, d):   *same date*
    (j)   You Brought a New Kind of Love to Me   (LP) Riff 659.014

Other issues: (a), (c) on (LP) Circle CLP18. (j) on (CD) Progressive PCD-7125.

NAT GONELLA with Ted Easton's Jazzband (Nat Gonella, tp, vo; Bob Wulffers, tp; Henk van Muyen, tb; Frits Kaatee, cl, ts-1; Dick Cary, p; Pim Hogervorst, bj; Jacques Kingma, b-g; Ted Easton, d):
J.P.S. Studios, Leiden, Holland — October 28, 1975

(a)	We Wish You a Merry Christmas	(LP) CNR 657.524
(b)	White Christmas	(LP) CNR 657.524
(c)	At Christmas (T.Easton/D.Cary)	(LP) CNR 657.524
(d)	Jingle Bells	(LP) CNR 657.524
(e)	I'll Be Home for Christmas -1	(LP) CNR 657.524
(f)	Winter Wonderland	(LP) CNR 657.524
(g)	Rudolph the Red Nosed Reindeer	(LP) CNR 657.524

(Gonella vo; Cary, p):   *same date*
    (h)   The Christmas Song   (LP) CNR 657.524

Most, if not all, of the trumpet work is by Wulffers.

Other issues: (a),(c) on (LP) CNR 141.371. Album title: *Wishing You a Swinging Christmas.*

DICK CARY with Ted Easton's Jazzband (Dick Cary, tp; George Kaatee, tb; Frits Kaatee, cl; Ralph Sutton, p; Pim Hogervorst, bj; Jacques Kingma, b; Ted Easton, d):
J.P.S. Studios, Leiden, Holland — October 30, 1975

(a)	Mandy Make Up Your Mind	(LP) Riff 659.014

(Dick Cary, tp, a-h, p; Frits Kaatee. cl; Koos van der Sluis, b; Ted Easton, d):

(b)	Save It Pretty Mama	(LP) Riff 659.014

(Cary, a-h, p; Bob Wilber, ss; van der Sluis, b; Easton, d):
(c)	What's New	(LP) Riff 659.014

(Cary, a-h, p; van der Sluis, b; Easton, d):
(d)	Sleighride in July	(LP) Riff 659.014

Despite the details on the Riff sleeve, (c) was almost certainly recorded November 4th, with Bob Wilber adding his part three days later, and it is unlikely that Ralph Sutton was the pianist. He left Holland for Italy on October 28. (d) may also have been recorded November 4. Album title: The Amazing Dick Cary.

Other issues: all titles on (LP) Circle CLP18; (b),(c),(d) on (CD) Progressive PCD-7125

DICK CARY (Dick Cary, p; Koos van der Sluis, b; Ted Easton, d): *same date*
(a)	Time on My Hands	unissued
(b)	Time After Time	unissued
(c)	The Nearness of You	unissued
(d)	Come Sunday	unissued
(e)	Someday	unissued
(f)	The Beginning of the End	unissued
(g)	Embraceable You	unissued
(h)	Thanks a Million	unissued

Cary says he recorded 12 titles and includes *Save It Pretty Mama*, listed above. Cary does not name the bassist. The following day (October 31) he and Easton were in the studio and "overlaid" on these trio tracks, with Easton adding vocals to three of the titles.

JIMMY McPARTLAND, DICK CARY with Ted Easton's Jazzband (Jimmy McPartland, co; Bob Wulffers, tp; Dick Cary, tp-6, a-h-1, a-tp-2, p, arr; Henk van Muyen, tb; Frits Kaatee, cl-3, bar-5; Pim Hogervorst, bj; Jacques Kingma, b; Ted Easton, d):

New Orleans Jazz Club, Scheveningen, Holland — November 3, 1975
(a)	Ostrich Walk	aDC -1,-3	(LP) Riff 659.031
(b)	I'm Coming Virginia	aDC -3,-5,-6	(LP) Riff 659.031
(c)	Davenport Blues	aDC -1,-3	(LP) Riff 659.031

(Dick Cary, solo piano): *same date?*
(d)	In a Mist	(LP) Riff 659 031

Jimmy McPartland was in hospital on November 3. He added his cornet parts the following evening in the JSP Studios. The Riff sleeve gives Ralph Sutton on piano for *Davenport Blues*, but he was in Italy and Cary is sure he overdubbed piano on this title. Recording date for *In a Mist* is uncertain.

Other issues: (a) also on (LP) Berec 770803

DICK CARY (Dick Cary, p, tp, a-h; Koos van der Sluis, b; Ted Easton, d):
JPS Studios, Leiden, November 4, 1975
The trio recorded 10 songs, "then overlaid mostly horn and some A.T. [alto trumpet?] with some duets. Left spots for Bob Wilber who arrives Friday [November 7]." Riff See *What's New*, October 30, 1975.

JIMMY McPARTLAND, DICK CARY with Ted Easton's Jazzband (personnel as for *Ostrich Walk,* November 3, 1975):

New Orleans Jazz Club, Scheveningen, Holland — November 4, 1975

(a)	Riverboat Shuffle	-1,-3	(LP) Riff 659.031
(b)	Louisiana	aDC -1,-3	(LP) Riff 659.031
(c)	At the Jazz Band Ball	-1,-3	(LP) Riff 659.031
(d)	Singin' the Blues aDC	-2,-3,-5	(LP) Riff 659.031
(e)	Clarinet Marmalade	-2,-3	(LP) Riff 659.031

Sleeve for Riff 659 031 quotes recording dates as October 30/31, but Cary's diary gives as above. Album title: Salute to Bix.

JIMMY McPARTLAND (Jimmy McPartland, co; Dick Cary, a-tp, a-h; Spiegle Wilcox, tb; Russ Mussieri, cl, ts; Joe Venuti, vl; Marian McPartland, p; Major Holley, b; Cliff Leeman, d):

TV Show, Plaza Hotel, Rochester, New York — perhaps November 1975

(a)	At the Jazz Band Ball	(VCR) Halcyon
(b)	Royal Garden Blues	(VCR) Halcyon
(c)	Blues at the Top	(VCR) Halcyon
(d)	China Boy	(VCR) Halcyon
(e)	Sweet Georgia Brown	(VCR) Halcyon
(f)	Avalon	(VCR) Halcyon
(g)	Nobody's Sweetheart	(VCR) Halcyon

The show was entitled "Jazz at the Top: Remembering Bix Beiderbecke." It was broadcast on station WXXI-TV and the presumed date for this was August 7, 1976. As Cary was not in New York during 1976 it is an assumption that possibly he stopped-over in NY while returning to Los Angeles after his European tour with McPartland. The show also included two piano solos by Marian McPartland — *In a Mist* and *Candlelights.*

UNKNOWN (Dick Cary, tp, a-h?; Abe Most, cl; Babe Russin, ts; Ray Sherman, p; George Van Eps, g; Ray Leatherwood, b; Nick Fatool, d):

Annex Studios, Los Angeles — March 22, 1976

"8 tunes for Glenn Shipley." Two sessions, 10-1 & 2-5.
Dick Cary's diary gives no other details.

TERRY MARETTI (?) (Bob Enevoldsen-v-tb; Dave Edwards, ss; Dick Cary, p?; Neil Levang, bj; Ray Leatherwood, b; Nick Fatool, d): *Annex Studios, Los Angeles — May 6, 1976*

One More for the Boys
Bi-Centennial Rag

From Dick Cary's diary — no other details.

The following recordings of December 1976 are taken from concerts broadcast during the Australian Jazz Convention, held that year in Brisbane.

MILEHAM HAYES with Dick Cary (Dick Cary, a-h?; Allan Murray, tp; Mileham Hayes, cl; Alan Birmingham p; John Cox, bj, g; John Reid, b; Ron Rae, d):

concert, Schonell Theatre, Brisbane — Dcember 26, 1976

(a)	Jeepers Creepers	(AC) Audio Alchemy
(b)	Doin' the New Lowdown	(AC) Audio Alchemy
(c)	Rosetta	(AC) Audio Alchemy

(d)	That Da Da Strain		(AC) Audio Alchemy
(e)	Riverboat Shuffle		(AC) Audio Alchemy

DICK CARY and his Convention Hotshots (Mileham Hayes, cl; Lachie Thomson, cl, as; Dick Cary, ?; others?): *concert, Schonell Theatre, Brisbane — December 26, 1976*
- (a) Shim-Me-Sha-Wabble
- (b) Sugar
- (c) Rosetta
- (d) Save It Pretty Mama
- (e) Wolverine Blues

DICK CARY and BOB BARNARD (Bob Barnard, tp; Dick Cary, p; others?): *concert, Schonell Theatre, Brisbane — December 26, 1976*
- (a) Panama
- (b) Six or Seven Times
- (c) You Took Advantage of Me (tp/p duet)
- (d) Irish Black Bottom

THE WORLD'S HOTTEST JAZZ BAND (Bob Barnard, tp; Ken Herron, tb; Mileham Hayes, cl; Dick Cary, p; Ed Gaston, b; Len Barnard, d): *Brisbane — December 27/28, 1976*

(a)	Jeepers Creepers		(LP) EMI EMC 2635

(add Ade Monsbourgh, as-1, ts-2):

(b)	Fingerbuster	-1	(LP) EMI ECM 2635
(c)	Doin' the New Lowdown	-2	(LP) EMI EMC 2635

(Cary, p; Gaston, b; Len Barnard, d):

(d)	Phineas Newborn Jr's Waltz		(LP) EMI ECM 2635

(Ken Herron, tb; Cary, p; Gaston, b; Len Barnard, d):

(e)	What Are You Doing the Rest of My Life		(LP) EMI ECM 2635

(Bob Barnard, tp; Monsbourgh, ts; Cary, p; Gaston, b; Len Barnard, d):

(f)	Save It Pretty Mama		(LP) EMI ECM 2635

(omit Monsbourgh):

(g)	I'm Coming Virginia	(take -1)	(LP) EMI ECM 2635
(h)	I'm Coming Virgina	(take -2)	(LP) EMI ECM 2635

(Barnard, Herron, Cary, Gaston, Barnard, plus Ade Monsbourgh, cl; Neville Stribling, bar):

(i)	Strut Miss Lizzie		(LP) EMI ECM 2635

(same, except Monsburgh out):

(m)	Bourbon Street Parade		(LP) EMI ECM 2635

(Barnard, Herron, Lachie Thomson, cl; Stribling, bs-sax; Cary, Gaston, Barnard):

(n)	Shim Me Sha Wobble		(LP) EMI ECM 2635

(same, plus Frank Johnson, tp; Stribling out):

(o)	Sunday		(LP) EMI ECM 2635

(p)	Way Down Yonder in New Orleans		(LP) EMI ECM 2635

ALL THE PRESIDENT'S MEN (Bob Barnard, tp; Dick Cary, p, ah; Ade Monsbourgh, v-tb, reeds; Mileham Hayes, cl; others):

afternoon concert, Schonell, Theatre, Brisbane — December 27, 1976

(a)	Jeepers Creepers	(AC) Audio Alchemy
(b)	Save It Pretty Mama	(AC) Audio Alchemy
(c)	Doin' the New Lowdown	(AC) Audio Alchemy
(d)	That Da Da Strain	(AC) Audio Alchemy

BOB BARNARD BAND (Bob Barnard, tp; Dick Cary,tp, a-h; Ade Monsbourgh, reeds, vo; Len Barnard, p; Gary Dunbier, b; Bob Watson, d):

evening concert, Schonell Theatre, Brisbane — December 27, 1976

(a)	My Monday Date	
(b)	Ain't Gonna Give Nobody None of My Jelly Roll	vAM
(c)	Exactly Like You	
(d)	The Jazz Parade	

This is probably a private tape rather than an Audio Alchemy cassette.

DICK CARY and BOB BARNARD (Bob Barnard, tp; Dick Cary, p, a-h -1; Chris Ludowyck, b; Bob Watson or Len Barnard, d):

evening concert, Schonell Theatre, Brisbane — December 27, 1976

(a)	The Man I Love		(AC) Audio Alchemy
(b)	New Orleans		(AC) Audio Alchemy
(c)	Them There Eyes	-1	(AC) Audio Alchemy
(d)	I'm Confessin'		(AC) Audio Alchemy
(e)	Someday (You'll Be Sorry)		(AC) Audio Alchemy

Cary does not play piano on (c).

BRISBANE JAZZ CLUB BIG BAND with Dick Cary (John Noble, Bob Barnard, Gene St. Ledger, Vince Hardaker, tp; Allen Robinson, Mike Causebrook, Joe Mills, tb; Mel Bongers, Rod Taylor, as; Jim McKenzie, Art Loxton, ts; Cec Shaw, bar; Dick Cary, p; Pat Roche, g; Horsley Dawson, b; John Harrison, d; Tony Ashby, leader; Roy Theoharris, director):

evening concert, Schonell Theatre, Brisbane — December 28, 1976

(a)	Mopsy		(CD) T&T 04

(same, except Cary, tp-1 or f-tp-2; Ray Clifford, ts; Graham Tait, p; added): ***same concert***

(b)	Embraceable You	-1	(CD) T&T 04
(c)	Cerulean Blue	-2	(CD) T&T 04
(d)	Bud's Blues	-1	(VHS)

(similar): ***same concert***

(e)	Blue Sue
(f)	Embraceable You
(g)	Jazz Blues
(h)	Over the Waves

some of these titles probably on (AC) Audio Alchemy. T&T 04 is a compilation. The video of the 1976 Convention was produced by the organisers.

DICK CARY and Friends (Dick Cary, tp, a-h, p; Frank Johnson, tp; Paul Furniss, reeds; Gordon Cummins, p; others?):

afternoon concert, Schonell Theatre, Brisbane -December 29, 1976

(a)	Echo of Spring	(AC) Audio Alchemy
(b)	Dinah	(AC) Audio Alchemy
(c)	Beale Street Blues	(AC) Audio Alchemy
(d)	Monday Date	(AC) Audio Alchemy
(e)	Struttin' With Some Barbecue	(AC) Audio Alchemy

(a) presumably a piano solo.

ADRIAN FORD BIG BAND (John Roberts, Les Crosby, Dick Cary, Bob Barnard, tp; John Bates, tb; Paul Furniss, Lachie Thomson, as; Terry Wynn, ts; Adrian Ford, p; George Woods, g; Laurie Buckland, b; Ian Hill, d):

concert, Schonell Theatre, Brisbane — December 30, 1976

(a)	Jumpin' at the Woodside
(b)	The Preacher
(c)	Two O'Clock Jump

This is probably a private tape, rather than an Audio Alchemy casstte.

GRAEME BELL, featuring Dick Cary (Dick Cary, Cliff Reece, tp; Ken Herron, tb; Paul Furniss, cl; Graeme Bell, p; Ed Gaston, b; Geoff Proud, d):

evening concert, Schonell Theatre, Brisbane — December 30, 1976

(a)	Fidgety Feet	(AC) Audio Alchemy
(b)	Keeping Out of Mischief Now	(AC) Audio Alchemy
(c)	Clarinet Marmalade	(AC) Audio Alchemy
(d)	Stormy Weather	(AC) Audio Alchemy
(e)	That's a Plenty	(AC) Audio Alchemy

ADE, BOB, DICK, ED, BOB, KEN (Bob Barnard, tp; Ken Herron, tb; Ade Monsbourgh, reeds; Dick Cary, p, a-h; Ed Gaston, b-g; Bob Watson, d):

afternoon concert, Schonell Theatre, Brisbane — December 31, 1976

unknown titles   (AC) Audio Alchemy

CONVENTION GUESTS (Bob Barnard, tp; Dick Cary, a-h, p-3; Ade Monsbourgh, cl-1; as-2; ts-3; Adrian Ford, p; Horsley Dawson, b-g; Ron Rae, d):

evening ? concert, Schonell Theatre, Brisbane — December 31, 1976

(a)	From Monday On	-2
(b)	Singin' the Blues	-2
(c)	Under a Blanket of Blue	-3
(d)	Royal Garden Blues	-1

(c) Ford out. *The Peanut Vendor* from this set is by Bob Barnard, with the rhythm section. This may be a private tape rather than an Audio Alchemy issue.

LACHIE THOMSON ORCHESTRA (Bob Barnard, tp; Lachie Thomson, reeds; Dick Cary, p; others?):

Brisbane — December 31, 1976

(a)	That Certain Motion (two versions)	unissued
(b)	Bugle Call Rag	unissued
(c)	You Ain't the One	unissued
(d)	unknown title	unissued

Recorded for an unknown record company — reported in Names & Numbers No. 34.

DICK CARY and Chicagoans (Dick Cary, tp-1, a-h-2, p-3; Klaus Bader, ss, as-4; Christian Hirschmann, p-5; Klaus Schultze, b; Peter Malinowsky, d):

Schlosskeller, Pforzheim, Germany — February 23, 1977

(a)	Ain't Misbehavin'	-3	(LP) AGM 7716
(b)	Do You Know What It Means to Miss New Orleans	-1,-5	(LP) AGM 7716
(c)	Avalon	-2,-5	(LP) AGM 7716
(d)	Echo of Spring		(LP) AGM7716
(e)	Nobodies (sic) Sweetheart	-2,-5	(LP) AGM 7716
(f)	Misty	-3,-4	(LP) AGM7716
(g)	I'm Coming Virginia	-3	(LP) AGM7716
(h)	Wrap Your Troubles in Dreams		

(d) is a piano solo by Dick Cary. (f) is by Bader, ss; Cary, p; Schultze, b. (g) is a duet by Baser, ss; Cary, p. Album title: Jazz Life.

DICK CARY (Cary, p; Chris Smildiger, b; Ted Easton, d):

J.P.S. Studio, Leiden, Holland — February 28, 1977

    8 titles recorded — "as tracks for future soloists like Buddy Tate and Roy Williams."   Riff unissued

(same personnel):   *J.P.S. Studio, Leiden, Holland — March 1, 1977*

14 titles, including:

Stealin' Apples	Riff unissued
Fingerbuster	Riff unissued
My One and Only Love	Riff unissued
"Jack O'Brien's tune" (probably If You'll Just Say)	Riff unissued

DICK CARY   *J.P.S. Studio, Leiden, Holland — March 2, 1977*

1. Added random trumpet and horns on songs recorded February 28 and March 1.
2. "I added alto horn to an album on which [Bobby] Hackett played 'side meddles.' This must have been done about three years ago." [Bobby Hackett recorded for Riff in 1973.]

Jim Turner says that Dick Cary heard the the phrase "side meddles" from Barney Bigard. "Once, Dick was playing horn alongside Bigard and heard him sort of noodling with the clarinet very quietly in a low register while someone else was soloing. Bigard said it came from New Orleans and the players there called it 'sidemeddling.' Dick thought that was great and began doing it himself."

OLD MERRYTALE JAZZBAND and DICK CARY (Dieter Bergmann, tp, vo; Jost Münster, tb, vo; Dick Cary, ah, ah&tp-1, arr, vo; Helmut Lamszus, cl; Bruno Lefeldt, p; Andreas von der Meden, bj, g-2, arr; Reinhard Zaum, b-g, sou-3, vo; Bernd Reiners, d):

Fabrik Zelt, Hamburg, Germany — March 4, 1977

(a)	Lonesome Road	-2	(LP) Polydor 2664 197
(b)	1919 March	-3	(LP) Polydor 2664 197
(c)	S-H-I-N-E	vJM	(LP) Polydor 2664 197
(d)	Roseroom (sic)	-3,-4	(LP) Polydor 2664 197

-4 von der Meden dubbed a second banjo part onto track (d).

(same personnel):   **Fabrik Zelt, Hamburg, Germany — March 5, 1977**

(e)	Someday	vRZ aDC	(LP) Polydor 2664 197
(f)	Get the Bucket	vDB&band	(LP) Polydor 2664 197
(g)	Swing Down to New Orleans (sic) (Cary)	vDC -2	(LP) Polydor 2664 197
(h)	Willie the Weeper	-3	(LP) Polydor 2664 197
(i)	When You're Smiling	vDB&band aDC	(LP) Polydor 2664 197

(Cary, solo piano):

(j)	Echos (sic) of Spring	(LP) Polydor 2664 197

(same personnel):   **Fabrik Zelt, Hamburg, Germany — March 6, 1977**

(k)	Original Dixieland One Step		(LP) Polydor 2664 197
(l)	Breeze	-1	(LP) Polydor 2664 197

(Cary, ah; Lefeldt, p; von der Meden, g; Zaum, b-g; Reiners, d):   **same date**

(m)	Please	aDC	(LP) Polydor 2664 197
(n)	Crazy Rhythm		(LP) Polydor 2664 197

Polydor 2664 197 is a 2-LP set. Cary not on all titles. *Swing Down to New Orleans* is so listed, although Cary sings *Swing Down in New Orleans*. Titles recorded in a large tent (fabrik zelt) which was being used while the main hall was being rebuilt after a fire.
March 6 was an afternoon session, prior to Cary flying to London.

It is not clear if Cary also recorded three piano solos, *Don't Answer* (March 4), *Who Was It Last Night* (March 5) and *Up the Podium* (March 6), and perhaps band numbers, *Do You Know What It Means to Miss New Orleans, Body and Soul, One and Only Love*.
Album title: Jazz Fabrik: Old Merrytale Live & Dick Cary.

THE JACK LESBERG SEXTET with Eddie Miller and Dick Cary (Dick Cary, tp, a-tp-1, arr; Bob Enevoldsen, vtb; Eddie Miller, ts; Ray Sherman, p; Jack Lesberg, b; Nick Fatool, d):
     Wally Heider Studios, Hollywood — October 28, 1977

(a)	Stomp Mr. Henry Lee		(LP) Famous Door HL120
(b)	But Not for Me		(LP) Famous Door HL120
(c)	Blues for Sydney		(LP) Famous Door HL120
(d)	The Preacher		(LP) Famous Door HL120
(e)	Blues for George	-1	(LP) Famous Door HL120
(f)	Come Rain or Come Shine		(LP) Famous Door HL120
(g)	Ballad for Eddie (Cary)		(LP) Famous Door HL120
(h)	Crazy Rhythm	-1	(LP) Famous Door HL120

Album title: Hollywood Swing.

KLAUS BADER'S CHICAGOANS with Dick Cary and Beryl Bryden (Beryl Bryden, vo; Dick Cary, tp-1, p-2, ah-3; Klaus Bader, as-4, ss-5; Jörg Reiter, p; Klaus Schultze, b; Peter Malinowski, d):
     Revolution Club, Pforzheim, Germany — November 6, 1977

(a)	Do You Know What It Means to Miss New Orleans	-1,-5	(LP) WSO Record 0101-1
(b)	After You've Gone	vBB -1,-4	(LP) WSO Record 0101-1

(c)	Mandy Make Up Your Mind	-3,-5	(LP) WSO Record 0101-1
(d)	Margie	-3,-4	(LP) WSO Record 0101-1
(e)	Please Don't Talk About Me When I'm Gone	vBB -2 *	(LP) WSO Record 0101-1
(f)	The Preacher	vBB -1,-4	(LP) WSO Record 0101-1
(g)	I Love My Man	vBB -3,-4	(LP) WSO Record 0101-1
(h)	Some of These Days	vBB -3,-4	(LP) WSO Record 0101-1

* omit Bader and Reiter.   Album title: Jazz Night at Revolution Club.

Other issues: all titles on (AC) with same catalogue number.

PUD BROWN'S TENOR FOR TWO (Dick Cary, tp-1, ah-2, p-3; Bob Havens, tb; Pud Brown, cl-4, ts-5; Eddie Miller, cl-6, ts-7; Bill Campbell, p; Nappy Lamare, g, vo; Monty Budwig, b; Shelly Manne, d):   *Capitol Studios, Hollywood — December 27, 1977*

(a)	Tenor for Two	-1,-5,-7	(LP) New Orleans Jazz LP-001
(b)	Swing Down in New Orleans (Dick Cary)	vNL -1,-4,-5,-6,-7	(LP) New Orleans Jazz LP-001
(c)	Gotta Be on My Way	-3,-7 **	(LP) New Orleans Jazz LP-001
(d)	That Old Gang of Mine	-2,-4,-7	(LP) New Orleans Jazz LP-001
(e)	Bayou Lafourche (Dick Cary*)	-2,-4,-5,-7	(LP) New Orleans Jazz LP-001
(f)	Down in New Orleans	-2,-4,-6,-7	(LP) New Orleans Jazz LP-001
(g)	What'll I Say Dear	-2,-4,-7	(LP) New Orleans Jazz LP-001
(h)	Congo Jazz	-2,-4,-6,-7	(LP) New Orleans Jazz LP-001
(i)	Yellow Dog Blues	-1,-4,-6,-7	(LP) New Orleans Jazz LP-001
(j)	Left Right Left	-2,-4,-7	(LP) New Orleans Jazz LP-001

* as "Dick Kay" on label. (g) correct title is: *What Can I Say Dear After I Say I'm Sorry.*
** omit Havens, Brown and Campbell. Album title: Pud Brown's Tenor For Two.

MICKEY FINN (Dick Cary, Cappy Lewis, tp; Bob Havens, tb; Jack Nimitz, Don Menza, reeds; Fred Finn, p; Mickey Finn, bj; John Guerin, Colin Bailey, d; --- Barnett, unknown):
Capitol Studios, Hollywood — January 5, 1978
From Dick Cary's diary — no other details

(perhaps similar personnel; Cary also on p): *Capitol Studios, Hollywood — January 6, 1978*
theme from Julia   -1

-1 featuring two pianos. No relevant session is found in "The Capitol Label Discography" (CD-Rom) by Michel Ruppli, Bill Daniels and Ed Novitsky.

B.B. KING (vo; with Dick Cary, tp; Bob Enevoldsen, vtb; Abe Most, cl; Eddie Miller, ts; Joe Sample, keyboard; Dean Parks, Roland Bautista, g; Stix Hooper, d):
Hollywood Sound Studios, Hollywood, January 11, 1978
00562   I Just Can't Leave Your Love Alone   (LP) ABC LP1061

Other issues: title also on (45) ABC 12412. Album title: Midnight Believer.

CHUCK CONKLIN'S ANGEL CITY JAZZ BAND (Chuck Conklin, co; Dick Cary, tp; Dan Snyder, Gordon Mitchell, tb; Joe Darensbourg, cl, vo; Wayne Songer, ts; Elaine Mitchell, p; Red

Murphy, g; Dolph Morris, b; Ike Candioti, d; Marge Murphy, vo):
Encino, CA — April 15, 1978

(a)	Sacramento Jubilee	vMM, JD	(45) Angel City Records ACR4501
(b)	Swing Down in New Orleans		
	(Cary)	vMM	(45) Angel City Records ACR4501

Dick Cary appeared with the Climax Jazz Band on the Peter Appleyard television show, in Toronto, Canada, on April 25, 1978. Two clips from this show can be seen on YouTube — *Magnolia's Wedding Day*, on alto-horn with the band, and *Crazy Rhythm*, on piano with Jim Buchanan, clarinet, and Peter Appleyard, vibes. Others in the band included Bob Erwig, co; Geoff Holmes, tb; probably Chris Daniels, b; Jack Vincken, bjo.

TOM JONES (vocal, with group including Dick Cary, tp; Bob Havens, tb; Abe Most, cl; John Fresco, reeds; John Norris, conductor): ***Los Angeles — February 10, 1979***

This was an overdub session to "add colour" to probably just one track by the singer, who may not have been present.

UNKNOWN BAND (including Dick Cary, tp-1; Roy Brown, unknown; Sol Gubin, d; Jack Elliott, arranger): ***Sunset Studios, Los Angeles — May 3, 1979***
What'll I Do?   -1

From Dick Cary's diary. No other details known. Cary recorded *What'll I Do?* for Hi-Hat Records, but an issued version has no trumpet present.

UNKNOWN BAND (including Dick Cary; Jack Elliott, arranger):
Wally Heider Studios, Los Angeles — September 25, 1979
From Dick Cary's diary. No other details known.

JAZZ AT THE OJAI FESTIVALS BOWL (Dick Cary, a-h; with, probably, Ray Sherman, p; Ray Leatherwood, b; Nick Fatool, d): ***Ojai Jazz Festival, CA — October 21, 1979***
Singing the Blues   (LP) Town Hall 27

Cary is not present on other tracks on this album. It is possible that the drummer is Alvin Stoller, not Fatool. This is believed to be the relevant concert.

DICK CARY'S JAZZ ALL STARS (Dick Cary, tp; Bob Havens, tb; Henry Cuesta, cl; Eddie Miller, ts; ----, p; ----, b; Nick Fatool, d; Danny Michaels, Dee Hendricks, vo):
Los Angeles — c. December 1979

(a)	That Great Big Friendly Town	
	(Chicago) vDM	(45) Mishawaka Records 5000
(b)	Saucy, Sassy, Saucy Sassy Sue vDH	
	(A. Trace-L.Abrams-D.Cary)	(45) Mishawaka Records 5000

Contract for (b) with Playhouse Music Co. signed December 12, 1979. Al Trace was the record producer. The address for Mishawaka Records was 79 W. Monroe St., Chicago, IL 60603.

PEE WEE ERWIN (Pee Wee Erwin, tp; Bob Havens, tb; Kenny Davern, cl; Eddie Miller, ts; Dick Cary, p; Ray Leatherwood, b; Nick Fatool, d):
United Western Studios, Hollywood — May 26–27, 1980

(a)	Farewell Blues	(LP) Qualtro music QM101
(b)	Blues My Naughty Sweetie Gives to Me	(LP) Qualtro music QM101
(c)	There'll Be Some Changes Made	(LP) Qualtro music QM101
(d)	Hindustan	(LP) Qualtro music QM101
(e)	Bye Bye Blues	(LP) Qualtro music QM101
(f)	Old Fashioned Love	(LP) Qualtro music QM101
(g)	Rose Room	(LP) Qualtro music QM101
(h)	It Don't Mean a Thing	(LP) Qualtro music QM101

(Erwin, tp; Cary, p): *same dates*

(i)	Monday Date	(LP) Qualtro music QM101

There are three unissued titles from these two sessions, as reported in sleeve note. Two other titles on the LP are duets by Erwin and Dick Hyman. Recording dates are shown on the album sleeve. Cary's diary for May is blank, but he gives this personnel and recording studio in his entry for June 2, 1980, together with the note, "Plane to LA," namely the flight from Sacramento — the Jazz Jubilee ended on May 26. The sleeve note says: "All five of the West Coast men had just returned from the .... weekend in Sacramento." This leaves a number of questions unanswered! Album title: Pee Wee In Hollywood.

DICK CARY with The Chicagoans (Dick Cary, ah, vo, arr; Klaus Bader, ss, ts-2, arr; Hans-Jurgen Bock, p; Klaus Schwartze, b; Bernd Schuchard, d):

Pforzheim, Germany — November 1/2, 1980

(a)	Sweet Georgia Brown -2,	(LP) WSO NR.0102J
(b)	Swing Down in New Orleans (Dick Cary) vDC	(LP) WSO NR.0102J
(c)	After You've Gone -2	(LP) WSO NR0102J
(d)	Love Is Just Around the Corner	(LP) WSO NR0102J
(e)	Sheik of Araby -2	(LP) WSO NR0102J
(f)	Nobody Knows You When You Are Down and Out	(LP) WSO NR0102J
(g)	I Got It Bad and That Ain't Good	(LP) WSO NR0102J
(h)	If I Had You -2	(LP) WSO NR0102J
(i)	Ellen (Dick Cary)	(LP) WSO NR0102J
(j)	Can't We Be Friends	(LP) WSO NR0102J
(k)	Shine	(LP) WSO NR0102J

(i) Bader out. (j) Bader, ts; Cary, p; only. Arrangements and routines by Cary and Bader. Cary has been listed as pianist on (a) and (i), perhaps by overdubbing.

Other issues: all titles on (AC) WSO, same catalogue number. Album title: Golden Jazz.

DICK CARY'S SEPTET (Dick Cary, tp-1, ah-2, arr; Bob Havens, tb; Tommy Newsom, Dick Hafer, ts; Ross Tompkins, p; John Heard, b; Nick Fatool, d):

Sage & Sound Studios, Hollywood — June 16, 1981

(a)	Everybody Loves My Baby	-1	(LP) Famous Door HL-140
(b)	What's That You're Playing? (Dick Cary)	-2	(LP) Famous Door HL-140
(c)	I Remember You	-2	(LP) Famous Door HL-140
(d)	You'd Be So Nice to Come Home To	-2	(LP) Famous Door HL-140
(e)	Dream of You	-1	(LP) Famous Door HL-140

(same personnel):   ***Sage & Sound Studios, Hollywood — June 22, 1981***

(f)	A Lovely Way to Spend an Evening	-2	(LP) Famous Door HL-140
(g)	Why Shouldn't I?	-2	(LP) Famous Door HL-140
(h)	It's Been So Long	-2	(LP) Famous Door HL-140

Other issues: all HL-140 titles on (CD) Progressive PCD-7125.
Album title: California Doings.

MAXIM SAURY (Dick Cary, tp-1, ah-2, Ftp; Bob Havens, tb; Maxim Saury, cl; Ray Sherman, p; Nappy Lamare, g, vo; Ray Leatherwood, b; Nick Fatool, d):

                         St. Alban's Episcopal Church, Westwood, CA — August 19/20, 1981

(a)	Saint Louis Blues		(LP) Black and Blue 33.211
(b)	Creole Love Call	-2	(LP) Black and Blue 33.211
(c)	Sweet Georgia Brown	-2	(LP) Black and Blue 33.211
(d)	Louisiana and Me	vNL -1	(LP) Black and Blue 33.211
(e)	Strike Up the Band	-1	(LP) Black and Blue 33.211
(f)	Big Noise From Winnetka		(LP) Black and Blue 33.211
(g)	Mood Indigo	-1	(LP) Black and Blue 33.211
(h)	When the Saints Go Marching In	vNL -1	(LP) Black and Blue 33.211
(i)	Rose Room	-2	(LP) Black and Blue 33.211
(j)	Together	-1	(LP) Black and Blue 33.211
(k)	C Jam Blues	-1	(LP) Black and Blue 33.211

(a) *Saint Louis Blues* (7:50) and (f) *Big Noise From Winnetka* (4:42) are features for Saury with Leatherwood and Fatool. The band joins in at the close of (a). On the Honey CD there are three titles by Saury, Sherman, Leatherwood and Fatool—*Swingin' in L.A., Summertime* and *Blues for Lucille.* The CD is credited to Maxim Saury with Bob Havens' All Stars.
All titles, except (i) *Rose Room*, on (CD) Honey CD214.
Album title (Black & Blue): Maxim Saury in Los Angeles. (Honey): Swingin' in L.A.!

> The Black and Blue sleeve shows the recording date as August 27, 1981, in Westwood. On the Honey CD it is given as August 19, 20, 1981 at St. Alban's Episcopal Church, Westwood. These date variations probably explain why the records have been listed elsewhere as separate sessions. In fact the band titles are the same. Cary's diary has no entry for August 27, but on the 19th he gives "Maxime (sic) 7:30 to 12:30" and on the 20th, "Maxime 7:00 to 12:00." Perhaps some of the Saury/Sherman/Leatherwood/ Fatool titles were recorded on the 27th? Floyd Levin's notes also refer to the titles being issued in France, but only now (1991) in the U.S.

> Russ Reinberg, on the Westlake Records website, says that sometime in the early 1980s he and Bob Havens sponsored a "pro bono" recording session which, presumably, remains unissued. Collective personnel was Dick Cathcart, tp; Betty O'Hara, tp, horn, vo; Bob Havens, tb; Russ Reinberg, cl; Dick Hafer, ts; Dick Cary, p; Dave Koonse, Larry Koonse, g; Ray Leatherwood, b; Gene Estes, d.

KEITH SMITH (Keith Smith, tp; 'Big Chief' Russell Moore, tb; Peanuts Hucko, cl; Dick Cary, p; Arvell Shaw, b; Barrett Deems, d):

                                concert, Bletchley Leisure Centre, England — October 17, 1981
                Struttin' With Some Barbecue   (CD) Let's Do It LDI- 4
Other issues: this title also on (CD) Lake LACD80

DICK CARY (piano solos): *same concert*
   (a)   Echoes of Spring   (CD) Jazztown 2303011-2
   (b)   Love's Stream   (CD) Jazztown 2303011-2

Other issues: both titles also on (CD) Hefty Jazz HJ114, which shows location as Milton Keynes. (b) shown as *Loves Dream*. Album title: The Wonderful World of Louis Armstrong.

FLAT FOOT STOMPERS (Ernst Eekstein, co; Trummy Young, tb, vo, Roland Müller, tb; Peter Bühr, cl, leader; Dick Cary, p; Werne Neidhard, bj; Uli Reichle, sou; Uli Fussenhauser, d):
                             Bauer Recording Studios, Ludwigsburg, Germany — March 20, 1982
                             Way Down Yonder in New Orleans   vTY   (LP) DMM SP8283

(Yank Lawson, tp; Ernst Eekstein, co; George Masso, Roland Müller, tb; Dick Cary, a-h, arr; Johnny Mince, bar; Peter Bühr, cl, leader; Al Klink, ts; Martin Giebel, p; Werne Neidhard?, bj; Bob Haggart, b; Uli Reichle, sou; Uli Fussenhauser, d):
                                          Ludwigsburg, Germany — October 17, 1982
   (a)   At the Jazz Band Ball   (LP) DMM SP8283
   (b)   Original Dixieland One Step   (LP) DMM SP8283

(omit Eekstein, Müller, Bühr, Giebel, Neidhard, Reichle; Mince on cl; Cary on p; add Carrie Smith, vo): *same date*
   (c)   I've Got The World On A String vCS   (LP) DMM SP8283

Other issues: (a),(b),(c) on (CD) Timeless CDTTD632.
Album title: Flat Foot Stompers and Friends.

THE CHICAGOANS (Wolfgang Trattner, tp, flh-3; Charly Höllering, cl; Klaus Bader, bar; Dick Cary, p-1, ah-2; Martin Giebel, p-4; Klaus Schultze, b; Hans-Peter Schucker, d):
                                               Stuttgart, Germany — late October 1982
   (a)   Fidgety Feet   -2,-4   (LP) BAD 170.250
   (b)   Black and Blue   -1   (LP) BAD 170.250
   (c)   Everybody Loves My Baby   -1   (LP) BAD 170.250
   (d)   Laura   -1,-3   (LP) BAD 170.250
   (e)   How Come You Do Me Like You Do   -2,-4   (LP) BAD 170.250
   (f)   Jazz Me Blues   -1?   (LP) BAD 170.250

Note: there are 3 other titles on this album from a live session, in the Dixieland Hall, Stuttgart, with Werner Lener on piano, and without Cary, whose presence on (f) is also uncertain. Cary arrived in Germany on October 13 and left on October 31. Klaus Bader recalled that the session took place sometime after his daughter, Laura, was born on the 15th. He believes it was held in "Studio at Zuckerfabric." Album title: Wanted.

BOB CROSBY ALL-STARS (Dick Cary, Dick Cathcart, tp; Bob Havens, tb; Peanuts Hucko, cl; Eddie Miller, ts; Ray Sherman, p; Ray Leatherwood, b; Gene Estes, d):
                                                              Hollywood — January 4, 1984
   (a)   March of the Bobcats   (VC) MMGVIDEO MMGV042

(Ray Leatherwood, b; Gene Estes, d; Dick Cary, whistling): *same date*
   (b)   Big Noise From Winnetka   (VC) MMGVIDEO MMGV042

The Hessions with the All-Stars (Martha Hession, vo; Jim Hession, p; replacing Sherman):
same date
    (c)   The Joint Is Jumping   (VC) MMGVIDEO MMGV042

Scatman Crothers (vo, g; with the All-Stars):
same date
    (d)   The Gal Looks Good   (VC) MMGVIDEO MMG042

Irma Thomas (vo; with the All-Stars):
same date
    (e)   Don't Mess With My Man   (VC) MMGVIDEO MMG042

Al Hirt and Bob Crosby (Al Hirt, tp; with the All-Stars):
same date
    (f)   South Rampart Street Parade   (VC) MMGVIDEO MMG042

Cary is not present on other titles on this video. Introductions are by Bob Crosby and Al Hirt.
MMG = Magnum Music Group.
Video title: America's Music, Jazz, Volume 2.

"Mac" McREYNOLDS Planes of Fame Orchestra (Don Smith, Jim Linahon, Gary Hartman, tp; Tim Hoff, Richard Berkeley, tb; Bob Uthe, b-tb; Mac McReynolds, cl; Ted Herman, Charlie Richard, as; Dick Hafer, Norm Smith, ts; Dick Cary, p, a-h-1, arr; Dave Koonse, g; Arnold Fishkin, b; Ron Jones, d; "Margaret-Jean" McReynolds, vo):
                      Sage & Sound Recording Studio, Hollywood — September 16/November 25, 1985
    (a)   Beautiful Friendship   vMJM   (LP) POF-001
    (b)   One Morning in May   (LP) POF-001
    (c)   People   (LP) POF-001
    (d)   Savoy (Stomping at the Savoy)   vMJM   (LP) POF-001
    (e)   Just the Way You Are   vMJM   (LP) POF-001
    (f)   Poor Butterfly   -1   (LP) POF-001
    (g)   Star Dust   vMJM   (LP) POF-001
    (h)   It's Been So Long   (LP) POF-001
    (i)   Smile   (LP) POF-001
    (j)   For Once in My Life   vMJM   (LP) POF-001

Cary is not on other three titles on album. It is possible that the September date was a rehearsal. Only identification for the album is "POF-001" on the spine; there is nothing on label or sleeve. No doubt intended for sale at the Planes of Fame museum in Chino, CA. On (f) a piano can be heard behind Cary's alto-horn solo; it may be Bobby Williams or perhaps overdubbing. Album title: Mac McReynolds Planes of Fame Orchestra.

JACKIE COON OCTET (Jackie Coon, fh, a-h-1, vo; Dick Cary, tp, atp-1, a-h-2, arr; Bob Havens, trombone; Dick Hafer, cl-3, ts-4; Dick Houlgate, bar; Dave Koonse, g; Herb Mickman, b; Gene Estes, d):   *Master Control Studios, Burbank, CA — February 4, 1986*
    (a)   Jazzin' Around   -4 vJC   (LP) Sea Breeze SB-1009
    (b)   Struttin' With Some Barbecue -1,-3,-4   (LP) Sea Breeze SB-1009
    (c)   Singin' the Blues   -2,-3   (LP) Sea Breeze SB-1009
    (d)   Willie the Weeper   -3 vJC   (LP) Sea Breeze SB-1009

Sleeve notes also show Houlgate playing flute.
Album title: Jazzin' Around

DOC CHEATHAM and his Swedish Jazz All Stars featuring Dick Cary (Doc Cheatham, tp, vo; Staffan Arnberg, tb; Claes Brodda, cl-1, as-2, ts-3, arr-4; Dick Cary, p, ah-7, arr-8; Mikael Selander, g; Göran Lind, b; Sigge Dellert, d):
Sandvik Studios, Stockholm, Sweden — May 6, 1988

880362-3	A Kiss to Build a Dream On	vDCh -1,-3	(LP) Kenneth KS 2062
880363-1	I Double Dare You	vDCh-1,-2	(LP) Kenneth KS 2062

(same personnel, except Göran Eriksson, cl-5, as-6; replaces Arnberg and Brodda):
same date

880364-3   Sweethearts on Parade   vDCh-6,-7   (LP) Kenneth KS2062

(same personnel, with Arnberg and Brodda returning):   *same date*

880365-1   Once in a While   vDCh -1,-4,-5,-6   (LP) Kenneth KS2062

(Cheatham, tp; Brodda, cl-1, as-2; Eriksson, cl-5, as-6; Erik Persson, ts; Cary, p; Selander, g; Ollie Brostedt, b; Dellert, d):   *same date*

880366-3	Our Monday Date	-1,-6	(LP) Kenneth KS2062
880367-1,-2	Dinah		(CD) Kenneth CKS3408

(Cheatham, tp; Eriksson, reeds; Cary, p; Selander, g; Brostedt, b; Dellert, d):
Sandvik Studios, Stockholm, Sweden — May 7, 1988

880368-1,-2	I'll Guess I'll Get the Papers and Go Home	(CD) Kenneth CKS3408
880369-1	Drop Me Off in Harlem	(CD) Kenneth CKS3408

(Cheatham, tp, vo; Arnberg, tb; Brodda, cl-1, as-2, ts-3, arr-4; Eriksson, as; Persson, ts; Cary, p, arr-8; Selander, g; Brostedt, b; Dellert, d):   *same date*

880370-3   I'm in the Mood for Love   vDCh -2,-4   (LP) Kenneth KS2062

(same personnel, except Selander out):   *same date*

880371-1   Jeepers Creepers   vDCh -2,-4   (LP) Kenneth KS2062

(same personnel, except Brostedt, g; Göran Lind, b):   *same date*

880372-4	Swing That Music	vDCh -2,-4	(LP) Kenneth KS2062
880373-3	Save It Pretty Mama	vDCh -1,-3,-6,-8	(LP) Kenneth KS2062

(Cheatham, tp, vo; Persson, ts; Cary, p; Brostedt, b):   *same date*

880374-1,-3   For All We Know   vDCh   unissued

(same personnel, plus Arnberg, tb; Brodda, cl):   *same date*

880375-1,-4   Swing Down in New Orleans
                (Cary)   vDCary   (CD) Kenneth CKS3410

A version of *Sweethearts on Parade* with Cary on piano is reported to have been recorded.
Other issues: titles on KS2062 also on (CD) Kenneth CKS3408.
Album title: A Tribute to Louis Armstrong.

DICK CARY & his Swedish All Stars (Dick Cary, tp-8, ah-1, p, arr; Jan Åkerman, cl-2, ss-3, as -10, vo; Claes Brodda, cl-4, ts-5, as-9, arr; Mikael Selander, g; Ollie Brostedt, b; Sigge Dellert, d):   *Sandvik Studios, Stockholm, Sweden — April 13, 1989*

890442-3   The Nearness of You   -2,-5,-8   (CD) Kenneth CKS3410

890443-3	Kinda Lonesome	vJA -2,-4,-8	(CD) Kenneth CKS3410
890444-2	Harvey	-3,-5,-8	(CD) Kenneth CKS3410

(add Bent Persson, tp, arr; Clas Göran Faxell, tp; Staffan Arnberg, tb; Erik Persson, ts; Bo Juhlin, tu): **same date**
890445-3	Rockin' Chair	-1,-8,-10	(CD) Kenneth CKS3410
890446-1	Love Is Like a Cigarette	vJA -9,-10	(CD) Kenneth CKS3410
890447-1	Kissing My Baby Goodnight	vJA -2,-4	(CD) Kenneth CKS3410

(*Rug Cutter's Swing* and *Take the A-Train* also listed as recorded at this session.)

(same personnel as 890442, except Göran Lind, b; for Brostedt):
Sandvik Studios, Stockholm, Sweden — April 14, 1989
890448-1	New Orleans	-3,-4,-8	(CD) Kenneth CKS3410

(Cary, p; Selander, g; Brostedt, b; Dellert, d): **same date**
890449-1	Little Old Lady		(CD) Kenneth CKS3410

(same personnel as 890448, plus Erik Persson, ts-6, bar-7): **same date**
890450-3	What Kind o' Man Is You?	-3,-5,-7,-8	(CD) Kenneth CKS3410
890451-3	One Morning in May	-1,-2,-4,-5,-6	(CD) Kenneth CKS3410

(Arnberg, tb; Åkerman, ss; Persson, ts; Cary, p; Selander, g; Brostedt, b; Dellert, d):
same date
890452-2	Snowball		(CD) Kenneth CKS3410

(Arnberg, tb; Persson, ts; Cary, p; Selander, g; Brostedt, b; Dellert, d): **same date**
890453-1	Skylark		(CD) Kenneth CKS3410

(Bent Persson, tp; Åkerman, ss; Brodda, cl, as; Erik Persson, bar; Cary, p; Selander, g; Brostedt, b; Dellert, d): **same date**
890454-2	Lyin' to Myself		(CD) Kenneth CKS3410

(Bent Persson, tp; Erik Persson, ts, Cary, tp, p; Selander, g; Brostedt, b; Dellert, d): **same date**
890455-3	Ev'ntide		(CD) Kenneth CKS3410

(Bent Persson, tp; Arnberg, tb; Brodda,. cl; Erik Persson, ts; Cary, p, ah; Selander, g; Lind, b; Dellert, d): **same date**
890456-4	Riverboat Shuffle		(CD) Kenneth CKS3410

All arrangements by Dick Cary, except for *Rockin' Chair* (Bent Persson) and *Kissing My Baby Goodnight* and *Love Is Like a Cigarette* (Claes Brodda).
Album title: The Wonderful World of Hoagy Carmichael.

RICK FAY and Friends (Jon-Erik Kellso, tp; Dan Barrett, tb, arr-1; Chuck Hedges, cl; Rick Fay, ts, ss-6, vo; Dick Cary, p-3, ah-4, arr-5; Howard Alden, g; Paul Scavarda, bj; Lou Mauro, b; Joe Ascione, d; Mat Domber, steam whistle-2):
Parc Studios, Orlando, Florida — December 29/30, 1991
(a)	I Double Dare You	-3,-4	(CD) Arbors ARCD19108
(b)	Blues (My Naughty Sweetie Gives to Me)	-3	(CD) Arbors ARCD19108

(c)	In the Dark	-3,-5	(CD) Arbors ARCD19108
(d)	Ballad For Eddie (Cary)	-3,-4,-5	(CD) Arbors ARCD19108
(e)	Can't We Be Friends?	-1,-3,-6	(CD) Arbors ARCD19108
(f)	Roll On, Mississippi, Roll On	-1,-2,-3,-6	(CD) Arbors ARCD19108
(g)	Possum Jump	-1,-3	(CD) Arbors ARCD19108
(h)	Tishomingo Blues	-3	(CD) Arbors ARCD19108
(i)	Plain and Simple vRF	-3,-6	(CD) Arbors ARCD19108
(j)	Echo of Spring (solo piano)		(CD) Arbors ARCD19108
(k)	Come Back Sweet Papa	-3	(CD) Arbors ARCD19108

(c),(d),(e) omit Scavarda. (f) Alden plays bj. (h) omit Alden; Scavarda plays g. (i) omit Kellso, Hedges, Alden. (k) Alden plays bj; Scavarda plays guitar, then banjo.
Somebody Loves Me, Manoir de Mes Reves and *Day Dream,* on this CD, are without Cary.
There is a video record of this recording session. Album title: Rolling On.

BARBARA LEA (vocal, with Dick Cary, p, arr; Dave Koonse, g; Putter Smith, b):
Dick Hamilton Studios, Los Angeles — September 28, 1992

(a)	Don't Smoke in Bed	(CD) Audiophile ACD119
(b)	Deep Summer	(CD) Audiophile ACD119
(c)	Think Well of Me	(CD) Audiophile ACD119
(d)	Born to the Bayou	(CD) Audiophile ACD119
(e)	Run for the Roundhouse, Nellie	(CD) Audiophile ACD119

Other titles on this CD are from a 1976 session without Cary.
Album title: The Devil Is Afraid of Music.

DICK CARY and His Tuesday Night Friends (Betty O'Hara, Dick Forrest, tp; Dick Hamilton, tb; Ernie Tack, b-tb; Abe Most, cl; Terry Harrington, ss, cl, ts Fred Cooper, bar, fl; Dick Cary, el-p, tp, arr; Dave Koonse, g; Herb Mickman, b; Jerry McKenzie, d):
Sunland, CA — May 4, 1993

(a)	Fritz	(Cary)	(CD) Arbors ARCD19132
(b)	Vallen's Waltz	(Cary)	(CD) Arbors ARCD19132

(same personnel, except Forrest out; Tommy Newsom, ss, cl, ts; added; Gene Estes, d; replaces McKenzie):
Sunland, CA — June 15, 1993

(c)	Ding	(Cary)	(CD) Arbors ARCD19132
(d)	Henry	(Cary)	(CD) Arbors ARCD19132
(e)	Kreik	(Cary)	(CD) Arbors ARCD19132
(f)	Bud	(Cary)	(CD) Arbors ARCD19132
(g)	Fugue	(Cary)	(CD) Arbors ARCD19132
(h)	Black Shadow	(Cary)	(CD) Arbors ARCD19132
(i)	Another January	(Cary)	(CD) Arbors ARCD19132
(j)	Thursday Blues	(Cary)	(CD) Arbors ARCD19132

(same personnel as June 15, except Barrett O'Hara, b-tb; for Tack; Jerry McKenzie, d; replaces Estes):
Sunland, CA — June 22, 1993

(k)	Pong	(Cary)	(CD) Arbors ARCD19132

(same personnel as June 22, except add Bob Summers, tp; Ernie Tack, b-tb; replaces Barrett O'Hara; Newsom out; Gene Estes, d; replaces McKenzie):
Sunland, CA — July 27, 1993

(l)	8th Avenue Rag	(Cary)	(CD) Arbors ARCD19132

(same personnel as July 27, except Newsom, reeds; added; Lee Callett, bar; replaces Cooper):

Sunland — August 10, 1993

(m)	Tuxford	(Cary)	(CD) Arbors ARCD19132
(n)	M & M	(Cary)	(CD) Arbors ARCD19132

Album title: Dick Cary & His Tuesday Night Friends Playing Dick Cary Originals.

The MERRY-GO-ROUND and HI HAT RECORDS

Over a period of nearly thirty years (1960 to 1987) Dick Cary recorded for Merl Olds, the owner of a round and square dance record company, variously Merry-Go-Round or Hi Hat. Many of these 45 rpm records were under Cary's name. There are insufficient details to be able to fit these issues into correct discographical order in the main discography. Therefore this attempt to document the Merl Olds records is shown separately.

PART ONE lists the known records by Dick Cary in numerical order. This information has been gathered from the Gemm website and from records in the Jim Turner and Derek Coller collections. Some labels state "Music by DICK CARY," and others "Music played by DICK CARY." Other issues have an instrumental track on one side which is repeated on the reverse, but with cues (ie: a caller giving the dance steps) added. No composer credits are shown, except on some later dance step inserts. Release dates are sometimes given on the labels and where known these are quoted in brackets after the titles.

Lazy Two Step		Merry-Go-Round 1	(rev: Memo Bernabei)
Ida / Swingin'		Merry-Go-Round 7	
Bittersweet		Merry-Go-Round 9	(rev:)
Cincinnati Two Step		Merry-Go-Round 10	(rev:)
I Ain't Got Nobody	#	Merry-Go-Round 44	(rev: same + cues)
Florida		Merry-Go-Round 59	(rev:)

this title also on Hi Hat 834.

Till the Well Runs Dry (2 parts)	[1966]	Hi Hat 330	
No Tears Milady		Hi Hat 349	(rev: same + cues)
Coney Island Baby		Hi Hat 351	(rev:)
Little Pedro		Hi Hat 352	(rev:)
Cryin' the Blues		Hi Hat 363	(rev:)
Unicorns	[9/68]	Hi Hat 365	(rev: same + cues)
Too Many Chiefs	[1/69]	Hi Hat 370	(rev: same + cues)
Look at Me Now		Hi Hat 371	(rev:)
American Boys		Hi Hat 379	(rev: same + cues)
Society Square		Hi Hat 444	(rev: same + cues)
Spaghetti Rag / Oh You Kid		Hi Hat 831	
Silver Dollar		Hi Hat 833	(rev:)
I Ain't Got Nobody / Fascination Rhythm	[1/67]	Hi Hat 834	
C'Est Si Bon / Lara		Hi Hat 835	(reissued on Hi Hat 960)
My Gal Sal / Road Runner Two-Step	[4/67]	Hi Hat 836	
Fence Me Not / Darling		Hi Hat 837	
Peg Leg / Call It Spanish	[6/67]	Hi Hat 838	
Centennial Baby / Possibilities		Hi Hat 839	
Sugarumba		Hi Hat 842	(rev:)
Wilkommen	[11/67]	Hi Hat 843	(rev: Gene Garf)
Good Morning / Rag Doll		Hi Hat 845	
Bramble Bush / Little White Lies		Hi Hat 846	
Good Times		Hi Hat 849	(rev:)

Around 'n Round		Hi Hat 850	(rev: Memo Bernabei)
Rosita	[1968]	Hi Hat 852	(rev: Memo Bernabei)
Molly 'n Me / Just As Much		Hi Hat 854	
Green Alligators / Daydream		Hi Hat 855	
Here Comes Charlie / Tango D'Ann		Hi Hat 856	
Sock It to Me / Just Pretend		Hi Hat 857	
Like I Love You / Waltz Along		Hi Hat 860	
Candy Kisses	[1969]	Hi Hat 861	rev: Frank Sterling)
Tuxedo Blues	[6/69]	Hi Hat 862	(rev: Frank Sterling)
Far Away Places / Take Me Along		Hi Hat 866	
Lillie's Back		Hi Hat 868	(rev: Alex Johnson)
Girl Watching / Yes Yes in Your Eyes		Hi Hat 869	
Cheatin' Heart / Silver Slippers		Hi Hat 874	
High Society		Hi Hat 877	(rev: Frank Sterling)
Baby Face		Hi Hat 879	(rev: Gene Garf)
Mama's Gone	[12/70]	Hi Hat 880	rev: Frank Sterling)
It's So Good / Shadows of Paris		Hi Hat 882	
Muscrat Ramble	[7/71]	Hi Hat 888	(rev: Jerry Vaughn)
Baby Mine		Hi Hat 889	(rev: Joe Leahy)
Beale Street Blues	[8/72]	Hi Hat 901	rev: Joe Leahy)
Glad Rag Doll / Summertime in Venice		Hi Hat 926	
Gospel		Hi Hat 931	(rev: Joe Leahy)
That's My Baby		Hi Hat 933	(rev: Joe Leahy)
Sweet Georgia		Hi Hat 935	(rev:)
Hot Pepper		Hi Hat 936	(rev:)
Certain Party / Love Is		Hi Hat 937	
Bitter Sweet / Brasilia		Hi Hat 939	
Apple Cider / Tango de la Luna		Hi Hat 941	
Baby Talk / Apron Strings		Hi Hat 946	
Lazy Swing	[4/76]	Hi Hat 947	rev: Del Kacher)
Cowboy Blues / Tattletale Cha-Cha		Hi Hat 964	
It Had to Be You		Hi Hat 967	(rev:)
Lovely / Orchids '79	[12/78]	Hi Hat 968	
Lonesome / Peachie Keen	[2/79]	Hi Hat 970	
Finesse / Pizazz	[3/79]	Hi Hat 971	
Nobody cares / Peppermint		Hi Hat 974	
San		Hi Hat 976	(rev:)
Sheik of Araby / Rocky-Fella		Hi Hat 978	(also on Roper 978)
Andrea		Hi Hat 979	(rev: Del Kacher)
Something Big / Donna		Hi Hat 980	
Cheatin' / Manhattan		Hi Hat 981	
Love Song / What'll I Do	[5/80]	Hi Hat 983	
Sheboygan / Swinging Sal	[8/80]	Hi Hat 985	
Cheatin' / Manhattan		Hi Hat 981	
Mississippi Mud / Moonlight Tango		Hi Hat 996	
Paper Roses		Hi Hat BB-001	(rev: The Hi-Hatters)
Angels		Hi Hat BB-002	(rev: Joe Leahy)
Button Up		Hi Hat BB-003	(rev: Gene Garf)
Blues Skies /			
Walking the Floor Over You	[4/82]	Hi Hat BB-004	

Dreaming	Hi Hat BB-005	(rev: Joe Leahy)
Country Style	Hi Hat BB-008	(rev: Gene Garf)
Tango Ecstasy	Hi Hat BB-010	(rev: Joe Leahy)
Christmas Bells	Hi Hat BB-011	(rev: Gene Garf)
Florida / I Ain't Got Nobody	Hi Hat BB-012	
Lilly's Back Again	Hi Hat BB-015	(rev: Frank Sterling)
Again	Hi Hat EN-019	(rev: same + cues)

<u>PART TWO</u> lists the recording dates and personnels for the Merl Olds sessions in which Dick Cary participated, as listed in the Cary diaries, though not all may have been released under his name. Some of the dates may be only dubbing sessions in which Cary was involved and it is even possible that one or more are live dates. It is known that Cary did play occasional country-and-western gigs. All titles were recorded in Los Angeles and will include sessions recorded for other leaders. Dick is present on all, but it is not always clear which instrument he played. Other musicians are multi-instrumentalists, so assumptions have been made about them.

November 7, 1960: square dance date for Jerry Vaughn (arranger, composer): Art Barduhn, tp; Milt Norman, g; Art Maury, d.
November 14, 1960: round dance date with Jerry Vaughn. No other details.
October 16, 1961: round dance records: titles only listed.

    Sheboygan *   Hi Hat 985 ?
    Loch Lomond
    Why Don't We Do This More Often

    * This title is on Hi Hat 985, which was released in 1980. Is it a late issue or different version?

October 25, 1961: 12–2— for Jerry Vaughn: "13 quickies" !
November 1, 1961: for Jerry Vaughn: "played mostly hammond organ—3 dubs."
December 15, 1961: for Jerry Vaughn: with Milt Norman, g; Art Maury, d.
May 7, 1962: for Jerry Vaughn: with Art Barduhn, tp; Tom Tedesco, bj; Art Maury, d.
February 11, 1963: for Jerry Vaughn: with Art Barduhn, tp; Walt Kunnecke, b; Howie Oliver, d. 4 tunes, and overdubs. International Sound Studios.
April 8, 1963: for Jerry Vaughn: with Art Barduhn, tp; Walt Kunnecke, b; Maury Harris.
May 22, 1963: round dance date—no details
July 2, 1963: for Jerry Vaughn at International Sound Studios: with Dick Cary, tp, a-h; Art Barduhn, tp; Stan Wrightsman, p; Walt Kunnecke, b; Art Maury, d.
August 17, 1964: for Jerry Vaughn: with Dick Collins, Art Barduhn, tp; Arine (?), cl; Nino (?), cello; Howie Roberts, g; Maurie Russell, d. 4 waltzes at H&R Studios.
December 16, 1964: for Art Barduhn ("now leader"): with Milt Norman, Neil Levang, g; Maurie Russell, d. 5 tunes & an overdub at Radio Recorders Studios.
January 11, 1965: for Merl Olds at H&R Studios: with Cary, tp, p, organ; Wayne Songer, cl, fl, as; Carol Kaye, Bud (?), g; Joe Leahy, presumably leader, arr.
January 5, 1966: Hi Hat record date at H&R Studios on Melrose: Art Barduhn, leader, with Carol Kaye, Neil Levang, Buddy (?), g; "Joe Leahy in control room."
April 12, 1966: Merl Olds date: Dick Cary scheduled band, with Frank Morocco (also known as Marocco), reeds; Jad Paul, p and/or bj; Carol Kaye, g.
April 9, 1968: Merl Olds date: Jim Bryant, Bill Newman (both guitarists, apparently), Ray Leatherwood, bass; Wayne Songer, reeds, Frank Morocco, reeds. "I brought vibes. The Waltz of Tears was quite pleasant. 2 overdubs, 3 square and 2 rounds."

January 6, 1969:	10 am for Merl Olds at Sunset. Art Barduhn, trumpet; Wayne Songer, reeds, Nick Bonney, Bob Gibbons, guitars; (Charles 'Chuck' ?) Berghofer, bass-guitar; Gene Estes, drums. Cary on piano? "We also did What Should I Do—my original for Merl's lyrics."
September, 1972:	"4 hours with Joe Leahy, a piano ('I'm to do some piano background tracks') and a click track. All Leahy's original tunes, lots of overdubbing." "Glad he's finally called me for something. Merl Olds had him call me once this year, early summer."
November 6, 1972:	3 hour session for Merl Olds.
July 19, 1973:	Rec.—Western—2:00 to 4:00, alto-horn.
August 14, 1973:	(Joe) Leahy 2:00 to 5:00—Cary on trumpet.
September 17, 1973:	"Merl Olds 10:00 to 1:00 p.m., P.D. Recorders—many square—all originals."
January 28, 1974:	"We (Bob Jung, cl, Charlie ----, tb; Jack Sperling, d; Ira Westley, b; and myself trumpet) started overlaying to tracks by banjo and piano. Boy Ayars was arranger. Ayars is also Liberace's conductor and plays piano."
February 5, 1974:	"Had to get cornet for a last minute date at RCA. Cipriano called me—also Dick Nash & Tommy Johnson—overdubbing again." [probably Gene Cipriano as; Dick Nash, tb; Tommy Johnson, b.]
April 3, 1974:	date with Merl Olds (Cary was not the leader).
July 30, 1974:	10 a.m. Merl Olds date at Del Kacher's. 6 squares with Wayne Songer, reeds; Al Vescovo, Ron Benson, g; Nick Fatool, d.
March 1, 1975:	Merl Olds date at Ron Ray [studios]. Wayne, Ron Benson, Nick F., & Al Vescovo. "6 things & 7 overlays." [Wayne Songer, reeds, Ron Benson, g; Nick Fatool, d; Al Vescovo, g.]
March 24, 1976:	"Merl Olds arrived with a tape made some years back by Joe Leahy. I must substitute horns for voices on 6 tunes & get Wayne Songer & will overdub twice. Then on 7th tune—only organ. Good little project."
April 17, 1976:	"Merl 9:30. Stolle's. Wayne & I had completed 6 overdubs—actually 12—by 11.35 so he left … Merl's 6 tapes from Joe Leahy came out very well. On the 7th tune, Always, the organ blended as if it had been recorded originally."
June, 1976:	"I overdub for Olds during this month."
November 2, 1976:	"Lengthy recording for Merl Olds at Del Kacher. (Wayne) Songer there. Some piano, some bass (Red) & some drummer with miles of soundtrack."
September 7, 1977:	a possible Merl Olds session.
August 2, 1978:	"Merl—9:30 am—P.D. Recorders. Shanahan, Eno, Ron Benson, Wayne. Overdubbing everything – 7 tunes came out well." [Bob Enevoldsen, tb; Wayne Songer, reeds; Ron Benson, g; probably Dick Shanahan, d;
May 3, 1979:	Sunset Studios at 7:00—Jack Elliott, Roy Brown, Sol Gubin [drums]. "Cornet on What'll I Do—best I ever was recorded." [A Hi Hat record of this tune was issued in 1980, but there is no cornet present.]
August 30, 1978:	"Merl—9.30 to 3.40—Stolle's—nine songs—24 overdubs … Wayne [Songer] & I played close to pitch."
October 15, 1979:	"10—Stolle Magn. for Merl Olds. Wayne, Chas & Jerry. Ordinary, fairly easy date of assorted Merlisms or Oldsies. Best was a quick added starter, Hard Hearted Hannah." [Wayne Songer, reeds; Charles Myerson, g; Jerry McKenzie, d.]
January 15, 1981:	Merl Olds, 10 to almost 6—Wayne & I each did 2 overdubs. [Gene] Estes, d; Ron Benson, g; Wayne [Songer], reeds, Bob Walters [probably vl/vbs].
November 23/24, 1981:	Merl Olds sessions scheduled. No other details.

January 11, 1982: at United Western Studios – a possible session for Merl Olds?
September 30, 1987: "Pete & Carol Metzger came over – planned Hi Hat – 8 tunes –
April *Showers* / *Silver Lining* / *Moonlite Swim* / *Tara's theme* /
Ever See a Dream Walking / *Heart & Soul* / *Again* (cha cha) /
Somebody Else (waltz)." The Metzgers were choreographers.
Again was issued on Hi Hat EN-019.

PART THREE is a listing based upon those records which have been heard by the compiler.

(tp; tb; cl; bj; b; d):	released January 1967
I Ain't Got Nobody	Hi Hat 834
(cl; p; g; b; d):	
Fascination Rhythm (actually *Fascination*)	Hi Hat 834
(tb; cl; vbs; bj; b; d):	released April 1967
Road Runner Two-Step	Hi Hat 836
(tp; tb; cl; p; bj; b; d):	
My Gal Sal	Hi Hat 836
(as; p; g; b; d):	released June 1967
Peg Leg	Hi Hat 838
(tp; cl; p; g; b; d):	
Call It Spanish (actually *In a Little Spanish Town*)	Hi Hat 838
(tp; acc; p; bj; b; d):	released November 1967
Willkommen (Welcome)	Hi Hat 843
(reverse by Gene Garf, *Put Your Little Foot*)	
(tp; cl/fl; acc; p; g; b-g; d): (Cary doubling tp & p?)	released September 1968
Unicorns	Hi Hat 365
(reverse is same music, with vocal cues added)	
(tp; acc; p; g; b-g; d: Cary probably both tp & p):	released January 1969
Too Many Chiefs	Hi Hat 370
(reverse is same music, with vocal cues added)	
(cl; p; g; b-g; d):	released June 1969
Tuxedo Blues (actually *Ballin' the Jack*)	Hi Hat 862
(reverse by Frank Sterling, *Holiday in Vienna (Holiday Waltz)*)	
(tp; tb; cl; p; g; b; d):	released December 1970
Mama's Gone (actually *Mama's Gone, Goodbye*)	Hi Hat 880
(reverse: by Frank Sterling, *Lola* (actually *Whatever Lola Wants*)	
(tp; tb; cl; b-g; d):	released July 1971
Muscrat Ramble	Hi Hat 888
(reverse by Jerry Vaughn, *Whispers*, actually *Whispering*)	
(tp; tb; cl; p; b-g; d):	released August 1972
Beale Street Blues	Hi Hat 901
(reverse by Joe Leahy, *The Melody of You*)	
(cl; b-g; d):	released April 1976
Lazy Swing	Hi Hat 947
(reverse by Del Kacher, *Humoresque in Two-Time*)	
(tp; tb; cl/as; p; b-g; d):	released December 1978
Lovely (actually *Lovely to Look At*)	Hi Hat 968

(tp; as; bar; acc; p; mandolin; b; d):
    Orchids '79   Hi Hat 968

(2 tp; 2 sax; p; org; d):   released February 1979
    Lonesome (actually *Are You Lonesome Tonight?*)   Hi Hat 970

(tp; tb; as/cl; p; b-g; d):
    Peachie Keen (actually *Georgia on My Mind*)   Hi Hat 970

(2 tp; 3 reeds; p; b-g; d):   released March 1979
    Pizazz   Hi Hat 971

(2 tb; 3 reeds; b-g; d): (Cary on trombone?)
    Finesse   Hi Hat 971

(as; p; g; b-g; d) .   released May 1980 *
    What'll I Do?   Hi Hat 983

*possibly recorded May 3, 1979, though Cary said he played cornet.

(tp; as; g; b-g; d): (piano not evident, so Cary, tp?; perhaps another sax present)
    Love Song   Hi Hat 983

(tp; tb; cl; p; bj; b; d):   released August 1980
    Swinging Sal (actually *My Gal Sal*)   Hi Hat 985

(as; p; g; b-g; d):
                                 released August 1980 but perhaps recorded October 16, 1961 ?
    Sheboygan   Hi Hat 985

(tp; 2 ? saxes (ts, bar); p; b; d):   released April 1982
    Blue Skies   Hi Hat BB-004

(tp; tb; as; cl; p; g; b; d):
    Walking (actually *Walking the Floor Over You*)   Hi Hat BB-004

(tp; tb; 2 or 3 saxes/cl; organ; b-g; d):   recorded c.October 1987
    Again   Hi Hat EN-019
                                (reverse is same music, with vocal cues added)

No release dates are known for the following:

(tp; cl; p; b-g; d): (piano not heard same time as tp; presumably Cary playing both)
    Ida   Merry-Go-Round MGR 007

(cl; bj; b-g; d):
    Swingin'   Merry-Go-Round MGR 007

(tp; tb; cl; bj; b; d):
    I Ain't Got Nobody   Merry-Go-Round MGR-044
                                (reverse is same music, with vocal cues added)

(tp; tb; cl; p; bj; b?; d):
    Country Style   Hi Hat BB-008
                              (reverse by Gene Garf, *Wouldn't You Know*)

See Chapter 16 for further background.

DICK CARY'S
RECORDED ARRANGEMENTS

The main discography includes all known recordings by Dick Cary as an instrumentalist, and it also attempts to show those titles which he arranged. The following is a list of recordings on which he did not play but to which he contributed arrangements/outlines/backgrounds. In contrast to the main discography, only basic details are shown, except when new information is available.

BENNY GOODMAN and his Orchestra (Benny Goodman, Carol Kaye, vo):
broadcast, Hotel Astor, New York City — July 27, 1943
  Thank Your Lucky Stars   vCK   unissued
Cary said he first heard his arrangement broadcast on July 22, 1943.

broadcast, New York City — October 13, 1943
  Do Nothing Till You Hear From Me   vBG   (Tx) AFRS ONS36
ONS = One Night Stand. Other issues: on (LP) Queen-disc 042, Magic AWE23.
Another version, from a broadcast of November 17, 1943, appeared on (Tx) AFRS ONS53 and (LP) Swing Treasury 103.

> The other arrangements which Cary made for Benny Goodman were: *You Better Give Me Lots of Lovin,' Honey / Coming in on a Wing and a Prayer / The Very Thought of You* (broadcast November 20, 1943) / *I Cried for You / Embraceable You / Put Your Arms Around Me, Honey* (broadcast August 17 & November 20, 1943) / *Who Did? I Did, Yes I Did!*

EDDIE CONDON'S JAZZ CONCERTS
Of the arrangements, or "backgrounds," which Dick Cary provided for the Eddie Condon Blue Network broadcasts, the following are given on air by Condon:
October 28, 1944   It's the Talk of the Town (vocal by Red McKenzie)
November 25, 1944   Old Folks (vocal by Lee Wiley)
December 16, 1944   There's a Small Hotel (cornet solo, Bobby Hackett)
January 6, 1945   Every Night (vocal by Jack Eberle)
January 13, 1945   How Long Has This Been Going On (vocal by Lee Wiley)
February 17, 1945   Time on My Hands (vocal by Red McKenzie)
March 3, 1945   Just Friends (vocal by Red McKenzie)
March 10, 1945   Can't We Be Friends (vocal by Red McKenzie)

Other titles which may have backings sketched by Cary include:
October 7, 1944   Someone to Watch Over Me (Lee Wiley)
October 14, 1944   Sweet Lorraine (Red McKenzie)
November 4, 1944   Through a Veil of Indifference (Red McKenzie)

THELMA CARPENTER (vo; with Bud Freeman and his Orchestra; The Delta Rhythm Boys, vo):
New York City — October 1945
  T-555-1   My Guy's Come Back   vTC, DRB   (78) Majestic 1017
  T-556-   These Foolish Things   vTC   (78) Majestic 1017

T-557-2	Hurry Home	vTC, DRB		(78) Majestic 1023

EDDIE CONDON and his Orchestra   *New York City — March 27, 1946*
- 73482-   She's Funny That Way   (78) Decca 23600
- 73483-   Stars Fell on Alabama   (78) Decca 23719

BILLY BUTTERFIELD and his Orchestra   *probably New York City — 1946*
-            Cheatin' on Me   (Tx) Capitol B-241

EDDIE CONDON and his Orchestra   *New York City — March 20, 1950*
- 75989-   Dill Pickles   (78) Decca 24987
- 75990-   Sweet Cider Time   (78) Decca 27106

(Jimmy Atkins, vo):   *New York City — March 22, 1950*
- 76000-   At the Jazz Band Ball   vJA   (78) Decca 24987
- 76001-   Jazz Me Blues   vJA   (78) Decca 27035

                                            New York City — September 26, 1950
- 76896-   Grace and Beauty   (78) Decca 27408

(date from Cary's diary. Some listings show October 2, 1950)

MAXINE SULLIVAN (vo; with orchestra of Bob Haggart: unknown tp; Hymie Shertzer, Art Rollini, Art Drellinger, Jerry (Jerome?), reeds; (Nick?) Parito, p?; ----, b; Mel Zelnick, d):
                                Beltone Studios, New York City — December 20, 1950
-            Restless   (78) Apollo 1178

Cary refers to the rhythm section as Parito/Quinn/Zelnick. If Quinn is the bassist, then Haggart conducts only. Hackett probably arranged the reverse of Apollo 1178, *Cry, Buttercup, Cry.*

HARRY LOOKOFSKY SEPTET (Peanuts Hucko, cl, b-cl; Harry Lookofsky, vl; Bobby Christian, vb; Buddy Weed, p; Benny Mortell, g; Ted Kosoftis, b; Morey Feld, d; Dick Cary, arr):
                         broadcast, ABC "Jazz Beat" show, New York City — c. April 1952
-            Night Life (Cary)   (CD) AB Fable XABCD-X013
-            Good Bait   (CD) AB Fable ABCD2-011/12

(same personnel):   *broadcast, ABC "Jazz Beat" show, New York City — April 24, 1952*
-            Love for Sale   (CD) AB Fable XABCD1-X013
-            Jealousy   (CD) AB Fable XABCD1-X013

HARRY LOOKOFSKY with the Buddy Weed Trio (Lookofsky, vl; Buddy Weed, p; Tommy Kay, g; Felix Giobbe, b; Morey Feld, d; Dick Cary, arr):
broadcast, ABC "Saturday Night Dance Session" show, New York City — November 8, 1952
-            Body and Soul   on acetate

(same personnel):*broadcast, ABC "Saturday Night Dance Session" show, New York City —*
                                                           November 22, 1952
-            Stardust   on acetate

TOMMY DORSEY and His Orchestra, featuring Jimmy Dorsey (Dick Cary, arr):
                                Pythian Temple, New York City — March 23, 1954
- (a)   Rhumba Montevideo   (D. Cary/B.Freeman)   (LP) Columbia CL1240
- (b)   The Time Is Right   (D. Cary/B. Freeman)   (LP) Columbia CL1240

Other issues: both titles on (CD) Avid AMSC1008

MAX KAMINSKY and his Windy City Six (Max Kaminsky, tp; Miff Mole, tb; Pee Wee Russell, cl; Joe Sullivan, p; Jack Lesberg, b; George Wettling, d; Dick Cary, arr):

New York City — April 11, 1955

(a)	Hot Time in the Old Town Tonight	(LP) Jazztone J-1208
(b)	A Tavern in the Town	(LP) Jazztone J-1208
(c)	Del Mar Rag	(LP) Jazztone J-1208
(d)	Stuyvesant Blues	(LP) Jazztone J-1208
(e)	Mix Max	(LP) Jazztone J-1208
(f)	Lonesome Road	(LP) Jazztone J-1208
(g)	Never Touched Me	(LP) Jazztone J-1208
(h)	Short Ties and Long Ties	(LP) Jazztone J-1208
(i)	At the Jazz Band Ball	(LP) Jazztone J-1208
(j)	Fidgety Feet	(LP) Jazztone J-1208

No composer credits given for the originals (d), (e), (g), (h).
Other issues: (a),(d),(f) also on (CD) Vintage Music Productions VMP0311.

EDDIE CONDON and His All-Stars   *New York City — April 22, 1955*

CO53234	At the Jazz Band Ball	(LP) Columbia CL719
CO53235	Louisiana	(LP) Columbia CL719
CO53236	Ol' Man River	(LP) Columbia CL719
CO53237	Fidgety Feet	(LP) Columbia CL719
CO53238	Jazz Me Blues	(LP) Columbia CL719

JIMMY McPARTLAND and his Jazz Band (Jimmy McPartland, tp; Cutty Cutshall, tb; Bill Stegmeyer, cl; Bud Freeman, ts; Marian McPartland, p; Sandy Block, b; George Wettling, d; Dick Cary, arr):

New York City — February 1, 1956

89304	Jazz Me Blues		(LP) Brunswick BL54018
89305	In a Mist	-1	(LP) Brunswick BL54018
89306	Way Down Yonder in New Orleans		(LP) Brunswick BL54018
89307	Sorry		(LP) Brunswick BL54018

-1 add Romeo Penque, oboe; George Berg, bassoon; for *In a Mist*.
Other issues: all titles on (LP) Decca DL8386, MCA 2-4110, and (CD) J&M J&MCD8007.

CHUCK GOULD   *Hollywood — April 28, 1956*

Cary scored "last part of waltz for [pianist] Tommy Todd for record date." Presumably Todd played the waltz at this recording session, held in the Capitol studios, but not for Capitol. Cary was at the session, no doubt as a spectator.

BUD FREEMAN'S Summa Cum Laude Orchestra   *New York City — July 8, 1957*

Dick Cary did "arrange" at least one title, *Prince of Wails*.

ETHEL SMITH at the Organ (Ethel Smith, hammond organ, with unidentified g; b; d; Dick Cary, arr):

New York City — August 11 (?), 1959

107888	Firebird Blues	(LP) Decca DL8955
107889	St. Louis Blues (Part 1)	(LP) Decca DL8955
107890	Swingin' Shepherd Blues	(LP) Decca DL8955
107891	Limehouse Blues	(LP) Decca DL8955

(same):   *New York City — August 19, 1959*

107966	The Birth of the Blues	(LP) Decca DL8955

| 107967 | Blue (and Brokenhearted) | (LP) Decca DL8955 |
| 107968 | Jazz Me Blues aDC | (LP) Decca DL8955 |

(Smith, hammond organ; unidentified tp (Dick Cary?); tb; cl, as*; g; b; d): **same date**
107969	Basin Street Blues	(LP) Decca DL8955
107994	Livery Stable Blues	(LP) Decca DL8955
107995	St. Louis Blues (Part 2) * aDC	(LP) Decca DL8955

(Smith, hammond organ; with unidentified g; b; d): **New York City — September 3, 1959**
108081	Funky Blues (Dick Cary-Ethel Smith)	(LP) Decca DL8955
108082	Take Me Along	(78) Decca 30991
108083	Fugue in Blue	(LP) Decca DL8955

Cary mentioned that he arranged 107968 and 107995, but it is probable that he arranged the ten titles between 107889 and 108081. His diary does not cover these particular dates. The two parts of *St. Louis Blues* play as a complete number, with a drum solo connecting the two.
Album title: Bouquet of the Blues

ETHEL SMITH (Hammond organ, with rhythm accompaniment: guitar, bass, drums):
New York City — June 1, 1961
110668	Love for Sale	aDC	(LP) Decca DL4145
110669	The Gipsy in My Soul	aDC	(LP) Decca DL4145
110670	I've Found a New Baby	aDC ?	(LP) Decca DL4145
110671	Honeysuckle Rose	aDC	unissued

(Ethel Smith, org; g; b; d): **New York City — June 15, 1961**
110677	Just One of Those Things		unissued
110678	Honeysuckle Rose	aDC	(LP) Decca DL4145
110679	Carinhoso		(LP) Decca DL4145

Other issues include: the above titles on (LP) Decca 7-4145 (stereo) & BrE LAT8391.
Album title: The Many Moods of Ethel Smith. It is unlikely that Cary provided arrangements for the June 9, 27, and 28, 1961 sessions, or for the big band date on June 15, 1961.

CHRIS CLIFTON and his All Stars (Chris Clifton, tp, vo; Charlie Fardella, Dennis Jones, tp; David Sager, tb; Jacques Gauthe, cl, as; Pud Brown, ts; Steve Pistorius, p; Frank Fields, b; Barry Martyn, d; Dick Cary, arr): **New Orleans — April 5, 1985**
	You Rascal, You	vCC aDC	(LP) GHB 190
	Sweethearts on Parade	vCC aDC	(LP) GHB 190
	Dinah	vCC aDC	(LP) GHB 190
	Someday, You'll Be Sorry	vCC aDC	(LP) GHB 190
	Mahogany Hall Stomp	aDC	(LP) GHB 190

All titles also on (CD) GHB BCD-190.

BOBBY GORDON ("Pee Wee's Song"): **Newport Beach, CA — September 10/11, 1993**
| | Muskogee Blue | -1 | (CD) Arbors ARCD19130 |
| | Pee Wee's Song | -2 | (CD) Arbors ARCD19130 |

-1 "head" arrangement from Dick Cary lead sheet.
-2 adaptation by Jon-Erik Kellso of Dick Cary arrangement.

THE ROYAL BLUE MELODIANS (Eddie Jansson, Svante Thuresson, vo):
concert, Karlstad, Sweden — September 23, 1993

930505-2	Let's Face the Music and Dance	vEJ aDC	(CD) Kenneth CKS3414
930506-2	How Deep Is the Ocean	vST aDC	(CD) Kenneth CKS3414
930527-2	Easy to Love	aDC	(CD) Kenneth CKS3414

Cary arranged a total of seven titles for this Swedish band. The remaining four, already recorded, are: *Say It With Music/A Pretty Girl Is Like a Melody/You Do Something to Me/All Through the Night.*`

JIM TURNER (solo piano): *West Baden, IN, February 5-7, 1994*

Sea of Cortez	(CD) Klavier KD77016
Seven Card Stud	(CD) Klavier KD77016
Waltz for Judy	(CD) Klavier KD77016
Gwenders	(CD) Klavier KD77016
Rialto	(CD) Klavier KD77016
Doctor Salkin	(CD) Klavier KD77016
Duisenpoot	(CD) Klavier KD77016
Idyl	(CD) Klavier KD77016
Forty-Seventh Street	(CD) Klavier KD77016

all Dick Cary compositions, transcribed by Jim Turner from pieces heard at rehearsals by the Tuesday Night Friends. Album title: The Dazzler.

DICK CARY's TUESDAY NIGHT FRIENDS (Dick Hamilton, tp-5, a-h-6, p; Jack Trott, tp; Betty O'Hara, tb, bar-horn, euphonium-1; Ernie Tack, b-tb; Abe Most, cl; Tommy Newsom, ss-2, ts, b-sax, cl; Terry Harrington, ts; Fred Cooper, bar, fl-3; Dave Koonse, g; Herb Mickman, b; Jerry White, d; Dick Cary, arr): *The Doing, Los Angeles — February 4, 5 & 6, 1997*

Catching Up	(Cary)	(CD) Klavier KD-77024
Late Sunday	(Cary)	(CD) Klavier KD-77024
White April	(Cary)	(CD) Klavier KD-77024
Sgt. Pee Wee	(Cary)	(CD) Klavier KD-77024

(same personnel, except Harrington out):

September Etude	(Cary)	(CD) Klavier KD-77024
Gramercy Park	(Cary)	(CD) Klavier KD-77024
Black and Blue	-3	(CD) Klavier KD-77024
Between Prone and Supine	(Cary) -5	(CD) Klavier KD-77024
December Song	(Cary)-5	(CD) Klavier KD-77024

(same personnel, plus John Bambridge, ts, cl-4):

Oofy	(Cary) -2	(CD) Klavier KD-77024
The Albatross	(Dick Cary-Jimmy McPartland) -5	(CD) Klavier KD-77024
Rialto	(Cary)	(CD) Klavier KD-77024

(same personnel, except Trott, Most out; Randy Aldcroft, bar-horn; in):

Shimmy Sha Wobble	-4,-6	(CD) Klavier KD-77024
Sea of Cortez	(Cary) -6	(CD) Klavier KD-77024
B-e-t-t-y O'-H-a-r-a	(Cary) -1,-6	(CD) Klavier KD-77024
Recado	-6	(CD) Klavier KD-77024

Album title: Catching Up.

DICK CARY'S TUESDAY NIGHT FRIENDS (Dick Hamilton, tp, a-h, p, dir; Jack Trott, tp; Dave Ryan, tb; Ernie Tack, b-tb; Abe Most, Phil Feather, Terry Harrington, Fred Cooper, reeds; Dave Koonse or Barry Cooper, g; Herb Mickman, b; Jerry White, d; all arrangements by Dick Cary):

The Doing, Los Angeles — April 18, 19, 21, 2000

My Inspiration	(CD) Arbors ARCD 19253
Warm for June (Cary)	(CD) Arbors ARCD 19253
The Sleepwalkers (Cary)	(CD) Arbors ARCD 19253
Harlem Speaks	(CD) Arbors ARCD 19253
Echoes of Harlem	(CD) Arbors ARCD 19253
Clarinet Gumbo	(CD) Arbors ARCD 19253
Sweet and Lovely	(CD) Arbors ARCD 19253
Fifty Six	(CD) Arbors ARCD 19253
Little Eddie's Song (Cary)	(CD) Arbors ARCD 19253
Caravan	(CD) Arbors ARCD 19253
Tent Blues (Cary)	(CD) Arbors ARCD 19253
It Don't Mean a Thing	(CD) Arbors ARCD 19253
I Didn't Know About You	(CD) Arbors ARCD 19253
Puttin' on the Ritz	(CD) Arbors ARCD 19253
Soft and Easy (Cary)	(CD) Arbors ARCD 19253
Struttin' with Some Barbecue	(CD) Arbors ARCD 19253
A-la-Carney (Cary)	(CD) Arbors ARCD 19253
Local Blues (Cary)	(CD) Arbors ARCD 19253
Down South Camp Meeting	(CD) Arbors ARCD 19253

Album title: Got Swing?

BOB HAVENS (tb, vo, arr; with 14-piece orchestra, including Jack Coon, tp; Morris Repass, b-tb; John Setar, Terry Harrington, Roger Neumann, John Bambridge, Fred Cooper, reeds; Dick Cary, Deane Kincaide, Curt Ramsey, Frank Scott, arr):

Dick Hamilton's Studio, Los Angeles — May 2006

Washboard Blues	aFS	(CD) BHCD6027-2
Can't Help Lovin' That Man of Mine	aDK	(CD) BHCD6027-2
Casanova's Lament	vBH aDC	(CD) BHCD6027-2
Roll On, Mississippi, Roll On	vBH aDC	(CD) BHCD6027-2
Mama's Gone, Goodbye	aDC	(CD) BHCD6027-2
In My Solitude	aDC	(CD) BHCD6027-2
Isle of Capri	aDK	(CD) BHCD6027-2
I Gotta Right to Sing the Blues	aDC	(CD) BHCD6027-2
Goody, Goody	aBH	(CD) BHCD6027-2
Darkness on the Delta	aCR	(CD) BHCD6027-2
Blue and Broken-Hearted	aDC	(CD) BHCD6027-2
Love Lies	aBH	(CD) BHCD6027-2
Tiger Rag	aFS	(CD) BHCD6027-2
Junk Man	aDC	(CD) BHCD6027-2
How Come You Do Me Like You Do	vBH aDC	(CD) BHCD6027-2
My Inspiration	aDC	(CD) BHCD6027-2

Album title: The King Swings

The author with Dick Cary.
Sunland, Los Angeles,
October 11, 1979

*(Photograph by and
courtesy of Bert Whyatt)*

Jim Turner

MISHAWAKA RECORDS
79 W. Monroe St. — Chicago, IL 60603
(312) 782-8854

Playhouse Music
Hiawatha Music
ASCAP
5000-B

Al Trace
(Producer)
Time: 2:21
(BP-385-B)

SAUCY, SASSY, SAUCY, SASSY SUE
(A. Trace — L. Abrams — D. Cary)
Dee Hendrick — Vocalist
DICK CARY'S JAZZ ALL STARS
featuring: Eddie Miller — Nick FaTool — Bob Haven
Henry Cuesta and more
STEREO

HI HAT
DANCE RECORDS
365
Released 9/68 (AJW)
Square Dance MUSIC
"UNICORNS"
Music Played by DICK CARY
Produced By MERL OLDS, Los Angeles, Calif.

ABC-PARAMOUNT
PROMOTION COPY
Pamco Music, Inc. (BMI)
2:09
NOT FOR SALE
45-9770
AMP 45-566

45-m 640

EVERYBODY LOVES PIERRE
(Costa)
DON COSTA
AND HIS ORCHESTRA AND CHORUS
A PRODUCT OF AM-PAR RECORD CORP.

COMMODORE
CLASSICS IN SWING
616 B
ANGRY
(A-4762-2)
April, 1944
(Mecum-Cassard-Brunies Bros.)

MUGGSY SPANIER AND HIS RAGTIMERS
Muggsy Spanier, Trumpet; Pee Wee Russell, Clarinet; Miff Mole, Trombone; Eddie Condon, Guitar; Dick Cary, Piano; Bob Casey, Bass; Joe Grauso, Drums

---

Merry-Go-Round
HI HAT ROUND DANCE RECORDS
FUN-LEVEL ROUNDS

Choreography by:
Dave & Jean Trowell

MGR-044
Instrumental
Produced by PETE METZGER

I AIN'T GOT NOBODY
Music By **DICK CARY**

The Indexes

Name Index to Biography

ABNEY, Don	257, 274, 290, 292, 293
ABRAMSON, Herb	98, 107
ABRUZZO, Tommy	117
ADAMS, Laura	446
ADAMS, Pepper	210, 231, 424
ADLER, Bob	267–68, 274
ADLER, Polly	268
AIRMEN OF NOTE	439
ALBERTINE(?), Charlie	129
ALBRIGHT, Frank	235
ALDCROFT, Randy	291, 436
ALDEN, Howard	358, 360, 370, 388, 409
ALESSI, Sam	441
ALEXANDER, Ashley	272, 372
ALEXANDER, Bill	234
ALEXANDER, Mousey	206, 209, 211, 214, 272
ALEXANDER, Van	317
ALLEN, Bob	327, 374
ALLEN, Dave	210
ALLEN, Fred	168
ALLEN, Henry 'Red'	33, 91, 112, 124, 127, 137, 153, 154
ALLEN, Leslie	82, 126
ALLEN, Mynell	113
ALLEN, Nicky (see ALLEN, Virginia)	
ALLEN, Red (see ALLEN, Henry 'Red')	
ALLEN, Rex	291, 333, 337, 339, 343–44, 346, 387
ALLEN, Rod	340
ALLEN, Scott	291
ALLEN, Steve	156, 281, 437, 440
ALLEN, Tony	363
ALLEN, Virginia	72–73, 79, 81–82, 83, 86–87, 90, 93, 95, 99, 106, 118, 120, 126, 134, 138–39, 148, 186, 214, 221, 233, 332
ALLEN, Walter C	204
ALLISON, Mose	440
ALLOTRIA JAZZ BAND	321
ALLRED, Bill	343
ALLRED, John	381, 395
ALLYSON, Karrin	440
ALPERT, Herb	264
ALSTON, Al	188
ALVIN, Danny	23–26, 28, 31, 33, 35–36, 38, 40–41, 54
AMES, Lionel	273–74
AMMONS, Albert	22
AMOS, Frank	300
AMSLER, Clyde	369
AMSTERDAM, Morey	170
ANDERSON, Dick	13
ANDERSON, Ed	228, 238, 253, 284, 288, 338–39, 344, 350, 365
ANDERSON, Ernestine	212, 293, 429
ANDERSON, Ernie	xv, 32, 48, 50, 52, 65–72, 79, 80, 90, 98, 101
ANDERSON, Janet (and sons)	311–12, 315, 317, 327, 329–31, 333, 337, 340, 344, 347
ANDERSON, Sonny	250
ANDREWS, Jim	215
ANDREWS, Johnny	102
ANDREWS SISTERS	17
ANGEL CITY JAZZ BAND	349, 383, 450
ANNABELLA	21
ANTHONY, Ray	438
ANTOLINI, Charly	371
APPLEWHITE, Charlie	158
APPLEYARD, Peter	384
ARCHEY, Jimmy	101, 106, 137, 157
ARDMORE Music Corporation	445, 447, 449
ARLEN, Harold	262
ARMSTRONG, Louis	xi, xvi, 32, 65–69, 71–75, 77–81, 85, 88, 91–93, 99–100, 102, 111, 133, 142, 157, 192, 193, 251, 273, 322, 342, 347, 428, 430, 432, 435, 440, 451, 461
ARMSTRONG, Louis (Tributes)	xii, 341–342, 347, 361–363, 364, 367, 373, 383, 389, 395, 421
ARMSTRONG, Lucille	88, 121
ARMY AIR FORCE BAND	440
ARNOLD, Buddy	402
ARNOLD, Jack	408, 410
ARNONE, Don	129, 156, 172, 206
ASBURY, Helen	34
ASBURY, Herbert	34
ASCIONE, Joe	409
ASH, Marvin	264, 287
ASHCRAFT, Squirrel	78, 88, 210, 212
ASHER, Bob	185
ASTON, Al	157, 188
ATKINS, Jimmy	97
AUGUSTYNOWICZ, Humbert	306
AULD, George	88, 99, 111
AUTON, Art	273
AUTREY, Herman	176, 211
AVAKIAN, George	35, 137. 161, 217, 457
AVALON, Frankie	282
AXEL'S DREAM BAND	321
AZZOLINA ————	50
BACIN, Bill	248, 256, 259, 262–63, 269, 283

570

BACKUS, Jim 262
BADER, Klaus 335–36, 356, 372, 443, 460
BADER, Laura 372
BAGGIANO, Joe 198
BAGLEY, Don 241
BAILEY, Bob 337, 339, 346
BAILEY, Buster 107–08, 141–42, 188, 190
BAILEY, Jessie (see BUSTER, Jessie)
BAILEY, Pearl 91, 290
BAIRD, Eugenie 44
BAIRD, Mike 327
BAKER, Cy 160
BAKER, Julie 201
BAKER, Richard 416
BALABAN, Red 203
BALDOCK, Kenny 325
BALL, George 347, 352, 360
BALLIETT, Whitney 79–80, 429
BAMBRIDGE, John 359, 366, 400, 410, 411, 416, 436, 440
BANCROFT, Anne 290
BARBARIN, Paul 213
BARBE, John 129
BARBER, Chris 310, 368
BARDOCK, Bunny 44
BARDUHN, Art 239, 297
BAREFIELD, Eddie 130–33, 136–37, 149, 153, 155, 158, 160, 170, 172, 174–75, 201, 204, 208–12
BARNARD, Bob 319–20
BARNARD, Len 319–20
BARNES, George 138, 172, 237, 271
BARNES, John 323–24, 370
BARNET, Charlie 99, 437, 440
BARNET ORCHESTRA 441
BARNETT, Anthony xv, 125
BARON, Jimmy 254, 257
BARRE, Lorraine 17
BARRELHOUSE JAZZBAND xvi, 302, 304–05, 321, 335, 336, 460
BARRELL, Ernie 288
BARRETT, Dan xv, 288, 331, 340, 347, 379, 387, 388, 408, 409
BARRETT, Sweet Emma 251
BARRIE SISTERS 36
BARRIS, Harry 74
BARTLEE, Ron 275, 442
BARTÓK, Béla 96, 424
BARTON, Jim 147
BARUFALDI, Joe 118, 146, 150, 199–201, 211, 214
BASIE, Count 9, 91, 99, 111, 132, 156, 164, 168, 176, 241, 279, 369, 405, 437, 438, 440, 442
BASSEY, Bus 241
BATES, Bob 281
BAUDUC, Ray 108–09, 148, 150, 249, 251

BAUER, Billy 142, 200, 202, 206–07, 208, 455
BAUGHN, Wilda 328
BAUTISTE, Dr. ---- 413
BEACH BOYS, The 438
BEACH, Frank 279
BEAMSLEY, Don 290, 299–300, 348
BEATRICE Music Corporation 444–47
BECHET, Leonard 235
BECHET, Sidney 31, 33, 66, 91, 96–97, 106, 137, 216, 459
BEE, Molly 262
BEEBE, Bill 11
BEGLEY, Ed 174
BEIDERBECKE, Bix 69, 157, 169, 171, 309, 408, 429, 436, 453–54, 459, 462
BEILMANN, Pete 231, 240, 242–44, 249–52, 257–58
BELAFONTE, Harry 105
BELDING, Ken 152, 159
BELL, Bill 196
BELL, Ernie 17
BELL, Graeme 320, 363
BELL, Kay 250
BELLSON, Louis 139, 267, 293, 436, 437
BENEDICT, Les 383, 417
BENEKE, Tex 78, 436, 437
BENFORD, Tommy 101, 131
BENJAMIN, Joe 200
BENNETT, Dave xv, 325
BENNETT, Ed 385
BENNETT, Tony 255, 262
BENNY, Jack 434
BERG, Billy 73–75
BERG, George 200
BERGER, Judy 251, 253–54
BERIGAN, Bunny 10, 369
BERK, Dick 354, 358, 369
BERKELY, Harold 3
BERLIN, Irving 393, 413
BERMAN, Marty 257
BERNARDI, Noni 294, 369, 396
BERNSTEIN, Dr. Alan 242
BERNSTEIN, Mathew Alan 242
BERRY, Bill 349
BERRY, Emmett 111, 148
BERT, Eddie 104, 211
BESSE, Ralph 102, 447
BEST, John 227, 257, 267, 272, 279, 288–89, 294, 300, 315–16, 327, 339–40, 347, 350–51, 357, 374, 378, 385
BETHERS, Steve 405
BETTS, Keeter 213
BIENERT, Gerd 306
BIGARD, Barney 14, 66, 72, 73, 79, 80, 133, 142, 207, 247–48, 253, 260, 262–63, 271, 284–87, 299,

571

	316, 332, 341–42, 362, 373, 428, 430, 438, 445–46, 458–59	BRITT, Jackie	266
		BRITTEN, Benjamin	392
		BROADBENT, Alan	412, 440
BIGARD, Dottie	142	BRONSON, Charles	66
BILLINGS, Bernie	18	BROOKMEYER, Bob	184, 195, 201, 209, 229, 398, 456
BILLINGS, Josh	82		
BISSET, Russ	378	BROOKS, Major Louis	74
BIVONA, Gus	228, 232–33, 357, 369, 442	BROOKS, Mel	290, 294
BLACK, Russ	232	BROOMFIELD, Bob	344
BLACKLOCK, Buddy	206	BROWN, Buster	407
BLAKE, Eubie	277, 282, 352, 428	BROWN, Clifford	165, 174, 417, 426, 434
BLAKENEY, Andy	253, 273, 316, 342	BROWN, Jim	209, 233
BLANC, Rick	405	BROWN, Jimmy	161
BLOWERS, Johnny	131, 133, 136–37, 142	BROWN, Jimmy	187
BODNER, Phil	156, 214, 312	BROWN, Les	279, 436, 438
BOEDDINGHAUS, David	414	BROWN, Marshall	212
BOHANNON, Hoyt	255, 365	BROWN, Mr. ----	7
BOLEN, Gene	214, 227, 235, 239, 249, 255, 381	BROWN, Norm	260
		BROWN, Pud	313, 337–38, 444, 446, 458–59
BOLGER, Ray	262		
BONANO, Sharkey	25, 251	BROWN, Ray	429, 438
BOND, Paul	441	BROWN, Roy	349
BONNEE, Don	228, 240, 249	BROWN, Ruth	98–99, 102, 106, 442
BONYTHON, Kym	245	BROWN, Vernon	45, 48, 57, 330, 344
BOONE, Pat	214, 442	BROWNLOW, Pete	11
BOOTH, Dianne	231	BRUNIS, George (Brunies)	24–26, 29–30, 33–38, 42, 57, 66, 97, 104, 129
BORCHER, Bill	328		
BOSE, Sterling	33	BRUNO, Sam	108
BOSTON POPS	368–69, 433	BRUNS, George	264, 461
BOSWELL SISTERS	6	BRYAN, Mike	103
BOUCHARD, Jerry	174	BRYANT, Ray	212–13
BOUGHTON, Joe	xv, 379–80, 394	BRYDEN, Beryl	335, 460
BOURNE, Dave	xv, 294, 298, 300, 379, 382	BRYNNER, Yul	137
BOURNE, Pat	294	BUCKNER, Teddy	260, 268, 316, 374
BOWDEN, Norman	260	BUDGE, Donald	187
BOWER, Roy	xv, 326	BUDWIG, Monty	338, 348, 383, 388
BOWERS, Joe	254	BUDZINSKI, Stella	3
BOWES, Major	48	BÜHR, Peter	356, 368, 372
BOWMAN, Dave	33, 46, 153, 163	BULL MOOSE PARTY BAND	349
BOYD, Dorothy Virgina (see ALLEN, Virginia)		BUNCH, John	313, 388
BOYNK, ----	12	BUNDOCK, Roland 'Rollie'	331, 369, 383
BRACEGIRDLE, Tony	323	BUNKER, Larry	235
BRADEN, Joe	365	BURGHOFF, Gary	359
BRADLEY, Jack	390	BURKE, Betty	273
BRADLEY, Tom	396	BURKE, Johnny	460
BRADLEY, Will	15, 98, 138, 436	BURKE, Sonny	241
BRADY, Dick	237	BURKE, Stan	325
BRADY, Pat	244	BURNETT, Ernie	442
BRAFF, Ruby	54, 64, 172, 191, 209–10, 217, 425, 429	BURNS, Buddy	235, 327
		BURNS, Ralph	205
BREDISE, Fred	64	BURNS, Roy	199, 211
BREDISE, Lou	64	BURRELL, Duke	342
BREGMAN, VOCCO & CONN, Inc.	449	BUSHELL, Garvin	137, 203–04, 209
BREWER, Roy	271, 282	BUSHKIN, Joe	19, 33–34, 56, 86–87, 92, 98, 105–06, 133, 156
BRIGGS, Bunny	91		
BRIGLIA, Tony	44	BUSSEY, Bus	292, 338
BRILEY, Jerry Lee	408	BUSTER, Jessie	xiii, xiv, xv, 232–33, 235–38, 242, 248, 250–54, 257–58,
BRISBANE JAZZ CLUB BIG BAND	320		

572

	261–64, 267, 273–74, 280, 281, 285, 290, 292–93, 295, 398, 400–01, 412, 420
BUTTERFIELD, Billy	xi, 25–26, 33, 43, 48–50, 56–57, 59–61, 95–97, 99–101, 104, 106, 108, 124–25, 133–34, 142, 158–59, 161–62, 189, 195, 199, 202, 277–78, 308, 313–14, 329, 359, 379, 437, 441, 450, 454
BUTTONS, Red	158
BYERS, Bill	164, 261
BYRD, Charlie	210, 213
BYRD, Donald	183, 231, 240
BYRNE, Bill	300
BYRNE, Bobby	16, 138
CACERES, Ernie	69, 96, 99, 104–05, 108, 133, 146, 177, 178, 180, 181, 185, 189, 194, 214, 398, 456
CACERES, Pinie	189–90
CAESAR, Jimmy	142
CAIAZZA, Nick	158
CAIN, Jackie	181
CALELLA, Sonny	114, 116, 156, 442
CALLAHAN, John	409
CALLENDER, Red	235, 250, 316, 341–43, 374
CALLETT, Lee	436
CALLOWAY, Cab	386
CAMARATA, Tutti	207
CAMERON, Ken	233
CAMPBELL, Bill	74, 227, 238–39, 273, 282–84, 290–91, 333, 338, 345, 351
CANDOLI, Conte	99
CANYON, Virginia	447
CAPITOL CITY JAZZ BAND	300, 313
CAPP, Frank	241, 349
CAREY, Frank	176, 210–12
CARISI, John	86–87
CARLE, Frankie	279
CARLIN, Fred	311, 328
CARLSON, Kay	234, 237–38, 242, 251, 255, 258, 263, 268, 274, 398–402, 442
CARMICHAEL, Hoagy	45, 73, 358, 393, 462
CARMICHAEL, Ian	365
CARMICHAEL, Judy	374
CARMICHAEL, Ralph	366
CARNEY, Harry	430
CARPENTER, Pete	231, 353
CARPENTER, Thelma	51–52, 91
CARROLL, Barbara	191
CARROLL, Buddy	286, 443
CARROLL, Joe	42
CARTER, Benny	164, 255, 261, 341–43, 402
CARTER, Bob	111, 155, 164, 210
CARTER Brothers	11–12
CARTER, Lou	45
CARY, Albert Ely	2, 4, 11
CARY, Helen	11
CARY, Janet	82, 106, 129, 162, 186
CARY, Jessie (see BUSTER, Jessie)	
CARY, Judy	13, 17, 39, 51–52, 55, 106, 112, 129, 151, 154, 165, 186, 216, 229, 242
CARY, Lois E.	3–5, 73, 168, 219
CARY, Lois Pierson (Durant)	2–6
CARY Music Library, The Dick	447
CARY, Phyllis A.	2–3
CARY, Renee	410
CARY, Rose	12, 16–17, 24, 31, 36, 39, 50–52, 55–56, 59, 62, 65, 67, 93, 106, 129, 151, 165, 221, 233
CARY, William 'Bill'	2–5, 410
CASA LOMA Orchestra	6–7, 44–45
CASAMENTI, Al	185
CASEY, Bob	103, 122, 129, 150
CASPAROFF, Joe	365
CASTLE, Del	128
CASTLE, Lee	32, 120, 124, 126, 128–30, 139–40, 144–45, 151, 441, 442, 444–45, 451
CATES, George	290
CATHCART, Dick	226–27, 231, 233–34, 240, 249, 359, 365, 370, 374, 377–78, 380, 382, 384, 385, 387–88, 397, 399, 420, 436
CATLETT, Sid	xi, 19, 31, 67, 68, 71–73, 75, 78, 79, 80–82, 88, 93, 99, 112, 117, 119, 239, 362, 373
CATRON, Johnny(?)	311, 315, 317
CAVALLARO, Carmen	44, 441
CAVANAUGH, Page	240
CAVETT, Dick	362
CENARDO, Doc	345
CERULLI, Dom	184, 195
CHALLIS, Bill	44–45
CHALPRIN, ----	442
CHAMBER Music Library	447
CHAMPLIN, Charles	380, 417
CHARLES Singers, Ray	205
CHARLES, Teddy	143, 157–58, 195, 216
CHASE, Sherry	361
CHEATHAM, Doc	141, 208–11, 389, 390, 406, 446, 461–62
CHESTER, Bob	11, 438
CHICAGOANS, The	321, 335, 356, 372, 460
CHICAGO SIX, The	378, 386, 406–07
CHILTON, John	57
CHISHOLM, George	361
CHRISTIAN, Buddy	125

573

CHRISTY, June	100		COOK, Joe	241
CLARK, Buddy	33, 436		COOKE, Mickey	363–64
CLARK, Garner	228		COON, Jackie	227, 247–49, 251, 261, 272, 358, 382, 403, 458, 461
CLARK, Mahlon	74, 249, 289, 315, 330–31, 379, 382, 386, 389, 436		COOPER, Ashley	318
CLARKE, Bill	371		COOPER, Bill	235, 239, 249
CLAUSEN, Alf	272		COOPER, Fred	275, 370, 378, 405, 417, 420, 436
CLAYTON, Buck	141, 163, 170, 174, 187, 212–13, 236, 244, 250, 258, 398, 452, 458		COOPER, Jackie	91, 294
			COPELAND, Arnold	102
CLAYTON-HAMILTON Hollywood Bowl Jazz Orchestra	436		COPLAND, Aaron	301
			COQUETTES, The	233
CLESS, Rod	32, 36, 48		CORB, Morty	71–74, 81, 267–68, 272, 289, 337, 340, 348–51, 367, 406
CLIFTON, Chris	342			
CLIMAX JAZZ BAND	341			
CLOONEY, Rosemary	91, 438, 440		CORBETT, Glenn	356
COAT, C.	227		CORDANA, Bob	175
COCHRAN, Steve	74		CORELLI, Carl	20
COHEN, Greg	394		CORNUCOPIA Publishing	201, 206, 447
COHEN, Porky	137		CORTESE, Dom	175
COHN, Al	185, 398, 456		CORVO, ————	12
COLE, Cozy	133, 160, 316, 341		CORWIN, Bob	273
COLE, Geoff	xv		COSTA, Bill	201
COLE, Nat 'King'	32, 110		COSTA, Don	112, 114–15, 121, 134–35, 174, 442
COLE, Natalie	436			
COLEMAN, Ornette	428		COSTA, Eddie	161, 206
COLLER, Phyllis	xvii		COUNTRYMAN, Lee	271, 300, 313, 327
COLLIER, Mike	326		COURT, Bill	286
COLLIER, Ralph	251, 262		COVINGTON, Warren	207
COLLINS, Dick	258, 297		COWARD, Noel	365, 389, 391
COLLINS, John	315		CRAIN, Jeanne	83
COLONNA, Jerry	58–59		CRANE, Mickey	157, 181
COLUMBO, Lou	54		CRAWFORD, Cheryl	34
COLTRANE, John	428		CRAWFORD, Jimmy	47, 142, 149–50, 153, 156
COLVILLE, Randy	326		CREASH, Bob	149
COMMANDERS, The	207		CREATH, Charlie	88
CONDON, Eddie	xi, xii, 14, 25–27, 29, 32–34, 36, 38–40, 43, 45–51, 54–57, 63, 85, 89–91, 93, 96–106, 110, 119, 122, 126, 130, 133–34, 136–37, 145–51, 153, 157–58, 162–65, 170–72, 175, 178, 195, 197, 198–99, 201–03, 205–06, 209, 211, 213, 215–16, 221, 229–30, 236–37, 244–47, 283, 304, 307, 318–319, 325, 356, 419, 426, 427, 429, 430, 431, 432, 435, 441, 442, 444–47, 449–51, 453–54, 456–59, 463		CRESTON, Paul	63, 87, 158, 162–63
			CRESTWOOD Music Publications	444–48
			CRIBARI, Joe	128
			CRIMMINS, Roy	370
			CROSBY, Bing	73, 97 132, 231
			CROSBY, Bob	8, 57–58, 72, 74, 227, 231, 255, 256, 268, 279, 286, 316, 327–28, 333, 350, 354, 374, 378, 384, 385, 397, 436, 437, 438, 440
			CROSBY, Israel	50
			CROSBY, Kathy Lee	349
			CROTHERS, Scatman	264, 337, 374
			CROW, Bill	xv, 163, 187–188, 208–09, 236–37
CONKLIN, Chuck	xiv, 331, 340, 370, 374, 383, 396, 400, 419, 444, 450		CRUMP, Charlie	xv, 361
			CRYSTAL, Jack	88, 172, 212
CONNIFF, Ray	45, 174, 436, 440		CUBETA, ————	62
CONNOR, Leonard	118		CUCKEL, Senator	237
CONNORS, Gene	342		CUESTA, Henry	294, 333
CONOVER, Willis	210		CULLUM, Jim	376, 418
CONTE, Joe	54		CULTER, Bill	124

574

CULVER, Rollie	228, 257
CURTIS, Benson	255
CURTIS, Gail	125, 173
CUTSHALL, Cutty	43, 96, 99, 104–05, 108–09, 120, 122, 130, 134, 138, 148, 156, 163, 186, 197, 201, 205, 209, 211, 229, 231, 236–37, 454, 456
DAGOSTINO, Joe	62, 441
DAILEY, Dan	33, 83
DAILY, Pete	328
DALE, Alan	132
DALE, Dick	233, 249
DALTRY, Joseph S.	8
DAMERON, Tadd	99
D'AMICO, Hank	48, 56, 63, 97, 133, 136, 149, 159, 162, 207, 213, 441, 442
DANCE, Stanley	198
DANIEL, Fats	201
DANIELS, Buzz	239
DANIELS, Jack	289
DARENSBOURG, Joe	234, 252–54, 262, 271–74, 282–84, 286–87, 291, 299–300, 311–13, 327, 331, 345, 354, 378, 428
DARKTOWN JAZZ BAND	307, 321, 460
DARLENE	202, 209
DAVENPORT, Cow Cow	54
DAVERN, Kenny	217, 236, 354, 359, 451–52
DAVIS, ----	340
DAVIS, Bette	329–30
DAVIS, Blind John	341
DAVIS, Bob	254, 401
DAVIS, Doug	343–44, 346–47, 349–50, 352, 356–58
DAVIS, Duke	17
DAVIS, Joe	140, 151
DAVIS, Mel	199, 202, 212
DAVIS, Miles	99, 174, 178, 181, 184, 194, 199, 250, 456
DAVIS, Quinn	367
DAVIS, Ray	154
DAVIS, Stanley	115
DAVISON, Wild Bill	24–28, 30–33, 41–42, 45–46, 49, 51, 54, 56–57, 66, 90–91, 93, 104, 106–08, 117, 120, 122, 127, 133, 136, 148, 151, 153, 158, 163, 165, 170, 199, 209, 231, 234, 260, 272, 308, 343, 356, 358, 374, 382, 425, 430, 450, 454
DAWN OF THE CENTURY RAGTIME ORCHESTRA	450, 458
DAY, Bobby	32, 441
DAY, Laraine	113
DEAN, Allan	129
De BÉRIOT, Charles	5
DEBUSSY, Claude	5, 115, 118, 190
DECHTER, Brad	383
DEE, Jimmy	132
DEEMS, Barrett	130, 331, 359, 361, 364, 374
de FAZIO, Joe	16, 441
DEFEBAUGH, George	227, 232, 234, 238, 261, 266, 313
DeFRANCO, Buddy	99, 111, 124, 128, 289
DEHNER, John	252
DEJAN, Harold	342
DELANEY, Joe	214
DELUIS, Dom	290
DEMERLE, Les	367
DEMPSEY, Jack	136
De NAUT, Jud	227
DENGLER, John	xv, 118, 174, 177, 178, 179, 181, 185, 189–91, 198, 219
DENNIS, Stan	44
DENVER, Tom	352
DePARIS, Sidney	50
DePARIS, Wilbur	50
DePEW, Art	234, 237–38, 242, 254–55, 257, 271, 275, 317, 331, 345, 401, 408, 410, 411, 442
DESBOIS, Bob	16
DESMOND, Johnny	299, 438
DEUTSCH, Dutch	328
DEUTSCH, Emery	14–15, 441
DeVITO, Frank	401
DeVITO, Harry	176, 209, 237, 388
DeVOL, Frank	281, 292
De VORGON, Barry	358
De VRIES, Johnny	34, 97, 156, 201, 447–48
De WEESE, Glen	238–39
DIAMOND, Lou	254
DI CARLO, Tommy	19, 441
DICKEN, Charlie	118
DICKENSON, Bob	58
DICKENSON, Vic	112, 126, 128, 141, 158, 162–63, 171–75, 187–188, 190–91, 209, 211–13, 215–16, 245–47, 250, 308, 343, 398, 452, 458
DIEHL, Ray	104, 107, 109, 111, 125, 136, 139, 149–50, 153, 155, 158, 160, 162, 172, 174, 177, 186, 214, 217
D'IMPERIO, Danny	368
DI NOVI, Gene	267
DIVA Big Band	439
DIXON, Joe	40, 64, 370
DODDS, Baby	66, 108
DOLNEY, Joe	401
DOMBER, Matt	408–10
DONAHUE, Al	19–20

DONALDSON, Bobby	146, 174, 200, 202, 206, 215			267, 288–89, 305, 328, 389,
DONIN, Bunny	351			393, 407, 419–21, 425, 430,
DONOVAN, Kathy	253			432, 434, 455
DOREY, Ray	43		ELLIOTT, Don	128, 145, 156, 188, 199
DORSEY, Jimmy	xi, 9, 69, 74, 95, 103,		ELLIOTT, Jack	349, 351
	106–11, 139–40, 164–65,		ELLIS, Herb	44, 238, 400
	173, 330, 434, 451		ELLSWORTH, Scott	xiv, 11, 67, 226, 267, 398,
DORSEY, Tommy	xi, 40, 69, 72, 74, 95, 108,			430, 432-33
	138–40, 151, 164, 173, 279,		ELMAN, Ziggy	9–10
	330, 369, 397, 432, 438,		ENDRESS, Gudrun	xiv, xv, 95, 232, 300, 306–
	442, 445–46, 452			07, 336, 398
DOUGLAS, Jim	363, 370		ENEVOLDSEN, Bob	xv, 29, 268, 272, 281–83,
DOUGLAS, Kirk	91, 131			285–88, 290–92, 312–14,
DOUGLAS, Mike	232			317, 329–34, 339, 341,
DOWELL, Saxie	441			343–44, 346, 348, 350–51,
DOWNER, Bill	42			353–54, 359–61, 365, 367,
DOWNING, Harden	17			369–70, 374, 386, 397,
DRAKE, Ron	363			399–402, 407, 413, 420, 437
DRAKE SISTERS, The	257		ENNIS, Skinny	440
DRELLINGER, Art	350		ERHMAN, Gus	353
DREW, John	202, 214		ERICSON, Ed	247
DROOTIN, Al	63–64, 452		ERTEGUN, Ahmet	98–99
DROOTIN, Buzzy	19, 63–64, 97–98, 103–04,		ERWIN, Pee Wee	23, 25, 117, 136, 172, 175,
	122, 125–26, 164, 174–75,			188, 209, 272, 328–29, 346,
	181–82, 185, 190–91, 192,			354, 395, 430, 439, 459
	193, 194, 198–200, 206,		ERWIN, Ward	254–55, 401
	208–10, 236–37, 398, 432		(c/f: IRVIN, Ward)	
DUCHIN, Eddie	59		ESSER, Bobby	257, 262, 311, 317, 329,
DUKES OF DIXIELAND, The	354			443
DULONG, Jack	238		ESTES, Gene	278–79, 292, 297–98, 317,
DUNBAR. Dixie	18			327, 330–31, 337, 339,
DUNCAN, Hank	96, 117			343–46, 348–51, 355, 358,
DUNHAM, Katherine	41–42			360, 366, 369–70, 374,
DUNHAM, Sonny	205–06			377–78, 379, 380, 382,
DURANT, Lucy	3			384–87, 388, 389, 394–95,
DURANT, Phil	281			397, 402–03, 407, 415,
DURANTE, Jimmy	150			420, 437
DURHAM, Eddie	11		EVANS, Doc	78, 92
DUVIVIER, George	359		EVANS, Gil	132, 184, 439, 456
			EVANS, Marion	158
EAGER, Alan	168		EVANS, Phil	230
EASTON, Ted	308–10, 322, 444, 453,		EVANS, Virgil	383
	459–60		EWELL, Don	201
EBERLE, Bob	128			
EBERLE, Ray	113		FAHEY, John	281–82, 437
EBSEN, Buddy	358		FAIN, Sammy	165
ECKINGER, Isla	394		FAIRWEATHER, Digby	453–54, 460
ECKLUND, Peter	394		FALES (?), Dick	137
ECKSTINE, Billy	100, 105, 272		FARLOW, Tal	120, 361
EDEN, Barbara	250		FARMER, Art	250
EDWARDS, Dave	274, 291, 293, 315, 383		FARRARO, ----	198
EDWARDS, Eddie	42		FARROW, Mia	288
EDWARDS, Teddy	254, 401		FATOOL, Nick	47, 227–28, 231–32, 242,
EKBERG, Anita	156			247–48, 250, 252, 256,
ELDREDGE, Tom	121			257–58, 261, 268, 270,
ELDRIDGE, Roy	14, 63, 97, 145, 236, 430			272–292, 293–94, 298–300,
ELLINGTON, Duke	7, 22, 33, 66, 113, 132, 189,			311–17, 327–34, 337–41,
	205, 218, 227, 239, 250,			344–48, 350–54, 357–61,

	369, 374, 381–82, 386–88, 390, 401, 459	FORREST, Dick	437
		FORREST, Helen	288, 299
FAY, Jack	103	FOSTER, Gary	354, 443
FAY, Rick	xiii, 249, 273, 286, 408–09, 444, 462	FOSTER, Pete	62
		FOSTER, Preston	249
FAYE, Alice	257	FOSTER, Pops	66, 101, 160, 162
FAZOLA, Irving	57	FOSTER, Stephen	457
FEATHER, Leonard	46, 66, 120, 128, 131, 145, 151, 169, 178, 199, 268, 272, 293, 301, 400, 426	FOUNTAIN, Pete	437
		FRANCIS, Panama	137, 160, 175, 236, 271–72
		FRANCK, Cesar	6
FEATHER, Phil	405	FRASER, Ian	258
FEETWARMERS, The	307	FRAZIER, George	34, 46
FEIERMAN, Jack	282, 300, 359, 437	FREDERICK Brothers	36
FEINGOLD, Jay	207	FREEDMAN, Steve	92
FEINSTEIN, Harold	143	FREEMAN, Arnie	36, 93, 183, 447–48
FELD, Morey	92, 104, 112, 119, 125, 150, 164, 191, 215, 261, 441	FREEMAN, Bud	8, 15, 18, 25, 32, 51–52, 63, 88, 93, 95, 119–20, 135–41, 145, 153, 159, 162–65, 169, 173–76, 180, 183, 185, 187–88, 196, 197, 199, 202–03, 205–06, 213, 245, 250, 301, 308, 352, 379, 388, 398, 402, 430, 431, 436, 444–47, 449, 452, 454, 456, 458
FELDMAN, Marty	294		
FENTON, George	441		
FERAND, Steve	327		
FERGUSON, Allyn	373		
FERGUSON, Maynard	118, 173, 440		
FERRANTE, Joe	119, 133		
FERRER, Jose	102		
FERRETTI, Andy	138		
FERRICKER, Marty	120	FRENCH, Bill	290–91, 298, 352, 354
FEUSTADO, Tom	183	FRENCHY (see TALLERIE, Pierre)	
FIELD, John	64, 153, 155, 158	FRESCO, John	347
FIELDING (ZARCHY), Andy	251–54, 257, 375	FRILEY, Vern	241
FIELDS, George	350	FRISHBERG, Dave	354, 358
FIELDS, W. C.	366, 433	FRISSELL, Jim	348
FINDLEY, Chuck	359	FROMICA, ----	62
FINE, Jack	215	FROST, David	363
FINEGAN, Bill	133	FROST, John	171
FINK, Larry	14	FRYE, Don	95, 103
FINN, Fred (Freda)	349, 353	FULCHER, Dr. O.E	271
FINN, Mickey	339, 349, 353	FULLER, Gil	440
FIORITO, Matt	13	FULLER, Jack	103, 112, 122, 137
FIREHOUSE FIVE + 2	232, 251	FULLER, Larry	101
FIRESTONE, Ross	451	FULTON STREET JAZZ BAND, The	314
FISCHER, Clare	398	FURNESS, Rolly	227
FISHKIN, Arnold	206, 380		
FITZGERALD, Andy	215	GABLER, Milt	26, 42, 44, 46, 92–93, 97, 215–16
FITZGERALD, Ella	91, 97, 436		
FLANAGAN, Ed	63	GAGE, ----	63
FLAT FOOT STOMPERS, The	356, 368, 371–72, 460	GALBRAITH, Barry	211
		GALE, Bill	138
FLEMING, Herb	131–32, 137, 199	GALLACHER, Ken	xiv, 46–47, 67, 179, 216, 239–40, 244, 247, 268, 274, 323–25, 430–32
FLESCH, Mike	126		
FLORENCE, Bob	257		
FLORES, Jess	242	GALLACHER, Moraig	xiv
FLORY, Med	436	GALLOWAY, Jim	359, 370
FONTANA, Carl	271, 339, 430	GARCIA, Henry	17
FORBES, Don	107	GARCIA, Russ	438
FORBES, Graham	124	GARDNER, Ava	110
FORD, Adrian	318	GARDNER, Hy	46
FORD, Art	100–01, 113, 202	GARF, Gene	262, 296
FORD, Paul	252	GARLAND, Ed 'Tudi'	253, 255, 262–63

GARNER, Errol	113	GOLDSTEIN, Lenny	21
GARROWAY, Dave	92–93	GOLSON, Benny	179, 189, 218
GARVEY, Jack	129	GOMEZ, Dick	349
GAS (?), Benn	351	GOMEZ, Phil	231–32
GASKIN, Leonard	206, 213, 447	GONELLA, Nat	308, 460
GASTON, Ed	310, 320, 351	GONZALES, Pancho	163, 276
GAUVIN, Aime	122	GOODALL, Bill	144, 153
GAY, Al	325, 363, 370	GOODENOUGH, Robert	305
GECKLER, Tommy	251	GOODMAN, Dodie	191
GEHRKE, Mike	305	GOODMAN, Benny	8–9, 11, 42–44, 57, 72, 74, 86, 94–95, 112, 124, 133, 142, 206–07, 279, 288–89, 328, 356, 386–88, 397, 428, 436, 437, 438, 439, 440, 441
GELBART, Larry	290, 294		
GELLER, Herb	165		
GENTILE, Al	62, 64, 110, 151, 154, 156, 158–60, 162, 170, 173, 187, 419, 441, 442		
GENTRY, Chuck	312	GOODMAN, Fred	43
GERSHWIN, George	87, 91–92	GOODWIN, Bill	74
GETZ, Stan	99, 157, 221, 439	GOODWIN, Henry	101
GIACCO, Mike	159, 173	GORDON, Al	12–13
GIACCO, Sal (?)	63	GORDON, Bobby	314, 394, 406, 452
GIBBS, Georgia	138	GORDON, Dexter	438
GIBBS, Terry	436	GORDON, Jim	xv, 331
GIBELING, Howard	111, 139	GORDON, Justin	289
GIBSON, Banu	xv, 413–14, 420, 443	GORDON, Max	107
GIBSON, Dick	258	GORME, Edie	114
GIBSON, Steve and the Redcaps	218	GORMLEY, Hap	236
GIEST, Monty	128	GORMLEY, Paul	383, 386
GIFFORD, Lee	112, 170	GOULD, Chuck	168
GIFFORD, Walt	155, 451	GOWANS, Brad	18, 25–31, 33, 38–42, 44–45, 53, 56, 63, 74, 93, 96–97, 148–49, 247, 427
GILBERT, Ed	231		
GILLESPIE, Dizzy	89, 128, 189, 191, 231, 239–40, 439, 451		
		GOZZO, Conrad	11, 241, 251
GIOBBE, Felix	97, 158	GRADY, Eddie	207, 273
GIRARD, Adele	157, 184, 267	GRAHAM, Eddie	408
GITLER, Ira	268	GRANZ, Norman	133
GITLIN, Irving	143	GRAUSO, Joe	96, 98, 108
GIUFFRE, Jimmy	201	GRAVES, Joe	375
GIUFFRIDA, John	62, 64, 90, 125–26, 131, 137, 151, 153–54, 162, 164, 186–87, 192, 193, 200–02	GRAVINE, Mickey	349
		GRAY, Glen	7, 44–45, 114, 221
		GRAY, Jerry	439
GLASEL, Johnny	107, 141, 158, 184–85, 201, 208, 213, 218, 236, 398, 426, 446, 456, 463	GRAY, Phil	257
		GRAY, Wardell	221
		GREAT PACIFIC JAZZ BAND, The	376, 392, 395–97, 410–11, 440
GLASER, Joe	67, 71, 72, 76, 78–79, 82–85, 133, 201, 229		
		GRECO, Buddy	134
GLASS, Manny	291	GRECO, Ken	345, 358
GLEASON, Jackie	136, 149, 175	GREEN, Byrdie	237
GLEASON, Ralph	75	GREEN, Dave	370
GLENN, Tyree	117, 131, 142, 148, 153, 160, 163, 174, 199, 453	GREEN, Harry	118, 131, 139
		GREEN, Jack	58, 142
GOBEL, George	374	GREEN, Johnny	7, 270
GODFREY, Arthur	146, 184	GREEN, Urbie	58, 142, 146–47, 157, 184, 343, 398
GODFREY, Murray (Gottfried)	62, 441		
GODLIS, Al	208	GREENBACH, Harry	75
GOLD, Sanford	99, 101	GREENE, Milt	165
GOLDEN, Lex	260, 443	GREENER, Dorothy	165–66
GOLDIE, Don	214	GREENLEAF, Fred	451
GOLDKETTE, Jean	69–72, 441	GREER, Sonny	132

GRENADA, Jim	441
GREY, Joel	165–66
GRIFFIN, Chris	138, 395
GRIFFIN, John	9
GRIFFIN, (Merv?)	287
GRIFFITH, Andy	284, 292, 338
GROSS, Walter	47
GROSZ, Marty	219, 379, 388, 394, 406
GUARNIERI, Johnny	69, 248–49, 268, 272, 314, 331, 343, 375, 426
GUBIN, Sol	349
GUMBINER, Jack	313
GUSSAK, Billy	215
GWALTNEY, Tommy	xv, 177, 178, 179, 180, 181, 189, 194, 439
HACKENBERG, Friedrich	xv, 305
HACKETT, Bobby	xi, xii, 16–19, 25, 29, 33–34, 39, 42, 45, 48, 63–64, 67–68, 85, 88, 90, 92, 97–100, 105, 115, 118, 125–26, 146, 149, 157, 175, 177, 178, 179, 180, 181–87, 189–92, 193–95, 199–200, 202, 206, 210, 217, 222, 229, 237, 274–75, 308–09, 314, 322, 382, 398, 426, 429, 431, 435, 437, 442, 444–46, 454–56, 463
HADEN, Charlie	216
HADLOCK, Dick	118
HADNOTT, Bill	238, 271, 352
HAESLER, Bill	318
HAFER, Dick	189–90, 192, 194, 208, 311–12, 315, 329–33, 352–53, 358, 360–61, 372, 378, 380, 382–83, 385, 398, 402, 417, 437, 455
HAGAN, Earle	276
HAGGART, Bob	45, 57, 67, 68, 119–20, 138, 236, 277–78, 311–12, 317, 328–30, 332, 348, 371–72, 374, 379, 384–86, 388, 406
HÄGGLÖF, Gösta	xv, 78, 389, 393, 413, 461
HAIG, Al	113, 431
HAINES, Connie	337, 340, 343
HALE, Teddy	98
HALL, Al	146, 174, 181, 185, 202–03, 205, 211, 215, 267, 447
HALL, Dan	232
HALL, Ed	31, 66, 89–90, 112, 120, 122, 128, 130, 134, 148–49, 156, 158, 215, 260, 362, 451, 454–55, 463
HALL, Herbie	206, 211
HALL, Joe	44
HALLETT, Mal	7
HALPERT, Bernie	235

HAMBRO, Lennie	133
HAMID, George	69–70
HAMILTON, Dick	369, 377–78, 380, 405, 412–13, 417–18, 420–21, 437
HAMILTON, Scott	379, 388, 431
HAMMICK, Valda	365
HAMMOND, John (writer)	9–10, 94, 124, 133, 212
HAMMOND, John (pianist)	172, 369, 397, 407
HAMPTON, Lionel	50, 72, 74
HANDEL, George Frideric	5
HANDY, George	32, 70
HANGOVER JAZZ BAND, The	372
HANLEY, Peter	xv
HANLON, Allan	117, 202, 209
HANNA, Jake	272, 313, 379
HANNAN, Tony	177, 178
HARALAMBOS, Tom	413
HARDAWAY, Bob	383
HARDEN, Ralph	262
HARMON, Charles	135, 138, 147, 152, 157, 159, 199, 207, 280
HARPER, ----	227
HARPER, Herbie	248, 254, 268, 271–74, 277, 281–83, 287–88, 292, 294, 299–300, 311–12, 314–15, 330, 332, 339–40, 359, 383, 400–01
HARRINGTON, Bob	54, 62, 107
HARRINGTON, Terry	286–88, 292, 294, 300, 315, 331, 400–01, 405, 420, 437
HARRIS, Albert	87, 347–48
HARRIS, Bill	63, 88, 124, 130
HARRIS, Chiz	352
HARRIS, Maury	290
HARRIS, Phil	257, 262, 264, 289, 311, 313, 374, 383, 386
HARRISON, Max	68, 169, 457
HART, Lorenz	450
HART, Mike	xv, 371
HARTE, Roy	264
HARTFORD, Huntington	165–69
HARTFORD SYMPHONY	4, 439
HASSO, Signe	126
HASTINGS, Lennie	325, 326
HAVENS, Bob	240, 249, 252, 254–55, 258, 263, 267, 272–73, 275, 281, 284, 286–88, 290, 293, 331, 333, 337–38, 340, 346–47, 354, 360–61, 367, 374, 376, 378–79, 382, 384, 385–87, 394–95, 401, 408, 410, 411, 437, 443, 459
HAWES, Hampton	168
HAWES, Pat	325, 326
HAWK, Ken	207
HAWKINS, Coleman	19, 153, 163, 170, 174–75, 188–90, 196, 197

HAWKINS, Dolores	142	HODGES, Earl	129
HAYES, Bill	406	HODGES, Johnny	148, 428, 430–32
HAYES, Buddy	240–41, 249	HOEFER, George	75
HAYES, Edgar	260	HOFFMAN, Dick	128
HAYES, Fowler	38	HOFFMANN, Franz	xv
HAYES, Gertie	17	HOGAN, Ben	187
HAYES, Joe	242	HOGAN, Claire	106, 111
HAYES, Mileham	318–20	HOGG, Derek	326
HAYES, Richard	129	HOHMAN, Jack	400
HAYMES, Joe	397, 440	HOLGATE, Dick	255, 338, 344, 353, 366, 369, 374, 378, 382, 399, 402–03, 438
HAYTON, Lennie	158		
HAZELDINE, Mike	xvii		
HEARD, J.C.	208–09	HOLIDAY, Billie	91, 111, 202, 389
HEARD, John	352, 360	HOLLOWAY, Stirling	252
HEBERT, Paul	226, 232, 235	HOLLYWOOD BOWL SYMPHONY	414, 420
HEDGES, Chuck	374, 408, 409	HOLMAN, Bill	440
HEFTI, Neal	139, 285, 343	HOLMES, Wally	241, 382, 406
HEIDER, Wally	351	HOLZFEIND, Frank	92
HEINDORF, Ray	270	HONEY, Dean	254
HENDERSON, Fletcher	11, 203–04, 387, 428, 455	HONEYWELL, Jack	207
HENDRICKSON, Al	290, 294, 299, 314, 340, 345, 350	HOOD, Bill	260
		HOOKER, John Lee	316
HENREID, Paul	329	HOPE, Bob	58, 249, 262
HENRY, Art	216, 219	HORNE, Lena	158
HENRY, Hank	235	HORRINGTON, Frank	23
HENRY, Haywood	153	HOWARD, Darnell	130
HERBERT, Arthur	170	HOWARD, Dave	276, 278, 294, 327
HERFURT, Skeets	378	HOWARD, Joe	270, 294, 299
HERMAN, Woody	9, 11, 14, 33, 42, 72, 91, 93, 97, 132, 156, 165, 437, 438, 441, 442	HOWARD, Mary Lou	34
		HOWELL, Beatrice	118
		HOYT, Charlie	62, 186
HERRON, Ken	320	HUBBELL, Paul	236
HERWIG, Lou	261	HUBBLE, Ed	96–97, 100, 102, 118, 122, 133, 136, 141, 144, 155, 158, 161–62, 170–71, 187, 199, 203, 206, 278, 406
HESSION, Jim	374		
HESSION, Martha	374		
HESTER, Stan	xv, 229		
HESTER, Steve	xv, 229	HUCKO, Peanuts	63–64, 67, 68, 69, 88, 98, 103–06, 108, 110, 119, 122, 124–25, 133–34, 150, 156, 162–64, 172, 197, 201, 236–37, 271, 273–74, 277, 279, 281, 283, 287, 289, 306, 308, 313–14, 328–30, 340, 344, 348, 352, 356, 358–59, 361, 364, 366–68, 374, 378, 384, 442, 443, 454
HETHERINGTON, Ron	363		
HICKOX, Barker	332		
HIGGINBOTHAM, Carl	186		
HIGGINBOTHAM, J.C.	63, 103, 170		
HIGGINS, ————	227		
HIGGINS, Billy	323		
HIGGINS, Bob	227, 249, 255, 256, 382, 407		
HIGH SIERRA JAZZ BAND, The	349		
HILBERT, Robert (Bob)	213, 247	HUDD, Roy	363
HILL, Bill	314–15, 333, 443	HUDSON, George	103
HILL, Chippie	88	HUGHART, Jim (or Ted)	354, 369
HINDEMITH, Paul	96, 135	HULME, George	xv, 99, 181–82, 194
HINES, Earl	7, 80–81, 83–85, 362	HUMPHREYS, Conn	44
HINTON, Milt	142, 148, 156, 162–63, 171, 175, 181, 197, 236, 271, 313	HUNSTEIN, Don	197
		HUNT, Pee Wee	118, 188
HIRT, Al	354, 374, 437	HUNTER, Lurlean	168
HOAGLAND, Everett	15	HUPFER, Nick	9
HOCKETT, Ron	457	HURD, Danny	140
HODES, Art	27, 33, 42, 54, 66, 101, 104	HUSTON, John	66

HUTCHENRIDER, Clarence	44	JONES, Jo	132, 157–58, 174, 186, 188, 205, 212–13, 215
HUTCHINSON, Ralph	130	JONES, Jonah	141, 157, 174, 191
HUTTON, Ina Ray	105, 233	JONES, Max	61
HYMAN, Dick	96, 104, 164, 375, 379, 388, 426	JONES, Quincy	142
		JONES, Sam	323
IADONE, Joe	135	JONES, Spike	48
ILLE, Marty	118	JONES, Tom	347
IND, Peter	207, 361	JORDAN, Al	257
INGERSOLL, Carol	101–02	JORDAN, Frank	344
INGHAM, Keith	323, 326, 394	JOSEPH, Don	70
INGLE, Doug	255	JOUARD, Paul	135, 138, 147, 152, 159, 168
INZINTARE, Pat	32		
IRVIN, Ward (probably ERWIN, Ward)	247	JOY, Teal	105
IVES, Red	13	JUIEZ, ————	387
JACKSON, Chubby	88, 214	KAATEE, Fritz	310
JACKSON, Cliff	33, 64	KAMINSKY, Max	19, 31, 34, 48, 53, 55, 57, 63–64, 88, 90, 95, 105, 112–13, 117–20, 125–26, 131–33, 136–37, 139, 141, 144–45, 147, 149–51, 153, 155–56, 158, 160–62, 170–72, 174–75, 185–86, 199–205, 211–13, 215, 217–19, 229, 236, 261, 308, 432, 444–46, 452–53, 457
JACKSON, Franz	50		
JACKSON, Milt	99, 133		
JACOBSEN, Gunnar	xv, 145, 216, 232		
JACQUET, Illinois	95		
JAMES, Harry	231, 234, 366–68, 372, 375, 381, 385, 431, 437, 438, 440		
JANIS, Conrad	xv, 162–63, 165–68, 170–72, 217, 383		
JAZZBERRY JAM	300	KANIN, Garson	105
JAZZBIRDS, The	439	KAPLAN, Alan	402
JAZZ MINORS, The	300, 372	KASHER, Del	370
JEAN, George	44	KASPAROFF, ————	413
JEFFRIES, Herb	13, 365, 438	KAUDER, Roland	305
JEFFRIES, Norm	311	KAWAI, Jyunichi	245
JENKINS, Al	227, 261, 290, 313, 328, 333, 351	KAYE, Carole	42–43
		KAYE, Danny	43, 72, 74, 366
JENNEY, Bob	185	KEECEY, Dr. John C.	412
JENSEN, John	349, 357	KEFAUVER, Estes	115
JENSEN, Kenny	235	KELLAWAY, Roger	307, 329
JEROME, Jerry	23, 45, 105, 112–17, 119–20, 124, 138, 142, 151, 156, 158, 160–61, 163, 200–03, 205, 209, 451	KELLEY, Peck	59
		KELLSO, Jon–Erik	408, 409
		KELLY, Pete	436
		KELLY, Wynton	195
JESSOP, David Marsh	xv	KENNEDY, Bob	156, 161
JOHN, Kenny	126, 127, 142	KENNEDY, John F.	232
JOHNS, Al	18, 441	KENNET, Earl	142
JOHNSON, Arthur	102	KENNEY, Sister	113
JOHNSON, Bunk	72	KENTON, Stan	72, 84, 118, 133, 168, 253, 283, 289, 438
JOHNSON, Frank	320		
JOHNSON, Gus	236, 312, 330, 356	KERR, Deborah	365
JOHNSON, James P.	48, 50, 63–64, 88, 163, 375, 433	KERSEY, Ken	162
		KERSHAW, Reverend	180
JOHNSON, Jimmy	17, 41, 69, 94, 132–33	KESSEL, Barney	56, 281, 283
JOHNSON, J.J.	111	KESSLER, Jerry	394
JOHNSON, Osie	200, 206	KEYES, Stan	374
JOHNSON, Tommy	254, 289–90, 358	KIFFE, Karl	155, 157–58
JOHNSTON, Freddy	13, 16	KIMMICK, Bob	232
JONES, Isham	9, 14	KINCAIDE, Deane	23, 128–29, 131, 237, 268, 271–74
JONES, Jimmy	200, 213, 261, 447		

KINCH, Don	264	LAMB, John	408
KING, B.B.	339, 347	LAMOND, Don	119, 124
KING, Jerry	238, 240–41	LANCERS, The	275
KING, Tom	343, 358	LANDERS, Muriel	165
KING Sisters, The	337	LANE, Francis	102
KINGS OF DIXIELAND, The	457	LANE, Johnny	283, 286–87, 290–91, 298, 314–16, 328–29, 333, 340, 349
KIPP, Jerry	227		
KIRBY, George	373		
KIRKPATRICK, Don	158	LANE, Ken	268
KITZMELLER, John	314	LANE, Lucille	268, 271
KLAVER, Hans-Georg	305	LANG, Eddie	69
KLEE, Harry	289	LANG, Irving	174, 186, 188, 208–09
KLEIN, Bernie	237	LANGLOIS, Jack	234, 299
KLEIN, John	240, 249	LANIN, Lester	157, 160, 162, 174, 204, 208–09
KLEIN, Manny	299, 343, 351		
KLEIN, Russ	240	LANNING, Lynn	xvii
KLIEVERT, Anna Leas	124	LaPORTA, John	141
KLINK, Al	40, 104, 133, 164, 371	LARKIN, Don	259
KLUGER, Irving	69	LARKIN, Lura	259
KNAPP, John	349	LARKINS, Ellis	172
KNAUER, Wolfram	xv	LA ROCCA, Nick	229
KNOPF, Alfred A.	xvi	LASALLE, Sid	346, 370
KNOX, Bertil	213	LASELL, Dr. ----	330
KOCH, Merle	387	LASKY, Al	255
KÖLBL, Peter	305–06	LAUDERMAN, Paul	62, 441
KONITZ, Lee	148, 189	LAUREL & HARDY	366
KOONSE, Dave	378, 380, 385–86, 389, 404, 405, 412–13, 417, 420, 438	LAVELLE, Rich	268
		LaVERE, Charlie	272, 287
KOONSE, Larry	383, 438	LAWLESS, Ed	256, 269
KORDA, Murray	292, 300	LAWRENCE, Baby	91
KORN KOBBLERS, The	136	LAWRENCE, Elliott	132
KOSTELANETZ, André	11	LAWRENCE, Steve	114
KOSTER, Howard	253	LAWSON, Bob	275, 283, 294, 338
KRAKOWSKA, Ilick	441	LAWSON, Don	299
KRAL, Irene	283	LAWSON, Yank	25, 128, 138, 277–78, 311–12, 317, 328–30, 332, 371, 406
KRAUS, Phil	117, 202, 206		
KREISLER, Fritz	306		
KRESS, Carl	34, 108–09	LAYLAN, Rollo	14
KRISTOFFERSON, Kris	366	LAYTON, Teddy	323
KRUM, Roger	xv	LAZAR, Jack	445, 449
KRUPA, Gene	19, 91, 98, 205, 442	LEA, Barbara	153, 171–75, 184, 205, 406, 412, 416, 455
KURNIK, John	407		
KWARSCYK, Illick	100	LEAHY, Joe	296
KYLE, Billy	142	LEATHERWOOD, Ray	xviii, 241–42, 248, 250, 257, 261–62, 268, 270, 272–79, 281–290, 292–95, 297–300, 311–17, 321, 327–30, 332–33, 337–41, 344–47, 349, 351–54, 357–61, 365, 367, 369–70, 372, 374, 377–78, 381–82, 387, 388, 400–03, 420, 438
LABELLA, Louis	138		
LACEY, Steve	141, 144, 155, 158		
LACY, Mike	353		
LADLEY, Bill	129		
LaFARGE, Jacques	442		
LAFATA, Eddie	333		
LAIS, John	232		
LAKER, Freddy	361	LEE, Peggy	436
LAMARE, Nappy	29, 72, 231, 234, 249, 256, 257, 268, 273, 280, 283, 289, 291–92, 294, 300, 312, 327–28, 338–39, 344–45, 361, 370	LEE, Sammy	260, 342
		LEEMAN, Cliff	26, 70, 126, 133–34, 136, 147, 157, 162–64, 172, 197, 211, 213, 215, 217, 231, 236, 245, 267, 271, 279, 311, 430, 432

LEGARE, Pete	249
LEGENDS OF JAZZ	428
LEIGHTON, Bernie	191
LEMON, Brian	325
LENER, Werner	307
LEON, Harvey	206
LEON, Ruben	289, 292
LEONARD, Eddie	130
LEONARD, Nellie Mae	136, 448
LESBINES, Tele	135
LESBERG, Jack	57, 64, 69, 99, 104, 119, 128, 133, 136, 155, 162–63, 170, 172, 205–08, 213, 215, 237, 245, 260, 271, 273, 311–12, 315, 334, 338, 356, 360, 368, 402, 444, 458–59
LESNIAK, ––––	64
LESNIAK POLISH BAND	441
LESTER, Jay	142
LETMAN, Johnny	209–10
LEUKHARDT, Bill	90, 97, 107–08, 118
LEVANG, Neil	240, 249, 254, 401
LEVIN, Dave	211
LEVIN, Floyd	xii, xiv, xv, 11, 91, 157, 226, 277, 316, 341, 378, 395, 399, 417, 462
LEVINE, Abe	22
LEVINE, Bobby	384
LEVINE, Sam	14
LEVY, Lou	17, 88
LEWIS, Buddy	231
LEWIS, George	424, 427
LEWIS, John	439
LEWIS, Mel	388
LIBMAN, David	438
LIDO, Bob	240–41
LIGHT, Enoch	32, 441
LIM, Harry	22, 28, 31, 334, 360, 431
LINCOLN, Abe	239, 249–50, 260–62, 267, 270, 283, 286, 291, 300, 313, 327, 329, 344, 347, 353, 357
LINDSEY, Mort	214
LINKE, Dick	284
LINN, Ray	279, 283, 288, 292, 298, 300, 337, 354, 356–57, 369
LIPKINS, Steve	104
LISTER, Joe	287
LODICE, Charlie	227, 249–50, 254–55, 401
LODICE, Don	247–48, 267
LOESSER Music, Frank	196
LOFTHOUSE, Pete	289
LOGAR, Frank	253
LOLATTE, Bill	109
LOMBARDI, Clyde	200, 202
LOMBARDO, Guy	134, 151, 264, 442
LONDON, Julie	438
LONG, Benny	208, 210–11
LONG, Slats	40
LOOKOFSKY, Harry	124–25, 130, 132, 136, 142(?), 161, 442, 445
LORD, Dick	201
LOUISIANA SHAKERS	342
LOVE, Carol	443
LOWE, Mundell	164
LOWELL, Buddy	236
LOWEY, Hal	65
LOY, Myrna	329
LUCAS, Al	45, 209
LUCAS, Johnny	168, 262, 300
LUCAS, Nick	292
LUCRAFT, Howard	314–15, 351
LUDWIN, ––––	408
LUNCEFORD, Jimmy	11, 47
LUND, Art	141
LUTCHER, Nellie	73
LYNCH, Reul	228
LYONS, Art	73, 248, 254, 268, 298, 317, 329, 340, 343–44, 352, 432
LYTELL, Jimmy	36
LYTTELTON, Humphrey	370
MACBETH, Carlton	268, 274
MACDOWELL, Edward	5
MACHITO	211
MACPHERSON, Dr. William	264, 266
MADISON, Rick	399
MADONNA	436
MAGERIAN(?), Leon	69
MAGGIO Music Press	444–47
MAGYAR, ––––	210–11
MAIDEN VOYAGE	439
MAINE, Kathie	292
MAKOWICZ, Adam	438
MALIN, Lou	291
MALTBY, Richard	263, 266
MALTZ, Bob	119, 122
MALVIN, Art	214
MANGANO, Silvana	137
MANNE, Shelly	85, 88, 168, 196, 267, 270, 338, 437
MANNING, Irene	124, 442
MANNING, Irving	88, 96, 98–99, 129, 160
MANONE, Wingy	74, 134, 263, 313, 450
MARABLE, Fate	88
MARAGO, Chief Jay	219
MARCHAND, Gene	154
MARETTI, Terry	313
MARGOLIS, Sam	161
MARGULIS, Charles	23, 441
MARIE, Rose	440
MARINO, Don	64, 121, 158, 207, 432
MARINO, Joe	340
MARIO ___ NATIONAL GUARD BAND	441
MARKS, Edward B.	170, 195–96, 229, 237, 444–47, 449

MARKS, Herbert 170–71
MAROCCO, Frank (sometimes Morocco) 257, 270, 285, 332–33, 356–58
MARQUETTE, Pee Wee 369
MARSALA, Joe 17, 34, 36, 49, 56, 63–64, 98, 136, 157, 185, 267, 406, 441, 450, 456
MARSALA, Marty 19, 25
MARSH, Warne 189, 290, 440
MARSHALL, Pat 290, 294–95
MARTIN, Arizona Cliff 114, 120
MARTIN, Freddy 95, 279, 439
MARTIN, Gale 400
MARTIN, Henry 90
MARTIN, Ray 210
MARTIN, Steve 348
MARTINEZ, Bonnie 418
MARTINEZ, George 226, 418
MARTYN, Barry xv, 80, 291, 316–17, 341–42
MARVIN, Lee 276
MARX Brothers 366
MARX, Chico 32
MARX, Groucho 332, 366
MASSO, George 311–12, 328–30, 371
MASTERS, Mark 440
MASTERS, Robert 323
MASTREN, Carmen 34–35, 134
MATARESE, Roc 88
MATLOCK, Matty 72, 74, 168, 227, 231, 234, 247–48, 255, 257–58, 259, 262, 264, 267–68, 270–71, 273, 275–76, 278, 294, 300, 344, 436, 457–58
MATTUCCI, Al 164
MATTUCCI, Dan 236
MAUCERI, John 414, 420
MAUDLIN, Jules 441
MAURO, Lou 409
MAURO, Ernie 137
MAXTED, Billy 25, 41, 103, 117, 119, 126, 127
MAXWELL, Jimmy 368
MAY, Billy 436, 438
MAY, Cliff 276, 287, 311, 340, 361
MAYNES, Frank 109
MAYO, Virginia 74
MAYORCA, Lincoln 437
McAMISH, Chas 70
McCALL, Mary Ann 348
McCARTHY, Joe 146, 289
McCLURE, Jack 286–87
McCOY, Clyde 278
McCORMICK, Dick 327, 351, 369
McCRACKEN, Bob 192, 193, 234, 242, 244, 249–52, 256, 260
McCULLUM, John 323
McDANIEL, Ernie 359

McDOUGALD, Roz 400
McEACHERN, Murray 235, 240–41, 272, 442
McGARITY, Lou 33, 43, 49, 72, 122, 133, 135–36, 154, 156, 172, 205, 207, 212–16, 237, 271, 430, 432, 454–57, 463
McGHEE, Howard 133, 168
McGREGOR, Don 219
McHARGUE, Rosy 438
McINTYRE, Mark 258
McKAY, Haifer 231
McKAY, Stu 118, 124, 442
McKAY, Ted 44–45
McKENNA, Dave 153, 209–10, 216–17, 236, 379, 424, 427, 431, 432, 457
McKENZIE, Charles 330
McKENZIE, Jerry 294, 299, 312, 340, 344, 370, 372, 383, 402–03, 406, 413, 438
McKENZIE, Red 49
McKINLEY, Ray 30, 32, 86, 110, 128, 150, 436, 441
McKORMICK, Dick 271
McKUSICK, Hal 132
McLEAN, Don 125
McLEAN, Ron 145
McMAHON, John xv
McMAHON, Mick 400
McMANUS, Al 215
McNAB, Malcolm 359
McPARTLAND, Jimmy 124, 128, 131–33, 142, 145–46, 158–59, 162–65, 169–71, 173–75, 180, 187–88, 190, 195–96, 197, 199, 201–03, 205, 211, 214–15, 217, 222, 224–25, 229, 237, 267, 302–10, 425, 426, 439, 442, 444–47, 449, 451–54, 459–60, 462–63
McPARTLAND, Marian (nee Margaret Turner; aka Marian Page) 147, 163–65, 169, 180, 183, 236, 262, 301, 310, 442, 453
McRAE, Carmen 164
McREYNOLDS, Mac 283–84, 288, 290, 294, 298, 314, 374, 379–83, 385, 402, 443, 461
McREYNOLDS, Margaret Jean 380
McRITCHIE, Greig 353
MEISSNER, Zep 253
MEISTER, Fred 383
MELHARDT, Axel xv, 303
MELINSKY, Dorothy 328
MENCKEN, H.L. 405
MERCER, Johnny 73–74, 126, 156, 216
METTOME, Doug 208
METZGER, Erich 306

MEVS, Janet (see CARY, Janet)			204–05, 209, 236, 361, 364
MEYER, Edward	217	MOORE, Freddie	106, 137, 214
MEZZROW, Mezz	117	MOORE, Garon	36
MICKMAN, Herb	292, 346, 348, 378, 380, 382, 385, 387, 405–06, 417, 420, 438	MOORE, Phil	72, 74
		MORELLO, Joe	163, 165, 171
		MORENO, Joe	329
MIDDLETON, Velma	73, 75, 133	MORGAN, Al	247–48
MIGLIORI, Francis	63	MORGENSTERN, Dan	458
MIHELICH, Ed	311, 356	MOROCCO, Frank (see Marocco)	
MILAN COLLEGE JAZZ SOCIETY	302, 306, 321, 460	MORRIS, Dolph	383
		MORRIS, Philip	142, 156
MILES, Billy	253	MORROW, Buddy	439
MILLER, Cassie	413, 443	MORROW, Liza	92, 283
MILLER, Eddie	xi, 231, 233, 247–48, 251–52, 255, 257–60, 272–73, 317, 321, 327–30, 332–34, 337–40, 344–45, 347, 350–54, 357–59, 361, 365–67, 369–70, 372, 374, 378–79, 381–82, 384–85, 387–88, 401, 424, 428, 438, 450, 458–59	MORTON, Benny	36, 93, 97, 154, 203
		MORTON, Jelly Roll	460
		MOSS, Leonard	350
		MOST, Abe	268, 276–77, 279, 281–85, 287–88, 292–95, 298–99, 311–15, 317, 327–32, 337–41, 343–53, 356–61, 365, 369–70, 372, 374, 378–79, 383, 385–88, 395, 399, 401, 403, 406–07, 416–17, 420, 438, 443
MILLER, Glenn	13, 40, 46, 128, 279, 288–89, 369, 440		
MILLER, Richard	xiv	MOST, Sam	279, 331, 358, 378, 386, 388, 406
MILLINDER, Lucky	69		
MILLS BROTHERS, The	6, 440	MOSTEL, Zero	91
MINCE, Johnny	271, 343, 371, 388	MOZART, Wolfgang Amadeus	102, 424
MINGUS, Charlie	120, 157–58, 205, 250, 437	MUCCI, Louis	104, 236
MINTZ, ----	412	MÜCKENBERGER, Dr. Heiner	xv, 76–77
MIRANDA, Eddie	62	MUDVILLE'S FINEST	343, 348
MITCHELL, Bill	252–54	MUELLER, Peter	342
MITCHELL, Dixie	238, 253–54, 274	MULLIGAN, Gerry	99, 157, 184, 209, 250, 436, 437, 452, 456
MITCHELL, Elaine	327, 331, 365		
MITCHELL, Gordon	238, 252–54, 262, 271, 274, 293, 313, 315, 327, 331, 339	MULLIGAN, Mary	213
		MULLINS, Diz	406
		MUNI, Paul	174
MITCHELL, Guy	115	MUNSTER, Jost	xv, 321
MITCHELL, Lennie	235	MURANYI, Joe	311, 452
MITCHELL, Ollie	241, 263	MURPHY, Earl	24–25
MITCHELL, Red	99	MURPHY, Jack	349
MITCHELL, Whitey	209	MURPHY, Jerry	384
MODERNAIRES, The	317, 391	MURPHY, Marge	311, 331, 333
MODERN BRASS QUINTET	351	MURPHY, Red	257
MOLE, Miff	25, 64, 89, 92, 155, 159, 203, 261	MURPHY, Turk	161, 245, 329, 427
		MURRAY, Max	259, 274, 284, 287, 327
MOLINELLI, Larry	14	MURRAY, Pete	363
MONDELLO, Toots	54	MUSSO, Vido	9
MONK, Thelonious	89, 157, 179, 189, 212, 216, 250	MUZZILLO, Ralph	23
		MYERSON, Charlie	271, 314–15, 327, 333, 346, 354, 365, 370, 401–03
MONROE, Vaughn	114		
MONSBOURGH, Ade	319–20		
MONTE, Pee Wee	234, 366	NAPOLEON, Joe	441
MONTGOMERY, Wes	439	NAPOLEON, Marty	50, 210
MOONEY, Art	15–16, 120, 441, 442	NAPOLEON, Phil	103, 126, 127, 163
MOONEY, Joe	63	NAPOLEON, Teddy	205
MOORE, "Big Chief" Russell	112, 124, 145, 157–58, 160, 174–75, 186, 188,	NATHAN, David	xv
		NBC Orchestra	436, 439, 440

585

NEIDLINGER, Buell	62, 162, 188		311, 315–16, 321, 330–33, 337–40, 344–46, 348–53, 358–61, 365, 369–70, 372, 378, 379, 380, 383–85, 388–90, 395, 399, 402–03, 405, 407–08, 413, 415, 417–18, 421, 439, 440, 442
NELSON, Don	408		
NELSON, Gene	118		
NELSON, Nancy	394		
NELSON, Rick "Cougar"	211, 346, 349		
NENTWIG, Dieter	xv, 303–04, 308		
NEPUS, Ira	273–74		
NEUMANN, Roger	287, 354, 383, 402, 417, 436, 438, 440	O'HARA, John	34
		OHMS, Freddie	162, 164
NEW ANGEL CITY JAZZ BAND, The	383	OLAY, Ruth	356
NEWBORN, Calvin	173	OLD MERRY TALE JAZZBAND	321–22, 460
NEWBORN, Phineas	173, 176, 264, 325, 427, 433, 461	OLDS, Merl	296–97, 352, 358
		OLIVELLA, Phil	103, 142, 155, 157, 160, 162, 174, 186, 188, 199, 208–09, 215, 217
NEWLEY, Anthony	258		
NEWMAN, Bill	262		
NEWMAN, Eddie	120	OLIVER, John	367
NEWPORT YOUTH BAND	212, 438	OLIVER, Myrna	416
NEWSOM, Tommy	294, 312, 314–15, 348–49, 352, 358, 360, 369–70, 378, 383, 397, 403, 405, 407, 414–15, 417, 420, 433, 438–39	OLIVER, Sy	47, 459
		OLTON, Irv	20–21
		OLTON, Whitey	20
		OMERON, Gweneth	88
		O'NEIL, Betty	442
NEWTON, J. (see PERRY, J. Newton)		O'NEILL, Tom	145
NEWTON, Frankie	64	OPPENHEIMER, Irving	102–03
NICHOLAS, Albert	54, 66, 131–32	ORCHARD, Frank	23, 31, 64, 99, 108, 122, 131–32, 136–37, 144, 147, 150–51, 441
NICHOLS, Bobby	78		
NICHOLS, Herb	209		
NICHOLS, Red	228–32, 442	ORENA, Charlie	405
NICHOLS, Roger	273	ORENDORFF, George	253
NICK, Al	147, 152	ORIGINAL DIXIELAND JAZZ BAND	29, 42
NIGHT BLOOMING JAZZMEN, The	349, 354	ORLINO, Eddie	201
NIXON, Richard	232, 267, 289	ORY, Kid	66, 74, 251, 424, 427, 428
NOBES, Roger	325	OSBORNE, Mary	107, 120, 395
NOONE, Jimmie	40, 290	OSBORNE, Will	41, 441
NORMAN, Bill	262	OSBOURNE, Ralph	400
NORMAN, Louie	290	OSTMAN, Ray	16–17
NORMAN, Milt	231	OSTROW, Stu	196
NORVO, Red	21, 112, 115, 120, 135, 314, 343, 361, 362, 436, 438	OVERTON, Hall	143, 156–57, 173, 184, 193, 195, 201, 212, 229, 264, 398
OAKIE, Jack	9	OWENS, Don	168, 250, 327–28
O'BRIEN, Jack	8, 16, 19, 24, 39, 59, 113, 391	OWENS, John	44
O'CONNELL, Helen	240, 440		
O'CONNOR, Donald	150	PAGE, Bill	260, 262, 443
O'CONNOR, Pat	111	PAGE, Hot Lips	19, 36, 63–64, 88, 90–91, 95–97, 101, 112, 118, 122, 124, 137, 442
O'DAY, Anita	438		
ODERS, Lennie	16		
O'FARRILL, Chico	94	PAGE, Marian (see McPARTLAND, Marian)	
OGAWA, Masao	245	PAGE, Walter	130, 134, 148, 164, 174, 430
OGLE, Red	44		
O'HARA, Barrett	xiii, xv, 231–32, 254, 333, 338, 340, 359, 361, 369–70, 402–03, 405, 414, 420, 439	PAICH, Marty	437
		PALEY, Charles	23, 441
		PALMER, Earl	250
O'HARA, Betty (nee Peterson)	xiii, xv, 62, 107, 126, 151, 154, 231–32, 235, 237, 239–41, 258, 266, 273, 275–77, 279–82, 286, 288, 291–92, 294–95, 298, 300,	PALMER, Jack	108, 442
		PALMIERI, Remo	313, 362
		PANASSIE, Hugues	83–84
		PANTO, Norman	359
		PARENT, Bob	192, 193

PARENTI, Tony	26, 57, 87–90, 93, 97, 101, 103–06, 170, 172, 175, 214, 229		PIOUS, Min	34
			PIZZARELLI, Bucky	271, 332, 394
			PLAYHOUSE Music Company	446–47
PARHAM, Truck	130		PLONSKY, Johnny	161, 184
PARIS, Norman	210		PLUNKETT, Brad	262
PARITO, Nick	112, 114, 147–48, 236		PODEWELL, Polly	227(?), 228(?), 388
PARKER, Charlie	89, 99, 105, 124, 155, 221, 436, 451		POE, David	349
			POLCER, Ed	379, 387, 388
PARKINS, Sam	208, 210		POLIFRANI, Fran	227
PARNELL, Rich	283		POLK, Lucy Ann	329, 443
PARRISH, Ben	126, 127		POLLACK, Ben	32–33, 239–40, 250, 255, 263, 436
PASHERT, Ted	133			
PASS, Joe	402		POOLE, Carl	23
PASTOR, Tony	183, 437, 442		POPILARDO, ----	292
PATRUNO, Lino	xv, 302, 306, 321, 322, 460		PORTER, Cole	413, 425
PAUL, Jad	238–39		PORTER, Jake	225, 341–42, 352
PAULSON, Art	36		PORTERFIELD, John	138
PAULSON, Bruce	298, 403		POST, Mike	353
PAYNE, Sonny	268		POWELL, Bud	99, 433
PECK, Bob	59–60		POWELL, Glenn	112–13
PEERLESS, Brian	xv		POWELL, Mel	33, 43
PELICO, Nick	72, 238, 286		POWELL, Specs	45, 64
PELIZZI, Pete	101, 108, 120, 442		POWELL, Teddy	447
PEMBERTON, Bill	101, 188, 190		POWER, Tyrone	21, 131
PENA, Ralph	402		PRATT, ----	19
PEPE, Howard	248		PRATT, Jimmy	441
PEPLOWSKI, Ken	394, 406, 439		PRESLEY, Elvis	331, 436
PEPPER, Art	221, 291		PREVIN, Andre	196, 392
PEPPER, Rufus	45		PRICE, Jesse	252
PEPPIE, Hal	254		PRICE, Ray	343
PERELMAN, Sid	34		PRICE, Ruth	235
PERI, Danny	158		PRICE, Sammy	40, 96
PERKINS, Bill	235, 254, 272, 295, 300, 311, 350, 402, 440		PRIESTLEY, Bill	168, 229, 447
			PRIESTLEY, Cricket	168
PERLMAN, Dave	235		PRIMA, Louis	42, 124
PERRY, J. Newton	283–86, 294		PRIMUS, Pearl	91
PERRY, Marilyn	283		PRING, Bobby	271
PERRY, Vince	240, 244, 257, 281		PRINTERS JAZZ BAND, The	302, 305, 321, 335–36
PERSHING, Devon	291			
PERSSON, Bent	389, 462		PRIVEN, Bernie	104
PESCI, Pete	157, 198		PROBERT, George	340, 354
PETERS, Bernadette	348		PROKOFIEV, Serge	417
PETERSON, Betty (see O'HARA, Betty)			PRUDENCE, Brian	363
PETERSON, Bob	133, 141, 145		PRUITT, Carl	200
PETERSON, Charles	36, 441		PUCHARD, Jean	292
PETERSON, Oscar	110, 135		PURNELL, Alton	262–63, 327
PETERSON, John 'Tweet'	13, 62, 107, 154, 419		PURNELL, Keg	151, 153, 155
PETTIFORD, Oscar	142		PURTILL, Moe	155
PHILLIPS, Flip	157, 272, 359		PUSSYFOOT STOMPERS, The	385
PHILLIPS, Harvey	192, 194, 208, 213, 236, 264, 399, 439			
			QUEALEY, Chelsea	35–36, 40–41, 45
PHILLIPS, John	78		QUEEN CITY JAZZ BAND, The	300, 313
PHILLIPS, Lloyd	106		QUEENER, Charlie	24, 27–28, 42, 93, 96, 98, 112, 117–18, 125, 145, 157–58, 186, 199–203, 205
PHILO, Steve	171			
PHYFE, Eddie	92, 96, 98, 118, 139, 141, 143–44, 150, 203, 271			
			QUINN, Anthony	93
PIERCE, Glenn	63		QUINN, Bob	16
PIERCE, Nat	156, 214, 272, 442		QUINN Sisters, The	92, 441

RAE, Johnny	203	RIDDLE, Nelson	288
RAEBURN, Boyd	69, 132	RIEMAN, Al	396
RAFFELL, Don	241, 244, 277, 292, 294, 299, 369	RILEY, Herman	402
RAINEY, Hugh	426	RILEY, Mike	88, 98, 103, 106, 108, 110, 450
RAKSIN, David	270	RILEY, Tom	235
RANCH, Billy	202	RINGLING BROTHERS	239, 276
RANCH, Harry	135	RINGWALD, Bob	291, 328, 337, 344, 381, 392, 395, 406–08, 410, 411
RANDO, Doc	72, 74		
RANEY, Jimmy	143, 184, 209, 215, 229, 398, 426	RINGWALD, Molly	395
		RISEMAN, Jay	19
ROPOLO, Leon	98	RIVER COLLEGE YOUTH BAND	443
RASEY, Uan	263, 294, 338	ROACH, Les	349
RAY, Buddy	240	ROACH, Max	165
RAY, Nat	94, 129–30, 134, 137, 159, 165–66, 172, 177, 181	ROBERTS, Caughey	248
		ROBIN, Jack	34
RAY, Roy	128	ROBIN, Leo	34
RAYE, Don	17	ROBIN, Shelley	92
RAYE, Martha	33	ROBINSON, Edwin Arlington	34
RAYMAN, Morris	41	ROBINSON, Les	279, 287, 292–94, 299, 312, 316, 329, 338, 340, 365, 385, 388
RAYNO, Don	125		
REDDIE, Bill	433		
REDFORD, Robert	288	ROBISON, Willard	189, 407, 412, 420
RED HOT PODS, The	335	RODBY, John	359
REED, Nancy	115	RODGERS, Richard	450
REHAK, Frank	137, 207, 212–13	RODMAN, Sigi	262
REICHENBACH, Bill	352, 403	RODNEY, Red	88, 105
REID, Bill	112, 119	ROGERS, Buddy	353
REID, Bob	286	ROGERS, Shorty	437
REIMEN, Al	xiv	ROGERS, Will	171, 183
REINBERG, Russ	346, 360	ROLLINS, Sonny	174
REINER, Carl	294, 348	ROLPH, Dick	382
REINHARDT, Bill	23, 31, 78, 169, 378	ROMANO, Tony	58
REINHARDT, Randy	394	ROMERO, Charlie	300
REINHARDT, Ruth	78, 169, 222	ROMOFF, ----	156
REITMEIER, Bob	358, 379, 388, 394	RONGETTI, Nick	25, 30, 33, 40
REMAL, Gary	392	ROOTIN, Roy	255
RENWICK, Bill 'Doc'	348	ROSA, Eddie	23, 353
RESNICK, Ephie	207, 215, 236	ROSE, Billy	117
REUBEN, Ronnie	237	ROSE CITY JAZZ BAND, The	314
REUSS, Allan	9, 282, 289	ROSEN, Jerry	165
REY, Alvino	436	ROSEWALL, Ken	276
REYNOLDS, Debbie	236, 270	ROSIE O'GRADY BAND	343
REYNOLDS, Fred	183, 195	ROSS, Arnold	313–14
REYNOLDS, Tommy	11–12	ROSS, Candy	211
RHODIS, ----	36	ROTELLA, Johnny	257, 352
RIBBLE VALLEY Jazzmen	323	ROTH, Irving	257
RIBBLE, Ben	155	ROUSSEAU, Ernie	63
RIBERA, Johnny	16	ROWAN and MARTIN	258
RICE, Sylvester	327	ROWLES, David	431
RICH, Buddy	19, 98–99, 433, 438	ROWLES, Jimmy	439
RICH, Dave	162	ROWLES, Stacy	439
RICHARDS, ----	159	ROY, Teddy	136, 151, 177
RICHARDS, Joe	16	ROYAL BLUE MELODIANS, The	393, 413, 453
RICHARDS, Red	199	RUBIN, Ron	xv, 326, 363
RICHARDS, Trevor	341	RUBIN, Stan	155, 160, 171–72, 174–75, 442
RICHARDSON, Jerome	200, 287, 292		
RICHMAN, Boomie	119, 214	RUDD, Roswell 'Ros'	215–16

RUFFO, Musky	443		SCHROEDER, Gene	54, 56–57, 63, 87, 96, 101, 104, 117, 122, 130, 132, 137, 146, 148, 170, 197, 202, 206, 211, 215, 454
RUGOLO, Pete	290			
RULE, Amy	xvi			
RUMSEY, Howard	277–78			
RUNYON, Damon	98		SCHROFF, Brodie	249
RUSHING, Jimmy	174, 245–46		SCHULBERG, Budd	252
RUSHTON, Joe	33, 74, 165, 228, 242, 247		SCHUMANN, Robert	102
RUSSELL, Andy	299		SCHWARTZ, Dick	144
RUSSELL, Bertrand	289		SCHWARTZ, Willie	294, 299
RUSSELL, George	235		SCOBEY, Bob	202
RUSSELL, Mary	93		SCOTT, Cecil	95, 137, 142, 157, 170
RUSSELL, Pee Wee	18–19, 24–28, 30–33, 36–40, 44–45, 53, 56, 92–93, 98, 103, 113, 120, 122, 129, 141, 148, 151, 155, 162, 164, 170–72, 174, 185–86, 203, 205, 209, 211, 213, 215, 218, 245–47, 250, 369, 398, 433, 444–46, 452, 458		SCOTT, Dick	209
			SCOTT, Frank	348, 356, 378
			SCOTT, Jerry	23
			SCOTT, Jimmy	107
			SCOTT, Paul	241
			SCOTT, Ronnie	323, 367–68
			SCOTT, Terry Lee	231
			SCOTT, Tony	99
			SCULLY, Al	17, 441
RUSSIN, Babe	299, 369		SEALEY, Paul	370
RUSSO, Andy	103, 186		SEDLAR, Jimmy	207
RUSSO, Ernie	62		SEDRIC, Gene	126, 165–66, 175
RUSSO, Sonny	209–11		SEGAL, George	290
RUTHERFORD, Rudy	213		SEGAL, Jerry	184
RYAN, Dave	405		SELCHOW, Manfred	xiv, xvi, 128, 247, 343
RYAN, George	58		SELDON, Paul	128
RYAN, Jack	231		SELLERS, Peter	363
RYAN, Kathy	405		SETAR, John	275, 286, 352, 402, 405, 439
RYE, Howard	xvi			
RYERSON, Art	156		SEVERINSEN, Doc	156, 433, 436, 440, 456
			SHACTER, Jim	89
SACHS, Aaron	136, 201, 211		SHANAHAN, ————	227
SAFRANSKI, Ed	70–71, 85, 105, 112, 118, 124, 268, 272, 274, 276, 278, 280–81, 284, 286, 288–89, 401		SHANAHAN, Dick	386
			SHAND, Terry	110
			SHANK, Bud	235, 241
			SHAPEY, Ralph	96–97, 102, 107
SAGE, ————	12		SHAPIRO, Art	267
SALAD, Sonny	100, 128		SHARD, Jerry	205, 207–08
SALKIN, Dr. ————	411		SHARP, Bill	408
SALT CITY FIVE	127		SHAVERS, Charlie	31, 140, 153, 173, 197, 209, 213
SALVADOR, Sal	184			
SAMPSON, Edgar	32, 87		SHAW, Artie	11, 19, 57, 66, 81, 110, 112, 279, 288–89, 432, 438, 440
SASSEN, Diane	377			
SATTERFIELD, Jack	23		SHAW, Arvell	73, 75, 79, 81, 88, 133, 137, 142, 172, 175, 361, 364
SAUNDERS, Sandy	364			
SAURY, Maxim	361, 458–59		SHAW, Dick	378
SAUTER, Eddie	21, 43, 57, 60, 86–87, 94–95, 128, 133, 145, 328, 387, 417, 419, 429		SHAW, George Bernard	174, 367
			SHAW, Len	408
			SHAWKER, Bunny	126, 135, 142
SAUTER-FINEGAN ORCHESTRA	133, 439		SHAY, Dorothy	97
SBARBARO, Tony (see SPARGO, Tony)			SHEARING, George	99, 165, 438
SCAVARDA, Paul	409		SHEEN, Micky	229, 252
SCHERMAN, Bo	xvi		SHELDON, Jack	387
SCHILLINGER System	87, 135		SHEPARD, Tom	289, 358
SCHNEIDER, Elmer 'Moe'	227, 231, 242, 247, 256, 257, 260–62, 457		SHEPHERD, Harry	176, 209
			SHERIDAN, John	179, 196, 394
SCHOEN, Vic	17		SHERIDAN, Lee	72

SHERMAN, Ray	xviii, 268, 273–74, 276, 278, 280–81, 283, 285–89, 292, 294, 298–99, 311–12, 315, 317, 327, 333–34, 338–41, 344, 346–48, 350, 352–53, 360–61, 369, 374, 378, 381, 383, 386–87, 388, 459
SHEROCK, Shorty	108, 288–89, 337
SHERWOOD, Bobby	33
SHIELDS, Larry	29, 40
SHIELDS, Roy	99–100, 102
SHIPLEY, Glenn	312
SHORE, Dinah	310, 436
SHRIVANEK, Eddie	242
SHROYER, Ken	299
SHURER, Russ	62, 64, 441
SIBELIUS, Jean	6
SIGNORELLI, Frank	32, 136
SILVER, Horace	173, 195, 231, 250, 440, 454
SILVERMAN, Mike	340
SILVERS, Chubby	160, 162, 186
SIMKINS, Benny	323, 326
SIMKINS, Pete	326
SIMMONS, Del	282, 311, 374
SIMMONS, Jim	199, 374
SIMMS, Lou Ann	205
SIMON, George	213
SIMPSON, Mike	255
SIMPSON, Ruth	136, 448
SIMS, Sylvia	156
SIMS, Zoot	104, 209, 398, 417, 431
SINATRA, Frank	34, 73, 110, 114, 436
SINDEN, Donald	365
SINES, Miff	126, 127, 214
SINGLETON, Zutty	34–35, 74, 88, 131–32, 162
SKEAT, Bill	325, 326
SKEAT, Len	325, 326
SLANSON, Ed	365
SLOAN, Belle	23
SMALL, ----	311
SMITH, Al	313
SMITH, Carrie	356, 371
SMITH, Carson	440
SMITH, Charlie	200–01
SMITH, Earl	233, 235, 238, 241, 248, 252, 402
SMITH, Ethel	94–95, 124, 211, 215–16, 229, 236, 442, 445, 447
SMITH, Gene	188
SMITH, Hal	xvi, 379, 394
SMITH, Jabbo	336
SMITH, John	xvi
SMITH, Keith	xii, xvi, 361–65, 421, 461
SMITH, Putter	358, 366, 407, 412–13, 415, 417, 440
SMITH, Stan	276
SMITH, Stuff	234, 239
SMITH, W. Eugene	xvi, 143
SMITH, Warren	72, 237, 239, 249, 254–55, 257, 259
SMITH, Willie "The Lion"	xi, 8, 22, 45, 48, 50, 96, 112–13, 118, 141, 157, 175, 179, 213, 229, 325, 433, 461
SMITH, Willie	402
SMITZER, Mike	254, 257
SMOGSVILLE SOCIETY ORCHESTRA, The	300
SNEAD, Sam	187
SNELL, Bob	271
SNODGRASS, James	338
SNYDER, Terry	138
SOHMER, Jack	207
SOLOMON, ----	200
SOLOMON, Doc	207
SOLOMON, Red	105, 161
SOMMERS, Bob	434
SONGER, Wayne	242, 254, 257, 276, 278–81, 296–97, 300, 311, 331–33, 337, 339–40, 344–47, 350, 352–53, 360, 401–02, 434
SONS of the PIONEERS	240
SOPER, Tut	92
SORKIN, Barney	273, 275
SOSNICK, Harry	46
SOUTH HUNTINGTON LONG ISLAND JUNIOR H.S. BAND	205
SOUTHERN SISTERS, The	114
SOUTHERN, Toni	121
SPANIER, Muggsy	19, 22, 25, 32–33, 42, 49, 87, 90, 92–93, 130, 217, 450
SPARGO, Tony (aka SBARBARO)	41–42, 103, 136, 186
SPDJ STARS	300
SPEAKERMAN, Hank	349
SPERLING, Jack	267, 290, 314–15, 330, 337, 346, 348, 367, 388, 407
SPIGA, Carlo	353
SPILKA, Bill	178
SPITZER, Dr. ----	412, 415
SPIVAK, Charlie	42
SPRINGSTEEN, Bruce	392
SPURRIER, Warner	231
ST. CYR, Johnny	252–54
ST. JOHN, Jay	260, 262
ST. LOUIS SYMPHONY	414
STACEY, George	23
STACY, Jack	344, 349
STACY, Jess	xii, 110, 289, 439
STAFFORD, Jo	74
STANDSBURG, Woody	240
STANLEY, Aileen	165
STANLEY, Bill	184, 206–07
STARR, Kay	378, 385, 440
STAVA, Bob	365
STEARNS, Marshall	190

STEELE, Ted	113–15
STEGMEYER, Bill	57–60, 135, 138, 170
STEIN, Lou	135, 271
STEPHEN, Warren	441
STEPHENS, Haig	34–35
STEPHENS, Phil	231, 271, 327, 344
STEPHENSON, Sam	xvi
STERN, Leonard	290
STEVEBURG, Stan	13
STEVENS, ----	227
STEVENS, Alan	xiv, 289, 325–26
STEVENS, Leith	238, 276, 442
STEVENSON, Allan	260
STEVENSON, George	172
STEWART, Ernie	136, 442
STEWART, Herbie	241, 268, 400, 402
STEWART, Angel	136
STEWART, Rex	12, 33, 63, 69, 185, 188, 198, 201, 203–09, 211, 215, 234–35, 238–39, 242, 247–48, 251–52, 254–55, 260, 402, 434, 442, 444–47, 451, 455
STITT, Dr. ----	353
STIVOLA, Eddie	16
STOCK, Jackson	406
STOLLE, Fred	276
STOLLER, Alvin	99, 292, 378
STONE, Bob	251
STONE, Dave	378, 383, 389, 397
STONE, Eddie	107, 114, 441
STONE, Floyd	238, 253–54
STORM, Mike	20
STOUGHTON, Jeff	133–34, 157, 199, 450
STOVER, Smokey	260
STRAVINSKY, Igor	70, 118, 369
STRAYHORN, Billy	158, 328, 419, 421
STRIBLING, Neville	320
STULCE, Fred	233
STUMPP, Bill	248, 328–29
SUDHALTER, Dick	xvi, 195–96, 217, 358, 440, 454
SULLIVAN, Joe	19, 26–27, 54, 89, 97, 117, 129, 141, 155
SULLIVAN, Maxine	91, 113, 118, 379, 384
SUMMA CUM LAUDE ORCHESTRA	15, 25, 431
SUMMERS, Bob	383, 440
SUMMERS, Del	358
SUPERSAX	436, 440
SURKIN, ----	280
SUTCLIFFE, Mike	320
SUTER, Paul	238
SUTHERS, Tom	244
SUTTON, Ralph	89–90, 93, 105–06, 108, 122, 123, 126, 136–37, 150, 162, 164, 173, 175, 266–67, 308–09, 312, 318, 343, 356, 458, 460
SUTTON, Sunnie	266, 458
SWINGING MOTHERS, The	233, 442
SYLVESTER, Robert	188
TABACKIN, Lew	402–03
TABELLA, Dr. --	223
TABOR, Bob	277, 311, 333, 340, 347, 359, 369, 381, 392
TACK, Ernie	399, 402, 405, 417, 420, 440
TACKUS, Bill(?)	209
TALBERT, Tom	440
TALLERIE, Pierre 'Frenchy'	81–82, 84
TALTER, John	147
TANZON, Jeannine	139
TARTO, Joe	126, 127
TASILLO, Bill	17, 441
TATE, Buddy	204–05, 212–13, 308, 322
TATUM, Art	xi, 7–8, 22, 26, 45, 73–74, 92–93, 110, 145, 168, 249, 264, 307, 318, 424, 428, 433
TAX, Mel	132
TAYLOR, Billy	174
TAYLOR, Billy, Jr.	213
TAYLOR ORCHESTRA, Jack	349
TAYLOR, Joe	17
TAYLOR, Lynn	183
TEAGARDEN, Addie	72, 83
TEAGARDEN, Charlie	108–10, 231, 434
TEAGARDEN, Norma	74, 148, 343
TEAGARDEN, Jack	xi, 63, 67–69, 71–74, 77–78, 79, 80, 83, 90–91, 101–02, 104, 111, 148, 150–51, 201, 362, 373, 424, 428, 434, 437, 438, 451, 459
TEDESCO, Tom	227, 239, 349
TEE PEE Music Company	445–47, 449
TEMPLIN, Ray	408
TERASSI, Lou	122
TERRI, Vince	275
TERRY, Clark	205
TERRY, Dave	205
TESCHEMACHER, Frank	32, 98
THIELE, Bob	131–32, 202
THOMAS, Bob	294, 298, 344
THOMAS, Danny	235
THOMAS, Irma	374
THOMAS, Joe	137, 142, 162
THOMPSON, J. Walter	156
THOMSON, Lachie	320
THORNE, Francis	204
THORNHILL, Claude	11, 405, 437
THOW, George	168, 290
TILTON, Martha	386–89
TIMBERLIN, Neil	186
TIMBRELL, Tim	238

TIMOTHY, Tim	86–87, 122, 135, 138, 141	VACHE, Warren Jr.	386
TINY TIM	264	VACHE, Warren Sr.	41, 395
TIZOL, Juan	190	VACHER, Peter	xvi, 146, 345, 364
TOBIN, Louise	314, 340	VAIL, Ken	xvi
TODD, Dick	185	VALLEE, Rudy	278, 292
TODD, Tommy	165, 168, 240	VALLESE, Rico	18, 72, 74, 88
TOENNIGES, Paul	257	VAN, Jerry	226
TOLE, Bill	317. 369, 378, 440	VANCE, Dick	211
TOMPKINS, Ross	360	VAN DYKE, Jerry	348
TOONAN, Tom	227	VAN EPS, Bobby	249
TORME, Mel	110, 120, 460	VAN EPS, George	227, 260, 380, 387
TORTOLLA, Johnny	18, 64, 238	VAN GELDER, Rudy	145
TOSHIKO, Akiyoshi	212, 403	VAN HEUSEN, Jimmy	460
TOTAH, Knobby	236–37	VARRO, Johnny	xvi, 145, 232, 352–53, 359, 367, 378–79, 382
TOUGH, Dave	8, 17, 42, 57, 391, 430, 432		
TOWNSEND, Irving	163	VAUGHAN, Sarah	91, 100, 438
TOWSLEY, Alice	125	VAUGHN, Billy	439
TRACE, Al	446	VAUGHN, Jerry	238–40, 296
TRACY, Jack	179, 210, 216	VENTURA, Charlie	99, 142
TRAEGER, Charlie	105, 107, 118, 157, 170–72, 174, 185, 217	VENUTI, Joe	42, 69, 257, 306, 316, 434, 443
		VERNON Music Corporation	444–47, 449
TRAILL, Sinclair	334	VERPLANCK, Billy	201
TRAPPIER, Art	95, 101, 103–04, 112, 118, 170, 172	VILLEPIGUE, Paul	54
		VINCENT, Ann	113, 119
TRATNER, Joan	299, 444, 446, 448	VINE, Johnny	16, 62–64, 90, 100, 102, 106–08, 122–23, 137, 150, 153, 155, 161–62, 170–71, 174, 186–87, 203, 205, 218
TRATTNER, Wolfgang	307		
TRAVIS, Ned	175		
TRAVIS, Nick	210		
TREMBLE KIDS, The	359	VOGT, Jack	209–10
TRISTANO, Lennie	105, 141, 189	VOLLEBRECHT, Nick	368
TROTT, Jack	275, 277, 281, 287–88, 293–94, 314–15, 329–33, 340, 353, 369, 383, 400–02, 404, 405, 413, 417, 440	VON ESSEN, Reimer	xvi, 302, 304–05
		VREELAND, Mike	408
		WADSWORTH, Jack	408, 410
TROTTER, Terry	400	WAGNER, Don	289
TROUP, Bobby	437	WAGNER, Dr. Joseph	87, 262–63, 266
TRUMBAUER, Frankie	69	WALDRUP, Don	443
TUCKER, Forrest	374	WALLER, Fats	7–8, 22, 33, 163, 289, 428, 433
TUCKER, Tommy	131		
TUDOR, David	87	WALLINGTON, George	162
TURNER, Big Joe	203	WALSH, Gene	240, 254
TURNER, Bruce	323, 326	WALTER, Cy	98
TURNER, Jim	xii, xiv, xvi, xvii, xix, 337, 365, 375–76, 381, 394–95, 405, 411–13, 418, 421, 440, 444–46, 448	WALTON, Cedar	323
		WARD, Brendan	207
		WARD, Helen	183
		WARD, Herb	92
TURNER, Margaret (see McPARTLAND, Marian)		WARD, Pat	164
TURNER, Sandi	418	WARE, Munn	103, 118–19
TURNHAM, Floyd	342	WARING, Fred	40
TYLER, Dr. George	264, 266	WARK, Doug	22
		WARREN, Fran	142
UKELELE, Johnny	255	WASHINGTON, Gene	238, 253–54, 271, 294
ULANO, Sam	207	WASHINGTON, George	234–35
ULYATE, Lloyd	283, 292, 294, 299, 358	WASSERMAN, Chuck	141
USSELTON, Bill	241	WATERS, Benny	127, 370
USTINOV, Peter	365	WATROUS, Bill	353
UWHILER, John	135	WATTERS, Lu	427
		WAX, Carole	284

WAYLAND, Hank	23, 88
WAYNE, Chuck	99, 201
WEAVER, Jack	317
WEBER, Al	340
WEBER, Gus	62, 173
WEBSTER, Ben	204
WEED, Buddy	125
WEEMS, Ted	6
WEIDLER, Arndt	xvi
WEIL, Bob	205
WEIN, George	130, 141, 213, 368, 452
WELK, Lawrence	239–40, 264, 274, 284, 287, 290, 293, 436, 437
WELLS, Bill	328
WELLS, Dickie	213, 215
WELLSTOOD, Dick	215, 217
WELSCH, Chauncey	378, 386
WELSH, Alex	323–25, 370
WERTH, George	241
WESLEYAN SERENADERS, The	8
WEST, Bernie	165–66
WEST, George	443
WESTLEY, Ira	239, 247, 250, 252, 260, 266, 294, 298–300, 327, 386, 402
WESTMAN, ----	12
WESTON, Paul	74, 440
WETTLING, George	45, 48, 57, 64, 67, 120, 122, 128, 133, 136, 141–42, 145, 148, 155–56, 159, 162-63, 170, 172, 175–76, 188, 190, 205–06, 214–15, 236–37, 430, 432, 447, 451
WHALEY, Doug	323
WHITAKER, Jack	366
WHITE, Hy	160
WHITE, Jack	22
WHITE, Jerry	405, 417, 440
WHITE, Josh	118
WHITE, Loray	165
WHITEMAN, Paul	14, 125, 147, 347, 414, 429, 442
WHITING, Margaret	440
WHITNEY, Jill	134
WHITNEY, Leonard	44
WHITWOOD, Jim	253
WHYATT, Bert	xii, xvi, 91, 225, 351–52, 404, 410–11
WICK, Ted	10
WILBER, Bob (variant misspelling "Wilbur")	xvi, 101, 117, 122, 141, 153–54, 158, 174–75, 184–85, 189–93, 198, 200–03, 205–08, 210, 212–13, 215–18, 220, 236–37, 261, 277–78, 306, 308–09, 346, 398, 426, 450–51, 455–56
WILDER, Joe	202, 379, 388, 394
WILEY, Lee	48–49, 91–92, 100, 126, 128, 130, 201, 230, 420, 435
WILKINS, ----	248
WILKINS, Ernie	139
WILKINS, Herb	249, 253
WILLARD, Clarence	14
WILLARD, Hal	30, 163
WILLEMS, Jos	xvi
WILLIAMS, Al	215
WILLIAMS, Bill	235, 271
WILLIAMS, Bobby	379
WILLIAMS, Cootie	43, 91, 97, 115, 231, 308
WILLIAMS, Curt	350
WILLIAMS, Denis	421
WILLIAMS, Fred	20, 67
WILLIAMS, George	439
WILLIAMS, Joe	250
WILLIAMS, John	369
WILLIAMS, Mary Lou	91, 120, 128
WILLIAMS, Roy	322–24, 370
WILLIAMS, Sandy	45, 101, 117
WILLIAMS, Teddy	342
WILLS, Lou	158
WILLSON, Meredith	196
WILSON, Bud	74
WILSON, Gerald	438
WILSON, John	104, 122, 185
WILSON, Teddy	7–8, 10, 124, 260, 271, 318, 336, 370, 431, 453
WINDHURST, Johnny	45, 56, 63, 70, 72, 74, 82, 89–90, 93, 96–97, 99–100, 102–03, 105–06, 108, 117–18, 122, 130, 133, 139, 144–45, 153, 155, 158, 161, 164–66, 168, 170, 184, 186, 203, 206, 435, 455
WINDING, Kai	99, 108, 271, 315
WINTERS, Shelley	270
WINTERS, Vi	240
WIPPLER, Elmar	307
WISWALL, Andy	179, 200
WITHERS, Googie	323
WOLFE, Edgar	126
WOLFE, Tom	260, 279, 284
WOLPE, Stefan	86–87, 96–97, 102, 106–07, 110, 121–22, 145
WOOD, Bill	227–28, 251, 271, 300, 313, 369, 383
WOODMAN, Britt	282, 292
WOODS, Phil	162, 213
WOODWARD Music, Inc.	445, 447, 449
WOOLEM, Dee	271, 281, 286–87
WORLD'S GREATEST JAZZ BAND	57, 277, 311, 329–30, 332, 371, 438
WORLD'S HOTTEST JAZZ BAND, The	319, 461
WRIGHT, Eugene	395
WRIGHTMIRE, Bob	356

WRIGHTSMAN, Stan	227, 231, 242, 250–52, 255, 257, 261–62, 273, 286, 297, 310, 324	ZABIDIS, ————	63
		ZACK, George	49
		ZAID, Herman	312
WYLER, William	329–30	ZAID, Sid	226, 231, 235, 257, 280
WYLIE, Allan	441	ZARCHY, Amy	252–54
		ZARCHY, Andy (see FIELDING, Andy)	
YAGED, Sol	88, 96, 103, 132, 156–57, 162–63, 176, 442	ZARCHY, Zeke	251, 268, 288, 299, 312, 320, 338, 340, 350, 365, 375–76, 382–83, 395, 401–02, 408, 440
YODER, Walt	227, 233, 240, 313, 333, 340		
YOUMANS, Vincent	414	ZELNICK, Mel	156
YOUNG, David X.	143, 157, 195, 201, 209–10	ZENTNER, Sy	440
YOUNG, Graham	292, 299–300	ZIMMERMAN, Art	xvi, 200
YOUNG, Lester	124, 437	ZIMMERMAN, Jack	112, 114, 119, 134, 150, 153, 157, 184, 200
YOUNG, Trummy	133, 142, 316, 359, 368		
YOUNG, Victor	435	ZITO, Jimmy	348
YUKL, Joe	278–79, 311, 349	ZURKE, Bob	7–8

Name Index to Discography

ABRAMS, Ray	495		BAUTISTA, Roland	544
ABRAMS, L.	545		BECHET, Sidney	487–91
ABRUZZO, Tommy	499		BELL, Bill	509
ACOCELLA, Gianni	535		BELL, Graeme	541
ÅKERMAN, Jan	550–51		BELLEROSE, Dick	492
ALBERTI, Giorgio	535		BENJAMIN, Joe	512
ALDCROFT, Randy	564		BENNETT, Ben	499
ALDEN, Howard	551–52		BENSON, Ron	557
ALEXANDER, Mousey	515, 523		BERG, George	509, 562
ALLEN, Dave	516		BERGHOFER, Chuck	527, 557
ALLEN, Henry 'Red'	488, 494		BERGMANN, Dieter	542
ALSTON, Al	491		BERKELEY, Richard	549
ALVIN, Danny	483		BERNABEI, Memo	554–55
ANDERBY, Nils Gunnar	479		BEST, John	530–31, 533–34
ANDERSON, Dick	526		BETTS, Keeter	519
ANDERSON, Ed	523		BICKLEY, Len	479
APPLEYARD, Peter	545		BIELDERMAN, Gerard	479
ARIE, Dr. Michael	479		BIGARD, Barney	486–87, 533, 542
ARMSTRONG, Louis	479, 480, 485–88, 548, 550		BIRMINGHAM, Alan	538
			BLAIR, Lee	522
ARNBERG, Staffan	550–51		BLOCK, Sandy	496, 562
ARNONE, Don	493, 495–96, 500–502		BLOWERS, Johnny	508
ASCIONE, Joe	551		BOCK, Hans–Jurgen	546
ASH, Marvin	526, 530		BODNER, Phil	516
ASHBY, Tony	540		BOLEN, Gene	525
ATKINS, Jimmy	488, 561		BONGERS, Mel	540
AUTREY, Herman	509		BONNEE, Don (?)	522
AYARS, Boy	557		BONNEY, Nick	557
			BOUGHTON, Joe	479, 500
BADER, Klaus	542–43, 546, 548		BOURGEOIS, Jess	526
BADER, Laura	548		BOURNE, Dave (Professor D.E.)	479, 534
BAGNOLI, Carlo	535		BRADLEY, Will	490, 499
BAILEY, Colin	544		BRODDA, Claes	550–51
BAIRD, Mike	534		BROSTEDT, Ollie	550–51
BALL, Ronnie	495		BROWN, Bill	479
BAMBRIDGE, John	564–65		BROWN, Dan	493
BANDINI, Al	499		BROWN, Pud	544, 563
BARDUHN, Art	556–57		BROWN, Roy	545, 557
BAREFIELD, Eddie	502		BROWN, Ruth	490
BARKSDALE, Everett	512		BROWN, Vernon	509
BARNARD, Bob	539–41		BRUCE, Bobby	533
BARNARD, Len	539–40		BRUNIS, George (Brunies)	481
BARNES, George	496, 498, 516, 519–20, 524		BRUNO, Jerry	497, 499, 503
			BRUNS, George	527
BARNETT, ——	544		BRYANT, Jim	556
BARRETT, Dan	551		BRYANT, Ray	519
BARUFALDI, Joe	513		BRYDEN, Beryl	543
BARZAGO, Renato	535		BUCHANAN, Jim	555
BASIE, Count	490		BUCKLAND, Laurie	541
BATES, John	541		BUDWIG, Monte	544
BAUDUC, Ray	491–92, 501		BÜHR, Peter	548
BAUER, Billy	509, 513		BURKE, Vinnie	513

BURNS, Ralph	516	COOPER, Fred	552, 564–65
BURRIESCE, Joe	519	CORTESE, Dominic	494, 497
BUSHELL, Garvin	506, 512, 515	CORTESI, Dan	499
BUSHKIN, Joe	489–91	COSS, Bill	512
BUTTERFIELD, Billy	481, 483–85, 490, 500, 505, 512, 514–15, 561	COSTA, Don	493–97, 503
		COTTLER, Irv	526
		COX, John	538
BYERS, Bill	516	CRANE, Mickey	484, 505
BYRD, Charlie	519	CRAWFORD, Jimmy	501, 520
BYRNE, Bobby	495, 499	CROSBY, Bob	548–49
		CROSBY, Les	541
CACERES, Ernie	482–83, 485, 489–91, 495–96, 504–07, 509, 519	CROTHERS, Scatman	549
		CROW, Bill	504, 510, 517, 524
		CRUMP, Charlie	479, 515
CADWAY, Phil	521–22	CUESTA, Henry	545
CALELLA, Sonny	493–94, 496, 502	CULVER, Rollie	523
CALLENDER, Red	524	CUMMINS, Gordon	541
CALLETT, Lee	553	CUTSHALL, Cutty	488–91, 494, 496–500, 502, 506, 509–15, 517–21, 562
CAMPBELL, Bill	525, 544		
CANDIOTI, Ike	555		
CANTOR, Mark	479		
CANYON, Virginia	501	D'AMICO, Hank	500
CARON, Fern	484	DANIELS, Bill	544
CARPENTER, Thelma	487–89, 560	DANIELS, Chris	545
CARUSO, Mary	496	DARENSBOURG, Joe	532–33, 544
CASAMENTI, Al	495–96, 503–07	DARKTOWN JAZZ BAND	536
CASEY, Bob	481–83, 488, 494	DARROW, Chris	533
CASTLE, Lee	499, 501, 503	DAVERN, Kenny	501, 521, 545
CATHCART, Dick	522, 524, 547–48	DAVIS, Joe	499
CATLETT, Sid	485–86, 488, 490–91	DAVIS, Mavis	534
CAUSEBROOK, Mike	540	DAVIS, Mel	516
CENICOLA, Phil	492	DAVISON, Wild Bill	481, 483, 487–88, 493, 498, 500
CERVANTES, Bill	484		
CHANEY, Jack	527–28	DAWSON, Horsley	540–41
CHARLES SINGERS, Ray	516	DEEMS, Barrett	547
CHEATHAM, Doc	499, 550	DEFRANCO, Buddy	494–95
CHERICO, Gene	531, 534	DELLERT, Sigge	550–51
CHRISTIAN, Buddy	561	DELTA RHYTHM BOYS, The	560
CHRISTY, June	490	DeNAUT, Jud	522
CINTI, Giancarlo	535	DENGLER, John	504–05, 509
CIPRIANO, Gene(?)	557	DESMOND, Johnny	490
CLAYTON, Buck	518–19, 525	DeVITO, Harry	521, 524
CLIFFORD, Ray	540	DICKENSON, Bob	484
CLIFTON, Chris	563	DICKENSON, Vic	479, 495, 499, 509, 518–19, 521, 525
CLIMAX JAZZ BAND	545		
CLOONEY, Rosemary	488	DIEHL, Ray	500
COHN, Al	507	DOMBER, Matt	529, 551
COLLINS, Dick	556	DONALDSON, Bobby	521
COMEGYS, Leon 'Jim'	515	DORSEY, Jimmy	491–92, 561
COMMANDERS, The	516	DORSEY, Tommy	561
CONDON, Eddie	481–83, 487–91, 494, 498, 500, 502, 506, 510–15, 517–19, 524–25, 535, 560–62	DRELLINGER, Art	488, 501, 561
		DREW, John	516, 522
		DROOTIN, Al	499
		DROOTIN, Buzzy	491, 494, 499, 507, 509, 513, 524–25
CONDOS, Steve	489		
CONKLIN, Chuck	544	DRUCKMAN, Joel	533
COON, Jackie	527, 532, 549, 565	DUNBIER, Gary	540
COOPER, Barry	565	DUNHAM, Kathryn	481

596

DUVIVIER, George	513		FUSSENHAUSER, Uli	548
EASTON, Ted	536–38, 542		GABLER, Milt	479, 484, 519
EBERLE, Jack	560		GALBRAITH, Barry	484, 5167, 521
EDWARDS, Dave	538		GALE, Bill	499
EEKHOFF, Hans	536		GARF, Gene	554–56, 558–59
EEKSTEIN, Ernst	548		GARROWAY, Dave	487
ELDREDGE, Tom	493		GASKIN, Leonard	506, 509, 512–14, 517–18, 521
ELLIOTT, Don	495			
ELLIOTT, Jack	545, 557		GASTON, Ed	539, 541
ELLSWORTH, Scott	532		GAUTHE, Jacques	563
ELTON, William	522		GENTILE, Al	502
ELVIN, Norman	484		GERSHWIN, George	489
EMERY, Bill	479		GIBBONS, Bob	557
ENEVOLDSEN, Bob	532, 538, 543–44, 557		GIBELING, Howard	492
			GIEBEL, Martin	548
ERIKSSON, Göran	550		GIFFORD, Walt	450, 499
ERWIG, Bob	545		GILLESPIE, Dizzy	495
ERWIN, Pee Wee	545–46		GIOBBE, Felix	561
ERWIN, Ward	527–28		GIRARD, Adele	507–09
ESTES, Gene	527, 547–49, 552, 557		GIUFFRIDA, John	513
			GLASEL, Johnny	507, 509–10, 519, 522
ETTORE, Remi	535			
EVANS, Marion	503		GLENN, Tyree	504–05, 509, 513
			GLOW, Bernie	495, 516
FAHEY, John	532–33		GODLIS, Al	516–17
FARDELLA, Charlie	563		GONELLA, Nat	536
FARTINA(?), Carl	533		GOODMAN, Benny	560
FATOOL, Nick	522–23, 524, 531–34, 538, 543, 545–47, 557		GORDON, Bobby	509, 563
			GORDON, Jack	509
			GOULD, Chuck	562
FAXELL, Clas Göran	551		GOULDING, Pete	479
FAY, Jack	491		GOWANS, Brad	481, 487–88
FAY, Rick	551		GRAUSO, Joe	482
FEATHER, Leonard	501, 512		GRECO, Buddy	497
FEATHER, Phil	565		GREEN, Byrdie	524
FEIERMAN, Jack	532–33		GREEN, Jack	484
FELD, Morey	484, 561		GREEN, Urbie	507, 516, 523
FERRETTI, Andy	499		GREENE, George	495
FIELD, John	499–500		GREENLEAF, Fred	501
FIELDS, Frank	563		GRIFFIN, Chris	499
FINLAY, John	530		GUARNIERI, Johnny	530
FINN, Fred (Freda)	544		GUBIN, Sol	545, 557
FINN, Mickey	544		GUERIN, John	527, 544
FISHELSON, Stan	498		GUSIKOFF, Al	509–10
FISHKIN, Arnold	549		GUSSAK, Billy	520
FITZGERALD, Andy	523		GWALTNEY, Tommy	504–05, 509
FLAT FOOT STOMPERS, The	548			
FORD, Adrian	541		HACKETT, Bobby	485, 489–91, 502, 504–05, 509–13, 523–24, 542, 560–61
FORD, Art	513			
FORREST, Dick	552			
FRANCIS, Panama	530, 551		HACKMAN, Bob	492
FREEMAN, Bud	498, 500, 502, 504–08, 510–15, 517–19, 525, 560–62		HAFER, Dick	509–11, 546–47, 549
			HAGGART, Bob	484–85, 488, 496, 499, 501, 503, 509, 548, 561
FRESCO, John	545			
FURNISS, Paul	541		HÄGGLÖF, Gösta	479
FUSSELL, Ben	492		HALE, Teddy	487–88

HALL, Al	500, 503, 505–08, 518, 520, 528–29		514–15, 524–25, 531–32, 547–48, 561
HALL, Ed	479, 494–95, 498, 500–02, 520	HULME, George	479, 512
		HYMAN, Dick	503, 509. 516, 546
HALL, Herb	509, 512–15, 520		
HALL, Jim	523	IPPOLITO, Frank	495
HAMBRO, Lennie	484		
HAMILTON, Dick	532, 552, 564–65	JACKSON, Cliff	489
HANLON, Allan	495, 499	JACOBSEN, Gunnar	479, 522
HANNA, Jake	523	JACOWSKY, Sid	495
HANSON, Jack	497	JAMESON, Peter	533
HARDAKER, Vince	540	JANSSON, Eddie	564
HARMON, Charles	497, 516	JEFFERSON, Hilton	512, 515
HARPER, Herbie	531, 534	JEPSEN, Jorgen G.	479
HARRINGTON, Terry	552, 564–65	JEROME, Jerry	493–95, 499, 501, 561
HARRIS, Bill	494		
HARRIS, Maury	556	JEWETT, John	534
HARRISON, John	540	JIRZIG, Eberhard	535
HARTMAN, Gary	549	JOHNSON, Alex	555
HAVENS, Bob	530–31, 544–49, 565	JOHNSON, Archie	484
HAWK, Marshall	484	JOHNSON, Frank	539, 541
HAWKINS, Coleman	511	JOHNSON, Osie	503, 506–07, 517, 521
HAYES, Clancy	527, 530–31		
HAYES, Mileham	538–40	JOHNSON, Tommy	557
HEARD, J.C.	489	JONES, Dennis	563
HEARD, John	546	JONES, Jimmy	517
HEDGES, Chuck	551–52	JONES, Jo	496, 501, 519
HENDRICKS, Dee	545	JONES, Ron	549
HENRY, Haywood	512, 515	JONES, Tom	545
HERMAN, Sam	495	JORDAN, Taft	515
HERMAN, Ted	549	JOUARD, Paul	497
HERRON, Ken	539, 541	JUHLIN, Bo	551
HESSION, Jim	549	JUNG, Bob	557
HESSION, Martha	549		
HI–HATTERS, The	555	KAATEE, Frits	536–37
HILBERT, Robert (Bob)	479	KAATEE, George	536
HILL, Ian	541	KACHER, Del	555, 557–58
HILL, Parke	516	KAMINSKY, Max	481, 483, 496–97, 500, 506, 509–10, 513, 518–19, 521–22, 562
HINTON, Milt	501, 504–06, 511		
HIRSCHMANN, Christian	541		
HIRT, Al	549		
HOCKETT, Ron	479, 515	KAUFMAN, Bernie	493
HOFF, Tim	549	KAY, Tommy	561
HOFFMAN, Dick	492	KAYE, Carol (guitar)	556
HOGAN, Claire	491–92	KAYE, Carole (vocal)	560
HOGERVORST, Pim	536–37	KEITH, Lyn	530
HOLGATE, Dick	549	KELLAWAY, Roger	527
HOLIDAY, Billie	514	KELLSO, Jon–Erik	551–52, 563
HÖLLERING, Charly	548	KELLY, George	512
HOLLEY, Major	538	KEMPER, Norbert	535
HOLMES, Geoff	545	KENNEDY, Charles	495
HOOPER, Stix	544	KENNEDY, Dave	534
HOPKINS, Ken	496	KESSEL, Barney	525
HORNER, Bob	484	KINCAIDE, Deane	531–32, 565
HOWARD, Joe	533–34	KING, B.B.	544
HUBBLE, Ed	499	KING, Jerry	525
HUCKO, Peanuts	485, 488–91, 493–501, 504, 509, 511,	KINGDOM CHOIR, The	488
		KINGMA, Jacques	536–37

KINGS OF DIXIELAND	524
KLAUER, Hans–George	535
KLEIN, ——	516
KLINK, Al	548
KNOX, Bertil	519
KOONSE, Dave	533, 547, 549, 552, 564–65
KOONSE, Larry	547
KOSOFTIS, Ted	561
KRAUS, Phil	494–95, 497, 499, 503
KRESS, Carl	491–92, 495, 501
KUNNECKE, Walt	556
LAMARE, Nappy	524, 527–28, 530–32, 544, 547
LAMOND, Don	494–95, 498–99
LAMSZUS, Helmut	542
LANE, Lucille	531
LANE, Tom	479
LA ROCCA, Mimi	492
LAWRENCE, Baby	489
LAWSON, Yank	499, 548
LAZARE, Jack	512–13
LEA, Barbara	503, 506–07, 510, 516, 552
LEAHY, Joe	555–58
LEATHERWOOD, Ray	530–32, 534, 538, 545, 547–48, 556
LEEMAN, Cliff	497–98, 500, 504, 509, 511, 517, 519, 521, 525, 528–30, 538
LEFELDT, Bruno	542–43
LENER, Werner	536, 548
LEON, Harry	513
LESBERG, Jack	485, 487–91, 495–96, 498, 500, 519–20, 524–25, 543, 562
LESTER, Sonny	518
LEVANG, Neil	538, 556
LEVIN, Art	534
LEVIN, Floyd	547
LEVINE, Bob	484
LEWIS, Cappy	544
LIBERACE	557
LINAHON, Jim	549
LINCOLN, Abbey	513
LINCOLN, Abe	527, 530
LIND, Göran	550–51
LINN, Ray	527–28
LODICE, Don	530–31
LOLATTE, Bill	491–92
LONG, Walter	490
LONGHI, Bruno	535
LOOKOFSKY, Harry	561
LORD, Tom	479
LOWMAN, Richard (see Hyman, Dick)	
LOXTON, Art	540
LUDOWYCK, Chris	540
LYON, Jimmy	506–07
MacBETH, Carlton	532
MALINOWSKY, Peter	542–43
MALONE, Kass	501
MALONE, Ray	490
MANNE, Shelly	544
MANONE, Wingy	497
MARETTI(?), Terry	538
MARINO, Don	519–20
MARSALA, Joe	481, 483, 507–09
MARTIN, Kenny	492
MARTIN, Ray	516–17
MARTYN, Barry	563
MASSO, George	548
MASTREN, Carmen	481, 497, 508
MATLOCK, Matty	524, 527–28, 530–32
MAURO, Lou	551
MAURY, Art	556
MAY, Billy	532
MAYNES, Frank	491–92
McEACHERN, Murray	531
McGARITY, Lou	481, 483, 493–95, 498–503, 510, 519–20, 524
McGOWN, Sonny	509
McKENNA, Dave	521–23
McKENZIE, Jerry	534, 552, 557
McKENZIE, Jim	540
McKENZIE, Red	483, 560
McKIBBON, Al	495
McPARTLAND, Jimmy	489, 495–96, 501, 504, 506, 509–13, 517, 519, 523–24, 535–38, 562, 564
McPARTLAND, Marian	509–10, 523, 538, 562
McREYNOLDS, Mac	549
McREYNOLDS, Margaret–Jean	549
MENZA, Don	544
MERCER, Johnny	487
MERKIN, Lester	495
MEROLA, Pat	508
METZGER, Carol	558
METZGER, Pete	558
MICHAELS, Danny	545
MICKMAN, Herb	549, 552, 564–65
MIDDLETON, Velma	486, 488
MILAN COLLEGE JAZZ SOCIETY	535
MILLER, Big	516
MILLER, Eddie	524, 532, 543–45, 548
MILLS, Joe	540
MINCE, Johnny	488, 548
MITCHELL, Bob	499–500
MITCHELL, Elaine	544
MITCHELL, Fred	525

MITCHELL, Gordon	544
MITCHELL, Jack	479
MOLE, Miff	482, 562
MONSBOURGH, Ade	539–41
MOORE, Russell 'Big Chief'	494, 547
MOROCCO, Frank (sometimes Marocco)	556
MORRIS, Debbie	516
MORRIS, Dolph	545
MORROW, Buddy	488
MORTELL, Benny	561
MORTON, Benny	515
MOST, Abe	533–34, 538, 544–45, 552, 564–65
MOST, Sam	534
MUCCI, Louis	501, 522
MÜLLER, Roland	548
MULLIGAN, Mary	517–18
MÜNSTER, Jost	542
MURPHY, Dick	492
MURPHY, Marge	545
MURPHY, Red	545
MURRAY, Allan	538
MUSSIERI, Russ	538
MYERSON, Charlie	531, 557
NAPOLEON, Phil	491
NASH, Dick	557
NEIDHARD, Werne	548
NEUMANN, Roger	565
NEWMAN, Bill	556
NEWSOM, Tommy	546, 552–53, 564
NICHOLS, Red	523
NIMITZ, Jack	544
NIVEN, David	479
NOBLE, John	540
NORMAN, Milt	556
NORRIS, John	545
NORRIS, (Miss) Lou	526
NORVO, Red	531
NUGENT, Peter	488
OBERSTEIN, Eli	493
O'BRIEN, Jack	542
O'CONNELL, Helen	525
O'CONNOR, Patricia	484
O'HARA, Barrett	552
O'HARA, Betty	502, 527–28, 547, 552, 564
OLDS, Merl	533, 554, 556–58
OLIVELLA, Phil	491, 521
OLIVER, Howie	556
OTTO, Bernd K.	535
OVERTON, Hall	507
PAGE, Hot Lips	489–90, 493
PAGE, Walter	498, 501–02
PALOTTI, Nick	492
PARIS, Norman	517

PARITO, Nick	493, 495, 561
PARKER, Charlie	494
PARKINS, Leroy	521
PARKS, Dean	544
PARRISH, Ben	491
PASS, Joe	534
PATRUNO, Lino	535
PAUL, Jad	556
PEARSON, Earl	484
PECK, Bob	484
PEER, Beverly	506–07
PEERLESS, Brian	479, 515
PEMBERTON, Bill	515
PENQUE, Romeo	562
PERRI, Dan	484
PERSSON, Bent	551
PERSSON, Erik	550–51
PETERSON, Bob	498
PHILLIPS, Flip	488, 531
PHILLIPS, Harvey	517, 519, 521–22
PISTORIUS, Steve	563
PIZZARELLI, Bucky	497
PLONSKY, John	507
POLIC, Ed	479
POLLACK, Ben	525
PORCARO, Joe	531
POTTER, Tommy	521
PRIMUS, Pearl	488
PROUD, Geoff	541
QUEENER, Charlie	513
QUINN, ——	561
RABEN, Erik	479
RAE, Don	538
RAE, Ron	541
RAFFELL, Don	534
RAMSEY, Curt	565
RANCH, Harry (Mr & Mrs)	498
RANDALL, Bill	517
RANEY, Jimmy	506–07, 520, 523
RATTI, Marco	535
RAY, Nat	504–05
REECE, Cliff	541
REED, Nancy	493, 495
REHAK, Frank	492, 510, 516, 519
REICHLE, Uli	548
REID, John	538
REINBERG, Russ	547
REINERS, Bernd	542–43
REITER, Jörg	543
REPASS, Morris	565
RESNICK, Eff	516
REUSS, Allan	526, 532–33
RICCI, Paul	496, 499
RICH, Buddy	488–89, 491
RICHARD, Charlie	549
RICHARDS, Red	515

RIEMPP, Dieter	536
RILEY, Mike	491
ROACH, Max	495
ROBERTS, Howie	556
ROBERTS, John	541
ROBINSON, Allen	540
ROBINSON, Les	534
ROCHE, Pat	540
RODGERS & HART	491
ROLLINI, Arthur	561
ROTELLA, Joe	532–33
ROTEN, Roy	534
ROYAL BLUE MELODIANS	564
ROYAL, Ernie	516
RUPPLI, Michel	479
RUSHING, Jimmy	525
RUSHTON, Joe	523
RUSSELL, Maurie	556
RUSSELL, Pee Wee	479, 482–83, 487, 493–94, 499, 504–06, 510, 517–19, 525, 562
RUSSIN, Babe	534, 538
RUSSO, Andy	491
RYAN, Dave	565
RYAN, George	484
RYERSON, Art	495
SAFRANSKI, Ed	494, 497, 520, 531–33
SAGER, David	563
SAKS, Norman	479
SALVADOR, Sal	507, 510
SAMPLE, Joe	544
SATTERFIELD, Jack	499
SAURY, Maxim	547
SCAVARDA, Paul	551–52
SCHNEIDER, Elmer 'Moe'	522, 524, 527–28
SCHROEDER, Gene	483, 494, 498, 500, 502, 509, 511–14
SCHUCHARD, Bernd	546
SCHUCKER, Hans–Peter	548
SCHULTZE, Klaus	542–43, 548
SCHWARTZ, Willie	534
SCHWARTZE, Klaus	546
SCHWARZ, Horst	535
SCOTT, Frank	565
SEDLAR, Jimmy	516
SEGAL, Jerry	507
SELANDER, Mikael	550–51
SELCHOW, Manfred	479
SELTEN, Frank	535
SETAR, John	565
SEVERINSEN, Doc	494–95, 520–21
SEYFFER, Siegfried	536
SHANAHAN, Dick	557
SHAND, Terry	492
SHAPIRO, Artie	530
SHAUGHNESSY, Ed	522
SHAVERS, Charlie	511, 519
SHAW, Arvell	486, 488, 547
SHAW, Cec	540
SHEEN, Mickey	512
SHERMAN, Ray	531, 533–34, 538, 543, 545, 547–49
SHEROCK, Shorty	492
SHERTZER, Hymie	561
SHIPLEY, Glenn	538
SHOPPEE, Tony	479
SIMEON, Omer	520
SIMMS, Dan	479
SIMMS, Lou Ann	516
SIMON, George	518
SINGLETON, Zutty	481
SMILDIGER, Chris	542
SMITH, Allan	515
SMITH, Bob	516
SMITH, Carrie	548
SMITH, Charles	513
SMITH, Don	549
SMITH, Ethel	519–20, 562–63
SMITH, Keith	547
SMITH, Norm	549
SMITH, Paul	499, 500
SMITH, Putter	552
SMITH, Warren	525
SMITH, Willie "The Lion"	512
SNYDER, Dan	544
SNYDER, Terry	493, 516
SOLOMON, Red	494, 516
SONGER, Wayne	527–28, 530, 534, 544, 556–57
SPANIER, Muggsy	479, 482–83, 487, 489
SPARGO, Tony	481, 491
SPERLING, Jack	527–28, 530, 557
STACY, Jess	483
STANLEY, Bill	507, 510, 516
STEGMEYER, Bill	484, 496, 499, 562
STEIN, Lou	493
STEPHENS, Haig	481
STERLING, Frank	555–56, 558
STEVENSON, George	512
STEWART, Rex	508–09, 512–16
STEWART, Slam	497
STIMMLER, Ludwig	536
STOLLE, (Fred?)	557
STOLLER, Alvin	545
ST. LEDGER, Gene	540
STOUGHTON, Jeff	497–98
STRIBLING, Neville	539
STUMPP, Bill	534
SULLIVAN, Joe	562
SULLIVAN, Maxine	561
SUMMA CUM LAUDE ORCHESTRA	502-05, 562
SUMMERS, Bob	552
SUTCLIFFE, Mike	479

SUTER, Paul	525
SUTTON, Ralph	490, 494, 528–29, 536–37
TACK, Ernie	552, 564–65
TAIT, Graham	540
TAKAS, Bill	518
TATE, Buddy	515, 519, 542
TAYLOR, Billy, Jr.	519
TAYLOR, Rod	540
TEAGARDEN, Charlie	491–92
TEAGARDEN, Norma	501
TEAGARDEN, Jack	485–86, 488, 501–02
TEDESCO, Tom	556
TERRY, Clark	516
TERRY, Dan	509
TERRY, Dave	516–17
THEOHARRIS, Roy	540
THIELE, Bob	497
THOMAS, Irma	549
THOMAS, Joe	515
THOMSON, Lachie	539, 541
THURESSON, Svante	564
TODD, Dick	507
TODD, Tommy	562
TOMELLERI, Paolo	535
TOMPKINS, Ross	546
TOTAH, Knobby	524
TOWN CRIERS, The	497
TRACE, Al	545
TRACY, Jack	519
TRAPPIER, Art	512
TRATTNER, Wolfgang	536, 548
TRAVIS, Nick	516–17
TROTT, Jack	564–65
TUCKER, Ben	523
TURNER, Jim	479, 542, 564, 566
ULYATE, Lloyd	533–34
UTHE, Bob	549
VAN DER SLUIS, Koos	536–37
VAN EPS, George	524, 528, 531, 538
VAN GELDER, Rudy	499, 503
VAN MUYEN, Henk	536–37
VAUGHN, Jerry	555–56, 558
VENUTI, Joe	527, 535, 538
VESCOVO, Al	557
VINCKEN, Jack	545
VON DER MEDEN, Andreas	542–43
VON ESSEN, Reimer	535
WALLACE, Guy	512
WALLER, Fats	489
WALTERS, Bob	557
WARD, Helen	489
WATSON, Bob	540–41
WAYNE, Chuck	513
WEBSTER, Paul	515
WEED, Buddy	488, 561
WEIL, Bob	516
WEIN, George	499
WEIR, Bob	479
WEISS, Sid	482–83
WELCH, ——	516
WELLS, Dickie	515
WELLSTOOD, Dick	517, 521
WESTBROOK, Chauncey	515
WESTERBERG, Hans	479
WESTLEY, Ira	527–28, 532, 557
WETTLING, George	481, 483, 485, 487–88, 493, 495–99, 501–06, 508–10, 512–14, 517–19, 524, 562
WHITE, Bozy	483
WHITE, Jerry	564–65
WHITNEY, Jill	497
WHYATT, Bert	479, 512, 515, 566
WILBER, Bob	479, 503, 507–10, 513, 515–17, 519–21, 523–24, 537
WILCOX, Eddie	520
WILCOX (Willcox), Spiegle	538
WILDER, Joe	516
WILEY, Cliff	484
WILEY, Lee	483, 488, 490, 560
WILLEMS, Jos	479, 485, 487
WILLIAMS, Bill	531–32
WILLIAMS, Bobby	549
WILLIAMS, Joe	523
WILLIAMS, Mary Lou	488
WILLIAMS, Roy	542
WILSON, Marty	499
WILSON, Teddy	488, 523
WINDHURST, Johnny	499, 503, 507
WIPPLER, Elmar	536
WOOD, Bill	523
WOODMAN, Britt	532–33
WOODS, George	541
WOODS, Phil	519
WOODWARD, Eric	479
WRIGHTSMAN, Stan	527–28, 532, 556
WULFFERS, Bob	536–37
WYLIE, Allan	484
WYNN, Terry	541
YAGED, Sol	510
YODER, Walt	525
YOUNG, Trummy	548
ZACK, George	484
ZARCHY, Zeke	533
ZAUM, Reinhard	542–43
ZELNICK, Mel	493, 561
ZIMMERMAN, Dick	534
ZIMMERMAN, Jack	493–97, 500, 507